DATE DUE

MAY 31 1972

MAY 15 1992 ENDS

JUL 1992

MICHIGAN INTERNATIONAL BUSINESS STUDIES

NUMBER 8

MICHIGAN INTERNATIONAL BUSINESS STUDIES NUMBER 8

INFLATION AND DEVELOPMENT IN LATIN AMERICA
A Case History of Inflation and Stabilization in Bolivia

George Jackson Eder

PROGRAM IN INTERNATIONAL BUSINESS
GRADUATE SCHOOL OF BUSINESS ADMINISTRATION
THE UNIVERSITY OF MICHIGAN
ANN ARBOR, MICHIGAN

PROGRAM IN INTERNATIONAL BUSINESS

Since 1961 the Graduate School of Business Administration of the University of Michigan has conducted a Program in International Business, made possible originally by a Ford Foundation grant to the University to support international studies in various fields. The chief use of the funds allocated to this School has been to enlarge the teaching program, with the aim of fulfilling the growing need for competent and informed persons to direct business operations abroad. It has also been possible to carry on a wider range of research and publication on questions related to foreign commerce. Results of the research are published in the *International Business Studies* series. Publications currently included in this series are listed below.

The Balance of Payments and Domestic Prosperity, by Paul W. McCracken and Emile Benoit, No. 1, 1963.

Leading World Stock Exchanges, by Wilford J. Eiteman and David K. Eiteman, No. 2, 1964.

Capital Markets of the European Economic Community, by Antonín Basch, No. 3, 1965.

Educating Asian Students for Business Careers, by James D. Scott, No. 4, 1966.

Management of International Advertising: The Role of Advertising Agencies, by Gordon E. Miracle, No. 5, 1966.

The Doctor, the Hospital, and the Patient in England, by Arthur F. Southwick, Jr., No. 6, 1967.

Stock Exchanges in Latin America, by David K. Eiteman, No. 7, 1966.

Dedicated to Juan Mamani and Joe Doakes

— to Juan Mamani, the forgotten man of the Bolivian Andes, who may be taken as the representative of all the nameless *peones, rotos, cacos, caboclos, favelados,* and *guajiros* of Latin America, exploited, deceived, and disillusioned by generations of *políticos* and *caudillos* of every political coloration conceivable

— and to Joe Doakes, the anonymous American taxpayer, whose hard-earned contributions to his neighbors in Latin America have so largely vanished in the quicksands of inflation, incompetence, and corruption.

PREFACE

This volume, a case history of monetary inflation and stabilization in Bolivia, reveals how relatively simple are both the causes of inflation in Latin America and the measures necessary to combat it, but at the same time how almost overwhelmingly complex are the practical obstacles in the way of stabilization. "If to do were as easy as to know what were good to do, chapels had been churches, and poor men's cottages princes' palaces."

There is no need here to dwell upon the subtle distinctions between the various theories of the causes of inflation, whether demand-pull, cost-push, or variants of those theories such as demand-shift; nor need we enter upon a discussion of the effect of prices and interest rates upon employment, or the relative advantage or disadvantage of either a stable or a gradually rising general level of prices.

In Latin America in general over the past two decades, and in Bolivia in particular, the inflationary process has been of the extreme variety that economists of all schools will agree is inimical to economic development. It has been attributable almost exclusively to a single cause — the action of the government in spending beyond its available resources and in borrowing the difference from the Central Bank, resulting in the printing of constantly increasing supplies of paper money to provide the Treasury with funds.

Monetary debasement, rather than monetary inflation, would be a more apt description of the process — a process that kings and governments have resorted to for centuries, lowering the gold or silver content of their coinage whenever they found that they could not, or did not dare, extort more money from their subjects or citizens through taxation.

In Bolivia, as elsewhere in Latin America, the extraordinary need for funds has for the most part originated in the well-intentioned desire of the government to promote the general welfare. With that aim, the government has constructed schools, hospitals, water systems, and highways beyond the nation's economic capacity to build or to maintain. It has attempted to speed the process of industrialization through government owned and operated power plants and industrial enterprises, with the intention of diversifying the economy and thus escaping the extreme fluctuations of prices and income endemic in "one-crop" or "one-product" countries. These sharp fluctuations in purchasing power are frequently referred to as "structural" causes of inflation. A general survey of the facts and fallacies of inflation in Latin America, now in course of preparation, will show, however, that while diversification is by all means a desirable goal and monoproductivity is frequently a structural cause of economic hardship, it has repeatedly been proved possible to maintain monetary stability in the face of the most extreme structural imbalance. This has certainly been proved true in the case of Bolivia.

It may be asked why we should study Bolivia. Simply because Bolivia is the only country in Latin America that has undergone a rampant inflation, more extreme than has been witnessed in any other country in the hemisphere, and yet has succeeded in putting into effect a monetary stabilization program that, with a single adjustment, has kept its currency stable in terms of dollars for the past nine years, and its internal price level relatively stable. In fact, domestic prices have been virtually stable with the exception of prices for services and rents, which have been gradually decontrolled with the return to a preponderantly free market economy. And it is believed that this study of the Bolivian inflationary and stabilization experience will be of general interest, *because the lessons learned in Bolivia are applicable,* mutatis mutandis, *to every other country of Latin America suffering from uncontrolled inflation.* As Ortega y Gasset writes in *Revolt of the Masses,* "The past will not tell us what we should do, but it will tell us what we should avoid." [1]

The very fact that monetary depreciation had reached such extremes in Bolivia, from 60 to 14,000 bolivianos to the dollar in four years, made it all the easier to analyze its causes and to trace its consequences. The sequence began with government attempts to relieve poverty by ever mounting expenditures for welfare and economic development, financed by the exhaustion of the nation's gold and foreign exchange reserves, by U.S. aid, and by borrowing from the Central Bank. The bank met the government demand for credit by constantly increased issues of unbacked paper currency, which in turn were followed by a drop in the foreign exchange value of the boliviano and higher and higher prices at home. Higher prices brought demands for increased wages and higher social security benefits, which were wiped out by the inflationary tide. At the same time, they raised the cost of government, increasing the deficits and making necessary still further borrowing from the Central Bank. Price controls were instituted, but these resulted only in shortages of goods, black-marketing, still higher prices, and a flight of capital, each consequence accentuating its antecedent cause in a vicious spiral that seemingly had no end. (The sequence is shown graphically in Figs. 1, 4, and 5 below.)

In desperation, the government called upon the United States for aid, which came in cash and commodities. But the cash was swallowed up in the deficits of the government and of a score of government enterprises, while the commodities largely found their way into the black market or were smuggled out of the country. The counterpart funds generated by U.S. aid became a major source of further inflation, while the distribution of cash and commodities aggravated Bolivia's chronic ills and provided "the most potent source of illegal enrichment" that had ever been known in the history of that nation.[2]

In the words of the American Under Secretary of the Treasury, U.S. aid had "gone down the drain," and the Assistant Secretary of State for Latin American Affairs added that sending aid to Bolivia under those circumstances was like trying to fill a "bottomless tub."

Finally, after long negotiations, the Bolivian government, faced with the threat that U.S. assistance would be cut off unless Bolivia put its house in order, "requested" the U.S. government to send a financial mission to stabilize the boliviano. Thus, I arrived in Bolivia on June 1, 1956, as an invited, but scarcely welcome, guest of the Bolivian government.

The assignment as described in the service contract drafted by the International Cooperation Administration (ICA) was "to assist and advise the government of Bolivia in its planning for national economic stabilization and its formulation of overall economic, fiscal, and budgetary policy," and specifically:

1. To serve as the head of a team of three men who would act as advisers to a national stabilization council that the Bolivian government had agreed to establish, and to advise that council on the national budget, credit structure, monetary system, economic and fiscal policy, and

related problems, "and the most effective ways of meeting such problems in order to control inflation"*
2. To serve personally as adviser to the President of the
   Republic
3. To advise the Bolivian government in planning a stabilization program, and in developing the organization,
   structure, and methods of operation of the Stabilization
   Council, as well as in drafting the decree which would
   establish the council [3]

Instructions were neither given nor requested as to the
means to be employed "to control inflation," nor as to how the
other functions of the assignment were to be carried out. It
seemed wiser to work out a plan of action after threshing out
the problems with the Bolivian authorities than to attempt to
define the procedures in advance with ICA, State, and Treasury
officials, a course which could only serve to circumscribe my
freedom of action.

Prior experience dating back to 1926 and extending up to
more recent years had given me a fairly comprehensive understanding of Bolivia's basic economic and monetary problems,
and by the time I accepted the ICA assignment on May 15, 1956,
I had already roughed out the steps necessary to combat the
dramatic drop in the value of the Bolivian peso since 1952 and
had planned the approach to take in my initial conversations
with the Bolivian government officials whom I was scheduled to
meet only a fortnight after my appointment.

Nevertheless, it must be admitted that I was hardly prepared for the utter chaos — fiscal, monetary, political, social,
and economic — which confronted me on arrival in Bolivia on
June 1, 1956. It was immediately apparent that, although my
basic approach to the task was sound, I would have to work
under a pressure of time that made careful analysis and preparation impossible.

Whatever had to be done must be done instantly. Any unnecessary delay would be more serious in its consequences than
any reasonable margin of error in the appraisal of the situation
or in my recommendations for action. There would be no time
for consultation with Washington until after I had drafted at

---

*The two remaining members of the mission did not arrive in Bolivia
until the end of the year, by which time the essential legislation creating
the Stabilization Council had been enacted and a forty-step stabilization
program drafted and cleared in La Paz and Washington. The full three-
man team was, however, available to help in the implementation of the
program (see Chapter 4).

least a preliminary program, and I must be prepared to discuss these tentative plans with Bolivian government officials and advise that government on the basis of hastily assembled and woefully incomplete facts and assumptions. It was a time for action, not for painstaking analysis and certainly not for adding a further volume to the shelf of unheeded U.S. government and U.N. reports on Bolivia's precarious economic position.

Thus, the immediate task was to draw up and obtain acceptance of a tentative stabilization program and to draft a decree creating a National Monetary Stabilization Council and defining its powers. This was done, and by December, 1956, the entire program, with all its necessary laws and decrees, had been whipped into shape, financed with a $25 million stabilization fund, and put into operation.

And then, by the simple expedient of removing the causes of inflation — doing away with price controls, abolishing all quotas and ration limitations, balancing the overall budget of the government and its deficitary enterprises, and prohibiting borrowing from the Central Bank and further unbacked issues of paper money — there occurred almost overnight the "miracle" of stabilization, the elimination of shortages of food and other supplies, the disappearance of the black markets and of smuggled exports of commodities. Prices, free to find their own levels in a free market, gradually dropped to 22 per cent below the prestabilization levels in just eight months, until the government thought for a time that it could return to its old ways and go back to an unbalanced budget, to borrowing from the Central Bank, and to printing more bank notes. Then prices shot up again until the government once more heeded the counsel of its monetary advisers. But this brief divagation from the precepts of the stabilization program, and its instant repercussions, merely served to reaffirm the analysis of the causes of inflation and to corroborate the effectiveness of the measures taken to combat it. Since then, for over seven years, the Bolivian currency has remained absolutely stable in terms of dollars, *with no restrictions whatsoever on the purchase or sale of foreign exchange.*

If it be objected that the Bolivian example has little relevance for other countries of Latin America where inflation has been less extreme and where, presumably, the remedies need not be so drastic or so sudden, it may be answered that wherever inflation has gotten out of control — as in Brazil, Argentina, Chile, and Colombia, for example — a surgical operation and not a palliative is called for. If the patient is to survive, the surgeon must cut, and cut quickly. As Edwin Walter Kemmerer once said, "The way to stabilize is to stabilize," and, so far as can be recalled, there has never been a case of uncontrolled inflation that has been successfully overcome by a process of gradual stabilization, say by reducing the inflationary rate from 100 per cent a year to 50 per cent, to 20 per cent, and finally to zero. The Brazilian experiment with gradual stabilization has not yet reached its goal.

More to the point, the maladjustments produced during a long period of uncontrolled inflation are so great, and the difficulties and distortions of readjustment so formidable that there is probably not a single country of Latin America with fortitude enough for the legislature, the administration, the labor unions, the general public, and the army to sit quietly by for a period of two or three years while the monetary or economic adviser assures them that all will be well if they follow his advice, but that they must be patient — and starve in the meanwhile. In stabilization, above all, "'twere well it were done quickly."

Or, if it be objected that Bolivia is not typical, that the extremes of illiteracy and economic backwardness outlined in this volume are without counterpart in any other country of this hemisphere, it may be answered that no country is "typical" — each has its own personality, its own admixture of good and bad qualities. But there is some advantage in studying an extreme example, where economic, social, and political ills have reached the ultimate stage, in order that one may more readily perceive the causes and consequences of the much milder problems in one's own country. Perhaps so radical a model may even serve as a warning of the dangerous direction of current trends closer to home. As one La Paz newspaper commented: "Bolivia stands as an example to other countries of Latin America of the disasters that follow from the nationalization of the sources of production."[4]

It is believed, therefore, that this study, in revealing both the simplicity and the complexity of currency stabilization and inflation in their most drastic manifestations, will prove useful to monetary stabilizers, economic advisers, government officials, students, and the general public in other countries of Latin America. Persons in the United States interested in Latin America, or in monetary, investment, and economic development problems — whether as students of the subject, as administrators of foreign aid, or as legislators or taxpayers — will also find it helpful.

So far as Bolivia is concerned, the volume serves a further purpose. It provides an authentic history, nowhere else available, of the causes and consequences of inflation in that country and of the nature, purposes, and course of the measures taken to combat it. It gives an account of the crises, disasters, triumphs, and shortcomings of the program, so that Bolivians may judge for themselves what persons and what policies are responsible for Bolivia's past and present difficulties, and what forces have worked most notably for Bolivia's welfare. Former President Hernán Siles-Suazo stands first and foremost as the man who carried on his shoulders the full weight of responsibility for the success or failure of Bolivia's monetary stabilization program, and whose courage, dedication, and determination carried the program through to ultimate success. Others are mentioned in the course of this narrative whose loyal cooperation in the arduous task of preparing, enacting, and carrying out the stabilization measures made it possible for President Siles to bring the program to its successful culmination. Bolivians, regardless of political party, owe a deep debt of gratitude to all those courageous, devoted, and patriotic men.

Others referred to in this volume whose policies were responsible for the inflation, or who attempted to block, destroy, or distort the stabilization program, may be adjudged by Bolivians to have played a less worthy role. I regret the necessity of mentioning them, but their actions have been so widely publicized that concealment would be futile, and this volume would fall short of being a history of stabilization in Bolivia if it failed to point out the antagonists as well as the protagonists in the drama.

To those who feel that this book paints an unduly grim picture of Bolivia, of its illiteracy, violence, and political shortcomings — the failure of the government-operated industrial enterprises and the ravages wrought by nationalization of the mines and a misdirected "agrarian reform" — it may be said that this is a history of inflation and stabilization, and that all those matters are inescapably germane to that history. The inflationary disasters, as well as the major obstacles to stabilization, were the direct consequences of politics and corruption, and political corruption is the one major vice in the Bolivian scene.

It is much as if one were to write of juvenile delinquency or racial intolerance in the United States. The picture, if honest, could not fail to be a grim one. Yet we know that there are many more things right about the United States than there are wrong, and that, although the negative side of the picture is unhappily true, it is by no means the whole truth nor the whole picture of life in the United States.

The same is true of Bolivia. If I were not writing of inflation, political ineptitude, and corruption, then no one book — not twenty books — would suffice to contain all that is good, admirable, and noble in that distressed country. And I can only hope that my many friends in Bolivia, knowing how hard and with what true affection I have labored for that country's good, will not only forgive my frankness but be grateful for my having given them a true and complete account of one of the most disastrous periods in Bolivian history.

The notes at the end of the book contain references to many who played an important part in the development of the stabilization program, names that would mean little to the casual reader or to one outside of Bolivia, but that serve to complete the history of the times. On the whole, it may be said that these reference notes contain little that would be of interest to the general reader, who may save time and annoyance by ignoring the numbered references in the text. Any notes that are thought to be of general interest appear as footnotes in the text itself.

G. J. E.

Ann Arbor, Michigan
1966

ACKNOWLEDGMENTS

In writing a book of this nature, an author almost inevitably leaves one of the pleasantest tasks for the last — acknowledging his indebtedness to all those who have helped him in his endeavors. With deep gratitude, then, I wish to express my appreciation to Floyd A. Bond, Dean of the Graduate School of Business Administration of the University of Michigan, and to D. Maynard Phelps, Acting Director of the Program in International Business, as well as to the Ford Foundation, for having made it possible for me to undertake this study as a member of the faculty of that school.

For their invaluable suggestions on structure, tone, style, and content I am indebted to Dean Bond and Professor Phelps, as well as to the following members of the faculty of the Graduate School of Business Administration: Robert W. Adams, Director (since June, 1965) of the Program in International Business; Paul W. McCracken, Professor of Business Conditions; Alfred W. Swinyard, Director of the Bureau of Business Research; Merwin H. Waterman, Professor of Finance; and J. Philip Wernette, Professor of Business Administration; and to Professors Alfred F. Conard and Eric Stein of the Law School. I am likewise grateful to Herbert F. Taggart, Professor of Accounting, and to Elman Service, Professor of Anthropology, for their careful perusal of those parts of the manuscript that are within their respective fields of special competence. Nor must I overlook the assistance of John D. O'Neill and Mrs. Jeanne Brownlow, whose painstaking editing and tolerance of my literary idiosyncrasies are much appreciated, as is also the cooperation of Mrs. Janet Williams Stuhlman, who typed the entire manuscript, and of Mrs. Mary B. Woolfenden and all her cheerful assistants in the duplicating department.

Beyond the confines of the University of Michigan, I am greatly indebted to Emilio G. Collado, Executive Vice-President and Director of Standard Oil Company, New Jersey, who was the first to suggest that I expand the area of my study to include inflation in Latin America in general and not in Bolivia alone, and who was kind enough to comment on certain sections of the manuscript; to G. A. Costanzo, Senior Vice-President of the

First National City Bank, New York, who read the manuscript from cover to cover and, with his colleague, Assistant Vice-President George J. Clark, gave me the benefit of his highly expert advice and suggestions; and to Dr. Dana G. Munro, President of the Foreign Bondholders Protective Council, Incorporated, who provided me with material and comments on the status of Bolivia's defaulted dollar bonds. I am also grateful to H. W. Balgooyen, Executive Vice-President, American Foreign Power Company, Incorporated; Donald J. Bevis, Senior Partner of Touche, Ross, Bailey & Smart; Victor C. Folsom, Vice-President and General Counsel, United Fruit Company; Lewis B. Harder, Chairman, International Mining Corporation; F. J. Gutchess, Executive Officer, General Services Administration; John D. J. Moore, Vice-President and General Counsel, W. R. Grace & Company; Herbert V. Prochnow, President, First National Bank of Chicago; Leroy D. Stinebower, Treasurer, Standard Oil Company, New Jersey; and Craig Thompson, Director of Public Relations, Gulf Oil Corporation, for their advice in connection with the original outline of this study or suggestions and material within their respective fields; and to many others, too numerous to mention here, whose contributions are acknowledged in the text or in the bibliography.

Finally, I must gratefully acknowledge the assistance of my wife, Marceline Gray Eder, who shared with me the joys and dangers of life in Revolutionary Bolivia, as well as a common deep affection for the Bolivian people; and of my son, Richard Gray Eder, a correspondent of the *New York Times* until recently in Latin America and now in Washington. Their perceptive comments have served to restrain to some extent the infelicities and irrelevancies of the original draft.

None of the views, statements of fact, or conclusions expressed in this volume is to be attributed to any of those whose help I here acknowledge. Their contribution has been chiefly in what has been omitted from the book rather than in what has been included, and that contribution has beyond question made this study more readable, more scholarly, more worthy of publication by the University, than it was in its original form. The views expressed are my own, and may not coincide with those held by others in the University of Michigan, the Graduate School of Business Administration, the Program in International Business, the Bureau of Business Research, or the Ford Foundation.

ABBREVIATIONS AND ACRONYMS

The following list does not purport to be complete. It omits abbreviations and acronyms that are so widely known as to require no explanation (U.S., U.N., etc.) or that are used only occasionally and are explained in the text.

AID	Agency for International Development (Washington)
BAH	Booz, Allen & Hamilton (Chicago)
Bs.	Bolivianos (the Bolivian currency until July, 1962, when the Peso Boliviano, equal to Bs. 1,000 was established)
CEPAL	Comisión Económica para América Latina (U.N. Economic Commission for Latin America; see ECLA)
CNSS	Caja Nacional de Seguridad Social (National Social Security Administration)
COB	Central Obrera Boliviana (Bolivian Workers' Confederation)
COMIBOL	Corporación Minera Boliviana (Bolivian Mining Corporation)
ECLA	Economic Commission for Latin America (U.N. agency based in Santiago, Chile)
EXIMBANK	Export-Import Bank of Washington
FAO	Food and Agriculture Organization, U.N. (Rome)
FBD	Ford, Bacon & Davis, Inc. (New York)
IBRD	International Bank for Reconstruction and Development (Washington — generally referred to as the World Bank)
ICA	International Cooperation Administration (Washington — predecessor of AID)
IDA	International Development Association (Washington; the "soft loan" affiliate of IBRD)

ABBREVIATIONS AND ACRONYMS

IDB	Inter-American Development Bank (Washington)
IFC	International Finance Corporation (Washington; the "hard loan" — private industry — affiliate of IBRD)
IMF	International Monetary Fund (Washington)
MNR	Movimiento Nacional Revolucionario (National Revolutionary Movement — the Government Party, 1952-64)
n.a.	Not available
USAID/Bolivia	Field office of AID in La Paz (successor to USOM/Bolivia)
USOM/Bolivia	U.S. Operations Mission (field office of ICA in La Paz)
YPFB	Yacimientos Petrolíferos Fiscales Bolivianos (Bolivian Fiscal Petroleum Deposits — the government oil company)

CONTENTS

I
THE BACKGROUND

II
BREAKING GROUND

III
DRAFTING THE STABILIZATION PROGRAM

IV
THE PROGRAM FINANCED AND ENACTED

V
SUBSEQUENT MEASURES

TABLES

FIGURES

I

THE BACKGROUND

1

THE LAND AND THE PEOPLE

The Land

Among the factors that have a bearing on monetary stability (as well as on economic development), human resources bulk so much larger than natural resources that it suffices to say with respect to Bolivia's natural endowments that the country possesses within its territory every form of wealth requisite for economic development. And these resources are found in an abundance that should, or at least might, make Bolivia one of the most prosperous countries of the world, with a currency as sound as that of Switzerland, to which it has often been compared by reason of its mountainous terrain.

By contrast, Switzerland, a country of monetary and economic solidity par excellence, is lacking in virtually all natural resources save mountains, water power, and fertile valleys; in all of these assets Bolivia so far excels her that it is an understatement to call Bolivia the "Switzerland of America."[1] Bolivia's mountains are the most formidable in the Western Hemisphere. The tallest peak (Illampú, 21,522 feet) falls some 1,000 feet short of Argentina's Aconcagua in altitude, but Bolivia's high plateau — the altiplano — lies between two massive cordilleras: the western range, separating Bolivia from Chile, with an average altitude of some 16,500 feet; and the Cordillera Real, separating the altiplano from Bolivia's eastern plains and Amazonian jungles, with an average altitude of 18,000 feet.

Overlooking the altiplano are five mountain peaks, one to the west and four to the east, all over 20,000 feet above sea level and all looming higher than Alaska's Mt. McKinley. The plateau itself is an amazingly level tableland, 520 miles in length and 80 to 100 miles in breadth, at 13,000 feet above sea level, or nearly as high as the peak of Switzerland's Mont Blanc (15,771 feet) or California's Mt. Whitney (14,495 feet).

On the plateau, at 12,500 feet, lies Lake Titicaca, partly in Bolivia and partly in Peru, the highest navigated lake in the world, occupying an area of some 3,500 square miles, or roughly three times the size of Rhode Island. Its depth has been plumbed at 1,500 feet. It drains into Lake Poopó, 200 miles to the south, and only a few hundred feet lower. Poopó itself has no visible outlet other than a small stream which disappears underground. It is hence a shallow, intensely saline lake of some 1,000 square miles in area, or perhaps half as much again during the rainy season, when it becomes approximately as large as the Great Salt Lake of Utah. South of Poopó are the dazzling white salt plains of Uyuni, which extend, with three lesser adjacent deposits, for some 3,220 square miles and constitute an important element in Bolivia's mineral wealth.

In all, Bolivia occupies an area of between 411,000 and 514,000 square miles (accurate figures are hard to come by in any matter relating to Bolivia) — roughly the size of Texas and California combined or, for European comparison, approximately as large as Spain and France together. Of this area, about 16 per cent is altiplano, cold and dry, and containing perhaps 70 per cent of the population. Some 14 per cent is steep and rugged valley land lying at altitudes of 5,000 to 12,000 feet, and having a temperate to subtropical climate with little to moderate rainfall. The remaining 70 per cent of the country, containing less than 14 per cent of the population, consists of the eastern plains (the llanos), which comprise (1) the Gran Chaco, bordering on Argentina and Paraguay, generally subtropical with little rainfall and lying at altitudes of 1,500 to 2,300 feet; (2) Santa Cruz, on the Paraguayan-Brazilian border, likewise subtropical but with more adequate rainfall and altitudes of 1,000 to 1,500 feet; and (3) the Beni, Bolivia's vast tropical plain and jungle land, watered and sometimes inundated by the Beni and Mamoré rivers and their tributaries, which flow into the Madeira River in Brazil and thence into the Amazon.[2]

In colonial times, Bolivia's total area was well over 900,000 square miles.[3] But she lost half her territory to Peru, Brazil, Argentina, Chile, and Paraguay in a series of disastrous wars that deprived her of her former access to the Pacific and left her dependent upon treaties for an outlet by river and rail to the markets of the world.*

*From the standpoint of monetary stability and economic development, the lack of a seaport is of no greater consequence than in the case of Switzerland, but Bolivia continues to claim her "right" of access to the sea, despite the fact that this right was lost in war with Chile and acquiesced in by truce as long ago as 1884 and by treaty in 1895. Since then, Bolivia has generally been referred to in Latin American literature as the only "mediterranean" country of Latin America (Paraguay being, of

Mineral resources

Beneath the surface of the land are found at least traces of practically every mineral known to man. According to Frederick Ahlfeld, the leading authority on the subject, Bolivia is one of the most highly mineralized areas in the world. In colonial days, silver was pre-eminent, and the Spaniards are reported to have had 350,000 llamas engaged in the transportation of silver from the mines. As each llama can carry a burden of some 50 to 130 pounds and travels anywhere from 6 to 18 miles a day, and as one Indian is accustomed to herding from 15 to 20 animals, it is easy to understand that in manpower, beasts of burden, and mineral wealth, Bolivia constituted the treasure house of Spain's colonial empire.[4] The royal mint in Potosí, in the heart of the mining region, made that city second only to Lima in wealth, at a time when La Paz, now the capital of Bolivia, was merely the center of the coca leaf trade and a llama-stop for the caravans carrying silver from Potosí to the seacoast at Arequipa.*

Today, silver accounts for less than 5 per cent of Bolivia's mineral output, with tin far in the lead, followed by tungsten and petroleum. In all, minerals constitute some 95 per cent of Bolivia's exports (tin, tungsten, petroleum, lead, zinc, silver, copper, gold, sulphur, bismuth, and others), with tin contributing around 70 per cent of the total.[5] The importance of mineral production as a source of foreign exchange and the drop in production since the nationalization of the major mines in 1953 are thus principal factors in Bolivia's present precarious economic situation. They were a major problem in the task of achieving and sustaining monetary stability. This aspect of Bolivia's economy is discussed at greater length in Chapter 3.

course, "mesopotamian"). Politically, no party dares drop the claim to *Bolivia irredenta,* and letters from Bolivia are currently postmarked: *Bolivia demanda su derecho de salida al mar* ("Bolivia demands its right of exit to the sea").

*Legally, the capital of Bolivia is Sucre, known successively in history as Chuquisaca, Charcas, and La Plata before being renamed after the Venezuelan general, Antonio José de Sucre, who was Simón Bolívar's second in command and the leader of the forces of independence in both Colombia and Bolivia. The Supreme Court still convenes in stately isolation in Sucre, but the actual seat of government — Congress, the presidency, and all the executive departments — is La Paz.

Agricultural and forest resources

From the viewpoint of the total economy, however, the land itself is Bolivia's greatest natural resource, rather than the minerals which lie beneath its surface. Farming, hunting, and fishing are far more important than mining, although pursued chiefly on a subsistence basis, so that the products of Bolivia's farms, fields, and forests enter the domestic market only to a limited extent, and account for little more than 2 per cent of the export trade. Nevertheless, 71 per cent of the economically active population is reported to be engaged in farming, 2 per cent in ranching, hunting, fishing, and the gathering of forest crops, and an additional 8 per cent in the processing industries, largely the processing of farm and forest textiles and food-stuffs. A total of some 80 per cent of the population is dependent directly or indirectly upon the soil as compared with 3 per cent engaged in mining and manufacturing put together.*

Even in the value of the output of the various sectors of the economy, agriculture bulks far larger than is generally realized. According to estimates made by the Economic Commission for Latin America, agriculture accounts for between 27 and 32 per cent of gross national product, and the latter figure includes, of course, the rather top-heavy figures for public works, government salaries, and the like. Eliminating "other sectors," which includes those categories as well as private construction and services, agriculture accounts for 39 to 45 per cent of the national output as compared with 35 to 39 per cent for mining

---

*Percentages are based on the population census of 1950, reported in Cornelius H. Zondag, *Problems in the Economic Development of Bolivia* (La Paz, USOM [Mimeographed, 1956], p. 217), but must be regarded as no more than rough approximations, as there is no way of reconciling widely divergent Bolivian statistics, whether from the same or from different sources. The general unreliability of Bolivian statistics is repeatedly stressed by the U.N. Mission of Technical Assistance to Bolivia in the Keenleyside report (United Nations, *Report of the United Nations Mission of Technical Assistance to Bolivia* [New York: United Nations, 1951], pp. 15, 19, 71, 89, 90, 112-14) and by the Economic Commission for Latin America in the ECLA report (Naciones Unidas, *Análisis y Proyecciones del Desarrollo Económico: IV — El Desarrollo Económico de Bolivia* [Mexico City: Naciones Unidas, 1958], pp. 1, 7, 14, 18, 19, 71, 73, 83, 251, 285). Experience shows that all Bolivian figures, and particularly those relating to the revenues, expenditures, or indebtedness of the government and governmental enterprises, should be written plus or minus as much as 50 per cent, with a considerably higher margin of error where foreign exchange values are concerned.

and petroleum combined, and this in the 1950-55 period when
tin prices were higher than in any previous period of the nation's history.[6]

The plateau region. In agriculture, as in mining, the altiplano and the adjacent valleys are the center of Bolivia's economy, containing nearly 90 per cent of the cultivated land and
some 86 per cent of the farm population, despite the fact that 90
per cent of Bolivia's potentially arable acreage lies in the eastern plains, and that the plateau region is the "highest, coldest,
and most inhospitable area in South America."[7]

The llama and llama-alpaca hybrids (*huarizo* or *mixti*) are
the only beasts of burden that can thrive at that altitude and on
the scanty vegetation that the altiplano affords, chiefly a harsh
grass some 12 to 18 inches high, known as *ichu*. Occasionally a
burro will be seen on the high plateau, but despite its greater
carrying capacity it is less useful than the llama, as it must be
fed and stabled at perhaps a thousand feet lower and hence many
miles away. Llama meat was a staple in the days of the Inca
empire, but is not much used today. Llama wool, however, is a
valuable item in the Indian domestic economy. The llama and
its less frequently seen cousin, the alpaca, make a further contribution to the plateau economy, as their dung supplies the
chief fuel (*taquia*) on these treeless plains.*

The only other fuels are the now scarce *tthola* and *yareta*
shrubs (which also furnish a sparse pasturage to the llamas and
other camelidae) and *kenua*, a stunted woody bush which has almost disappeared in recent years. The use of llama dung for
fuel, and the failure to use human excrement as fertilizer, as it
is used in the Far East today and was used in Europe until recent times, has broken the replenishment cycle of nature, and
is generally correlated with the soil depletion of the altiplano.[8]

The chief crop of the altiplano is the potato. The Spanish
word for potato (*papa*) is of Quechua origin. Potatoes, together
with cocoa beans, tobacco, quinine, rubber, coca leaves (from

---

*Other Camelidae of the Bolivian plateau are the small, generally
wild guanaco, whose wool, hides, and meat are used, although of little or
no commercial value, and the still smaller and quite rare vicuña whose
soft lustrous pelts and fine silky wool are highly priced. Vicuña wool is
half the diameter of sheep wool; of extremely short fiber, and consequently
low tensile strength. The yield of usable wool averages only $\frac{1}{4}$ lb. per
animal which makes vicuña one of the world's most expensive textile
fibers, used almost entirely for export today. In Inca times it could be
woven only by the Virgins of the Sun and for royal use.

which cocaine is extracted), all indigenous to Bolivia, are among the New World's many gifts to the Old, and the potato is the major article of diet of the inhabitants of Bolivia's plateau region. It is eaten largely in the form of *chuño,* a bitter and rotted form easily stored in a dry climate, prepared by soaking the potatoes for a week in water, then exposing them to the alternate heat of the sun and the freezing temperature of the night until they are rotten, when the moisture is trodden out and the potatoes left in the air to dry hard. The *tunta* is a more refined form, less bitter than *chuño,* and somewhat like a boiled chestnut in flavor.

The second major crop of the plateau, and the most highly prized article of the Indian diet, is *quinoa,* a grass somewhat similar to goose-foot or pigweed, with a seed comparable to millet. It is eaten like rice or in a porridge, or else fermented to make *chicha.*

Canihua, the seeds of which are roasted and used like corn meal, is of less importance, but these three plants, together with some corn (maize) and barley, form practically the sole edible crops and the principal diet of the altiplano farmer.[9]

The valleys. The drop from the altiplano to the valleys is as fantastic as an imagined journey through the mountains of the moon. From the cold mountain pass on the outskirts of La Paz, at an altitude of over 15,000 feet, one descends in less than 70 miles to the steaming jungles of the *Yungas* (an Aymara word applied only to the valleys near La Paz) at 4,000 feet. To describe the terrain as rugged gives only a faint conception of the stupendous cliffs and precipes at every turn of the narrow road. The descent from Cochabamba is almost equally precipitous, and the abrupt conjuncture of dry mountain cold and moist semitropical air from the valleys leaves the pass blanketed with fog from 4,000 to 11,000 feet. It is "the land of the cloud forest," of weirdly misshapen trees, of lichen and dense undergrowth.

In the *Yungas* the chief crop is coca. Eighty per cent of the revenue of the region is derived from the cultivation of that plant, whose leaves are chewed by the Indians of the altiplano in a juicy quid *(acullico)* mixed with *quinoa* ashes. The Indians used this sedative to allay their hunger and dull their senses for centuries before the white man learned to extract cocaine from the leaves or to combine the cocaine-free residue with cola as a beverage. Tobacco, cocoa beans, coffee, oranges, and bananas are also grown.

Further south, in the valleys extending from Cochabamba down to the Chaco plains, the crops are more varied and include potatoes, wheat, barley, alfalfa, fruit, and corn, the last consumed chiefly in the form of a strong fermented drink (*chicha*) made from chewed cornmeal (*muko*). Cochabamba was once the center of a rich dairy country until the "agrarian reform" brought about the slaughter of most of the dairy cattle.

Leaving the valleys and coming to the eastern plains, one comes to the Chaco region on the Argentine and Paraguayan border. It is plagued by locusts and drought, by erosion from misguided attempts at cultivation, and by overgrazing by the cattle and goats that roam the unfenced prairies.[10]

At the northernmost section of the eastern plains, "the Beni," as both the region and the river are known, lies at the headwaters of the Madeira branch of the Amazon water system. On the Beni plains, horses and cattle — unknown in South America until brought there by Spanish Jesuit missionaries in 1675 — constitute "the main and almost the only negotiable wealth of the region." Following the expulsion of the Jesuits in 1767, however,

> the cattle and horses of the Beni were regarded as an unlimited reservoir of natural wealth... to be exploited for the enrichment of the government, the official and the merchant. For close on to two centuries a veritable war of extermination has been conducted against them. Government officials descended like vultures upon the Beni with every encouragement to make a rapid, if not an honest, fortune at the expense of the livestock there.... The cattle were hunted and slaughtered wantonly for the hides, or the fat, and the carcasses were left to rot upon the plains.... The breeding ranches instituted by the Jesuits did not long survive their departure and for a century and a half no serious attempt has been made to preserve or improve the stock.[11]

Despite these depredations, estimates of the cattle population in the Beni, prior to the slaughter that took place during the "agrarian reform," run anywhere from one million head to over three million.[12] Horses and mules are still reasonably plentiful although there is no longer a surplus for export.

In the tropical jungles of the Beni — the "Green Hell" of Bolivia — rubber and Brazil nuts are the principal commercial crops. Although the lumber resources of the Beni, and of Santa

Cruz to the east and south, are said to have a value of some $25 billion, from which it is claimed that ten million dollars' worth of timber a year could be cut without deplenishing the forests,[13] persons with practical commercial experience have learned to be skeptical of the allegedly limitless resources of any tropical forest area where the extreme diversity of forest growth, coupled with labor scarcities and high transportation costs, makes large-scale lumbering operations generally impractical.

The most important section of the eastern plains is that of Santa Cruz, extending to the borders of Brazil and Paraguay. Of all Bolivia's underdeveloped agricultural areas, that region would appear to offer the greatest immediate potentialities. Rice, sugar cane (80 per cent of which was consumed in the form of rum before the 1956 stabilization measures), corn, yucca, cotton, peanuts, citrus and other fruits, and vegetables are all grown in that area.[14]

Other natural resources

Such are Bolivia's major natural resources, the riches of the land and of the subsoil, including petroleum and other underground "juices of the earth" — *los jugos de la tierra,* to use the old Spanish term. The many great rivers and lakes are bountifully supplied with many varieties of edible fish, but for the most part the Bolivian Indian is not a fisherman, and the difficulties of transportation and the absence of refrigeration make it difficult to obtain fresh fish except to a limited extent in the immediate vicinity of the lakes and in the altiplano markets above La Paz.

The lakes, rivers, and mountains provide Bolivia with potential sources of hydroelectric power in an abundance far beyond any foreseeable needs, although not beyond the visionary dreams of Bolivia's economic planners, as will be seen in the survey of some of the causes of the country's inflationary problems. In the mining areas and at the centers of population, where electricity is urgently required for power and light, the expansion of privately owned power companies has been throttled by rate structures that barely allow for current operating costs, with little or no margin for depreciation and none for a return on the investment; so that, all in all, Bolivia's power resources have been as badly misused as her land and mineral resources.

The mountains and rugged valleys have served to separate

the country into completely isolated compartments, racially, socially, politically, and economically. Transportation, as Harold Osborne says, is not merely one problem among many, "but the one problem upon which all else depends."[15] The attempt to link so diverse an area as Bolivia into one political and economic unit by costly and patently uneconomic railways and highways has proved to be one of the major causes of Bolivia's inflationary problems, as will be seen in the course of this study.*

Other aspects of the Bolivian economy, aside from the human and natural resources — i.e., manufacturing, construction, trade, banking, service industries, foreign trade, the balance of payments, and such shadowy concepts as the Bolivian gross national product, etc. — will be dealt with incidentally as they impinge upon the subject of monetary inflation, its causes, consequences, and cure. †

The People

The earliest inhabitants of the Bolivian altiplano are generally believed to be the Uru, Chipaya, and Pukina tribes,

---

*A U.S. Embassy official, perhaps exhilarated by the altitude, made himself *persona non grata* by repeating the oft-quoted statement that there is no economic justification for Bolivia's existence and that the people and country would be better off if split on natural lines between Chile, Peru, Brazil, Argentina, and Paraguay (*Time*, February 27, 1959; *New York Times*, March 3, 1959; March 4, 1959). This was denied by the State Department but reaffirmed by H. R. Luce. As a result of the *gaffe*, a mob did $50,000 of damage on the embassy and wrecked the U.S. information offices in Cochabamba and Oruro (*New York Times*, March 4 and March 5, 1959). Any such suggestion is, of course, politically untenable today, and overlooks 140 years of history.

*Readers desirous of a more detailed treatment of the Bolivian economy will find the most complete surveys in the ECLA report, which was written in April, 1957, although not published until 1958; in the U.S. Army *Area Handbook for Bolivia* (1963); and, above all, in the mimeographed Zondag report, dated November 19, 1965, and Cornelius H. Zondag, *The Bolivian Economy, 1952-65*. Other studies of a high standard of excellence are the Bohan report (*Report of the U.S. Economic Mission to Bolivia*, 1942); the Keenleyside report (*Report of the United Nations Mission of Technical Assistance to Bolivia*, 1951); and the books by Harold Osborne (*Bolivia: A Land Divided*, 1964); and Olen E. Leonard (*Bolivia: Land, People and Institutions*, 1952).

clustered around Lakes Titicaca and Poopó and probably related to the Arawak Indians of the Caribbean. Somewhat later, apparently, came the Aymara, who occupied practically the entire altiplano of Bolivia and are ancestors of most of the Bolivians of today.* The eastern plains of the Beni and Santa Cruz were inhabited by the Moxos, definitely of Arawak origin, and the early Spanish settlers in that region called the entire area north of the town of Santa Cruz, and embracing northern Cochabamba, Moxitania. Further south, in the Chaco and across the Paraguayan and Argentine borders, lived the Guaraní, but relatively few of their descendents remain in present-day Bolivia.[16]

The Quechua tribe occupied a comparatively small area in the valleys of the Peruvian altiplano until the era of the great conquest under the Inca Pachacuti around 1450 A.D., but in less than a hundred years they had conquered the entire territory from Ecuador to Chile and Argentina and built the great Inca Empire whose wealth so excited the amazement and greed of the Spanish conquistadors.

The Quechua tongue was analogous to that of the Aztec in northern Mexico in that it was the language of a comparatively small conquering race and was later adopted by the conquered tribes. At the time that Pizarro and Almagro overthrew the Inca Atahualpa in 1532 by a combination of treachery, courage against overwhelming odds, and fratricidal strife between rival claimants to the Inca throne, there were at least seven distinct language groups in northern and western Bolivia, five on the Bolivian-Brazilian border, and five more in the Chaco and elsewhere in Bolivia. Quechua, however, gradually became the lingua franca of most of the Andean area, although Aymara survives around Cochabamba and other pockets throughout the altiplano. In the "Green Hell" of the Beni, the Arawak language groups survive among the relatively sparse population, but elsewhere on the eastern plains Spanish is virtually the only language spoken, thanks to the educational efforts of the Jesuit missionaries.

The Franciscans and Dominicans likewise had extensive territories allotted to them for their missionary efforts, but the

---

*Official and semiofficial figures show 1,165,040 Quechuas and 862,840 Aymaras, but this division is based on language (the only feasible census criterion) rather than race. Forest Indians are estimated at 87,000. (United Nations, *Report of the Commission of Enquiry on the Coca Leaf* [Lake Success, N. Y.: U.N. Economic and Social Council, 1950], p. 55; Zondag, p. 20.)

Jesuits were the most successful in educating their charges, protecting them from exploitation by the whites, and developing their agriculture, cattle raising, and crafts, on a communal or mission-centered basis, to the point that the textiles, artifacts, fruits, and other products of the Moxos were famous throughout western South America for their high quality.[17]

With the expulsion of the missionaries, this paternalistic protection and peaceful way of life came to an end. The Creole (i.e., American-born) descendants of the Spanish colonists in Santa Cruz and other towns mixed freely with the Indian women and one would be hard put to find in the Santa Cruz or Moxos regions today Indians of the type that inhabited the area in the colonial era.*

Yet even today, the inhabitants of Santa Cruz, whether of Spanish or mestizo (white and Indian) ancestry, look down upon the dark-skinned inhabitants of the altiplano, at the same time that they resent their political and economic hegemony. For their part, the political leaders in La Paz, who proudly proclaim themselves Indo-Americans rather than Latin Americans, are at all times keenly concerned at the possibility of a separatist movement in Santa Cruz and the Beni, which they fear is encouraged by their Brazilian neighbors.

Officially, some 53 per cent of Bolivia's population (3,013,000 according to the 1950 census; 4,136,400 in 1965) is of pure Indian ancestry; 15 per cent is white; and some 32 per cent cholo. (This is the altiplano term for mestizo, although it is sometimes used for Indians of the town as distinguished from those of the country.) Ethnic distinctions, however, tend to be blurred, and give way to comparatively rigid social strata from which the individual can only extricate himself by dint of superlative political or financial achievement. When an Indian woman "passes" to the higher chola stratum, it is known as taking the skirt (*poner falda*), much as one would speak of a novitiate nun's

---

*A Basque, "who spent fifteen years of holiness in that region as administrator of the Society of Jesus over the Moxitanians" describes the natives: "In general the men are of medium build, the women below medium. Their naked bodies are dark in color, the whole body very well formed. They are speedy, agile, in no wise deformed by labor. Indeed one never sees hunchbacks or any other kind of bodily deformity.... The leaders are for the most part graceful and it would not be easy to find a fat man." (Francis Xavier Eder, S.J., *Descriptio Provinciae Moxitarum in Regno Peruano*, Budapest: Typis Universitatis, 1791 (posthumously published), Book IV, Chap. I, p. 214.)

taking the veil. The transition is a matter of considerable pride to the family as well as to the new chola. One frequently sees an Indian woman of the purest strain, handsome in the typical derby-shaped hat, shawl, and half-dozen heavy wool petticoats (*polleras*), walking with her daughter who wears a simple modern skirt and blouse, her right to pass as a chola vouched for by her perhaps dubious mestizo paternity. The derby-shaped hat (in former years a Borsalino but now a soft felt of local manufacture) is found in the Titicaca and La Paz region. In Cochabamba a stiff, heavily starched, chalk-white hat shaped like the tall hat worn by the Pilgrim fathers is used. There is a similar diversity in men's headgear, from the felt hats modeled after the helmets of Pizarro's conquistadors used near Sucre to the knitted woolen helmets of the altiplano. Altogether, according to Elena Hosmann (*Ambiente de Altiplano* [Buenos Aires: Editorial Peuser, 1945], p. 48) there are over three hundred distinct regional costumes in Bolivia, and doubtless there are as many varieties of tribal customs and usages.

A Bolivian scientist, classifying the population on the basis of social strata, estimates the population as 70 per cent Indian, 25 per cent cholo, and 5 per cent "literate" (preferring this term as more accurate than "white"). Another estimate based on official and semiofficial data places the Aymara and Quechua population at 2,027,880, which, with the 87,000 forest Indians, would likewise mean an Indian population of some 70 per cent of the total.[18]

From the standpoint of a monetary stabilization or economic development program, literacy is, of course, of high importance, and even though the majority of the people in government speak some Quechua or Aymara (generally the former) the difficulty of communicating in writing with the great majority of the population poses an almost insuperable obstacle to political, social, and economic unity and advancement. At least 80 per cent of the population is illiterate, even though anyone who can write his own name is counted as literate. The agricultural population is almost entirely illiterate, and according to Richard Patch, only 6 per cent of the "Indian" population — meaning those who have not "passed" to cholo status — speak any language other than Quechua, Aymara, or another Indian tongue.[19]

As to racial origins and their possible bearing on monetary stabilization and economic development, I prefer to leave it to more qualified observers to determine whether, in fact, there

is any such thing as a "racial trait," or whether the characteristics generally observed among the Andean Indians are in reality environmental, cultural, historical, or the consequences of
faulty diet and education. Whatever the origin of such traits,
however, they do exist, and they do have a direct and indeed an
overwhelming bearing on the possibility of attaining the political
maturity and cultural, social, and economic progress which are
prerequisites of *permanent* monetary stability and material
advancement. Hence, these traits warrant discussion in the
present study as a basis for understanding the problems of
stabilization.

Ellsworth Huntington, for example, has said:

> It is literally true ... that the more an Indian is paid the
> less he will work. If one day's pay will buy two days' food,
> he will work half the time.... The experiment has been
> tried again and again, and there is practically universal
> agreement as to its result. The most considerate employ-
> ers of tropical labor agree with the most inconsiderate in
> saying that in general it is useless to attempt to spur the
> Indians by any motive beyond the actual demands of food
> and shelter.[20]

Huntington was speaking of the Guatemalan Indian, but,
judging by observations in Central as well as in South America,
and from conversations with both American and Latin American
employers of Indian laborers (the North Americans are the
more charitable in their judgment), I find that the Indian of the
Bolivian altiplano is even more inclined to loaf — to work only
under the stress of hunger — than the Indian of Central America.* Cornelius Zondag, writing for the U.S. Operations Mission, states that, in general, the Bolivian Indian will work only
60 per cent of the time, and the United Nations (Keenleyside)
report points to the exhorbitant expenditures on alcohol, coca,
and *fiestas* as a cause of "decreased labour efficiency, a high
degree of labour absenteeism, and thus of lower income."[21]

Olen E. Leonard of the U.S. Department of Agriculture,
who writes with manifest empathy for the Bolivian Indian, says
that

---

*Bolivian labor worked only 119 days in 1954 and 136 days in 1958.
A Bolivian paper editorializes on "the fervent cult of idleness." (Minister
of Labor, *El Diario*, February 24, 1959; editorial, *ibid.*, July 24, 1958.)

many of the poorer people in Santa Cruz spend money at
these festivals ... that could contribute substantially to improving their economic and living status throughout the
year. It is no exaggeration to say that enough money is
spent on such festivals and *fiestas*, by the majority of these
families, in 10 years to buy sufficient land and equipment
to guarantee the family a secure and comfortable existence.
So important do the people consider these festivals that it
is not at all uncommon for them to sell their last head of
livestock to obtain needed money to participate.

In Chullpas Valley (Cochabamba), Leonard found that the Indians' average expenditures on alcoholic beverages amounted to
about 30 per cent of what they spend on food, and, although no
statistical studies seem to have been made, it is widely believed
that on the altiplano where expenditures for *fiestas*, alcohol, and
coca are conspicuously higher than in either Chullpas or Santa
Cruz, as much as half of the family budget is spent on these
three items, even allowing for the value of foodstuffs consumed
on a subsistence basis. [22]

    The majority of investigators, chiefly Bolivian and Peru-
vian, believe that coca chewing is highly detrimental, mentally,
physically, and psychically, and that it has not only affected the
individual (which to the lay observer would seem obvious), but
that "it has led to a general degeneration of the Indian race"
(which may or may not be true). Other Latin American scien-
tists hold that coca is not the problem, but that the Indian is
congenitally "oligophrenic" (mentally deficient) and lazy. [23] In
support of the latter observation, Bolivians have pointed out
that the Inca rulers and officials traditionally greeted their
subjects with the Quechua salutation *Ama sua ama llulla ama
kella* — "Do not steal. Do not lie. Do not loaf."

    Under the stress of that injunction, agricultural production
per capita and per acre reached its peak of efficiency under the
Inca rule, with drainage, irrigation, soil replenishment through
enforced periods of fallowness, and terracing of the mountain
sides on an impressive scale, much of it antedating the Inca
regime and much still remaining today although the land has
since become exhausted.

    It was an efficiency, however, produced by the iron rule of
the master over the serf,* or at best of *misqui y huasca*, the

---

*It has become usual in recent decades to refer to the Empire of the
Incas as "socialist," rather than as feudal, and that is perhaps correct if

combination of "honey and lash," reward and punishment, which forced the utmost out of the Indian workers and enabled them to achieve apparently a higher standard of living than they have ever enjoyed before or since, while their rulers and priests lived in the luxury so eloquently described by Prescott and Garcilaso de la Vega.[24]

The recurrent drunkenness, lying, thieving, and indolence of the Bolivian Indian and cholo are traits witnessed in incident after incident, frequently amusing and in any event scarcely deserving of censure, considering the rigors of life on the altiplano, the dire poverty, and the apparent futility of further exertion where not only men and women but the very soil itself are exhausted. The one question germane to the possibility of economic development and permanent monetary stability is whether the torpor, laziness, and hopeless outlook of the Indian are ineradicable characteristics, either congenital or produced by generations of coca-chewing, or whether they are the product of environment and dietary deficiency. †

----

the term socialist is used as it is commonly used in Latin America. The clue is found in the introduction of *L'Empire Socialiste des Inka,* by Louis Baudin, which has been translated into Spanish by the Bolivian José Antonio Arze (Louis Baudin, *El Imperio Socialista de los Incas,* trans. José Antonio Arze [Santiago, Chile: Empresa Editora Zig-Zag, 1955]), and is widely quoted as an ideological argument to prove that socialism is of native growth and not an import from Europe. Louis Baudin defines socialism as "opposed to individualism, and implying the substitution of a rational plan of organization for the spontaneous equilibrium arrived at by the action of personal interests and the free play of competition, the plan implying a certain community ownership of property. A PLANNED AND AUTHORITARIAN SYSTEM WHICH NULLIFIES INDIVIDUAL PROPERTY RIGHTS, such is the definition of socialism which we request the reader to accept as a premise" (p. 10). Baudin goes on to compare the Inca rule with that of ancient Egypt. With that definition, the Inca regime may perhaps properly be described as socialist, but it was a system imposed by a conqueror over subject tribes, highly authoritarian, and highly regimented. The Incas, it is true, did not attempt to interfere with local tribal customs or impose their language or culture; they did impose tribute and taxes with an iron rule, and it might be contended that they gave Bolivia the best government it has ever had, and that best suited to the temperament of the Bolivian Indian. Cf. Bertrand Flornoy, *Cuzco, ou le Socialisme chez les Inka* (Paris, La Nef, 1946).

†Zondag has calculated that the average daily food intake in Bolivia may be as low as 1,221 calories (Zondag report, pp. 155, 266), and it is recognized that the diet on the altiplano is far below the average. The Keenleyside report (pp. 89-90) gives a figure of 1,612 calories per capita

In this connection, I recall being told by experienced mine operators, on my first visit to Bolivia in 1941, when the mines were still under private ownership, that the Bolivian miner, under competent supervision, was at least the equal of his counterpart in Peru and Chile and, equipment considered, as good as the average miner in many other parts of the world.

Even more vividly, I recall visits with President Paz-Estenssoro to agricultural developments in Santa Cruz in 1956, where farmers, unmistakably Indians from the altiplano, were hewing out a new way of life for themselves and their families in a temperate or semitropical climate under the auspices of one or another of the various conflicting agencies charged with the task of colonization. Here, to one's astonishment, were highland Indians, smilingly and proudly eager to show the visitors their scrupulously clean little houses and carefully tended plots of land, while their children were romping and laughing in the garden as happily as ever children have played since time began. To anyone who has lived in the altiplano, the transformation was incredible. On the highland, the sight of the stolid, unsmiling faces of the Indians, devoid of the faintest glimmer of expression save possibly that of resentment, suspicion, and deep brooding anger, hangs oppressively over the altiplano and brings home to the foreigner the reason for Bolivia's "perpetual secret terror, the lurking dread of an Indian uprising" which has dwelt in the minds of the ruling classes since the great insurrection of Tupac Amaru in 1781. [25]

Then, too, when one reads of "racial oligophrenia," one is forced to recall the extraordinary rise from poverty to wealth of Simón Patiño, a cholo of markedly Indian physiognomy, who was certainly neither stupid, nor lazy, nor without ambition.*

(equal to 2,000 calories on an adult male basis) for La Paz, stressing a relatively high meat consumption and an almost total lack of milk, fresh fruit, and vegetables in the diet. Other estimates run from 1,500 to 2,000 calories, not counting some 500-800 calories daily in alcohol (Harold Osborne, *Bolivia: A Land Divided* [3d ed., London: Oxford University Press, 1964], p. 100). Perhaps, though, the Bolivian Indian is an amazingly tough specimen of humanity well adapted to the struggle for survival, and perhaps his 5 feet 2 inch frame, and his habit of just squatting in apparently complete stupor when tired, do not call for much more than a 2,000-calorie intake. Whether or not there can be any economic progress on such a diet, however, is a pertinent question.

*According to the accepted saga, Patiño, a partner in a small firm with another Bolivian, Sergio Oporto, accepted a mine deed in payment of

And one recalls too a former Bolivian Ambassador to Washington, claiming pure Indian ancestry, handsome, intelligent, and an
able and effective representative of his country; the President
and other members of the Stabilization Council, some of them
of largely Indian origin and all of the highest intelligence and as
hard-working a group of men as could be found anywhere; the
labor leaders, school teachers, representatives, senators, and
party leaders, virtually all of them mestizos, and certainly not
lacking in intelligence although many of them had had little or
no formal education.

Admittedly, I had no contact or means of communicating
with the torpid, sullen, coca-chewing Indians who passed through
the streets like beings from another world, "a survival," as
Keenleyside says, "only partially assimilated of pre-Columbian
America." [26] But, from my stay in La Paz, I can recall much
ignorance and considerable mendacity and thievery, yet certainly no more stupidity than could be found anywhere else in
the world. As for laziness, for many of the Bolivians, not to be
lazy under the Revolutionary Government, with full pay for no
work, would indeed be stupid.

And so, with the courage born of ignorance, I venture a
layman's opinion that the major barriers to the economic advancement of the Bolivian Indian, within the limits of his capacity, are historical and political rather than racial. To put it
another way, Bolivia has shown its capacity to produce men of
intelligence and energy; it has a superabundance of natural resources; and it is only ignorance, and the incompetence and
corruption of its leaders, that have held it back.

------

a debt to the partnership. Oporto considered the mine worthless, and
compelled Patiño to buy out his half share for 5,000 bolivianos, dissolving
the partnership. Patiño thereupon, out of a job, started to work the mine,
and on the Patiño estate may be seen the seven-ton boulder with which
Patiño and his wife crushed the tin out of the ore by rocking the boulder
back and forth on a slab of hard stone, using long poles inserted into holes
in the boulder in order to provide leverage, and shoving pieces of ore
under the boulder as it rocked back and forth (the apparatus is known as a
quimbalete). In one of his few inaccuracies Zondag writes: "Simon Patiño
crushed ore with his wife" (p. 108), which would seem to be an unintended
tribute to her physical toughness. In any event, she lived to bear him
progeny who have married royalty and, as heirs to what was once the
richest tin mine in the world, are conspicuous exemplars of Veblen's theory of the leisure class. The most authoritative account of Patiño's rise
to fortune, however, gives a somewhat different version: Manuel Carrasco, *Simón I. Patiño, un Prócer Industrial* (Paris: Jean Grassin, 1960).

So far as coca-chewing is concerned, the United Nations Commission of Enquiry on the Coca Leaf has reached the conclusion that, while coca-chewing is undeniably harmful and may develop into an addiction rather than a habit, there is no proof that it is productive of racial degeneracy. Further, the degenerative stigmata, deformities, and other congenital abnormalities observed among the coca-chewing Indians of Bolivia and Peru are more likely to be the result of alcoholism, chronic starvation, or syphilis, than of cocaine addiction.[27] In any event, those Andean Indians who have been transplanted to the lowlands have seemingly lost any desire or need for coca (they reacquire it, however, if they return to the altiplano).*

*The older Andean colonists in the lowlands have shown an average gain of eleven pounds; illness has been negligible despite the change in altitude and climate; and alcoholism has decreased (Agnes Nelms Lockwood, *Indians of the Andes* [New York: Carnegie Endowment for International Peace, 1965], p. 390). Whether or not the children born in the lowlands will exceed their parents in stature as a result of better diet remains to be seen, but the average height of the altiplano male Indian is only 5 feet 2 inches while that of kindred tribes in the lowland is 5 feet 3 inches to 5 feet 5 inches (Morris Steggerda, "Anthropometry of South American Indians," in *Handbook of South American Indians* [Washington, D.C.: Smithsonian Institution, 1950], Vol. 6, pp. 63-68).

THE 1952 REVOLUTION AND THE MNR

The history of the Spanish conquest, the struggle for independence, and the subsequent 140 years of government, republican in form but despotic in fact, is too well known, and too far removed from the subject of this study, to warrant a recital. It is admirably condensed in Harold Osborne's *Bolivia: A Land Divided*, which, like other volumes in the series published by the Royal Institute of International Affairs, manages to convey in a remarkably brief compass an authoritative compendium of the country's geography, people, history, government, and economy, with a purity of style and felicity of expression seemingly unattainable by the generality of American authors.*

The war with Paraguay in 1931-35, as a result of which Bolivia lost the greater part of the disputed Chaco territory and her outlet to the Atlantic via the Paraguay River, is of more immediate significance because the majority of Bolivians attribute most of their economic, political, and social difficulties over the past thirty years to the consequences of that conflict. More objectively, however, Osborne concludes that the economic consequences were minor but that "recovery from the moral effects of the war was slower and it left in its wake a lasting sense of exhaustion, bitterness, and frustration." [28]

One reason, not generally known, why the Chaco settlement was less disastrous for Bolivia than it might have been is that the Bolivian government had in its possession, as a consequence of its seizure of the Standard Oil properties in 1936, a part of the confidential geological surveys made by that company (Bolivia acquired the complete surveys in 1942). With this information, the Bolivian negotiator at the Chaco Peace Conference in 1938, by dint of the most astute and persevering diplomacy,

*For a more detailed history, Alfredo Ayala's *Historia General de Bolivia* (La Paz: Ed. Don Bosco, 1958) is a standard text, while *Nueva Historia de Bolivia* by Enrique Finot (2d ed. La Paz: Gisbert y Cia, 1954) attempts a sociological viewpoint. *The Emergence of the Republic of Bolivia*, written by Charles W. Arnade (Gainesville, Fla.: University of Florida Press, 1957), is unique in its objective approach but only carries down to 1825 when "Bolivia began her life as an independent nation... at the threshold of a terrible and frightening history" (p. 205).

managed to have the line of demarkation between the two countries so drawn that all known oil deposits lie on the Bolivian
side of the border, an achievement not unlike Benjamin Franklin's triumph in the Treaty of Paris in obtaining the Mesabi
range and Isle Royale for the United States. As a consequence,
Union Oil Company reportedly spent some $15 million in its
later explorations in the Paraguayan Chaco and encountered
nothing but dry wells, while Bolivia's oil development is the one
bright spot in the economic spectrum.

Origins of the Revolution

More pertinent to the present study is the Bolivian Revolution of 1952 and its aftermath. In fact, the whole history of the
galloping inflation in Bolivia began and ended under the Revolutionary Government, and some of the most pressing problems
confronting Bolivia today are the consequences of that regime.
This is not written in criticism, as the basic troubles lie deep
in the roots of Bolivian history and many of the problems created or accentuated by the Revolution are merely the inevitable
consequences of the social, political, and economic conditions
and blunders of the past.

The 1952 Revolution had its origins in the formation of the
Movimiento Nacional Revolucionario in 1941, financed with
German money supplied "by Nazi and Argentine agents operating from bases in Argentina" (as is stated in the memoirs of
Secretary Cordell Hull), as well as through the German Embassy, German Club, and Trans-Ocean press agency in La
Paz.[29] The objective of the movement, from the Nazi viewpoint,
was the establishment of a strategically located, pro-German
government, hostile to the United States, and closely allied to
the pro-Nazi government of Juan Domingo Perón in Buenos
Aires. The program of the MNR, as the party is still called,
was published in June, 1942, and was violently and expressly
anti-Semitic, antiforeign, and demagogic, calling for "extirpa-
tion" of all private monopolies and the death penalty for speculators, smugglers, and bribe-givers.* At about the same time

---

*To Bolivia's illiterate Indians and mestizos, as a consequence of the
MNR propaganda, all Jews were foreigners and vice versa and equally to
be hated as the cause of all their misery. I recall going through the market in La Paz in 1943 with my wife and a strikingly blond and beautiful

that the MNR was formed, a secret society of army officers was created, known as RADEPA, short for Razón de Patria (The Cause of the Fatherland), similar in concept and structure to the GOU cabala in Argentina which brought Perón to power on June 4, 1943. GOU is variously spelled out as Grupo de Oficiales Unidos (Group of United Officers) and Gobierno, Orden, Unidad (Government, Order, Unity).

The Bolivian conspiracy struck on December 20, 1943, two weeks after the constitutional President, Enrique Peñaranda, had issued a long-delayed declaration of war against Germany, Italy, and Japan. A military junta was set up under RADEPA leader Major Gualberto Villaroel, who, like Perón, was virtually unknown except to his fellow officers in the army cabala. A cabinet was formed, largely dominated by members of the MNR. Under those circumstances, elections for Congress were held in July, 1944, and Congress promptly "elected" Villaroel as President (Article 84 of the Constitution provides for direct election of the President by the electorate).

After a two-year reign of terror, punctuated by kidnappings, tortures, and sudden raids and incarcerations by police officers, a counterrevolution broke out and a mob invaded the presidential palace on July 21, 1946, and murdered the unfortunate Villaroel, who had been deserted by all but two of his MNR and RADEPA companions. Most of the others had fled to Argentina, where they remained in exile until it was judged safe to return. The lamp post on which Villaroel was hanged has since become a venerated monument of the MNR.

A civilian junta was then set up composed of a former judge, Tomás Monje-Gutiérrez, two university professors, and a representative of labor. Six months later, general elections were held. The victor, Dr. Enrique Hertzog, defeated his opponent, Luis Fernando Guachalla, by only 443 votes. There then occurred an event unique in Bolivian history and virtually unheard of in Latin America: the loser congratulated his opponent and urged the public to support the elected government in the interest of national unity.

Two years of constitutional and relatively peaceful government ensued, during which the MNR and other opposition parties

---

American girl, born in Bolivia, and hearing an old chola market woman scream at the latter: *"Judía"* (Jew), to the accompaniment of menacing glares from the other cholas. Such is the force of the zenophobia stirred up by the Nazis, MNR, and communists, which persists to this day.

were permitted freedom of action and of the press, with the result that, in Congressional elections held in May, 1949, the MNR obtained a decisive victory. A few days later, President Hertzog, who was ailing, turned the reins of government over to Vice-President Mamerto Urriolagoitía who, highhandedly and without color of law, placed the newly elected Senator from Potosí, Juan Lechín-Oquendo, under arrest.

Lechín was the "Maximum Leader" of the Mine Workers' Federation (Federación Sindical de Trabajadores Mineros de Bolivia) and an official of the Workers' Revolutionary Party (Partido Obrero Revolucionario or POR), which was an outgrowth of the Tupac Amaru, an ultranationalistic secret society formed in Argentina by a group of Bolivians, who had fled from Bolivia at the time of the Chaco War. It was officially affiliated with Leon Trotsky's Fourth International, and its political objectives — important because they represent the never-repudiated principles of the MNR — were set forth in November, 1946, in the "Declaration of Pulacayo" which proclaimed, among other things

> ... the proletariat is the social revolutionary class par excellence and ... the mine workers are the most advanced and combatant sector of the national proletariat.... The workers must cooperate in bringing about the indispensable bourgeois-democratic revolution, for the purpose of eliminating all vestiges of feudalism and freeing the country from economic imperialism. But the bourgeois-democratic revolution must be regarded as only a step toward the proletarian revolution. True democracy can only be brought about through the dictatorship of the proletariat.... [The workers must] eliminate the system of private property ... must not [compromise with their] class enemies or with the representatives of Yankee imperialism ... must demand the institution of a sliding scale of wages, so that wage rates would automatically move upwards with every rise in the cost of living ... must equip themselves to run the mines effectively without the assistance of the owners ... must arm themselves to the teeth against the armed bourgeoisie [the Army].... Direct mass action, especially through strikes and the occupation of the mines, is the principal means by which the revolution of the workers can be secured.... Every strike must be started with the intention of converting it into a general strike ... (translation from the U.N. Keenleyside report).[30]

With the arrest and deportation of Lechín, the miners at Patiño's Catavi mine went out on strike and captured a number of American mine engineers as hostages. The Army attempted to free the hostages, and the miners retaliated by killing two of the Americans, wounding two others, and raping the wife of one of them. The Department of State expressed its displeasure, and there followed the "Massacre of Catavi," with a reported 40 dead and 83 wounded, presumably including both miner and Army casualties.

The MNR thereupon joined forces with the Trotskyite POR and, apparently with funds and weapons from Argentina, succeeded in overthrowing the civilian authorities in Santa Cruz, Cochabamba, Oruro, Potosí, and Sucre. Víctor Paz-Estenssoro, later to become President of the Republic, was made chief of the Revolutionary junta.

The rebellion was suppressed, however, and Urriolagoitía served out most of the remaining two years of his term in comparative peace. Meanwhile a coalition of trade unions and leftist parties known as COSPI (Coalición de Organismos Sindicales y Partidos de Izquierda) was formed by the MNR, POR, and PIR (Partido de la Izquierda Revolucionaria), a Communist-oriented party headed by José Antonio Arze-Murillo, who had once taught in New York's Communist Party Jefferson School and was the erudite translator of a book on socialism under the Inca Empire. The PIR was later dissolved, its members splitting between the MNR and the Partido Comunista Boliviano.*

*As is usual in Latin America, the Partido Comunista Boliviano is the only party which is openly and avowedly communist, following the party line to the letter. In 1952, it was Stalinist, later Khruschevist, and at present there is dissension within the ranks as a consequence of the apparent split between Peking and Moscow. To a Communist Party member, except when Moscow decrees a people's coalition (*frente popular*), a deviationist from the party line is more to be abhorred than a member of the *bourgeoisie*, who is despised rather than hated. Hence, conversely, the members of the Trotskyite POR and the socialist (as defined in the footnote on p. 16n) PIR, and the members of the MNR (who in private conversation and in their speeches for home consumption are avowedly socialist or Marxist and violently anti-imperialistic and anti-Yankee) can honestly declare that they are anti-communist. Many of them sincerely believe that their brand of socialism is the best insurance against communism and the best assurance of "democratic" rule, by which they mean government by an authoritarian state acting as the representative of the masses. The MNR, while Nazi in its inception and in the source of its

This leftist alliance was reinforced in May, 1951, three days before the election, by a coalition between the MNR, the Communist Party, and the Mine Workers' Federation (FSTMB), on a platform which bound them to the following line of actions:

1. To support the Paz-Siles ticket (the Communist Party had originally proposed Lechín as candidate)
2. To oppose the "oligarchy" and "Yankee imperialism"
3. To unite the people and the workers in a single organization of trade unions (which later developed into the COB, the Confederación Obrera Boliviana, that governed Bolivia jointly with the MNR from 1952 to the end of 1964)
4. To support the Communist Party in its struggle against the United States
5. To nationalize the mines, take over all foreign-owned properties, and put through an "agrarian reform"
6. To ensure a victory by the MNR, *whether by election or by force*
7. To guaranty the Communist Party full political rights, although it would not take part directly in the government *because of reasons of international "discretion"*

There were five other less significant points of like tendency in the program, all published in the La Paz press.

In the elections, on May 5, 1951, the Víctor Paz-Estenssoro and Hernán Siles-Zuazo ticket got 43 per cent of the votes (Paz claims he got 79 per cent). The four candidates of the right, center, and left of center, including the government candidate, together received 53 per cent of the votes. Article 88 of the Bolivian Constitution requires the President to be elected by an absolute majority, failing which Congress must choose a President from among the three leading candidates. The Congressional elections had overwhelmingly supported the government

---

initial financing, is distinctly nationalistic and socialistic in the Latin American sense of the term, as was, of course, the National Socialist (Nazi) party in Germany. To those Americans who believe in the primacy of the individual rather than in the supremacy of the state, and who use the term democracy loosely when they mean a republic, the Latin American definition of the words communism, socialism, and democracy, is confusing, and they are likely to believe that the MNR government in Bolivia was "liberal," which it was not, in any sense of the term. As the Bolivian socialist, Vicente Mendoza-Lopez, states: "Bolivian socialism means the disappearance of individualistic liberalism" (*Las Finanzas en Bolivia y la Estrategia Capitalista* [La Paz: Escuela Tipográfica Salesiana, 1940]).

party, which had a nearly two-to-one lead in Congress over the MNR, the remaining parties having only a few scattered votes. Thus, President Urriolagoitía might have safely entrusted the decision to the legislature without imperiling his party's position, and should constitutionally have done so. Instead, perhaps under the fear of pressure from Paz-Estenssoro's militant plurality, Urriolagoitía abdicated and turned the government over to a military junta, contrary to his obligation under the Constitution.

There followed, as was to be expected, a period of plotting and conspiracy until finally, on April 9, 1952, the rebellion broke out, with the police force, carabineers, and the armed forces of the MNR and communists lined up against the army, which was outnumbered, disarmed, and disorganized by the desertion of the Minister of Government. During the course of the conflict, the minister hedged his bets by then deserting the rebels, and Siles, a lawyer and university professor, took command and led the Revolution to a successful conclusion. With the surrender of the Army regiments in La Paz and Sucre, the struggle was over, and Paz-Estenssoro returned from Argentina to assume the Presidency, although without the constitutional requirement of election by Congress. Siles, at all times loyal to his comrades in the MNR, stepped down from the command to assume the Vice-Presidency, while Lechín, retaining his leadership over the Mine Workers' Federation, was appointed Minister of Mines and Petroleum.[31]

Such, in sum, was the origin of the Revolutionary Government of 1952, which remained in power until 1964 under the leadership of the Paz-Siles-Lechín triumvirate (for the aftermath, see Part VII). This background is presented as factually and succinctly as possible, inasmuch as, without some comprehension of the political forces and personalities behind the present situation, it is impossible to understand the events leading up to the galloping inflation of 1952-56, and the problems of stabilization and their aftermath.*

*For a more detailed account of the origins of the MNR and of events up to May, 1956, the reader is referred to *Un Pueblo en La Cruz* by Alberto Ostria-Gutiérrez (2d. ed., Santiago, Chile: Editorial del Pacífico, 1956), translated as *The Tragedy of Bolivia* by Eithne Golden (New York: Devin-Adair, 1958), condensed and toned down for American consumption. Although the book is partisan and vehemently opposed to the MNR, it is on the whole accurate so far as I have been able to check its factual contents.

There have been three presidential elections in Bolivia between 1952 and 1966, all held under an August 2, 1952, decree which, for the first time, gave Bolivia's illiterate majority the right to vote. Answering the criticism of Bolivian conservatives that illiterates are unqualified to vote intelligently, a Chilean journalist commented with some wisdom and more wit that if, in 300 years, the literate governing class had been unable to teach the Indians how to read or write, it was high time to give the Indians a chance to govern and teach themselves.

There was and could be no organized opposition to the candidate of the MNR, with many of the leaders of the opposition parties in exile, and with freedom of the press curtailed either by the sacking and suppression of some newspapers or by the fear of reprisals against those independent papers which continued publishing. Even so friendly an author as R. J. Alexander writes in *The Bolivian National Revolution:* "So far as the author knows, no Communists were jailed by the Paz Estenssoro or Siles administrations ... a few P.O.R. members were jailed in 1953, but they were soon released ... Paz took a much sterner attitude toward the right-wing opposition."[32]

But quite apart from those limitations, there can be no doubt that the MNR enjoyed the support of the great majority of the Bolivian people and, with universal suffrage, the illiterate masses were able for the first time to express their views. Elections were thus a matter of negotiation within the inner circles of the MNR, and the election itself meant merely the confirmation of the choice of the party leaders.*

In the first election under the auspices of the MNR, in June, 1956, there was no question as to who the presidential candidate

---

For a diametrically opposite viewpoint, "frankly sympathetic" to the MNR but attempting to be objective, the reader is referred to Robert J. Alexander's *The Bolivian National Revolution* (New Brunswick, N.J.: Rutgers University Press, 1958), which I have drawn on for much of this material, particularly from pp. 29-31, 37, 41, 215, and 224-41. Biographies of the Revolutionary triumvirate are to be found in the *New York Times,* June 6, 1960, and October 26, 1962 (Paz); April 21, 1959 (Siles); December 14, 1963 (Lechín).

*In November, 1956, at one of the Stabilization Council meetings, Dr. Siles asked me for an explanation of the functioning of our voting machines. I explained at length, concluding, perhaps with some show of pride, that the machines enabled us to know the results of the election within hours after the close of the balloting. Dr. Siles, with his always delightful sense of humor, commented that that was primitive — "In Bolivia, we know the results of the elections before we hold them."

would be — Hernán Siles-Zuazo, the hero of the 1952 Revolution, supported by Paz-Estenssoro, Lechín, and all factions of the party. Because of the necessity of continued U.S. aid, and Lechín's openly anti-American posture, Ñuflo Chávez-Ortiz, the Minister of Agriculture and leader of the peasants' militia, was chosen by the MNR as the vice-presidential candidate. Lechín was content to accept the presidency of the Senate, but continued as head of the Mine Workers' Federation, commander of the miners' militia, and one of the three most powerful figures in the party directorate of the MNR and in the controlling council of the COB.

The elections took place almost without incident,* and Dr. Siles was duly inaugurated on August 6, 1956, with the acclaim of the vast majority of the Bolivian masses, but not strictly in accordance with the Bolivian Constitution, which provides for a four-year lapse before a Vice-President can be elected as President or re-elected as Vice-President (Art. 85). Dr. Paz-Estenssoro was appointed Ambassador to the Court of St. James's. (For the results of the 1960 and 1964 elections, and events down to and since the *coup d'état* of November 3, 1964, see Chapter 21.)

The Legacy of the Revolution

The basic problems in the Bolivian situation in June, 1956, when I was charged with stabilizing the currency, were largely consequences of the 1952 Revolution although, as in the case of the galloping inflation of 1952-56, most of them had their origins deep in Bolivian history. The violence and cruelty set forth in Ostria-Gutiérrez' *Un Pueblo en la Cruz* was nothing new to that troubled country, and corruption in government, accentuated as it was by the multiple exchange rates and

---

*In the polling places in and around La Paz, it was a moving sight to witness the enfranchised Indians waiting in almost interminable lines to exercise their right to vote, with the same stolidity and patience with which they squatted and waited in equally extended lines to exercise their right to eat. In the voting lines, however, there was no selling of places in line. Indians, cholos, and whites waited in the same long lines to the ballot boxes where they deposited their colored slips of paper to denote their party, for there could be no question of reading printed names or even symbols; a pink, blue, or white slip sufficed to designate their choice, and to ensure party regularity.

controls of the inflationary period, was by no means a Revolutionary development.

Illustrative of the pervasiveness of the abuses under the multiple exchange rate system, and of the problems faced by the council, is an incident that occurred at a meeting on July 2, 1956, with four high officials of the Bolivian government to discuss the first draft of a decree establishing the National Monetary Stabilization Council. Because of the tremendous burden of work to which the council members would be subject, in addition to their regular duties as members of the Cabinet, etc., the draft proposed that the *voting* members of the council (i.e., the Bolivian members) should receive a fee of Bs. 100,000 for each full meeting attended, with a maximum of Bs. 5,000,000 a year (say $700 at the then rate of Bs. 7,000 = $1). The requirement of a *full* meeting was stressed in view of prior experience with directors' meetings elsewhere in Latin America where a director would make an *acta de presencia,* collect his fee, and depart immediately because of an urgent meeting with a cabinet minister or other reason. The conferees laughingly agreed that this was a necessary proviso in Bolivia as well, but one of those present suggested that it would not look well for a council bent on reducing government expenditures to commence by giving themselves attendance fees. This argument was cut short by another conferee who said tersely: "Shut up! When Dr. Eder finishes his work we shall not be able to import a truck a month and live comfortably on the proceeds."

What this meant was that the highest officials in the Bolivian government had been accustomed to importing a truck each month at the official rate of Bs. 190 per dollar. A $6,000 truck could be bought for Bs. 1,140,000, equivalent to about $160 at the then rate of exchange. It could then be sold for the equivalent of perhaps $10,000. At most, only two of the conferees would conceivably have been involved in such transactions, although it was implied (and later confirmed) that at least a dozen others of equal rank had engaged in similar operations. The truck transactions were undoubtedly *legal* under the peculiar legislation then in force and were not inconsistent with prevailing ethical standards in Bolivia. My dismay at this revelation, however, must have been evident to President-elect Siles, who was one of the conferees, as he plucked me by the sleeve and whispered that he would like to see me later at his office. At that meeting, Dr. Siles gave assurance that one of the first acts of his administration would be to do away with this whole business of *camiones y cupos* (trucks and "quotas," meaning by the latter the foreign exchange and import quotas which enabled the recipients, among other abuses, to black-market a large proportion of the U.S. aid commodities). These abuses were eliminated by the stabilization measures which were repeatedly heralded as a "return to morality" — the word "return" perhaps implying an overly optimistic view of pre-existing conditions.*

Since colonial times, as Osborne says, the remuneration of a government official has always been "too small in relation to his duties to offer any temptation to honesty... There has too often been a feeling from ministers downward that as the tenure of office is likely to be uncertain and short, the profits of office must be rapid and sure."[33] This condition, unfortunately, has held true throughout the greater part of Bolivia's history. A U.N. report states that higher salaries and assurance of tenure would not succeed in raising ethical standards.[34]

On the other hand, after many months of intimate association with the members of the Bolivian National Monetary Stabilization Council, I say without reservation that those members who served on the council continuously from its first session through June, 1957, were, without exception, men of unimpeachable integrity and of the highest devotion and loyalty to their country's interests. In view of the attacks that have been made upon some of them by their compatriots, I consider it a duty to history to say that Bolivia may well be proud of those citizens and of others, too numerous to mention, in Congress, in the

---

*Some readers may question whether this and numerous other specific examples of corruption, incompetence, violence, etc., are not too personal to be included in a study which attempts to be objective. The reason for their inclusion is that in all too many reports on Latin America, violence, corruption, and so forth are referred to in general terms that tend to minimize their importance. These specific instances of which I have personal knowledge are deemed essential to bring home to the reader the environment under which the stabilization measures had to be enacted and carried out. The enemies of monetary stabilization in any country where inflation has run rampant (at least in Latin America) are the government officials and their associates who were responsible for the inflation and profited from its opportunities (see Patch, "Bolivia: U.S. Assistance in a Revolutionary Setting," in *Social Change in Latin America Today* [New York: Council on Foreign Relations, 1960], p. 132). Names are omitted, here and elsewhere, as it would be unfair to single out for opprobrium a few cases to which I can testify in person, when such cases are not the exception but the norm.

Cabinet, and in various government enterprises, who cooperated with the council in its task of stabilization.

The militia and the Co-Gobierno

Another political heritage of the Revolution was the virtual emasculation of the army and air force which were reduced to some 6,500 career personnel and a few thousand conscripts, and transformed into the "Army of the National Revolution" *whose loyalty was sworn to the MNR party.* Its weapons were largely turned over to, or seized by, the "peoples' militia,"* consisting chiefly of an estimated 40,000 men in the peasants' (*campesinos*) militia under the command of Ñuflo Chávez-Ortiz; anywhere from 10,000 to 50,000 men — the figures vary according to the year and the informant — in the miners' militia headed by Juan Lechín-Oquendo; and perhaps 20,000 in the MNR militia who were loyal to Siles. There were also some 2,000 men enrolled in the railway workers' militia, and about 3,000 in the factory workers' militia.[35] The carabineers, a national constabulary of perhaps some 2,000 officers and enlisted men, had supported the Revolution and were permitted to retain their weapons. Of all these forces, the miners' militia undoubtedly enjoyed a preponderance of power in 1956 by reason of the discipline of a hard core of some 10,000 men, and the ability to muster a comparatively well-armed, well-trained force in Oruro, La Paz, or elsewhere on the altiplano, in a minimum space of time. The municipal police forces were unarmed and negligible as instruments of law and order. †

*Elimination or infiltration of the armed forces, and their replacement by a "people's militia," has been a common ploy of the communist or proto-communist parties in Latin America since World War II, as was witnessed in Cuba under Castro. It was attempted by Brazil's "left-wing radicals" who proposed to arm several key union groups in Rio de Janeiro, Brasilia, and elsewhere, prior to the Army *coup d'état* that overthrew President João Goulart (Juan de Onís, *New York Times,* April 15, 1964). Thus, in recent years, it has been the Army which has played the unaccustomed and unsuitable role of a bulwark of democracy against subversion in various countries of Latin America, e.g., Argentina, Brazil, Peru, and, in 1964, Bolivia.

†As an example of the power of the militia, in September, 1956, following a press conference in which I announced my conviction that Bolivia would succeed in stabilizing its currency, the American Embassy received reports that there would be a "demonstration" to impress both me and the government that the miners were in charge. At the insistence of the

Allied with this circumstance was the fact that the government was no longer the simple structure of Congress, the Presidency, and the Judiciary, envisaged in the Constitution, but a government in which power was in theory equally divided between the constitutional authorities and the COB (the Bolivian Workers' Confederation). Officially, it was a Co-Gobierno or, as its enemies called it, a COB-Gobierno. Certain ministers (e.g., mines and petroleum, and labor) were appointed by and owed their allegiance to the miners' Federation under Lechín and not to the President; others (e.g., agriculture and rural affairs) were appointed and controlled by the peasants' union under Ñuflo Chávez. The balance of power shifted from one side to another from time to time, but in Oruro and the mining area there was no doubt that Lechín was in control, while Ñuflo Chávez proclaimed before his downfall: "Siles may govern in La Paz, but east of the Andes I am the law," even threatening to have the President thrashed if he should venture into Santa Cruz.[36]

Other institutional factors resulting from the 1952 Revolution presented a further stumbling block in the path of stabilization and economic recovery. First and foremost, of course, was the inflation itself and the steps taken to combat it, with all the unhappy consequences emanating from those measures, including the perversion of the functions of the Central Bank. There were also the government mining corporation (COMIBOL), which took over the mines confiscated from private ownership; the Mining Bank; the government petroleum corporation (YPFB); the Bolivian development corporation; the Social Security Administration (CNSS); agrarian reform; and U.S. aid; all these institutions either owed their existence to the Revolution or were fundamentally changed as a consequence of it. Each of these institutional factors will be discussed in turn to complete the background picture against which the problems of monetary inflation and stabilization must be viewed.

---

chargé d'affaires, my family and I spent the night in the Embassy residence. That evening two trucks full of armed members of the militia threw sticks of dynamite around the square facing the Embassy. I chatted with the miners, most of whom were drunk, and suggested that they throw their dynamite into the square away from the buildings. The striking fact is that the Army and police, with full knowledge of what was to occur, never appeared on the scene, and the President later told me that if he had intervened there would have been broken heads instead of merely broken windows.

Inflation and its consequences

Even prior to the Revolution, the Bolivian currency — the boliviano — which had been quoted at Bs. 2.40 to the dollar at the close of World War I, had fallen in successive stages until, by the beginning of 1952, it reached an official rate of Bs. 60 to the dollar and a free market rate of Bs. 210, despite the futile attempts of one government after another to peg the money to successively increasing official rates of exchange.[37] It remained, however, for the MNR to bring the debasement of the currency to a rampant stage, and by July, 1956, the value of the boliviano at the "street rate" reached a low of Bs. 14,000.[38]

Actually, however, an infinite number of exchange rates existed, varying from the free rate of Bs. 14,000 to the official rate of Bs. 190 to the dollar. Víctor Paz-Estenssoro,* the first President of the Revolutionary Government, had attempted to stay the inflation in May, 1953, by enacting a series of so-called "stabilization measures" on the advice of the United Nations advisors to the Central Bank and Ministry of Finance, viz.:

1. Devaluation of the boliviano from Bs. 60 to the dollar to Bs. 190
2. Creation of a "Stabilization Office" †
3. Establishment of a free market for the purchase and sale of foreign exchange in transactions not covered at the official rate (principally for the invisible items of trade such as tourist expenditures, etc.)
4. Foreign exchange surcharges of 50 per cent or 100 per cent of the CIF value of imports
5. Price-fixing on basic foodstuffs
6. Rent controls
7. Drastic restrictions on credits to the private sector
8. Wage increases to compensate for rising living costs‡

*Throughout the book, the hyphen is used (although this is not the general practice), to avoid confusion for the reader not accustomed to Spanish double names in which the father's surname is placed after the baptismal name, followed by the mother's family name. Thus, it is correct to refer to President Paz, but never to President Estenssoro.

†The function of this office, under the direction of the Superintendent of Banks, was to stabilize prices and wages. Its powers were solely advisory, and it was foredoomed to failure in the absence of a fundamental approach to the problem of monetary depreciation, which would attack causes rather than consequences.

‡Wage increases by government decree are usual in Latin America. In Bolivia, from March, 1954, to July, 1956, wages had been increased by

This series of decrees, as President Paz explained, was designed (1) to put a halt to what he termed a galloping inflation, (2) to ensure the profitable operation of the mines taken over by the government from the private owners, and (3) to encourage gold mining and private saving by the minting of gold coins to be exchanged for gold ore and dust at a modest seignorage charge. At the same time, the decrees were expected to replace the "chaotic and completely irrational" system of differential rates of exchange with a single rate — the *cambio único* — and, in the President's words, to eliminate the business speculators, corrupt government officials, and grafters (*coimeros*) who thrived on that system.[39]

Brave words! But from May, 1953, until the end of the presidential term in August, 1956, decree followed decree in stages of increasing severity, in the vain attempt to put a stop to what was by then a truly galloping inflation with no end in sight. In the course of that three-year period, the Bolivian exchange system reached a situation that the U.N. Economic Commission for Latin America could only characterize as "anarchy, with disastrous consequences for the general economy of the country."[40]

For example, the commodities and equipment donated to Bolivia by the U.S. government were, under contracts signed between the two governments, supposed to be sold by the Bolivian government to the public at prices reasonably close to world market prices, and the proceeds held as "counterpart funds" to be used for economic development and other mutually agreed purposes. The Central Bank was required to hold 70 per cent of the counterpart funds for Bolivian government uses; 15 per cent was for U.S. government use in Bolivia; and 15 per cent was set aside for "Cooley Act" (P.L. 480) loans to U.S. investors or exporters.

Instead of pricing the goods at fair prices, however, the Bolivian government computed the dollar value of these products at the official exchange rate or at multiples of that rate far below the actual free market rate of exchange. The *average* rate of conversion for the creation of counterpart funds worked

---

successive decrees 48 per cent, 70 per cent, 60 per cent, and 40 per cent (Zondag report, p. 172), and in each case, as President Siles was accustomed to say, wages went up by the staircase while prices went up on the elevator.

out at Bs. 217 in 1954 (free rate: 1,890); Bs. 362 in 1955 (free rate: 4,260); and Bs. 810 in 1956 (free rate in June: 7,360).[41]

To cite a specific example, in mid-1956 the cost of imported rice placed in La Paz was about $130 per metric ton (6 cents U.S. a pound). The Ministry of Economy would sell this rice to the government mining corporation and other privileged agencies or private companies at Bs. 510 to the dollar, or Bs. 66,304 ($9) a ton. It sold to other middlemen at Bs. 876 to the dollar or Bs. 114,000 ($15.50) a ton. The intention was that the middlemen would sell the rice to the public at Bs. 130 a kilo (Bs. 130,000 a ton), which would work out at $0.008 a pound, but, as the black market export price was five times this figure, very little of that rice ever reached the public.[42]

Other rates of exchange were also prevalent. To stimulate exports of products other than minerals, exporters were given certificates which permitted them to import various kinds of merchandise, in part at the official rate and in part at the auction rate of exchange. The subsequent profits on the import operations, even at the auction rate of exchange, were such as to amount in effect to a subsidy on imports (which, in Bolivia's economic situation, should have been curtailed) and to stimulating exports of certain commodities at prices that represented a loss to the economy as a whole.*

As an example, one exporter shipped whole Brazil nuts from Bolivia's tropical jungles to Cochabamba by a Bolivian government airline, which operated at a heavy loss despite the

---

*Under decrees promulgated in March, November, and December, 1955, exporters of rubber, brazil nuts, cocoa beans, and lumber were permitted to import machinery and other capital goods up to the value of 40 per cent of their exports (and general merchandise up to a like percentage), at the auction rate of exchange which they were permitted to purchase from the Central Bank in advance, knowing that, by the time the goods were actually imported, their value in bolivianos would be far higher than their boliviano cost. The remaining 20 per cent would be in foodstuffs of prime necessity, imported at the official rate of exchange and saleable to licensed middlemen at controlled prices, at which point the goods would largely be diverted to the black market. Exporters of other products were permitted to import 60 per cent in capital goods and 40 per cent in general merchandise, at the auction rate, and to dispose of the goods in the free market. In both cases, import permits were transferable up to July 21, 1956, when the privilege of transferability was annulled by decree. (Zondag, chap. iv; annex, pp. 1-3.) As a consequence of this decree, importers and exporters largely lost interest in these "compensation" transactions, with the result that export smuggling increased, particularly in the case of shipments of forest products to Brazil.

subsidy of gasoline and supplies purchased at the 190 rate. The outer pods, which are the size of a coconut, were cracked in a "factory" in Cochabamba, and the nuts in the inner shells in the form familiar to consumers in the United States, were exported for sale in world markets at prices far below the real cost of transportation. The exporter thus privileged to engage in this operation would make his major profit by using or selling his import certificates. Manifestly, a product as bulky, heavy, and cheap as whole Brazil nuts cannot support the cost of air transportation at normal freight rates.

An elaborate system of foreign exchange surcharges was set up to offset in part the windfall profits resulting from importations at the 190 or other privileged rate. The surcharge, known as a *revertible* because the exchange profit "reverted" in part to the government, took the form of a payment made by the importer to the Ministry of Economy subsequent to importation of the goods into Bolivia. This surcharge was intended to bring the landed price of the merchandise up to world market levels and thus discourage its re-export. In effect, it was a sales tax. However, as the amount of the payment was fixed by the Ministry on each transaction, the opportunity for favoritism and special privilege was not lacking, with the result that some importations were made without *revertible* payments while other imports of similar merchandise carried heavy charges.[43] Long delays in payment of the *revertibles* by the importer were equivalent to an interest-free loan from the government to the importer, while the rapid depreciation of the Bolivian currency meant that the importer could ultimately pay the tax for practically nothing. The list of debtors to the Central Bank was virtually a roll call of Bolivia's leading *políticos* and their agents. The system, inaugurated in mid-1954, was abolished in March, 1956, and replaced by simple surcharges, but unpaid *revertible* accounts continued to hamper the stabilization plans throughout the remainder of the year and well into 1957.

The government oil company (YPFB) received a so-called "subsidy" by being given Bs. 1,600 per dollar on its exports, which was above the Bs. 190 official rate but far below the number of bolivianos the YPFB should have received in a free market. The government mining corporation likewise got a subsidy rate of Bs. 1,010, while the private miners, who were compelled to export their output through the government mining bank were given a subsidy rate of Bs. 1,310, which was largely diminished in practice by the reportedly dubious assessments of the metal content of their ores and other sharp practices attributed to the bank.[44]

What with the various rates of exchange, charges and sur-charges applicable to different classes of exports and imports (and varying among different exporters and importers depending upon their respective positions of privilege), and the "compen-sation" system of profitless exports linked with profitable im-ports at the privileged exchange rates, there were literally hundreds of rates of exchange in force by mid-1956, applicable to the visible and invisible transactions in Bolivia's balance of international payments, in lieu of the single rate of exchange — the *cambio único* — promised by President Víctor Paz-Estenssoro on introducing the "stabilization" measures of May 14, 1953.*

To forestall a continuing rise in living costs, the govern-ment imposed a series of new rent and price controls and a prohibition on foodstuff exports, accompanied by drastic crimi-nal penalties which, if they could have been enforced, would have led to the incarceration of a sizable portion of the Bolivian population. Instead, they led merely to an intensification of the speculation, graft, and corruption previously noted by the Pres-ident, and on a scale and pervasiveness probably never before known in the history of the country.

As smuggling for export proved safer and more profitable than local black-marketing, not only staple commodities such as sugar and flour entered the stream of contraband, but even bread — some 200,000 loaves a day — was smuggled from La Paz by car, truck, and grass-thatched canoe, across Lake Titicaca to Peru, possibly the only instance in history where so bulky and perishable a commodity as bread has ever entered the smuggling trade on such a scale. But with the legally controlled price in Bolivia at Bs. 30 a loaf (actually an oversize roll weighing about a fifth of a pound, or 90 grams) and free market prices equivalent to Bs. 500 a loaf across the border in Peru, such smuggling became inevitable. It is estimated that some 40,000 head of cattle and some 20,000 sheep, with a total value of around $4.2 million, were smuggled out of the country each year, while imports of cattle, mostly coming from Argentina

*See W. John R. Woodley, "Multiple Currency Practices," *Fund and Bank Review: Finance and Development,* III (June, 1966), 113-17 for a discussion of the unfavorable effects of a multiple currency system, in general, by an International Monetary Fund economist.

under barter treaty arrangements and consisting largely of previously smuggled Bolivian cattle, amounted to approximately $4.3 million per annum.*

The Foreign Minister gave the council a specific example of tractors imported for government use on short-term credits at the Bs. 190 rate and then smuggled immediately out of the country for perhaps a 3,000 per cent profit, while the Minister of Mines reported on shipments of tin smuggled to Brazil, in both cases with the connivance of high political leaders.

A traffic check on the Santa Cruz to Corumbá railway revealed that 95 per cent of the freight carried from Bolivia to Brazil on this line consisted of articles of prime necessity, including coffee, sugar, rice, hides, and imported powdered milk, smuggled out of Bolivia in return for medicines and textiles which likewise entered into the black market trade, thanks to the exchange rate differentials. At least one-third and possibly as much as two-thirds of U.S. aid was black-marketed, and food scarcities in Bolivia by mid-1956 were acute, approaching the famine conditions that prevailed in 1953 at the inception of the aid program. †

The miners, however, were able to purchase U.S. aid commodities and other imported goods at the commissaries of the government mining corporation (COMIBOL), in an amount equivalent on the average to double the value of their wages, and those purchases were made, not at the official rate of Bs. 190 to the dollar, but at the equivalent of Bs. 60 to the dollar, which

---

*I saw a drove of cattle entering the country from Argentina at Yacuiba in July, 1956 (presumably legally and at the official exchange rate of Bs. 190), and not far east of there, at Villazón, another herd being driven back into Argentina (presumably illegally and at a considerable profit), the steers practically following their own tails in what may be called a graphic illustration of a vicious circle.

†Senators Mike Mansfield (Democrat, Montana) and Bourke B. Hickenlooper (Republican, Iowa), both of whom had visited Bolivia in 1956, submitted a perceptive and informative joint report in which they denounced the lack of adequate controls over the disbursement of U.S. aid and stated that an unknown but substantial percentage of U.S. foodstuffs, ostensibly destined to relieve starvation in Bolivia, was being smuggled across the border to Peru (*El Diario,* March 12, 1957; U.S. Congress, Senate, *Technical Cooperation in Andes Countries of South America,* 85th Cong., 1st Sess., 1957). The estimate that between one-third and two-thirds of U.S. aid was diverted to the black market (either sold locally or smuggled abroad) was made unofficially in June, 1956, by Ross Moore, Chief, USOM/Bolivia.

was the official rate of exchange at the time the Revolutionary Government first came into power in April, 1952. (Under the May, 1953, "stabilization" decrees, Bs. 190 was to have been the sole official rate of exchange, but the miners threatened violence if prices were raised at the commissaries, which were thus forced to continue pricing goods at the Bs. 60 rate.)

The mining corporation's losses on these purchases, representing the difference between the Bs. 60 rate and the Bs. 190 or other official rate that the corporation was compelled to pay, amounted to 50 per cent more than the total payrolls. The merchandise that the miners were thus able to purchase at a fraction of the true value (for example, a pound of meat for $\frac{1}{7}$ of a U.S. cent per pound, of flour for $\frac{1}{18}$ of a cent, of rice for $\frac{1}{19}$ of a cent, and of sugar for $\frac{1}{14}$ of a cent) was for the most part sold by them almost immediately to the black marketeers and smugglers who, with the middlemen for U.S. aid and dealers in import quotas at the Bs. 190 rate, formed the hard core of the political supporters of the MNR.[45]

Foreigners and the well-to-do could, with difficulty, purchase a limited supply of food at black-market prices, for example, Bs. 8,000 to 10,000 a kilo for beef of incredibly poor quality and of random cut, as Bolivian butchers commence slicing and chopping at one end of the animal, and end at the other, with no niceties of sirloin, rib, flank, or chuck. Even at the free market rate of exchange, this worked out at some 54 cents a pound which, considering the quality of the meat and the amount of bone and fat, was higher than the New York price at the time. Many butchers had no scales, and scales were seldom accurate, so that buyers often bought more thumb than meat. Chickens, eggs, bread, and fruit were more easily come by in the Indian markets out of town, and occasionally an Indian would trudge down from the altiplano with a dead lamb around his neck for sale; but all these rather questionable comestibles were offered at prices certainly not below those of the New York markets.[46]

For the poor — and in 1956 that included conscientious government officials, university professors, and the vast majority of the middle and upper classes, as well as most laborers and salaried employees — black-market prices were prohibitive. For those not enjoying the luxury of the below-cost commissaries — in other words, for all but perhaps 80,000 out of some 600,000 heads of families — the government provided posts in the markets and at various places throughout the major cities where meat, bread, sugar, cigarettes, and other commodities, in part the bounty of U.S. aid, could be purchased at well below world market prices.[47]

The amount of such supplies available was so low, however, that the most striking sight to greet the eye of the visitor to La Paz in June of 1956 was that of people patiently waiting in endless lines at every place of sale, knowing that long before the end of the line was reached the supply of whatever commodity was on sale would be exhausted.

A new profession arose in 1955 and 1956, that of *coleros*, persons whose sole occupation was to wait on queues (*colas*), not knowing nor caring what merchandise might be on sale at the head of the line, but merely that it was sure to be something that could be eaten, smoked, or worn, and hence resold at a profit or, even simpler, that the *colero's* place on line could be sold to some anxious and more prosperous latecomer. Thus, in a country where increased production was the crying need, the majority of the Indian farmers and potential laborers living near the urban centers of population found that they could spend their time more profitably and with less exertion as *coleros*, smugglers, or black-market middlemen than as workers in the fields, mines, or factories.[48]

Less apparent to the casual observer, but at the root of Bolivia's monetary difficulties, lay these factors:

1. An increase in government borrowing, chiefly from the Central Bank, from Bs. 2,730 million net at the beginning of 1952 to Bs. 90,450 million on June 30, 1956
2. A consequent increase in the money supply from Bs. 6,920 million to Bs. 112,990 million over the same period
3. An increase in living costs from a base of 100 to either 1,945 or 3,593, depending upon which index is used
4. An increase in the "free market" dollar quotation from Bs. 190 to Bs. 7,360, rising shortly thereafter to Bs. 14,000 to the dollar
5. A drop in gold and foreign exchange reserves from $34.5 million to a stated figure of $1.6 million which, on investigation, proved to be a minus quantity
6. A $30 million flight of capital
7. An increase in current indebtedness abroad from $4.5 million to between $48 and $65 million, and in the total foreign debt from $300 million to upwards of $500 million (see Chapter 8)

The nexus between government borrowing and the rise in bank note circulation is graphically shown in Figure I, which also reveals the comparatively negligible importance of credits to the private sector (the difference between total borrowing and government borrowing). There can be no doubt about what was cause and what was effect. The Central Bank could certainly not compel the government to borrow, but the government could and did compel the Central Bank to lend, and, since the bank had exhausted all other resources, it was forced to issue bank notes. This in turn resulted in an increase in deposits and hence in total money supply, which is the sum of note issue plus deposits.

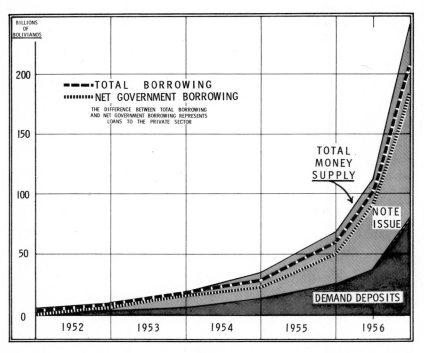

Fig. 1. Government and private borrowing and the money supply. (Source: *International Financial Statistics* [Washington, D.C.: International Monetary Fund].)[49]

Manifestly, any attack on the Bolivian inflationary problem that failed to put a stop to government borrowing and the issuance of printing press currency was doomed to failure, and that is why the 1953 "stabilization" measures devised by President

Paz, with the aid of the U.N. and the IMF, proved as useless as a bladeless knife without a handle.

Figure 1, be it noted, reveals only a part of the inflationary pressure from the government sector, as it omits the exhaustion of the nation's gold and foreign exchange reserves, almost entirely a consequence of government spending. The link between the rise in note circulation, living costs, and foreign exchange rates is brought out in Figures 4 and 5 (Chap. 6).

This was the picture in mid-1956 — not as it appeared to anyone at the time, for no one in the Bolivian or U.S. governments, or in the Central Bank, had more than a faint conception of the full impact of Bolivia's financial misadventures — but as it appeared to a painstaking observer in November, 1956, with the benefit of considerable hindsight and much digging into facts, figures, and fallacies.[50]

But, by the spring of 1957, the National Monetary Stabilization Council had learned to its dismay that the Central Bank had placed its guaranty on at least $33 million of dollar obligations with no record in its books of account — not $22 million as Zondag of the USOM had reported, nor $12 million as the Bolivian government and the Central Bank had claimed when they applied to Washington for a stabilization loan. It was also found that there were $20 million in short-term credits outstanding but not previously accounted for; that, all in all, most of the figures which the council had been forced to accept as factual in 1956 with respect to the finances of the government and the government-owned mines and other enterprises proved to be even more misleading than in the case of the Central Bank guaranties; that, in short, the picture was one of utter financial chaos resulting from a combination of basic economic and political shortcomings accentuated by incompetence, corruption, misdirected U.S. aid, fiscal and monetary mismanagement, and the utter impossibility of proper accounting under a system of multiple foreign exchange rates and controlled prices.

GOVERNMENT ENTERPRISES

Central Bank

The Banco Central de Bolivia was one of five central banking institutions established in South America between 1922 and 1928 on the advice of the economic mission led by Edwin W. Kemmerer. Their general functions, although not the details of their organization, were modeled on those of the Federal Reserve System in the United States.

It will be recalled that the primary objective of that system when it was established in 1913 was to provide the United States with an elastic supply of money and credit, meaning one that would contract as well as expand with the legitimate needs of business, agriculture, and industry. The chief mechanism used to achieve this objective was to permit member banks to discount "eligible paper" (i.e., drafts at up to ninety days' tenor, backed by actual commercial transactions) at the regional Reserve Bank, and at the interest rate set by the bank which, in turn, was permitted to issue Federal Reserve notes in an equal amount in order to provide the cash funds required by the borrowing bank.[51]

In 1916 the Federal Reserve Act was amended to permit the regional Federal Reserve Banks to make advances against notes issued by member banks, secured by eligible paper, or by bonds or notes of the U.S. government, which the member bank might hold in its portfolio. The discount process continues to fulfill a key function in the U.S. Federal Reserve System today, but open market operations, i.e., the purchase and sale of government obligations, have become of primary importance, and the original objective of Federal Reserve policy has been expanded to include the not always compatible goals of economic growth, high employment, and price stability, in the face of government deficits, wage demands, and other pressures.

Other amendments, chiefly in the Banking Acts of 1933 and 1935, and changes now pending before Congress, have permitted the system to evolve in step with changing times, as was its original concept. The fact that the powers of the Federal Reserve System were not availed of in 1928-29 to curb overexpansion, nor in 1930-31 to curb overcontraction, so that elasticity became a factor in prolonging the boom and accentuating the slump, may be attributed to the *zeitgeist* or to the illness and death of Governor Harrison, but this does not detract from the validity of the various mechanisms entrusted to the system.[52]

In Bolivia (and elsewhere in South America) elasticity of the paper currency was the desideratum, that is, a note issue that would expand and contract to meet seasonal and other exigencies, and would be based on actual business operations, with overexpansion and overcontraction curbed by a strong central bank — not a note issue that could be expanded at the will of the government but with no built-in mechanism for contraction. The dangers in Bolivia (and other South American nations), as Kemmerer and his Bolivian and American advisers recognized, would arise not so much from speculation in the private sector as from structural weaknesses inherent in "one-crop" countries, and in government demands for credit which arose generally when a government was too weak or too lacking in courage to impose taxes sufficient for its needs.*

These demands for credit might either take the form of government pressure on the commercial banks to purchase government bonds or notes, in which case the banks would borrow from the Central Bank or of direct government pressure on the Central Bank itself, which might be compelled to grant credits to the government in open account or to purchase government securities without effective limitations.

To minimize the likelihood of these pressures' materializing and to bring the currency base closer to reality, the Kemmerer mission recommended, and the Bolivian government enacted, the following measures in addition to the creation of the Central Bank under the law of July 1, 1928: (1) establishment of the gold exchange standard in lieu of the gold standard, thus saving the expense of storing gold in Bolivia or abroad, and permitting the Central Bank to earn interest on its foreign hard currency deposits; (2) a new budget law of May 3, 1928, which did away with extraordinary or nonbudgetary expenditures of

*The term "structural" had not yet been used in this sense but, if anyone thinks the idea was invented in the past decade, he is underestimating the perspicacity of all the economists, statesmen, and financiers who have labored over the past fifty years to diversify Latin American production. Their efforts have not been entirely in vain, but economic laws — including the law of comparative advantage — are not easy to repeal.

the government and required all revenues and expenditures to be placed in a single, balanced budget; and (3) a series of tax measures designed to enable the government to live within its income. At the same time, the Bolivian peso was revalued at 18 pence, or Bs. $13\frac{1}{3}$ to the pound sterling by the law of July 14, 1928 (the previous par had been 19.2 pence or £ 1 = Bs. 12.50).[53]

In recognition of the fact that one of the most serious obstacles to balanced budgets and government fiscal planning in Bolivia, and indeed to private planning and economic development in general, was the country's almost sole dependence upon world demand and prices for tin, the central focus of all the Kemmerer mission planning was the encouragement of agriculture and cattle raising, and Central Bank credit policy was intended to be directed with that end in mind.[54]

The timing of these measures could hardly have been more unfortunate. In anticipation of the Kemmerer program, the government had floated a $14 million, 7 per cent bond issue in the United States in February, 1927, at $98\frac{1}{2}$ per cent of par, and, following the program, in September, 1928, had issued a further $23 million of 7 per cent bonds at $97\frac{1}{2}$ per cent of par. With a world-wide depression coming virtually on the heels of the Kemmerer mission, before either the Central Bank or the government had had a chance to consolidate its position, world tin demand and world tin prices slumped disastrously, and the value of Bolivia's metal exports dropped from $44 million in 1929 to $8 million in 1932. There was simply no way in which Bolivia could have continued to meet service charges on its foreign debt, but, to make matters worse, revolution broke out in June, 1930; the government defaulted on its bonds in January, 1931; England went off the gold standard in September, 1931, so that Bolivia's change from the gold standard to the gold exchange standard (which seemed quite justifiable in 1928) meant a loss of one-third of the value of its sterling reserves. To cap the climax, the disastrous Chaco War with Paraguay broke out in June, 1932.

With this accumulation of disasters, the Central Bank was forced to revert to the practices of its predecessor, the Banco de la Nación Boliviana, and extend short- and long-term credits to industry and commerce, not backed by actual business operations, and, even worse, to speculators, thus facilitating the flight of capital.* Still more ominous for Bolivia's future, the government turned increasingly to the Central Bank for "temporary" advances and, following the Chaco War, acquired 100 per cent ownership of its shares, with the result that the bank, despite legal limitations on credits to the government, became in fact little more than a printing press that churned out bank notes as fast as the government needed them.[55]

It was not until 1940, after the outbreak of World War II, that the dollar value of Bolivia's metal exports exceeded the 1929 level (it has kept well above that level ever since). The Central Bank managed to replenish its gold reserves and, by 1945, had built them up to unprecedented levels, keeping its funds largely in gold rather than in dollars or sterling, in view of its unfortunate experience in 1931. Under the Revolutionary Government, however, these reserves were soon depleted, and the Central Bank pledged its last eleven tons of gold for a loan from Manufacturers Trust Company of New York, originally for $9.5 million, later raised to $11 million. By 1954 it had become evident that Bolivia would be unable to repay the loan, and it would have been absurd, as the president of the Central Bank pointed out, for Bolivia to continue to pay storage charges to the Federal Reserve Bank of New York for custody of the gold, and at the same time pay Manufacturers Trust $320,000 a year for interest on the loan. The gold was therefore sold, the loan repaid, and, by June, 1956, the country's gold and foreign exchange reserves were nil — a minus figure, in fact, as it later turned out, despite the fact that no indication of this state of affairs could be gathered from the published statistics of the Central Bank.[56] †

The Central Bank of Bolivia had ceased to exist — at least as a central bank. The building remained intact; the law creating the bank had not been repealed; but pressure from the government from above for forced loans, and from the union of bank employees from below, preventing any accounting controls

*One of the chief reasons for replacing the Banco de la Nación Boliviana with the new Banco Central de Bolivia was that the Kemmerer mission considered the commercial operations permitted by the charter of the older institution incompatible with the functions of a central bank, and this has been amply substantiated by the later history of the Central Bank.

†Later, in 1957, the Central Bank sold Bolivia's last 87 bars of gold to the Federal Reserve Bank of New York (34,669 ounces worth approximately $1,213,000) and in 1959 disposed of 450 tons of copper coins (about $300,000), whose metal content far exceeded their face value.[57]

or employee discipline, had crushed any vestige of independence of action, leaving the bank a mere vehicle of unmanageable inflation. The president of the bank stuck to his post out of a sense of loyalty and in the hope that some day, surely, the bank could be restored to its proper functions, as in fact it was, with the enactment of the monetary stabilization measures in which the president of the Central Bank himself played so vital a role.

COMIBOL — The Government Mining Corporation

At the time of the MNR *coup d'etat* in 1952, the mining industry occupied a position of such overwhelming preponderance in the Bolivian economy that 95 per cent of the country's exports, and hence of its foreign exchange resources, were derived from that industry. Over 70 per cent of that amount came from exports of tin. Export taxes on minerals accounted for 42 per cent of the revenues in the 1950 government budget, and represented from 18 to 23 per cent of the gross value of the ore. The companies were compelled to turn over to the Central Bank constantly increasing percentages of the gross value of their tin concentrate exports. By the close of 1954, this percentage had reached 70 per cent of the value after deducting transportation and smelting charges. The remainder was said to be barely sufficient to cover foreign currency costs and a modest dividend to the stockholders, an estimate which may or may not be a true one.

Together with import duties on mining equipment and supplies, and income and other taxes on the mining industry and its shareholders, it is probable that between 65 and 75 per cent of the government's revenues were derived directly or indirectly from mining.[58] Furthermore, three companies alone — Patiño Mines & Enterprises Consolidated, Inc. (a Delaware corporation), Compagnie Aramayo de Mines en Bolivie (a Swiss corporation), and Mauricio Hochschild, Sociedad Anónima Minera e Industrial (a Chilean corporation) — accounted for close to 70 per cent of total mineral production and exports, a concentration of economic power that had been a sore point in Bolivian politics for at least three decades prior to the Revolution.

One of the charges levied against the industry was its "centrifugal tendency," that is, that its profits were spun off and exported instead of being reinvested in the country. An objective analysis of the facts on which such charges might be based is found in the reports of the three-member Permanent Fiscal Commission for Bolivia, two of whose members were appointed on the recommendation of the bankers who arranged the 1922 loan to the Bolivian government. According to the commission, the industry showed net earnings for 1926 of $9,800,000 (Bs. 26,878,000 converted at 36.5 cents per boliviano), "of which the greater part must have left the country to pay dividends." [59] However, on an investment, reported by the commission, of over $135 million (Bs. 370,808,000), of the mining companies in actual operation in that year (i.e., excluding those which had invested money but had gone bankrupt or were no longer operating), these earnings represented a return of less than $7\frac{1}{4}$ per cent, which would not appear to have been an unduly burdensome drain on the country's resources, even if the greater part of such earnings had in fact been remitted abroad in dividends. Furthermore, it is obvious that, at least in earlier years, the Big Three must have attained their impressive size chiefly by ploughing back into Bolivia a very substantial part of their earnings (debt capital was relatively minor), considering that Simón Patiño and Mauricio Hochschild commenced operations on shoestrings, while José Avelino Aramayo and the lesser operators were men of relatively modest means.

Nevertheless, the fact remains that, in the decades immediately preceding the Revolution, conditions of political instability, onerous taxes and foreign exchange regulations, plus the threat of ultimate confiscation, afforded so little incentive for investment in Bolivia that the mining companies attempted to withdraw an ever-increasing percentage of their profits from the country, and spent the minimum possible amount in exploring and developing new sources of ore. As a consequence, even before the Revolution, the percentage of metal content in the existing veins had steadily declined, and geological exploration and the blocking out of new areas had come virtually to a halt.

By 1950, when the Keenleyside study was made, Bolivian mining was already in a precarious position; mine labor was rebellious and worked effectively for only 40 to 50 per cent of its eight-hour shifts; [60] and the steady political trend to socialism pointed either to eventual expropriation of the mining companies or to their piecemeal erosion by higher taxes, higher wages, lower labor productivity, and increasing government intervention.* Seizure of the Big Three mines in 1952 may therefore be viewed as having been historically inevitable. In view of the nature of the government that came to power in that year, the seizure took the form of confiscation rather than expropriation, which implies a constitutional taking of private property for a public use, by virtue of law, and upon payment of prompt and adequate compensation determined by an impartial court of law. †

The decree of October 31, 1952, "nationalizing" the Big Three companies, fixed their aggregate value at Bs. 304 million, plus $16.8 million in foreign exchange assets. This would probably not have been out of line with the Bs. 371 million valuation placed on the entire mining industry in 1926 by the Permanent Fiscal Commission, had it not been that the boliviano, at the free exchange rate, had meanwhile depreciated to one-thirtieth of its 1926 value, and was destined shortly to drop to one five-thousandth of that value. Converted to dollars at the 1926 rate of 36.5 cents, the government valuation would give a total value of $128 million for the Big Three properties. The net book investment in the Patiño properties on December 31, 1951, *in depreciated currency* was $18,531,000 or $15,928,000, depending upon whether the conversions from boliviano assets are figured at the then official rate of Bs. 60 to the dollar, or at the so-called "free" rate of Bs. 100. None of these figures necessarily

---

*Labor-management relations were not as uniformly critical as is generally depicted. Keenleyside reports that at the Aramayo mines "a really friendly and harmonious atmosphere appears to exist as between management and the organized workers." At least one of the Aramayo mines provided assistance to the workers to purchase land for part-time cultivation and as an investment against retirement (Keenleyside report, p. 97). This situation was confirmed in the Stabilization Council by a knowledgeable member of the MNR Cabinet. The Patiño group maintained the Fundación Universitaria Simón Patiño, a foundation that sent Bolivian students to Europe for study, and established the most modern hospital in Bolivia, where free medical and dental service was given to all workers and their families, as well as six day schools and one night school with 1,200 students (Herbert S. Klein, "The Creation of the Patiño Tin Empire," *Inter-American Economic Affairs*, XIX [Autumn, 1965], 17).

†One of the first acts of the Revolutionary Government was to dismiss the members of the Supreme Court and to replace them with persons loyal to the MNR. The district courts were similarly purged shortly thereafter (Message to the Nation, President Paz-Estenssoro, December 31, 1952; see Ostria-Gutiérrez, pp. 203-4 [*The Tragedy of Bolivia*, pp. 127-8]).

represents fair value at the time of taking. Net income for the three years prior to the taking averaged slightly over 10 per cent on net book investment, and dividend payouts represented practically 100 per cent of earnings.[61] The unilateral government valuation of the Patiño properties, fixed by the "nationalization" decree, was $2,918,921 plus Bs. 260,255,334 plus £ 87,657, which would have given a total value of some $7.5 million, at the time, prior to the extreme depreciation of the boliviano. On that basis, the valuation for the aggregate Big Three properties might perhaps be placed at around $10 million.

The government, however, claimed that the entire boliviano value was more than offset by taxes and foreign exchange payments allegedly due by the companies to the government and the Central Bank, and particularly by the dismissal pay owed by the companies to the workers for their having gone out of business. The miners, of course, had been immediately transferred to the rolls of the government mining corporation (COMIBOL), with no loss of pay, so that the indemnity for dismissal represented an unearned bonus that won the workers' enthusiastic approval of the nationalization measures.

The companies, however, were not lacking in means of defense. Because of the low metal content and complex composition of the Bolivian ores, there were few smelters in the world equipped to handle the concentrates economically. For years, Bolivian tin had been refined chiefly by Williams, Harvey & Co., Ltd., of Liverpool, who managed to reduce smelting costs by combining it with the high-content concentrates from the Straits Settlements. The lowest-quality Bolivian concentrates were smelted by Capper Pass & Son, Ltd., in Yorkshire, and by the U.S. government-financed Longhorn Tin Smelter in Texas City, Texas. The contract with the Texas smelter expired in 1945, but, as a disguised subsidy to Bolivia, the plant was kept operating at a loss until January 31, 1957.[62]

Patiño owned a substantial interest in Consolidated Tin Smelters, Ltd., which in turn owned Williams, Harvey & Co., Ltd. It was not difficult, therefore, for Patiño to have that company withhold from the COMIBOL shipments a proportion of all tin refined, as a deposit against whatever settlement might ultimately be reached with the Bolivian government. On June 10, 1953, this arrangement was embodied in a formal agreement with Bolivia, whereby an agreed percentage of revenues, on a sliding scale, was withheld from all shipments from the former Patiño, Aramayo, and Hochschild properties. Up to July 1, 1956, when I arrived in Bolivia as the first member of the U.S. Stabilization Mission, $9,611,658 had already been withheld and paid under that arrangement ($3,080,286 for Patiño; $1,783,175 for Aramayo; and $4,748,196 for Hochschild), without any definite agreement having been reached as to the total indemnization due for seizure of the mines.

From the companies' viewpoint, the retentions, at the rate of 5 per cent on the proceeds from the smelting (when the price of tin is between $1.06 and $1.215, plus 1 per cent for each 6 cents over that price, or $2\frac{1}{2}$ per cent when the price is between $0.90 and $1.06), have represented less than a reasonable return on their investment pending a definitive agreement on compensation, so that in their view these payments have not diminished the sum that they claim to be due. The payments to Patiño, for example, for 1953-56, would represent a return of $5\frac{1}{2}$ per cent per annum on the net book investment, and would be 40 per cent less than average dividend payments reported in Moody's for the years 1949-51.

From the government viewpoint, this contention is outrageous, and the powerful miners' union has made it clear that it would not agree to any settlement whatsoever with Patiño *et al*. On the other hand, confiscation of the mines, and failure to reach a negotiated fair settlement, interposed a serious deterrent to the return of Bolivian capital from abroad and to the investment of any foreign capital other than that provided by the U.S. government and the international lending agencies, thus greatly increasing the obstacles in the way of achieving and maintaining monetary stabilization.

Far more serious, however, as obstacles to monetary stabilization and economic development were the complete disorganization of the Big Three mining enterprises as a result of the dismissal or departure of virtually all the experienced technical and managerial staff, Bolivian and foreign; the inexperience and incompetence of government management; and, above all, the utter lack of discipline of labor as a consequence of the establishment of the *control obrero*. This was control by the workers, a system under which representatives of the mine workers' federation were assigned as commissars throughout the mines and administrative offices of COMIBOL, with absolute power of veto over all management decisions other than in "technical" matters. Suffice it to say that, under this system, all questions turned out to be economic, labor, or social problems, which fell under the jurisdiction of the FSTMB commissars. There were no problems that were exclusively "technical."

The term "lack of discipline," used by practically all writers on Bolivia, fails to convey the degree of anarchy that has prevailed since the Revolution. Cornelius Zondag, the economist for the U.S. Operations Mission, has tried to describe its meaning by citing: (1) the case of one large mine where a quarter of the workers are out on sick leave at all times although the medical staff can find no trace of illness; (2) the full thirty-day annual sick leave insisted upon for all workers by the *control obrero* regardless of need; (3) the constant disappearance of ore and equipment, and particularly the theft of shovels which must later be bought back by COMIBOL on the black market; (4) the absolute impotence of foremen and managers to enforce any disciplinary measures or to dismiss workers even for theft or assault; and (5) the fact that, on December 30, 1955, COMIBOL employed 34,500 "workers" (many more above ground than below) and produced 23,484 tons of tin in 1955, whereas the three private companies had employed 17,990 workers, as of December 31, 1949, and had a 1949 output of 34,662 tons. The drop in production was not, however, entirely attributable to the workers. For years prior to the Revolution, ore content had been dropping off steadily, and insufficient funds were devoted to new exploration and blocking out new veins, owing to the lack of incentive and the fear of confiscation. In the first year of government ownership, production actually increased as the mines were stripped of all their most accessible reserves. In fact, the worst effect of government ownership has been that it has tried to "plunder" the mines — the German economic term, *raubwirtschaft* — rather than to work them to the long-term economic advantage of the country. [63]

Investigation of the COMIBOL accounts and conferences with management revealed absolute chaos in the accounting department and large-scale corruption in the purchasing department, abetted by two of the highest officials in the Bolivian government (see pp. 391ff), as well as the confessed inability of the president of COMIBOL to cope with the situation because of the *control obrero* and the intervention of the Minister of Mines.*

---

*This is not by reason of incompetence. Bolivia could not have found, in Bolivia or abroad, a better qualified man to run its nationalized mines than the late Raúl Gutiérrez-Granier, a man of integrity and ability, to whom the country owes an unpaid debt of gratitude. His knowledge of the

To cite a specific example, the mines issue new waterproof boots to the miners when the old ones are worn out, and the same pairs of worn-out boots are turned in again and again, week after week, by one worker after another, while the new ones are openly black-marketed. The life expectancy of any manager who attempted to interfere with this trade would have been short indeed. The "lack of discipline" since the Revolution was not confined to government industry. I have seen a locomotive wrecked in a gulley, because the workers let it go careening down a steep hill with no driver or brakeman, just in a spirit of exuberant destruction.

The foregoing should suffice for the present to give a picture of the country's chief industry, and practically sole source of foreign exchange, under the control of the Co-Gobierno and the *control obrero*. The consequences of COMIBOL's accounting shortcomings on the monetary stabilization program are related in Chapter 17.

The destruction of this once prosperous industry through government mismanagement was unquestionably the most serious mistake made by the Revolutionary regime. COMIBOL deficits, however, were not the cause of the precipitate depreciation of the currency, as most people in government and in the Central Bank believed. Quite the contrary; if the nation's accounts had been properly kept, without the confusion produced by multiple rates of exchange, and particularly the absurd official exchange rates, it would have been clear that COMIBOL's excess of cash receipts over cash expenditures was the only thing that enabled Bolivia to survive the cash deficits of the petroleum corporation, the Development Corporation, and the railways. The proof of this statement is set forth at pp. 116ff.

One matter, however, that has never been publicized is the effect of government mismanagement on the real earnings of miners employed by COMIBOL. At a meeting in the Presidential Palace on February 16, 1957, just two months after enactment of the monetary stabilization decrees, President Siles attempted to impress President Eisenhower's special personal representative, General Lawton Collins, with Bolivia's urgent

---

Bolivian mining industry dated back to his long-term connection with the Aramayo and W. R. Grace & Co. operations, and he was one of the many high Bolivian officials who attempted to cooperate with the Stabilization Council in the face of insuperable odds.

need for increased U.S. aid.* Siles cited in support of his contention the fact that the Bolivian miner earned less than a dollar
a day — "a starvation wage." To quote wages in dollars was to
ignore of course, the fact that the miners received far higher
wages when the mines were operated by Patiño, Aramayo, and
Hochschild.

The fact is that, according to a study made by Ford, Bacon
& Davis, Inc., the large private mines paid a daily (per shift)
wage of $2.61 in 1950, consisting of a cash wage of $2.09, plus
the equivalent of $0.90 in losses from below-cost sales to the
workers from the companies' stores, plus $0.43 in other fringe
benefits. The U.N. reports (Keenleyside and ECLA) would place
the total at between $2.55 and $5.91 per diem.[64] By mid-
November, 1956, on the eve of stabilization, the average wage,
plus the actual value to the miners of the below-cost commissary privileges, and including bonuses and fringe benefits,
amounted to 83 cents U.S. a day. In terms of purchasing power,
the 1950 wage was probably close to five times the value of the
aggregate wage, including commissary privileges, paid to the
miners on the eve of stabilization; this figure gives a measure
of the consequences of government ownership (see pp. 222-24).

With stabilization, the miners were given a basic wage of
Bs. 7,500 per day. At the initial stabilization rate of Bs. 7,750
to the dollar, this gave the wage of "less than a dollar a day" to
which the president had referred. However, the total average
wage, with bonuses and fringe benefits, was Bs. 15,802, or
$2.04, which was more than COMIBOL could afford to pay, con-
sidering that twice as many employees were producing only
two-thirds as much tin as had been produced under private
management.

The Mining Bank and the Private Mines

While the nationalization of the Big Three properties constituted the major disaster of the Revolutionary regime, the
destruction of the small and medium-sized mining enterprises

---

*To this, General Collins replied: "Neither a borrower, nor a lender
be; For loan oft loses both itself and friend, and borrowing dulls the edge
of husbandry." As an unofficial translator, I had to put this into Spanish —
not an easy text for extemporaneous translation, as any Spanish scholar
must admit.

by the government and the government Mining Bank was even more serious from the standpoint of the number of wage earners involved. The Big Three had employed some 18,000 miners (raised to nearly 35,000 under government management), whereas the remaining mines gave employment, prior to the Revolution, to at least 50,000 workers, some estimates running as high as 70,000. Ford, Bacon & Davis, Inc. gives an estimate, for the entire industry in 1955, of 70,500 miners, which would indicate that employment in the private mines had shrunk to some 35,000 workers.[65]

The medium-sized mining enterprises varied in size from operations employing fewer than 100 miners to comparatively large and once prosperous concerns employing over 1,000 workers. The small mines included outcroppings worked intermittently on a family basis by peasants or part-time mine employees, up to operations almost large enough to be classified as medium-sized. The classifications were fixed from time to time by the Ministry of Mines, on the basis of output, for the purpose of determining the degree and nature of government regulation and of the mine's obligatory dependency on the government Mining Bank. According to the FBD report, excessive government controls, direct and hidden taxes, social legislation, the breakdown of labor discipline, and the withholding by the Central Bank or by the government Mining Bank of over 40 per cent of the proceeds of the gross sales of the private mines, made it "impossible for legitimate private enterprises to be economically self-sustaining." As a result, the "mortality trend" in private mining was shown by the reduction in the number of medium-sized enterprises from 22 to 16 between 1953 and 1956, and by the fact that 1,600 mines, formerly productive, had closed down despite high world metal prices.[66]

According to the same report, however, tin production in the private mines could have been doubled within a five-year period, adding over $20 million a year to the Bolivian economy, if Bolivia had been prepared to offer investors a sound investment climate comparing favorably with that afforded by neighboring countries. This would have meant a complete reversal of government policies and of the current burdensome labor legislation. The capital needed to place the industry on a sound basis was estimated at approximately $7.5 million a year over the following five years. If the climate and capital were forthcoming, Ford, Bacon & Davis believed that the predicted decline in output of the exhausted nationalized mines could be compensated by the expansion of private operations.[67] This was a long-term outlook, as in 1956 COMIBOL accounted for 75 per cent of total Bolivian mineral output, and the private mines for the remainder; but by 1963 the FBD prediction had almost materialized (Table 16).

To a large extent, the problems of the private mines were attributable to the operations of the Mining Bank under the Revolutionary regime. The bank had originally been chartered in 1936 as a private institution, operated for the benefit of the small and medium-sized mines. It was expected to serve as an agency for the economical financing of purchases of equipment and supplies, and for the sale of concentrates in world markets at prices more advantageous than could presumably be obtained through the ore buyers (*rescatadores*), who had theretofore had a *de facto* monopoly of the business. These intermediaries were charged, justly or unjustly, with taking advantage of the smaller producers, both in the prices paid for the tin or other metals purchased, and in the statements of account showing the net metal content of the concentrates and the expenses incurred.

The Mining Bank was converted into a government bank in 1939. After the Revolution, a decree of June 2, 1952, gave it an absolute monopoly over the purchase and sale of all mineral products, and over the purchase of mine equipment and supplies, for all mines other than those operated by COMIBOL. According to the FBD report, the "arbitrary, bureaucratic, and technically incompetent interference" of the bank was largely responsible for the fall in Bolivian mineral production. Added to administrative mismanagement, however, the accounts rendered by the bank to the private mines were "nowhere near" what the law provided, going so far as to charge expenses incurred by the bank in bolivianos by converting them into dollars at the official Bs. 190 rate, meaning that an item costing Bs. 1,000 (say 10 cents at a current rate of Bs. 10,000) would be billed to the mine at $5.25. In all, the Mining Bank took from the private miners 67 per cent of the *gross* value of their exports in 1954, and 78 per cent in 1955, which left a net return of zero for the private operator.[68]

On the purchasing side, abuses were equally widespread although less damaging. As an example, Zondag cites the case of miners' helmets sold by the bank for Bs. 3,500 that were worth Bs. 785.[69] Examples could be multiplied *ad nauseum* — charges by the mine officials of extortion and forced bribery were commonplace, and the bank was easily the most hated agency of the MNR government.

YPFB — The Government Petroleum Corporation

Yacimientos Petrolíferos Fiscales Bolivianos (Bolivian Fiscal Oil Deposits) had its origin in the confiscation by the Bolivian government of the concession rights and properties of Standard Oil Company (N.J.). Standard had taken over a concession originally granted to Richmond Levering & Co., Inc., of New York, and, with that and other concessions obtained directly from the Bolivian government, had made extensive exploratory surveys in the early 1920's under Bolivia's first petroleum law of June 20, 1921. By 1930, Standard had brought the Bermejo, Catatindi, Sanandita, and Camiri fields into production, and had set up small refineries at the two latter fields.*

The risk capital of Standard having proved the existence of oil reserves or potential oil reserves over a large area of Bolivia, a wave of nationalism set in, and the government created the YPFB as an exclusive monopoly by decree of December 21, 1936, confiscating the Standard property rights and cancelling its concession in the following year. After long negotiation, in 1942, Standard managed to obtain payment of $1,750,000 in partial compensation for the cost of the invaluable geological surveys, exploratory studies, and maps it had made, but not for its capital investment nor for the risks it had undertaken.[70]

The importance of the Standard surveys to Bolivia in the Chaco peace conference negotiations has already been referred to. Their value to YPFB is demonstrated by the fact that there is not a single area that has been brought into production by YPFB up to the present time that had not previously been laid out and marked for drilling, or drilled, by Standard Oil. Modern drilling and production methods, and present-day deeper drilling, account for the rise in production since 1954.[71]

YPFB has been fortunate, in comparison with other Bolivian

---

*The refineries were simple topping plants. The Bolivian crude comes from the ground amazingly pure. On a visit to Camiri with the then chief engineer, Eduardo Hinojosa, I was permitted to draw off a tumblerful of crude which was allowed to settle for a moment or two. Aside from a little over an eighth of an inch of clean yellow paraffin at the bottom of the glass, the remainder was as clear and light as pure gasoline. In answer to the inevitable question, Hinojosa stated that he had driven a car using the crude, with the paraffin strained off, in lieu of gasoline. Hinojosa and Gulf Oil Company engineers stated that if the Bolivian oil could be transported in sufficient quantities to blend with the California asphalt-base oil, it would command premium prices.

government enterprises, not merely in starting off with the Standard properties and surveys, but in having had expert management early in the course of its operations under the guidance of Eduardo Hinojosa, an American-trained Bolivian petroleum engineer, formerly employed by Standard Oil. Mr. Hinojosa quickly built up a staff of Bolivian engineers, likewise trained in the United States, with the result that morale has been exceptionally high and, from the operations viewpoint, the enterprise has been comparatively successful.[72]

Financially, however, it has been a different story. No one in the Bolivian government, and probably no one outside the government, certainly not in the YPFB management, realized that it was YPFB and the Development Corporation, not COMIBOL, that were principally responsible for the galloping inflation from 1952 through 1956. This fact was reported to the president and fellow Stabilization Council members at the council meeting of October 5, 1956. All previously available government accounts had computed foreign receipts and expenditures at the official exchange rate of Bs. 190 to the dollar or some other completely unrealistic rate, with boliviano and dollar entries hopelessly commingled. Consequently, these accounts showed practically all government departments and agencies with their accounts in balance, except for COMIBOL, which had to borrow again and again from the Central Bank simply because the bank paid COMIBOL in bolivianos at official rates of exchange for the dollar and sterling proceeds of COMIBOL's exports. With the accounts properly analyzed, at realistic, hypothetical rates of Bs. 4,000, 5,000, and 6,000 to the dollar, the principal culprits in Bolivia's inflation, to the amazement of the council members, were the Bolivian Development Corporation, YPFB, the government railways, the government airline (LAB), and U.S. aid, approximately in that order. The COMIBOL *cash surplus,* however, did not mean profits and, conversely, the YPFB *cash deficit* was largely for capital investments which might or might not be economically justifiable.

With drilling equipment and supplies coming into the country at the official rate of exchange, and depreciation charged on the basis of book value likewise computed at that rate, it was not difficult for YPFB to show apparently satisfactory financial results, particularly as no one in the corporation had had sufficient training or experience in corporation accounting and finance to interpret an income statement nor to understand the difference between cash requirements and income. No depletion was charged until 1956, depreciation at the Bs. 190 rate was meaningless, and the income accounts and balance sheets were hopelessly distorted by artificial foreign exchange rates. No account of cash requirements and cash flow was kept, with the result that the corporation never had any working capital, used up whatever cash it did have on capital expenditures, and was compelled to borrow again and again from the Central Bank to meet its payroll and other current expenses, frequently borrowing dollars and repaying in bolivianos at the Bs. 190 rate, instead of at twenty to seventy times that rate.

Thus, oil was produced on an encouraging scale, but the economic resources of the country were being drained at a faster rate than the oilfields. Pipe lines were purchased from Brazil at prices higher than they could have been bought elsewhere, the cost being disguised by the exchange rate and by arrangements for the purchase of Bolivian oil in "treaty dollars" that could only be exchanged for Brazilian goods at exorbitant prices. As an example of unrealistic accounting, in 1955 YPFB bought 20 tank cars, worth over $15,000 each, and paid for them through the Central Bank at the boliviano equivalent of $675 each. In fact, by the end of 1955, as a consequence of this Alice in Wonderland accounting, all but $6.3 million of the YPFB investment had been written off, and the $6.3 million unamortized remainder was down in the books for the boliviano equivalent of less than $160,000 at the 1956 stabilization rate! [73] With the investment shown at virtually nil, and depreciation computed on that figure, it was natural for the YPFB management and the government to think they were making money, while actually the corporation was losing money, and the nation its foreign exchange reserves, hand over fist.

Fortunately for Bolivia's economic development, the policy of the U.S. government at the time was opposed to financing government petroleum operations that could be undertaken by private capital. Hence, as a result of continued shortage of funds, and constant pressure from Washington, Bolivia agreed to forego its government monopoly, and ICA contracted with the New York law firm of Schuster & Davenport to draft a new Petroleum Code calculated to attract foreign investment. The code was completed, and issued in decree form on October 26, 1955, but failed to bring in private risk capital until it was finally enacted into law by Congress on October 25, 1956, thanks to the insistence of the Stabilization Council. As a consequence of that law, a number of companies commenced preliminary exploration work early in 1957, and private production capacity has now far outstripped that of the YPFB.

While petroleum production will continue to be of importance to the Bolivian economy, there is little hope that it can take the place of the declining output of the nationalized mines. According to the ECLA report, which gives a summary of the situation in 1957, high transportation and other costs in Bolivia, together with the relative sparsity of known oil reserves, result in a unit investment cost of some $4,000 per barrel per day of production, against comparative costs of $2,800 in the United States, and $2,500 in Venezuela.[74]

A further deterring factor was that, under a 1938 treaty with Brazil, Bolivia had set aside up to 1,300,000 hectares of its potentially richest oil lands for exclusive exploration, production, and marketing by Brazil, in order that Brazil might, from the proceeds of the development of this area, be repaid with interest for its construction of the railroad from Santa Cruz to Corumbá on the Brazilian-Bolivian border. Brazil has "thus far not commenced exploration in the area despite the lapse of time,"[75] and despite the fact that Bolivia turned over to Brazil the maps and studies acquired through confiscation of the Standard properties. Nor can Bolivia expect to reap much benefit from these potential resources if the Brazilian government is no more successful in developing the area than PETROBRAS, the Brazilian government oil monopoly, has been in Brazil.

Bolivian Development Corporation

The Bolivian Development Corporation had been created in 1943 for the purpose of establishing "self-liquidating" projects, i.e., enterprises which would, when completed and in operation, be turned over to private enterprise. In point of fact, however, even prior to the inception of the Revolutionary Government, the United Nations reported that "its assets have become frozen in loans to the government for road construction and for a number of other projects which have not proved self-liquidating" and it "has become a holding company saddled with assets of doubtful value."[76]

Most of the Development Corporation's "assets" and projects were an inheritance from previous improvident administrations. Under the MNR government, however, the galloping inflation and ever-widening gap between the actual free market

rate of exchange and the wholly unrealistic official rate gave
free rein to a degree of profligacy in governmental spending
that had never theretofore been witnessed.

In the early years, the corporation's dollar and boliviano
expenditures had been kept separately, and it was not impossible, although by no means easy, to ascertain with some degree
of accuracy the amount of money that had been expended on at
least the major projects under its control. In October, 1956,
however, the corporation turned over to the Stabilization Council, in answer to its reiterated demands for information, seven
huge volumes of accounts, and it was then discovered, first,
that the corporation had made no accounting entries later than
June 30, 1955, and, second, that, since January 1, 1953, the
dollar and boliviano expenses had been hopelessly commingled.
As the former had been converted into bolivianos at the rate of
Bs. 190 to the dollar while the true rate of exchange ran as high
as Bs. 14,000 at its peak, the totals were meaningless. This is
not to imply that the change in accounting methods was instituted with fraudulent intent. To the contrary, the action was
apparently taken on the advice of independent public accountants
given, however, at a time when the boliviano was relatively
stable. On the other hand, a 1954 decree required the dollar
and boliviano budgets to be again segregated, and this was never
done, at least with respect to the entries in the accounting
records. [77]

The Bolivian Development Corporation projects included a
$10 million sugar mill built at three times the cost at which a
private mill of equal capacity could have been constructed, and
located in the middle of a swamp on the advice of U.N. experts
so that 2,800 piles had to be sunk for the foundation at an added
cost of some $250,000 or more; a $50 million highway from
Cochabamba to Santa Cruz, on which annual interest and maintenance charges work out at $170 to $215 per truck trip for the
traffic handled, and which a later $60 million highway to be built
between the same points will render obsolete; a number of colonization projects for Andean Indians, Japanese, Okinawans,
Italians, and Central European Mennonites, laudable in purpose
but economically unremunerative; a politically inspired irrigation project at Villa Montes in a practically unpopulated area
with soil so badly eroded that it would take at least fifty years
for the project to become remunerative; a cattle-breeding project stocked with culls from Brazilian herds so malformed and
diseased that a USOM expert stated that if those bulls were

crossed with native stock it would set back the Bolivian cattle industry for two generations; a powdered milk plant in Cochabamba with practically no local milk available because the cattle had been killed off as a result of the "agrarian reform," and virtually no market for the powdered product; various electric power projects in excess of the country's needs or resources, which could have been more efficiently constructed and operated by private enterprise to the extent that they were economically justifiable; and a cement plant at Sucre, politically inspired and built with funds illegally diverted from earthquake relief in an area containing less than 3 per cent of Bolivia's population within a 200-kilometer radius. Because of the continuing importance of these projects in the Bolivian economy, a fuller account is given in Appendix IV.

There was not a single project undertaken by the Development Corporation that could be justified on economic grounds. But it was not until later that the Stabilization Council had even a clue to the full impact of Bolivia's development expenditures on the country's finances. The council never did receive — at least not up to June, 1957 — any accounts of the corporation's actual expenditures subsequent to June 30, 1955, and those accounts, as stated above, were useless, since there was no way of segregating local expenditures in bolivianos, and dollar expenditures entered in the books at the Bs. 190 rate. In November, 1956, however, as the result of a detailed investigation of government budgets, the Stabilization Council managed to obtain a 1956 budget from the Development Corporation which, *for a single budget entry,* did separate the local and foreign expenditures. Table 1 (p. 64) sets forth the corporation's budgeted income and expenditures as they appear in the corporation's official accounts, with all foreign expendutures computed at the Bs. 190 to the dollar rate.

The official 1956 budget shown in Table 1 was not too alarming in the magnitude of its deficits, which the Bolivian Development Corporation had assumed would be met by the Central Bank as a charge against the general fiscal accounts, as in previous years. The last line for "unspecified projects and expenses" was small enough to escape unnoticed, as in fact it did until the Stabilization Council's investigation. Upon investigation, it developed that that one item concealed an expenditure of $5,188,191 which, at the official exchange rate, was less than one billion bolivianos (say $165,000), but at the rate of Bs. 6,000 to the dollar, which was a fair average for the 1956 year, turned out to be over 31 billion bolivianos — *twice as much as the entire Development Corporation deficit according to the official budget.* If the remaining Development Corporation projects, aside from those financed by U.S. aid, concealed a similar proportion of foreign expenditures — in dollars, sterling, or "treaty dollars" — as may well have been the case, then a further $22 million of disbursements would be concealed in the Development Corporation budget. And that budget, prepared prior to stabilization, was based on budgets and expenditures for prior years. The council never was able to get the facts, but the possibilities for extravagance, which the accounting methods made it impossible to control, and even for peculation, were undoubtedly there. In view of the highly political nature of the Development Corporation and its major projects, the members of the Stabilization Council were inclined to suspect the worst, in the light of the incident related at page 30 and the facts later developed with respect to COMIBOL purchases (p. 392). In any event, it was impossible to ignore the fact that the Development Corporation was the major factor in Bolivia's fiscal disorders.

TABLE 1

Bolivian Development Corporation Budget for 1956*
(In Millions of Bolivianos with Dollar Expenditures at Bs. 190 to the Dollar)

	Income	Expenditures	Deficits
Guabirá sugar mill	. . .	2,161	2,161
Cochabamba-Santa Cruz highway	. . .	5,584	5,584
Other roads	. . .	1,419	1,419
Colonization projects	. . .	506	506
U.S. aid for these projects	664	664	. . .
Villa Montes irrigation project	. . .	1,001	1,001
U.S. aid for this project	180	180	. . .
Reyes cattle breeding project	. . .	429	429
Miscellaneous projects	. . .	2,157	2,157
U.S. aid for these projects	140	140	. . .
Other unspecified projects and expenses	488	3,131	2,643
	1,472	17,372	15,900

*Summarized from a report prepared in the Ministry of Finance (see pp. 156ff).

Other Government Enterprises

Aside from the mining and petroleum corporation, and those enterprises operated by the Bolivian Development Corporation, the only enterprises of major significance (from the viewpoint of monetary stabilization) were the railways and airlines and the three government banks (previously discussed).*

Railways

Out of a total of some 2,000 miles of railroads, 815 miles were owned and operated by private companies: the Peruvian Corporation, which owns the line from La Paz to Guaqui on the shores of Lake Titicaca, connecting with a steamship line across the lake, and thence by rail to the Peruvian ports of Matarani and Mollendo; and the Antofagasta (Chili) & Bolivia Railway Co., Ltd., and its subsidiary, the Bolivia Railway Company, which together provide Bolivia with an outlet to the Chilean ports of Antofagasta and Mejillones.

Between them, the Bolivian lines and the Peruvian Corporation handle well over 80 per cent of the freight and passenger traffic in Bolivia.[78] So long as they remained under private ownership, they presented no problem from a fiscal point of view, although prior to stabilization, the private railways were permitted, in common with the government lines, to import equipment and supplies at the official rate of exchange, thus adding to the concealed deficits in Bolivia's international accounts.

The government-owned and operated lines, with a total mileage of over 1,100 miles, have always constituted, and will continue to constitute, a serious fiscal problem, not merely because of inefficient management, inadequate rates, and bad labor conditions but, basically, because for the most part the

*Zondag (pp. 29, 178) adds the universities to the list of governmental enterprises, as well as several factories owned outright by the government or by "mixed companies" owned partly by private investors. The financial and other arrangements of those enterprises, as related by the members of the Stabilization Council and discussed in the press, are so unsavory that, in the absence of any direct knowledge of their operations, it is deemed best to pass over the subject, particularly as it has no bearing on monetary stabilization except to the extent that the participants may have subtracted funds from the Bolivian economy at a time when the need for those funds was most pressing.

amount of traffic fails to warrant their existence. An exception is the 67-mile railway built by the Patiño mines, which was confiscated by the government and turned over to COMIBOL. [79]

In the 1956 budget, converting the dollar amounts into bolivianos at the rate of Bs. 6,000, the government railways showed a deficit of Bs. 20,255 million. Of this deficit, Bs. 15,000 million was accounted for by the peculiar rate structure of the Arica-La Paz Railroad, the Bolivian section of which is owned by the Bolivian government, and the Chilean section by Chile. Under a 1904 Treaty of Peace and Friendship between the two countries, the line was built by Chile and completed in 1913, and the Bolivian section was turned over to Bolivia in 1928. Under that treaty, all passenger and freight revenues, other than for ore, were to be divided on a 60/40 basis, with Chile getting the lion's share to compensate for higher operating costs on the more rugged Chilean section.

This arrangement was considered equitable at the time, but, unfortunately for Bolivia, it was provided that currency conversions would be made at the *official rates of exchange,* and, as previously explained, the official rate for the boliviano in 1956 was still Bs. 190 to the dollar even though the actual value had dropped to as low as Bs. 14,000 to the dollar. This meant that when Bolivia collected Bs. 14,000 in freight for the Chilean section, it had to turn over to Chile not one dollar but $73.50. This was at the extreme point of the inflation and is theoretical inasmuch as no payments were made at that time, so far as was known. However, according to Mr. Rey Álvarez, the U.N. railway expert in Bolivia, freight rates in hard currency in 1956 were forty times higher on the Chilean section than on the Bolivian, which gives an idea of the absurdities caused by perpetuation of an artificial rate of official exchange in the face of an actual decline in the real value of the currency. [80] This discrepancy was, of course, automatically wiped out by stabilization, which made the official value of the Bolivian peso whatever value it might have on the free and only exchange market. From the standpoint of the Bolivian economy, and hence of monetary stabilization, the international railways constructed for Bolivia by Brazil and Argentina constituted an even greater drain on the economy than the Chilean or other government-operated lines.

The Brazilian line is that which links Corumbá, on the Brazilian side of the Paraguay River, with Santa Cruz. It was built and (until July, 1964) was operated by a Mixed Bolivian-Brazilian

Railway Commission under a treaty of February 25, 1938. Construction materials, rolling stock, equipment, and supplies were virtually all purchased in Brazil or through Brazilian suppliers, and the cost, according to the Mixed Commission, added up to some £ 224,000 in sterling, plus over one billion cruzeiros, plus some $10 million in dollars, against which total Bolivia had a credit under the treaty of £1 million sterling. The Economic Commission for Latin America calculated the total cost at some $27 million, while Zondag placed the indebtedness at $45,864,000 as of December 31, 1955. No agreement had been reached, however, up to the time of stabilization, as to the conversion rates to be applied and, with the subsequent depreciation of the Brazilian cruzeiro, all except the dollar and sterling indebtedness would have been virtually wiped out. At the time of stabilization, the cruzeiro was quoted at 1,200 to the dollar, which would place the total debt at $11.5 million, and, as it turned out, an agreement was reached between the Brazilian and Bolivian authorities on July 23, 1964, fixing the indebtedness at $11.8 million.

Despite this attrition of capital costs under the new agreement, with the debt payable over 20 years from 1970, and interest at $3\frac{1}{2}$ per cent per annum from 1965, the railway may be expected to prove a continuing burden on the Bolivian economy, as the entire traffic in both directions does not warrant maintenance and operation of a 400-mile railway between the two countries.*

The payments to be made under the new agreement are to be used by Brazil for development projects in the Bolivian zone served by the railroad. Brazil is thus relieved of the mounting railroad deficits while retaining its interest in that area. Bolivia hopes to cut costs by dismissing the 1,200 railway employees, and having the line run by the army, which can hardly be more than a temporary expedient.[81]

The Argentine line extends from Yacuiba, on the Bolivian side of the Chaco frontier with Argentina, to the village of Boyuibe, some 125 miles away. To celebrate the "completion" of the railroad to Boyuibe, it was necessary for tractors to drag the locomotive to a building called the "railroad station," as the tracks had not yet arrived. As ECLA states: "Construction is

---

*For an amusing and revealing account of the operations of this once-a-week Blunderland railroad, see Trevor Armbrister, "Watch Out — Here It Comes!" *The Saturday Evening Post,* February 27, 1965, p. 75.

proceeding very slowly." Meanwhile the railroad goes from nowhere to nowhere.

Eventually, it is supposed to extend another 370 miles to Santa Cruz, passing through the oil region of Camiri, but, even then, the Economic Commission for Latin America sees very little possibility of developing any substantial traffic. The commission was unable to obtain any information as to the cost of the railway to date, or its total prospective cost, although the Director General of Railways ventured an estimate of some $30 million expended on the Yacuiba-Boyuibe sector. Unless this figure conceals expenses that do not show up in the railway assets, it would appear high, considering that the entire debt to Argentina had been consolidated at $20,890,000 in a protocol of February 11, 1955, and that construction on the railway had been negligible since that date.[82] With interest at 3 per cent, that debt would have amounted to $22,088,000 by December, 1956, at the outset of stabilization.

Equipment and supplies for this railway are purchased in Argentina; construction and operation are under a Mixed Bolivian-Argentine Commission under a treaty of February 10, 1941; and interest rates are 3 per cent on Bolivia's debit balances instead of $3\frac{1}{2}$ per cent in the case of the Brazilian-built line. In other respects the Argentine agreement is similar to the Brazilian agreement except that there is no tie-up to a petroleum concession.*

---

*Bolivian cabinet ministers, and members of the Stabilization Council, on various occasions, expressed their dissatisfaction with the Brazilian agreement and, at one discussion on ways and means to lighten the burden on Bolivia of trading with Brazil in "trade agreement dollars," one official expressed the opinion (to which his colleagues immediately assented) that Brazilian "imperialism" was one of Bolivia's most pressing problems and that in the background of every trade discussion with Brazil there was the ever-present threat of a Brazil-fostered separationist movement in Santa Cruz and the Beni. Not long after, at a Brazilian Embassy reception, the Brazilian Ambassador took me aside to say that it would be most unfortunate for U.S.-Brazilian relations, and for Brazilian cooperation in any future war, if I persuaded Bolivia to alter the trade agreement currency arrangement or the petroleum concession, "in a region where Brazil possesses a natural geographic hegemony." Some months later, a Brazilian senator charged that U.S. oil interests, and Henry Holland in particular, had used their influence to prevent Bolivia from permitting PETROBRAS (the Brazilian oil monopoly) to carry out petroleum operations in Bolivia in an area where Brazil had monopoly rights by treaty. Mr. Holland denied the charge.[83]

Airlines

The only important airline offering domestic service in Bolivia prior to stabilization was Lloyd Aereo Boliviano, S. A. (LAB). This was originally a private enterprise, founded in 1925 by Bolivian investors, and affording the only convenient means of transportation of freight and passengers to and from some of Bolivia's more isolated areas. Later, it was taken over by the government as a "mixed company," with the government owning 59 per cent of the stock, Pan American Grace Airways 20 per cent, and other shareholders, chiefly the original Bolivian investors, the remainder.

Its traffic in mid-1956 consisted largely of contraband flown into or out of Bolivia by smugglers, plus such uneconomic freight as shipments of beer to Bolivia's Amazon region and Brazil nuts from that area. Low freight (and passenger) rates were made possible by the purchase of aviation gasoline at the official rate of exchange, and other subsidies, totalling in all $3.1 million in foreign exchange for the years 1955-56.[84] In the 1956 budget, recomputed at a Bs. 6,000 rate of exchange, LAB showed a deficit of Bs. 10.5 billion. The stabilization measures did away with uneconomic freight and passenger tariffs and left LAB insolvent, as it had in fact been for many years, although its true condition had been disguised by subsidies.

There were other equally uneconomic air transport services, including the air freight and passenger services offered by Military Air Transport (TAM); YPFB (the petroleum corporation); the Bolivian Development Corporation; two subsidized meat packing plants (Ballivián and Los Andes); and COMIBOL (the mining corporation).[85] These lines had all enjoyed the same privilege of purchasing aviation gasoline at the official exchange rate and were at least as heavily subsidized, in proportion, as LAB; so they too were faced with the problem of readjustment following stabilization. Pan American-Grace Airways, Inc., Braniff International Airways, and the subsidized Chilean, Brazilian, Argentine, and Uruguayan government airlines, were engaged almost exclusively in international service, and their operations presented no problem to the Monetary Stabilization Council.

Social Security

In Bolivia, as in many Latin American countries, social security and similar payments have increased in recent decades to the point where they represent a wholly disproportionate part of the sums available for total labor costs, in some cases even exceeding actual wage payments. To a large extent, this rise in social security, pension, and analagous payments can be attributed to inflation. With currency depreciation, amounts paid into pension or other funds in previous years provide only a pittance instead of a pension. Thus, there is continuous pressure from labor for higher and higher contributions and payouts. Chiefly, however, the disproportionate rise in social security and allied payroll costs has been attributable to the fact that practically the entire cost of such benefits has been borne by the employer, not the employee, and hence there has been no limit to the demand by demagogic labor leaders and politicians for higher and ever higher social security contributions and payouts. Such payouts have become one of "the conquests of labor," and the laboring man has been too ignorant to realize that the cost is not paid by the employer but is added on to the cost of every article he buys and, moreover, that every peso that the employer pays into the social security fund means one peso less that he can afford to pay in cash wages.

The abuses of labor legislation in general are stated in the U.N. report:

> It may be said in general that Bolivian *general* labor legislation has been hastily drafted. It is based not so much on a serious study by competent persons of actual conditions of work in Bolivia and the particular needs of the Bolivian worker, as on a study of labour legislation in other countries ... and on a desire to confer benefits on the workers in accordance with the authors' own conception of abstract justice. Bolivian labour legislation thus appears advanced and generous, but the impulses of the legislators have in many cases outrun possibilities of practical application. A number of the provisions at present in force are calculated to do more harm than good to Bolivian industry and even to its workers.... It may be doubted whether all this legislation has resulted in any real improvement in the workers' standard of living, whether it has contributed to the formation of an efficient and responsible labour force, and whether it has brought about any increase in the productivity of the country's industries.[86]

The foregoing was written prior to the 1952 Revolution. Since then, largely as a result of the activities of a U.N. expert in social security matters, total payroll costs for cheap housing, hospital and health benefits, industrial accident risks, plus pensions and old age and disability insurance and other fringe benefits, either enacted by law or imposed by labor contracts, have been increased to as high as 120 per cent of direct basic wage payments in some industries, exclusive of the below-cost commissary benefits. The Stabilization Council did its best to change this situation but was able to make little headway. In the end, as will be seen, the government mining corporation was simply unable to bear this added cost, and social security came close to wrecking the COMIBOL and government budgets, and with it the monetary stabilization program. As it is, the exaggerated social security structure remains one of the major deterrents to economic development in Bolivia today.

The stabilization program was not, of course, blocked by this factor. It merely meant stabilizing at a less favorable rate than would otherwise have been the case; paying lower real wages than would otherwise have been possible; raising prices; burdening the 90 per cent of the population who are not covered by social security; and precluding or retarding any substantial economic recovery.

Agrarian Reform

It is probable that no country in Latin America was so much in need of agrarian reform as Bolivia in 1952, yet certainly there was no Latin American country where confiscation of private property for purposes of agrarian reform was less necessary or justifiable.

Until 1945, when a first feeble attempt at reform was made under the administration of President Villaroel, the payment of wages for agricultural services was *virtually unknown* in Bolivia. Even then, the Villaroel decree remained largely a paper law, and things went on much as they had before.

The Inca and pre-Inca Indian communities on the altiplano, in which a million people had once lived in a state of relative well-being and complete self-sufficiency, had long since deteriorated, with the progressive exhaustion of the soil and the lack of Inca discipline, to the point where the surviving communes were barely able to scratch out of the earth a subsistence far below any decent standards for human life. The better lands under cultivation were held chiefly in large estates, and on these the majority of Indian farmers lived as sharecroppers or tenants under conditions that are frequently compared with those of feudal serfs in medieval Europe. Actually, rural conditions in Bolivia in 1952 were probably worse than in Western Europe in the Middle Ages, at least so far as diet and economic conditions in general are concerned, and the comparison is apt only in the sense that the Indians were in fact serfs tied to the land, often under the domination of an unsympathetic manager acting on behalf of an absentee landlord.[87]

According to the Economic Commission for Latin America, the semifeudal system of land tenure was the principal reason for the decadence of Bolivian agriculture, and for the continuation of primitive methods of cultivation, not only on the tiny plots of land which the Indian croppers or tenants were permitted to work for themselves, but on the landlords' properties as well.[88]

The land tenure system undoubtedly contributed to the primitive agricultural methods, the low productivity, and the miserable conditions in which the majority of the rural Indian population lived. However, the principal deterrent to a more progressive agricultural system was that the government for generations had attempted to improve the living conditions of the miners and urban population by imposing artificial price controls on food and importing or facilitating the importation of foodstuffs and agricultural raw materials from abroad. Food imports entered the country at privileged foreign exchange rates and at prices so low that Bolivian agriculture simply was not in a position to compete. With this subsidized competition, and with the general uncertainties of the political climate and a deteriorating currency, there was no incentive for large landowners to invest additional money in improving production but, on the contrary, every incentive to hold idle land as a defense against further monetary depreciation.

This is borne out by the immediate increase in agricultural production that occurred whenever prices were permitted to rise under the forces of supply and demand, and, conversely, the immediate drop in production whenever price controls were reimposed. Food imports amounted to between $23 million and $27 million a year, and some 40 per cent of all imports into Bolivia consisted of foodstuffs or agricultural raw materials, all of which could and should have been produced at home and would have been produced locally had it not been for the misguided policies of one Bolivian government after another.[89]

In any event, the desperate situation of the Indian population, whether attributable primarily to the land tenure system or to errors in government policy, made agrarian reform a historical necessity and, the nature of the Revolutionary Government being what it was, confiscation of private property became the means to that end.

There was no conceivable economic need for confiscation of existing farms. Probably not more than 400,000 hectares — at the most 654,000 hectares — of land were under cultivation out of a total of from 21 to 33 million hectares of potentially cultivable land.[90] Much of this land, probably most of it — facts and figures in Bolivia are never better than probabilities — was owned by the government. The remainder was owned by private investors as a hedge against currency depreciation with no intention of putting it into production in the foreseeable future. A simple and easily applied system of land taxation (for example, that proposed at p. 337), and a stable currency, would have forced most of this private land onto the market in a relatively short time, certainly no longer than it would take to train the Indians for farm ownership and operation. Even lack of transportation was not a serious obstacle, for within 100 kilometers (62 miles) of La Paz there was ample vacant land which, if cultivated, could have more than supplied the city and surrounding area with most of its food requirements. Improvement and proper maintenance of existing roads rather than construction of new highways was all that was needed to bring these potentially rich farming regions into easy communication with the capital. The same was true of other major population centers of the country.[91]

But confiscating existing farms, rather than bringing new areas into cultivation, seems to have been the aim of the MNR and associated Trotskyite and communist leaders. At no time during my stay in Bolivia did I hear any of the protagonists in the Bolivian agrarian movement speak of increased agricultural production as the goal of the "reform," but solely of the "crimes" of the *latifundistas*, the large landowners.

The lines were clearly drawn at the FAO Latin American seminar on agrarian problems held in Campinas, Brazil (May 25 to June 26, 1953), which inspired the Bolivian Decree-Laws 3464 and 3471 of August 2 and August 27, 1953. At that conference, the proposals studied were split in accordance with two opposing ideologies: (1) the Uruguayan thesis, according to which expropriation should be resorted to only in those cases where the land is unimproved and where expropriation is essential for social stability and to meet the legitimate needs of potential beneficiaries — in such case, expropriation must be subject to payment of the fair value of the property taken; and (2) the theory, founded on the Mexican precedent, under which all real property is considered to belong to the nation, and the government only recognizes private property rights where the property fulfills a function useful to society as a whole, subject to the standards laid down by government planning and agrarian reform regulations — in such case, all large estates (*latifundios*) must be abolished and, if compensation is paid, it may be payable in worthless or near-worthless government bonds for an amount based on tax assessments.[92]

But the exponents of the Mexican thesis were (and are) dedicated men and well organized. A young Mexican, Edmundo Flores, had published an impassioned study (he calls it "angry") of agrarian reform in 1951, and Thomas F. Carroll, then with the U.N.-FAO and now an official in the Inter-American Development Bank, decided Flores was "the right man to organize the Land Tenure Seminar in Campinas." Flores was sent on a mission to every one of the Latin American governments to obtain delegates. There he gave lectures and met with government officials in Bolivia and elsewhere. "Suddenly," as he puts it, "I was asked to join the United Nations Mission in Bolivia as an adviser to the government on land reform matters." Another IDB official, Casto Ferragut, at a University of Wisconsin conference, characterized the consequent Bolivian agrarian reform as "a progressive step urgently required by the nation in order to achieve the most rapid social and economic development possible," while Carroll put the matter in proper perspective by stating: "Along with the Mexican and Cuban reform, the Bolivian agricultural transformation is one of the very few that can be regarded as 'true agrarian reform.'" Flores agreed with Carroll "that the Mexican, Bolivian, and Cuban reforms are in the same family — *and I think we're going to have some more.*" The IDB land reform activities are financed by the United States through the Social Progress Trust Fund; the strategy was revealed by Carroll: "You pick your agencies carefully and then you don't worry too much about integration. This is the strategy... Our concern is to choose agencies and individuals we trust... We picked the *Corporación Boliviana de Fomento* for this job."[93] (See pp. 61-64 and 606 for sidelights on the competence of that agency.)

Thus, with the FAO indoctrination at Campinas, it was

natural that the Bolivian decree-laws, drafted largely by Alberto d'Avís and Arturo Urquidi-Morales under the chairmanship of Hernán Siles-Zuazo, should follow the Mexican thesis. All rights to personal service running with the land, whether under a sharecropper or tenancy system or otherwise, were abolished; the ancient Indian communal holdings were recognized or re-established; cooperative ownership was favored; and broad powers were placed in the hands of peasant unions enforced by the armed peasant militia. In theory, large agricultural enterprises which employed modern methods and machinery, as distinguished from the hacienda, with its absentee landlord, were to be spared expropriation. In actual fact, however, the peasant unions and armed militia had, and exercised, the physical power to seize such lands, and the Indians settled in as squatters, killing the livestock and in some cases the owners as well.*

In such cases, no compensation was paid, and, even where compensation was payable, it was to be in the form of 25-year bonds, with noncumulative interest at 2 per cent, payable at maturity. Up to 1957, apparently, no such bonds had yet been issued; and, in fact, they would hardly be worth having, with the boliviano quoted at Bs. 11,880 to the dollar (the new peso, worth Bs. 1,000, is quoted at P. 11.88 to the dollar), and no telling what it may be worth two decades hence. It is true that, by Decree 3298 of January 16, 1953, *seven months prior to the agrarian reform measures,* landowners were given an opportunity to revalue their properties for tax assessment purposes at a minimum of five times the previous assessment.[94] But the quintuple revaluation would have offset only an infinitesimal part of the devaluation of the boliviano, at the official rate of exchange in January, 1953, and would have been wholly confiscatory in 1956 or later.

*The slaughter of livestock and the flogging and murder of landowners by squatters, peasant trade unions, and rural militia, were so commonplace that specific citation is superfluous. As to the consequences of communal ownership, the Zondag report cites the case of one Indian community, awarded an imported, pure-bred ram as a prize for high production, which celebrated the award in a huge fiesta with barrels of alcohol, with the result that the ram "ended up ignominiously in the stomachs of those attending the party" (p. 18). See Dwight B. Heath, "The Aymara Indians and Bolivia's Revolutions," *Inter-American Economic Affairs,* XIX (Spring, 1966), pp. 31-40, for a report on the independent, not to say anarchic attitude of the peasants at the present time.

Aside from the destruction of dairy herds, particularly around Cochabamba and Sucre, and the general despoliation of farm property, including the consumption of seed potatoes and faulty irrigation practices that turned once fertile pastures into salt flats, one of the most unsettling consequences of the agrarian reform was the complete insecurity of land titles. The agrarian decree-laws provided that any Indians whose ancestors had worked on Indian communal lands, or as sharecroppers or tenants, up until the year 1900, could claim a parcel of that land on the testimony of two witnesses as to the tenancy of the ancestor in 1900. In Bolivia, it is a wise child who knows his own father, and this provision opened up wide vistas of litigation or political influence. There was no practical limit to the claims of the so-called *ex-comunarios,* many of whom were living in the cities and had no intention of going back to the farms of their putative ancestors, but were violently insistent on claiming their rights so that they could return to town as "absentee landlords, no better than those before the 1952 Revolution."[95]

The anthropologist Dwight B. Heath[96] reports, after a year's study in Bolivia that, in those cases where the land has in fact been distributed to individual owners, many of the farmers, "freed from the restricting schedule of work for the landlords ... accede to a temptation to rest from their lifetime of labor." Even those who diligently till their land produce chiefly for subsistence, and have "little surplus product to take to market." To allow the pooling of resources, and encourage greater efficiency, five agrarian cooperative farms were established in the first five years following enactment of the Agrarian Reform Law, but all five ventures failed, and the administrators and officers of the cooperatives shirked their duties and were reported to "cheat and steal openly."*

According to Lockwood, writing for Carnegie Endowment

---

*Heath reports that the bulldozers used by Point IV for clearing land on the eastern plains scraped "off humus and rich topsoil as well as trees and brush, exposing the sandy substratum which is readily leached of any nutriment ... during torrential seasonal rains." Small wonder, then, as Heath reports, that the Indian members of one Quechua commune "blockaded the road when they heard that a truck convoy was to bring tractors, plows, harrows, and other machinery," resulting in a barrage of stones, with one man stabbed and several shots fired. The Point IV administrators wrote the incident off as communist-instigated, but Heath is inclined to attribute it to the Indians' resentment of the attempted violation of the sanctity of *Pachamama,* the divine Earth-Mother. (See Chapter 4 for further discussion of Point IV.)

for International Peace, agricultural production on the large estates which, prior to the agrarian reform, provided the bulk of the market-directed output, sank to 20 to 30 per cent of the pre-1952 level.* Even though the individual Indian farmer was probably better off than formerly, as he was able to consume the entire output of the land, the reduced output meant that the economy of the country as a whole suffered, and that practically all agriculture was on a subsistence basis, thus increasing the need for foodstuff imports to prevent starvation at the mines and in the urban centers.[97]

It was not only the large estates that bore the brunt of land "reform," but Bolivian agriculture as a whole, including the once prosperous medium- to large-sized family farms that, in Bolivia, were usually the most productive units. Lawlessness and the destruction of property rights resulted in a disastrous reduction of cultivated acreage. President Siles reported that the area planted in corn had dropped from 104,000 hectares in 1950 to 45,000 hectares in 1955, and that potato planting had dropped from 84,000 hectares to 40,000 hectares in the same period. On the same occasion, he announced that his administration had distributed 5,000 land titles under the agrarian reform program, from August, 1956, to the end of May, 1957, as compared with 7,000 titles issued in the three preceding years. By December, 1957, he stated, it was hoped to complete the program with the distribution of 30,000 land titles in all.[98]

The "agrarian reform," therefore, because of its impact on the domestic economy and particularly because of the consequent demand for foreign exchange for foodstuffs and other agricultural imports, was one of the major problems faced by the Monetary Stabilization Council, second only in its harmful consequences to the nationalization of the tin mines.

There are certain processes, however, which are irreversible, and, as in the case of the confiscation of the mines, I never attempted nor even considered suggesting a reversal of the "agrarian reform." In the long run — perhaps, optimistically, in fifty years or more, judging by the length of time it has taken Mexico and Russia to realize that collective farming is

*The FAO and the U.S. advisers in the Inter-American Agricultural Service (SAI) place the drop in agricultural production at 40 per cent, but this figure refers to agricultural output in the entire economy, both subsistence and market-directed, whereas the 70-80 per cent drop cited in the text refers to the decline in production caused directly by the seizure of the large estates (cf. Zondag, p. 40; ECLA report, p. 249).

less productive than individual enterprise — it may even be that the change in the Indian from a feudal serf to a submarginal subsistence peasant will provide some measure of social and political stability which is at present lacking.[99]

What I did advocate with the support of the head of the U.S. Operations Mission, was to call a halt at some definite date to all further seizures of land, whether by squatters or under color of law, and the issuance of definitive land titles without delay to all who were presently working on the land. Likewise advocated, and in some measure procured, was closer cooperation between the Bolivian authorities in charge of the agrarian reform and colonization programs (chiefly the Development Corporation and the Ministries of Agriculture, Rural Affairs, and War) and the United States — managed Highways Service and the Inter-American Agricultural Service that were doing such a creditable job in improving agricultural methods, in advising on supervised credits, and in local road construction and maintenance. President Siles' announcement of the expected termination of land distribution in December, 1957, may perhaps be in part attributable to these efforts, as in the same speech the President announced his arrangements with Point IV for supervised credits and assistance for the development of four-hectare (ten-acre) family truck farms in the valleys adjacent to La Paz and Cochabamba.

4

UNITED STATES AID TO BOLIVIA

Loans and Grants

Among the factors that contributed to Bolivia's galloping inflation from 1953 through 1956 was U.S. aid, including both grants and loans as well as commodity shipments under Public Law 480.* U.S. aid had become institutionalized and incorporated into the Bolivian economic structure to such an extent that, in the years 1955 and 1956, American taxpayers were contributing nearly three times as much to Bolivian government revenues as the Bolivian taxpayers (Fig. 16, p. 596).

Without U.S. aid, the Revolutionary Government could not have survived, according to President Paz-Estenssoro, referring to the economic assistance agreement entered into on November 6, 1953, and to the $13,766,136 in cash and $37,336,857 in foodstuffs and other products received from the United States up to the end of his presidential term in August, 1956.[100] There is in fact little doubt that, had it not been for U.S. aid, the MNR regime would have collapsed, as was asserted repeatedly by State Department and Embassy officials in justification of the continuance of that aid, and despite the manifest miscarriage of its purposes. Thus, for better or worse, the U.S. government must bear a share of the responsibility for perpetuation of the political and economic conditions described in the foregoing pages. Whether it was in fact for better or for worse must depend upon one's judgment as to the probable alternatives.

On the debit side of U.S. aid must be placed its contribution to the inflationary process, the corruption engendered by the method of its distribution, the ruin of agriculture and private enterprise in general, and the squandering of some $60 million (up to June 30, 1956; by now $360 million) in badly managed,

*It would be idle to distinguish between grants and loans in the case of loans made at nominal rates of interest, particularly when it was evident — even in the case of the Export-Import Bank loans — that Bolivia would continue to meet interest and principal payments only for so long as it could hope to receive even greater amounts in new loans and grants (see p.436n).

basically uneconomic government projects, enterprises, and imports, which have added to Bolivia's problems instead of solving them. (This side of the picture is discussed at length in Chapter 24, pp. 595ff.)

Point IV Program

On the credit side, on the other hand, must be placed the splendid cooperation given under the direction of the U.S. Operations Mission in the field of what is known as Point IV or technical assistance. Starting on a small scale in 1942 as a public health project, U.S. technical assistance had developed by 1956 into a program, in general well-administered, that cost the U.S. taxpayer approximately $3 million a year (compared to $24 million a year in "economic aid"). The Point IV program embraced the following phases which are set forth at some length in view of their impact on economic development and hence, in the long run, on monetary stabilization.

Inter-American Agricultural Service

The Servicio Agrícola Interamericano (SAI), founded in 1948, was originally operated under the direct supervision of the Ministry of Agriculture. It was later found that it could act more efficiently as a virtually independent agency under the aegis of USOM, with only a nominal regulatory connection with the Ministry. Since then, it has been the principal agency in Bolivia for improving the lot of the Bolivian farmer. It conducts agricultural and livestock research; operates down-to-earth extension services going direct to the individual farmers and Indian communities; and provides seeds, insecticides, breeding stock, tractors, and farm equipment.*

---

*In connection with the loan of tractors and mechanized equipment, SAI recommended that the machinery pool be turned over to private enterprise and that emphasis be placed on more and better draft animals, particularly mules, as being better adapted to Bolivian conditions than mechanical traction (Zondag report, pp. 94-5). Certainly, there was more broken-down mechanical equipment than equipment in operation, and a Bolivian colleague advised that the Bolivian farmer and laborer will never repair or take care of anything that he does not own and has not paid for: "A gift plant never takes root" (*Planta regalada no prende*). That pungent phrase can be applied to every aspect of U.S. aid and not merely to agri-

The 1954-55 fiscal year report of the SAI shows that the 39 "county agents" of the SAI held 6,412 method demonstrations for adults in that year with an attendance of 271,838, and had enlisted 2,024 members of the Bolivian equivalent of 4-H clubs, as well as showing demonstration moving pictures with an attendance of 136,173.[101] A summary of Bolivian Point IV activities from 1942 through 1960 reports that there are 36 offices and 115 employees in the SAI extension services and that the agricultural experiment station at La Tamborada (near Cochabamba) and the agricultural school at Muyurina (near Santa Cruz) have been turned over to the Bolivian government, thus carrying out the original intention of the program. They are now operated respectively by the University of San Simón and by Catholic missionary agricultural experts.[102]

One invaluable service of the SAI has been training personnel of the government Agricultural Bank to handle supervised credits, in which USOM employed the services of a private agency, the International Development Services.[103] The activities of this agency, observed at close range, gave proof that there is no more effective means of promoting immediate and fruitful economic development — paying off in the course of a single crop year — than a program of carefully supervised credits to individual farmers, ranging perhaps from twenty-five to several hundred dollars, coupled with equally careful grassroots assistance to the individual farmers and communities. The men employed by International Development Services, and by SAI in general, were for the most part dedicated men and experts in their respective fields — not "book experts" but men capable of shearing a sheep (or llama), building a hen house, or engaging in laboratory research on hoof and mouth disease (*aftosa*). The high standards then maintained by the agricultural and highway services in Bolivia are a tribute to the then Chief of the U.S. Operations Mission, the late Ross Moore, inasmuch

---

culture. Osborne (p. 96) points out that the "only two products of industrial civilization which have penetrated to any extent to the Indian communities are sewing machines and tin chamber pots," and although one may note the avidity with which the Indians, but more particularly the cholos, seize upon other more sophisticated industrial products — bicycles, electric blenders, power saws, trucks, tractors — it is also apparent how quickly these are broken and how seldom repaired. So long as such equipment is given or loaned to the Indians or cholos, or sold at below-cost prices, it will "never take root" and will not add one iota toward helping Bolivia to become self-supporting.

as results observed in other countries in Latin America leave
much to be desired. On the whole, however, "technical aid,"
particularly in agriculture, has been much more intelligently
administered than direct government-to-government economic
aid.

Highway service

The Servicio Cooperativo Boliviano-Americano de Caminos
(SCBAC) commenced operations in 1955 as an integral part of
the Ministry of Public Works and Communications. Like the
SAI, it was manned by capable and dedicated professionals, and
the results of its activities in feeder road construction, repair,
and maintenance, were almost immediately productive at a minimal expenditure of taxpayers' money. According to calculations made by the SCBAC, the cost of running a truck over the
average Bolivian road could be reduced by over 60 per cent by
proper highway maintenance and repair. The average life of a
truck could be doubled, with an estimated saving of some $6
million a year in truck imports alone, without counting the savings in tires, gasoline, and the like. Four decades ago, Commissioner of Public Roads Thomas H. Macdonald used to say
that good roads are expensive, but that it costs more if you
don't build them. This is as true in Bolivia as it is in the
United States, provided that the volume of traffic warrants the
cost.

The maintenance and improvement of existing roads is far
more important for Bolivia's economic development than the
construction of new highways, although there is a need for
feeder roads (in most cases, meaning merely the improvement
of existing roads), of from five miles up to perhaps sixty miles
in length, from potential farming areas to the principal cities
and to railheads. Even with present farming methods, such
roads could bring enough presently uncultivated arable lands
within easy reach of the major markets to make Bolivia self-
sufficient. With improved farming methods, Bolivian agriculture could be revolutionized, leaving a surplus available for
foreign as well as domestic markets.[104] Superhighways, on the
other hand, with a vehicular capacity far beyond any conceivable need, contribute little to economic development in Bolivia
but impose an annual carrying charge for maintenance and capital costs far in excess of the country's capacity to pay.

Other services

Other *servicios* operated by USOM, less immediately germane to the field of monetary stabilization, were the Public Health Service (Servicio Cooperativo Interamericano de Salud Pública, known as SCISP) and the Education Service (Servicio Cooperativo Interamericano de Educación — SCIDE) which, among other things, had contracted with the University of Tennessee to assist the University of San Andrés in establishing a center of instruction in public administration, and helped to establish four normal schools staffed with instructors trained by SCIDE and graduating 150 teachers a year.[105]

Other services provided under the aegis of USOM, although not dignified with the formal cooperative form of organization designated as a *servicio,* included a civil aviation mission, police and armed forces missions, and assistance in colonization projects. The services of the American advisers on the Stabilization Council were likewise provided under an ICA contract with Bolivia (USOM was the Bolivian office of ICA).

ICA also assisted Bolivia by arranging for the drafting of a workable Petroleum Code under contract with Wortham Davenport, senior partner of the law firm of Schuster & Davenport, and for the investigation of Bolivia's mining industry under contract with the engineering firm of Ford, Bacon & Davis, Inc., both of which developments have already been referred to. The engineering services of Tippetts, Abbett, McCarthy & Stratton were employed by ICA to design and supervise construction of a bridge over the Piray River as well as to supervise the Cochabamba-Santa Cruz highway and other projects, while the services of Thompson-Cornwall, Inc., were used on those construction jobs as well as for the construction of a number of highways and other projects.[106] Neither firm, of course, is responsible for the fact that the Cochabamba-Santa Cruz highway fails to serve a useful economic purpose commensurate with its cost, nor for the fact that many of the other jobs on which they were employed have proved to be a burden rather than a benefit to the Bolivian economy.

II

BREAKING GROUND

5

STRUCTURAL PREREQUISITES

So much space has been devoted to a description of the Bolivian background before even approaching the subject of monetary stabilization in Bolivia because the historical, political, social, and economic events leading up to the inflation of 1952-56 were amazingly complex, while the concepts and procedures of the monetary stabilization program itself were disarmingly simple. Yet a grasp of underlying conditions is essential in order to understand why certain measures indispensable in the case of Bolivia might prove inappropriate in the case of some other country, and why other measures which would appear logical and appropriate in another environment could not possibly be applied in Bolivia.

In any monetary stabilization program the first step, of course, is to determine the causes of the antecedent depreciation of the currency, and the steps that might be *feasible* for putting a stop to the inflationary spiral. Stabilization, like politics, is the art of the possible, not the quest for the ideal. Nevertheless, it may require the reversal of many of the measures previously taken by the government responsible for the inflation. Thus, a monetary stabilization program undertaken by a new government, which has come into power by election or revolution and has broken completely with the past, would present fewer problems than in the case of Bolivia, where the government of Hernán Siles-Zuazo, which took office in August, 1956, was merely a continuation of the Revolutionary MNR regime of President Víctor Paz-Estenssoro.

There were no doubts in my mind about the prime cause of the inflation — briefly, spending by the government and government enterprises in excess of their means, with deficits financed by the Central Bank through the issuance of additional paper currency. The obvious remedy for this situation was simple, but, of course, it meant the repudiation, at least tacitly, of virtually everything that the Revolutionary Government had done over the previous four years. Hence, my first task was twofold: (1) to expose the fallacies propounded by the "structural" economists and neo-Keynesians (defined at p. 475 n), who for four years had misled the MNR government; and (2) to convince the new administration that stabilization would only be possible with an almost complete change in course from a controlled to a free market economy — save for the irreversible blunders of a misguided agrarian reform and nationalization of the mines.

Within six weeks from my arrival in Bolivia, I was able to present to an organizing group consisting of the President, the President-presumptive, and their respective advisers (1) a combined agenda and time schedule, (2) an outline of the basic concepts of the proposed monetary stabilization program, and (3) a draft decree setting up the National Monetary Stabilization Council.*

A month later I prepared a series of forty points for discussion with ICA, State, Treasury, and IMF. With the benefit of the suggestions of those agencies, this scheme was later expanded into the "Fifty-Step Plan" of September 25, 1956, that constituted the first Stabilization Program presented to the Bolivian government and served as the basis for enactment of the legislation of December 15, 1956, and subsequent measures.

While this may give the impression that the stabilization program was virtually a one-man creation, such an impression would be wholly erroneous. It is true that the other members of what should have been a three-man U.S. Financial Mission did not arrive until after the Fifty-Step schema of the stabilization program had been completed. But the fact is that the final program was the work of many hands. The Fifty-Step Plan was discussed and revised, step by step and word by word, by the members of the Bolivian National Monetary Stabilization Council with the expert cooperation of a special mission from the International Monetary Fund headed by Dr. Gesualdo A. Costanzo.

---

*The organizing group varied in its membership from meeting to meeting, but consisted basically of President Víctor Paz-Estenssoro; the Vice-President and future President-elect, Hernán Siles-Zuazo, and his principal adviser, Miguel Gisbert-Nogué, Executive Vice-President of the National Coordinating and Planning Commission; and myself. Foreign Minister Manuel Barrau-Pelaez who, as the official intermediary with the American Embassy, had set up the initial conference, attended the first meeting. The President of the Central Bank, Franklin Antezana-Paz, and Finance Minister Alberto Mendieta-Álvarez were later added to the group. The principal economic adviser of President Paz, Arthur Karasz (a member of the U.N. Technical Mission), attended all except the initial meeting, while Ñuflo Chávez-Ortiz, Vice-President-elect and leader of the peasant militia, was present at the final revision of the basic decree creating the National Monetary Stabilization Council.

That mission arrived on the scene on October 14, 1956, and it is no exaggeration to say that the program could not have been drafted in time to be of any use without their assistance.*

Before we could get down to a discussion of stabilization principles, however, there were certain structural prerequisites which were essential to the formulation and successful operation of a stabilization program and which I outlined briefly to the President at our initial interview.[1] These were incorporated in a draft decree which I prepared for presentation at the first meeting of the organizing group, originally scheduled for June 28 but postponed until July 5, 1956, in accordance with a cable from the Department of State which stated that the decree must first be cleared with the Department. This unexpected requirement of prior clearance — the draft decree had, of course, been cleared with the American Embassy — came close to wrecking the stabilization plans at their inception. President Paz left La Paz on July 6, and Dr. Siles left for Brazil shortly after. Had the meeting been delayed a single day more, the decree would never have been enacted, as the former was reluctant to assume any responsibility and the latter refused to take the double responsibility for enactment of the decree and for carrying out the stabilization measures. That would have precluded any possibility of stabilization, as Congress could never have been persuaded to pass a law in workable form. Fortunately, the

---

*It had been my original intention to make specific reference throughout this volume to the many invaluable contributions to the stabilization program made by the IMF and, in particular, by Dr. Costanzo and by John R. Woodley, who remained in Bolivia from December, 1956, until after my departure in mid-1957. It was thought that, by quoting *in extenso* from the suggestions and comments of those gentlemen in the meetings of the Stabilization Council which they attended, two purposes would be served: (1) credit would be given where credit was due; and (2) it would deemphasize my role in creating and helping to carry out the stabilization program. Officials of the International Monetary Fund felt, however, that, as an international agency, its representatives must be free to express their views without incurring the risk of subsequent quotation or attribution. In deference to that viewpoint, I have refrained from direct quotation of the views of IMF officials or citing their attendance at council meetings, except as reported in the press. I must, however, if this is to be a complete history of the Bolivian stabilization program, give recognition to their indispensable collaboration in the creation and implementation of that program. Needless to say, the International Monetary Fund is not responsible for any statements of fact or opinion appearing in this volume, other than such material as has been taken from official publications.

intervention of the Ambassador and of Assistant Secretary of State Henry Holland, who cabled me that I would have full freedom to negotiate the text of the decree, saved the situation at the eleventh hour, although with the discourtesy of postponing a meeting with the President when he *knew* the draft decree was ready and was anxious to expedite it. It is an untenable position for an economic adviser to have the host government put on notice that his advice is subject to clearance from Washington. Thanks to Henry Holland's comprehension, this situation did not recur.

A translation of the decree, as finally enacted, is included as Appendix I, with annotations showing the changes in substance from the original draft. The draft decree began with a quotation paraphrased from the report to Bolivia's Constitutional Assembly of 1826: "Up to now, Sir, we have fought for the liberation of the people; henceforth we must fight to establish and maintain their economic welfare." The Bolivian conferees thought the quotation apt for the Revolutionary Government, and *simpático,* and it helped get the discussions off to an amicable start, despite the untimely intervention of Washington.

Planning an Effective Monetary Stabilization Council

The following conditions were postulated as a *sine qua non* for the success of the plan:

1. That a stabilization council be created at the earliest possible moment with substantially the powers set forth in the draft.
2. That the President of the Republic be designated President of the Council (Appendix I, Art. 2). This was essential in order that every measure proposed by the council would carry the full weight of the President's backing and authority. In monetary stabilization, no decision is ever based on purely technical or strictly economic reasoning. Every decision and every measure has political implications. In some cases, the broadest political, social, and economic consequences hinge on its adoption and form. In the Latin American countries, only the President (or dictator) has the power to carry through, against all extraneous political or military pressures, a politico-economic measure to which he has pledged his

support. If a measure proposed by me for the Bolivian stabilization plan proved unacceptable to the President, whether by reason of his own misgivings or because of the objections of the MNR or COB, it was up to me either to convince the President of its soundness or, better yet, to devise some appropriate and acceptable alternative. Once the council, under the chairmanship of the President, had approved a measure, however, the weight of his prestige should presumably suffice to carry it through the Cabinet. That this did not prove true in all cases was attributable to the President's minority position in the *Co-Gobierno* Cabinet.

3. That, as Executive Director of the Council, I be permitted to attend all meetings, as the Spanish phrase goes *con voz pero sin voto,* with voice, but without vote (Appendix I, Art. 2).[2]

4. That all ministries and government enterprises be required to submit to the president of the council, within thirty days, complete details of receipts and expenditures, separately in bolivianos and dollars, for each of the preceding four years and for the first six months of 1956, showing the rates of exchange used for conversions, as well as a statement of all outstanding obligations or commitments which would involve the expenditure of funds. Meanwhile, and thereafter from the date of the decree, any new obligation or commitment assumed by any government ministry or enterprise without express authorization of the council would be null and void. The phrase "null and void" was objected to by the Finance Minister at the second reading by the organizing group, but President Paz replied: "That is the key to the whole problem," adding that the worst factor in the inflation had been that there was no unified control over spending (Appendix I, Art. 6).[3]

As it turned out, none of the ministries or agencies submitted the data required, and COMIBOL, YPFB, and the Development Corporation continued to enter into new commitments without consulting the council. Nevertheless, these requirements proved their worth in curbing expenditures and commitments. A weapon of this kind may be useful even though it is only brandished and never used.

5. That no new bank notes be issued by the Central Bank nor credits granted to the government or any governmental agency or enterprise without the *unanimous*

prior approval of the council,* and that such approval be given only after a report had been submitted by the "appropriate Technical Adviser," (meaning the adviser on Central Bank matters, Ernest Moore, who was not appointed by the Bolivian government until early 1957; meanwhile the responsibility of submitting a report devolved upon the president of the Central Bank).† The word "unanimous" was desirable as otherwise some of the members of the council might play politics by voting against a measure which might prove unpopular.

6. That Congress enact a law empowering the President, on the advice of the Monetary Stabilization Council, to issue decrees with the force of law and to take such measures as might be necessary to carry out the objectives of the monetary stabilization program. A translation of this law is given in Appendix II, together with comments showing the variations from the original draft.

Without the emergency law, the stabilization program would have proved impossible. If the stabilization measures had to be enacted by the legislature, it is certain that political pressures would have altered them so fundamentally that, instead of a coordinated, well-integrated stabilization program, the country would have been faced with nothing but a continuation of the preceding confusion. Furthermore, it would have been a physical impossibility to have planned, drafted, and pushed through Congress, within any reasonable period of time, all the measures which were essential to the stabilization program. It was

*The successful Greek currency stabilization law carried a similar provision (Law 1015, February 27, 1947, Art. 2); I added the closing phrase, after the asterisk, in order to deter hasty action.

†As the note issue and credits to the government and government agencies continued to increase, not only between August, 1956, when the council was created, and December 15, 1956, when the stabilization measures were passed, but for several months thereafter, it is proper to absolve the president of the Central Bank of all responsibility for that development. The stabilization measures — at least the essential ones — all had to be enacted simultaneously. There had to be a complete and instantaneous break with the past, but the issuance of bank notes and credits to cover payrolls and certain other prior commitments could not be shut off like water at the tap, else the chaos of inflation would have been succeeded by the chaos of stabilization, and the entire program would have been discredited. Instead, all such inflationary forces were thenceforth duly reported to the council, and restricted within the closest possible limits. With this, the inflationary flood was reduced to a trickle and kept under control.

clear, for example, that it would take months to work out a complete revision of the customs tariff, and there were many other loose ends which the council realized would have to be tied up in the course of the coming year, but which it simply could not tackle by December, 1956. All that the council could hope to accomplish by the end of the year was to take the initial steps — sufficient to get the program under way — leaving the remaining measures, and any necessary amendments to the initial measures, for later enactment following a shakedown period. To have left these additional measures and amendments to the mercy of Congress would have been to subject the President and the council to irresistible political pressures and log-rolling.

This explanation of the necessity for emergency powers is inserted for the benefit of those readers who are not familiar with Latin American constitutional law and custom and who might feel that this meant "delegation run riot." The necessity was never for a moment questioned by the President or his advisers, nor by the press or general public, nor would it be viewed askance in any Latin American country under similar circumstances. The Bolivian constitution expressly provided for such emergency powers.

The only ticklish problem was to obtain the acquiescence of Congress in the manifest attenuation of its own powers and the diminution of the pecuniary advantages that accrue with power. The President charged me with the task of convincing the inner circles of the MNR and COB, and finally the Congress, of the need for these emergency powers and, by necessity, of explaining to each of these groups in turn the origin of the preceding inflation and the steps that the council intended to take to stabilize the currency. I was reluctant to engage in propaganda for the program before political groups and had hoped that the President and the Bolivian members of the council would assume that task. In their judgment, however, the intervention of an outside "expert" added the weight of a presumption of objectivity, and they concluded that, had it not been for these "political" speeches and frank answers to all questions, neither the emergency law nor the stabilization program could have passed.

These talks entailed answering their questions extemporaneously. Some of these questions were extremely penetrating, while others — particularly from the Trotskyite or communist members of Congress — were clearly intended to be merely disruptive. The latter questions were left to be answered in

angry repartee by others in the audience with whom members
of the council had spoken in advance to ensure having some
well-informed supporters at each meeting. (Moral: One must
learn communist tactics in order to beat them at their own
game.)

The foregoing six points embraced the indispensable structural prerequisites which were embodied either in the decree
creating the Stabilization Council or in the enabling act. Certain other points which were recommended in order to facilitate
the work of the council, but which were perhaps not absolutely
essential to its operations may be mentioned.

Essential and nonessential government functions

With a view to establishing priorities in expenditures (and
at the same time stressing that inflation was largely attributable to the government's having entered fields more properly
cultivated by private industry), the draft decree sought to distinguish between (1) essential governmental functions (defense,
foreign affairs, etc.), in which the council's intervention would
be limited to recommending the greatest possible economy;
(2) indispensable social obligations which private capital will
not meet (the "infrastructure" of schools, roads, public health,
etc.), in which the council would be charged with seeing that
expenditures and commitments did not exceed the government's
resources, including U.S. aid; and (3) those functions which,
given a proper investment climate, could be fulfilled by private
initiative (industrial, commercial, financial, utility enterprises,
etc.), in which the council would seek ways of attracting private
capital, thus leaving the government free to use its sparse resources in fields where private investors would not venture.

The State Department cable had suggested elimination of
this entire article, at which the President exclaimed that this
was the very marrow of the entire decree, and the one part that
would convince the public that the government really meant to
do something about inflation. Gisbert* was entrusted with re-
drafting the article in such a way as not to reflect upon the past
activities of the government, yet preserving the three-way

*In Bolivia, Gisbert would be referred to as "Ing. Gisbert" (Engineer
Gisbert). With no pretense of consistency, engineering titles are omitted,
but the "Dr." for all lawyers is retained in conformity with common usage
in most countries of Latin America.

division of governmental functions — indispensable, desirable, and dispensable. (Appendix I, Arts. 4 and 5.) [4]

Supervision of legislation

The original draft provided that decree-laws and other measures could be proposed to the Stabilization Council by the Executive Director or by any of the council members, and that such measures would be considered by the council following a report to be made by the Executive Director (Appendix I, Art. 3). It was obvious that various measures might be proposed by the members (perhaps by the President himself) from time to time, and that they might be voted upon and passed before the Executive Director had had time to study their implications and propose a tactful and acceptable alternative. This provision was a way of imposing some measure of control by bottleneck, inasmuch as the Executive Director would have neither vote nor veto. Too much important legislation in Latin America is improvised, and many of Bolivia's difficulties were traceable to decrees enacted in haste and repented at leisure. The State Department had suggested elimination of this safeguard in its entirety, but the conferees unanimously supported it, and agreed that the Executive Director could be most useful as a scapegoat (*cabeza de Turco**).[5] As a matter of fact, this proved to be one of my chief functions, as I was able to bear the brunt of attacks that would otherwise have been directed against the President.

Similarly, to forestall improvised legislation by Congress, and following a suggestion made by President Paz, the draft decree provided that the President would turn over to the council for its study all bills of an economic nature passed by Congress. The council would then recommend a veto or not, depending upon the availability of funds and the implications of the bill with respect to monetary stabilization. The Department of State had recommended elimination of this provision on the ground that a limitation on the President's powers would be meaningless, as he could veto a bill or not as he saw fit. This

*A Turk's head. During the Moslem invasions, the Spaniards would raise a captive's head on a pole to draw the arrows of the Saracens. By extension, a Turk's head is the rope ball which protects a ship's side from lighters or tugs, or which was used in tournaments for lancers to tilt at, in other words, a whipping boy or scapegoat.

was elaborating the obvious, but the equally obvious advantage
to the President of interposing the council as a scapegoat between an ill-considered measure of Congress and the disagreeable necessity of a Presidential veto seems to have escaped the
Department. The President, President-elect, and Gisbert, later
joined by the Vice-President-elect Ñuflo Chávez, discussed the
matter, and agreement was reached in the form shown in Appendix I.[6] In the redraft, the Executive Director and his colleagues on the U.S. Financial Mission were made advisers to
the Senate and House committees on financial, budgetary, and
similar matters (Appendix I, Art. 7). This was wrong in principle. An economic adviser should not be required to serve two
masters, but the President and President-elect insisted upon it
and, as it turned out, neither the Senate nor the House ever consulted the U.S. Mission.

Stabilization Council membership

The original draft, in addition to having the President as
President of the Council and the Finance Minister as Vice-
President, proposed that the Bolivian members should include
the Minister of Foreign Affairs, the Minister of Economy, and
the heads of the Central Bank and the Planning Commission.
The conferees at the first meeting of the organizing group had
insisted on inclusion of the Minister of Mines, to which I objected that the Minister of Agriculture and other ministers
would then wish to be included, and the council would become
unwieldly. The real reason for the objection, however, was
based on the advice of the Embassy that the Minister of Mines
under the COB-MNR "Co-Government" would be a labor representative picked by Lechín and the miners' federation and that
it was essential to have the council represent *national* and not
factional interests. The objection was overruled, but it served
to keep down the size of the council, as President Paz had also
suggested including the Minister of Peasant Affairs (a Trotskyite) and the presidents of the Mining Bank and COMIBOL. The
latter two would have been an invaluable addition; the Trotskyite
would have been a disaster. As it turned out, the Minister of
Mines proved to be an indispensable member of the council.

The original draft had provided that the other ministers,
and the various agency heads, could attend council meetings
when matters of particular interest in their fields were to be
discussed, and that in such cases they would have "voice but not

vote." In the end, it was decided that Cabinet ministers would be admitted to council meetings, with the right to vote in matters affecting their respective departments, or without vote in other matters, and that other government officials (which would include officers of COMIBOL, YPFB, and other agencies) could be invited by the President to attend meetings, but without vote (Appendix I, Art. 2).

FALLACY AND FACT

Two out of three Bolivians — in the government and out of the government, bankers, businessmen, Marxists, conservatives — attributed the plight of the Bolivian peso to the Chaco War. This seemed amazing, as the Chaco War had ended over twenty years before and, from the viewpoint of monetary stabilization in 1956, was about as relevant as attributing Bolivia's economic underdevelopment to the fact that South America had been isolated from the rest of the world for 70,000,000 years, until the close of the Pliocene period. Certainly, if the Chaco War *were* the cause of the hyperinflation, there was nothing that could be done about it, and not much point in having a U.S. stabilization mission. On further reflection, however, this popular impression appears to contain at least a kernel of truth for, as Osborne says, the Chaco defeat "left in its wake a lasting sense of exhaustion, bitterness, and frustration," [7] and it is true that in Bolivia there prevailed an attitude of hopelessness and helplessness that I had never before encountered in any Latin American country.

Structural Theories

An equally depressing view was taken by other interlocutors. In their opinion, Bolivia's monetary troubles were due to the fact that the country was almost wholly dependent on tin production and prices — to structural forces in the economy. Again, if this were true, there was not too much that the mission could do to remedy the situation, although, as will be seen later, the revival of agriculture as a consequence of the monetary stabilization program did in fact serve to redress the balance to a considerable extent. The structuralists were about equally divided between those who attributed the current troubles to allegedly low world prices for tin (and some of these spoke darkly of a conspiracy between the English and Americans to keep prices down) and those who cited lower production as the cause. The latter were split between those who blamed the drop in production on the "lack of discipline" on the part of the miners and those, chiefly in the government, who blamed the international tin quotas or the lower tin content of the ores and the exhaustion of the mines. In some cases, the depletion of ore had reached a point where the tailings of past operations had a higher metal content than the veins being currently mined.*

As to tin prices, however, current prices were *not* low by any reasonable standards of the past, although they had dropped since the years of the Korean War. As to production, while it was true that the miners were simply not working as hard as formerly and that many of the mines had long since become unprofitable, the solution could not be supplied by a monetary stabilization council. It was to be found, if at all, in courageous action by political and labor leaders, and in new exploration and development, following the recommendations in the nine-volume Ford, Bacon & Davis report, which proved to be too damning of the consequences of the Bolivian Revolution to be either published or followed.[8]

Monetary Theories

Neither war nor prices nor production, nor other structural causes, however, appeared to suggest the true origin of inflation in Bolivia, or to point the way to a solution. Certainly, it is true that a "one-crop" country is more subject to the extremes of boom and bust than a country with a more balanced economy, but those experienced in Latin American affairs may recall that Cuba, a one-crop country par excellence, managed to maintain her currency at par after the "Dance of the Millions" had ended, when sugar dropped from 23.2 cents a pound to 4.7 cents, between May and November, 1920, and continued the downward plunge in 1921 to well below the cost of production. It may be recalled too that Germany after two wars, and Japan after one, both far more devastated internally and by

---

*The structuralists insist, in Bolivia as elsewhere in Latin America, that the country's troubles are all due to forces beyond its control — international commodity prices and demand, lack of capital, etc.; e.g., Memorandum II, "Economic Development of the Republic of Bolivia," presented by the Ministry of Foreign Affairs in December, 1954, to justify Bolivia's request for U.S. aid. This is a comforting doctrine — if something is beyond one's control, one cannot be blamed for misfortune. But an honest *mea culpa* might be more conducive to tackling the job of putting matters right.

loss of territory than Bolivia, had succeeded in stabilizing their currencies, and that the Haitian gourde and the Central American currencies had long been maintained at par throughout decades of internal strife, at least as sanguinary and destructive as Bolivia's war with Paraguay.

Of all Bolivia's analysts, only two, Drs. Humberto Fossati and Franklin Antezana, seem to have pinpointed the true and virtually sole cause of Bolivia's galloping inflation — the chronic deficit in the national budget, financed by borrowing from the Central Bank, which in turn was forced to issue ever-increasing quantities of bank notes to provide the funds.[9] Perhaps there were others who shared that view, but if there were, their opinions did not come to the Stabilization Council's attention.

Cornelius H. Zondag, the economist for the U.S. Operations Mission, likewise recognized that the cause of the runaway inflation was to be found in the increase in circulation resulting from governmental deficits. His report contains charts showing the simultaneous rise in circulation, living costs, and the free market quotation for dollars. However, not having access to the facts which the council was later in a position to obtain, Zondag attributed the excess spending chiefly to the credits granted to COMIBOL, the government mining corporation. This was a natural conclusion based on a study of the Central Bank accounts, and one which was shared by Dr. Antezana, president of that institution.[10]

Zondag correctly showed that the inflation had given rise to a vicious capital flight which in turn engendered further inflation, and that price controls had been absolutely useless in checking the rise in prices, leading only to black markets which escaped all controls.[11] At the same time, he pointed out that the propensity of the Bolivian Indian to hoard paper money had to some extent tempered the inflationary pressures. This phenomenon is corroborated by Osborne and Keenleyside. In 1950, before the inflation was rampant, it was estimated that between 20 and 40 per cent of the entire note circulation was hoarded.[12] Whether or not this percentage would hold true at the height of the inflation would be difficult to say, but one Bolivian attorney told of the death of a client of his, a cholo, reputed to be wealthy, who died leaving a great quantity of paper money that, judging from the dates of some of the bank notes, represented savings of well over $10,000, but which were worth less than $100 at the time of his death. It was said that this situation was typical, although generally on a smaller scale.

The Economic Commission for Latin America likewise attributes the galloping inflation from 1952 through 1956 to government expenditures, plus a program of government "investments," that together called for resources in excess of its capacity, and hence required financing through Central Bank credit. ECLA points out that, to a lesser extent, the municipalities and departments, as well as the national government, had recourse to the Central Bank for credit, but that loans to independent government agencies, and above all to the mining corporation, were the principal source of inflationary pressure. The responsibility of the private sector in the inflationary process, they concluded, was less than that of mining and the public sector. This conclusion is borne out by tables in the ECLA report which show aggregate private bank loans of Bs. 5,836 million, as of June 30, 1956, and Central Bank loans to the private sector, on the same date, of Bs. 5,991 million. Governmental borrowings from the private banks were minor. At the most, then, credits to the private sector totalled Bs. 11,827 million. By contrast, Central Bank loans to the government sector (at the nearest comparable date shown in the ECLA report) amounted to Bs. 204,604 million.[13] In other words, judging by bank note circulation and bank credit, the private sector was responsible for only 5.5 per cent of the inflationary pressure.*

However, this figure overlooked the inflationary pressure of U.S. economic aid through the printing of currency to take care of counterpart fund requirements (between Bs. 12 billion and Bs. 30 billion), all of which must be charged to the government sector, and, of even greater importance, the sale of foreign exchange by the Central Bank at the official rate of Bs. 190 to the dollar. By far the greater part of these sales was to the government sector, chiefly the Development Corporation and YPFB (COMIBOL may be ignored here, as Central Bank profits on foreign exchange generated by COMIBOL exceeded its losses on sales of exchange to COMIBOL). It is these sales at the Bs. 190 rate which, more than any other factor, served to wipe out Bolivia's entire gold and foreign exchange reserve.

It would seem evident that if a Central Bank loan to a government enterprise is inflationary, then a Central Bank gift to

---

*Figures published by the Superintendency of Banks (Estadística Bancaria) show Central Bank loans to the government and independent agencies, as of June 30, 1956, of Bs. 124.5 billion, which would bring the private sector percentage up to 8.7 per cent.

that enterprise is equally inflationary; and the sale of dollars for Bs. 190, when the market rate of exchange was between Bs. 4,000 and Bs. 14,000, was manifestly a gift. Parenthetically, the "loans" may also be considered as gifts, for a loan, where there is neither the intention nor the capacity to repay, is a gift masquerading as a business transaction.

Considering all factors, therefore, it was reasonable to conclude that the government was responsible for at least 90 per cent and perhaps as much as 98 per cent of the inflation in Bolivia from 1953 to mid-1956. If this were true (and by hindsight it proved to be), the concept of a stabilization program to remove the cause of the inflation was relatively simple, as will be seen by the discussion in Chapter 7.*

Exposing the Fallacies

First, however, it was necessary to convince the leading figures in the government — President Paz, President-elect Siles, Lechín, Chávez, and their advisers — that the runaway inflation was due to government spending, financed through the Central Bank and the printing press. It was necessary to wipe out all their preconceptions and misconceptions and, in effect, convince them that they alone were to blame for Bolivia's present troubles. The term "first" at the beginning of this paragraph connotes some sort of sequence, and, in logic, the proof of the cause of the monetary depreciation would have to precede the search for a remedy. In actual fact, everything had to be done simultaneously — the planning for the creation of a

*This is as good a place as any to explain that where I speak of stabilization of the Bolivian currency, I have in mind stabilization in terms of dollars (or gold). Manifestly, a stable currency should be one that is stable or relatively stable in terms of purchasing power. I was at one time a crusading advocate of a "managed currency" (see George Jackson Eder, "Effect of Gold Price Changes upon Prices for Other Commodities," *Journal of the Royal Statistical Society,* CI [1938], 173-87), and I still believe in the possibility and desirability of monetary management. But to have aimed at a managed currency with the objective of price stability in a country as structurally imbalanced as Bolivia would have been wholly unrealistic. Stability in terms of foreign exchange, in hard currency or gold, *was* attainable, and would bring with it a far greater stability in internal and external purchasing power for Bolivia's currency than had existed for nearly three decades. This was the goal.

monetary stabilization council, the proof of the origin of the inflation, and the outline of a stabilization program — in order to inspire the organizing group with the *absolute conviction* that a solution was feasible, simple, and sure.

There may have been doubts at times as to whether the government would take the measures necessary to carry out the stabilization program, but I had no doubts as to its success if it were carried out. It was essential to adoption of the plan that this conviction be indelibly impressed upon the government and upon such public opinion as counted in the operation, meaning the labor unions, the MNR, Congress, the press, and the business community, roughly in that order of importance.

In preparation for this task of marshalling the facts into a convincing argument, I had assembled a mass of statistical data going back to 1897 in the case of tin prices, and back to 1918 for bank note circulation, quotations for the boliviano, etc. Fortunately, I had two U.S. Department of Commerce publications, long since out of print, and these contained foreign exchange data which it proved impossible to obtain in Bolivia. By the end of June, these figures had been completed, and a series of relatives worked out by slide rule, necessitating conventional adjustments at each point where one series of figures ended and a new series commenced.

But it was essential to have the data available, not merely in statistical tables, which would have been unintelligible to the audience that it was necessary to convince. The many adjustments and computations, mathematically valid, would have looked like a manipulation of the facts to suit the argument, and it must be borne in mind that the gist of that argument was that the government and the MNR are to blame for the hyperinflation, and here is the proof. It was a task for a lawyer arguing to a jury against all the inbred prejudices of the jurymen, not an academic presentation by an economist or statistician, replete with the usual disclaimers of *ceteris paribus* and "on the other hand."

Hence, I condensed the material into four simple charts prepared with a felt pen, each broad enough to carry conviction and to slur over statistical inaccuracies, and containing no more material than could be readily comprehended. To avoid complications, on the first chart (Fig. 2 here), the 1918 par of 38.93 cents was used for the boliviano, without revaluation to the 1927 par of 36.5 cents. The breadth of the line graph obviated the need for adjustment. For one of the charts, a semilogarithmic chart would have been more logical, but this was tried out on an associate who failed to understand why the figures at the side were not uniformly spaced. That then was out, so the charts were traced on simple squared paper. Photocopies of the charts and of the supporting statistical data and computations (which would not be read at the meeting, but which would be passed out to carry impressive evidence of ample preparation) were ready for presentation at the July 5 meeting of the organizing group, but since that meeting was taken up with discussion of the draft decree establishing the Stabilization Council, the charts were held over for the July 12 meeting, following a week's trip around the country in the company of President Paz and members of his entourage, the American Ambassador, the head of the U.S. Operations Mission, and others.

The showdown — meeting of July 12

The circumstances of the meeting could hardly have been less auspicious. The President had opened the session by stating that its purpose was to discuss the emergency measures that had to be taken *instantly* to prevent a further drop in the value of the boliviano, until such time as the National Monetary Stabilization Council could be formed. He announced that he had obtained lists of people who were buying dollars in the free market, with no legitimate need for dollars, and he recommended that the names be published, and penalties imposed.

Sr. Gisbert (the Planning Commission head) pointed out, however, that free market operations were not illegal, and that penalties would therefore be inequitable. Karasz (the U.N. financial adviser) stated that the rise in the boliviano price for dollars was three times the rise in circulation, so that it could not be attributed to the increase in the note issue, but to the fact that people were using the free exchange market for purposes for which it was not intended when the 1953 "stabilization" decrees were enacted; that the intention of the 1953 decrees was that the free market would be used only to pay for the legitimate invisibles in the balance of payments. To put a stop to this abuse, he recommended that all free market foreign exchange purchases be considered *income* and taxed accordingly, unless the buyer could prove a legitimate transaction. With that, he submitted a series of decrees he had prepared in advance of the meeting, providing for:

1. Taxation as *income* of foreign exchange purchases on the free market, or from dealers.
2. Seizure by the Central Bank of merchandise imported at official or special exchange rates with foreign exchange derived from certain agricultural or mining exports. The bank would then pay the exporter the dollar value, give the importer an allowable percentage profit in bolivianos, sell the merchandise on the market, give 50 per cent of the profit to the Treasury, keep 25 per cent, and give 25 per cent to the bank employees' benefit fund.*
3. Restriction of free exchange operations by banking institutions to a total of Bs. 20 million (say $2,000 at the prevailing exchange rate) for each bank, out of their own capital; depositors' money could not be used for that purpose.
4. Restriction on the use of "excess production" foreign exchange by the private mines to the purchase of imports for their own use (i.e., under existing regulations, if a mining company produced ore in excess of previous production, it could keep 80 per cent of the foreign exchange from this excess, and use it for imports or sell the privilege to others; this right was now to be made nontransferable).
5. Prohibition of transfer to third parties of the right to import goods at the official rate of exchange against exports of agricultural and livestock products.

The Finance Minister concurred with these proposed measures and stated that the Superintendent of Banks could trace the flight of capital through the free market, as well as imports of merchandise with foreign exchange bought on that market. Gisbert held that any such controls would be futile, to which Dr. Siles replied that inasmuch as all the classical economic remedies had been tried in the attempt to stop the drop in the boliviano, and had failed, and neither of the experts present (Karasz and Eder) had any other suggestions, it was essential to enforce effective punitive measures, if necessary at bayonet

*As the bank would have to compute its dollar cost on the absurd Bs. 190 rate, this would convert the confusion to chaos. "Oh, what a tangled web we weave when first we practice to deceive," and the author of "Lochinvar" had never heard of official and multiple exchange rates when he wrote those words. But if buying foreign exchange — *outgo* — is *income*, anything is possible.

point or with jail sentences, in order to prevent improper merchandise imports and the flight of capital.*

Karasz stated that his proposed measures would accomplish that purpose; that the cause of the drop in the boliviano was the failure of Bolivia to increase its production to keep up with consumer demand; and that, until production could be increased, it was necessary to put controls on consumption. The discussion continued, with many suggestions for controls and punitive measures, until finally the President stated that the proposed measures would be enacted by decree, and asked if all agreed, turning to me as he spoke, for some indication of agreement, as, up to that point, I had taken no part in the discussion.

In reply, I stated that perhaps I should speak out, lest silence be taken to indicate approval, and continued with the following observations: that no system of controls or punitive measures could be effective in stemming the drop in the boliviano; that Bolivia's experience since 1953, and experience in every country of the world, showed that price controls, foreign exchange controls, and other controls have always proved ineffectual; that as soon as controls are instituted, there is either a shortage of merchandise, or black markets, contraband, and corruption, or all four together; and that any attempt to substitute government restrictions for free supply and demand in a free society is doomed to failure.

The mere fact of publication of the Stabilization Council decree would in itself strengthen the boliviano even though no stabilization measures could be taken for many months, as speculators would assume that, when stabilization came, it would be at less than the then current rate of Bs. 9,000 to the dollar, and they would be afraid to be caught with their pants down (the Spanish expression was somewhat cruder). Furthermore, I would prefer not to be associated with any additional control measures, as this might create a false impression as to the steps I intended to recommend and thus prejudice the

---

*It was generally believed that the free exchange market was the major outlet (*el gran puente*) for the flight of capital. Actually, free market transactions were insignificant, and the major channels were the smuggling of exports, the under-invoicing of declared exports, and the over-invoicing of imports. Most of the traffic was conducted by the *politicos* who ran the destinies of the country, or by their close associates, so that any control was impossible.

ultimate success of the program; that perhaps it might be well for me to outline the policies I expected to recommend to the council, once it was set up, in order that the conferees might judge whether any of the measures they now intended taking would be inadvisable.

The President stated that Karasz's measures would in any event be enacted, as the need was urgent, but that they would all like very much to hear my plans.*

The causes of the Bolivian inflation

Before coming to any conclusion as to what ought to be done to arrest the drop in the boliviano, I explained, I wished to be sure that the true causes were known, and, as there were no long-term statistical data available, I had compiled my own. I thereupon launched into the following exposition of the facts, based upon the charts and tables which were passed around the table, as the discussion proceeded.

The first chart (Fig. 2) showed that the present plight of the boliviano could not be attributed to the Chaco War, as seemed to be the general impression in Bolivia, inasmuch as the dollar value of metal exports, which was a measure of Bolivia's economic capacity to keep its currency on a par with the dollar, had since risen to levels far higher than at any time prior to that war. The low value of exports during the Chaco War period was due not so much to that war as to a worldwide depression, as shown by the far greater drop in the value of U.S. production of metals. (The chart presented at the meeting contained a third line showing the value of U.S. metal production. In later expositions to other groups, and in the chart reproduced here, that graph has been eliminated in order to simplify the presentation.) Figures were then cited to show that, although tin prices and total metal exports had slumped to some extent since the high point reached during the Korean War, both

*The decrees were promulgated on July 20 and proved completely ineffective although they caused considerable consternation in business circles. A delegate from the Chamber of Commerce complained that business had been led to believe that I would recommend increased freedom of trade, not further restrictions and penalties, and they were concerned at the turn of events. At a Stabilization Council meeting two months later the Minister of Economy reported that the decree had caused more difficulties than the inflation itself.

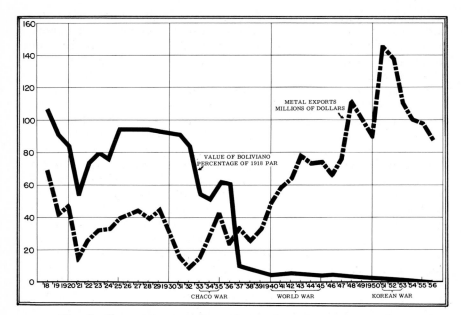

Fig. 2. Economic capacity and monetary depreciation. (Source: Central Bank Bulletin and other sources.) [14]

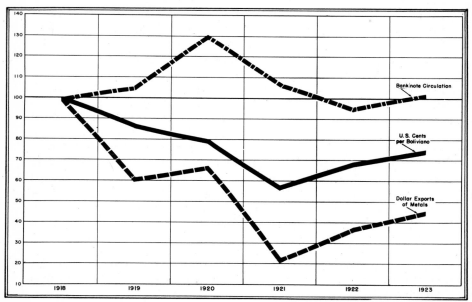

Fig. 3. Monetary depreciation, 1918-23. (Source: Central Bank Bulletin.) [15]

tin prices and the dollar value of Bolivia's metal exports — the source of 90 to 95 per cent of its foreign exchange — had been greater over the past six years than at any previous time in Bolivia's history; and that, if Bolivia could keep its currency above par in 1918, with $69 million of metal exports, it could certainly do so in 1956, with $90 million.

There were objections that the purchasing power of the dollar in 1956 was less than in 1918; that Bolivia therefore had to import more dollars' worth of goods now than then; and that it was the balance of payments rather than the value of exports that was the vital factor. To this, it was replied that Bolivia would be better off if the boliviano had been maintained at par with the dollar even though the 1956 boliviano, like the dollar, might buy less than the 1918 boliviano; that it would have been well within Bolivia's power to maintain parity with the depreciated dollar;* that Bolivia did not actually *need* to import more in 1956 than in 1918; and that the chief reason for its present high import level was an erroneous financial policy that would be referred to later, namely, maintenance of a wholly artificial rate of exchange of Bs. 190 to the dollar. With respect to the balance of international payments, Bolivia was no longer paying interest on its foreign debt and, on the other hand, was receiving $20 million a year in U.S. aid, so that certainly, so far as Bolivia's economic capacity was concerned, there was no reason for the boliviano to be worth less in terms of dollars in 1956 than it was worth in 1918, except for reasons which would be made clear from the charts which would now be shown.

Figure 3 was then handed out to show that there could be periods, such as had occurred in 1918-23, when a drop in the dollar value of metal exports was indeed responsible for the drop in the value of the boliviano. It was stated that it would perhaps have been possible in 1919, had the nation been better prepared, to have maintained the value of the currency in spite of the drop in exports, but that what had actually happened was that, during World War I, metal prices and Bolivia's exports had been unusually high, and Bolivian merchants had placed orders for merchandise well in excess of normal needs, but had been unable to obtain shipments in view of war conditions. As soon

---

*Compared with the high point during the Korean War, the "terms of trade" for Bolivia were worse in 1956, but compared with any "normal" period, Bolivia was better off. There was no need to go into this point at the meeting.

as the war was over, U.S. manufacturers started filling those orders, and the Bolivian market was flooded with merchandise precisely at a time when metal prices, and the world demand for metals, had slumped disastrously, and Bolivia did not have enough dollars to pay for its orders.*

Then, in 1920, raw commodity prices had crashed and the crisis all over Latin America was the worst in recent history — much worse than in 1929-30. Bolivian tax collections dropped, and the government was forced to turn to the then National Bank for help, with the result that there was a 30 per cent increase in paper money circulation and an even greater drop in the value of the boliviano. With a return to sound financial policies, however, bank note circulation was brought down to normal by 1923. The boliviano started to recover, and held reasonably steady from 1924 until the next world depression of 1929, as was shown by the first chart.

When Figures 4 and 5 were handed around, there were gasps of astonishment from everyone around the table except from Dr. Antezana-Paz who was fully aware of the influence of bank note circulation on the value of the Bolivian peso. Figure 4 showed that there was obviously a close relationship between the increase in bank note circulation and the drop in the value of the boliviano, but it was explained that the chart covered too long a period, with too many diverse factors present, to be of much value as a guide to the present.

Turning to Figure 5, it was stated that the increase in bank note circulation, and consequently in the total money supply, which included bank deposits, was attributable solely to the fact that the government, and the various governmental agencies and enterprises, were spending far in excess of their means, and compelling the Central Bank to lend or give them the money, which it could only do by issuing more bank notes. The graph showing total money supply was dropped from the charts used in later speeches, as it was too difficult to explain that bank deposits should be added to bank note issue to show the total. On several occasions, the argument was advanced that bank deposits represent savings and are therefore counterinflationary.

---

*The situation was the same in 1919-20 in every country of Latin America. American exporters cannot escape all blame for the 1920 crisis when they filled orders placed months or years previously, knowing that the slump in commodity prices would affect their customers' capacity to pay.

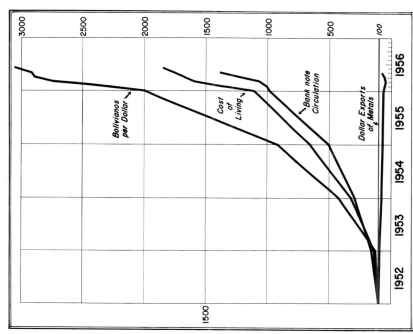

Fig. 5. Monetary depreciation, 1952-56.
Index 1951=100. (Source: Central Bank Bulletin.)[17]

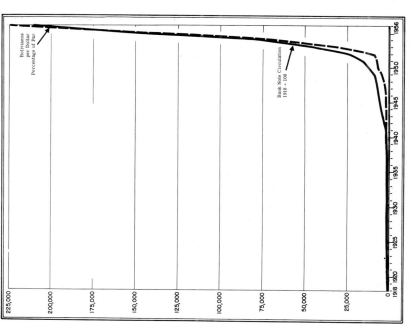

Fig. 4. Bank note circulation and monetary
depreciation. (Source: Central Bank Bulletin and
other sources.)[16]

"Keep it simple" is sound advice in economic as well as in legal argument.*

Dr. Antezana-Paz nodded his head in complete agreement, in answer to the unspoken questions of the remaining conferees who turned to him for comment. (Figure 1, shown at page 42, gives proof that government borrowing was responsible for at least 90 per cent of the increase in the money supply, but the data were not then available. However, no one in government or out ever questioned the fact that it was the government sector whose borrowings, chiefly from the Central Bank, had compelled that bank to increase its issues of paper money.)

The most vicious feature in Bolivia's financial policy, it was emphasized, was the maintenance of the completely artificial rate of Bs. 190 which, when applied to the agricultural products furnished under U.S. aid, or imported from Argentina or Brazil, had virtually strangled Bolivian agriculture, which could not meet such ruinous competition. As a result, Bolivia was now importing some $20 to $25 million of farm products that she could, and should, produce herself. The Bs. 190 rate also meant that the government did not have enough counterpart funds to build roads, schools, etc., and had to run a deficit in its fiscal accounts; that smuggling, black-marketing, and corruption were completely out of control; and that there was not a department, agency, or enterprise of the government that had the faintest idea of what it was really spending, as dollar expenditures were entered in their accounts at Bs. 190 to the dollar when they really ought to be entered at perhaps Bs. 4,000, 5,000, or 6,000 to the dollar, and accounts were shown in balance when in reality there were huge deficits that had to be financed by the Central Bank through the issuance of paper money.

This, it was concluded, was the true and practically sole cause of the plight of the boliviano. But the very fact that monetary depreciation was so clearly attributable to erroneous financial, foreign exchange, and price policies made it possible to claim, with absolute conviction, that the boliviano could be stabilized. It was imperative, however, that the measures

*If Figure 5 looks familiar to monetary experts, that is not surprising. It is in fact almost identical to James Harvey Rogers' chart "Exchange, Prices and Circulation in Germany, 1918-23," showing that exchange rose most sharply, prices next, and circulation least. Because of the trillion-to-one magnitude of the German inflation, Professor Rogers plotted logarithms of the items (*The Process of Inflation in France, 1914-27* [New York: Columbia University Press, 1929]).

recommended by the Stabilization Council should not be improvised, precipitate, or piecemeal — a great many steps had to be taken simultaneously, or chaos would result.

By this time, all the conferees, with the exception of the U.N. adviser, were ready to accept without question this explanation of the true origin of the inflation, and had caught the contagion of my *absolute conviction* that stabilization of the currency lay within their grasp. The suddenness of their conversion to these views, which ran counter to everything that the Revolutionary Government had said or done for the past three years, can only be explained by the fact that, in spite of all they and others had said about the Chaco War, low tin prices, and the neo-Keynesian argument that spending and printing paper money is not inflationary if used for investment, they knew instinctively that the printing press lay at the root of all their troubles.

At this point, Dr. Siles interrupted to ask how soon the council would be in a position to make its first recommendations because, if something were not done quickly, he would soon be dangling from the same lamp post on which Villaroel had been hanged. To this, it was replied that definitive action could hardly be expected before the end of the year and that, although the general plan of action was clear (which I proceeded to outline, as set forth below, pp. 128ff), it would be necessary to investigate the many laws and decrees that would have to be amended or repealed, and that I was handicapped in that ICA had as yet been unable to find the two other advisers who would complete the U.S. Financial Mission.

The facts on government expenditures

While nearly three more months were to pass before the Stabilization Council could obtain even an approximation of the facts about government expenditures in dollars and in bolivanos, those facts were an essential part of the effort to wipe the slate clean of prevailing misconceptions as to the true origins of the inflationary process, and they are therefore recorded in this chapter dealing with fallacy and fact in the Bolivian inflation.

With the exception of two of the Planning Board economists, apparently everyone in Bolivia, including even the well-informed president of the Central Bank, blamed COMIBOL for the huge and ever-increasing issues of paper money. This was true, regardless of whether they believed that the paper money issues were the *cause* of the inflation, or whether, like the U.N. adviser, they believed that increased bank note circulation was merely a *consequence* of the inflation. As that gentleman put it at the July 12 meeting of the organizing group, to attempt to stop the inflation by ceasing the issuance of bank notes would be like trying to control a heat wave by breaking the thermometers, and he cited the classical story of the municipal authorities in Paris obliterating the high-water marks on the Seine embankment because the people were terrified by the impending threat of a spring flood.

The belief that the mining corporation deficits were responsible for the rise in bank note circulation was held, not only among Bolivians, but by everyone in the American Embassy and in Washington, and is found in the three authoritative reports on the Bolivian economy of the era — that of Zondag for the U.S. Operations Mission, and the two U.N. reports of Keenleyside and ECLA.

No other conclusion could possibly have been drawn from the published and unpublished accounts of the Central Bank showing the continuing credits to COMIBOL and the concomitant issues of paper money to provide the funds to meet those credits. And yet it was hard for me to believe that this could be true. I had no illusions as to COMIBOL's making a profit, for there could be no doubt that COMIBOL was losing money hand over fist; but there is a vast difference between profits on the one hand and cash flow on the other. It just did not seem possible that Bolivia (and hence COMIBOL) could be receiving more dollars for its tin and other metal exports than it had ever received in the days of the tin barons, and yet be spending so much more than it received as to leave a deficit in its cash accounts that would call for billions of bolivianos of credit from the Central Bank.

Somewhere in the never-never land of multiple exchange rates, it seemed sure, was to be found the explanation. And, if that could be discovered, it should show too what agencies of government were in fact responsible for the billions of Central Bank credit, the billions of bank note circulation, and the hyperinflation.

Assembling the data. Thus, in the first agenda and stabilization time table, presented to the organizing group on July 17, I asked the President to issue orders to the heads of all government departments, agencies, and enterprises to assign a high official in each unit to provide complete details of their receipts and expenditures, separately in dollars and bolivianos, for the past four years and for the first six months of the current year, as was called for in Article 6 of the draft decree which was to establish the Stabilization Council (Appendix I).

Dr. Humberto Fossati, an economist employed by the Planning Commission, was assigned the task of procuring and assembling the data and was given full authority to call upon the Comptroller General, the Central Bank, and the various government departments, agencies, and enterprises for their cooperation. I drew up for Fossati the exact form in which the material was needed, with its related supporting data. Six weeks later, Fossati showed me the full results of his investigation — practically nil and totally useless. *Information on government and government enterprise expenditures, broken down into boliviano and dollar accounts, was simply not available for any period between January, 1952, and September, 1956.**

The Economic Commission for Latin America, with greater facilities and more time at its disposal, reports:

> It is not an easy task to analyze the fiscal accounts in Bolivia. The organization of public finance and the accounting methods are extremely complicated and confused. Together with the taxes and other revenues received by the central government, departments and municipalities, there are other charges collected by independent agencies, or even by government bureaus, which do not show up in the budget or in the accounts of the Ministry of Finance. Thus, alongside the general budget there has in fact been another independent budget administered by the Ministry of Economy.... Taxes on oil and its derivatives, including those collected for the benefit of the central government as well as those established for the benefit of the departments or specified

*This is no reflection on Dr. Fossati. His ability and his status in government circles were such that, if anyone was in a position to obtain the material needed, he certainly was. Dr. Siles had recommended Fossati for the post of Secretary General of the Stabilization Council and later, on August 2, 1956, he informed me that he was considering naming Fossati Minister of Finance, but refrained from doing so, doubtless for reasons that are set forth on page 165n. The following month, however, the President of the Central Bank informed me that he would probably be replaced by Fossati, and this was confirmed by other sources. The appointment failed to materialize at the time, but in 1963 he was appointed Central Bank President by President Paz-Estenssoro. Thus, his standing with at least two wings of the MNR party was undoubtedly of the highest, and his ability was beyond question.

agencies, are collected and distributed by the Government
Petroleum Corporation. The same is true of other taxes,
such as traffic taxes and fines, certain excises on sugar,
etc.... The confusion is even greater with respect to expenditures. The general budget in fact includes only the
current administrative expenses of the central government
and certain minor investments. The most important investments are in charge of independent agencies, and their
financing has come from various sources, such as United
States Government aid, the proceeds of taxes received by
the Ministry of Economy, and loans from the Central Bank.
None of these accounts shows up in the general budgets nor
in the financial statements of the central government....
There is no relationship between the annual figures of the
Comptroller General's Office and those of the Central
Bank....[18]

The hardest thing in a monetary stabilization program, or
in any government planning in Latin America, is to get the facts,
and it still seemed expedient to get the facts first, and to act
second. As a last resort, I decided I could make do with a
breakdown of the 1956 budget, if that could be obtained, knowing
full well that any relationship between government budgets and
government receipts and expenditures would be tenuous at best.

The Finance Minister thereupon assigned two competent
officials of the ministry to the task of compiling the data, and on
September 24, at a joint meeting with the Minister and Dr. Fossati, I gave them an outline of my requirements. In less than a
fortnight, the preliminary results were ready, sufficiently detailed for discussion at the October 5 meeting of the council.[19]
By the first week in November the work was completed, in the
shape of six desk-size tabulations showing the 1956 budgeted
receipts and expenditures, in dollars and bolivianos, separately
as well as combined at three different hypothetical rates of exchange (4,000, 5,000, and 6,000 bolivianos to the dollar), for
every department of the government, broken down by bureaus,
and for virtually every government agency and enterprise.

A condensed summary of the tables at the Bs. 6,000 rate,
which proved to be the closest to reality for the 1956 year, is
given in Tables 2 and 3, omitting the separate entries in bolivianos and dollars and showing only the combined totals, as well
as condensing the accounts of the minor departments and entities.

It must be borne in mind that the figures in Tables 2 and 3
represent budget estimates only. The apparent deficits of some

TABLE 2

Budget Analysis for 1956: Government Departments

	In Millions of Bolivianos
Revenues (with dollar revenues converted at Bs. 6,000 rate)	
Custom duties	41,327
Taxes	29,033
Posts and telegraphs	833
Consular fees	2,060
Boliviano proceeds of U.S. aid*	11,610
Other	187
Total revenues	85,050

Expenditures	According to Budget (includes dollar expenses at Bs. 190)	Recomputed (with dollar expenses at Bs. 6,000)	
Foreign affairs	4,058	13,093	
National defense	7,167	12,647	
Education	14,074	16,108	
Peasant affairs	13,415	15,080	
Subsidies	3,242	53,661	
Social services	6,233	6,233	
All other	35,937	39,806	
Total expenditures	84,126	156,628	156,628

Deficit (Revenues less expenditures; dollars computed at
Bs. 6,000 rate)   71,578

*The government accounts could only show the boliviano proceeds of U.S. aid, as the commodities which formed the greater part of that aid were sold at arbitrary prices based on the Bs. 190 or other artificial rate, and the intermediaries (*políticos,* black marketeers, and smugglers) reaped the difference between those prices and the actual values.

71 billion bolivianos in the accounts of the government departments, and of some 50 billion bolivianos in the accounts of the government agencies and enterprises, were in themselves meaningless. Actual receipts in both cases fell far short of budget estimates,* while actual expenditures (except probably

*For example, actual metal exports in 1956 amounted to $90 million, which, at the Bs. 6,000 rate, would equal 545 billion bolivianos, while COMIBOL and the Mining Bank (exports from the private mines) receipts shown in Table 3 were budgeted at 640 billion bolivianos.

TABLE 3

Budget Analysis for 1956: Government Agencies and Enterprises
(In Millions of Bolivianos with Dollar Items Converted at Bs. 6,000)

	Total Receipts	Total Expenditures	Net Surplus	Net Deficit
Social security and pension funds	20,282	26,094	...	5,812
Central Bank	4,261	7,241	...	2,980
Mining Bank	125,158	69,019	56,139	...
Bolivian Development Corporation*	1,472	...	...	...
Known expenditures	...	47,515	...	...
Estimated additional expenditures	...	132,000	...	178,043
COMIBOL (mining corporation)	514,419	335,487	178,932	...
Civil Aviation Administration	378	2,700	...	2,322
Lloyd Aereo Boliviano (airline)	11,034	21,499	...	10,465
YPFB (petroleum corporation)	32,956	97,877	...	64,921
Railways	7,500	27,755	...	20,255
Point IV *Servicios*	24,467	24,395	72	...
All other †	5,444	6,099	...	655
Totals	747,371	797,681		
Net deficit	50,310		50,310	

*The known expenditures of the Bolivian Development Corporation, as well as all other figures shown in the table, except the estimated additional expenditures of that corporation, were compiled by the Ministry of Finance from the accounts of the respective agencies. In the case of the Development Corporation, the commingling of boliviano and dollar expenditures made it impossible to arrive at the actual total budgeted expenditures except for a single item (see p. 63). The estimated additional expenditures ($22 million) are based on the assumption that dollar expenditures for the remaining items would be in the same proportion as for that item.

†Despite all efforts, no information could be obtained from six government agencies and enterprises, all of a deficitary nature. The receipts shown do not include subsidies from the national government, listed in Table 1, nor bank credits (chiefly from the Central Bank).

in the case of the Development Corporation) so far exceeded the figures shown in the table that, instead of an apparent aggregate deficit of some 122 billion bolivianos, there was a total deficit in 1956 that may be estimated at between 150 and 200 billion bolivianos. This necessitated Central Bank credits to COMIBOL, the Mining Bank, YPFB, and the Bolivian Development Corporation alone, of over 100 billion bolivianos in 1956, corresponding roughly to the 109 billion boliviano increase in net bank note circulation between December 31, 1955, and December 31, 1956.[20]

The importance of the tables lay not in their totals, but in the fact that, for the first time, they revealed what departments, agencies, and enterprises of the government were responsible for the inflationary process, *according to their own budget estimates for 1956,* which they had based on their 1955 accounts. Every member of the Stabilization Council realized, of course, that there was probably not a single department, agency, or enterprise that lived within its budget.

To say that presentation of the preliminary data at the October 5 special meeting of the council occasioned surprise would be an understatement.[21] But it was not until the November 2 and 5 meetings of the council that the completed tables could be presented, and by that time the Stabilization Council was so busy going over the Fifty-Step schema and preparing a definitive stabilization outline for presentation by the Central Bank to the IMF on behalf of the Bolivian government, that there was no time for studying past receipts and expenditures, or any 1956 budget antedating the stabilization program. All that mattered at that point was to compile a completely new budget for 1957, and for the remainder of 1956, based on the conditions that would prevail after the stabilization measures had been enacted.

Nevertheless, the preliminary view of the data contained in these tables did serve an indispensable function in reorienting the thinking of the members of the Stabilization Council. For the first time, they could see that government subsidies which, in the regular government accounts, showed up at only Bs. 3 billion — less than 4 per cent of total expenditures — actually were the largest item in the budget, accounting for more than a third of the total. And these subsidies included such items as $1.5 million in foreign exchange to a "cell" of the MNR political party which had been shown in the official accounts at Bs. 285 million ($47,500) at the official exchange rate, and had thus escaped detection. And, for the first time, they had convincing proof that it was not COMIBOL, but the Development Corporation, YPFB, the government subsidies, and the government railways and airline that were primarily responsible for the cash deficits which made necessary the continuing new issues of bank notes. They knew that these bank note issues in turn accounted for the decline in the value of the Bolivian currency, both in its internal purchasing power and on the foreign

exchange market. U.S. aid was also a major factor in the inflationary process (p. 122), but this fact is not shown in the
budgetary figures.

With that proof, which ran counter to all their preconceptions, there was no further room for argument as to the causes
of the galloping inflation and, by the time Dr. Gesualdo A.
Costanzo of the IMF Mission attended his first meeting with the
Stabilization Council on October 30, 1956, the council members
had accepted the Fifty-Step plan in principle, and were ready to
revise it and whip it into final shape with the able assistance of
Dr. Costanzo and his staff of experts. Furthermore, as they
saw that foreign exchange dealings by the government and its
agencies had been the crux of the crisis, they were prepared to
accept the concept of a *foreign exchange budget* for the government and all the governmental enterprises, leaving those in the
private sector free to buy or sell all the foreign exchange they
wished, with no restrictions other than the limitation of their
own pocketbooks, tied down by rigorous restrictions on bank
credits.

It must be noted that the cash surplus shown in the
COMIBOL budget in Table 3 did not mean that the company
would be operating in the black. It was emphasized at the October 5 meeting that cash flow makes no allowance for depreciation, depletion, exploration, and development, or for the payment of capital charges on the nationalized mines, and that
COMIBOL had allowed its machinery and equipment to deterio-
rate to a critical extent. Even more grave, it had used up its
high-grade ores and brought its remaining reserves close to
the point of exhaustion, with consequent lower ore content and
higher production costs. It had failed to use its cash surplus to
explore and block out new reserves and, in sum, it had been
consuming its capital, and its operations had impoverished and
were continuing to impoverish the nation to an alarming extent.

With respect to the Mining Bank, its sizable net cash surplus in the budget represented, not a gain for the nation, but a
measure of the extortion practiced by the bank against the small
and medium-sized mines which had been practically driven out
of business. Again, it was emphasized that this surplus was a
budgeted one, not an actual one, and would not in fact be
achieved. None of the conferees was surprised at this conclusion, as the Mining Bank was known to be the most corrupt and
oppressive of all the government enterprises.

On the other hand, the heavy cash deficit shown by the

adjusted budget of the YPFB might not represent losses, but new capital investment. Whether or not the government petroleum corporation was in fact operating in the black could not be determined from the available figures. From the standpoint of printing press inflation, however, it was not net income but the excess of cash disbursements over cash receipts that mattered. For that reason, I recommended that YPFB capital expenditures be postponed — with only the most urgent exceptions — for perhaps another three months, by which time the stabilization plan would be under way and it would be possible for Bolivia to apply to the World Bank for a long-term loan to meet her investment needs, provided that an agreement had been reached on the foreign debt and on payment for the nationalized mines, and provided that Bolivia was in a position to substantiate the necessity of the loan and the prospective return on the investment.

The effect of the government subsidies (which were largely awarded on a political basis), and of the Development Corporation and government railway and airline deficits, was apparent from the tables, and this served to stiffen the opposition of the council members to an expansion of those enterprises. In the case of the social security and pension funds, the total budgeted expenditure of Bs. 26 billion, and not the net deficit of Bs. 5.8 billion, could be taken as the measure of their share in inflation, for the total expense had to be shouldered chiefly by the government and would inevitably be reflected in the bank note issue. (Social security charges were borne almost entirely by "big business," and big business was principally government.)

Inflation and U.S. Aid

The impact of U.S. aid on the inflationary process, through the printing of paper money to meet the counterpart fund requirements, was more difficult to determine. This point was not brought up at the October 5 meeting, as the stabilization measures would remove the pressure from that source and there was no point in emphasizing the responsibility of the U.S. government for Bolivia's predicament.

In theory, Bolivia obtained the counterpart funds in bolivianos from the sale of U.S. aid commodities and, even though from one-third to two-thirds of these commodities found their way to the black market and were smuggled out of the country, there should theoretically have been no inflationary increase of bank note circulation from that operation. The Ministry of Economy would be receiving payment from the distributors, thus withdrawing bank notes from circulation, and would invest the funds in supposedly constructive projects, at which time the notes would again be placed in circulation with no increase in the total outstanding. In practice, however, the U.S. aid commodities were sold to *políticos*, black marketeers, and smugglers, who were charged in bolivianos at a fraction of their real value, so that, in the 1955-56 fiscal year for example, Bolivia had to provide Bs. 16,303 million in counterpart funds, and received only Bs. 7,799 million from sales. The difference had to be made up by the Central Bank-printing press route. Furthermore, the ministry allowed many of the accounts to become so far delinquent that, in mid-1956, some of the 1953 sales had not yet been paid for. In other cases, the Central Bank was compelled to extend credit to the distributors, and a good share of the Bs. 7.5 billion of Central Bank credits to the private sector represented overdue accounts due from the *políticos* and their friends. It is estimated that, in all, between Bs. 12 billion and Bs. 30 billion of counterpart funds in the 1955-56 fiscal year were supplied through the printing press.[22] Net bank note circulation on June 30, 1956, amounted to Bs. 70.6 billion, which gives some concept of the thrust of *a single year* of U.S. aid on the printing of paper money, and hence on the inflationary process.[23]

The fact that U.S. aid of slightly over $60 million from July, 1953, to June, 1956, generated counterpart funds of only Bs. 30.7 billion,[24] or an average rate of Bs. 500 per dollar, means that these operations were less inflationary, so far as bank note circulation was concerned, than they would have been if sales had been made at realistic rates — say Bs. 550 in June, 1953, Bs. 1,500 in June, 1954, Bs. 2,764 in June, 1955, and Bs. 6,765 in June, 1956.[25] The difference made possible the profits to the *políticos* and others. From the other side of the ledger (the supply of commodities as against the money supply), U.S. aid was price-deflationary to the extent that a part of the aid commodities remained in the country and were either black-marketed or sold legitimately to the public at lower than world market prices. On the other hand, such sales added to Bolivia's troubles by removing any incentive to domestic agriculture.

Only Bs. 4.4 billion of the 1953-56 counterpart funds were invested in capital projects (the remainder disappearing in the deficit between government expenditures and revenues), so that

even if the counterpart money projects had been remotely remunerative — and most of them were not — there would have
been only a slight offset against the inflationary effect of the
counterpart arrangement.[26]

Fallacious Solutions for the Hyperinflation

Intimately linked with the prevailing fallacies as to the
causes of Bolivia's inflation were the fallacious *solutions* propounded by various government officials and advisers to the
government. Karasz's basic recommendation of hard work and
increased productivity would, of course, have been the proper
solution, if it had been possible for production to outdistance
government extravagance under the multiple exchange rates and
other discouraging conditions prevailing in Bolivia. On the
other hand, his suggestion (made in August, 1953, in connection
with the visit of Milton Eisenhower) that the Export-Import
Bank of Washington or the International Monetary Fund lend
Bolivia $7.5 million to be used to pay off current foreign in-
debtedness would have solved nothing and, to the contrary,
would have perpetuated the evils it was intended to cure.[27] This
loan, as Karasz put it, would have been used for the same purpose as a $300 million loan made to Brazil a few months previ-
ously, and the so-called "stabilization loans" to Brazil had
proved to be money thrown away, contributing nothing toward
halting the inflation. A similar loan to Bolivia would have been
equally futile and extravagant, yet Karasz's idea of the purpose
of a "stabilization fund" — that it was money to be spent, rather
than held in reserve to iron out temporary or seasonal fluctuations in the foreign exchange supply and demand — continued to
prevail in Bolivia until 1956 and later.

The thought that all Bolivia's problems, of economic growth
as well as of monetary stabilization, could be solved by borrowing, was the most persistent of the fallacies that hampered the
enactment and operation of the stabilization program. One government enterprise after another — YPFB, COMIBOL, the railways, etc. — came forward again and again with a complete
"solution" for their difficulties: a supplier's credit for one,
two, or three years which would enable them to buy twenty locomotives or *absolutely indispensable* drilling equipment with no
cash outlay. A problem postponed was a problem solved, and if
something could be bought on credit, there was smooth sailing

ahead with no thought for the storm clouds on the horizon. Even after enactment of the decree establishing the Stabilization Council, when it was illegal for any government department or entity to contract new obligations without the prior approval of the council, YPFB and other agencies violated the law without a qualm, leaving the council to deal with the creditors as best it could.

As late as October, 1956, when Bolivia was in the midst of its negotiations with IMF and the U.S. government for a stabilization loan, the President himself proposed that Bolivia borrow $1.5 million from Venezuela for urgently needed equipment for COMIBOL, YPFB, and the schools.[28] It was to be a "political," not a "commercial" loan, at "easy" interest rates, i.e., with no regard for the sound business principle that nations, like individuals, should buy on the basis of price, quality, service — tangible factors that go with the merchandise — and not be misled by the meretricious virtues of easy credit terms or the factitious exigencies of a two-nation reciprocal balance of payments.

Another solution to Bolivia's monetary difficulties was proposed by the economists of Bolivia's National Planning and Coordination Commission. Inasmuch as monetary depreciation had been caused by the overissuance of paper money, they argued, it could be cured by having the United States lend Bolivia enough dollars to buy up, and withdraw from circulation, all outstanding bank notes in excess of such amount as would be required to restore the boliviano to a reasonable parity.[29]

When I reported this proposal at a conference in Washington as illustrating the lengths to which monetary absurdities can be carried, only Henry Holland of all the conferees appeared to be amused, and it was later learned that one of the State Department officials present at the conference had actually put across a similar plan in Greece. With the approval of the State Department, he had used U.S. funds to buy up Greek bank notes which the Greeks blithely and obligingly continued to print until finally, on the advice of a Treasury Department officer, Dr. Gesualdo A. Costanzo, the Greek government was persuaded to put through a proper stabilization program with dramatically effective results. The lesson of the Greek disaster, however, seems never to have penetrated, for later this same State Department official on a visit to Bolivia, after stabilization, suggested using part of the stabilization fund to buy up and retire several billion boliviano bank notes.*

A less absurd but completely unworkable solution was proposed by a high official in the Finance Ministry consulted at the specific request of the President. According to that gentleman, Bolivia's troubles were due to her failure to reinstate the tithe (*diezmo*) collected in Inca and colonial days as a 10 per cent tax in kind on the farmers. Such a tax, he claimed, would produce a revenue of $50 million a year in potatoes, corn, and other farm products, which could then be sold by the government. This would be enough to pay all government expenses, balance the budget, and put a stop to the inflation by making foodstuffs so abundant that prices would drop. Total government expenditures, including the deficits of government enterprises, were placed at only $38 million in the 1957 budget agreed to by the Stabilization Council. The U.S. Operations Mission, however,

*In Germany, it is true, the phenomenally effective June 21, 1948, currency reform did embody the plan proposed by Joseph M. Dodge of "siphoning off" excess cash holdings and, in effect, the quantity of money in circulation was reduced by 93.5 per cent. That plan in itself, however, did nothing more than to proclaim that the mark was now worth only 2 pfennig, but it proved effective because of Ludwig Erhard's insistence on a balanced budget and a return to a free-market economy, abandoning all price and other controls and ending "once and for all the whole complex of State controls of the economy" (Ludwig Erhard, *Prosperity Through Competition* [New York: Praeger, 1958], pp. 5, 12). But, in Germany, there had been fifteen years of "suppressed inflation," with "exceptionally severe control measures ... including the death sentence" to prevent or limit the rise in prices, and the danger lay in the vast amount of spending power in the hands of the general public when those controls were removed. In Bolivia, the sole cause of the inflation and the greatest threat to stabilization lay in government spending beyond its revenue resources and, as Jacques Rueff points out, it "would be an egregious error to expect such techniques" as the cancellation of bank notes and bank deposits to serve as a cure where the inflation has been "suppressed" by strict rationing and price control, and where practically the sole problem is that of government deficits (*The Age of Inflation* [Chicago: Regnery, 1964], pp. 88-89). And the Dodge-Erhard scheme was to wipe out excess money supply by exchanging the old *Reichsmarks* for the new *Deutschemarks* at the rate of 100 to one (with certain equitable exceptions), not by giving away good U.S. dollars for worthless paper. But, as Kemmerer has said: "Popular familiarity with money ... makes everyone a monetary expert ... without being handicapped by any knowledge of the elementary principles of economics or the facts of monetary history" (Edwin Walter Kemmerer, *Kemmerer on Money* [London: George Routledge & Sons, Ltd., 1934], p. viii).

scoffed at the idea that a 10 per cent tax on agriculture could yield $50 million when the most optimistic estimates of agricultural production did not run over $100 million. [30]

Moreover, the chief flaw in the scheme was that the tax collectors would not last very long if they were sent out among Bolivia's well-armed Indians to collect a tithe of their production. This seemed rather a drastic way of solving the overpopulation problem. The President had planned to announce the proposed tax in his inaugural address, but dropped the idea on my suggestion that announcement of a new tax on agriculture would be untimely. [31]

Another suggestion, advanced with considerable pertinacity by a well-informed Embassy official was that the measures adopted in Peru on the recommendation of the Klein & Saks Mission should be applied in Bolivia. The difficulty was that stabilization measures, tailor-made for Peru, were not necessarily the most appropriate for use in Bolivia. Particularly unsuitable were the Peruvian precedents of *gradual* removal of price controls and the complicated restrictions on foreign exchange under which exporters, in lieu of receiving dollars for their exports, were given Central Bank certificates, valid for 60 days and usable only to pay for imports and certain restricted categories of accounts. This is not in criticism of the Klein & Saks recommendations. It is merely that stabilization plans must be made to order, not hand-me-downs, although the basic essentials of every *successful* stabilization plan following hyperinflation are identical, whether in Bolivia, Peru, Germany, or Greece. The successes and shortcomings of such plans in one country provide an indispensable guide for similar planning in other countries.

The situation in Bolivia was such that a surgical operation was called for rather than protracted therapy, and a *gradual* approach to stabilization was out of the question. Furthermore, in the Bolivian environment, fewer restrictions were needed, not more restrictions, on the theory that every restriction means corruption — the more restrictions, the more corruption. Wisdom in such matters, as is so often true, is epitomized in a proverb widely heard in Latin America: *La ley es una tela de araña y solo los bichos grandes se escapan* (The law is a spider web and only the big bugs escape). [32] Any "expert" who ignores the popular wisdom does so at his peril.

Chiefly, however, my reaction to the Embassy advice was that I did not wish to commit myself to, or even discuss, any plan of action only ten days after arrival in Bolivia. I wished to get the facts, as many facts as possible, before contemplating any given plan of action, and unfortunately all of the well-meaning and undeniably intelligent advisers who besieged my office during the first two months in Bolivia were long on advice but extremely short on facts.*

*When Hjalmar H. G. Schacht, as Currency Commissioner for the Reich, stabilized the German mark, he was "inundated" with recommendations and requests for specific action, "overrun" by callers, and harried by businessmen, economists, and government officials in endless "committee meetings and conferences... all of which were concerned with currency questions, and were anxious to express themselves." Schacht, unable to carry on with his work in the face of constant interruption, reports that he made "an end of all such meetings and discussions outright." *The Stabilization of the Mark,* trans. Ralph Butler [New York: Adelphi, 1927], p. 97). This solution was neither feasible nor desirable in Bolivia.

BASIC CONCEPTS OF THE PROGRAM

The causes of hyperinflation in Bolivia were so clear and the maladjustments caused by that inflation so extreme that it was fairly simple to formulate, at least in outline, the basic concepts of an effective stabilization formula. As Wilhelm Roepke says: "The greater the degree of monetary depreciation, the simpler becomes the analysis of its causes."[33] And the cure is equally simple.

First and foremost, there would have to be the elimination of the unrealistic official exchange rate of 190 bolivianos to the dollar, and of all other official rates such as the Bs. 1,200 currently being paid to COMIBOL (in July, 1956) on its exports of metals, the Bs. 1,500 received by YPFB, the Bs. 560 per dollar paid by meat importers, and so forth — in other words, establishment of a single exchange rate for all transactions, including the conversion of the dollar price for U.S. aid commodities into bolivianos.

There could be two ways of accomplishing this: (1) to fix a definitive rate, based on so many grams of gold or so many U.S. cents per Bolivian peso, and announce "This is it"; or (2) "to let the peso find its own level," which is the not too accurate expression in current use for a currency which, in theory at least, is left free to fluctuate in accordance with the laws of supply and demand.

In the Bolivian case, there was probably little choice. The inflationary process had gone on for so long, and there were so many unknown or imponderable factors in the situation, that it was next to impossible to determine exactly what rate of exchange could be established *and maintained* that would work a minimum of injustice to debtors and creditors and allow the economy to develop to the best of Bolivia's scanty abilities.

If the value of the boliviano were set too high, that is, if a rate of say Bs. 4,000 to the dollar were fixed and it turned out that all the unknown factors of supply and demand called for a rate of say Bs. 6,000 — perhaps because of an unforeseen drop in the price of tin — then the following consequences might be expected to ensue: imports would be overencouraged, speculators would hasten to convert their bolivianos into dollars at the favorable established rate, there would be a flight of capital, the stabilization plan would collapse, and a new rate would have to be fixed that would in all likelihood be less favorable than that which might have been originally established and maintained, perhaps Bs. 7,000 or Bs. 8,000 to the dollar.

If, on the other hand, the value of the boliviano were set too low, that is, at a rate lower than the maximum that might have been successfully established and maintained, it would mean that Bolivia would be handicapped by having to pay exorbitant prices in bolivianos for necessary imports and that domestic living costs in bolivianos would rise because of Bolivia's dependence on imports for certain commodities. The incentive that might theoretically be given to foreign investment by reason of low wages (in terms of dollars) would be too slow in making itself felt to alleviate the immediate distress.*

Normally, in a stabilization program, one attempts to determine the *parity* rate of exchange, i.e., that rate of exchange which, if fixed, would place the country's commodity price

---

*In an economy whose exports are entirely, or almost entirely, raw materials, the effect of the exchange rate on exports is generally negligible, within fairly broad limits. Tin prices, for example, are set in London and New York, in shillings or cents. Whether the Bolivians set the value of their currency at Bs. 4,000 or Bs. 6,000 to the dollar will not affect the number of shillings or cents that London and New York are willing to pay for a pound of tin, as this depends on world supply and world demand for that metal. Of course, the boliviano price might be set so low as to give no incentive in Bolivia for production or export, and this has occurred within my experience in dealing on the commodity markets in the case of minor commodities such as hides, *tagua, babassú,* etc., but never in the case of a major export. Then, again, the exporting country may be in a position to control the world market price, temporarily or perhaps for fairly extended periods, as in the case of coffee. But these are exceptions. Basically, raw material and foodstuff prices are set at the market place, not at the farm or mine, and, in the case of the basic commodities of international trade, the price is fixed in the world market in dollars or sterling, and that price is not affected by whether the exporting country decides to set the value of its currency at five to the dollar or five thousand to the dollar. I demonstrated this statistically at a round table discussion chaired by George F. Warren, at the 97th Annual Meeting of the American Statistical Association, New York City, December 31, 1935. My paper, "Effect of Gold Price Changes Upon Prices for Other Commodities," (*Journal of the Royal Statistical Society,* CI, Part I [1938], 173-87) was based on the behavior of prices for *all* major basic commodities in the principal world commodity markets, following the devaluation of sterling in 1921, and of the dollar in 1933.

levels at a parity with the rest of the world, in other words, a rate that would be neutral so far as encouraging or discouraging imports, exports, investments, and the invisible components of the country's balance of international payments. The theory of a "purchasing power parity of exchange" dates back to John Wheatley (*An Essay on the Theory of Money...*, 1807), but its later revival may be attributed to Gustav Cassell (*Money and Foreign Exchange after 1914,* and other works.)

Conservatively, the expert stabilizer would take a pessimistic view of future world commodity demand and prices, make an allowance for factors unknown or imponderable, and then fix the exchange rate on the low side to discourage unnecessary imports, encourage investment, and, above all, to avoid the necessity of a second stabilization move at a later date which might shake public confidence beyond repair.

In Bolivia, however, with its background of smuggling, black marketing, and the anarchy of multiple exchange rates, there was simply no way of knowing in advance what rate of exchange would be proper, i.e., productive of the minimum disturbance to the economy. Thus, there was probably no choice — there could be no fixed rate to begin with, and the boliviano would have to "find its own level."

This was not my initial goal. Basically, it seemed to me that Kemmerer was right when he wrote that "the way to stabilize is to stabilize." Thus, my first proposal was to fix a firm rate of say Bs. 6,000 to the dollar, *and maintain that rate.* Long experience in international trade and investment, and in manufacturing, utility, and agricultural operations abroad, had emphasized the disturbing effects of fluctuating exchange rates on the domestic as well as on the international economy. Experience showed too that there are few governments that can be trusted to *manage* their currencies for any length of time, and certainly none of the less developed countries in Latin America had demonstrated such ability. So long as it is easier to let the currency depreciate rather than raise taxes, and so long as it is more politically pleasant and personally profitable to increase government expenditures rather than reduce them, managed currencies and fluctuating exchange rates will always be disastrous. Nevertheless, the conditions prevailing in Bolivia were unique, and it seemed wise to accede to the viewpoint of the Treasury and other competent advisers that the better solution for Bolivia was to stabilize temporarily on a fluctuating basis, and then to stabilize permanently and *de jure* on a gold or dollar basis as soon as that might be possible. This might take a year or more.*

But even such a plan does call for ascertainment of the initial rate of exchange at which the stabilization program will be put into effect, and the expression "to let the currency find its own level" is a euphemism. Actually, as will be seen, the Central Bank must add a considerable measure of control to a supposedly free and fluctuating market by standing ready to buy or sell exchange at a rate which it hopes will iron out temporary fluctuations, deter speculation, and prevent a flight of capital. The important thing is to avoid any political interference with that process, any attempt to keep prices down or gain prestige by strengthening the local currency, any attempt to go counter to underlying market forces, or any attempt by the government to meet its deficits by borrowing from the central or other government bank or by short-term borrowing of any nature.

In deciding upon an initial rate of exchange for Bolivia, which would be the basis on which all computations for the government boliviano budget and foreign exchange budget would have to be made, there was available a tentative estimate of the *parity* rate of exchange made by Cornelius Zondag, the economist for the U.S. Operations Mission. This was, so far as is known, the only such estimate that had been made, and although Zondag released it with considerable misgivings, inevitable in the light of the dearth and unreliability of statistical data, it was at least something to go on.[34] His computations worked out at

---

*One writer on the subject, while opposing a floating rate, as a permanent policy, "hastens to add that he would not be opposed to fluctuating rates as a *transitional* device to cushion the shock of a sudden restoration of currency convertibility... or to enable a country which has stabilized its internal financial position to seek a new parity at which to peg its exchange rate more realistically. Nor would he oppose, even as a more permanent arrangement, a spread between gold points moderately wider than that now permitted under the Fund arrangement" (i.e., 1 per cent each way). (Arthur I. Bloomfield, *Speculative and Flight Movements of Capital in Postwar International Finance* [Princeton, N.J.: Princeton University Press, 1954], p. 83.) The classical argument for a floating rate policy to curb exchange speculation is given by Frank D. Graham, "Achilles' Heels in Monetary Standards," *American Economic Review*, XXX (March, 1940), 16-32.

Bs. 3,696.86 to the dollar, as of June 30, 1956, but Zondag advised that Bs. 4,000 would probably be more realistic.*

There was, however, another factor to consider in the case of Bolivia. If all artificial rates of exchange were to be eliminated, and if we were to do away with all sales of goods from company commissaries to the miners at below-cost prices computed at those exchange rates, then the miners' wages would have to be increased considerably, because a large part of their real wage was derived from their ability to buy those commodities at absurdly low prices, either for their own consumption or for black-marketing.

A basic premise was that the government would continue to operate COMIBOL. It was therefore essential that, in spite of the wage increase, COMIBOL operate at a profit — a real profit, taking into account depreciation, depletion, new exploration, taxes, and capital charges to pay for the nationalized mines — else Bolivia would once again succumb to the spiral of government deficits, borrowing, and printing press inflation. If the miners' wages, including the compensation for the loss of commissary privileges, could be calculated, then — somewhere between the June, 1956, parity of Bs. 4,000 and some unknown higher rate — a rate could be computed which would allow COMIBOL to operate in the black. It was merely a question of subtracting from COMIBOL's gross dollar receipts, her gross expenses, including capital charges, taxes, etc., and dividing the difference among the employees. If COMIBOL employed too many miners, and if the miners produced less than they should, which was the case, there would be less for each miner. If the amount available for wages worked out at say $1 a day per miner, and if the miners demanded a wage of Bs. 6,000 a day, the exchange rate would have to be Bs. 6,000 to the dollar; if

---

*Later, following stabilization, ECLA worked out a series of exchange parities from 1938 through February, 1957, arriving at a figure of Bs. 2,815 for June, 1956, rising to Bs. 8,670 by December, and dropping to Bs. 8,020 in February, 1957, after stabilization (ECLA report, Table XXXI, p. 298). Their estimates, however, are based on official price data which were meaningless prior to stabilization because most sales were not made at official prices, and Zondag's figure of Bs. 4,000 seems closer to the true parity in mid-1956.

they demanded Bs. 10,000 a day, the rate would have to be Bs. 10,000.*

There was no way to escape this equation, unless COMIBOL produced more tin, or dismissed half its miners, most of whom had been taken on since nationalization of the mine, or unless world tin prices increased — and it would have been foolhardy in 1956 to count on such a windfall.

Of course, the higher the rate of exchange, and thus the higher the miners' wages in bolivianos, the higher their real wages would be, because domestic prices could be expected to climb rather more slowly than would be warranted by the rate of exchange. On the other hand, the higher the miners' wages and the higher the rate of exchange, the worse off the rest of the population would be, because of higher domestic prices and because of Bolivia's dependence on imports for many articles of prime necessity. Basically, the closer we could keep to the Bs. 4,000 rate (assuming that to be the true parity) the less harm would be done to the population as a whole. The miners represented less than 3 per cent of the economically active population, and were already in a privileged position, so that it was the duty of the Stabilization Council not to increase their advantages at the expense of the underprivileged 97 per cent. †

*It is interesting that no one in Bolivia, and no outside commentator, appears to have guessed precisely how the initial stabilization rate was arrived at, the general assumption among the economically literate being that it was based on a tremendously complicated analysis of theoretical parities. One commentator, the President of the Economic Committee of the House of Representatives, "revealed" that the rate was determined as follows: There were 174 billion bolivianos in circulation; the stabilization fund was $25 million; dividing one into the other gives an exchange rate of BS. 7,800, with 100 per cent backing in dollars. (Alberto Mendoza-López, Última Hora, La Paz, February 14, 1957). No one ever noticed the mistake in arithmetic (that method would have given a rate of Bs. 6,960), or pointed out that the initial stabilization rate was Bs. 7,700-Bs. 7,750 (buying and selling), or that the total circulation was Bs. 160 billion, and the net in the hands of the public Bs. 148.8 billion. True, I did aim for a 100 per cent gold or dollar reserve to commence the stabilization program, but the Treasury and other competent advisers, including my own colleague, Ross Moore, thought I was being unduly conservative. The fact that the stabilization reserve did in fact provide a 100 per cent reserve was purely fortuitous, and was not the origin of the Bs. 7,700 rate.

†This sounds like the classical wages-fund theory — if one group gets higher wages, other groups must necessarily get lower wages or be unemployed; i.e., if labor unions get more for their members, other workers must bear the burden (cf. John Elliot Cairnes, Some Leading Principles of

On the other hand, it was inevitable that the miners would demand higher wages when their commissary privileges were cut off, so that plans had to be based on a much higher rate than the hypothetical parity rate of Bs. 4,000. This was one of the reasons why the government was asked to break down its accounts on the basis of three hypothetical rates of exchange — Bs. 4,000, Bs. 5,000, and Bs. 6,000. The other reason was to avoid tipping off speculators in the event that the computations leaked out, which was almost inevitable.

The first basic element in the original schema was therefore the establishment of a single realistic rate of exchange, and calculation of an acceptable compensation to the miners and other workers for elimination of the cheap food and other supplies priced at artificial exchange rates.

The second basic ingredient in the plan would be to consolidate the budget of the government and all governmental agencies and enterprises and to reach an overall balance, so that there would be no further borrowing from the Central Bank. This meant that there would have to be a fundamental revision of the tax system, and improved tax administration, in order to increase revenues, as there was bound to be a limit to how far expenditures could or would be cut. General tax revision, for the most part, could wait, but an immediate change in customs duties to an ad valorem basis (i.e., a percentage of import prices) would have to be enacted simultaneously with the stabilization measures themselves. The existing system was partly ad valorem and partly specific. With the depreciation of the boliviano, the specific duties — so many bolivianos per unit or per kilo — were meaningless, and the whole system was complicated by surcharges, and by import permits tied up with certain exports, as well as by the so-called *revertibles* — a system so complex, and which changed so constantly, that it would only confuse the reader to describe its functioning at this point.[35]

The third essential part of the plan was the simultaneous elimination of all restrictions and controls on foreign exchange transactions; of all subsidies, restrictions, and controls on imports and exports, other than customs duties; and of all controls

Political Economy Newly Expounded [London and New York: Harper's, 1874], pp. 258-60; and Alfred Marshall, *Principles of Economics* [8th ed., London: Macmillan Co., 1925], pp. 822-29). There is no intention of arguing the validity of that theory as a universal proposition, but, given the unique circumstances prevailing in Bolivia, it was undoubtedly valid at that time and place (see p. 172).

on prices, except for rent controls which should be relaxed and removed gradually as housing became available. The reason for abolishing all controls, apart from the conviction that a free market economy is the only viable system in a free country, was that controls never had worked and never would work in Bolivia, and would result only in black-marketing and smuggling that would wreck the stabilization program.[36]

These three elements, then, formed the gist of the scheme outlined to the organizing group at the July 12, 1956, meeting. Other features of the plan included a foreign exchange budget, which was essential to keep down government expenditures in dollars; temporary curbs on bank credits to the private sector to prevent speculation and the flight of capital; settlement of the foreign debt and payment for the nationalized mines; establishment of a stabilization fund; and other measures. Personally, I never regarded a stabilization fund as an essential element in the plan, except for psychological reasons which made it in fact indispensable. To the Bolivians, however, it was the sugarplum for which they were willing to swallow the disagreeable purge prescribed as a cure.

At this initial discussion, the essential thing was to leave the President and other conferees not merely with the *hope* that monetary stabilization could be achieved — for they had been given such hopes in 1953, when a Stabilization Office was established on the recommendation of the United Nations and the International Monetary Fund, which loaned the Central Bank $2.5 million for stabilization purposes.[37]

Hopes were not enough. In order to obtain passage of the measures envisaged as essential for the achievement of monetary stabilization, it was necessary to inspire the conferees, not with mere hopes, but with the absolute conviction that if the measures recommended were enacted, stabilization would be the inevitable result.

My talk before the President and organizing group concluded with the suggestion that, after the *de facto* stabilization had proved its worth, it would be appropriate for Bolivia to pass to *de jure* stabilization, probably at the rate of 500 or 1,000 bolivianos for each unit of the new currency that would be established at the time. The new currency could be known by some new name, in the same way that Chile had changed from the peso to the condor; but, in order to avoid having the workers and farmers feel cheated at receiving say three pesos a day in wages in lieu of the three thousand bolivianos previously received, it might be a good idea at first to print both the old and the new denomination on the paper money. This idea, I added, was suggested by the current Bolivian bank notes which were engraved *Cien* (100) *Bolivianos* and, in smaller type, *Diez* (10) *Bolívares*. None of the conferees had ever noticed that peculiarity before and, drawing some bills from their billfolds, they agreed that the precedent would be useful.*

To end the conference on a lighter note, after the rather tense moments following my refusal to be associated with the emergency measures taken at the meeting, I suggested facetiously that, just as the Argentine currency is known as the *PESO M/N,* meaning *Moneda Nacional,* the new stabilized Bolivian currency could be called *Moneda Nacional Real* (real national money), and abbreviated *PESO/M.N.R.* Alternatively, if the group felt that some people might object to the use of M.N.R. (the Revolutionary party), and inasmuch as the Peruvian money was known as *Soles,* the Bolivian currency might be called *Siles.* These sallies were successful in removing the tension, so that the conference adjourned with the warm feeling that the Bolivian officials and their new American adviser were all working in harmony toward a common goal, despite the rather harsh statements which I had felt bound to make at that meeting with respect to the causes of the inflation and the implied criticism of the emergency measures adopted.

An Agenda and Time Table for Action

To strengthen the conviction in the minds of the members of the organizing group that they could and would succeed in stabilizing the Bolivian currency — and it is not too much to say

*The double denomination derives from a law of July 11, 1928, which authorized minting 10- and 20-boliviano gold coins, to be known as the "Bolivar" and "Double-Bolivar," on the analogy of the U.S. "eagle" and "double-eagle" which are equally unknown to the present generation in the United States. It is scarcely surprising that the conferees had never read the text of their bank notes. Not one American in a thousand has ever noticed that the U.S. one-dollar bills bear the inscription "In God We Trust," but that one dollar is the limit of that trust; or that, whereas the old dollar bills used to certify that "there is on deposit in the Treasury of the United States of America One Dollar in Silver Payable to the Bearer on Demand," the new bills merely state that "The United States of America Will Pay to the Bearer on Demand Ten Dollars." This is about as inane a promise as a government could make. Payable in what — more paper dollars? These anomalies are being corrected on the newer Federal Reserve notes.

that *nothing* could have been accomplished in Bolivia if confidence had been lacking — I prepared an agenda and time table for the stabilization program, complete to the last detail and with dates for each discussion, decree, law, action, and press release, up to the date of final stabilization. This document was presented to the organizing group at their next meeting on July 19. The time table served the further purposes of ensuring that no step in the preliminary planning would be overlooked and of keeping the organizing group steadily on the task, focussing their attention on the many details that had to be scheduled and carried out in sequence, in order to achieve the goal of stabilization within a reasonable time. Any detail delayed or overlooked would stretch out the entire plan, and the agenda was in essence a Critical Path Method outline such as is used in manufacturing, or the Program Evaluation and Review Technique (PERT) called for by alphabet-prone government agencies in defense contracts.

Such a schedule is common business and legal practice in any matter that must be closely timed and scheduled, but it was a novelty in Bolivian government procedure. There, as elsewhere in Latin America, important measures are too often improvised rather than planned, and presentation of the agenda produced a favorable impression — for the first time we were working together as a team with a scheduled and known objective.

Clearance of the Plan by Lechín and Chávez

The July 19 meeting of the organizing group was attended, for the first time, by the Vice-President-elect, Dr. Ñuflo Chávez-Ortiz, who, it will be recalled, was the leader of the peasant league and militia. The meeting was taken up entirely with the revision and final approval by Paz, Siles, and Chávez of the decree that was to establish the National Monetary Stabilization Council.

These were three of the four leaders of the Bolivian Revolution. There remained only Juan Lechín-Oquendo, reputed to be the most powerful of all in view of his command of the miners' federation and militia and his position as "maximum leader" of the Bolivian Workers' Confederation (COB). So, immediately following the meeting of the organizing group, Chávez, Gisbert, and I met for an all-afternoon discussion, where we were joined by Dr. Samuel Marín-Pareja, the intimate friend and legal adviser of Lechín. Step by step, we went over the program together, and particularly the plan to make up for the loss of the miners' cheap commissary privileges by increased wages and to establish a single, free rate of exchange high enough to enable COMIBOL to operate without a loss.

Only after the plan had thus been cleared with Dr. Marín did Lechín consent to participate in its approval. On July 30, therefore, a second meeting was held at the house of Dr. Marín, attended this time by Juan Lechín, Ñuflo Chávez, Fernando Pou-Mont (a former Minister of Finance), our host, Eugene Gilmore (the Economic Counsellor of the Embassy), and me. There it was made plain that the program had already been cleared, not only by the Bolivian conferees but by the leaders of the COB and MNR as well, as Dr. Marín opened the meeting by declaring that the decree creating the stabilization council would be signed by President Paz-Estenssoro that week before the new Congress convened.

Nevertheless, we ran over the salient points of the program in complete and at times vociferous agreement, Lechín saying jovially: "What a pity Dr. Eder was not here three years ago" (when the ill-fated U.N. "stabilization" plan was adopted). I even ventured to tread on dangerous ground by suggesting that, once the currency was stabilized and the workers' wages increased, it would be possible to reduce social security and similar charges to a more reasonable percentage of total payrolls, and yet give the workers more substantial benefits, in solid money, than they were receiving at the time. The two lawyers, Marín and Pou-Mont, as practical businessmen, agreed enthusiastically. Chávez and Lechín, as practical politicians, did not commit themselves, although they seemed to be in agreement.

After those two crucial conferences, enactment of the stabilization program was assured, with the four leaders of the Revolution aligned solidly behind it. The honeymoon did not last long — but it was enjoyable while it lasted. The groundwork for the stabilization structure was laid. The process of its construction and completion will be related in the following chapters.

III

DRAFTING THE STABILIZATION PROGRAM

8

PRELIMINARY DISCUSSIONS

The decree establishing the National Monetary Stabilization Council was issued by President Paz-Estenssoro on August 4, 1956, to the general acclaim of the press in Bolivia and abroad (Appendix I). On August 6 Dr. Hernán Siles-Zuazo was inaugurated President of the Republic. Two days later I was en route to New York and Washington, charged by the council with the task of undertaking "exploratory discussions" to determine what, if any, financial aid Bolivia might hope to obtain in furtherance of a monetary stabilization program.

I neither wanted nor was I authorized to seek firm commitments from private bankers or from government agencies, nor could I make commitments on behalf of the council. Such commitments would have to be made and received by Bolivian officials acting as representatives of the Bolivian government or of the Central Bank. The objective was much narrower — to obtain an informal statement from the U.S. government and, if possible, from intergovernmental and private financial institutions, to the effect that they would be willing to discuss the possibility of financial arrangements, *provided* that Bolivia manifested its firm intention to stabilize the currency by taking certain preliminary steps suggested to the organizing group and accepted by them in principle, as outlined in the preceding chapter. Such a statement, *with no commitments,* would provide the leverage that would be needed later to obtain enactment of certain rather drastic measures, necessary for monetary stabilization but hardly popular or politically easy.

Basic Measures Discussed in Washington and New York

The first step was to draw up a mimeographed "draft for discussion" — a set of forty measures, which it was believed might serve as a starting point for negotiations between the Bolivian government and prospective lenders in the United States, including perhaps the U.S. government, the Federal Reserve Bank of New York, the International Monetary Fund, and possibly a syndicate of commercial bankers.

The measures were grouped by subject matter rather than chronologically in order to simplify discussion point by point. Ultimately, after agreement had been reached on each subject, the measures would have to be rearranged in time sequence to constitute a workable stabilization program. These forty points embodied the basic concepts of the stabilization plan which had been accepted in general outline by the Bolivian organizing group, as set forth in Chapter 7.

These proposed measures were discussed at length with officers of the State and Treasury Departments, the International Cooperation Administration, and the International Monetary Fund, as well as with a number of leading bankers in New York.[1] Various minor changes were suggested as a result of these discussions, and certain areas that were touched on only in outline were further explored and blocked out. In essence, however, the basic concepts of the stabilization plan presented to the Bolivian organizing group and set forth in this "Forty-Point Draft for Discussion" were carried forward into the "Fifty-Step Plan" described below in Chapter 9, and ultimately enacted into law on December 15, 1956.

The only significant points of discrepancy between the two outlines were: (1) that the original plan had proposed a 100 per cent reserve against circulation and deposits, to be built up out of the proceeds of a 2 per cent tax on foreign exchange operations; and (2) that it contemplated stabilization at a fixed rate of exchange. The Treasury and New York bank officials, as well as other qualified advisers, including Ernest Moore of the U.S. Financial Mission, considered the 100 per cent reserve too restrictive. With great deference to their judgment, I am of the opinion that my understanding of the Bolivian government was correct, and that the 100 per cent reserve should have been required until Bolivia had proved its ability to live within its means by repaying the stabilization fund. As it turned out, the stabilization loan did in fact provide a 100 per cent reserve but this was fortuitous, and, as there were no enforceable restrictions, it was eventually frittered away. As to stabilizing at a fixed rate of exchange, I readily conceded that a fluctuating rate would be needed until a sufficient period of time had elapsed to determine a viable rate for permanent stabilization.

As a result of the discussions, it became clear that the stabilization financing would have to come principally from ICA and IMF, possibly with some additional funds from the Treasury and the New York banking group.

The principal reasons for my attempting to obtain private as well as governmental participation in the stabilization financing — say $5 million in private funds out of a total of $25 to $30 million — were that it was thought that this would be useful in later attracting private investment to Bolivia, and that it seemed certain that no stabilization measures would be *permanently maintained* unless Bolivia were safely headed in the direction of a free enterprise economy, and thereafter effectively and permanently enjoined from any further expansion of government enterprise. It would be impossible to expect an international agency such as the IMF to place an effective curb on the business activities of one of its member states. The U.S. government had virtually confined its loans and grants in Latin America to those on a government-to-government basis, practically to the exclusion and certainly to the detriment of private enterprise, and a curb on government expansion could hardly be expected from that source. Thus, the only hope of persuading Bolivia to live up to its stabilization commitments would be to have private banking institutions participate in the financing, even though they would probably demand to be placed on a last-in, first-out (LIFO) basis, or at least *pari passu* with the Treasury, which is traditionally a LIFO lender. There would be no difficulty in getting Bolivia to agree in advance to conditions that would ensure a return to a free enterprise economy — the difficulties would only arise after the loan was obtained.

The Bondholders Council and Bolivia's Foreign Debt

In addition to the conferences in Washington and with the bankers in New York, I conferred with the president of the Foreign Bondholders Protective Council, Inc., Kenneth M. Spang, and Dana Munro, a director.*

*The council had been founded in 1933 as a nonprofit-making institution "at the request of the Secretary of the Treasury, and the chairman of the Federal Trade Commission" (this was prior to creation of the SEC, which took over the FTC functions in the field of defaulted foreign bonds). In 1937, a "Board of Visitors" consisting of William O. Douglas, then chairman of the SEC, and Herbert Feis, then adviser on international economic affairs of the Department of State, reported that the council was the "appropriate permanent agency" for the protection of holders of defaulted foreign governmental bonds, and since that time, the council, while not an official body, has been recognized by SEC and the State Department as the

Bolivia had reached an agreement with the council in 1948 for a settlement on the defaulted dollar bonds, of which $59,422,000 were then understood to be outstanding in the hands of the public. The government, however, had taken advantage of the low prices for the bonds, occasioned by its default in payment of interest and amortization in 1931, and had repurchased $2,678,000 of the bonds in the 1930's. It had subsequently acquired a further $466,000, apparently since 1953, so that the total outstanding at the close of 1956, when the stabilization program was enacted, had been reduced to $56,278,000. Defaulted interest on the outstanding amount, which totalled approximately $72,600,000 in 1948, had risen to approximately $107,810,000 by December, 1956.[2]

The Bolivian Congress had passed a law on October 5, 1950, approving the 1948 agreement with the Stabilization Council and authorizing resumption of debt service, but no payments had ever been made under that arrangement. With the advent of the Revolutionary Government in 1953, the 1950 law was but one of many that had been written in water. I therefore outlined the current Bolivian political and economic situation to the council officers, and expressed the view that circumstances were so much more critical than in 1948 or 1950 that Bolivia would undoubtedly ask more favorable conditions for resumption of debt service than had been agreed to in 1948.

At the same time, I disclaimed any authority to negotiate, and proposed that, if a group of commercial bankers proved to be interested in participation in a monetary stabilization loan, it might be appropriate for that group to negotiate a settlement on the bonds. Munro and Spang were too courteous, apparently, to express their dismay at that suggestion, but their views were later communicated through the State Department. The Bondholders Council, quite understandably, prefers to deal directly with defaulting governments. An intermediary was proposed solely in the thought that it might accelerate an agreement. Consequently, and in accordance with the Department's views, I suggested to President Siles that he appoint a representative to negotiate with the council on behalf of the Bolivian government. This was done.

---

appropriate agency for that purpose. Munro was a former Chief of the Division of Latin American Affairs in the Department of State, at the same time that I held the post of Chief of the Latin American Section in the Bureau of Foreign and Domestic Commerce (1926-32).

The publicly held dollar bonds were by no means the only foreign debt of the Bolivian government, but, incredible as it may seem, the National Monetary Stabilization Council was never able to obtain a complete and accurate statement of Bolivia's total foreign debt outstanding in 1956, nor even an accurate statement of the amounts due and payable in 1956 and 1957 — an even more vital element in planning a monetary stabilization program. Figures there were in abundance, but not facts, and it appeared that on every occasion where it was attempted to delve below the figures to arrive at the facts, we discovered to our dismay that they were neither complete nor factual. Table 4 is an attempt to present a statement of Bolivia's foreign debt, as of the close of 1956, at the initiation of the stabilization program. On that basis, the foreign debt may be placed at somewhere between $300 million and $500 million.

TABLE 4

Bolivian Foreign Debt, December 31, 1956

Item	Range of Estimates*	
	Low	High
Dollar bonds outstanding in the hands of the public (p.144)	$ 56,278,000	$ 56,278,000
Interest in default (p. 144)	107,810,000	107,810,000
Union Allumettière bonds outstanding (p. 204)	356,000	356,000
William Harvey, Ltd., loan under buffer stock agreement (p. 187n)	4,000,000	4,000,000
Due as contribution in tin to buffer stock (p. 187n)	1,000,000	1,000,000
Due under bilateral trade agreements (p. 218)	6,025,000	6,025,000
Debt to Export-Import Bank (p. 412)	34,500,000	34,500,000
Due to Argentina for railway construction (p. 68)	22,088,000	30,000,000
Due to Brazil for railway construction (p. 67)	12,000,000	27,000,000
Suppliers' credits (p. 216)	50,869,000	65,000,000
Nationalized mines (p. 444)[†]	0	135,000,000
Total	$294,926,000	$466,969,000

*Discussions of these estimates are to be found in the text at the pages shown above in parentheses.

[†] The low figure is the estimate of the Minister of Mines; the high one is that of the Permanent Fiscal Commission.

The recognized internal debt was nil or negligible, depending on one's viewpoint. Any internal indebtedness incurred prior to the Revolution was virtually wiped out by the inflation. The entire internal debt of the national, departmental, and municipal governments, and of governmental agencies and enterprises, in bonds, loans, and current account, as of June 30, 1953, totaled Bs. 5,165 million, which, at the then rate of Bs. 191.90, was equivalent to $26.5 million.[3] In December, 1956, that pre-Revolutionary debt (debts were not repaid, but increased in the interim) was worth $430,000 prior to stabilization, or $670,000 after stabilization. By the close of 1956, governmental internal indebtedness had risen to over 200 billion bolivianos,[4] equivalent to $17 million prior to stabilization, or $26 million after.* Virtually the entire indebtedness was owing to the Central Bank or some other governmental bank. In other words, it was an indebtedness from the government or one of its agencies to another government agency; and, as it was never contemplated that it would be repaid, it may be said that the internal debt was, in fact, "nil or negligible." In any event, it had no bearing on the process of monetary stabilization, except with respect to the bearing of debt service on budgetary equilibrium. For the national government, internal debt service for 1957 was budgeted at Bs. 12.5 billion (6.2 per cent of total expenditures); for COMIBOL, Bs. 2 billion (0.4 per cent); and for YPFB, Bs. 7.4 billion (5.5 per cent).

The Noncommittal Commitment

After nearly four weeks of discussion in Washington and New York, including a formal interdepartmental conference in the office of Assistant Secretary of State Henry Holland, the State Department drafted an official statement of "minimum prerequisites for a Bolivian stabilization program," approved by State, Treasury, and ICA.† I was authorized to show this

*The internal debt figures make no allowance for such amounts as might be due for the confiscation of properties taken under the agrarian reform, whether by government seizure or by squatters. The *recognized* indebtedness for such seizures would in any event be negligible in amount in view of the basis of valuation used, and the depreciation of the boliviano.

†The first two weeks were consumed largely in the usual Washington "run-around," until I finally broke through bureau barriers and conferred directly with Assistant Secretary Holland at State, and Under Secretary

statement to the bankers in New York and, thereafter, to President Siles and other members of the National Monetary Stabilization Council.

There were no commitments of any kind in this document — merely a statement, unsigned by anyone, of those measures that Bolivia should take *prior* to any stabilization program. These prior steps were:

1. Enactment of a new ad valorem customs tariff with criminal penalties for smuggling or false declarations
2. An over-all government and government enterprise budget, balanced without borrowing from the Central Bank, and computed at my suggested hypothetical rates of 4,000, 5,000, and 6,000 bolivianos to the dollar, coupled with a statement of anticipated post-stabilization price and wage levels
3. Establishment of quantitative credit controls and new reserve requirements
4. An agreement with IMF on a stabilization program, following a study to be made of Bolivia's situation by a special mission which would be sent to Bolivia by the IMF

Burgess and Assistant Secretary Overby at Treasury, and arranged for the interdepartmental conference. Meanwhile, at least three and possibly more memoranda were exchanged between the various State Department bureaus and divisions and circulated to at least 20 persons in State, Treasury, and ICA, prior to the meeting. The gist of the memoranda was that the various agencies and bureaus should present "a united front" on the 40-step plan, that it was premature to consider stabilization in Bolivia, that there was little indication of any "will to stabilize" on the part of the Bolivian government, and that more time must be devoted to a tax study before going ahead, etc. Following the meeting, at least four memoranda were immediately interchanged between the various bureaus and divisions, interpreting and misinterpreting my comments and giving recommendations for action or for delaying any action whatsoever. These scripts produced another round of memos, supporting, rebutting, or criticizing the other memoranda, and it is understood that probably some sixteen memoranda were exchanged as a consequence of this one meeting. See testimony of Secretary Rusk, Under Secretary Lovett, and former Ambassadors Briggs and Bruce on the perils of "layering" (communications must run the gauntlet of 7 or 8 "layers" between the Secretary and the desk officer); the "killed in committee" technique; and the multiplication of work because of overstaffing (Briggs' testimony that he could get more work done with half the staff); U.S. Congress, Senate, *Administration of National Security, Hearings*, Part 2, 88th Cong., 1st Sess., 1964 pp. 131-33; Subcommittee Study, pp. 5-8.

5. An increase in Bolivia's free foreign exchange reserves by $1 million (from less than zero)
6. Evidence that Bolivia was increasing its reserves at the rate of $300,000 a month
7. Conclusion of a "satisfactory" arrangement for resumption of payments on the foreign debt
8. A mutually acceptable agreement negotiated with the Patiño group covering compensation for nationalization of their properties*
9. Enactment of a law providing that takings of private property shall be subject to prompt, adequate, and effective compensation
10. Enactment of a fair mining and fair investment code
11. Effective action to carry out a reorganization plan for COMIBOL
12. Participation by a New York banking group in any stabilization program financing that might be undertaken by ICA, IMF, and the Treasury

A truly tough stand by Washington, such as outlined above, would have been most desirable provided it were combined with a stabilization program and an agreement to provide a stabilization fund to ensure the success of that program. But some of the foregoing steps were completely unrealistic, and to require that they be taken *prior* to enactment of a stabilization program was to delay the unpostponable and to demand the impossible.

There was, however, a slender reed to grasp for encouragement in the shape of a memorandum drafted jointly by me and the State, Treasury, and ICA conferees, but likewise unsigned. In that memorandum I was instructed that I must adhere verbatim to its terms as "guidance for possible oral statements" to the bankers, to Bolivian government officials, and to the press. This statement would have been precisely what was needed, had it not been for the other memorandum, which was just too cagey for comfort, and evaded a decision that could not be avoided.

Statement to the press

The following is a translation of the interview that appeared in the press in La Paz on September 21, 1956.[5] It follows the

_____

*Patiño Mines & Enterprises Consolidated, Inc., was the only one of the Big Three that included a substantial American interest, and hence the only one that could legitimately ask U.S. protection.

original "guidance" as closely as it was possible to translate from English to Spanish and back to English.

During my visit to the United States I had the opportunity of holding informal conversations with many officials of the U. S. government, of the International Monetary Fund, and of various commercial banks.

We talked about the prospects for stabilizing the Bolivian currency and economy. These conversations were necessarily of a purely preliminary nature, because there is a great deal that Bolivia will have to do, a great deal that Bolivia must prove itself willing and able to do, before any definitive stabilization program can be discussed in detail, and before we can ask for that reasonable measure of foreign financial support which will be useful when the final stages of stabilization are reached.

I must emphasize the fact that my conversations were of a purely formal and exploratory nature, but at the same time I found a very great interest in the United States in the problem of stabilizing the Bolivian economy and currency. Of course, I was not authorized to make, nor did I make, any commitment, nor was any commitment made by those with whom I spoke, but I was told in effect that if the National Monetary Stabilization Council were to formulate a realistic stabilization program, and if the Bolivian government were to adopt and carry out the essential elements of that program, the way would then be cleared for formal and official discussions with U. S. government agencies, with the International Monetary Fund, and with private commercial banks.

I wish to make it clear that the kind of assistance which would be appropriate in support of a stabilization effort in Bolivia would not be additional grant aid to enable Bolivia to pay for imports or to finance development projects. It would consist in the creation of a dollar reserve which Bolivia would be determined not to dissipate but to maintain as support for a currency which would retain a realistic and stable value in the country and abroad.

I would like to repeat what I have said on other occasions: I am completely confident that Bolivia has the economic capacity to stabilize its currency so that it will have and maintain a realistic and stable value here and in world markets. With that objective, I have drawn up a complete and coordinated program, and am prepared to recommend to the President and to the National Monetary Stabilization Council certain steps that are essential as a necessary preliminary to the later coordinated stabilization measures which, in my judgment, should be taken. Those proposed steps will be submitted to the council as soon as they can be drafted in appropriate form. Meanwhile, I beseech all Bolivians to have patience, to realize that a condition which has developed over a period of years cannot be cured overnight, and that any hasty action which might not coincide with the full coordinated program could be seriously detrimental, and might even make impossible the fulfillment of the council's mission.

In conformity with the objectives of that mission, Bolivia has invited the International Monetary Fund to send a mission to La Paz which is expected to arrive early in October. I shall be working very closely with the members of that mission and it will be of the utmost importance that we jointly formulate in concrete terms the measures deemed essential for the rehabilitation of the Bolivian financial and monetary situation.*

Report to the council

On the morning following my return to La Paz, I had a long conference with the president of the Central Bank, who brought me up to date on developments during my absence. These were, chiefly, a 40 per cent across the board wage increase to all employees of the banks, industry, mines, and railways, in fact, of virtually all major groups with the exception of employees of the national government, states, and municipalities. As a consequence, there had been five meetings of the Stabilization Council, chiefly for the purpose of authorizing further Central Bank credits to COMIBOL to meet its payrolls; note circulation had increased; and prices had risen. Foreign exchange, which, prior to the wage increase, had shown some improvement based on stabilization expectations, had slumped to Bs. 11,000 to the dollar, and the market was in near panic.

Later that morning there were conferences with the

---

*The statement closed with a courteous plea for patience and forbearance, to give me time to work on the program with a minimum of interruption. It was carried in the press but is omitted here because of its length and because only the Spanish version would be of assistance to economic advisers elsewhere in Latin America.

American Ambassador and with Embassy officials, who were brought up to date on developments in Washington and on plans for immediate action.

That afternoon a full report was made to President Siles and Gisbert, in private conference, on the results of the exploratory mission in the United States, and, on the following day, I attended my first meeting with the National Monetary Stabilization Council, in a session that lasted from 9:00 p.m. until 2:00 a.m. the following morning.

As three of the council members were newly appointed,* the account of the discussions in Washington and New York commenced with an outline of the causes of the Bolivian inflation and the general plan for a stabilization program, already familiar to the other members. The first task, I said, would be to draw up a complete stabilization program, commencing with the preliminary stage, and embracing those measures that, in accordance with Washington's views, would have to precede the stabilization measures proper. It was hoped to have the program completed within a week, which would give the council an opportunity of studying the essential elements of the plan so that, as soon as the International Monetary Fund mission arrived, the council and the IMF mission could jointly draft a definitive program with a minimum of delay.

Meanwhile, I asked for copies of the minutes of the previous meetings held in my absence, to bring me up to date. At the same time, I suggested that future minutes be confined to a bare statement of the matters discussed, and the text of the resolutions adopted, without detailing the arguments and votes pro and con. This would accord with usual business practices, and would eliminate the possibility of later discord, with some members of the council perhaps pointing to the minutes to evidence their opposition to some particular resolution that later proved to be unwise or politically objectionable.

The head of the Planning Board, himself a businessman, opposed that suggestion on the ground that what was suitable for business was by no means appropriate in government, and that he would want his arguments on every measure, pro or con, set

*I.e., the new Ministers of Finance, Economy, and Mines, respectively, Hugo Moreno-Córdova, Carlos Morales-Guillén, and Jorge Tamayo-Ramos. The other council members, President Hernán Siles-Zuazo, Central Bank President Franklin Antezana-Paz, Foreign Minister Manuel Barrau-Peláez, and the Executive Vice-President of the National Planning and Coordination Commission, Miguel Gisbert-Nogué, were all old friends.

forth in full; also, that he might very well wish to publish them later to prove that he had supported or opposed some particular point. The Ministers of Mines, Finance, and Economy agreed with that proposal, and the council therefore asked the acting Secretary to prepare duplicates of all minutes for the individual, discretionary use of the members of the council.*

With the smell of panic and potential political disturbances in the air, the council requested that I again enlist the support of the other forces in the Co-Government, so, on September 19, it was arranged for me to dine with Juan Lechín and the U.S. Commercial Attache, Charles Bridgett, at the house of Samuel Marín (see p. 138 for account of previous meeting with Marín, Lechín, *et al.*).

Again the results of the mission in Washington and New York were outlined, and assurances of full cooperation were received from Lechín. Over the course of the following week, there were conferences with the Finance Minister and the U.N. adviser in the Ministry, Jean Peset; with the chief of the U.N. Mission in Bolivia, Alejandro Oropeza-Castillo; with the then British Ambassador, Sir John Lomax; with former President Víctor Paz-Estenssoro; with one of the two most notorious of the persons who had reportedly engaged in scandal-tinged contracts with the government, this meeting having been arranged at the instance of a political figure whom there is no point in naming;† and with a dozen other persons. To each of these persons, the stabilization plans were outlined in greater or lesser detail, in most cases not going beyond the announcement already made to the press. In return, suggestions were received which, even if not always disinterested, were nevertheless invaluable.

*This was done, and the minutes of that meeting and of subsequent meetings were distributed in due course. Some months later, the acting Secretary, Rubén Darío Villena, had copies made of the earlier minutes, and distributed them to the council members. In the preparation of this volume, I have used the minutes to refresh my memory as to dates and the sequence of events, but have based the book chiefly upon my personal diaries, notes, and recollections, in considerably greater detail than is reported in the minutes and, in many cases, in the absence of minutes, as there were a number of meetings and "rump sessions" in the presidential palace with no secretary present.

†A meeting was arranged with the other equally publicized government contractor in November, 1956.

Rioting in the Streets

The crisis continued, however, for political as much as for economic reasons, and on the following day riots ensued. Three members of the police force were killed by the mob, allegedly in a demonstration against high food prices; many more were injured; the Illimani radio station (government-owned) and *La Nación* (the government-oriented newspaper) were set on fire; a state of siege was declared; and, over the course of the next four days, three hundred rioters were reported arrested.[6]

President Siles summoned me to a private conference at the presidential palace, literally sick at heart at the turn of events. He stated that machine guns were mounted on the palace roof, and could easily have dispersed the mob with a hail of lead, but that he simply could not bring himself to shed the blood of his Revolutionary comrades who had brought him to power — the Bolivian psychology was such that if he opposed force with force, it would lead to a massacre, whereas if he continued firm in his purpose, without using force, the affair would soon be forgotten. He outlined the political situation at length, and stated that his only goal was to enact a sound monetary stabilization program — that as soon as that end had been attained, he intended to resign. I pointed out to him that enactment of a program was not enough — that the success of the program would depend on its enforcement, and that it was just as important for the President to campaign in person for the program *after it was enacted* as it was for him to have the measures enacted.*

*Again and again, the President gave way to periods of extreme depression in private conferences — which is hardly surprising in the light of the situation in Bolivia. On one occasion, shortly after stabilization, the President, his head bowed down in his hands, exclaimed that the MNR had committed so many "stupidities" *(estupideces)* that there seemed to be no way out of the dilemma. I attempted to reassure the President as to the certainty of success of the monetary stabilization plan, and added that in every social revolution — the French, the Russian, etc. — there had been stupidities and excesses. Mistakes were not a monopoly of the Bolivian Revolution. On the occasion of this particular conference, it seemed that spiritual as well as economic and political reassurance was needed, and I sought the aid of Monsignor Humberto Mozzoni, the Papal Nuncio and one of the most brilliant minds in La Paz, to bring the message of *sursum corda*. From that time on, the stabilization program was frequently spoken of by the President, and repeated in the council and the press at large, as a "moral revolution" as well as an economic revolution. And,

But more of that anon. The story has been allowed to run
ahead of itself to point up the far from auspicious circumstances
under which the drafting of the stabilization program was begun.
I have already related how my family and I were greeted by
dynamite on the night of September 27, and I might add that on
September 16, the very night of our arrival in La Paz, when my
wife and I went out for a brief ride, there was a rain of bullets
between the hotel and the central square that made it seem expedient to return to shelter.

---

indeed it was, for it meant, for a brief time at least, "a return to morality," and the elimination of the corruption, black-marketing, and smuggling
that had accompanied the hyperinflation of 1952-56. And, in the final
crucial days preceding stabilization, it was the Bishop of La Paz, and the
Apostolic Vicars of Bolivia's hinterland, who exhorted their flocks to support the stabilization program with all their hearts (p. 242).

9

THE FIFTY-STEP PLAN

My usual practice in drafting documents for use in Latin America is to write them first in Spanish and then translate them into English, thus ensuring greater accuracy and tact in the communication of ideas and avoiding the appearance of translation. But the monetary stabilization program was drawn up first in English, as it was essential to transmit it to Washington with the minimum possible delay to make certain that it contained nothing that might in any way jeopardize State, Treasury, ICA, and IMF support.

The three stages of the Fifty-Step Plan — prestabilization, stabilization *de facto*, stabilization *de jure* — are transcribed in Appendix III (pp. 626ff) with comments in italics outlining the cabled suggestions received from the State Department on Stage I, as well as the action taken by the National Monetary Stabilization Council in its meetings between October 30 and November 16. The gist of the plan is contained in the *Four major areas for action* at pp. 181-85.

This Fifty-Step Stabilization Program is in essence the program that was ultimately enacted in the shape of the December, 1956, decree-laws and subsequent decree-legislation. But even those suggested measures which failed of enactment for one reason or another might very well have constituted a valid part of a Bolivian stabilization program, had it not been for the inexorable pressures of time and politics. They are thus deserving of consideration by anyone charged with formulating a similar program for any other country of Latin America, with such modifications as might be appropriate in each case.

Acceptance of the Fifty-Step Plan by the Government

A number of copies of the Spanish draft of the Fifty-Step Plan were delivered to the Finance Minister as soon as it was completed. On the evening of October 4, 1956, the President summoned a meeting of the full Stabilization Council, excluding only me, for the purpose of a free discussion of the proposals among the Bolivian members. Invited to the meeting, in addition to the council members, were Juan Lechín, Ñuflo Chávez, Mario Tórres (Lechín's right-hand man in the miners' federation, later appointed Minister of Mines), José Cuadros-Quiroga (Minister of Agriculture, and Executive Secretary of the Political Committee of the MNR), and the two economists of the National Planning and Coordination Board, Humberto Fossati and Domingo Alberto Rangel. (See p. 165 n for comment on the ideological background of those two economists.)

The following evening, President Siles summoned me to attend a rump session of those members of the Stabilization Council who were at the same time Cabinet members, i.e., the Ministers of Finance, Foreign Affairs, Economy, and Mines. The President then stated that a meeting had been held on the previous evening, on his initiative,* and that the Fifty-Step Plan had been approved in general, but that there were still a few points on which they would like further clarification, viz.:

1. The Minister of Economy objected to the immediate elimination of the Bs. 190 rate in the government accounts, on the ground that it would mean an increase in foodstuff prices and thus be inflationary. It turned out that he was afraid that if his Ministry were compelled to continue selling at prices calculated at that rate, or any other official rate, but was charged at the Bs. 3,500 rate, which was recommended for use during the interim period until Stage II (stabilization) was reached, the Ministry would show a deficit. I pointed out that it was necessary to avoid raising prices to the public during Stage I (until wages were also raised and compensation paid for the loss of cheap commissary privileges), and that it was the "give-away" plan and not the bookkeeping that was inflationary. In any event, this was purely a temporary expedient, and admittedly a bad one. The other conferees agreed that food prices could not be raised during the interim period but that the government

*This did not coincide with the information given me that morning by the Subsecretary of Press and Information who, of course, did not know that the President would be giving a different version. According to that official, the October 4 meeting had been called at the insistence of Juan Lechín, and he gave the names of those persons attending. He added that the meeting had been a stormy one but that President Siles had won the battle and had presented an ultimatum: He would either carry out the stabilization program — or resign.

should not continue to deceive itself with false accounting. They attempted to convince their colleague but
without success.
2. The Minister of Economy balked at reducing imports.
The country simply *had* to have twelve more locomotives, a considerable number of freight cars, and so on
through a long list of "absolutely indispensable" materials. I could only reply that, unless the government
demonstrated its willingness and ability to balance its
budget and reduce imports below exports, with a $4-$5
million excess to cover debt settlement and build up a
reserve, it might as well abandon hope of stabilization
or of foreign aid for that purpose. Again, the Minister
refused to be convinced by his colleagues and, in fact,
throughout his brief stay on the council he proved to be
a rather reluctant participant in the stabilization program. In his view, the government's needs were ineluc-
table and simply could not be limited by financial capacity, an attitude that has accounted for inflation not only
in Bolivia but in every other country of Latin America
where the government has dominated the economy and
debased the currency.
3. The President asked what projects of the Bolivian Development Corporation would have to be abandoned, to
which I replied that the decision was one of policy which
the President and his associates would have to make.
The sole essential was to have total real expenditures
amount to less than total real income, both in bolivianos
and in foreign exchange. I added that the sugar mill,
cement plant, and rice mill might be sold to local private capital, and that foreign private capital had expressed itself as willing to undertake expansion in the
hydroelectric power field, provided there were assurance
of adequate rates, monetary stability, and a favorable
investment environment.
4. I had mentioned that the only tax measure that could
bring quick budgetary relief would be the reorganization
of import duties. The Finance Minister agreed, but
stated that he believed duties should range from 10 per
cent to 200 per cent rather than be limited to 100 per
cent, as suggested in the Fifty-Step Plan. To this I
replied that the Finance Minister was the expert in that
field, and that my only suggestion was to keep the structure simple, and not make the tax so high as to encourage smuggling.

5. The Finance Minister then asked what I would think of a capital levy on all business and all property as a means of bringing in immediate revenue, to which I replied that such a tax would discourage any possible new investment. The Minister explained that he meant only a single levy to be applied once, and never again, but I answered that investors would have no confidence that the levy would not be repeated again and again.

6. President Siles asked whether it would be incompatible with the proposed program for the government to borrow $1.5 million from a neighboring country, that it would be a purely *political* loan that would not cost over $\frac{1}{2}$ per cent interest, and "would not have to be paid back." I replied that the preliminary period had as one of its aims to determine Bolivia's ability and determination to live within its means; that if it balanced its budget by borrowing, it would not be living within its resources, but further mortgaging its future; that if the United States and IMF were considering lending Bolivia money for a stabilization fund, the government must not further increase its indebtedness by borrowing elsewhere; that if any country offered a loan at $\frac{1}{2}$ per cent interest, there must be ground for suspicion, as money simply could not be had at that rate; that if the thought that the loan would never have to be repaid meant that Bolivia would be getting equipment and not money, and that it would have to make repayment in exports, it should be doubly on its guard, as Bolivia had lost in all such barter deals, and I cited chapter and verse; that Bolivia should stick to the policy of selling only for hard currency, and buying where it can buy best and cheapest, not being deceived by barter deals or apparently cheap credits. The President and Minister of Foreign Affairs seemed unable to grasp that borrowing was no solution; that equilibrium in the budget or balance of payments achieved by borrowing was no demonstration of the country's determination and ability to stand on its own feet. Later, it turned out that the deal would have been with Venezuela, and that it was being engineered by one of Bolivia's leading political personalities; I am unable to say precisely what personal interest, if any, that person might have had in the operation, but Bolivians may be able to figure that out for themselves (see pp. 169, 176).

7. The Foreign Minister stated that, contrary to my statement that Bolivia should not count on any increase in

U.S. aid, Milton Eisenhower had promised Bolivia a huge increase in aid shipments.[7] To my question as to whether a definite commitment had been made, the Minister replied that Eisenhower had made a definite promise "to do all within his power" to obtain the increase, but that the Minister had noticed a reluctance to make a definite commitment until after the elections because of possible political repercussions. It was hard to visualize the results of the November elections in the United States hinging on an increase in U.S. aid to Bolivia, but I confined myself to suggesting that they had better make their plans on the basis of what Assistant Secretary Holland had specifically told all of them, viz., that unless Bolivia stabilized its finances and its currency before June, 1957, it would be extremely difficult to convince Congress to "throw any more money down the drain" by continuing U.S. aid to Bolivia. I quoted Holland's words to them verbatim; Holland had used the same language in talking to Juan Lechín at a private meeting in the U.S. Embassy residence, in my presence. As a matter of fact, it was only this firm stand (abandoned after Holland's retirement) that made possible the stabilization program.*

These were the only points raised at the conference and, as it was after midnight, the President suggested that the meeting be continued on the following day when they could go over the program point by point in a full council meeting.

Conversations and Commitments

In reporting this meeting to Washington, and with reference to Milton Eisenhower's alleged promise of additional aid, I stated that any increase at that time in the U.S. "give-away"

---

*Holland's resignation was effective August 31, 1956. President Eisenhower, however, requested that he make his services available to advise Milton Eisenhower on matters affecting the Organization of American States (New York Times, September 1, 1956, p. 9). In that semiofficial position, he was most helpful on a subsequent trip to Bolivia in April, 1957. His retirement was unfortunate from the viewpoint of the Bolivian program, as he was the only man in Washington who not only had a thorough grasp of the Bolivian situation, but at the same time sufficient authority and independence to make a decision and make it stick.

program would make stabilization absolutely impossible. The Bolivian government was so reluctant to take the politically difficult step of balancing the budget, so eager to find an easy way out, that Bolivia's representatives, when meeting with representatives of the United States, would seize on the slightest and most innocent expression of interest, or even the raising of an acquiescent eyebrow or a courteous and evasive cough, as assurance absolute of unlimited and unrestricted aid.

An example of this occurred a few weeks later, at a luncheon given by the head of the U.S. Operations Mission to introduce the members of the Stabilization Council to Drs. Costanzo and Saenz of the IMF mission. At that meeting, a high Embassy official, who should have known better and hence shall be nameless, asked out of the blue, "just for purposes of discussion," what the effect would be if U.S. aid, instead of $25 million a year, were to take the shape of an outright grant of say $100 million. The effect was electric — this would be the way out of all Bolivia's troubles; stabilization would be simple, and Bolivia could go ahead with all its development projects, with ample money for the mining and petroleum corporations. Never a thought was given to the fact that a year later Bolivia would be back again for more, as its problem was not a lack of money but the utter inability of the government to manage what money it had.

This conversational gambit disrupted my plans for months and was certainly a factor in making it impossible to trim the Bolivian budget as much as it should have been trimmed, for neither the Finance Minister nor President Siles could believe that such a question had been asked "just for purposes of discussion" (see p. 456).*

This tendency to take the word for the deed, this eagerness to assume that the slightest expression of interest is the equivalent of a binding commitment, is so pervasive in Latin America that only someone as well versed in Latin American psychology

---

*Ambassador de Lesseps Morrison points out a similar instance in Chile where Deputy Assistant Secretary of State Richard Goodwin made a statement that was accepted in good faith by the Chilean government as a definite promise to send a U.S. mission to Chile to offer aid and credits. Goodwin "vehemently denied that any such promise had come from him or that he had made any such arrangements," but *traduttore traditore* (translators are traitors), and Goodwin was unable to negotiate except through an interpreter. *Latin American Mission*, p. 221.

and as fluent in Spanish as Henry Holland can hope to deal with Latin American governments without misunderstanding, and utter an unmistakable "no" without offense.

The greatest mistakes in U.S. relationships with Latin America had been caused by the intervention of well-meaning amateurs, with only a "hotfooted transient's" knowledge of Latin America. This is the expression used by Milton Eisenhower, who writes that this "brand of reporter specializes in the one-night stand, stopping in a capital city only long enough to pick up a bit of palace-guard gossip," and not having enough "time to develop the knowledge and perspective so essential to accurate, well-balanced, meaningful news stories and interpretive articles." Eisenhower's ability and his relationship to the President enabled him to make a substantial contribution to inter-American goodwill, although his judgment on Latin American economic development, policies, and politicians was as fallible as that of any other tourist. His involvement as a director in President Kennedy's "Tractors for Freedom" ransom scandal (ultimately involving a $55.9 million blackmail payment to Castro), along with such other well-intentioned neophytes in Latin America as Eleanor Roosevelt, Walter Reuther, and Richard Goodwin, is sufficient to preserve his amateur standing.[8]

Milton Eisenhower, more than any other man, was responsible for U.S. aid to the Revolutionary Government of Bolivia, beginning with his visit to that country in June, 1953, at a time when the fate of the Revolution hung in the balance, as President Paz-Estenssoro himself admitted. The Bolivian government, during Paz's second term, gave official recognition to Eisenhower's role in making possible the Treaty of Economic Assistance of November 6, 1953.[9]

His influence on U.S. Latin American policy in general is borne out by numerous references in his book, *The Wine Is Bitter*, and is perhaps best illustrated by the fact that, on one occasion, a career Assistant Secretary of State for Latin American Affairs told me with ill-concealed chagrin that, if I wished to speak with the Secretary of State on a matter connected with Latin America (which was the purpose of the call), I had better get in touch with either Milton Eisenhower or Richard Nixon, because he himself had not been able to see the Secretary for weeks.

The United States has been fortunate in having had in charge of its Latin American affairs many persons who were true "pros" in that area, some of them career officers, and others presidential appointees, and virtually all of them highly qualified to advise the Secretary of State and the President in our Latin American relationships. The trouble has come when the White House has ignored these professionals, and used what Ambassador Ellis Briggs characterizes as "latter-day circulating Magellans" to pilot it through the difficult channels of Latin American policy, producing "either bewilderment or havoc abroad and not infrequently both."[10]

Organizing the Council for Action

On October 6, the Stabilization Council went over the Fifty-Step Plan from beginning to end, but it was decided that, as the mission from the International Monetary Fund was expected to arrive shortly, it would be best to delay detailed discussion — and certainly a decision on any points of the program — until after arrival of that mission.

The first of the remaining members of the U.S. Financial Mission, Ernest O. Moore, had arrived in La Paz on October 8, and on November 16 the mission was completed with the arrival of Roger Freeman. They attended their first National Monetary Stabilization Council meeting on November 19, 1956.*

Moore had a record of thirty-five years' experience in commercial and central banking, including over twenty years with the Federal Reserve Bank of New York and five with the Bank for International Settlements in Basle. Over the previous three years he had served as economic and financial adviser to the Haitian government and to the *Banque Nationale d'Haiti*. Following enactment of the stabilization measures, his practical knowledge of central banking proved invaluable to the mission, and to the council, and it was unfortunate that he had not arrived early enough to play a part in formulating the program. Once

*Moore's absence from the prior council meetings was by his own choice. With Dr. Costanzo representing the IMF mission and with me representing the U.S. Fiscal Mission, he felt that it might have appeared that there was a superfluity of foreign experts if he had also taken part in the twenty-five meetings (October 5 through November 16) at which the Fifty-Step Plan was discussed and whipped into final shape. Then too Moore would have been at a disadvantage in that the remaining conferees were all familiar with the plan and its background, while he was not, although he was briefed as fully as possible on all developments.

the stabilization decrees were enacted, however, all banking and central bank matters were left entirely in Moore's hands and in those of John R. Woodley, the representative of the International Monetary Fund. Moore remained in Bolivia for four months after my departure and carried on alone as Acting Executive Director and sole U.S. representative on the council, until his own departure in October, 1957.

Roger Freeman was the adviser in tax matters, with a background in business and, later, as a special assistant to the governor of the State of Washington where he reorganized the tax administration, and handled welfare, budget, and fiscal matters in general. He had come recommended by the Treasury Department and was undoubtedly highly competent, and indeed brilliant, in his field; but, unfortunately, his lack of fluent Spanish made it difficult for him to participate in the rapid-fire discussions at the council meetings. He soon became disgusted at the constant frustration of seeing one sound tax proposal after another defeated or hopelessly emasculated by political intromission or plain ineptitude. He left La Paz in April after a little more than five months on the job, leaving a serious gap in the fiscal mission, as tax reform should have been one of the most important contributions to the task of increasing government revenues and thus balancing the budget.

As it was, I was forced to take charge of the long process of a complete revision of customs tariffs and devoted considerable time to the elimination of nuisance taxes and to the question of social security taxes, matters that Freeman could have handled more effectively had he been fluent in Spanish. A much needed reform in the real property tax system, proposed by me, and an effective income tax, proposed by Freeman, went by the board solely because there was no one who had the time, the fluency in Spanish, and the persuasiveness to put the measures across. This was unfortunate, as it would have been simpler to reorganize the tax laws and administration under the temporary emergency powers of the monetary stabilization program than at any other time, before or since, in Bolivia's history.*

*This experience points up the necessity, in Latin America at least, of having economic, monetary, fiscal, and tax advisers who are thoroughly equipped to negotiate in Spanish (or Portuguese). ICA erred in sending an expert with no prior experience in a Latin American environment where frustration is the norm, and *paciencia* the proverbial remedy. One other factor which quite understandably added to Freeman's frustration and exasperation is the fact that ICA had assured him that he would be one of

The U.S. Mission was thus completed, or soon to be completed, prior to the arrival of the IMF mission, but, with so much work to accomplish in so short a time, it became more than ever necessary for the Executive Director to nominate a Secretary General for the Monetary Stabilization Council, who would rank as a full-fledged member of the council, appointed by its voting members (Decree, Art. 2, p. 747). The nominee had to be *persona grata* to the U.S. Embassy as well as to the President and the other council members, and at least not personally obnoxious to Juan Lechín or Ñuflo Chávez. At the same time, he would have to be a person with whom I could work in the most intimate and confidential relationship, as he would be the only one on whom I could depend, day after day, for advice from the Bolivian point of view, and for all the many details that must be attended to in managing even as small an office staff as was envisaged for the council.

At the first meeting with President-elect Siles, on June 20, 1956, I had asked for advice as to a suitable candidate, and shortly thereafter Dr. Siles had suggested the names of Humberto Fossati and Domingo Alberto Rangel, both employed at the time by the National Planning and Coordination Commission. He stated that he would send those gentlemen around to see me, as they had prepared a study of Bolivia's financial problems for the commission, and it would be helpful if I would collaborate with them in working out a stabilization program.

The Fossati-Rangel study turned out to be the only study, Bolivian or American, that showed any grasp whatsoever of the effect of the Bs. 190 rate on the COMIBOL operations. It was, however, highly theoretical in parts, as I informed Dr. Siles on August 2, 1956, owing to the writers' manifest lack of understanding of accounting and finance.

On conferring with the American Embassy, I was informed emphatically that neither person would be suitable because of their ideological backgrounds. I was forced to explain this as tactfully as possible to Dr. Siles at our next meeting, pointing

---

three experts of equal rank. Ernest Moore confirmed that he too had been given a like assurance, but he realized that someone had to head the mission; that I had already completed the stabilization plans before his arrival; and that only one man could have the title and authority of executive director. Even in the matter of providing office space, Freeman was unaccustomed to the procrastination that an old Latin American hand learns to overcome as a matter of course, and cramped quarters added to his discomfiture.

out that it was necessary to have the entire confidence of the Embassy in view of the likelihood that U.S. financial aid would be required in any stabilization program.

I added that I had been favorably impressed by Fossati, and by a newspaper article written by that gentleman, but that a book by Rangel on the oil companies in Venezuela revealed such an intemperate anti-American bias that it would be impossible to work with him. Dr. Siles replied that, so far as Fossati was concerned, it was true that he understood he had formerly been an Italian Communist, but that he was one no longer, and that, with respect to Rangel, every Latin American intellectual is brought up to be anti-American when young, and Rangel would be a useful addition to the council.*

Nevertheless, Dr. Siles recognized that if Bolivia hoped to get financial support from Washington the Executive Director could not possibly nominate a candidate who was *persona non grata* to the Embassy, and it was not until the end of October that a suitable candidate could be found, fulfilling all the difficult requirements for the post of Secretary General of the National Monetary Stabilization Council. As it turned out, the council was fortunate in finding a man so well fitted to the task as Dr. René Otero-Calderón, a lawyer then employed by the Inter-American Agricultural Service (SAI) under the aegis of the U.S. Operations Mission. Dr. Otero was formally appointed by the council on October 30, 1956, and his loyal cooperation in the council work, and my association with him, remain among the pleasant memories of my work in Bolivia. (Dr. Otero is at

---

*Regardless of whether or not Fossati had ever been or was still a communist, there was certainly no trace of it in his article in *El Diario*, July 31, 1956, nor in his later Bolivian writings. With respect to Rangel, there has seldom been so virulently anti-American a book as his *Venezuela: País Ocupado* (La Paz: Editorial Juventud, 1955). A proposed Bolivian investment code, drafted by Rangel, which Dr. Siles sent me in October 1956, was prefaced with the statement that Bolivia's situation was analogous to that of China, North Vietnam, Egypt, etc., and should be guided by precedents in those countries. It may be pertinent to point out that Rangel, formerly a fellow-member of the Acción Democrática in Venezuela with Rómulo Betancourt and Alejandro Oropeza-Castillo, head of the U.N. Mission in La Paz, later became the head of the "Venezuelan Movement of the Revolutionary Left," which was "Marxist, violently anti-Betancourt and aggressive in its support of Premier Fidel Castro" (*N. Y. Times*, March 4, 1960, and October 21, 1960), "virtually indistinguishable ideologically from the Communist Party" (Robert Jackson Alexander, *The Venezuelan Democratic Revolution* [New Brunswick, N. J.: Rutgers University Press, 1964], p.80).

present a member of the staff of the Inter-American Development Bank in Washington.)

In addition to the three U.S. advisers and the Secretary General, the National Monetary Stabilization Council staff consisted of a stenographer, a typist, and a messenger — not too large a group for efficiency, and not too heavy a financial burden on the U.S. government.* It was not as large a staff as it should have been for the task of bank and credit reform, tax reform, reorganization of the tax administration, revision of budgetary methods, a thorough reform of accounting methods and controls in government enterprises, and an overall comptrollership of government revenues and expenditures. As a consequence, none of these tasks was accomplished except in cursory fashion, and in this sense the U.S. stabilization mission fell short of preparing the groundwork for an adequate and permanent monetary stabilization program.

It is my considered opinion that an adequate monetary stabilization or economic development task force cannot be created by AID or any other U.S. government agency through hiring experts on a piecemeal basis, as was done in Bolivia. Only a thoroughly competent advisory organization, such as was built up by Kemmerer forty years ago in eleven successful financial missions, or by Klein, Saks & Company, which did a commendable job in Peru and Chile (despite political shortcomings), can

_____

*Economy does not appear to be the invariable goal in U.S. operations abroad. One day, I found on my desk a requisition with a note from the Embassy: "Please sign and return immediately." The requisition was for file cabinets, typewriters, adding machines, supplies, etc., things for which there was absolutely no use in the Council. On investigation, it turned out that, because Moore and Freeman did not appear until the end of 1956, expenditures were far below the budget, and an alert ICA official explained that if we went below the budget in the 1956-57 fiscal year, it would be hard to increase appropriations in the coming year. With my taxpayer nerves on edge, I refused to sign, but later was informed by a career Consul General from another post that this was S.O.P. (standing operating procedure); that the State Department, toward the close of each fiscal year, sent out circular letters, discreetly worded but unmistakeable in meaning, to the effect that unless the Consulate or Embassy spent its entire budget, it would probably be cut in the coming year. That this state of affairs is not confined to AID or to the State Department was demonstrated when a retired admiral, employed by my former company, was enraged to find that the department of which he had charge had failed to spend its entire budgeted allotment, and told his comptroller, with accompanying profanity, that this would never be allowed in the Navy and that it was the most stupid thing he had ever heard of.

unite the requisite number and quality of experts in a true team, some of whose members might be employed in any given task for only a few months, while others might remain for two or three years or more. It is true that there have been a number of advisory firms employed by ICA or AID whose records have been scandalously ineffectual, but examination of the political background of such missions would generally explain why they were chosen in the first place, and why their reports are superficial, their accomplishments negligible. The World Bank and IMF missions have been first rate in every respect, while the UNESCO and ECLA missions have been well staffed and can be justly criticized only on ideological grounds, or on the ground that some of their economists have only theoretical rather than practical experience (with certain notable exceptions). The lesson to be learned from the Bolivian experience, in the matter of organization, is that an economic or financial mission should be headed by an experienced practical expert or by an established and reputable advisory organization, and that the team should be chosen by that expert or organization under contract. Government salaries and regulations make it impossible to pick an adequate team on other than a contract basis.

The Council and IMF Mission Complete the Program

The special mission promised by the International Monetary Fund arrived in La Paz on October 13, headed by Gesualdo A. Costanzo, formerly an economist in the U.S. Treasury Department and chief architect of the successful Greek stabilization plan of 1947.

The mission staff buckled down immediately to the task of compiling, collating, and digesting the mass of statistical and other information and misinformation available on the accounts, budgets, and indebtedness of the government and government agencies and enterprises, taxes and tax revenues, production, prices, wages, social security payments, price and rent controls, money and credit, foreign exchange receipts and disbursements, trade and barter arrangements, and other matters germane to a monetary stabilization program. Their office, in the board room of the Central Bank, was conveniently accessible both to me and to the president of the bank, through whose office they were able to obtain most of the available material, which was more impressive in quantity than in reliability.

The preparatory work of the mission, much of which they had commenced in Washington, was so effectively organized that by the time Costanzo attended his first meeting of the Monetary Stabilization Council on October 30 he was prepared to outline his plans and to start asking questions.

Asking questions is the alpha — and sometimes the omega — in work of this nature. Fortunately, in this case, the work progressed from questions to answers to decisions. Meanwhile, Costanzo and I had found that we could work together in complementary harmony and had reached a tacit understanding that all differences of opinion should be ironed out in private. Thus, the Stabilization Council never witnessed the unedifying spectacle of two "experts" disagreeing in public. In fact, the press reported that the true "miracle"* of the times was that there were two experts who were in complete agreement. [11]

To emphasize that harmony and strengthen the hand of the Stabilization Council Costanzo in his first press interview stated that he had complete confidence that the Bolivian authorities would find the solution to the problem of monetary stability because the measures that had been proposed (the fifty steps) were sound, and the public was willing to cooperate: "If I were not optimistic as to monetary stabilization in Bolivia, I would not be here." [12]

Dr. Costanzo had received the Fifty-Step Plan nearly a fortnight prior to his departure from Washington and had had time to go over it with his colleagues in the International Monetary Fund. At our first discussion together, it was agreed that Stages I and II should be telescoped, eliminating some of the impossible conditions that had been imposed by the State Department as conditions precedent to a loan. This would reduce Stage I to the matter of assembling the necessary factual data to back up Bolivia's petition for a loan from the IMF, Treasury,

---

*The reference to a "miracle" was to my first press conference in which I asked the public to have patience and explained that conditions which had existed for so long could not be remedied overnight but that, once the stabilization measures were decided upon and enacted, the stabilization would come so quickly as to seem almost a "miracle" (see editorial, *El Diario*, La Paz, September 22, 1956). Thereafter, until the almost instantaneous "miracle" of stabilization did actually occur, certain left-wing papers sneeringly referred to me as the "Miracle Man" *(milagrero)*, which Henry Holland later turned into a compliment in speaking of the "miracles" that did take place as a consequence of stabilization (Appendix VI).

and ICA, and probing the extent and firmness of Bolivia's determination and ability to take the steps necessary to achieve stability. This proposal of telescoping the plan, even though it was merely a hope, with no certainty of approval in Washington, was most welcome to the President, who had received from political circles some reactions to the Fifty-Step Plan that were not entirely encouraging.

Political clearances

The President summoned me to a private conference on October 16 to outline these political reactions. The Fifty-Step Plan had been considered at the October 11 Cabinet meeting where it had been agreed, after long debate, that stabilization was absolutely essential and that the program *must* be carried out. There were only two major points which the President would like me to reconsider, although he stated that if no concession could be made on those points he was prepared to go ahead on the strength of my opinion as an expert.

The points that had aroused the most intense political opposition were: (1) the suggestion that the private miners should be free to use the services of the government Mining Bank or not, as they saw fit; and (2) that social security charges should be reduced to 5 per cent, divided equally between employers and employees. The President stated that he would set up appointments with Lechín, Chávez, and the Minister of Labor to discuss those matters, and that he would also like me to talk with the Minister of Education.

The President then asked if the position I had taken at the October 5 meeting with respect to a "political" loan from Venezuela (p. 158) could be modified, emphasizing that interest rates would be low and that the loan could be paid off in fifteen years (at the previous meeting the President had stated that it would never have to be paid off, which appeared to be a barter arrangement). To this, I replied that if the loan were for the importation of absolutely essential equipment that would increase production for export, if the equipment were competitively priced and properly designed for the job, and if Bolivia would not be entering into onerous commitments for interest or amortization or for bartering, there might be no basic objection; but that, inasmuch as Bolivia would be negotiating with the IMF and other agencies for a stabilization loan, it would be essential to check with those agencies first, as they might be working on the basis of what they thought to be Bolivia's maximum borrowing capacity, so that any additional borrowing might jeopardize a stabilization loan.

The President then broached two further matters: (1) the investment code that had been drafted by Rangel (see p. 165 n for comments); and (2) a statement which the President understood I had made at a meeting of the Directors of the Central Bank to the effect that the government had been subsidizing a "cell" of the MNR to the extent of $1.5 million a year for the past three years, a statement which, "of course, could not be true."

With respect to the latter, I stated that I had merely quoted the statement made by the Minister of Economy in answer to an interpellation from Congress and had told the Central Bank directors that the stabilization plan would require the elimination of many government subsidies, especially if they involved foreign exchange, such as that particular subsidy.

The President picked up the phone to verify the facts, and the Minister of Economy confirmed that for the past three years the MNR "cell" in question had in fact received considerably over $1.5 million a year for imports at the official rate of exchange ($1,687,000 in 1954; $2,638,000 in 1955; $2,310,000 in 1956). The President reassured me that the "cell" had since gone out of business, and said, in extenuation, that others had received the same privilege, including certain commercial houses.*

The President thereupon read parts of a speech which he was to deliver over the radio the following day, dealing with

---

*The "subsidy" consisted in giving the "cell" dollars at the Bs. 190 rate. At the then current rate of about Bs. 10,000 to the dollar, this would mean a profit of $1,472,000 on $1.5 million. The "cell" in question was for "economic activities," of the MNR and was the private preserve of one of Bolivia's top political figures. The subsidy afforded an ideal way to build up a fortune outside of Bolivia. American taxpayers may be pleased to know that the $6,635,000 which were eventually shown to be involved in this operation represented only a small fraction of the U.S. aid that went down the drain, before and after stabilization. If anyone thinks that such practices are confined to Bolivia, he must be wholly innocent of what is going on in other countries of Latin America where multiple exchange rates are in force, the only difference being that, in Bolivia, such operations were on a relatively minor scale. By this time, the reader will probably not be surprised at the intensity of the opposition that later developed against the stabilization program from certain sources, nor will he be surprised that the same politicians who opposed the program were still doing business up to the end of 1964, although they were forced to figure out new angles for their operations.

monetary stabilization. As the newspapers had been editorial-izing on the "sacrifices" that the workers must be expected to make with the advent of stabilization, I suggested that the Pres-ident might state expressly that the stabilization program did not imply a *régimen de sacrificios* for the workers; that the in-crease in prices of certain subsidized commodities would be accompanied by an appropriate increase in wages; and that meanwhile the workers must be patient and not demand any in-crease in wages until the stabilization measures could be taken. The President was delighted with this suggestion and said that he supposed wages might perhaps be increased 10 per cent to compensate for the loss of cheap commissary privileges. I had in mind an increase of well over 100 per cent, but said merely that it would have to be very much greater than 10 per cent, as the compensation would have to be adequate; that the Ford, Bacon & Davis mission was working up some figures; and that undoubtedly Lechín would come up with figures higher than FBD. It was important, however, not to exaggerate the com-pensation as this would mean stabilizing the currency at such an unfavorable rate as to prejudice other sectors of the econ-omy — the ideal would be to demand *no further sacrifices* and to grant *no further privileges*. This concept was incorporated in the President's speech.

The President then telephoned the Minister of Mines, who stated that the average daily wage of the miners was Bs. 1,700 and that, if the cheap commissaries were eliminated, they would have to receive an additional Bs. 3,000 a day. It later developed that the basic wage was approximately Bs. 2,250, not Bs. 1,700, and, in the end, the miners were given an additional Bs. 3,950 for the loss of commissary privileges, plus Bs. 1,300 given to all wage earners for rising living costs.

Social security. In outlining the background of Bolivia's prestabilization economic problems, mention has been made of the extraordinarily high cost of social security and of the fringe benefits that, in Latin America, are usually grouped with social security under the general head of "social charges" (*cargas sociales*) and "social benefits" (*prestaciones sociales*). At the conference with the President, it was explained that it was es-sential to reach some reasonable arrangement in this matter, since if the existing high percentage rates were applied to the increased wages that the council would have to authorize to make up for the loss of cheap commissary privileges, all pay-rolls would be enormously increased. This would directly affect the government budget and the budgets of all government enterprises, and hence the rate at which the boliviano might ultimately be stabilized.

To simplify the economics of the situation, and avoiding the questionable aspects of the wage-fund theory (p. 133 n), the case of Bolivia's largest enterprise, COMIBOL, was cited. The price for COMIBOL's products was fixed in world markets, so that it would be impossible to compensate for added social charges by adding them to the selling price. Taking current figures, for example, COMIBOL had available from its gross sales, after deducting all expenses other than payroll, some $12 to $15 million a year left over to pay the 35,000 miners, roughly a dollar a day. Thus, a decision would have to be made as to whether it would be better to pay the miners 50 cents a day in wages and 50 cents in "social benefits," or $1 a day in wages and nothing for "social benefits," or some compromise figure between those two extremes. (Note that the stabilization plan gave the miners a base pay of nearly $1 a day in wages alone, but this was predicated on the government's firm commitment to dismiss 6,000 unnecessary and idle miners, a promise that was repeated again and again but never kept.)

Tentatively, the Fifty-Step Plan gave a figure of 5 per cent of wages for all "social benefits," of which $2\frac{1}{2}$ per cent would be paid by the employer, and $2\frac{1}{2}$ per cent by the worker. Actually, those percentages were solely for bargaining purposes, in the expectation of doubling the figure payable by the employer, the important principle being that the worker should pay at least one-third of the cost so as to impose some limit on future demands.

President Siles understood the gravity of the matter but considered the problem to be such a hot one, politically, that he requested me to pull the chestnuts out of the fire in personal discussions with the Minister of Labor and Juan Lechín.

The discussion with the latter appeared on its face to be fruitful. At a meeting on October 17, 1956, in the office of Vice-President Ñuflo Chávez, Lechín stated that he had long advocated reducing "social costs" by 50 per cent, since he realized that, if those costs were too high, wages would be lower. Furthermore, he considered that the administrative costs of the social security program were so excessive that the worker got very little benefit in return. At the same time, he quite properly pointed out that charges would have to be higher than in the United States, because the workers in Bolivia were neither able nor accustomed to saving part of their income, and the government had to be more paternalistic; also that the businessman's viewpoint was not necessarily the best for the country, as the businessman would naturally prefer to pay high wages and have happy workers, with no regard for the disabled and overaged, while the government simply had to look out for those who were too ignorant to look out for themselves. When I backed down from the proposed $2\frac{1}{2}/2\frac{1}{2}$ per cent basis, to a $5/2\frac{1}{2}$ per cent basis, raising wages to compensate for lower social costs, Lechín appeared to consider that reasonable, and stated that he would consult the manager of the National Social Security Administration.

The meeting with the Minister of Labor was less promising, as the Minister was new on the job, and had no direct knowledge of current social benefit costs nor of those proposed in a bill then pending before Congress, while the U.N. expert who was present at the meeting became so enraged at the idea of placing any limit on future social costs that he launched into what seemed to be a furious stream of Marxian dialectic that made discussion impossible. I therefore concluded by merely requesting exact figures under the current law, and budget estimates under the proposed law, of total collections for each item of social benefits, and total expenditures under the same heads, segregating administrative overhead, amounts actually received by the workers in cash and in hospital care, the investment of funds, and other details. The Minister backed this request as reasonable, but the facts were never supplied, either prior to stabilization or later. Such facts as could be obtained indicated that the workers recouped less than 10 per cent of what had been paid in (pp. 402-3). Following the meeting, the manager of the National Social Security Administration, who was likewise present, succeeded in mollifying the U.N. adviser, and they both agreed to explore certain possibilities suggested as a means of reducing the overall burden of social benefit charges.

In the end, the struggle for more reasonable social security charges proved to be the major defeat in the monetary stabilization program. Our efforts did, it is true, bring about a reduction in the housing tax from 14 per cent to $5\frac{1}{2}$ per cent, and in the family allowance from 13 per cent to $8\frac{1}{2}$ per cent. (The housing tax was a lottery to which employers were forced to contribute, on the chance that one worker in a thousand might get a house, while the cost of the family allowance was an average, as the actual family "subsidy" depended on the size of the family of each worker.) The proposed new old-age pension contribution of $8\frac{1}{2}$ per cent was enacted. In all, therefore, the new rates, enacted as part and parcel of the stabilization measures, totalled 35 per cent of the basic wage as against the pre-existing $39\frac{1}{2}$ per cent, or the 48 per cent which would have been effective after passage of the pension bill before Congress.*

The major point, however, was lost, that the rates should be applied to the basic wage prior to stabilization and not to the new wages authorized in the stabilization decree, which included compensation for the loss of below-cost commissary privileges and additional compensation for increased living costs. To take the extreme example, that of the miners, this meant social

---

*Bolivian authorities speak of social charges being equivalent to 80 per cent of the basic wage. However, one must be wary of accepting the amount of Latin American "social benefits" and "social charges" at face value, as labor unions and employers alike tend to lump under "social charges" all labor costs other than the basic wage. Many of these costs are paid directly to the worker and form a part of his cash wage, while others are fringe benefits, such as medical care, severance pay, and unemployment payments, called for either by law or under labor contracts. In Bolivia, following stabilization, the charges that may properly be considered analogous to social security, inasmuch as the payments are made by the employer to the National Social Security Administration, are sickness and maternity $5\frac{1}{2}$ per cent; professional risks (accident, etc.) 7 per cent; old age and death pensions $8\frac{1}{2}$ per cent; family subsidy $8\frac{1}{2}$ per cent; cheap housing $5\frac{1}{2}$ per cent. This adds up to 35 per cent. It is true that Article 39 of Decree 4538 (the principal stabilization decree of December 15, 1956) refers to the employers' contribution as 30 per cent, "according to actuarial figures." Those figures are highly theoretical, as $7\frac{1}{2}$ per cent is supposed to be paid by the workers but *must* be paid by the employer even if he fails to collect from the workers and, in general, only $2\frac{1}{2}$ per cent is paid by the employees; the charge for professional risks runs from 3 to 12 per cent, and presumably the 30 per cent total figured by the Social Security Fund assumes a $4\frac{1}{2}$ per cent average, which was on the low side. Other "social charges," not included in the 35 per cent, amounted to anywhere from 60 per cent to 85 per cent of payroll, so that the total such charges added up to 95 per cent to 120 per cent of the basic cash payroll, *exclusive of cheap commissary privileges,* prior to stabilization. After stabilization, the percentages were applicable to the increased basic cash payroll which allowed for elimination of the subsidized commissary. These additional "social charges" included: bonus based on length of service (average) 15 per cent; profit-sharing (often payable even where there were no profits) $8\frac{1}{2}$ per cent; Christmas bonus $8\frac{1}{3}$ per cent; "Sunday pay" (paid, but not worked) $16\frac{2}{3}$ per cent; paid vacation (2 weeks to 1 month; average cost) 6 per cent; severance pay (average cost) $8\frac{1}{3}$ per cent; lay-off pay (average cost) 2 per cent; hospital and medical care — this varied from a simple first aid clinic to relatively costly hospital facilities, such as those at the major mines.

benefit charges of 35 per cent on the new aggregate wage of Bs. 7,500 a day, in lieu of 48 per cent on the former wage of Bs. 2,250 per day.

Defeat on this front did not, of course, mean defeat of the stabilization program, but it did mean the continued impoverishment of the Bolivian people. To this day, social security and analogous charges, beyond the capacity of the Bolivian economy, constitute one of the two major obstacles to economic development, the other being, of course, the continued drain imposed by government deficits.

The Mining Bank. The background of the government Mining Bank, and the system whereby all private mines were compelled to use the facilities of that bank, both for the export of their ore and the purchase of imported equipment, has been set forth at p. 57. In the Fifty-Step Plan, it was proposed that the use of the bank's services be made voluntary in consonance with the free economy which was envisaged as the solution to Bolivia's problems. The President had asked that the matter be cleared with Lechín. Hence, at the same meeting with Lechín and Chávez at which the question of social security costs was discussed, this proposal was reiterated with the explanation that voluntary dealings would compel the bank to improve its administrative efficiency, and thus bring its settlements of account on ore shipments in line with those of competitive ore buyers (*rescatadores*), and with direct sales abroad by the larger operators.

At first, Lechín and Chávez placed emphasis on the crookedness of the *rescatadores,* who, according to prevailing opinion, were accustomed to render false accounts of metal content, prices, and expenses. To this I replied that the Mining Bank then had nothing to fear; the miners would deal with the person or bank that they found most reliable. Finally, in the course of a friendly and enlightening two-hour discussion, Lechín stated in all frankness that the Mining Bank had built up such a reputation for crooked dealing, charging high prices for imports, and falsifying the accounts on exports that, if the miners were free to choose, the Mining Bank would be forced out of business. This, Lechín concluded, could not be allowed to happen for political reasons; i.e., too many politicians had their fingers in the pie.*

*At a Stabilization Council meeting in November, 1956, the Minister of Economy likewise gave voice to the popular antipathy to the *rescata-*

The final outcome was that, under the December 15 stabilization decree, the small miners were compelled to continue selling their output through the Mining Bank, while the medium-sized mines were permitted to export directly. "Medium-sized" included all the larger enterprises, except the nationalized mines formerly operated by the Big Three. Presumably, operators of middle-sized mines were too well informed for the bank to take advantage of them. In any event, this compromise seems to have been politically acceptable although unfair to the small miners. On imports, the miners, large and small, were given leave to buy where they wished, but here again the scales were tipped in favor of the larger producers, as the small-scale miners could only get credit through the Mining Bank and were virtually compelled to make their purchases from it.

Conferences and speeches

The meeting with the Minister of Education, Fernando Diez-de Medina, had been arranged by President Siles, but the Minister opened the conversation by saying that the President was not to be held responsible for what he was about to divulge.

The Minister proved to be an enormously *simpático* person, Bolivia's outstanding literary figure, "left-wing" of course, and intensely loyal to the President. The gist of his remarks was that the President and Finance Minister had been badly buffeted around at the Cabinet meeting of October 11, which had been called to discuss the Fifty-Step Plan, but that in the end the battle had been won, and that I must stick to my guns in every respect — must help to strengthen the President's determination by acting as a "tough North American" and not vacillate like a polite *latino*. In the course of an hour's conversation, the Minister stated that a certain high political figure (whom he named)

---

dores, stating that Hochschild had made a fortune as a *rescatador* at the expense of the miners. He was not impressed with the argument that, if the Mining Bank did a better job for the miners than the independent *rescatadores*, it would get the business, and, if not, it did not deserve it. On the other hand, at a later meeting, the Minister of Mines, Tamayo, stated that the miners had no confidence in the Mining Bank; Dr. Sologuren called it an "octopus"; and Dr. Antezana and Sr. Gisbert stated that the only way to increase mining production was to allow the *rescatadores* to compete freely with the Mining Bank. In that event, the bank would go out of business, which would be an equitable solution to one of Bolivia's problems.

was making a trip to Venezuela with two objectives in mind: (1) to evade responsibility for any action taken by the President;* and (2) to carry on certain personal financial negotiations in that country, a political revelation whose significance can be appreciated by reference to pages 158 and 169.

All during this time, and extending from mid-October to the middle of November, at the President's request, I had engaged in a series of speeches or conferences with labor leaders and political and other groups for the purpose of clarifying the objectives of the stabilization program and the measures that would be taken to achieve those aims. At all these meetings, the charts referred to at pages 108 and 111 (Figs. 2-5) were used to portray graphically the causes of the hyperinflation, from which it was an easy step to explain the measures that had to be taken to stabilize the currency and eliminate the abuses originating in the inflation and in the multiple foreign exchange rates. The Fifty-Step Plan was merely a draft for discussion, and its circulation was limited to a restricted group. Hence, the speeches did not go into detail, but stuck to the general principles outlined in the initial meetings with Drs. Paz and Siles, and these were adhered to from beginning to end of the stabilization planning.

The first such conference followed a buffet supper at the house of the U.S. Labor Attaché. This gave an opportunity to meet the heads of the chauffeurs' (transport workers) union and other powerful labor organizations on an informal basis that paved the way for a discussion of stabilization problems.[13] The chauffeurs' union leaders later proved to be the first to announce their unqualified support of President Siles and the stabilization program.

There followed a succession of speeches, among others, to the following groups: Board of Directors of the Central Bank (October 15); Bolivian Mine Workers' Federation (October 26); National Federation of Teachers (October 30); National Manufacturers Association (November 5); Central Political Committee

---

*The personal courage of President Siles may be gauged by the fact that, on the day the stabilization measures were enacted, the other top leaders of the Revolution were out of the country. On two occasions Dr. Siles referred grimly to the lamp post in front of the presidential palace from which President Villaroel had been hanged and said that he and I might follow suit as a consequence of the stabilization program. Nevertheless, he stood his ground. I told the President that I personally had very little taste for that sort of thing and hoped not to participate.

of the MNR (November 7); National Mining Association (November 9); Federation of Printers (November 10); the Senate (November 10); Federation of Factory Workers (November 12); Confederation of Bank Employees (November 16); members of the Cabinet (November 20); etc.[14] Each group in turn withdrew its demands for wage increases ranging from 100 per cent to 200 per cent (factory workers), and announced their support of the President, and of the program, in some cases publicly, in others through private communication with the President or ministers. A letter which I addressed to the Finance Minister at his request, explaining why the factory workers of Cochabamba could not be allowed a wage increase, proved equally effective, and their wage demands too were withdrawn.

With the approval of the Stabilization Council, a decree was then issued during the first week of November, announcing 40 per cent wage increases to school teachers and other public employees. Later resolutions granted 15 per cent increases to workers in the private mines, and to bank, printing plant, and retail employees. These increases, while inflationary, were absolutely necessary, not only to bring those groups more nearly in line with the miners and factory workers, but to relieve a situation bordering on starvation. It was announced that these would be the only wage increases permitted; that the council and IMF mission were working on the final preparations for the stabilization plan; and that any further labor demands might prevent enactment of that plan.[15] * At the request of the council and of the Minister of Labor, I addressed a memorandum to the latter, explaining why no further wage increases could be granted, thus emphasizing the usefulness of a foreign adviser as a political scapegoat.

At the same time that the wage freeze was announced, a

---

*The 15 per cent increases were by resolution of the Ministry of Labor, with the approval of the Stabilization Council, in order to avoid getting Cabinet approval or the publicity of a presidential decree. All other wage demands were flatly rejected. It was not easy to hold the line. At one council meeting, the municipality of La Paz requested permission to increase municipal wages 150 per cent and the Minister of Economy saw no objection to the increase if the city had the funds. The council members objected that if the request were granted, there would be another round of wage increases for all other workers and the proposal was voted down. At another meeting the President suggested that, inasmuch as all wage increases were to be prohibited, manufacturers should be required to pay an extra month's wage each year. It was objected that this would be just as inflationary as a wage increase, and this proposal too was rejected.

freeze on all prices was decreed. No one on the Stabilization
Council had any expectation that such a decree could be enforced but, politically, it apparently proved essential to declare
a freeze on prices simultaneously with the freeze on wages.*

In a moving plea for public support, President Siles announced that he would resign from the presidency rather than
take any step that might adversely affect the position of the
workers and that the stabilization measures would not involve
any greater sacrifices than the workers had already made. It
was essential that no wage increases be granted for the present,
except to those who had not received raises since February,
1956, but, as soon as the stabilization program was put into
effect, there would be simultaneous wage increases for all
workers throughout the country. He threatened that anyone who
was hoarding merchandise for later sale, or speculating in dollars, would have some very disagreeable surprises coming.
The very vagueness of the threat probably made it more effica-
cious than if the consequences had been spelled out.[16]

*This decree was not authorized by the council (as it should have been
under the law establishing the council), but by the Cabinet. Nevertheless,
the preamble to the decree contains the usual "with the favorable opinion
of the National Monetary Stabilization Council, etc." (Decree dated November 8, 1956, El Diario, November 11, 1956.)

10

ORGANIZING THE PROGRAM

At Dr. Costanzo's first meeting with the Monetary Stabilization Council, on October 30, 1956, it was decided to break down the Fifty-Step Plan into four major areas, which were discussed at length, before getting down to a detailed discussion of the fifty steps in later meetings. The discussion provoked a lively exchange of questions and comments.

The first comment was from the Minister of Economy, who pointedly remarked that the outline now under discussion differed from the Fifty-Step Plan in the matter of timing, and particularly in that a million-dollar reserve was no longer insisted upon as a condition precedent. The telescoping of Stages I and II was explained as a question of mechanics; the fundamental point was that Bolivia must demonstrate its determination and ability to take the measures necessary for stabilization. The original plan had been drawn up some time ago when the Departments of State and Treasury, as well as the commercial bankers, had stipulated a prior million-dollar reserve, whereas the current working outline was based on the assumption that nothing must be allowed to delay enactment of the stabilization measures. It was suggested that, in the hope of enacting the stabilization measures on November 24, Bolivia should aim to complete its stabilization proposals by the middle of November and then immediately send its representative to Washington to obtain the approval of the International Monetary Fund as a basis for the financial support of the IMF and other Washington agencies.*

*This tight scheduling (admittedly optimistic) served to instill confidence and keep the council on its toes, precisely as the agenda and time schedule had done at a previous stage of the planning. Dr. Costanzo had planned to leave Bolivia with a draft of the stabilization measures on November 14 but postponed his departure until November 16. The president of the Central Bank and I left La Paz on November 21; the plan was presented to IMF on November 23, and final loan negotiations were concluded December 7. The plan was enacted December 15, 1956.

The Four Major Areas of Action

The four major areas of action, as they developed during the course of discussion, may be summarized as follows:

1. *The mining corporation:* Determination of a rate of exchange at which COMIBOL could operate without loss — say, tentatively, Bs. 6,500 to the dollar.
   a. Elimination of the below-cost company stores *(pulpería barata)*.
   b. Wages to be raised to compensate for elimination of the subsidized stores — say, tentatively, an increase of 150 per cent.
   c. COMIBOL to be required to pay a graduated royalty or export tax, say beginning at 10 per cent when the price of tin was 80 cents U.S. and rising with any increase in tin prices.

2. *Foreign trade:* Complete freedom of imports, exports, and foreign exchange.
   a. The rate of exchange to be left free to fluctuate according to supply and demand factors. It might rise to about Bs. 7,000, or, if the Central Bank were losing reserves, it might raise its dollar selling rate even higher during the initial period until such time as a definitive rate could be fixed. At that time, a new currency might be established.
   b. No controls over exports or imports in the private sector, except for export taxes and customs duties, which might be fairly high on luxury goods.
   c. Complete control over exports and imports in the government sector; government enterprises must turn over to the Central Bank 100 per cent of the foreign exchange received for their exports, and must purchase from the Central Bank the foreign exchange needed for imports, *within the ceilings fixed by the foreign exchange budget.* (It was later agreed that COMIBOL might retain 40 per cent of its gross foreign exchange earnings to meet its payments abroad.)

3. *Removal of price controls:* Complete freedom for the private sector to fix prices at will; the following limitations, however, to remain in force.
   a. U.S. aid commodities to be priced on the basis of cost, converted at the new foreign exchange rates.
   b. YPFB (the government petroleum corporation) to sell its products locally at realistic prices, i.e., at

prices sufficient to cover all expenses properly calculated.

c. Commercial rentals to be free of all controls; residential rentals in the lowest brackets to remain subject to temporary rent controls.

d. Wages to be raised to compensate for the rise in living costs as a result of the elimination ot price controls and subsidized food sales, and based on a careful study of working class living costs and consumption; thereafter, wages to be frozen for one year, following which readjustments could be made to fit the situation.

4. *Government budgets:* A unified general budget, and a unified foreign exchange budget to be drawn up to include the government and all governmental agencies; both budgets to be balanced on the basis of a realistic analysis of anticipated receipts and expenditures.

a. The general (domestic or boliviano) budget to be balanced by new ad valorem import duties; new taxes on mineral exports; the proper use of counterpart funds computed at realistic exchange rates (say, with half the funds frozen to deter inflation and half used to meet permissible counterpart expenditures); and reduction of expenses, particularly of the independent government agencies.

b. The foreign exchange budget to be based on ceilings assigned to the various government departments and agencies, within an aggregate limit determined by a realistic estimate of expected foreign exchange receipts; the government use of foreign exchange to be reduced as much as possible, allowing the remainder for the private sector.*

c. An analysis to be made of all governmental short- and medium-term debts; those falling due in 1957 to be renegotiated on a ten-year basis; no further indebtedness to be incurred by the government or any governmental agency.

---

*The assignment of only the residual foreign exchange to the private sector would work no hardship in Bolivia where the government and governmental enterprises dominated the international sector of the economy. Only the government use of foreign exchange was to be controlled. The private sector would be free to use any balances or credits it had or could obtain abroad, without restriction.

Discussion of these four points centered at first on the increase in living costs that would result from establishing the rate at Bs. 6,500 and eliminating the subsidized sales of foodstuffs at the Bs. 190 or any other official rate. The Minister of Mines contended that it would be necessary to raise the miners' wages from Bs. 1,500 a day to Bs. 8,000. Raising wages was, of course, a mere formality. Labor's aggregate real purchasing power would depend upon how much the country produced; not on any juggling the council might do with money or prices or wages or foreign exchange rates.

The Finance Minister presented tables purporting to show living costs based on consumption, by commodities, of workers in La Paz and Cochabamba. It was at once objected that the consumption figures apparently represented what the workers would like to consume, or what someone had figured out would be the ideal consumption pattern, as they showed higher consumption (particularly of sugar and meat) than in much more prosperous countries, even higher than in the United States.* Probably the high "consumption" figures were in part due to the inclusion of imports of U.S. aid foodstuffs and other subsidized imports from Argentina, which were not actually consumed in Bolivia but smuggled out of the country.

It was agreed that tables of consumption and prices would have to be compiled as accurately as possible, in order to determine what additional percentage compensation would be appropriate to offset expected higher living costs. The most difficult part of such calculations would be to determine what portion of a worker's wage was spent in purchasing food at official prices and what portion was spent for food and other commodities at black-market prices — a rather hopeless but necessary attempt to arrive at certainty by aggregating a vast number of uncertainties. The question of the actual composition of the laboring man's diet and living costs continued to plague the council, and the statistical table that was used to justify the wage increase finally granted showed an alleged food consumption which was a far cry from the U.N. and other figures showing the starvation diet of the Bolivian masses.

*At a later meeting, the Minister of Economy stated that Bolivian annual consumption of sugar was 21.8 kilos per capita (48 lbs.). In Peru, a major producer of sugar, consumption was 9 kilos. (Note: U.S. consumption is around 96 lbs. per capita, but 49 per cent is for industrial use, which is negligible in Bolivia. *Farr's Manual of Sugar Companies* [34th ed., New York: Farr and Co., 1958], pp. 15, 263.)

Fortunately, however, — and this is a fact that no one in Bolivia realized — it made little difference whether or not these computations were accurate or whether the additional compensation was equitable. The only important consideration was whether or not the wage earners would be satisfied. Whether they got a 50 per cent increase or a 150 per cent increase, their real wages, in terms of purchasing power, would be the same — they would still have only as much food and other commodities to consume as they were willing and able to produce. As there was sure to be grumbling, no matter how high the wage increase, it was more important for our ears to be attuned to the decibels of squawk than it was to worry about the accuracy of the computations we were forced to use.

The only limitation — and this our Bolivian confreres fully recognized — was that the higher the wage increase, the higher the price level would be, and the lower the value of the boliviano. This, manifestly, would work an injustice to the farmers and all those who did not benefit directly from the wage increase. As there were only about 150,000 to 300,000 wage earners who would get increases, out of a working population of perhaps 1,300,000,[17] it would be a case of the tail wagging the dog. In economic theory, the wage increases would be a mere formality and any inequities between various sectors of the population would be ironed out over the long run. As a practical matter, however, "in the long run we'll all be dead," and in Bolivia one's life expectancy might be fairly short with the armed militia of the farmers, miners, and MNR ready to iron out any supposed inequities.

In arriving at a foreign exchange rate for the boliviano, the closer we could come to Zondag's purchasing power parity of Bs. 4,000 (p. 131), the better off the great majority of the Bolivian people would be. The excessively high compensation that would obviously be demanded for the loss of cheap commissary privileges, however, made this rate impossible, and the best that could be hoped for was somewhere in the neighborhood of Bs. 6,000 to Bs. 8,000. The inaccuracy of available statistical material was such that it would have been difficult to determine where within that range would be found the figure that was least disturbing to the general economy. There was another factor to be considered, however, and that was that it would be less disturbing to public confidence, and hence less dangerous to ultimate stabilization, to use the Bs. 8,000 figure, and later discover that market forces were pushing the value of the boliviano up, than to attempt to stabilize at Bs. 6,000 and later find we could not hold it.

The ideal, therefore, would be to grant the minimum possible wage increases, in order to keep budget expenditures down and make it possible for COMIBOL to operate without a loss and for Bolivia to compete in world markets — and yet place the value of the boliviano as close as possible to the Bs. 8,000 limit, which would tend to curtail unnecessary imports, encourage investment, discourage capital flight, and reinforce the boliviano.

Prestabilization Wage Adjustments

In the course of the discussion on wage demands, the President stated that the factory workers were insisting on an immediate 200 per cent wage increase; that it was clearly a case of the Communists and Trotskyites in the rank and file of the workers' unions who were trying to sabotage the stabilization plans; and that the union leaders, far from leading the unions, took their orders from below (from the *bases,* as the rank and file were called). Within a week, nine more formal wage demands had been filed, from bank employees, retail clerks, and others. The council agreed that no wage increases could possibly be granted except for the 40 per cent increase to all government employees, and 15 per cent to certain other groups. This raise would fall far short of putting the government workers on a level with the miners or factory workers, but it would at least give them a percentage increase that was their due.

The President was strongly inclined to exclude the elementary and secondary school teachers and university professors from the 40 per cent increase to be granted to all other government employees, on the ground that the teachers and professors worked only a few hours a week. Dr. Antezana, himself a professor of economics, argued that it was unfair to judge by classroom hours alone, as teachers spent as much time preparing their class work and correcting papers as they did in class, but the President took the view that the teachers and professors were reactionaries, had always opposed the Revolution, and it would be an injustice to give them the same wage increase as other loyal government employees. (At a later meeting, Lechín was to take the same stand, with considerably more heat.)

At this, for the first and only time, I intervened in what was purely a political decision for, from the ‚viewpoint of stabilization, it made not the slightest difference whether the teachers and professors got a 40 per cent increase or not. They had no armed militia to enforce their rights; the increase would undeniably be inflationary; and, if they were all starved into doing some more *immediately* productive work, it might even conceivably help the stabilization program. But some elementary school teachers were so poor that, for breakfast, they had nothing but dry bread and a cup of hot water. Coffee was prohibitive, and even burnt corn, which was the common substitute for coffee, was too expensive.

To my own surprise, I found myself pleading passionately for the school teachers, for the men and women who would mould the coming generation of Bolivians, and in whose hands lay the future of the nation. Finally, I hit on the one argument that carried weight with the council — that for the government to grant a 40 per cent wage increase to all government employees, but expressly excluding the school teachers and university professors, would be looked upon so gravely by the press and public opinion in the United States that it might jeopardize the financial assistance that would be required for stabilization, and would certainly weigh heavily against Bolivia in future aid negotiations. This ended the discussion except for the question of the retroactivity of the increase, and it was finally decided to make the increase retroactive to August 1 for all government employees, including the teachers.

Capital Obligations: *The Tin Pile and the Foreign Debt*

Another problem came up, not included in the four-point outline of the principal areas of action for stabilization, namely, Bolivia's commitment to contribute to the buffer stock of tin held in England for the purpose of supporting world tin prices. According to the Foreign Minister, Bolivia would have to contribute a further six million dollars' worth of tin (approximately 3,000 tons) to the stock pile over the next three years. The Minister of Mines suggested that the tin pile contributions could be considered equivalent to building up a gold reserve, but this suggestion was vetoed on the basis of my statement that Washington placed great weight on the formation of adequate reserves by the Central Bank at the earliest possible time.* We

---

*Bolivia did at one time have a currency based on tin (Decree of May 25, 1932), with the number of bolivianos per pound sterling varying ac-

all agreed, however, that, while the tin pile could not be regarded as a substitute for the creation of Central Bank reserves, the contribution of some two million dollars worth of tin a year to the buffer stock could be taken as proof of Bolivia's ability and determination to put aside that much from its export resources, and as evidence that the country might be expected later to add an equivalent amount to its gold and dollar reserves.

Two further matters had to be disposed of, not covered in the four-point outline: (1) the necessity of reaching an agreement with the Foreign Bondholders Protective Council for resumption of payment on Bolivia's dollar bonds outstanding in the hands of the public; and (2) as soon as possible, an arrangement with the former owners of the nationalized mines for payment of the value of the seized properties.

The President asked whether, if Bolivia made a settlement on its foreign debt, it would be possible to borrow from the World Bank and was assured that the IBRD would in fact be very much interested in considering Bolivian applications for loans as soon as Bolivia had reached an agreement with the bondholders. The President then declared that, under those circumstances, if Bolivia could borrow substantial amounts from the World Bank, it would be worth while to make comparatively minor payments on the foreign debt. *

---

cording to the sterling price of tin. In theory, there would be no reason why a country could not have a tin currency, or a silver currency, instead of a gold or gold exchange currency, but the purpose for which the tin buffer stock was being accumulated, and the controls over that stock, made it unsuitable for consideration as a substitute for a gold or foreign exchange reserve (reference to 1932 decree from Mendoza-López, pp. 153-54). So far as can be determined from conflicting figures, Bolivia's 1956 contribution to the buffer stock was supposed to have been $5 million and, under an agreement negotiated by ex-President Paz-Estenssoro in his role as Ambassador to the Court of St. James's, Williams, Harvey & Co., Ltd., had advanced $4 million, repayable in 1957. The agreement was illegal, as it had been made without consultation with the Stabilization Council but, according to the IMF 1958 *Annual Report* (International Monetary Fund, *Annual Report* [Washington, D.C., 1958], p. 115), Bolivia contributed a further $8 million to the international buffer stock in 1957 and $2 million in 1958.

*This was the attitude that persistently prevailed in Bolivia. There was no recognition of any legal or moral obligation to repay the money that thousands of bondholders throughout the United States had loaned to the Bolivian government, but merely a realization that, by paying a small amount, Bolivia could hope to borrow a much larger amount (see p. 436). The same was true with respect to payments on the Export-Import Bank

The interest of the World Bank in Bolivia was confirmed at a later meeting by Gisbert, who had discussed the possibility of a loan in Washington with Eugene Black and others, and had been assured that the bank would send a mission to Bolivia as soon as a settlement on the bonds had been reached and the budget balanced, so that Bolivia's borrowing capacity could be appraised.

Priorities

Following the October 30 and 31 meetings, at which general agreement was reached as to the principles on which the stabilization program must be based (within the four major areas of action delineated), the council embarked on a series of nineteen daily or twice-daily meetings, from November 1 through November 16, with representatives of each of the major government enterprises and political factions. In the course of these hearings, the council reviewed each of the points in the Fifty-Step Plan and reached definitive decisions for action or postponement.

Logically, the first matter to be settled was the wage adjustment to be made by the mining corporation, and the rate of exchange determined by that adjustment, as outlined in the first of the four areas of action. Logically, too, this was the first matter tackled in discussions with COMIBOL and the Ford, Bacon & Davis mission.[18] But, as a decision was not reached on this crucial question until the eleventh hour of the final meeting, the council first made its definitive determinations on each of the following subjects, and then concluded its deliberations with the vital problem of COMIBOL.

---

loan, and on supplier credits for supplies purchased by the YPFB — debt payments were viewed solely as a means to further borrowing. That this attitude was not confined to the Revolutionary Government is seen in the attempt of an earlier administration to settle the Bolivian debt by cancelling all defaulted interest, reducing future interest to 1 per cent, and repurchasing the outstanding bonds, then quoted at less than 4 per cent of par, at an average price of 13 per cent of par. The sole purpose behind even this confiscatory proposal was that it would "place the credit of the country in a favorable position to reopen the doors of American banks" for future financing. See statement by former Finance Minister Vicente Mendoza-López, and report to President Busch by Mauricio Hochschild, confidential agent charged with negotiating a settlement of the debt (Mendoza-López, pp. 314, 319, 320).

Wage Decisions for Organizations Other Than COMIBOL

As a basis for a rough estimate of the increase in working class living costs after stabilization, for wage earners other than the COMIBOL employees, a compilation was made (Table 5), with the figures furnished chiefly by the Ministers of Finance, Economy, and Mines. The table purports to show the average consumption of the principal commodities entering into

TABLE 5

Anticipated Increase in Living Costs as Result of Stabilization
(In Bolivianos — Based on Estimated Expenditures of
Factory Workers in La Paz)

Commodity	Estimated Monthly Consumption	Price before Stabilization*	Estimated Price after Stabilization	Necessary Compensation per Unit†	Necessary Compensation per Month†
Sugar	5 kgs.	85	575	490	2,450
	5 kgs.	*650*	575	(75)	(375)
Meat	5 kgs.	1,200	3,000	1,800	9,000
	5 kgs.	*3,000*	3,000	...	...
Rice	3 kgs.	730	1,200	1,070	3,210
	3 kgs.	*2,100*	1,200	(900)	(2,700)
Bread	200 loaves	30	160	130	26,000
	100 loaves	*100*	160	60	6,000
Edible oil	½ bottle	650	3,750	3,100	1,550
	½ bottle	*3,200*	3,750	550	275
Lard	1 kg.	900	3,200	2,300	2,300
	1 kg.	*4,400*	3,200	(1,200)	(1,200)
Kerosene	30 liters	30	120	90	2,700
Spaghetti	5 kgs.	830	1,350	520	2,600
	5 kgs.	*1,300*	1,350	50	250
Coffee	1 kg.	*4,000*	5,000	1,000	1,000
Net necessary monthly compensation					53,060
Net necessary daily compensation					1,768

*Free market prices (prior to stabilization) are in italics; all other prices represent the official prices fixed by the Ministry of Economy for sale at company stores and at official distribution centers.
†Amounts in parentheses represent lower estimated prices after stabilization.

the market basket of a typical factory worker in La Paz, divided between those commodities which the worker could purchase in the factory store or at price-controlled distribution centers and those which he would have to buy in the workers' markets which were at partly price-controlled and partly black-market prices.

Admittedly, there was no such thing as a typical factory or a typical worker. Some factories had fairly well-stocked company stores, although not to compare with the COMIBOL and railroad commissaries, while other factories seldom had any goods for sale. Then too, La Paz was not typical of the country at large, and all of the figures, for prices as well as for consumption, were little more than guesses. Nevertheless, they were the guesses of men well qualified to make a knowledgeable estimate. They erred if anything in favor of the working man; that is, they tended to exaggerate the working man's quantitative consumption as well as the percentage of that consumption supplied at subsidized costs. There could be little doubt, moreover, that consumption of sugar, for example, had been greatly stimulated by artificially low prices and that, when all commodities were sold at realistic prices, the consumption of sugar and certain other commodities would tend to decline.*

Any estimate of what the new prices would be for the various commodities after stabilization was purely in the realm of fantasy. It will be noted that, in the table, all the commodities currently sold at subsidized prices were expected to rise, which was a foregone conclusion, but that free market prices for sugar, rice, and lard were expected to decline (shown in parenthesis). This proved to be the case and, in fact, within five months after stabilization, most prices were substantially lower than the anticipated new prices shown in Table 5. In all, according to the table, the living costs of a worker with "typical" prestabilization commissary privileges could be expected to rise some Bs. 1,768 a day.

Now, in the course of the preliminary discussions on

---

*As an example of the influence of price subsidies over the inflationary years, *imported* sardines had become a standard item of diet. The miners could obtain a can of sardines at one-fifth of a cent a can, and in the free-price Indian markets, the sardines were sold from open cans at a fraction of a cent per sardine. They cost the government, wholesale, 25 cents U.S. a can (FBD report, vol. 3, p. 82). At one point in the council discussions, Lechín had stressed how important it was for the workers to be able to buy sardines at the same price after stabilization as prior to stabilization, but fortunately he did not insist on that point.

COMIBOL wages and foreign exchange rates, it had been decided that the COMIBOL employees would get a wage increase
of Bs. 5,250 a day and that of this amount Bs. 3,950 would be
for the loss of commissary privileges and Bs. 1,300 for generally increased living costs. Further, it was decided that the
Bs. 1,300 increase would be given to all workers without distinction, on the theory, as President Siles put it, that all workers had the same vital needs even though they were not earning
the same wage. It was perhaps as good a theory as any other
but, it will be noted, the decision cannot be supported by the
figures in Table 5.* If anyone were asked to defend the logic of
the distribution of the wage increases, he would have to fall
back on the logic of bowing to the inevitable — the paramount
pressure of political power. In strict logic, and in economic
theory, no wage increases were needed, and any increases given
were meaningless, as has been pointed out.

In sum, nevertheless, if the factory workers' living costs
could be expected to increase Bs. 1,768 per diem, and if Bs.
1,300 were to be assigned as a general living cost increase to
all *wage earners,* that left Bs. 468 to be attributed to the loss of
pulpería privileges. Hence, the factory workers were granted
Bs. 450 on that account.

With as little logic, and as scanty statistical support, the
railway workers and the miners in the private mines were allowed Bs. 1,350 per diem for the loss of commissary privileges,
except for workers at the Fabulosa mines and at the International Mining Corporation mines, who were placed in the same
category as the COMIBOL miners. (The initial decision had
been to leave the private mine operators free to negotiate compensation for the elimination of the subsidized commissaries on
a mine-to-mine basis, but before the stabilization decrees were

*If the reader wishes to take the trouble to make the computation, he
will see that the increased costs shown in Table 5, for commodities previously purchased at controlled prices, aggregate Bs. 1,660 a day, while the
net increase for other commodities (deducting price declines from price
rises) is Bs. 108 a day. Assuming that workers who previously had had no
cheap commissary prices were to purchase the same amounts of each
commodity as the factory workers, but all at free market prices, their
living costs would go up Bs. 473 a day, and not the Bs. 1,300 which they
were allowed. This, however, would have been inequitable, as the workers
who had no commissary privileges were already the most underprivileged
workers in Bolivia.

enacted it was realized that this would have meant endless strikes and strife.)

At one meeting the Minister of Mines proposed a poststabilization minimum wage of Bs. 2,700 (i.e., the prestabilization minimum of Bs. 1,000 plus the 40 per cent general wage hike, plus Bs. 1,300), but it was pointed out that fixing a minimum wage might bring unemployment. The reason I opposed the proposal was that any discussion of a minimum wage would inevitably hinge on a minimum *salario vital* or living wage (i.e., the minimum needed to provide a family with the minimum subsistence intake of calories, proteins, etc.), and the U.N. experts had computed minimum subsistence diets on the basis of aspirations or theoretical ideals without taking account of Bolivia's current economic capacity. Hence, I suggested that it would be impossible to make a minimum wage study for at least six months after stabilization, and the pre-existing minimum wage was allowed to remain, plus the Bs. 1,300. In effect, this tended to lower the real minimum (as it omitted the 40 per cent general prestabilization wage hikes) and thus probably tended to prevent unemployment.

As evidence of the inequities in Bolivia's poststabilization wage scales, some 35,000 civil servants were budgeted with a total payroll of Bs. 79.3 billion a year (average $293 per annum at the stabilization rate of exchange), while some 28,500 COMIBOL miners (i.e., 34,500 less the 6,000 scheduled to be dismissed) were budgeted with direct payroll costs of Bs. 122.3 billion (average $555 per annum). Note that the COMIBOL figure works out at Bs. 11,800 a day (on the basis of 365 days in the year — the miners actually worked less than 200 days in the year but were paid for 365), compared with the *average basic wage* of Bs. 7,500 authorized by the council.

Both figures are exclusive of social security and fringe benefits. This same imbalance in favor of the miners existed prior to stabilization, and it would be hard to say whether it was increased or diminished by stabilization. Probably the former is true, inasmuch as the *políticos* were inclined to favor the side with the heaviest artillery.

According to the ECLA report, the wages of government workers had declined so drastically between 1952 and 1956, compared with the rest of the working population, that in the latter year there were only 13 employees earning over Bs. 100,000 a month, in terms of 1955 purchasing power ($32.50 a month). The purchasing power of the wage of the average civil servant in 1955 was stated to be little more than half that in 1950, with perhaps a slight gain in 1956. Factory wages were reported to have been 15 per cent lower in purchasing power in 1955 than in 1951, and the loss was attributed to gains of workers in other sectors of the economy (notably the miners) and not to increased profits of the employers. (The disparate dates used for comparison are those given in the ECLA report, figures for other years not being available.)[19]

Government Enterprises Other Than COMIBOL

YPFB

One of the most difficult problems confronting the Stabilization Council was the question of trimming the budget of the YPFB, or government petroleum company. So far as the Stabilization Council could judge, the petroleum company represented Bolivia's only chance, at least in the near future,* of escaping its almost total dependence on tin exports as a source of foreign exchange. Up to that time, YPFB's only exports had been to Argentina and Brazil, and for those exports Bolivia received, not foreign exchange, but barter rights of dubious value, to import merchandise from those countries at prices well above world market prices.

The petroleum company management, however, was convinced that, if it could complete its pipe line to the Pacific, it would bring in foreign exchange in amounts that would more than justify the cost of the investment. Furthermore, of all the government enterprises, YPFB appeared to be the only one that was competently administered, and which gave some promise of fulfilling the high hopes of its managers. The USOM had been particularly impressed by the ability of the general manager, an American-trained engineer formerly employed by Standard Oil Company (N.J.), who had built up a staff of enthusiastic young engineers, likewise trained in the United States. This group of Bolivian engineers ran an operation which, *from the technical operating viewpoint,* seemed to disprove the general

---

*The new Petroleum Code had just been approved by Congress, and it would be at least five years before any new private oil company could get on an export basis.

rule that government management in Bolivia was incompatible with operating efficiency.

The problem was that, in order to complete the Pacific pipe line and bring the company's production up to the point where its construction would be warranted, further investments would be needed far in excess of Bolivia's available foreign exchange resources. The YPFB management brought two budgets to the Stabilization Council, one showing its original plans for expansion, calling for foreign exchange expenditures of over $25 million in 1957, while the second, "cut to the bone" as an aid to Bolivia's monetary stabilization program, contemplated a $14 million outlay (which included $2 million for aviation gasoline for the government airline).

The YPFB management was told that Bolivia's available exchange resources would only permit foreign exchange expenditures of $10 million. Finally, after four long sessions with the YPFB representatives, the council ruled that YPFB could be allowed $10.8 million for its own needs in 1957, plus $1.8 million for aviation gas. The company perforce accepted this decision, but sent a formal notice warning the council that it would not be responsible for the consequences — that this reduction would mean postponing its production plans for five years. The contention that a one-year budget cut would mean a five-year delay was difficult to follow, particularly as Gisbert had reported that YPFB could expect assistance from the World Bank within one year, provided it showed evidence that it was not operating on a deficit basis. The reduction in capital expenditures imposed by the council was only $1.2 million, and President Siles commented with some asperity that this was a time to assume responsibilities and not to dodge them.

Confidence in YPFB management was further shattered by the fact that, despite the council's express warnings that there must be no further short- or medium-term borrowing by YPFB to make good the curtailment of its dollar capital expenditures, a letter was received from one of the company's largest suppliers to the effect that the YPFB management had stated that it was going ahead with its plans for expansion, and would require five-year credit terms on all equipment purchases. This was not only a violation of the law — the decree establishing the Monetary Stabilization Council had prohibited any credit operations without prior approval by the council — but, throughout the discussions between the council and the YPFB management, it was clear that the latter simply did not grasp the fact that purchasing capital equipment on short- or medium-term credit did not solve any problems but merely created new ones.

Later investigation of YPFB accounts revealed that all their budgetary projections justifying the profitability of new investments were based on purchases at the fictitious official rate of exchange of Bs. 190 to the dollar and on depreciation figured on those values. The management's understanding of corporation accounting and finance was practically nil. Thus, it would seem that even YPFB, which it had been hoped would prove a paragon of government enterprise, was merely another example of the fact that Bolivia would have been better off if all productive activities had been left entirely to private enterprise.

Another question that came before the council in connection with YPFB was that the company had outstanding some $3 million in notes payable to foreign equipment suppliers for orders already en route or in port, with another $2 million pending approval of the Finance Minister. If those bills were not paid, the council was told, YPFB would be unable to buy on credit in the future. This equipment, of course, had all been budgeted by YPFB in bolivianos at the rate of Bs. 190 to the dollar.

There was no problem there, YPFB was informed. It would merely have to pay the Central Bank for its foreign exchange at whatever stabilization rate might be established, say at Bs. 6,000 to the dollar, if that proved to be the rate finally settled upon, and it could find the bolivianos to pay the bank by raising prices on its domestic sales from the current controlled levels to realistic prices based on actual costs. This was agreed to by the council and, on that basis, it was decided that kerosene prices, for example, would be raised from Bs. 30 a liter to Bs. 320,* with similar increases in the price of gasoline and other products, exclusive of the tax which it was agreed would be placed on those products. On that basis, it was expected that YPFB could not only balance its budget but would show a surplus of Bs. 7.4 billion, according to figures submitted by YPFB to the council. Once the stabilization loan had been obtained, however, this triple agreement — on prices, the restriction of credits, and the budgeted surplus — was forgotten when the chauffeurs' union óbjected to higher gasoline prices, and when the public complained of the higher price for kerosene. [20]

---

*This does not tally with the Bs. 120 price shown in Table 5, which had been drawn up prior to the decision on YPFB.

Government railways

Another major government enterprise whose affairs were reviewed by the Monetary Stabilization Council was the *Ferrocarriles del Estado*. The Director General of Railways appeared before the council at two meetings, accompanied by the Ministers of Public Works and of Labor, as well as by the President of the Senate. At the first meeting, the general stabilization plan was outlined and the Director General was asked to work out a completely new tariff schedule for passengers and freight for each of the government lines, that would enable the railways to operate without a loss and without subsidies. Computations were to be based on the hypothesis of a foreign exchange rate of Bs. 6,000 per dollar for all imports and for calculating domestic purchases of fuel and other supplies which the railways were at present buying at artificially subsidized prices, and assuming a 50 per cent increase in direct and indirect labor costs. At the same time, it was suggested that discrepancies in the various rate schedules, that had arisen during the inflationary period, might be ironed out so as to present a more logical tariff structure as a whole.

At the second meeting, the Director General stated that the railway budget could be balanced with increases varying from 70 per cent to 136 per cent on the various lines.* The council authorized him to proceed on that basis, and advised that no foreign exchange could be supplied for new equipment in 1957. Gisbert assured him, however, that the World Bank could be counted upon for equipment financing if operating results were such as to warrant financial assistance.

The Director General of Railways was of inestimable value to the council in working out appropriate rate adjustments with the private railways, to be put into effect at the time of

---

*According to ECLA, the detailed rate schedules in the various categories showed increases of 46 per cent to 313 per cent for general freight, and as high as 103 per cent to 516 per cent for the transportation of petroleum products. *With no investigation of the cost of rendering service,* ECLA concluded from these increases, and from the fact that higher freight rates would mean higher commodity prices, that the rates should be lowered (ECLA report, pp. 224-32). This is precisely the kind of superficial reasoning that had caused the deficits in government enterprises, and was a major factor in the Bolivian inflationary experience. The "experts" seldom seem to grasp the fact that fixing rates or prices below cost is no gain to the economy, but a loss because of the resultant distortion of supply and demand.

stabilization, with the understanding that all such adjustments, of government as well as of private railway rates, would be tentative until sufficient time had elapsed for a proper appraisal of poststabilization costs. [21]

Bolivian Development Corporation

The projects managed by the Bolivian Development Corporation have been outlined in Chapter 3, as well as the budgetary deficits which pinpointed it as the major contributing factor in Bolivia's rampant inflation. At the request of the Finance Minister, I analyzed this situation in considerable detail at a series of council meetings attended by the President of the Development Corporation who was naturally upset by this analysis, which he took to be a personal affront to his integrity.*

I took pains, however, to explain that my recommendation not to advance a further six billion bolivianos requested by the corporation was no reflection on the honesty of the management, but was based solely on three factors: (1) that the Development Corporation had never furnished the data on receipts, expenditures, and budgets, in dollars and bolivianos, called for in the decree of August 4, 1956, and that this made all obligations entered into by the corporation since that date illegal; (2) that the

---

*Following the first council hearing on the Development Corporation, the American Ambassador summoned me to say that the president of the corporation took the recommendation to turn down his unsubstantiated request for a Bs. 6 billion credit as a reflection on his honor, threatening to shoot me on sight. At the Ambassador's request, I wrote a letter stating that it was not my intention to impugn anyone's integrity but that I opposed the credit on financial grounds. I continued to oppose further credits, and some time later the Development Corporation president stalked into the Central Bank, reportedly livid with rage, and laid a large automatic pistol down on the desk of one of my colleagues, and again repeated the threat. But a fortnight later, he appeared before the council to support an equally unsubstantiated demand for funds, which I again opposed without incident. The whole affair was most regrettable, as the president of the corporation was a likable person and an intimate friend of former President Paz-Estenssoro. On the other hand, stabilization would have been impossible if friendship were a bar to proper accountability. A detailed analysis of the corporation projects which I presented to the council, supplemented by later information, is given in Appendix IV, inasmuch as the operations of that agency, ill-conceived and worse-managed, were then and continue to be a major obstacle in the path of economic development and a permanent drain on U.S. aid funds.

council had no way of knowing what had become of the $50 million to $100 million already spent by the Development Corporation, nor what the corporation intended doing with the Bs. 2 - Bs. 6 billion it was then requesting; and (3) that any additional credit provided by the Central Bank could only be created by the issuance of bank notes which would be directly inflationary.

As a result of these hearings, it was decided to cut the corporation's foreign exchange budget for suppliers' credits, from the $4.5 million requested to $1.1 million, and to cut down domestic expenditures gradually from Bs. 1.4 billion a month in December, 1956, to Bs. 400 million in December, 1957. In the end, however, the corporation was permitted a budgetary deficit of Bs. 47.7 billion to be financed by subsidies included in the general government budget. Criteria for abandoning certain projects, and for stretching out other projects, were laid down. In general, all work on projects that were not 75 per cent completed was to be suspended. On that basis, President Siles ruled that only two projects should be carried on with budgeted funds, namely, the Sucre cement plan and the Cochabamba-Santa Cruz highway, and two with Point IV counterpart funds, namely, the colonization projects and feeder roads to the main highways. Foreign exchange for service of the Export-Import Bank loan was budgeted at $3.9 million for 1957, and it was agreed that, if negotiations made possible postponement of that payment, the funds would not be used for Development Corporation projects but would be assigned in accordance with recommendations to be made by the Stabilization Council — a commitment that was soon forgotten.[22]

Mining Bank

The general agreement reached with respect to the Mining Bank, in discussions with Juan Lechín and Ñuflo Chávez, has been outlined at p. 175. The representatives of the bank (a completely new management had been installed since the scandal-tinged days of the previous administration) appeared before the Stabilization Council, and the following detailed bases of operation were agreed upon, and enacted, as a part of the stabilization program:

1. Basically, all mineral exports other than those of COMIBOL to be handled by the Mining Bank, but the medium-sized mines to be free to export directly if

they could obtain prices higher than those quoted by the bank.

2. All private producers to receive payment in foreign exchange, whether or not their exports were handled by the bank, and to be permitted to dispose freely of such exchange, less charges for the bank's services in the case of shipments made through the bank.

3. On direct shipments by the medium-sized mines, the producers to contribute 10 per cent of net exchange proceeds for repayment of the Williams, Harvey & Co., Ltd., loan covering their share of Bolivia's contribution to the buffer tin stock.

4. Royalties to be paid by the private mines on gross metal exports at the same rates as the royalties fixed for COMIBOL, and in lieu of all other taxes on exports or mining profits.*

5. On shipments made by the Mining Bank, the repayment to Williams, Harvey & Co., Ltd., must be made by the bank, the bank to be reimbursed by the government, and the government to take title to the tin.

6. The bank to be prohibited from making further use of pending supplier credits or to open new credits without the express approval of the council ($17 million credits already outstanding).

7. The Mining Bank deposits in the Central Bank (some Bs. 5 billion) to be frozen, and the Mining Bank credits to private miners to be restricted to not over current levels.

8. The Mining Bank to be allowed $1.8 million in foreign exchange in the 1957 budget, of which $1.3 million would be for repayment of suppliers' credits, and the remainder for equipment, salaries, and laboratory fees.

9. All foreign exchange receipts would be turned over to the Central Bank and all exchange required would be purchased from the Central Bank.

10. The Mining Bank to reduce its personnel by 30 per cent (the General Manager had testified that only 300 employees were needed in all, but that the bank had been compelled by political pressure to take on 229 additional employees); the 30 per cent reduction in force was agreed to but not enforced.[23]

---

*An exception was made for small-scale placer and similar gold mining operations which were to be tax free. The president of the Mining Bank informed the council that the 10,000 inhabitants of the village of Tipuani were practically dependent upon such mining for their cash in-

Government airline

LAB had its 1957 foreign exchange budget cut to $1.5 million from the $2.3 million originally called for. The extent of the cut on the boliviano accounts of the company can be appreciated when compared with dollar expenditures of $1.5 million in 1955 and $1.2 million in the first ten months of 1956, when the line was permitted to purchase aviation gasoline and equipment in bolivianos at the Bs. 190 rate. Under realistic foreign exchange rates, a balanced budget was impossible, the airline being manifestly uneconomic, but the LAB was required at least to live within a maximum deficit of Bs. 1.7 billion.

All other government industrial enterprises and agencies were given a total subsidy from the general budget of Bs. 2.1 billion and were required to live within that budget. They were allowed $1.1 million in foreign exchange.

National Social Security Administration

The question of social security costs was discussed at four council meetings, and all members of the council, as well as Lechín, who was present at two of the meetings, agreed that the charges were exorbitant. It was suggested that, inasmuch as it was agreed that living costs would probably rise some 20-30 per cent after stabilization, the National Social Security Administration (CNSS) should be able to get along with a 20-30 per cent increase in its total revenues, plus a comparatively modest amount to cover its own increased payroll, and that the present was not an appropriate time for the CNSS to *increase* its services and demand higher revenues than in the past. At the final meeting, however, the best that could be arranged was that the 14 per cent for housing, the 13 per cent for family subsidy, and the 7 per cent workmen's compensation (accident compensation in hazardous employment) would be applied to the November 30, 1956, money wage, while the $5\frac{1}{2}$ per cent sickness and maternity and the $8\frac{1}{2}$ per cent for old age and death benefits under the new

---

come and that their annual production was about 100 kilos. This would be worth about $112,000 and, even if production were several times that figure, it would scarcely be feasible to collect royalties. Although these facts and figures are probably no more reliable than others in the Bolivian picture, the $11 per capita annual income can be explained by the fact that the placer miners were subsistence farmers and that mining represented their *cash income.*

law then pending in Congress would be based on the poststabilization wages.[24]

On the eve of my departure for the United States to assist in the final arrangements for the stabilization loan, however, the general manager of the CNSS and his U.N. adviser came round breathless to the house to advise that it would be impossible to base any percentages on prestabilization wages (this was probably true, as a practical matter). They suggested instead that the low-cost housing contribution be reduced from 14 per cent to $5\frac{1}{2}$ per cent and the family subsidy from 13 per cent to $8\frac{1}{2}$ per cent. They stated that they were authorized by President Siles to say that, if there was no objection, the law would be amended in that way. I replied that I had no power to approve or disapprove but that, if they gave me their absolute assurance that the change would mean no increase in the payroll of the government or government enterprises, I would have no reason to oppose their proposal, and would pass it on to Washington.* This was done, and the amendment was so enacted in the December 15 stabilization decree.

The Government Budget

With the effective cooperation of the Finance Minister, it was not difficult to obtain budget figures for 1957 government expenditures and estimates of the revenues expected to be produced by the new tax measures decided upon in the Stabilization Council meetings.

As it turned out, however, some of these tax measures were not enacted in time to produce the full revenue anticipated, and others were so emasculated by the Cabinet that they hardly paid the cost of collection. COMIBOL proved remiss in payment of its expected royalties, and the Ministry of Economy fell so far behind in presenting the facts and requisitions for U.S. counterpart funds that that source of revenue likewise fell short of the mark. On the expenditure side, fortunately, the

*In the case of the COMIBOL miners, the arrangement proposed by the CNSS would mean an increase of some 50 per cent in social security costs in view of the much higher poststabilization wage, assuming, of course, that COMIBOL carried out its obligation to dismiss 6,000 idle workers — a commitment that was not fulfilled. This increase might conceivably be offset by the decrease in costs on a substantially larger number of civil servants.

government departments were so bewildered by the processes of stabilization that, in the first semester of 1957 at least, they also fell short of the expenditures to which they were entitled.

Thus, the 1957 budgetary figures set forth in Table 6 are meaningless as estimates of actual results, which is not surprising when the prestabilization state of chaos in government finances is borne in mind, and when any predictions as to the effect of stabilization on 1957 revenues and expenditures were largely in the realm of the unknown. The figures did have meaning, however, in the sense that they represented the Bolivian government's best possible estimate of 1957 results and were presented by the government and the Central Bank in support of their request for stabilization financing. Thus, there was the weightiest possible moral obligation for the Bolivian government to see that its 1957 revenues fulfilled the budgetary expectations, and that its 1957 expenditures fell within the limits of actual revenue collections — an obligation which should have been more binding than the usual budgetary estimate.

In a sense it is misleading to place the 1956 budget figures alongside those for 1957, as the 1956 figures were pure fiction, owing to the commingling of boliviano and dollar accounts at various artificial rates of exchange. It was impossible for the Finance Minister or the Stabilization Council to obtain more than fragmentary figures for actual expenditures and revenues. In Table 6, the 1956 budget shows all dollar receipts and expenditures converted at the rate of Bs. 6,000 to the dollar, which may be reasonably representative of average actual free rates during that year. The budget thus shows substantial surpluses for the government mining corporation and the Mining Bank. Bear in mind that these are budget estimates only, and further, that they are estimates of cash flow, with no allowance for depreciation or depletion; they would bear no resemblance to a statement of profit and loss, if it were possible to prepare such a statement, which it is not. In the 1957 budget, these surpluses are replaced, in part, by the budgeted royalties on mineral exports. The budgeted deficits of YPFB, the railways, and various other government enterprises in 1956 were, it was hoped, eliminated in the 1957 budget, in which dollar receipts and expenditures are converted at Bs. 7,000, the rate the Stabilization Council had tentatively in mind at the time the budget was prepared.

In the 1956 figures, only a fraction of the $20 million of U.S. aid is shown (Bs. 25.5 billion, or about $4.4 million), the

TABLE 6

Government Budget Before and After Stabilization
(In Billions of Bolivianos)

Item	Dollar Converted at Bs. 6,000 1956	Dollar Converted at Bs. 7,000 1957
REVENUES:		
COMIBOL (Mining Corporation — net cash surplus)	178.9	. . .
Mining Bank — net cash surplus	56.1	. . .
Other government enterprises and agencies	.3	. . .
Royalties on mineral exports	. . .	57.5
Customs duties and taxes	41.3	52.5
Excise taxes	29.0	44.5
Income taxes	. . .	4.0
Consular fees	2.0	2.0
Post and telegraph taxes	.8	3.0
Other tax revenues	11.8	13.1
U.S. aid counterpart funds	25.5	105.0
Total revenues	345.7	281.6
EXPENDITURES:		
Government departments	78.5	139.1
Wages	Not	79.3
Social security	broken	12.9
Foreign exchange	down	26.3
Other		20.3
Debt payments	3.3	43.3
External	2.6	30.8
Internal	.8	12.5
Subsidies (chiefly to universities from earmarked taxes)	78.2	19.0
Deficits of government enterprises	153.6	51.5
National Social Security Fund	5.6	. . .
Central Bank	3.0	. . .
Bolivian Development Corporation	46.0	47.7
Civil Aviation Board	2.3	. . .
LAB (government airline)	10.5	1.7
YPFB (government petroleum corporation)	64.9	. . .
Government railways	20.3	. . .
All other government enterprises and agencies	1.0	2.1
U. S. aid counterpart fund projects	24.9	15.0
Contributions to technical assistance	23.8	5.0
Other projects	1.1	10.0
Total expenditures	338.5	267.9
SURPLUS	7.2	13.7

difference being accounted for by artificial exchange rates, and swallowed up in the capacious maw of the black marketeers and *políticos*. In the 1957 budget, it was hoped to "sterilize" (i.e., to postpone the use of) perhaps as much as 50 per cent of the U.S. aid counterpart funds as a deterrent to further inflationary pressure.

The external debt service shown in the 1957 budget included $1.4 million of interest payable to the Export-Import Bank of Washington (postponed by later negotiation), and $3 million payable on account (pending a settlement of the amount due) to Patiño, Aramayo, and Hochschild for seizure of their properties. The amount budgeted for external debt service in 1956 was for payments on the $2 million of 20-year, 7 per cent bonds given to *Union Allumettière,* the Belgian subsidiary of Krueger & Toll's *Svenska Tandsticks Aktiebolaget* in a penumbral deal under which *Union Allumettière* received an absolute monopoly on the manufacture, importation, and sale of matches in Bolivia. Interest and amortization continued to be paid on this loan ($355,867 outstanding at the close of 1956), despite the complete default on Bolivia's publicly held bonds, one of the many inequities against which I protested in vain.

Tax measures

Revenue measures loomed large in the preparation of the 1957 budget, as the old system of taxes would be practically meaningless after stabilization. The council, and particularly the Finance Minister, had to start virtually from scratch in preparing a completely new tax system in a period of a few weeks. The customs import duties, for example, were down in the 1956 budget at Bs. 2 billion (say $333,000), but the old specific duty rates were supplemented, as the boliviano depreciated, by a series of constantly changing surcharges that were budgeted at Bs. 33 billion. Export duties, which once constituted the major part of the Bolivian government revenues, were also budgeted at the ridiculously low figure of Bs. 2 billion, as a result of the steady erosion of the value of the boliviano.

Since the council had no time to prepare an adequate schedule of import duties, it was forced to take the ready-made schedule that had been drawn up by the U.N. advisers, with a few necessary changes made by the Finance Minister, even though every member of the Stabilization Council realized that the new schedule was completely unsuited to prevailing conditions, and would fall short either as a revenue measure or as a protective barrier.[25] The Bs. 52.5 billion of customs duties budgeted for 1957 was based largely on the expectation of a thoroughgoing revision of tariff schedules early in 1957. All other taxes, surcharges, and foreign exchange subsidies on imports were abolished.

On mineral export royalties, the council had laid down a general rule that tin, for example, would pay a tax of 10 per cent when world tin prices were 90 cents, and on a sliding scale when prices were above or below that level, the intention being to split any profits from higher prices fifty-fifty between the mines (including COMIBOL) and the government. Other minerals would be taxed in the same way. It was left to the Ministers of Finance and Mines, however, to work out a viable schedule of export taxes or royalties with COMIBOL and the Mining Bank, in order to ensure adequate revenues without crippling either COMIBOL or the private mining industry. Separate schedules were drawn up for tin, wolfram, antimony, copper, lead, zinc, and silver. Gold royalties were embodied in the concession contract of the sole large concessionaire, and small-scale gold production was left tax free. Each schedule, other than for gold, was on a sliding scale of royalties, dependent not only on the price of the metal, but on the metal content of the concentrates that were exported. For example, tin concentrates of 60 per cent metal content or over would pay a 3.6 per cent tax at the price of 80 cents per pound, 10 per cent at 90 cents, 18 per cent at $1.10, etc. Concentrates containing 20 per cent tin would pay 0.35 per cent to 2.4 per cent within the same price extremes. These tables were approved by the council and enacted simultaneously with the principal stabilization decree.[26]

A major improvement embodied in that decree was that all earmarked taxes formerly levied on metal exports for the benefit of the universities, departments, municipalities, and other entities, were abolished. In their stead, all recipients of such taxes were allotted subsidies based on 1955 tax collections plus a 30 per cent bonus.

Although the 1957 budget shown in Table 6, and presented to the IMF and other lending agencies, contains no provision for export taxes on other products, the council approved a series of export taxes, ranging from 3 per cent to 15 per cent on a list of fourteen categories of agricultural and forest products and certain manufactured goods. In this case too, the earmarked taxes on such exports were replaced by subsidies based on 1955 collections plus 30 per cent.[27]

The elimination of earmarked taxes was one of the original goals which met with a considerable measure of success. The council did away completely with the earmarked taxes on exports and imports where they amounted, in effect, to a tax on foreign exchange. The gross receipts from earmarked taxes had fallen from 70 per cent of total national tax revenues in 1953 to 30 per cent in November, 1956, but the reduction was attributable entirely to the erosion in the value of the boliviano and the continuous introduction of new, unencumbered taxes. The number and variety of earmarked taxes had continued to grow apace, and a single commodity or service might be burdened with a dozen different earmarks in favor of football clubs, political "cells," labor cooperatives, or other organizations, each earmarking infinitesimal in amount because of the depreciation of the currency, but extremely onerous both to business and government because of the disproportionate cost of collection and distribution. The major beneficiaries of these earmarkings, however, were the universities, and in their case there was at least the plausible, nonpolitical reason of university autonomy in favor of the system (see p. 430 for later difficulties in this connection).

There was a limit to the number of tax measures that the Finance Ministry could prepare, and the Stabilization Council could consider, during the last frenetic weeks of preparation for the stabilization decrees, and the only other tax measure enacted simultaneously with the stabilization decrees was one which had little fiscal importance, but which the President put in the category of bread and circuses — elimination of the multiple taxes on public spectacles (theaters, moving pictures, sports events, etc.), which sometimes doubled or tripled the cost of tickets. These taxes were replaced by a single 25 per cent tax on all tickets, which did away with all exemptions for charitable events, real or spurious. Again, the earmarked taxes were replaced by subsidies based on 1955 distributions plus 30 per cent, and the municipalities were authorized to enact new taxes up to an additional 5 per cent on the sale of tickets in lieu of the many municipal taxes previously charged.[28]

Other tax reforms envisaged in the 1957 budget — including excises on alcoholic and other beverages, petroleum products, and tobacco; income taxes; consular fees; communications taxes; and a tax on the revaluation of assets — were left for discussion and enactment at the earliest possible date in 1957, as was also the most needed tax reform of all — a completely revised real property tax structure.

The Foreign Exchange Budget

At least as important as the general government budget in drafting the Bolivian stabilization program was the preparation of a foreign exchange budget showing what Bolivia — the nation as a whole, and not merely the government — could reasonably count upon in the way of foreign exchange receipts in 1957, and the allotment of those receipts to the various users of foreign exchange.*

So great was the preponderance of the Bolivian government and government enterprise in the nation's international trans- actions, however, that the foreign exchange budget proved to be practically a governmental budget, with only residual amounts allotted to the private sector. So long as this situation did not extend beyond 1957 — and the council could not possibly make its projections beyond that year — it was not of major moment.

Individuals and companies would be free to use whatever bolivianos they might possess to purchase as many dollars as they could afford. The stabilization fund would be more than ample to attend to any conceivable contingency. Even if the private sector controlled the entire amount of bank deposits and note circulation, which was far from being the case, and even if the public used its last boliviano in buying foreign exchange, the fund would not run short unless a shortage were caused by gov- ernmental extravagance. Furthermore, the private sector would be free to use its bank accounts and other assets abroad to bring in merchandise in unlimited amounts. One of the reasons for not being more generous in the allotment of foreign ex- change to the private sector was precisely the intention and hope that stabilization would in fact mean the use or repatria- tion of private flight capital, provided the political situation were such as to encourage private enterprise.

The purpose of a foreign exchange budget, in short, was neither to hamper nor, on the other hand, to provide facilities to the private sector, but to put a brake on the spending of govern- ment departments and enterprises which had for the past five years indulged in an unrestricted spending spree, encouraged

*Readers may wonder why there is no statement here of the balance of international payments, actual or prospective. A 1954-55 statement was compiled, based on a statement prepared by the Central Bank, but the data are so fragmentary and inaccurate that they are not worth repeating. In an appropriate case, much useful information can be gleaned from such a statement by one familiar with their compilation and shortcomings.

TABLE 7

The National Foreign Exchange Accounts

Item	In Millions of Dollars		
	Actual 1955	Actual* 1956	Budget 1957
EXCHANGE RECEIPTS			
COMIBOL (Mining Corporation)	60.2	56.7	54.9
Mining Bank	17.1	19.5	5.0†
Private mines	...	...	9.1†
YPFB (petroleum corporation)	2.3	2.4	5.1
Other sources	1.7	1.9	2.0
U.S. aid	21.3	20.0	18.5
Total receipts	102.6	100.5	94.6
EXCHANGE EXPENDITURES			
Government sector			
Government departments:			
Ministry of Economy	32.6	31.0	...
Other ministries	2.7	3.3	3.0
Other government bureaus	.3	.2	.8
Departments, municipalities, and universities	.1	.1	.1
Government enterprises:			
COMIBOL			
Suppliers' credits	.3	1.3	1.7
Machinery and operating expense	13.6	14.0	17.0
Payments on account for confiscation of mines	2.9	3.0	3.0
Buffer tin stock agreement	...	...	4.0
Mining Bank			
Suppliers' credits	.1	.9	1.3
Machinery and operating expense	2.7	5.2	.5
Sales of foreign exchange	2.5	4.1	6.0‡
YPFB			
Suppliers' credits	5.2	5.8	3.2
Other	6.0	4.3	9.4
Bolivian Development Corporation			
Suppliers' credits	.7	.6	.7
Payments on Export-Import Bank loan	3.6	3.8	3.9
Other	.9	.8	.4
LAB (government airline)	1.5	1.4	1.5
Other government enterprises	.8	.7	1.1

TABLE 7 *(Continued)*

Item	In Millions of Dollars		
	Actual 1955	Actual* 1956	Budget 1957
Other debt repayment:			
Suppliers' credits	.3	1.5	2.4
Long-term debts	...	.4	1.0
Tin agreement loan	...	...	1.0
Miscellaneous	2.3	1.8	.2
U.S. aid	21.3	20.0	18.5
Total government sector	100.4	104.2	80.7
Private sector			
Private mines	...	...	8.9
Private railways	4.7	3.2	3.4
Other private companies	1.8	1.3	1.3
Total private sector	6.5	4.5	13.6
Total expenditures	106.9	108.7	94.3
Surplus (or deficit)	(4.3)	(8.2)	.3

*Annual rate, based on January-October figures.

† This is on the assumption that the medium-sized mines would elect to ship direct, and that their exports would account for approximately 65 per cent of the exports of the private mines. (Figures for 1955 exports from Ford, Bacon & Davis, Inc., *The Mining Industry of Bolivia* [La Paz: FBD, 1956], vol. IV, p. 5).

‡ The foreign exchange budget data compiled by the Ministry of Finance and Central Bank showed $19.7 million sales of foreign exchange by the Mining Bank but, of this, $3.5 million was for commissary imports on behalf of COMIBOL which, in the above table, has been added to the COMIBOL operating expenses. Of the remainder, $8.9 million has been arbitrarily allotted to the private mines on the assumption that the medium-sized mines, exporting direct, would use 90 per cent of their exchange receipts (i.e., after deducting the average 10 per cent royalty) for machinery and operating expenses abroad. Assuming that miscellaneous private companies would need $1.3 million, as in 1956, the remaining $6 million is allotted to the Mining Bank, part of which would be for exchange expenditures arising out of previous years' operations.

by the fact that their foreign purchases, for the most part, could be bought at the rate of Bs. 190 to the dollar.*

Table 7, therefore, shows an unhealthy imbalance between foreign exchange expenditures allotted to the government and private sectors in 1957 and, at the same time, a decidedly healthy reduction of $14 million in total foreign exchange expenditures, although foreign exchange receipts were expected to diminish by only $6 million.

Furthermore, in 1955, the Bolivian government and government enterprises had mortgaged the future by purchasing $20 million of merchandise on suppliers' short- and medium-term credits, and, in 1956, $26 million, so that the reduction in foreign exchange transactions and commitments in the 1957 foreign exchange budget may be placed at $40 million compared with 1956. This was the crux of the stabilization program. Bolivia had to learn to live within its means.

*The use of a foreign exchange budget is a fairly recent development (see E. R. Schlesinger, *Multiple Exchange Rates and Economic Development* [Princeton, N. J.: Princeton University Press, 1952], p. 8). It would not be appropriate, except as a guide, in a free market economy. In an economy as dominated by the government as Bolivia's, and in any stabilization program where monetary depreciation has resulted from government spending, however, the use of a foreign exchange budget for government expenditures is as essential as a cash flow projection for corporate enterprise. Bolivia's first foreign exchange budget had been introduced by U.N. advisor Arthur Karasz (Henry S. Bloch, *Report of the U.N. Technical Assistance Administration* [La Paz: UNTAA, 1954], p.19). (Hectograph.)

11

THE FINAL HURDLES

Suppliers' Credits

To anyone schooled in business or banking, the anarchy prevailing in the government and in the government enterprises in their purchases on short- and medium-term suppliers' credits passed all understanding. The COMIBOL, YPFB, Bolivian Development Corporation, and other government enterprises, simply purchased whatever they wished from their foreign suppliers, and, if the purchase did not fit within their available cash resources and the Central Bank could not be persuaded to extend further credit, they simply gave a promissory note for the amount due (sometimes in the form of an acceptance on a bill of exchange, or on a series of notes or bills of exchange maturing on successive dates). Where the seller was reluctant to accept such promise of payment, and this proved to be true in well over 50 per cent of the cases, the note or bill of exchange was sent to the Central Bank for its *aval* (a guaranty in the form of an endorsement, customary in Civil Law countries).

To put a stop to this unrestricted borrowing, for there were no controls or limitations on the various government enterprises other than the prudence of the suppliers, the August 4 decree, establishing the Monetary Stabilization Council, contained a provision calling on each government ministry, enterprise, and agency to submit a complete statement of all outstanding obligations, and expressly forbidding any such entity to enter into new obligations of any kind without the authorization of the council, under penalty of nullity. The government ministries were subject to the control of the Finance Minister, at least in theory, so that excessive suppliers' credits were less of a problem than in the case of the government enterprises.

Confusion in the Central Bank

A chance remark by the president of COMIBOL aroused the suspicion that the mining corporation, and perhaps other entities, might in fact still be buying on credit. No statements of past credit operations had ever been submitted, and no one ever "cracked down" on the delinquent agencies. On the following day, therefore, I accompanied the President of the Central Bank to see what form of check could be made through the bank's records, at least of those credits which bore the bank *aval*.

The Mining Corporation ledger sheet was called for. The ledger, however, proved to be the typical bound and notarized *Libro Mayor* called for in the Latin American Commercial Codes, which date from the middle of the nineteenth century (although most banks and business firms in Latin America now supplement the huge legal volumes with modern or reasonably modern loose-leaf accounting records). Furthermore, the balancing entries for December 31, 1955, had not yet been made in that volume, and no entries had been made since that date. This was on October 26, 1956! There was, of course, the loose-leaf statement of deposits and withdrawals in current account — the typical checking account statement — but that gave no clue to the Mining Corporation's signature on a note or acceptance on a bill of exchange that would involve neither a deposit nor a withdrawal. What, I inquired, of the bank's record of the *avals* it had given? Surely there must be a constant accounting of the Mining Corporation's obligation to the bank for its *avals,* and of the bank's contingent liability to the suppliers? No, there was no record of the latter, and no book entry of contingent assets and liabilities, commonly found at the foot of the balance sheets in Civil Law countries as *contrapartidas* (identical offsetting entries).

But, I was assured, the bank had a very complete record of all the credits it granted to its customers, including the *avals* on the notes and bills of government enterprises. This "record" proved to be a number of simple file folders, each containing a batch of loose letters and memoranda. The former were generally informal requests from the Mining Corporation for the bank to increase its credit by so many million bolivianos or to place its *aval* on a series of bills of exchange, in accordance with a telephone conversation or some other form of communication with the President of the Republic. The letter was in each case initialed by the President of the Central Bank and by the bank's accountants. The memoranda were generally nothing more than small sheets of paper signed by the President of the Central Bank with an annotation that the President of the Republic had instructed him by telephone to extend the credit or sign the *aval*.

The young man in charge of these papers also kept, in an

ordinary file card box — not in a file that could be wheeled into the vault — a set of 6- x 9-inch cards, one for each borrower, showing the debit balance of the borrower, apparently entered once a week, and, in the upper right-hand corner, an undated pencilled notation of the latest authorized credit limit of the borrower, with previous limits scratched out. There was no record of the *avals,* and there appeared to be very few letters or memoranda in the file requesting the bank to place its *aval* on a document — fewer than might have been expected.

Riffling through these papers, I came across a strange letterhead — Corporación Boliviana de Fomento (the Development Corporation), instead of Corporación Minera de Bolivia (the Mining Corporation). A simple error in filing, I was told; but, going through the papers more carefully with the president of the bank, I found in the COMIBOL folder half a dozen Development Corporation memoranda or letters, requesting and authorizing the extension of credit, and each appeared to have been taken into account as a charge against the annotations of the Mining Corporation credit limits at the head of the card, although this was difficult to determine.

Under these circumstances, I suggested that, if the Development Corporation credit authorizations were in the Mining Corporation's file, the contrary might also be true. In fact, the credit authorizations and the debit and credit entries in the accounts of the two enterprises might be scattered among any of the hundreds of accounts kept by the bank — there was no way of knowing whether any of the accounts was correct. This was impossible, I was told; the similarity of names of the two corporations made an occasional error inevitable, but the error would always be caught. The customer would catch the mistake!

It occurred to me that this explained precisely why the President of COMIBOL was so insistent on refusing to deposit all COMIBOL's foreign exchange in the Central Bank — the bank never kept the accounts straight.* Later, the council was to

---

*It was largely because of the undeniable shortcomings of the Central Bank that the council was compelled to depart from its basic principles, and permit COMIBOL to retain 40 per cent of its gross foreign exchange earnings which were needed for payments on the buffer stock loan, for payments on account of the indebtedness to Patiño, Aramayo, and Hochschild, and for other payments abroad. COMIBOL had been retaining 40 per cent prior to stabilization, so that we had suffered a complete defeat on this point. Later, at council meetings in March, 1957, the Assistant Manager of the Monetary Department of the Central Bank, Victor Romero,

learn that COMIBOL never got its accounts straight either, and for the same reason. The bank's accounts were so muddled up, and there was simply no way for the management to exercise any authority over the employees under the MNR government, or even to dismiss them for incompetence, disobedience, or embezzlement.*

We turned to the Development Corporation accounts. The debit balance shown on the file card exceeded by many millions of bolivianos the credit limit pencilled in the upper right-hand corner. I mentioned that the credit limit had been increased by Bs. 2 billion at the October 17 meeting of the council. With that, the young man in charge of the cards erased the figure he had down as the credit limit, and put in the new figure — just on my

---

admitted that he had given incorrect information to the Stabilization Council on the COMIBOL account, because of the delay in posting vouchers received from the banking department of the bank. To anyone accustomed to banking procedures, it seemed incredible that any vouchers would remain unposted on the very day of original entry, but here were checks cashed and deposits made, apparently 30 days earlier, and still not entered in the accounts!

*The president of the Central Bank stated that since 1953 it had been impossible for him to discipline the bank's employees in any way, or even to investigate what they were doing. The labor union, backed by the Minister of Labor and by President Paz, would not permit any "interference" by the president of the bank or department heads with the employees. On one occasion, I chanced to count the huge pile of bank notes — well over a million bolivianos in five to one hundred boliviano notes — that were given in exchange for the $100 check that I generally tendered for cash to meet household expenses. I noticed that practically each package of bills would be a few bolivianos short; none of the packages had too many bolivianos. I commented on this fact to the president, who stated that he, too, was accustomed to cash his checks without counting the bale of money received in return. The president then summoned the manager, and I sent a $100 check down to the teller's cage, as customary. Together we counted the packages. Again, there were shortages running to about 5 per cent of the total — no overages. The president was indignant and said he would summon the teller, but I persuaded him not to, much to the manager's relief. "What good would it do?" I asked. Could he fire the teller? Wouldn't his authority be diminished if he proved the teller was a thief, and then was unable to discipline him? So far as I was concerned, it was like getting an exchange rate of Bs. 12,350 to the dollar instead of Bs. 13,000, and I was not inclined to press a complaint. And there the matter was left. This anecdote illustrates the extremes to which a country can arrive where the government runs everything, and the labor unions run the government, a situation which many of the nations of this hemisphere are fast approaching without realizing the dangers.

say-so! The debit balance still exceeded the amount of the authorized credit. The president of the bank checked with the statement of account for the Development Corporation. The overdraft was even higher — if the bank's records could be relied upon. The president of the bank then asked my advice — should he stop payment on all checks? I replied that he had better be absolutely sure of his facts, that the way the bank's records were kept, there might be some credits that should have been entered in the Development Corporation account that had not been entered, or some debits entered that did not belong there, but that, in any event, it would seem expedient to telephone the President of the Development Corporation.

The president of the bank was so disturbed, however, by the revelations of the shortcomings in the bank's accounting controls, and by his knowledge, as an economist, that the Development Corporation was the agency chiefly responsible for Bolivia's inflation, that he put through a stop payment order on the following day on all checks of the Development Corporation. The repercussion was violent. The Development Corporation accounts were in far worse disorder than those of the Central Bank, but its check book, at least, had been kept up to date, and it had a record, and proof, of large deposits that apparently had never been entered in its account in the Central Bank. The Development Corporation had *not* overdrawn its credit. The bank was compelled to put a notice in the papers "lamenting" its failure to pay the corporation's checks on Saturday, October 27, 1956, and stating that they would be paid on presentation. [29] *

The Central Bank was given time to compile the necessary data on outstanding short- and medium-term credits on which it had given its guaranty, and at the November 9 meeting of the council Dr. Antezana was asked for a complete table of such credits, listed by purchasers, suppliers, and maturities, so that

*The foregoing narrative, and that which is to follow, may seem to cast doubt on the abilities of the president of the bank, Dr. Franklin Antezana-Paz. As a matter of fact, Antezana was a capable economist, trained at the Sorbonne, a man of intelligence, the soul of integrity, and one of the true, self-sacrificing heroes of the stabilization program. He was neither a trained accountant nor banker, but there was no one in Bolivia better qualified than he for the post which he had filled honorably for many years, a credit to his country in the many international banking conferences which he attended. The fact is that even such highly qualified men as the president of the Mining Corporation were completely unable to enforce any discipline on their accounting staffs, and were helpless under the rules imposed by the Revolutionary Government.

the council might have an idea of what payments would be falling due each month. The information was not yet available, but by the end of November, when the Central Bank and Bolivian government presented their formal request for stabilization financing to the international Monetary Fund, they stated that the *total* foreign exchange obligations of the Central Bank amounted to $12.6 million.

The council never was able to obtain the complete tally of guaranties given by the Central Bank on suppliers' credits, but by June, 1957, we had managed to unearth, with the assistance of the President of the Central Bank, some $28 million of promissory notes and bills of exchange containing the *aval* of the bank. Of these, $5.4 million had been accepted by the bank with no record of the date of maturity, the dates having been left in blank. The notes, of course, remained in the possession of the various suppliers, so that the bank had no way of knowing when it might be called upon for payment!

As to the total of suppliers' credits, including those which did not have the Central Bank *aval*, the Bolivian government, in its request to the IMF and other agencies for financial assistance, had placed the total at $20 million issued in 1955 and $26 million issued in the course of 1956, from which should be subtracted $9.9 million paid off in those two years, leaving a net of approximately $36.1 million. Part of these obligations undoubtedly bore the Central Bank *aval*, although this did not appear in the record.

Finally, by June, 1957, following an attachment placed by creditors on the Central Bank depositors in New York banks, as a consequence of the default on obligations guaranteed by the bank (see p. 414), a statement of government and government-guaranteed obligations to overseas suppliers was compiled which appeared to be reasonably complete, showing a total outstanding of $50,868,999 (Table 11, p. 412).[30]

This figure, if accurate (which it was not), would tally fairly closely with the $48.7 million ($12.6 million plus $36.1 million) reported to Washington, although it seems probable that the $15.4 million understatement in the Central Bank obligations may have reflected a similar state of disorder in the accounts of the Bolivian government as a whole, which might mean that outstanding suppliers' credits may have run upwards of $65 million.*

*On the other hand, during a visit to New York in December, 1956, I found evidence that the Bolivian government and government enterprises

As previously stated, the August 4, 1956, decree establishing the Stabilization Council and outlawing all credits not approved in advance by the council by no means put an end to such borrowing. The YPFB, the railways, and COMIBOL were the most flagrant violators of the law, and during my December, 1956, trip to the United States, I was shown a letter from COMIBOL to one major supplier, dated September 28, 1956, falsely stating that, as an autonomous agency of the government, it was empowered to enter into credit operations without the guaranty of the Central Bank.

Treaty Obligations

Perhaps even more detrimental to the country's economy than the spate of suppliers' credits were the treaty obligations which were of two kinds — the indebtedness to Brazil and Argentina for railway construction, described in Chapter 3, and the bilateral trade agreements with Argentina, Brazil, and Chile. Under the latter agreements, negotiated by the Revolutionary Government between 1953 and 1955, Bolivia was required to ship its products to those countries at prices, computed in dollars, at approximately world market levels.

The accounts, however, were not payable in actual dollars, but kept in clearing accounts between the Bolivian Central Bank and the central banks of those countries in what were called "treaty dollars" (*dólares convenio*). The treaty dollars could be cashed by Bolivia only by receiving such goods from the treaty countries as those countries were willing to supply under the agreements, and case after case was discovered where the prices charged on such imports were two to eight times the price for comparable merchandise from Europe, Japan, the United States, or Canada, including shipping charges.*

During the prestabilization era, this state of affairs had been disguised by the multiple currency rates. Bolivian exporters had a market for their goods, some of which could not have been sold profitably at world market prices, and they were

_____

had certain bank deposits in New York of which they were not even aware; if I had not dug up this information, in all probability, the funds would never have been found or made available.

*The extreme example of electric heaters from Argentina may have been unique. Knowledgeable importers and officials stated that two to four times competitive world prices would be the usual range.

either paid by the Central Bank in actual dollars or were allowed to purchase imports against the treaty dollars at the official rate of exchange of Bs. 190 to the dollar, thus deriving their profits from the imports. Even where the importer was compelled to pay as much as eight times the world market price for merchandise, its importation at a foreign exchange rate that might have been one-fiftieth of the true value (depending upon the date of payment) left ample margin for a profit so generous that those who were permitted to participate in the trade were in many cases those with the best political connections.

The balances outstanding under these bilateral trade agreements, at the time of stabilization, were not large — $5,374,000 owing to Argentina, $117,000 to Brazil, and $496,000 to Chile — but there was no record of how much shoddy merchandise Bolivia had imported at exorbitant prices over the previous four years under the treaties.* When stabilization came, the problem assumed major importance. No one was going to be foolish enough to import manufactured goods from Argentina, Brazil, or Chile, that could be purchased cheaper or better in West Germany or elsewhere, and the ABC nations demanded payment of the outstanding debts either in merchandise, under the treaty, or in actual dollars. Practically the only product that Bolivia was in a position to supply to Argentina in any quantity under the treaty was petroleum, and Argentina lacked transportation facilities for such shipments.

At a meeting at the Foreign Office between the Stabilization Council members and officials of the Ministry of Foreign Affairs, held the very afternoon that the IMF mission returned to Washington to prepare the way for the stabilization financing, the Foreign Ministry was insistent that the outstanding indebtedness be paid as soon as the stabilization fund was available, while I was equally insistent that a debt of over $6 million (which later grew to $8 million) in fictitious treaty dollars could not be settled in real dollars. As I was scheduled to leave for Washington shortly to assist my Bolivian colleagues in negotiating stabilization fund financing, and would certainly not have been a party to obtaining good dollars to pay off questionable

*There was also $38,000 due under a treaty with Spain that had terminated in 1955, and similar agreements with Paraguay, Uruguay, and Yugoslavia existed, but no balances were outstanding. A Peruvian trade agreement (YPFB) called for payment in real dollars (see Zondag, p. 62).

debts, my views prevailed, but the matter came up to plague the
council again in 1957 (p. 418).

Control of Bank Credit

As has been seen, the part played by the private sector in
the 1953-56 inflation had been minimal, so that it must have
seemed inequitable that the stabilization measures imposed
drastic credit restrictions on the private banks and business.
And this was precisely at a time when it was essential to stimulate private agriculture, mining, industry, and trade, in order
to speed recovery from the disaster of the previous four years,
which had stripped the private sector clean of capital resources.

Nevertheless, had private credit been unrestricted, the
contemplated stabilization fund would have been soon depleted.
Speculators would have been quick to use bank loans to buy
the dollars that would be freely available under the new economic regime, and a flight of capital would have obliterated the
stabilization fund and nullified our efforts to stabilize the currency. Hence, credit restrictions were inevitable, although as
soon as possible after stabilization had proved itself a success
the council did its best to bring down interest rates and make
credit easily available, under proper safeguards, to every sector of the productive economy.

Meanwhile, simultaneously with the stabilization measures,
credit controls had to be drastically tightened by improving the
administration of the previous 40 per cent bank reserve requirement, by requiring the banks to keep an additional marginal reserve of 50 per cent against any increase in their
deposit liabilities, and by introducing qualitative credit restrictions prohibiting the banks from making consumer and construction loans or other loans which would not contribute immediately to speeding up production.[31] The maximum ratio of
total deposits to capital and reserves, however, was by necessity increased from five times to seven times, and the Superintendent of Banks was charged with regulating the revaluation
of bank assets in order not to freeze credits at virtually zero.

All government accounts and U.S. counterpart funds were
transferred from the banking department of the Central Bank to
the monetary department, and control of the reserve requirements and credit restrictions of the banking department, as
well as of the commercial banks, was vested in the Ministry of

Finance (through the Superintendency of Banks), subject to the advice of the Stabilization Council.[32] So far as the council was concerned, this phase of the stabilization process was left almost entirely in the hands of O. Ernest Moore, the banking member of the U.S. Financial Mission, who worked very closely with the president of the Central Bank and with John R. Woodley of the IMF mission.

As one feature of the prestabilization measures, the auctions of dollars on the free exchange market were cut down from six days to three days a week and, in the last two weeks preceding stabilization, were abolished altogether in order to reduce speculative activity. Such a measure, of course, could not have been effective for very long, as it would merely have substituted a black market for the legal auction market, but for a brief period it served to put a damper on speculative movements in the immediate prestabilization period.

Return to a Free Market Economy

The essence of the stabilization program was a return to a free market economy, at least in the matter of freedom from price controls, foreign exchange controls, and controls on imports and exports. It was a constant battle, however, and one that had to be waged continually against those who could not conceive of any economic system not controlled by the government.

At the very last meeting of the Stabilization Council prior to the return of the IMF mission to Washington, Juan Lechín returned to the attack and expressed the fear that, under such a system, there would be a flight of capital and not enough dollars left in the stabilization fund to satisfy the needs of legitimate industry, as the dollars would at once be taken by speculators and importers of luxury products. My reply was that any controls would, on the contrary, lead to the flight of capital. I pointed out the failure of controls in Bolivia and in every other country where they had been attempted — and, conversely, the relative prosperity of those countries where controls had been abandoned.

The example of Greece was cited where, after stabilization and the elimination of controls, $10 million of flight capital had returned to the country in the first month and $50 million in the first year as a result of the simple fact that businessmen in

Greece needed the dollars for use in their business and could not obtain the money on credit. Lechín continued to insist that exporters must turn over their foreign exchange to the Central Bank, or at least a good part of it, and that restrictions and controls must continue on imports, exports, and prices. With rising ire, he declared that the stabilization program had been drawn up in haste, without giving a proper opportunity for criticism.

At that, I pointed out that we had just four hours left before the IMF mission went back to Washington, either with a program or without one. If Bolivia wished to continue to follow the path it had taken for the past three years, it could do so, and the currency would continue to depreciate, but if it wanted to stabilize the currency, and if it wanted to count on the continuation of U.S. aid, it would have to take another path.* Lechín, with great emotion, then made the following declaration to the council:

> I am a part of the government, and the action of the government will be my action and, although I may not be in agreement, I shall cooperate with all my strength and decision, and not merely in a passive attitude. Mr. Eder may be sure that not only I, but likewise all of the labor union leaders of the MNR, will take that attitude because we have placed our confidence in Dr. Siles and we have more confidence in his decisions than in our own proposals.

At that, I stated that Lechín's attitude was one that did him honor. Thus ended the resistance to a free market economy — until after stabilization.

COMIBOL, Foreign Exchange, and Wage Rates

The data requested from the Ford, Bacon & Davis mining survey mission in June, 1956, never materialized. This information was wanted as an independent check on whatever figures might be received from the COMIBOL management as to the rate of exchange that would be necessary for COMIBOL to

---

*Henry Holland had authorized me to make such a statement, and had himself made the same statement to Lechín in my presence, as well as to Presidents Paz and Siles. How far the United States has strayed from the path of fiscal responsibility will be seen in Chapter 24.

operate without a loss, and as to the compensation that should
be paid to the miners for the loss of their subsidized commissary privileges. As it turned out, however, the lack did not
prove crucial, as the compensation was in the end determined
on a political, rather than on a statistical basis, as will be
seen.*

A blow-by-blow account of the struggle to reach a viable
agreement on this fundamental question, such as is set forth in
the minutes of the eight council meetings at which the COMIBOL
problems were discussed, reveals an amazing disparity, not
merely of opinion, but with respect to the basic facts of the
miners' wages, the amount of the incentive bonuses for added
productivity, the effect of social security charges, the cost of
the cheap commissary privileges to the mining corporation, the
value of the commissaries to the workers, and, in fact, with
respect to every factor germane to the questions before the
council.

The confusion was worse confounded because the COMIBOL
management and the Minister of Mines, in all their discussions,
made payroll computations in dollars, *but in fictitious dollars,*
as COMIBOL actually paid the workers only Bs. 1,800 for each
"dollar," whereas the current rate of exchange was approximately Bs. 10,000 to the dollar.† Thus COMIBOL claimed that

---

*The Ford, Bacon & Davis report, dated December 3, 1956, but not
available until after the turn of the year, estimates that the miners were
able to add from 30 per cent to 50 per cent to their income by selling in
the black market the goods that they got from the mine commissaries.
This impartial estimate, based on careful study, must be borne in mind in
evaluating the Bs. 3,950 compensation for the loss of commissary privileges awarded to the miners by the Stabilization Council, in comparison
with their total prestabilization pay of Bs. 3,727 (see Table 8). (FBD report, vol. 3, p. 82.)

† In former times, when the mines were operated by Patiño, Aramayo,
and Hochschild, the companies likewise made their computations in dollars
in order to have a reasonably stable currency of account. Their revenues
were in dollars or sterling, and, by fixing wage rates in dollars and making
payment in bolivianos at the current rate of exchange, they could assure
the mine workers of a reasonably stable *real wage.* It was not until the
advent of the MNR government, however, that the gap between the actual
rate of exchange and the rate at which the miners were paid reached such
an extreme that the workers' *real wages* were worth less than a fifth of
their nominal wages. The really tough problem, which the government
never dared to face when the currency was stabilized and there was only
one rate of exchange, was to explain to the miners that they had been
cheated for four years and would have to accept lower dollar wages than
they thought they had been getting.

it was paying the workers a basic wage of $1.25 which, with
bonuses, made an alleged average direct wage of $2.20 a day.
This was further confused by the fact that a 13 cent arithmetical
mistake was included in that figure, and that the alleged average
pay should have been $2.07. In actual fact, however, COMIBOL
was paying a basic wage in bolivianos of Bs. 2,250, or a total
wage of Bs. 3,727 a day, worth 37.2 cents, and not $2.07 or
$2.20. This is shown in Table 8.

TABLE 8

Prestabilization Daily Wages Paid by COMIBOL*

Item	Alleged Pay in "Dollars"	Actual Pay in Bolivianos	True Dollar Equivalent at Bs. 10,000
Average base pay	$1.25	Bs. 2,250	22.5 cents
Average contract and incentive bonuses — 25 per cent	.31	562	5.6
Sundays when miners were paid but did not work — 16.7 per cent	.21	375	3.7
Average overtime pay — 15-25 per cent range	.30	540	5.4
	$2.07	Bs. 3,727	37.2 cents
Error in COMIBOL computations	.13		
Average pay claimed by COMIBOL	$2.20		

*Exclusive of social security or the value of the below-cost commis-
sary privileges. Computations based on data submitted to the Stabilization
Council in November, 1956, by the COMIBOL management.

The value to the worker of the cheap commissary privileges was placed by the council, after study by the technical
staff, the Minister of Mines, and COMIBOL, at Bs. 3,950 a day.
This figure was accepted by Lechín and was undoubtedly on the
high side (see p. 222 n). That gave a total prestabilization
wage, including commissary rights, of Bs. 7,677, worth 77 cents
U.S. To this must be added certain social security costs paid
by COMIBOL (family subsidy and housing), amounting to 27 per
cent on the Bs. 2,250 base pay, or Bs. 607.50, so that the aggregate *prestabilization* wage, including special charges and the
value *to the workers* of the commissary privileges, may be
placed at 83 cents U.S.

Under the stabilization decree, the workers were allowed
Bs. 2,250 basic wage, plus Bs. 3,950 compensation for the loss

of cheap commissary privileges, plus Bs. 1,300 for the estimated rise in living costs as a result of the elimination of price controls, or an announced new base pay of Bs. 7,500. But they were further allowed an average 35 per cent for contractual and incentive bonuses, an average 40.7 per cent for Sundays and overtime, and an average 35 per cent for sickness and maternity, professional risks, old age and death pensions, family subsidy, and cheap housing, all these percentages being computed on the new rate base. That gave a total addition to base pay of Bs. 8,302, bringing the *poststabilization* aggregate wage to Bs. 15,802. At the stabilization rate of Bs. 7,750, this was equivalent to $2.04 in comparison with the prestabilization remuneration of 83 cents.*

Apparently, no one connected with COMIBOL or with the mining industry nor anyone in the government could grasp the fact that the miners *never had been paid* dollar salaries, and that when they received their prestabilization base wage supposedly of $1.25, all they got in reality was Bs. 2,250, which was actually worth $22\frac{1}{2}$ cents. Obviously, if COMIBOL insisted on tying the miners' wages to real dollars, after stabilization, in amounts that simply were not available, COMIBOL would have a constant deficit, and stabilization simply could not be achieved. It was difficult enough for us on the Stabilization Council to keep the facts straight in our own minds, and if COMIBOL had sought deliberately to mislead themselves and the council, they could hardly have chosen a more effective means than to discuss wages in terms of hypothetical dollars.

This is not intended in criticism of the COMIBOL top management. The three witnesses who appeared before the council on behalf of COMIBOL were among the most intelligent and cooperative of all those whose testimony aided the council in its task — they were the COMIBOL President, Raul Gutiérrez-Granier, at one time manager of the W. R. Grace interests in Bolivia; the general manager, Goosen Broesma, a highly qualified mining engineer from the Netherlands, and formerly chief engineer of the Patiño mines; and a director, Mario Vernaza, a

---

*Note that management, labor, and government would all be inclined, when referring to the aggregate payroll cost of Bs. 15,802, to refer to the Bs. 7,500 as "wages," and to the remainder as "social charges," equal to 110 per cent of the wage. Under American usage, all but the last 35 per cent would be considered "direct payroll costs," and thus social security and analogous costs (Bs. 2,625) would only be 20 per cent of direct payroll (Bs. 13,177).

private mine owner, who was able to advise the council on the private mines as well as on COMIBOL affairs. All three, however, were misled — as others in Bolivia and elsewhere have been misled — by the confusion of monetary depreciation and a multiple foreign exchange rate system.

Finally, however, after a series of council meetings attended by three top representatives of COMIBOL and private conferences with the COMIBOL management and with the head of the Ford, Bacon & Davis mining survey mission, together with a tremendous amount of staff spadework, the council and the COMIBOL management agreed on the following tentative bases:[33]

1. The miners to receive a base wage of $1.25 a day, computed at Bs. 6,000 to the dollar, i.e., Bs. 7,500, which would include compensation for lost commissary privileges and for stabilization (meaning the expected rise in living costs resulting from elimination of price controls).

2. COMIBOL budget computations to be made on the basis of 90-cent tin and a Bs. 6,000 exchange rate, with no guaranty that this exchange rate would be maintained, and the express understanding that a change in rate would not alter the agreed Bs. 7,500 base wage.*

3. COMIBOL to dismiss 5,000 (later placed at 6,000) supernumerary workers within three months, and not to rehire any; it would be allowed up to Bs. 10 billion of budgeted funds for severance pay, part of which might be provided from counterpart funds, possibly to the extent that dismissed workers were relocated on cooperative or other agricultural projects.

4. COMIBOL to be allowed to use up to $3 million for exploration and development in 1957, to be taken, however, only if world tin prices exceeded 90 cents a pound, and from the proceeds of such excess. In other words, that item was not included in the 90-cent budget. †

*The likelihood of a Bs. 6,500 rate, and the possibility of a Bs. 7,000 rate, were pointed out (either of the latter rates or any higher rate would, of course, increase COMIBOL's profits). The Bs. 6,000 rate, however, was to be used in COMIBOL's computations in view of the impossibility of preventing a leak and because it was desirable to minimize COMIBOL's profits, if any, in order not to stimulate a demand for exaggerated wage adjustments.

†COMIBOL had asked $5 million for exploration, or slightly less than 10 per cent on *net* export receipts, i.e., after deduction of smelting, refining, and shipping charges. Exploration and blocking out new areas had

5. COMIBOL to pay an average royalty of 10 per cent on *gross* export receipts.
6. COMIBOL to turn over to the Central Bank its *net* export receipts (estimated at $73.7 million gross, less $18.8 million smelting, refining, and transportation), and to be allowed foreign exchange expenditures of $3 million for payments to the ex-owners of the nationalized mines, $4 million contribution to the tin stock, $1.7 million to repay suppliers' credits, $13.5 million for equipment, and $3.5 million for commissary purchases.
7. COMIBOL to balance its budget with no further supplier credits or other borrowing.

With these bases of agreement blocked out, and new boliviano and foreign exchange budgets prepared for COMIBOL and for the government sector as a whole, the council held a further series of meetings attended by Juan Lechín-Oquendo, President of the Senate; Renán Castrillo, President of the Chamber of Deputies; Abel Ayoroa-Argandoña, Minister of Labor and Social Security; and José Cuadros-Quiroga, Minister of Agriculture.* The purpose of these meetings was to obtain the political clearance that would be necessary to ensure that the proposed measures would be supported by the "Co-Government" (the Executive, the MNR, and the COB).

The discussion at these meetings was heated and disorganized, with the conferees breaking up into three or more discussion groups around the Cabinet table. The Minister of Mines (Tamayo) and the head of the Planning Commission (Gisbert) were on my left, working steadily on facts and figures in

---

been virtually nil during government operation of the mines, and existing veins had petered out to such an extent that the majority of the mines could not be operated profitably. In some cases the metal content of the ores being mined was less than that of the tailings from previous operations. Under Bolivian conditions, a well-managed tin mining operation would devote a minimum of 15 per cent of net export receipts to new exploration and development, so that the $5 million (10 per cent) was skimpy, and the $3 million could only be justified as a temporary expedient made necessary for stabilization purposes.

*The President had advised that Cuadros-Quiroga would attend the council meeting, as he was President of the Political Committee of the MNR, and he and Castrillo would offset any possible opposition by Lechín and Ayoroa, who represented the COB. I suggested, however, that Cuadros should appear in his capacity as a member of the Cabinet (which was authorized by the decree establishing the council), rather than in his political capacity.

consultation with Dr. Costanzo, while I engaged in whispered conversations, first with that group and then with President Siles on my right. This gave an opportunity for suggestions, discreetly whispered to the President, to be relayed to Lechín and the other political conferees, who were wildly arguing and gesticulating on the opposite side of the table, so that I was relieved from intervening directly in any politically tinged dispute.*

In the course of those meetings, among other things, Lechín stated that, provided retirement benefits were granted and measures taken to relocate some of the supernumeraries, there would be no problem in COMIBOL's dismissing from five to ten thousand workers within three months, but COMIBOL must be given definite instructions not to rehire any of the workers dismissed and not to take on any additional workers. If only three to four thousand workers were dismissed, there would not even be the social problem of relocation. It was in the end stipulated that COMIBOL must dismiss six thousand workers in three months in order to give somewhat greater latitude in the matter of social security and other expenses.

It was also decided that the additional wage to be granted the miners (and other workers) above their prevailing base pay, to compensate for the adjustments that would be caused by stabilization, should be broken up into two parts — one, an adjustment to compensate for the loss of commissary privileges, and the other for generally increased living costs resulting from the removal of price controls. It was further decided that these

---

*At one point in the first session, for example, I whispered to the President that a bill pending in Congress, which would make membership in a Masonic society a crime and whose passage was reportedly assured, would produce unfavorable reaction in the United States that might jeopardize Bolivian financing. I pointed out that George Washington and Simón Bolívar were both Masons. The President called Lechín over, explained the situation, and Lechín assured us that the bill would be killed, which it was. At another point, I reminded the President *sotto voce* that the wage Lechín was demanding for the miners was higher than the salaries received by the Cabinet ministers. The President, without involving me, passed on this comment to the political trio arguing across the table, and Lechín, livid with rage, shouted "That is no argument" *(Eso no es argumento)* and was furious for the rest of the meeting. After adjournment, the President stated that he had had to grip the arms of his chair to control his anger and that he did not know whether he would be able to keep his temper much longer, but was trying to prevent his personal feelings from interfering with the stabilization program.

adjustments should be stated in flat amounts rather than as percentages, in the first place to obviate a considerable area of dispute as to what constituted the basic wage, and in the second place to favor the lower-paid workers, whose vital needs, as President Siles pointed out, were the same as those of the higher-paid employees.

The estimates of the loss to the miners from the elimination of the cheap commissaries and the anticipated rise in living costs were upon the crudest possible basis. We had what was thought to be a fairly reliable account of the volume of each of the major classes of goods sold at the COMIBOL commissaries, and the loss to COMIBOL on such sales, the latter being the difference between the absurdly low price paid by COMIBOL for its supplies and the still lower prices charged to the workers. Discrepancies discovered later in the COMIBOL accounts, however, probably imply that even those figures, ostensibly the most reliable we had to work with, should probably have been written plus or minus 50 per cent.

The loss to COMIBOL on those sales was of no relevance to our computations, but the total quantities at least provided an ostensible ceiling to the total claimed purchases by the miners. The prices the miners paid, however, were not uniform at all mines, and the quantities of goods available for purchase varied from windfall quantities at some mines to relatively scanty supplies at others. We knew — so far as any figures could be relied upon — that the miners were buying goods from the commissaries for amounts over *double* the amount of their total pay. Thus it was obvious that only a small part of such goods was for their own needs and that the remainder was disposed of to the black marketeers who swarmed around the company stores like flies around a stable. What part was sold, and what consumed, and what profit the miners made on their sales to the black marketeers could not be ascertained by statistical means, and the council was fortunate in being able to rely on Minister of Mines Tamayo, whose personal knowledge of the mines and miners exceeded that of anyone else in the government. While Tamayo was undoubtedly conscientious in his compilation and weeding out of the facts and figures, it is certain that his figures erred, if anything, in favor of the miners, that is, that they tended to exaggerate the profits made by the miners on the company stores. Certainly, his estimate of the value of the cheap commissary privileges was far in excess of the Ford, Bacon & Davis estimate. On the other hand, it is equally certain that the "guesstimates" compiled with Tamayo's assistance were at least as reliable as any statistical or accounting data received from COMIBOL or from any other governmental source.

Once a total additional compensation of Bs. 5,250 had been stipulated for the COMIBOL workers, the council agreed with Lechín's view that the greater part of this compensation should be attributed to the loss of commissary privileges, and a much lower portion to the expected rise in living costs. Lechín's views were colored by his desire to secure greater benefits for the miners than for any other group, while the council's views were colored by the fact that a great many workers — in particular the government employees — had no commissary privileges and thus it would be easier to balance the budget if the living cost compensation were not too exaggerated. Also, it was felt that in point of fact the general rise in living costs would be negligible (see Table 5, p. 189).

In the end, compensation for commissary privileges was placed at Bs. 3,950, and living cost compensation at Bs. 1,300, the latter being given not only to COMIBOL but to *all* wage earners other than domestic servants and a few other unregulated employees who had no armed militia, no labor leaders, and no enforceable rights in the Bolivian labor hierarchy.

In the matter of social security and similar charges, which were estimated at over 20 per cent of direct payroll costs (including bonuses, overtime, etc. as part of the payroll), I came back again and again with the suggestion that the National Social Security Administration should either be given the higher percentage rates they were asking (based, however, upon the Bs. 2,250 prestabilization wage) or else have their percentages substantially cut if they were based on the Bs. 7,500 poststabilization wage. This proposal, if adopted, would have solved the problem of the COMIBOL deficit, would have made possible a substantial real wage increase, and would have removed any difficulty in the payment of export royalties by COMIBOL. Everyone at the meeting agreed with the view that social security charges were too high and bore no relationship whatsoever to benefits received. Lechín pointed out, however, that it would be dangerous to decrease the vested rights of the workers in their high percentage social security "benefits," and most of the other Bolivian conferees agreed that if the percentages were reduced, the miners would think that management was being favored at their expense — even though management was the government. President Siles had told the council members that there could be no "realistic stabilization program unless the miners were satisfied," and the council was wise enough not to let common sense push beyond the limits of realism.

My stubbornness, however, paid off in three respects: (1) Lechín expressed a willingness to give the miners somewhat lower increases in wages rather than reduce the social security percentages, and he agreed to the increases above mentioned rather than the substantially higher figures he had originally insisted on; (2) he agreed that it was better to stabilize at Bs. 7,000 or even higher, if necessary, and later come down, if possible, rather than attempt to stabilize at Bs. 6,000 or Bs. 6,500 and perhaps be forced upwards; and (3) he accepted without comment President Siles' emphatic "No!" in answer to the Finance Minister's query as to whether stabilization at the Bs. 7,000 or higher rate would mean that the added compensation for loss of commissary privileges and higher living costs would have to be increased.

Bolivian and U.S. inflation compared

In discussing the boliviano-dollar cross rate, Lechín raised the quite logical question of the stability of the dollar itself, and said that he understood there had been considerable inflation in the United States as well as in Bolivia. I confirmed Lechín's understanding, and stated that, from 1940 to 1953, but chiefly during the Truman administration from 1945 to 1953, wholesale commodity prices had gone up over 100 per cent; in other words, the value of the dollar had fallen 50 per cent in purchasing power (see Fig. 6 for graphic representation of this inflation). Since that date, under the Eisenhower administration, prices had risen only a fraction of one per cent, and the dollar was practically stable. If Bolivia had maintained its currency stable in terms of dollars, I added, it would, of course, be much better off than it was in 1956. Its currency would be as sound as any currency in the world, and better than most. Nevertheless, if, after stabilizing, Bolivia had any doubts as to whether the dollar would be maintained at par in terms of gold, it could fix the value of its currency at so many grams of gold, 900 fine. It could also keep its reserves in gold instead of in dollars, with the disadvantage, however, that it would then be paying storage charges instead of receiving interest.

Figure 6, showing the Bureau of Labor Statistics index of

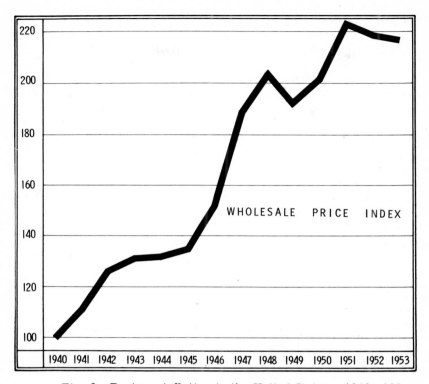

Fig. 6. Postwar inflation in the United States. 1940 = 100.
(Source: Bureau of Labor Statistics.)[34]

wholesale commodity prices converted to a 1940 base, with
prices rising 116 per cent from 1940 to 1953, brings out dramatically the fact that inflation in the United States, even during
a period when the dollar lost 54 cents of its purchasing power
in little more than a decade, simply cannot be compared with
what took place in Bolivia. A Bolivian chart, showing the drop
in the boliviano from 40 cents U.S. to Bs. 14,000 to the dollar,
and drawn on the same scale as Figure 6, would require a chart
800 feet high — almost twice as high as the dome of St. Peter's
in Rome. The dislocations produced by the Bolivian inflation
were at least commensurately greater.

    With my admission that the United States too had been
plagued by inflation but that the dollar was currently fairly
stable, Lechín withdrew his objections to the proposed cross
rate.

The last straw

Thus, final agreement on every vital point in the stabilization program was reached, literally at the eleventh hour — it was noon on November 16, and the IMF mission was scheduled to leave for Washington in a matter of hours. All agreements had been wrapped up, and briefcases were bulging with documents supporting Bolivia's petition for financial assistance from the International Monetary Fund.[35]

At that point, the Minister of Mines announced that COMIBOL's representatives were waiting in the anteroom and had to be heard on a matter of paramount importance. He stated that, whereas the council had agreed to a base wage of $1.25 plus an average of 25 per cent for contractual incentive bonuses, the miners insisted on $2.20 plus an allowance of 35 per cent for bonuses, and the higher bonuses were absolutely essential if production were to be maintained. (Note that here again the discussion is based on the false assumption that the miners' wages are paid in dollars.) There was sufficient margin for flexibility in our computations so that, if the exchange rate were fixed at Bs. 7,000 instead of Bs. 6,500, and if other conditions remained the same, the 35 per cent bonus could be granted, but we had received the definite impression, from conversations with the COMIBOL management, that COMIBOL was at the same time endeavoring to escape payment of all royalties, the contributions to the buffer stock, and compensation to the former owners of the nationalized mines.

COMIBOL's president, accompanied by the general manager, then entered the room, and explained that he had called a meeting of the managers of all the corporation mines, and had presented to them the proposals to which he had agreed at the previous council meeting. The mine managers had decided that the proposed wage increases would not be acceptable to the miners, and that it would be necessary to increase the Bs. 2,250 base salary by 64 per cent, or Bs. 1,440, for higher living costs plus Bs. 9,000 for the loss of subsidized commissary privileges, a total base salary of Bs. 12,700 in lieu of the Bs. 7,500 agreed upon.*

---

*With the 35 per cent production bonuses, and fringe benefits, this would mean an aggregate average pay of Bs. 26,759, or $3.82 a day at the Bs. 7,000 rate then being discussed. There simply was not that much money available from Bolivia's tin exports, even if the mines had been as efficiently operated as they were under Patiño, Aramayo, and Hochschild.

The presentation was considerably obscured by the constant reference to wages and bonuses in terms of "dollars," but the gist of it was clear — not only must the higher salaries and bonuses be paid, the council was told, but COMIBOL could only count on making 5 per cent profit on its commissary sales instead of the 10 per cent they had previously computed (the rest of the 10 per cent mark-up would be expense). The company could therefore not support the burden of royalties in addition to its contributions to the buffer stock, and the government would have to assume any obligation to the former mine owners. Gutiérrez-Granier presented the alternative courteously, but as an ultimatum — either COMIBOL could pay royalties or it could pay into the buffer stock, but not both. Again I advanced the alternative of bringing social security charges down to viable limits, but again to no avail.

At that, I then declared — and this too was a courteous ultimatum — that the council had done all within its power to present a workable stabilization plan; that the IMF mission was leaving for Washington in a matter of hours and that, if it could not return with a definitive and workable plan, we might as well give up any thought of stabilizing the currency; that the council had consulted with people representing all agencies and enterprises of the government, and with representatives of the private sector, reaching the figures and conclusions which, up to a moment ago, had been accepted by everyone present; that it would have been possible to ask the workers what salaries they would like to have and give them as many thousands of bolivianos as they wished, but the rate of exchange would then have to be fixed at many more thousands of bolivianos per dollar, to the detriment of the nation as a whole; that the council thought the proper way to proceed was to base its computations on the opinions of the members of the council and of such well-qualified and competent persons as the council might call upon to testify; and that they had not expected the witnesses who appeared before the council to take the council decisions back to the mine managers or others to be voted upon.*

*Some of the mine managers were men of reasonably independent judgment but, under the Control Obrero (control by the workers), created by decree of December, 1953, the managers were under the thumb of a sort of commissar, elected annually by the miners, and having the right of veto over all management action except (solely in theory) in technical matters (FBD report, vol. 3, pp. 73ff). At this point, the reader may well wonder at my high opinion of the competence and loyalty of the three top

Lechín then declared that this was a serious problem, that at the Bs. 6,000 rate the basic salary would have been $1.25, but that at Bs. 7,000, it would only be $1 — a fact that he was well aware of only a few minutes earlier, before he knew that the mine managers thought the workers would not accept the remuneration he had previously agreed to.

After some further discussion, the proposal previously discussed was presented as final — the council could accept the Bs. 7,500 basic wage previously agreed upon but could allow a 35 per cent incentive bonus, at a Bs. 7,000 rate of exchange. This suggestion was approved unanimously by the council in the presence of Lechín, who left the conference room shortly thereafter, and the meeting adjourned at 1:00 p.m.

The stabilization program was at long last completed!

---

figures in the COMIBOL management. I can only reply that my confidence in those gentlemen is based on subjective factors that defy analysis. In my judgment, all three were loyal to the government enterprise under their management and anxious to place it on a basis for successful operation. This was true of the majority of witnesses who appeared before the council and it was up to the council to sort out the national interest in monetary stabilization from the special interest of each of the government enterprises and agencies.

IV

THE PROGRAM FINANCED AND ENACTED

12

THE STABILIZATION LOAN

Dr. Costanzo and the other members of the International Monetary Fund mission departed from La Paz on November 16 to prepare the ground for Bolivia's request for financial assistance. The measures embraced in the Fifty-Step Plan referred to in Chapter 9 had been whipped into shape in the form of specific decrees — in outline only, but sufficiently precise to serve as the basis for the anticipated financing. To preclude any possible rumors of a discrepancy between the original plan and the draft approved by the council, which the IMF representatives were carrying back to Washington, the Finance Minister, in answer to the point-blank question as to the relationship between "the Eder Plan" and "the IMF Plan," announced to the press: "Their opinions are absolutely identical. Their recommendations coincide in every way."[1]

This was correct. There was no IMF Plan and never had been, and, by the time the conferences between the IMF representatives and the council had drawn to a close, there was no longer any Eder Plan, but solely the National Monetary Stabilization Council Plan, adopted by the President of the Republic and his fellow council members as the official program of the Bolivian government. Aside from the minor adjustments referred to in the preceding chapters, on which agreement was unanimous, the only basic departure from the Fifty-Step Plan was that the latter contemplated establishing the conditions that would be essential for long-term economic development, while the plan on which we were now agreed hewed to the line of monetary stabilization. There was no time for more. Even a fortnight's delay might have been fatal, and it was better to grasp what was within our reach than to strive for the unattainable.

Final Preparations at the Council

On the day following the departure of the IMF mission, the President of the Central Bank drafted a letter to be presented to Per Jacobsson, Director General of the International Monetary Fund, outlining Bolivia's proposed program and requesting that the IMF, the U.S. government, and private banks cooperate by subscribing to a stabilization fund of approximately $30 million, of which some $10 million would be immediately available, and the remainder made available on a stand-by basis.[2] The draft had been approved by the Stabilization Council, including, of course, the President of the Republic and the Minister of Finance.

The following days were taken up with preparations for my trip to Washington and New York as advisor to the two Bolivian council members who would be their government's official representatives in the negotiations. There were meetings with the head of the U.S. Operations Mission in Bolivia, the Economic Counsellor of the Embassy, and the second secretary charged with economic matters;[3] a private conference with President Siles; and a final predeparture meeting of the Stabilization Council, attended for the first time by the two other members of the U.S. Financial Advisory Mission. There, the Minister of Mines and the President outlined the political developments of the morning, following which the council discussed the ten items on the agenda, including, among other matters:

1. The framework of the decrees needed to put into effect the various measures agreed upon for the first phase of the stabilization program. As a matter of policy, it was decided that as many of the measures as possible should be incorporated in a single stabilization decree. This would emphasize the fact that it was an integrated measure, and that no one part of it could be altered without affecting the whole. Dr. Santiago Sologuren, the legal adviser of the National Planning Commission, was charged with drafting the decrees in proper legal form.

2. A bill, then under discussion in Congress, imposing an additional ½ per cent tax on all sales, and earmarked for the Bolivian Workers Federation (COB), which, with the National Revolutionary Movement (MNR) and the government, formed the *Co-Gobierno* that ruled the country. I pointed out that such a tax, not included in the stabilization plan and earmarked for a political party, might jeopardize acceptance of the plan, and the President stated that he believed he could block its passage.

3. The Minister of Mines again expressed the view that COMIBOL could not afford to pay royalties on exports and pointed out that this view was shared by the U.N. mining expert, André Gratacap, and Peter Antonelli of

the Ford, Bacon & Davis mission. With all deference to
the opinions of those authorities as experts in mining
matters, I stated that it was up to the council to decide
on matters of economics and taxation; that the mines had
presumably been nationalized for the benefit of the Bolivian nation and not for the personal benefit of the miners; that, if Patiño, Aramayo, and Hochschild had been
able, during decades of much lower tin prices, to enrich
their owners and yet pay an average export tax of 12 per
cent, contributing some 80-85 per cent of total government revenues, COMIBOL should certainly be able to
pay an average 10 per cent tax *and no other dividends.*[4]
FBD had recommended an income tax as an alternative
to royalties, but the council agreed that the COMIBOL
accounts would always be so arranged that there would
be no net income and hence no tax. Finally, I advised
the council that, if Bolivia wished to carry out the stabilization plan, it simply had to have this revenue and
there was no other way to collect it. The council then
agreed that the royalty rates should be adjusted on a
double sliding scale according to world market prices
for the various metals, and according to the metal content of the concentrates shipped; also that COMIBOL and
the Mining Bank might be given a further hearing with
respect to a suitable scale of royalties, so long as there
was no departure from the principles already agreed to
that might jeopardize the amount of revenues budgeted
in the stabilization plan.

4. Criminal as well as civil penalties were recommended
for the new customs tariff decree, and it was agreed that
the tariffs would be announced as temporary, as the
council members recognized that the proposed schedules
were unsuitable and would discredit the council if there
were not some disclaimer. They realized that temporary rates would be disruptive both to the Customs Bureau and to commerce (which they were), but that it
would do no harm to hamper imports for a month or two.

5. A draft measure was presented to the council for a 2
per cent tax on all purchases and sales of foreign exchange. Admittedly, central bank experts would in principle be opposed to a tax which in any sense could be
regarded as a tax on foreign exchange, or which widened
the admissible IMF *agio* between sales and purchases of
foreign exchange (one-half per cent on each side of parity). Nevertheless, Bolivia's situation was so excep-
tional, with less than zero reserves, that it was believed

essential to start building up a 100 per cent reserve
against note issue as soon as possible. The private
bankers were fully in agreement on that point, and it was
hoped that the Treasury would approve, and the IMF acquiesce. After discussion, the council unanimously
agreed to include this measure in the stabilization decree, but: (a) to waive the tax on exports during the 1957
year (because COMIBOL would have to contribute $5
million to the buffer stock and loan); (b) to reduce the
tax to 1 per cent on imports in that year; and (c) to keep
the tax at 2 per cent on all other purchases of foreign
exchange. The theory was that the tax was high enough
to tend to discourage capital flight yet not so high as to
encourage evasion.

My predilection for the foreign exchange tax was based on
the highly successful Cuban tax of 5 per cent on all exchange
transactions which had enabled that country to recover from the
debacle following collapse of the "Dance of the Millions" in
1920-21. The Cuban tax was, of course, abolished as soon as it
had served its purpose. Ultimately, Bolivia did enact the 2 per
cent tax on foreign exchange, in somewhat different form that
apparently was adjudged compatible with Article VIII of the IMF
regulations (see p. 584).

Other council meetings followed the departure of our financial mission to Washington. In the course of those meetings,
the measures which had been left with the council were gone
over one by one by the council's legal adviser, Dr. Sologuren,
discussed, clarified, made more precise, and agreed to, leaving
to Dr. Sologuren and the Minister of Finance the herculean task
of whipping them all into final shape in the form of decree-laws
in time for the stabilization date. The council also reached a
final decision (not without considerable opposition from the
COMIBOL representatives, joined by the Minister of Mines) that
COMIBOL must live up to the wage and royalty arrangements
previously agreed to as an indispensable part of the stabilization plan. They also decided that, if the bank employees insisted
on an immediate wage increase under the guise of a leveling-off
(*nivelación*) of wages, they must be denied any additional compensation in the stabilization decree for increased living costs
(they did insist, and the later increase was hence denied).

Congress confers emergency powers on President

On November 20, an informal meeting of the council

members was held at the Finance Ministry, and that afternoon I addressed the President and the full Cabinet, outlining in considerable detail the stabilization plans and prospects. Following the meeting, the President, with the approval of the Cabinet, sent Congress the draft of the law, approved by the council a month earlier, which granted the President, with the advice of the Stabilization Council, full power to enact by decree, with the force of law, such measures as might be necessary to carry out the purposes of the stabilization program (see Appendix II).

That evening, a reception was given in the presidential palace, mutual compliments exchanged, and toasts drunk to the success of our mission. On the following day, the President of the Central Bank and I left La Paz for Washington to raise the $25-$30 million. The head of the Planning Commission, who was the other Bolivian member of the mission, remained behind to take part in the Stabilization Council meetings of November 27 and 28, but joined us in Washington later.

Maintaining public confidence

A $25-$30 million loan was not a large operation in comparison with the corporation financing in which I had participated as counsel, but it was the first time I had ever attempted to borrow money on behalf of a borrower whose record was a history of bad faith and broken promises and whose credit, if any, must be based solely on the hope that a single man, President Hernán Siles-Zuazo, not immune to bullets, would have the courage and ability to impose standards of good faith and responsibility on what was perhaps the most corrupt, incompetent, and opportunistic group of politicians that had ever ruled the destinies of the nation.

The return trip to the United States in the company of Dr. Franklin Antezana-Paz, President of the Central Bank, gave me ample opportunity to wonder whether the appearance of unquenchable optimism which I had flaunted in all my speeches and press interviews, and which had been commented upon again and again by the press, might not have been temerarious.[5] On the other hand, if I had admitted the slightest doubt as to the immediate success of the stabilization program, if I had hedged my assurances with a prudent hem or an uncertain haw, every labor union in the country would have insisted on an immediate increase in wages, and all hell would have broken loose.

Meanwhile, those who remained behind were engaged in a

series of talks to labor leaders and the press, all for the one purpose of instilling confidence on the part of the public that the stabilization program would go through and should be supported. President Siles, the Ministers of Finance, Mines, Economy, and Labor, all came out with resounding appeals to the press and public to support the program. The labor leaders and the National Manufacturers Association, meeting in Cochabamba, did likewise. Juan Lechín-Oquendo and his alter ego, Mario Torres-Calleja, who, at the time they spoke, had the full text of the stabilization plan, urged the miners' federation, the COB, and the Revolutionary Youth of the COB, to give the stabilization program their full support, which is of interest in the light of Lechín's later attempt to sabotage the program on the ground that he was not aware of its substance. [6]

The Bishop of La Paz, and the Apostolic Vicars of the Beni and of Chiquitos, Bolivia's distant hinterland, perhaps influenced by the Papal Nuncio, Monsignore Humberto Mozzoni, who had long ago been enlisted in the struggle (p. 153n) exhorted their flocks, as their Christian duty, to support the laws enacted or to be enacted to restore monetary stability, and to "beware of those who engage in illegal operations, smuggling, fraud, and speculation in articles of prime necessity, and who trade on the sweat and blood of their brethren."[7]

Finally, and significantly, Senator Mike Mansfield, who visited Bolivia the first week of December, made it clear in a press interview that Congressional support of further U.S. aid to Bolivia would hinge on Bolivia's carrying out the stabilization program, that this would be true regardless of whether the next administration were Republican or Democrat, and that, in this respect, his views were identical with those of Senator Bourke H. Hickenlooper, who had visited Bolivia earlier in the year. The timeliness and pertinence of these remarks speaks highly not only of the senators' grasp of the problems of stabilization but of the sound practical briefing they must have had from Ambassador Gerald Drew who accompanied them on their visits to President Siles.[8]

Proposed sale and confiscation of gold

Scarcely had Dr. Antezana and I arrived in Washington and paid our respects to Bolivian Ambassador Victor Andrade, than the Bolivian Embassy received a cable from the Finance Minister asking our opinion, and that of the Monetary Fund, as to the government's selling some $178,000 in gold bars and some $812,000 in gold coins, held by the Mining Bank, in order to meet certain urgent obligations.* The Stabilization Council, we were informed, was inclined to authorize the sale, subject to our approval. Almost simultaneously, the State Department received a cable from the U.S. Embassy in La Paz, addressed to me by Ernest Moore, stating that he had informed the council that, in his opinion, in which Roger Freeman concurred, it was much more urgent to take over, and sell, some $1,250,000 of gold held by the three private commercial banks in La Paz; that this gold should be "nationalized" prior to stabilization, at the rate of Bs. 190, as otherwise the banks would receive the profit. In the case of the National Bank, the cable stated, the gold holdings amounted to nearly $1 million, and the profit would be close to Bs. 7 billion, or more than the bank's entire balance-sheet assets.

As to the latter suggestion, it was hard to see how the council could possibly justify seizure of this gold. Payment at the rate of Bs. 190 when the current rate was around Bs. 10,000, and when we expected to stabilize at Bs. 7,000 or higher, would be little short of confiscation. It meant, in effect, that the Bolivian government would be paying less than $1 an ounce (Bs. 6,650) for gold that was patently worth $35 an ounce. Approval of this action would have justified a similarly confiscatory settlement for the seizure of the nationalized mines or any

---

*The gold bullion was gold acquired by the Mining Bank directly from the small and medium-sized mines. The gold coins were minted by the Revolutionary Government under Decree of May 14, 1953, one of the ill-fated and counterproductive "stabilization" measures enacted on the advice of the U.N. advisers and approved by the IMF (Franklin Antezana - Paz, *La Política Monetario de Bolivia* [La Paz: Banco Central de Bolivia, 1954], p. 42). The coins bore no denomination, but merely their weight in grams of fine gold content: 3.5, 7, 14, and 35 grams, respectively, the largest coin being somewhat larger than the pre-Roosevelt $20 gold piece, and worth approximately $39.40 in terms of the gold value of the current dollar. The intention was to deliver these coins to the miners in exchange for their gold ingots or dust, subject to a small seignorage charge, as a means of stimulating production and deterring the illicit export of gold, inasmuch as the coins were to be freely exportable. The scheme collapsed along with the other 1953 "stabilization" measures, and the government was stuck with over $800,000 of coins which cost more than their gold value because of the charges of the Paris mint, but were worth less because of the apparently high base metal content (the coins have a dull appearance, unusual in gold coins).

other property. On the basis of conferences with Dr. Antezana and others in Washington, the Bolivian Ambassador was asked to send the following cable in reply (in Spanish, paraphrased from the coded message*):

> EDER AND OTHERS CONSIDER CONFISCATION COM-
> MERCIAL BANK GOLD UNDESIRABLE AND REPERCUS-
> SIONS ABROAD WOULD BE UNFAVORABLE[9]

Later it developed that at the Stabilization Council discussion, Foreign Minister Barrau had objected to Moore's proposal on the ground that it would be regarded as a further instance of "nationalization" on the part of the government; that Finance Minister Moreno objected that any provisions for the revaluation (and taxation) of such assets should wait until after stabilization; and that Gisbert had reminded the council that it had not yet reached a decision as to the taxation of paper profits arising out of the revaluation of assets. No Bolivian member of the council supported the idea of seizing private holdings of gold at the price of Bs. 190 per dollar.

As to the other suggestion, that the government sell some $990,000 of gold coin and bullion held by the Mining Bank in order to meet pressing obligations, no one from the United States or in Washington had been aware of the fact that the bank held that gold — it was just one of the many things not previously divulged to the council — and we could not understand why any obligations which were not "urgent" a week earlier should suddenly have to be paid immediately, just prior to stabilization. To be frank, it smelled too much of paying off some of the more malodorous suppliers' credits before the stabilization measures went into effect. After consultation, Dr. Antezana, as President of the Central Bank, cabled the Finance Minister that Washington would not be pleased if the Bolivian government used hitherto unrevealed assets to pay off debts whose urgency had not previously been disclosed, precisely at the moment when Bolivia was seeking some $25-$30 million from the IMF and other agencies.

---

*This and all other telegrams are quoted from paraphrased notes. Because of security requirements, no verbatim copies are available.

Conclusion of Financial Arrangements

As has been indicated, the International Monetary Fund was the chosen agent for determining the creditworthiness of the Bolivian government. Neither ICA nor the Treasury Department would contribute to the stabilization fund unless the IMF determined that the stabilization plan was feasible and would be carried out, and unless it was willing to risk its own funds in the program. Any contribution by the private bankers would be dependent upon the participation of the Treasury.

International Monetary Fund

On November 29, as scheduled, Antezana appeared before the IMF Executive Board and read a carefully drafted statement, previously approved by the council, outlining Bolivia's plans for monetary stabilization, expressing the gratitude of the government of Bolivia for the assistance rendered by Dr. Costanzo and me,[10] and requesting the cooperation of the IMF, without, however, mentioning any specific sum as the amount that would be required from the IMF or other entities.

A "Stand-by Agreement," in the usual IMF form, was agreed to by Dr. Antezana on behalf of the government of Bolivia and of the Central Bank, but neither this document nor any other contract was signed by either party. Under IMF procedures, the terms of the "Stand-by Agreement" remain confidential, although embodied in the minutes of the Executive Board meeting and read by representatives of the various governments whose delegates were members of the board at the time.*

*This peculiar procedure — "peculiar" in the sense that it is not customary in commercial practice nor, indeed, in intergovernmental loans (see Treasury Department arrangement, p. 251) or in World Bank loans where a formal, meticulously drafted contract is called for — is set forth by way of exposition and not of criticism. From the IMF viewpoint, the formal multilateral treaty entered into by all participating nations constitutes an agreement to abide by the rules of the IMF, as binding as any written contract covering a specific loan. A contract would be no more easily enforced and might be less flexible so far as subsequent changes in interest rates, stand-by fees, maturities, etc., are concerned. However, it would have been convenient (in Bolivia, at least) if the material prepared by the IMF staff on the basis of official Bolivian data and agreements had been presented by the Bolivian government, *and signed,* together with a contract committing Bolivia to the representations made in that document and to the undertakings set forth in its stabilization plan. As it

In substance, the agreement meant that Bolivia could borrow up to $7.5 million from the IMF, in addition to the $2.5 loan already outstanding, and that $5 million would be immediately available, and $2.5 million within 30 days. Interest would be charged at the IMF sliding scale of 2 to 4 per cent per annum on any amounts actually drawn down against this credit, while a stand-by fee of $\frac{1}{4}$ per cent per annum would be charged on any amounts not drawn, meaning that Bolivia would only pay interest on such amounts as were actually required and borrowed.*

Neither the interest nor the stand-by fee was specified in the "Stand-by Agreement," these rates being established from time to time by the Executive Board of the IMF, with binding effect on all borrowers.[11]   Later, after the ICA financing had been determined, it was arranged that Bolivia's drawings on the IMF funds would be *pari passu* with its drawings on the ICA credit, the difference being that the IMF credit would eventually have to be repaid, whereas the ICA credit was a gift. The ease with which these terms were imposed and amended is an example of the flexibility of the IMF procedure.

Shortly after the board meeting, the chairman informed Dr. Antezana of the favorable decision of the board which was confirmed in writing on November 30, subject to the routine four-day waiting period for possible objections.

---

was, again and again in the course of Stabilization Council meetings, mistakes in the factual material in that document — inevitable in view of the lack of data and pressure of time — and allegedly incorrect conclusions or impossible commitments as to living costs, wages, etc., were blamed on the IMF mission, instead of being acknowledged as errors on the part of the Bolivian government. As for treating the terms of the "agreement" as "confidential," while it is true that this may obviate unfair political criticism that the agreement was unduly onerous (which it was not), it would seem that the citizens of the borrowing nation, as well as the taxpayers of the lending nation or nations, have a right to know *all* the facts concerning any loan which may affect their interests — and this applies to the loans made by AID, the Export Import Bank, or the U.S. government, as well as to the loans made by the IMF, IBRD, or IDB.

*It has been stated that stand-by arrangements are an invention of the International Monetary Fund (see George Nicoletopoulos, "Stand-by Arrangements," *Finance and Development*, III [December, 1964], p. 193), but long before the fund first adopted this procedure in February, 1952, I had acted as counsel in banking operations under which interest was charged only on amounts actually drawn under the credit while a stand-by fee was charged on undrawn balances, and no originality is claimed for this procedure.

International Cooperation Administration

The IMF financing arranged, Dr. Antezana, Gisbert, and I conferred with a Dr. Adams,* who was charged with making the final decision on the details of the ICA financing. The amount ($10 million) had already been arranged in my previous discussions with State and ICA, both on this trip and in September, and the expectation was that ICA would make the funds available on a loan and stand-by basis. To our surprise, and to the delight of Gisbert and Antezana, however, Dr. Adams stated that the funds would be placed at the disposal of the Bolivian government *as a grant,* to be used in the form of "Procurement Authorizations" for merchandise which would be imported either by the Bolivian government or by government enterprises. Of the total ICA contribution to the stabilization fund, $5 million would be made available immediately after enactment of the stabilization decree, then tentatively set for December 15, 1956. To make the funds available for stabilization purposes — and it was understood that they were not to be used for any other purpose — the following procedure would be used:

> As each shipment of merchandise was paid for by ICA under Procurement Authorizations, the Bolivian Central Bank would use the foreign exchange (which it would otherwise have used to pay for these imports) to make remittances to New York banks for deposit to its account, thus creating a stabilization fund. As there was over $5 million of merchandise for government account already in Pacific coast ports in Peru or Chile, that amount, Dr. Adams explained, could be "P.A.'d" immediately, and it would be expected that the remaining $5 million would be "P.A.'d" before April 30, 1957. The dollars would be remitted by the Central Bank to New York when and as proceeds from the export of tin, etc., became available, meaning that the total $10 million should be remitted before the end of March, 1957. The second $5 million would carry the further restriction that the merchandise shipments would have to be within the limitations of the Bolivian fiscal and foreign exchange budgets presented to Washington and that the funds

---

*This is not his name, but I have preferred to follow a policy of not divulging names where it might cause embarrassment, except in those cases where the identity of the person is so widely known, in Bolivia or the United States, that it would be absurd to use a pseudonym.

must not be used for additional imports, nor for new governmental projects or activities but strictly for stabilization purposes, as in the case of the initial $5 million.

As an alternative, in the event that the "P.A." arrangement proved too cumbersome under the complex legal provisions governing U.S. aid, Dr. Adams stated that it might be possible for the Central Bank to obtain dollars from ICA, through USOM/Bolivia, *pari passu* with its drawings against the IMF credit, and in proportion to the relative amounts of the ICA and IMF credits. In other words, as Dr. Adams put it, for every $17,500 of dollars that the Central Bank sold to the public in Bolivia, it could go to the USOM disbursing agent in La Paz and get a check for $10,000 in exchange for $10,000 worth of bolivianos which it would have received from the public. At the same time, it could draw down $7,500 under the IMF credit. The Bolivian currency delivered to USOM would be held for U.S. account and could be distributed as counterpart funds subject to the usual restrictions governing the use of such funds. To avoid inflationary pressure, however, these funds would be largely sterilized or, if used, other counterpart funds would be proportionately frozen, subject to USOM control as well as to the restraining influence of the Stabilization Council. The dollar funds, on the other hand, could be freely used for the same purposes as the IMF or Treasury funds, i.e., for the stabilization fund.

As Dr. Adams pointed out, the only difference between the dollar funds derived from ICA and those derived from IMF or the Treasury would be that the ICA funds would never have to be repaid, while the remaining funds would be in the form of a loan. However, the IMF credit would not be repayable with ICA funds but with funds derived from Bolivian exports.

ICA reneges. Unfortunately, the negotiation with ICA was not to be concluded so easily. Almost on the eve of our mission's return to Bolivia, the Treasury Department called me on a matter of the utmost urgency. In answer to a cabled inquiry from Ambassador Drew and the chief of USOM/Bolivia, Dr. Adams had cabled on December 4 to the effect that no ICA funds could be made available to Bolivia so long as Bolivia had any remaining foreign exchange resources of its own. This was entirely contrary to our understanding and to that of the Treasury or State Department. The cable was stated to be confusing and ambiguous, but Treasury and State reported that they would be negotiating with Dr. Adams, in the hope of persuading him to return to what they understood was the arrangement originally proffered. Late that evening (Saturday, November 8), however, the Office of the General Counsel of the Treasury Department reported that they had been unable to budge Dr. Adams from his position.

Following that phone call, I tried in vain to reach Dr. Adams or W. Randolph Burgess, Under Secretary of the Treasury, that evening and on Sunday, inasmuch as I was scheduled to leave Washington on Monday morning's plane and had received cables from U.S. Ambassador Gerald Drew and from President Siles stressing the urgency of the situation in Bolivia and insisting that I must not under any circumstances delay my departure. On Sunday, therefore, I drafted a letter in longhand to Dr. Adams, which was left at the Treasury Department for photostating and distribution to Treasury and State. In that letter, I attempted to exercise all the powers of persuasion that a lawyer is trained to use — avoiding any trace of blame, recrimination, or criticism — in the hope of persuading Dr. Adams to find some viable solution to the dilemma. The very essence of the stabilization program was that Bolivia must demonstrate conclusively its determination and capacity to rebuild the foreign exchange resources which had been dissipated over the past three years. If no ICA funds could be made available so long as Bolivia had any funds of its own, the failure of the stabilization program was certain.

Only enough of this incident was communicated to Dr. Antezana and Gisbert — red tape, bureaucracy, ironing out of details — so that, if the worst came to the worst, they would not be completely unprepared. At the same time, it would have been a mistake to alarm them unduly by revealing what had actually taken place, inasmuch as the consequences for Bolivia and for them personally, if ICA aid were not forthcoming, would be too overwhelming to contemplate.

Actually, it seemed impossible that a man as intelligent as Dr. Adams would fail to see the consequences of the position he had taken. In my letter, I took all the blame for the "misunderstanding" — although the State and Treasury officials were equally misled and amazed by Dr. Adams' position — thus leaving Dr. Adams a way of retreating with dignity. Furthermore, it seemed almost sure that we would have some heavy artillery on our side, if the need arose: the Under Secretaries of State and Treasury, Hoover and Burgess, as well as U.S. Ambassador

Drew. The staff at Treasury and State were fully aware of the background, and of the dangers if ICA backed down from its original offer, and would be prepared to advise their chiefs accordingly. Hence, in reporting to the President and council on arrival in La Paz, I was again compelled to outline the difficulties, but I took care to avoid alarming them by divulging the full facts, which Gisbert and Antezana would certainly have regarded as a breach of faith on the part of ICA.

Fortunately, all's well that ends well and, whether because of my plea to Dr. Adams or because State or Treasury came to the rescue, ICA finally agreed to go along on a *pari passu* basis with IMF under a somewhat less complex arrangement than originally proposed, i.e., as IMF had already advanced $2.5 million, ICA matched that amount immediately, and, from then on, contributions to the stabilization fund were made on a fifty-fifty basis, as loans from IMF, as grants from ICA.

Treasury Department

In contrast to the unbusinesslike procedure at ICA, the financial arrangements at the Treasury Department were conducted as efficiently and graciously as they would have been handled by any first-rate private banking institution.*

The Under Secretary of the Treasury, W. Randolph Burgess,

---

*To the Bolivian representatives, raising $10 million, as part of the $25 million stabilization fund, was a very serious business indeed. The whole future of their country hung in the balance. Yet, instead of being received by the director of ICA, or by an Under Secretary of State, we were kept waiting half an hour in the office of a lower level ICA employee who *hoped* that Dr. Adams would have time to see us — this despite the fact that the appointment had been set up in advance. Finally, we were taken to a small office where we sat on hard wooden chairs while Dr. Adams pondered aloud whether there might be some way in which ICA could let Bolivia have the money for the stabilization fund. One might have supposed that this could have been thought out in advance, as it was not a question of negotiation — I had concluded the negotiating over the course of many previous meetings — but of determining what method would be most expedient under the provisions of the laws governing ICA loans and grants. Antezana and Gisbert were made to feel like a couple of improvident farmers trying to borrow $100 to buy fertilizer. One need not advocate throwing money away, but so long as the U.S. is giving away taxpayers' money, why cannot it be done with a little graciousness? The French manage to make a minimal amount of aid create a maximal amount of goodwill by just this added ingredient of courtesy. Perhaps, *savoir faire* is in fact untranslatable.

a distinguished economist and banker, and the Assistant Secretary and Executive Director of IMF and IBRD, Andrew N. Overby, likewise with an impressive financial background, greeted Gisbert and Antezana with the cordiality and courtesy to which they were entitled as representatives, respectively, of the Bolivian Government and of the Bolivian Central Bank. On their return to Bolivia, both gentlemen spoke warmly of their reception at the Treasury Department, which goes to show that it is not impossible to operate a government department effectively yet graciously.

A draft of the proposed Treasury contract had been furnished a week in advance, providing an opportunity to iron out a few minor questions with representatives of the Office of the General Counsel of the Treasury Department prior to the formal meeting for execution of the agreement, which took place on Friday, December 7. Burgess had kept abreast of the negotiations with the private bankers (see below at p. 253), and, since he realized that it would be impossible to complete the loan arrangements in New York and yet catch the Monday plane back to Bolivia, he had very considerately had two contracts prepared, one for $5 million — in the event that it was thought advisable to complete the private financing, say early in 1957 — and the other for $7.5 million.

There was no question in our minds that the larger amount would be in every sense preferable. From a strictly financial viewpoint, $22.5 million would have been ample, but President Siles had been counting on $25 million, hoping for $30 million, and the uneven amount would have seemed to denote a failure of our mission, an inauspicious beginning for a stabilization program that was bound to encounter many difficulties in the course of its execution. So... the agreement was executed, by Dr. Antezana for the Central Bank and by Gisbert for the government of Bolivia, for the amount of $7.5 million, subject to the following conditions:

> The contract was in the form of a stand-by arrangement, executed December 7, but dated "as of" December 1. It was to be effective for two years, but would not enter into effect until Bolivia had enacted the stabilization measures agreed to and had deposited with the Department of State appropriate evidence of that fact and of the powers of the signatories under the laws of Bolivia. This formality was attended to in due course by the Bolivian Ambassador.

The funds would not be available: (1) unless the IMF funds were completely exhausted (under the *pari passu* arrangement, this meant that the ICA credit would also be exhausted); (2) unless Bolivia had taken and was taking such steps as might be necessary to ensure monetary stabilization; and (3) unless sufficient advance notice were given to the Treasury Department so that the Treasury could verify compliance with the two other provisions. This meant, in effect, that — barring an unforeseen emergency — the Treasury funds need never be drawn upon, since, if Bolivia faithfully carried out all the measures she was required to take under the stabilization program, and if Treasury were alert to any deviations, there would never be any need for more than perhaps $3-$7 million of stabilization fund support. The Treasury stand-by credit was needed, however, to establish public confidence in the stabilization program, and that confidence was required, first, to obtain enactment of the plan, and, second, to ensure its success.

Under the circumstances, the stand-by arrangement was more economical for Bolivia than an outright loan, as interest would be charged only on such amounts as were actually drawn down, and meanwhile, Bolivia would only have to pay a carrying charge of $\frac{1}{4}$ per cent per annum on such part of the credit as remained unused. Interest on any amounts used would be at 4 per cent per annum in 1957 and 5 per cent in 1958. Any amounts drawn by Bolivia under this credit would be deposited by the Treasury with the Federal Reserve Bank of New York in a special account in the name of the Central Bank of Bolivia while the equivalent amount in bolivianos would be turned over to the Treasury but deposited in the Central Bank in the name of the Federal Reserve Bank of New York, as Fiscal Agent of the United States. The issuance and deposit of the boliviano bank notes would not be inflationary, as they would not be used. Repayment would be made *pari passu* with repayments under the IMF payment, and proportionately to the amounts drawn under the Treasury and IMF credits. The repayment would be made by taking one-third of any increment in the gold and foreign exchange resources of the Central Bank, and of the government of Bolivia, subsequent to the date of the Treasury's first purchase of bolivianos.

Judging by the scepticism expressed at State, ICA, IMF, and in New York, as to the likelihood of a Treasury loan, this $7.5 million stand-by credit was in fact one of the authentic "miracles" of the stabilization program.

Private commercial banks

As soon as possible after making a preliminary report to ICA, State, IMF, and the Bolivian Ambassador, and before the negotiations in Washington were concluded, I had gone to New York to confer individually and at a joint meeting with a number of private commercial banks, in the hope of forming a syndicate that might be willing to participate in financing a Bolivian stabilization fund on the same basis as the U.S. Treasury.[12]   Obviously, the banks could not be expected to make a firm commitment in advance, but the president of one of the banks did advise that the "New York banks will be very glad to come along" in the event that IMF and Treasury — particularly the latter — participated.*

Hence, as soon as IMF had approved the loan, and ICA and Treasury support was assured, I returned to New York. At this time, one of the smaller banks approached made a definite offer of $300,000, and another a definite offer of $500,000, while one of the larger banks agreed to furnish $1.5 million, provided Bolivia demonstrated its ability to build up its foreign exchange resources at the rate of $300,000 a month over a reasonable period. There is little doubt that commitments could have been obtained for at least $2.5 million, and probably for $4 to $5 million, without restrictions other than those imposed by the Treasury.   The alternative $5 million Treasury contract provided that it would be willing to come in *pari passu* with the private banks. It turned out, however, that, in the case of Bolivia's principal banking correspondent, the Vice-President who would have had to pass on the agreement was not in town, while another large bank with which I had discussed the matter would make no commitment in the absence of the primary banker, although there is good reason to believe that it would have participated in the operation, if there had been time to complete the syndicate. However, the Treasury contract was not signed until Friday, December 7, and our mission was compelled to return to La Paz on Monday, so that there simply was no time remaining in which a deal could have been made with the private banks prior to stabilization.

*Letter from Ralph S. Stillman, President, Grace National Bank of New York, September 5, 1956. Mr. Stillman was one of New York's best informed financiers in the Latin American field, and I shall be forever grateful to him for his encouragement and assistance in the Bolivian venture.

The operation could, of course, have been concluded after enactment of the stabilization measures on December 15, 1956, and one of the bankers interviewed wrote that he would be glad to take upon himself the responsibility of forming the syndicate. But, with the Bolivian currency backed more than 100 per cent by the $25 million fund already committed, there could be no justification for a further, unneeded, stand-by credit of $5 million at an annual carrying charge of $25,000 (the usual private bank fee at the time was $\frac{1}{2}$ per cent). In the light of Bolivia's subsequent actions, and the failure of the United States to insist upon Bolivia's fulfilling its obligations, it is just as well that the bankers did not participate.

Foreign Bondholders Protective Council, Incorporated

In accordance with the arrangements previously made with the Foreign Bondholders Protective Council, Incorporated, Gisbert and I visited the council on December 6, where Gisbert, duly authorized as the accredited representative of the Bolivian government, agreed to the following conditions for resumption of service on Bolivia's publicly held bonded debt:

> Accumulated unpaid interest through the first half of 1957, amounting to $107,810,000 on the $56,278,000 of bonds outstanding in the hands of the public, would be reduced to $5,627,800, and funded by exchanging each old $1,000 bond for a new $1,100 bond in 1962, and meanwhile surcharging them for that amount. Interest would be payable on the entire debt then outstanding at the rate of $\frac{1}{2}$ per cent of principle for interest payments due during the second semester of 1957;* at the rate of 1 per cent per annum for the four subsequent semiannual interest payment dates; $1\frac{1}{2}$ per cent per annum for the next four payments; 2 per cent per annum for the following four payments; and at the rate of 3 per cent per annum for all payments due the second half of 1963 and thereafter. Provision was made for sinking fund payments, with Bolivia retaining the right to accelerate amortization. [13]

*This would cover interest coupons due July 1, September 1, October 1, and November 1, 1957, on the four outstanding series of bonds. The first payment would be $5.50 per new $1,100 bond (see FBPC, Inc., Press Release, June 17, 1958).

From the Bolivian point of view, this arrangement, while following the general lines of the stillborn agreement reached in 1948, was more favorable than the 1948 settlement. Some $110 million of defaulted interest was funded for $5.6 million in new bonds, in lieu of some $70 million so funded under the 1948 agreement. Then too, the 1948 settlement provided for interest payments at 1 per cent per annum for 2 years; $1\frac{1}{2}$ per cent for 2 years; 2 per cent for 2 years; and 3 per cent after the sixth year; while interest under the 1956 agreement would not rise to 3 per cent until after $6\frac{1}{2}$ years.

Unfortunately, resumption of interest under this arrangement was delayed as a result of political intervention and, even after interest payments were resumed, they were again defaulted in September, 1960 (pp. 522, 577), on both occasions in violation of Bolivia's obligations under the monetary stabilization plan, and on both occasions frustrating any possible financial assistance by the World Bank.

Other financial arrangements

Gisbert took advantage of the anticipated resumption of debt service on the Bolivian bonds to renew his acquaintance with Eugene Black and other high officials of the International Bank for Reconstruction and Development. He found that they had been following Bolivia's proposed stabilization program with keen interest and had been delighted to learn of Gisbert's negotiations with the Foreign Bondholders Protective Council, Inc., inasmuch as, under World Bank policies, no loans were made to any country which was in default on its public obligations. Bolivia was the only country in Latin America thus barred from World Bank assistance, and Black promised to send a mission to Bolivia early in 1957 to study possible ways in which they could assist in financing Bolivian development projects.

Unhappily, this mission was delayed by reason of political interference with the debt arrangements and, what with the subsequent new default and other evidence of Bolivian financial ineptitude, it was not until July, 1964, that the World Bank or any of its subsidiaries extended credit to Bolivia.

Gisbert also visited the Export-Import Bank of Washington and made arrangements with Mr. Lynn U. Stambaugh, First Vice-President and Vice-Chairman of that bank, to reduce Bolivia's payments to the bank by $2 million for 1957, $2.3 million for 1958, and $2.5 million for 1959, a total reduction of $6.8

million for the first three crucial years of the stabilization
program. The ultimate maturity of the debt to the Export-
Import Bank was extended from 1971 to 1974. These arrangements were completed by Gisbert, and it remained merely for
the Bolivian Development Corporation and the YPFB to execute
the new agreements covering their respective debts.

13

THE FINAL DRAFT

While our mission was busy making final arrangements with the various financial institutions in New York and Washington, the remaining Stabilization Council members, but in particular Finance Minister Hugo Moreno-Córdova and the newly appointed legal adviser, Dr. Santiago Sologuren, were equally busy in La Paz reshaping the measures into the form of decrees. Gisbert had remained in La Paz for the council meetings of November 27 and 28 to help in the drafting process, and there were no more meetings until December 10, the day before our return from Washington.

Postponements and Amendments

Meanwhile, however, on the morning of December 1, 1956, the following telegram was received from the Minister of Foreign Affairs through the Bolivian Embassy in Washington (translated and paraphrased):

TO TRANSMIT TO EDER. THE PRESIDENT OF THE REPUBLIC AND THE NATIONAL STABILIZATION COUNCIL WOULD LIKE TO KNOW YOUR OPINION ON THE ADVISABILITY OF POSTPONING ENACTMENT OF THE STABILIZATION MEASURES UNTIL DECEMBER 15 STOP THEY BELIEVE IT ADVISABLE TO AWAIT YOUR RETURN TO LA PAZ IN ORDER TO PUT FINAL TOUCHES ON PROVISIONS OF DECREES AND FURTHERMORE BECAUSE DURING THE WEEK OF DECEMBER 9 TO 15 THERE WILL BE AN IMPORTANT NATIONAL CONGRESS OF FACTORY WORKERS AND IT WOULD BE EXPEDIENT TO AWAIT CONCLUSION THAT CONGRESS BEFORE PROMULGATING DECREES

Originally, it had been hoped to have the stabilization measures enacted on November 24, and the initial computations of probable bank note circulation and of the dollar-boliviano rate of exchange had been determined with that date in mind. By the middle of November, it appeared that it would be essential to postpone the date to December 1, and Ambassador Drew joined me in cabling to Washington, emphasizing the extreme urgency of the Bolivian political and financial situation in the hope that State, ICA, Treasury, and IMF would set their sights for that date and be prepared to act as soon as our mission arrived in Washington. Delays in La Paz, as well as in Washington, had forced a further postponement, and a week later Finance Minister Moreno announced to the press that the stabilization measures would be enacted between December 6 and 10.[14]   Meanwhile, of course, there was no way of stopping the continued issuance of bank notes to meet payrolls and other current expenses. In all, the note issue had risen from Bs. 75 billion on June 30 to Bs. 109 billion on September 30 and Bs. 160 billion by the close of 1956 (see Fig. 1, p. 42, and supporting data at p. 707, n 49).   With each increase in circulation, the calculated margins of safety grew narrower, making an increase in the dollar-boliviano crossrate inevitable.

Thus, when the cable was received from La Paz, I communicated first with my colleagues and then with Treasury, State, and other agencies in Washington, and, before the day closed, was able to send the following cabled reply (translated and paraphrased), likewise through the Bolivian Embassy:

REPLYING YOUR TELEGRAM EDER STATES QUOTE IN EVENT POSTPONEMENT INEVITABLE BECAUSE OF POLITICAL AND SOCIAL REASONS IT WILL NOT AFFECT FINANCIAL AID ALREADY OBTAINED STOP NEVERTHELESS ANY DELAY WILL AFFECT THE RATE OF EXCHANGE IN VIEW OF ADDITIONAL UNBACKED CURRENCY ISSUES STOP OBVIOUSLY ANY INCREASE OF WAGES AS A CONSEQUENCE OF THE FACTORY WORKERS CONGRESS OR ANY FURTHER POSTPONEMENT FOR SIMILAR REASONS WOULD HAVE UNFAVORABLE REPERCUSSIONS AND WOULD DETRACT FROM THE PRESTIGE OF AND CONFIDENCE IN THE STABILIZATION PROGRAM UNQUOTE

Gisbert, who, in addition to his position as a member of the Stabilization Council and active head of the Planning Commission, was president of a well-managed woolen textile plant in La Paz, had warned of the dangers that could arise out of the meeting of factory workers, and reported that the union leaders were planning to demand an immediate and substantial wage increase which would inevitably start off another round of increases for the miners, transport workers, and others. This was the reason for the *caveat* in the above telegram, but we all agreed on postponement, if President Siles thought it essential.

It may be pointed out that these national conventions of labor leaders often get out of hand and are generally swayed, not by the wisest or highest-ranking leaders, but by the most impassioned orators and, as President Siles had once warned, by Trotskyites and communists who are well trained for just such purposes. After the labor congress was over, it was reasonable to expect that there would be less difficulty in persuading the major labor leaders of the wisdom of supporting the stabilization program, and there was no doubt that the rank and file — unless misled by extremist agitators — would back the President.

Correcting the Bolivian drafts

In the meantime, the draft decrees prepared by Finance Minister Moreno and Legal Adviser Sologuren had been received through the Bolivian Embassy, and I had made numerous changes in style and substance to make certain that they conformed, over-all and in detail, with the agreements reached in the Stabilization Council, and that they were so meticulously worded that there could be no possibility of later misinterpretation or evasion.*

The proposed decrees were then checked with Antezana and Gisbert and with the Washington agencies, and Gisbert arranged with the Bolivian Ambassador to have the drafts, with my interlinear and marginal corrections (too numerous to be cabled), flown back to La Paz on December 1 by Germán Rovira, the Bolivian Commercial Counsellor.

The changes in language as well as in substance were so

---

*Latin American legislation is, in general, hastily drafted, and there is seldom that meticulous attention to details of phraseology and consistency that make American legislation so difficult for the layman to understand, yet, in general, so precise in substance. The courts in Latin America will generally construe any doubtful point of law in favor of the government, so that there is not usually the same compunction for extreme accuracy of expression that is expected in the United States. In this case, however, it would be the government itself, under political pressure, that would be seeking to evade the more onerous or restrictive provisions of the law, so that I made it my business to close every possible loophole in the interest of the stabilization program.

numerous and *seemingly* so trivial and captious that they might well have offended the susceptibilities of those who had worked so hard, and under such pressure of time, to draft the decrees. To obviate this, the following telegram (translated and paraphrased) was sent through the Bolivian Embassy, likewise on December 1:

> I CONGRATULATE MORENO SOLOGUREN ADMIRABLE DRAFTSMANSHIP PROPOSED DECREE STOP THE CHANGES MADE BY US WHICH ROVIRA IS BRINGING ARE THE RESULT OF RECOMMENDATIONS OF WASHINGTON AGENCIES STOP A DECREE SHOULD BE PREPARED PROVIDING UNIFORM ROYALTIES ON EXPORTS OF COMIBOL AND THE PRIVATE MINES HIGH ENOUGH TO PRODUCE THE REVENUES BUDGETED STOP THE DECREE COVERING CUSTOMS DUTIES ON IMPORTS SHOULD ELIMINATE EARMARKED TAXES AND REPLACE THEM WITH SPECIFIC BUDGETED SUBSIDIES STOP CORDIAL REGARDS EDER

Earmarked taxes

The budgets approved by the Stabilization Council with the assistance of the IMF mission had made provision for all expenditures that the government was capable of financing, and had provided for revenues believed to be adequate to that end and as high as it was believed the country could bear without wrecking the economy. There was no margin of taxpaying capacity available for additional earmarked taxes, no surplus fat in the government budget which would permit subtracting a fraction of existing taxes to be earmarked for nonbudgetary purposes, and no other way of financing unbudgeted expenses without inflation.

It was fortunate that the stricture against customs earmarkings was incorporated in the above cable, for it later developed that Congress had passed a number of other bills during our absence, all providing for specially earmarked taxes for supposedly vital public works — water supply, sewers, etc. Fortunately, too, President Siles, seeking to justify a veto of those bills, had asked Roger Freeman of the U. S. Fiscal Mission for his opinion as a tax expert with respect to the advisability of earmarked taxes, and Freeman had given him a seven-page memorandum explaining why earmarking was considered undesirable in fiscal theory and practice.*

It is true that Freeman, in addition to recommending direct government subsidies to the departments and municipalities in lieu of earmarking, had advocated broadening the powers of the local authorities to impose taxes of their own and empowering them to issue bonds to finance local public improvements. [15] These recommendations, however, were so foreign to the Bolivian political structure that there was no likelihood that any action would be taken, or even attempted, prior to our return. Thus, on the one question that was immediately germane, that of earmarking, the U.S. Financial Advisory Mission presented a united front.

Revaluation of assets

Another matter that fortunately came to our attention at this time was a copy of a decree, ready for the President's signature, and apparently approved by the Finance Minister, which would have called for the obligatory revaluation of all fixed assets of business at the arbitrary rate of Bs. 6,000 to the dollar, subject to a 3 per cent "royalty" on the increase in value as compared with the book value of the asset.

In other words, if a company had purchased equipment three years earlier for $10,000, when the boliviano was quoted at Bs. 190 to the dollar, and the equipment had therefore been entered in the company books at Bs. 1.9 million, it would have to be revalued at Bs. 70 million, and the 3 per cent tax on the paper "profit" would be Bs. 2,043,000. Such a rate of tax, if applied to all company assets, would confiscate the entire book capital; if any substantial part of its fixed assets dated back to 1953 or earlier, the company would be forced out of business. The distortions arising during a period of rampant inflation are such that they cannot be safely corrected by a seemingly reasonable tax on paper profits (see p. 368 for later attempts to tax such "profits" at from 5 per cent to 50 per cent).

*In his reply, Freeman had commented that the constitutional veto time had long since expired, but he was told that *such minor details were of no consequence.* (His memorandum, December 6, 1956). Had the original draft of the decree establishing the Stabilization Council been adopted, there would have been no danger of hasty and unsound legislation jeopardizing the stabilization program (see Appendix I., Art. 7, note).

Following an exchange of views with Dr. Antezana, Gisbert, and Washington officials, the Bolivian Ambassador was therefore requested to send the following cable (translated and paraphrased):

THE WASHINGTON AGENCIES AS WELL AS THE UNDERSIGNED HAVE OBJECTIONS OF A FUNDAMENTAL NATURE WITH RESPECT TO CERTAIN PROVISIONS OF THIS DECREE WHICH WILL BE EXPLAINED ON MY RETURN STOP THE LAW CAN BE ENACTED PRIOR TO JANUARY FIRST STOP EDER

The drafts corrected and politically approved

Between December 1 and 10, Dr. Sologuren and Finance Minister Moreno buckled down to the task of putting the draft decrees in shape and, on the latter date, the President summoned a meeting of the Stabilization Council, including Dr. Sologuren and Moore and Freeman of the U.S. Financial Advisory Mission. To ensure political support from both houses of Congress, Dr. Renán Castrillo, President of the House of Deputies, and Juan Lechín, President of the Senate, were both invited; both attended the meeting, the latter taking an active part in the discussion.

In the course of a three-hour meeting, the conferees went over the stabilization measures, article by article. On one point raised by Lechín — as to whether elimination of "all other subsidized services" in the mines included the free firewood, electricity, and moving pictures, as well as the subsidized commissaries — it was agreed, provisionally and pending our return from Washington, to cut out the phrase "all other subsidized services." As a matter of principle, and to prevent expansion of the system of free supplies, the firewood and electricity should have been supplied at cost plus 10 per cent, but it was hardly expedient to make an issue of *this one point* which Lechín considered vital.

On two other points raised by Lechín, the President suggested that they must await the return of Dr. Eder. The two points were (1) that, in lieu of having COMIBOL pay Patiño, Aramayo, and Hochschild for nationalization of the mines, the money could come from U.S. aid, a suggestion which Lechín stated had been favorably received by former U.S. Ambassador Sparks (this seems unlikely, but there may have been a misunderstanding on the point); and (2) that it had been agreed that the miners' wage would be $1.25 (U.S.), plus compensation for the elimination of commissary privileges, but that later this was reduced without consulting COMIBOL. Minister of Mines Tamayo explained that this arose out of raising the rate of exchange from Bs. 6,000 to Bs. 7,000 and added, quite inexplicably, that at the 7,000 rate COMIBOL would be unable to pay royalties. Actually, the higher the dollar rate, the greater COMIBOL's profits should be, so long as they did not insist on calculating salaries in dollars.

On every other article in the stabilization measures, Lechín either agreed without question, or else acquiesced after discussion, as in the case of the Mining Bank where he pointed out that the stabilization decree would mean that the bank's monopoly would terminate and that it would henceforth act merely as an agent for the private mines, but he added that he was not insisting on amending the draft decree but was merely pointing out its consequences.

Report to the President and council

At 10:15 a.m. on December 11, Gisbert, Dr. Antezana, and I returned to La Paz in triumph, met by the Minister of Finance and other high officials of the government and of the U.S. Embassy, as well as by crowds of people and the ever-alert gentlemen of the press, pencil in hand, ready to take down the authentic news of the stabilization fund, rumors of which had already filtered down to La Paz. One of the first reports to reach Bolivia was a United Press dispatch from Washington, dated December 10, and signed by a young reporter, Henry Raymont, who was later to win distinction for his work in Cuba and elsewhere for the *New York Times*. He reported a $27.5 million stabilization fund (which was fairly close to the mark), and said that the boliviano would probably be stabilized at between Bs. 7,000 and Bs. 9,000 to the dollar (which was correct).

Parrying the questions of the reporters with the remark that the expressions on our faces would tell them whether or not the mission had been a success,[16] I drove directly to the presidential palace to report the results of our mission to President Siles, who was delighted with our achievements, but quite despondent over the political turmoil that had prevailed in Bolivia during and since the Congress of Factory Workers.*

He denounced the leaders of the COB as ingrates, pursuing their own selfish ends instead of cooperating with the stabilization program and with the National Revolutionary Movement to which they owed their existence. "Whenever the workers want something," he exclaimed, "they go out on strike. Now they are going to find, if they refuse to support me, that I am going out on strike too." It was hard to imagine what the President had in mind, and the explanation did not dawn on me until later, when the President actually did go out on strike — a hunger strike!

A council meeting was scheduled for that afternoon at 5:30 p.m.; it lasted until 9:00 p.m. Thereafter the council met in daily sessions for eight successive days. One meeting lasted for twelve uninterrupted hours, which were spent chiefly in ironing out the problems of the Mining Corporation that had already been settled before, again and again, and in making the final arrangements for the stabilization decrees, dated and supposedly enacted on December 15, 1956, but, by grace of a special three-day week-end holiday, corrected and recorrected over the weekend, right up to the eve of the reopening of business on December 19. Many crucial problems were discussed and decided during the course of those heavy-laden meetings — social security; the Mining Bank; import duties; export royalties; taxes on income and on revaluation of assets, alcohol and liquor, sales, admissions, rents, etc.; railroad, bus, and public utility rates; and other matters — but the only problem that immediately threatened to wreck the entire stabilization program was the ever-recurring problem of COMIBOL.

*The government paper, *La Nación*, published a front page editorial the day of our return to La Paz, denouncing a demonstration by a group of workers on the previous day and making, *inter alia*, the following comments: "The National Revolutionary Movement, governing through the mandate of the national majorities, is the first party in the history of the country which has been characterized by the free exchange of ideas in the domestic sphere.... Nevertheless, it is necessary to point out that excesses in the right to criticize positions and actions may be taken advantage of by forces outside the party and enemies of the working classes. All criticism should be restricted to that which is useful to the party.... The MNR is a party which can take legitimate pride in practicing democracy in its purest sense.... This sense of democracy makes it an imperative necessity for its party members to respect the opinion of their leaders...." This illuminating editorial is illustrative of the fact that "democracy" does not necessarily mean the same thing in all countries, but that it is all things to all men.

Mining Corporation

The Minister of Mines and the representatives of the COMIBOL management again appeared before the Stabilization Council, with new statements of account, to "prove" that COMIBOL could not pay royalties to the government; that the miners would not tolerate the wage "reduction" from an alleged, but fictitious, $1.69 a day to $1.07 a day, which would be imposed by the stabilization decree; and that, in lieu of a Bs. 19.2 billion cash surplus after taxes, that had been shown in the statements given by the Bolivian government to Washington, there would be a substantial cash deficit.

In the COMIBOL accounts, and in the statements presented to the lending agencies, this Bs. 19.2 billion figure was referred to as "net profit after taxes." In reality, it was nothing more than net cash flow, as there was no allowance for replacements, and, on the other hand, a substantial provision for the contribution to the buffer stock and for a part payment to the owners of the nationalized mines, both of which items were in the nature of capital expenditures and would not appear in a proper profit and loss account. From the viewpoint of the Stabilization Council, our immediate interest was in *cash revenues and expenditures,* although, from the longer term view of economic development, *net income,* properly computed, would have been important. The $1.69 wage cited by the Minister and the COMIBOL management is composed of the supposititious $1.25 base pay, plus an average incentive bonus of $0.31, *plus an error in the COMIBOL computations of $0.13.* See pages 222-24 for a full explanation of this "dollar" wage aberration.

Again and again during the three-day discussion of the COMIBOL accounts, the Minister of Mines and the President, as well as the COMIBOL management, would insist that the council must recognize the "realities" of the situation, yet they never seemed to grasp the reality that COMIBOL *never had paid* the miners' wages in dollars and that, in actual fact, the so-called $1.69 was paid to the miners at the rate of Bs. 1,800 to the dollar, or approximately Bs. 3,000 a day, which was then worth about 30 cents U.S. Nor could they grasp the reality that the stabilization fund financing was based on the figures that the government of Bolivia itself had presented to the lending agencies, showing balanced budgets for COMIBOL and the government, the latter being based on the expectation of Bs. 50.7 billion in royalties from COMIBOL; and, furthermore, that

COMIBOL simply did not have the wherewithal to pay the miners a base wage of $1.69 a day in hard currency.

They continued to blame the discrepancies in the accounts: (1) on the fact that their original calculations had been made at the rate of Bs. 6,000 per dollar, whereas in the statement presented to the IMF a Bs. 7,000 rate was used, without increasing wages proportionately;* and, (2) on an error made in computing their social security costs on their 1956 payrolls without allowing for the increase in the miners' base pay, under the stabilization decree, from Bs. 2,250 to Bs. 7,500.

The social security problem was in part "solved" by calling in the head of the National Social Security Administration (CNSS) who agreed that the subsidized housing tax on employers could be reduced and, more important, stated that CNSS could take care of COMIBOL's medical services for 5 per cent instead of the 16 per cent budgeted by COMIBOL. At a previous council meeting, the CNSS General Manager had stated that the Social Security Administration, because of its more efficient organization, could perform all the medical services rendered by COMIBOL for Bs. 6 billion a year in lieu of the Bs. 23 billion budgeted by COMIBOL. The council had no illusions as to the efficiency of the CNSS administration, but there was no doubt as to the utter incapacity of the COMIBOL administration, despite its capable president and general manager. The main reason for the potential economy of operation was that COMIBOL kept a full staff of doctors, supplies, etc., at each mine, ready for emergencies but usually idle, while CNSS planned to have a minimal staff at the mines, plus hospitals available in town.

Despite the doubts once expressed by the President of COMIBOL, who had said it would be "murder" to let the fund handle the medical services, this was agreed to, on paper at least. In practice, it later appeared that this arrangement merely meant a partial duplication of services — services paid for to the CNSS, and services actually rendered by COMIBOL at the mines.

*This, was, of course, the essence of the stabilization plan, that wages be fixed in bolivianos; that the dollar crossrate be fixed at a point that would enable COMIBOL to pay those wages and prevent a flight from the boliviano; and that the wages be frozen regardless of the crossrate. When, finally, the rate was fixed at Bs. 7,700 to the dollar, it meant a Bs. 51.6 billion windfall for COMIBOL on its export receipts, not calculated in the figures given to Washington. This alone should have been enough to cover royalties.

Despite the pressure of the Minister of Mines, of the COMIBOL management, and of the President himself, I could make no concession to reality — in Latin America, being "realistic" generally means bowing to political expediency and failing to face economic reality. Fortunately, I was strongly backed by four other members of the council: Gisbert, Antezana, Moreno, and Morales.

At last, thumbing through the statements of account presented by COMIBOL at the meeting, but which were not read, on the presumption that they would support the management's contentions, I discovered that the real reason for the deficit shown in the new budget statements was not a question of wages and the exchange rate, but was due to the fact that, in lieu of dismissing 6,000 surplus miners within three months, as COMIBOL and the government had promised, they were planning to dismiss 2,500 in the first semester of 1957 and 2,500 in the second. This — plus the fact that, at best, COMIBOL could only hope to make a net profit of Bs. 3 billion on its commissary sales, instead of the Bs. 10 billion originally budgeted, and that social security costs would be higher than their original miscalculation — accounted for the increased expenditures that would wipe out the previously budgeted Bs. 19.2 billion surplus.

I therefore suggested that, if the President considered that the political situation and social unrest over the past fortnight made it impossible to go ahead with the original plan to dismiss 6,000 miners without delay, it was probable that the lending agencies would understand, but that this development must be reported to Washington and that it might affect the rate of exchange. This was agreed to by all the conferees, and it was decided to enact the decree as originally drafted and to insist that COMIBOL adjust its expenditures accordingly.

This may illustrate the difference between flexibility in bowing to the inevitable, yet refusing to give way in matters of principle. If the prospective monetary stabilizer cedes ground whenever he is told that some measure is politically or socially impossible, then stabilization will probably also prove impossible; but if certain facts are accepted (as we accepted continuing government operation of COMIBOL), it will always be possible to mould a stabilization program to fit those facts, *provided that fundamental principles are not ignored.* On these, the stabilizer must be inflexible; stabilization is not a popularity contest.

The Initial Stabilization Decrees

We were committed to enact the essential stabilization measures on December 15, which was a Saturday, and each day's delay would mean the issuance of more bank notes to meet government payrolls and other unpostponable expenditures. The principal decree was completed on December 14, but it was evident that other essential first-day measures (customs duties, etc.) would not be ready until December 16, and the Cabinet could scarcely be bludgeoned into enacting all the decrees on Sunday, aside from the time necessary to print them and hand out releases to the press.

The transition to a free market economy (at least so far as prices, foreign exchange, imports and exports were concerned), after three decades of a controlled economy, was likely to be chaotic enough in the first few days of open markets, without the added confusion caused by no one's knowing what the stabilization measures actually were. Hence, the council agreed that at least the principal decree must be handed to the press on Sunday, and that on that night the President should make a radio address to the nation explaining the substance of the measures, and calling on the public to give the government its full support. It was decided to close the banks on Monday and Tuesday and to reopen the foreign exchange market on Wednesday, December 19. Dr. Antezana would explain the decrees to the bankers over the long weekend, and on Wednesday, the Central Bank would sell all the dollar exchange that might be called for at such rate as it would announce the day before, at the same time offering to buy all the foreign exchange that might be offered, likewise at the announced rate, reserving the right to raise or lower rates at will, but not to restrict sales or purchases.[17]

The four essential stabilization decrees, all bearing the official date December 15, 1956, were enacted with the force of law under the enabling act of November 22, 1956 (Appendix II). The separation of the three auxiliary decrees from the stabilization decree itself made it possible to amend the former as the need arose, without conveying the impression that piecemeal modification of the latter would be permissible. The full text of the decrees is contained in the 28th *Annual Report* (1956) of the Central Bank (Banco Central de Bolivia, *Informe Anual* [La Paz, 1956], pp. 105-22).

Decree 4538: The Stabilization Decree [18]
(actually enacted December 16, 1956)

Chapter I removed all restrictions and controls on
foreign exchange; established a single rate of exchange for
the Bolivian peso in terms of U.S. dollars, applicable to all
foreign exchange transactions in *devisen* or *valuta;* stipulated that the Central Bank would fix the rate at which it
would buy and sell freely convertible *devisen* to the government, government enterprises, commercial banks, exchange houses, and the public.

Chapter II provided that anyone could export and import domestic or foreign merchandise freely, without permits, paying only the established import and export duties
or royalties, and obtaining consular invoices and statistical
forms, subject only to restrictions imposed by international
agreements (e.g., opium, etc.) or government contracts
(e.g., petroleum concessions, etc.) or laws affecting the
artistic treasures of the nation; exports and imports subject to international treaties to be governed by such treaties so long as they remain in force; exports of the national
and municipal governments, and of government enterprises,
to be sold for dollars or freely convertible currency (except as otherwise governed by treaty), and the *devisen,* less
expenses, to be sold to the Central Bank; *devisen* from
other exports (i.e., in the private sector) to be sold to the
Central Bank, private banks, or authorized exchange houses,
and to be freely disposed of; governmental imports to be
limited to the most urgent necessities, subject to the foreign exchange budget and under the control of the Finance
Ministry and Central Bank; subsidized imports and subsidized import prices to be abolished, except that the Ministry of Economy might continue to import basic necessities
until private commerce could supply the market; the private mines to be free to import, at their option, through the
Mining Bank, through private importers, or directly; customs duties to be computed at the rate of exchange prevailing at the time of payment even though the merchandise
may have arrived in customs prior to the date of the decree.

Chapter III provided for elimination of all controls
over the prices of goods and services, except that the national government should immediately authorize rate increases for government, municipal, and private utilities
sufficient to cover operating expenses, depreciation, and a
fair return on the present value of the investment, such

rates to be provisional and to be readjusted within not over six months; the system of *revertibles* to be abolished except with respect to imports made prior to the date of the decree.

Chapter IV abolished the subsidized commissaries in the national mines and increased the miners' wages by Bs. 3,950 a day in compensation, plus Bs. 1,300 "for the change in the exchange rate" (with certain specified exceptions); COMIBOL to fix commissary prices at cost plus 10 per cent under Law of November 6, 1945; the production bonus to be limited to 50 per cent of actual profits from increased production; COMIBOL to be allowed to dispose of its foreign exchange for its requirements only within the limits of the foreign exchange budget; COMIBOL to pay the same royalties on exports as the private mines.

Chapter V provided that the Mining Bank would be the sole ore buyer *(rescatador)* within Bolivia, and that the small mines must sell their production exclusively to the Mining Bank, but that the medium-sized mines might freely export their production direct when the prices offered by the Mining Bank were less than they could obtain from a foreign buyer; existing sales contracts for the medium-sized mines to be transferred to them, and such mines to assume the buffer stock obligations; the Mining Bank to pay all producers in free foreign exchange, less expenses; gold to be exported through the Mining Bank except as otherwise provided by contract;* the Mining Bank to be required to purchase and sell foreign exchange through the Central Bank, and its deposits to be frozen except as authorized by the Finance Ministry on the recommendation of the Stabilization Council; contributions to the buffer stock on shipments made by the Mining Bank to be paid by the Central Bank and the tin to be held for account of the government; *remanentes* arising out of prior sales of ore to the Mining Bank to be paid to the producers in dollars at the exchange

---

*As a consequence of continued irregularities in the operation of the government Mining Bank, although $2.35 million of gold was sold to that bank in 1963 by some 48 small mines organized as cooperatives under strict controls, it is estimated that $2.5 million was sold illegally to other buyers for higher prices (*Hispanic American Report,* XVII [August, 1964], 548). It would be difficult to estimate how far the Mining Bank monopoly on the exports of small mines has reduced production of other minerals which are more difficult to smuggle out of the country. The contract referred to is one entered into with a subsidiary of South American Gold & Platinum Company (now merged with International Mining Corporation).

rate in effect at the time of payment, and all pending sales of ore and supplies to be at the current exchange rate.

Chapter VI abolished the subsidized commissaries in the private mines, and government and private railways, the workers to be paid Bs. 1,350 a day for loss of that privilege, plus Bs. 1,300 "for the change in the exchange rate" (with certain specified exceptions); factory workers and others who had previously had subsidized commissaries to be paid Bs. 450 and Bs. 1,300, respectively; and government and other workers (except for bank employees and domestic servants) to be paid only the Bs. 1,300 "for the change in the exchange rate."

Chapter VII provided for a 200 per cent increase in residential rents (four rooms and over), and 400 per cent in business rentals.

Chapter VIII provided for an all-inclusive budget for the national government and all national government enterprises and agencies, surpluses of such enterprises and agencies to go to the national Treasury, and deficits to be paid for by the Treasury within budgetary limits; all governmental borrowing from the Central Bank to cease; the foreign exchange budget of the nation to include the entire government sector and private sector (but no restriction on the latter); and any surplus in the government foreign exchange budget to go: (1) up to $3 million per annum to COMIBOL, for exploration and development, out of any increased revenues arising from tin prices in excess of 90 cents a pound; (2) up to 50 per cent of the surplus to go to the Central Bank to build up a monetary reserve; (3) the remainder to be used as decided by the Cabinet on the advice of the Stabilization Council.

Chapter IX authorized the Finance Ministry, through the Superintendency of Banks, to fix the legal reserve ratios of the banking (commercial) department of the Central and other government banks, and of private banks, as well as the ratio between deposits and capital-plus-reserves; all governmental accounts, including U.S. aid counterpart funds, to be transferred from the banking department of the Central Bank to the monetary department.

Chapter X provided that employers would pay the National Social Security Administration 30 per cent of the amount of the *new payrolls* for illness and maternity, professional risks, old age, disability, death, family subsidy, and cheap housing (this was an actuarial estimate, leaving the actual percentages to be computed in each case — deplorable draftsmanship, but time was pressing); the employees' contribution likewise to be computed on the *new payrolls;* the new payrolls to include the cheap commissary and "foreign exchange compensation"; all wages to be frozen for one year in both the government and private sectors; vacancies in the civil service to be filled only with the authorization of the Finance Ministry; neither the government nor any government enterprise to be permitted to enter into any credit contract for the supply of materials and equipment without prior authorization of the President of the Republic; the Central Bank to be prohibited from guaranteeing any bill of exchange or other credit instrument without approval of the Cabinet and on the advice of the Stabilization Council. All laws, decrees, and legal provisions contrary to the present decree repealed.

Decree 4539: Import Duties[19]
(actually enacted December 19, 1956)

This was the new customs tariff. It provided for criminal penalties as well as fines; for the same rates of duty to be paid by the government, government enterprises, and municipalities, as by the private sector (certain merchandise, such as military equipment could, in theory at least, only be imported by the government, and was free of duty).

Decree 4540: Mineral Export Royalties[20]
(actually enacted December 26, 1956)

This decree established sliding scales of export taxes or royalties on ore exports.

Decree 4541: Miscellaneous Export Taxes[21]
(actually enacted December 16, 1956)

This decree imposed export duties on hides (10 per cent), cattle on the hoof (12 per cent), horses and mules (15 per cent), meat (10 per cent), wool (15 per cent), other animal products (5 per cent), rubber (6 per cent), Brazil nuts and almonds (10 per cent), boards (5 per cent), ties and posts (10 per cent), timber (15 per cent), coca leaves (10 per cent), coffee (10 per cent), other vegetable products (8 per cent), gold and silver manufactures (5 per cent), vicuña textiles and manufactures (5 per cent), alpaca and llama textiles and manufactures (3 per cent), other manufactures (5 per cent). (Note: I was opposed to these export taxes, but deferred to the strongly held convictions of the other council members.)

Establishing the Rate of Exchange

The only problem remaining, which had to be left to the eleventh hour, was the crucial one of fixing the opening rate of exchange. At a meeting of the council on December 13, the President had stated that a very serious problem for him would be created if the rate were higher than Bs. 7,000 to the dollar; that he had to cope with the anxiety and responsibility of making a decision in the face of the opposition of the Vice-President and President of the Senate (Chávez and Lechín); and that the council must be "realistic" and recognize that if the rate were fixed above Bs. 7,000 he could not get the support of his Cabinet. I pointed out that the principal reason for requiring a higher rate was not an error in the IMF calculations, as the Minister of Economy insisted, but the delay in promulgating the stabilization decrees, which had meant continued issues of bank notes. I further urged that we be realistic and recognize that the situation was no longer that which existed when Washington had approved a loan, with a rate of exchange then tentatively established at Bs. 7,000 to the dollar.

It was pointed out that there had been a seven-day delay in issuing the decrees; an increase in COMIBOL salaries (which had come up at the same meeting); and a continued rise in bank note circulation. If, in spite of those circumstances, the Bolivian government insisted on maintaining the Bs. 7,000 rate, the impression in Washington would be that it was the Bolivian government that was not being realistic. The rate of exchange, it was emphasized, was not something that could be fixed arbitrarily but must obey the forces of supply and demand.

That did not end the matter. Two days later, on December 15, the President attempted to impress me and one of my colleagues with the gravity of the situation from a political point of view. I assured him that I fully realized his difficult position, but that the note circulation had expanded from Bs. 136 billion, at the time the Bolivian petition was presented in Washington with a proposed rate of Bs. 7,000, to Bs. 165 billion. On a mathematical basis, Washington might decide that the rate would have to be Bs. 8,500, whereas, taking all factors into consideration, my colleagues and I were thinking of something like Bs. 7,800.*

Faced with the possibility of an even higher rate, the President gave up the struggle and in the end it turned out that, although Lechín at first berated Siles and the council for fixing the rate as high as Bs. 7,750, when the initial computations had been made at Bs. 6,000, he was denouncing the council a year later for not having fixed the rate even higher, and he actually drove it up to between Bs. 11,000 and Bs. 12,000 as a result of his wage demands for the miners. Thus it seems evident that, regardless of the rate, Siles' enemies would not have been satisfied. On the other hand, it is certain that, if the President had insisted on maintaining a fixed Bs. 7,000 rate despite changing circumstances, the Treasury would have refused to go ahead on its stand-by arrangement, and probably ICA and IMF would have followed suit.

At the final Stabilization Council meeting, on the eve of the opening of the banks and of the foreign exchange market, after full discussion of all aspects of the matter, the council adopted an opening rate of Bs. 7,700 on dollar purchases and Bs. 7,750 on dollar sales. The Central Bank issued an announcement, dated that same day (December 18), which appeared in the morning papers on December 19, announcing that it would buy and sell foreign exchange at those rates at the commencement of operations, without requiring import or export permits or any other formality, except for filling out a simple statistical application form. A ten-point spread was allowed as a wholesale rate for transactions between the Central Bank and the private banks and exchange houses, i.e., rates of Bs. 7,710 and Bs. 7,740.[22]

We were in business. Monetary stabilization was an accomplished fact!

---

*This was a simple slide-rule computation which I made in front of the President to carry conviction. Obviously, the computation of a viable rate of exchange — one that would protect the fund and make possible a balanced COMIBOL and government budget and balance of payments — is not as simple as that. My use of a pocket slide-rule, however, appeared to be a justifiable simplification to prevent almost certain disaster, as there could be no doubt whatsoever as to Washington's attitude.

14

STABILIZATION ACHIEVED

Even before the first stabilization decrees appeared in the papers on December 17, the President's Sunday night radio address to the nation brought forth pledges of support from labor and other groups in all sections of the country. The press throughout the rest of that week was full of declarations of "adherence" to the stabilization program, from the unions of chauffeurs, farmers, cooks, miners of various mining "cells," and oil company workers, as well as from the National Manufacturers Association, the National Chamber of Commerce, and others. [23]

The President's speech outlined the course of the inflation which, had it been left unchecked, would have brought the boliviano to 25,000 to the dollar by the end of the year, a development which would havè meant a still higher cost of living for the working classes. He stressed that there was *no other way* to stem the inflationary tide than that adopted by his government, and he expressed his gratitude to the government and people of the United States, to the International Monetary Fund, and to me personally for our cooperation in finding a solution. Finally, he besought the loyal support of all Bolivians for the program, admitting, to his regret, that stabilization would not immediately improve their lot but that at least it would not worsen their situation and that the only ones who would suffer from the change would be the speculators, the *cuperos,* the smugglers — all those who had been accustomed to "living in idleness, trafficking in prices and confusion." [24] (*Cuperos,* from *cupo* or quota, are persons who, through privilege or graft, receive or deal in permits for food, imports, or U.S. aid commodities.)

From Hell to Christmas

From the moment the markets opened on Monday — when "all hell broke loose," as a U.S. Embassy official put it — to Christmas eve, the following Monday, by which time the "miracle" of stabilization had taken place, events had run the gamut from panic to hope, from the first two days when it seemed that all was lost, to the advent of a new "renaissance of faith," as one of the La Paz papers described the event.[25] Truly, monetary stabilization is no sport for the faint-hearted!

The markets open

On Monday, in all the Indian markets in La Paz, and in similar markets throughout the country, the air was charged with expectancy and uncertainty. Only two days before, as narrated in Chapter 1, the city's supplies of food and other necessities were virtually nonexistent, except at the official trading posts where meagre stocks of meat, bread, cigarettes, or other commodities could be purchased at the absurdly low official prices, provided one had the fortitude to wait two hours in endless queues in the hope that *perhaps* some stock might still be available by the time one reached the front of the line. Or one could buy a place in line from the *coleros,* the professional waiters-in-line who had been squatting on the pavement all night long for just that purpose. Then, of course, there were the black markets where, if one had the cash, it *might* be possible to find a fly-covered chunk of meat at Bs. 8,000-Bs. 10,000 a kilo (say 40-50 cents a pound), or some other commodity at equally outrageous prices.

With the almost overnight transition from a controlled to a free market economy, would food be available in the market stalls?   And at what prices?   The old, subsidized prices — Bs. 240 per kilo of meat (say 1 cent a pound) or Bs. 30 a loaf of bread (say 3 loaves for 1 cent) — were out of the question. Would the shopkeepers continue to charge the old black-market prices and, if so, would the Indian and chola housewives stand for it? Would prestabilization chaos be followed by poststabilization riots and bloodshed? We did not have to wait long for an answer.*

---

*Of course, it is simple to say that the transition might have been made easier by a proper use of the radio and press to explain to the public the causes of the inflation, the measures that were being taken to end it, and the consequences that could be expected, immediately and over the long run. Undoubtedly, that is what a monetary stabilizer should advise the government to do, but for months I had been butting my head against a wall of political caution, and was unable to persuade the President to engage in a campaign of explanation — which would, of course, have publicly discredited everything the MNR Government had done in the previous four years. Where a stabilization program is initiated by a government that has broken with the past, a public information campaign might be easier,

The Tuesday morning papers carried the story — flour, tea, sardines, canned milk, rice, tinned meat, oats, bran, tires, all beginning to come out of the dealers' stores and from under the shelves under the influence of free prices, timidly at first and at prices approaching the previous black-market levels. One paper reported, with a show of confidence which it could hardly have felt, that prices would undoubtedly go down under the influence of supply and demand, that the larger merchants had full confidence in the ultimate results of the stabilization program, but that there was an undeniable feeling of uncertainty among the general public.[26]

At the Stabilization Council meeting that day, the Finance Minister reported that on Monday there had been an attack on the shopkeepers in the *Mercado Lanza,* one of the two largest Indian markets in La Paz, not by the housewives, but *by the smugglers.* Apparently, the shopkeepers, who were accustomed to receiving U.S. aid commodities and other subsidized merchandise from the *cuperos* and political traffickers, and to selling the merchandise to the smugglers for shipment to Peru or Chile, now found that they could get better prices by selling directly to the public without the danger and graft involved in black-marketing or smuggling. The smugglers, deprived of their livelihood, retaliated in force.*

---

as it would not be operating under those inhibitions. The two occasions when President Siles did address the public proved most effective, but there was never any consistent program of information in support of the stabilization measures, either by the President or by members of his Cabinet, and this may be adjudged one of the shortcomings of the stabilization program.

Or one might argue — not very convincingly — that a tapering off policy rather than an abrupt end to galloping inflation might be easier to take. "The answer...is that a gradual approach is fraught with more danger than sudden stabilization" (Dorrance, "The Effect of Inflation Upon Economic Development " [*IMF Staff Papers,* March, 1963], p. 29). The termination of a period of hyperinflation is bound to produce serious imbalances, tensions, and hardships, which are more pronounced the longer the antecedent era of inflation, and the more exaggerated the distortions of that period. No nation can be expected to endure a protracted period of painful readjustment, whereas a sharp break from hyperinflation has an almost anaesthetic effect. No nation, so far as can be recalled, has ever successfully terminated a rampant inflation by a gradual approach, and in Bolivia it simply would not have worked.

*A few days later, our cook — a splendid, pure Indian type, and a former active member of the smugglers' league (engaged in the transportation of bread and other merchandise across Lake Titicaca to Peru) — asked

The Minister of Economy reported to the council that he had worked out the prices at which the Ministry could sell the stocks of commodities — U.S. aid and other — that it had on hand, for example, meat at Bs. 4,000 a kilo, bread at Bs. 300 a loaf, but that he was afraid the distributors to whom the Ministry sold might charge exorbitant prices, and he wondered if the Ministry should impose controls on the resale prices.* My reply was that the only prices that should be fixed were the prices at which the government itself sold commodities or rendered services and the rates for public utility services, and that these prices and rates should be high enough to cover costs, as the council had agreed. All other prices should be left to the forces of supply and demand. The council should remain absolutely firm on that point because, if it started to cede ground in one instance, it would have to give way in others, and the country would soon be back where it was between 1953 and 1956.

The council members knew from experience that controls do not work, that they lead only to corruption and black-marketing, and I ventured the prediction that, within three or four months at the most, there would be an abundance of supplies of every kind, and at substantially lower prices. This prediction was based on four factors: (1) that the 35 per cent or more of commodities which were being smuggled out of the country under the artificial price system would no longer be exported, meaning an *immediate* 50 per cent increase in available supplies; (2) that "demand" in the economic sense means *effective demand* and that, at current prices, the bulk of the population did not have enough money, even with the increase in

---

me to speak with a friend of hers at the gate. It then turned out that the friend was a smuggler in distress, with a stock of cigarettes that he had purchased only a week before from a *cupero* who refused to take back the merchandise. He had sold a few cartons on Monday at a profit, but now people could buy cigarettes anywhere at less than he had paid the *cupero*. Considering the cook's many friends in the smuggling trade, I could scarcely take over the poor fellow's stock in trade at cost, as he begged me to do, so I suggested that he sell out as fast as he could and get into some other line of business.

*The ministry had been accustomed to turn U.S. aid flour over to certain politically favored bakers at the absurdly low official prices, receiving bread which it sold to favored dealers for distribution. This was the principal source, not only of the smuggled and black-marketed bread, but of the flour that entered the market illegally for consumption or export, for probably never before in history has so much flour produced so little bread.

wages, to convert their desires into effective demand; (3) that with everyone in the country free to import whatever he wanted from wherever he wanted, prices could not long remain above world market levels, plus transportation; and (4) that, with the Indians unable to earn a living as *coleros* or smugglers, they would soon return to their farms and start producing crops.

There was little hope of an early recovery of local industry as an immediate source of increased supplies, as most of the local manufacturers had been dependent on imported raw materials at impossibly low, subsidized prices. There were exceptions, of course, and those industries which were capable of competing in a free market economy could be counted upon to do so.

Manuel Gisbert, himself a manufacturer, supported these arguments, and said prices would level off over the next 30 days. Ernest Moore, of the U.S. Financial Advisory Mission, likewise spoke from experience of the futility of price controls, but suggested that prices be published and conspicuously posted in order to step up competition. The idea of posting prices as a means of stimulating competition was later taken up enthusiastically by Ernest Moore's namesake in the U.S. Operations Mission, Ross Moore. Such action would be desirable wherever possible, although the local political environment and mores must, of course, be taken into account.

The council members were reluctant, however, to go ahead with that proposition, doubtless because, to them personally, the new price levels seemed so outrageously high that they felt it would be impolitic even to recognize their existence. However, they all, including the Minister of Economy, agreed that any form of price control would be "counterproductive" and that, if the stabilization program were to succeed, the free market economy must be given a chance.*

---

*"Counterproductive" — *contraproducente*. What a common and useful word this is in Spanish — something that produces an effect contrary to what one intended. Yet "counterproductive" does not appear in Merriam-Webster's *Third International*, and there is no satisfactory substitute. As in the case of *simpático*, which is equally untranslatable into English, it must be admitted that every nation's language provides the words that are most essential to its needs, and certainly in the Hispanic countries — the most *simpático* people in the world — the word *contraproducente* is indispensable, for their governments are always committing some blunder that is desperately counterproductive.

By Tuesday afternoon, certain organs of the press were dubious of the outcome — the change to free prices had been too sudden, people were alarmed, and the government as well as the Stabilization Council should consider taking emergency measures to bring real prices into harmony with real wage levels. [27] Where such a course would lead us — whether we tampered with prices or tampered with wages — may well be imagined.

The Embassy alarmed

The following day, Wednesday, December 19, which was the day the banks reopened after the two-day bank holiday, I was summoned to the U.S. Embassy for a full-dress conference on the problems arising out of the stabilization measures. The CIA representative at the meeting reported rioting in the market places; in some cases the Indian and chola women, outraged by the new price levels, had got out of hand and assaulted the shopkeepers. There was unrest and uncertainty everywhere. The labor attaché reported that labor union leaders were dissatisfied with the wage increases, and that there was mounting discontent from the rank and file. The Economic Counsellor of the Embassy suggested that price controls be instituted and a number of features of the stabilization program abandoned. Following the summing up from his staff, the Ambassador concluded that *something* had to be done immediately, the situation could not be allowed to get out of hand — and he turned to me to ask what I proposed doing.

To say that I was astounded would be putting it mildly, but I was not dumbfounded. I explained vehemently and *in extenso* that, after a quarter of a century of price controls, it was too much to expect a return to a free market economy in the space of forty-eight hours without some friction, and that the only thing I proposed to do, so far as prices were concerned, was to await developments. Meanwhile, the Stabilization Council had a great many urgent matters to occupy its time, including the passage of a number of tax bills and other measures that we had under consideration. I added that the Bolivian members of the council had considered, and rejected, the idea of price controls the day before, and had resolved to go ahead with the stabilization program *exactly as drafted* and as presented to the IMF and other agencies as a basis for their financial assistance. I added that I had no power to vote at the council, but merely to give advice, and I certainly did not intend to advise departing from the program the very day that we had put it into effect with the reopening of the foreign exchange market, particularly as it was absolutely certain that Washington would withdraw its support if there were any fundamental change in the stabilization arrangements. With that, I turned to the head of the U.S. Operations Mission and asked his opinion as to what the position of the ICA in Washington would be if Bolivia were to impose price or any other controls at this time, and thus abandon the basic principles of the stabilization program.

Ross Moore rose loyally to the occasion and, whereas I had doubtless contributed more heat than light to the discussion, and had been so impertinent as to advise the Ambassador that "the best thing to do is to do nothing, and not to panic," Moore managed to calm the gathering storm and to persuade the conferees that it would be advisable to wait another forty-eight hours at least, and that Washington might look askance at any recommendations to alter the program the very day it went into effect.

Later, on April 3, 1957, on the eve of the Ambassador's departure from Bolivia, when the stabilization program had proved a success, the Ambassador told me that he had sent the State Department a "bushel of suggestions," gathered from all members of the Embassy staff, as to what ought to be done; but, he added, they never paid any attention to his message. That, at least, was one case where the State Department technique of euthanasia by committee (see p. 146n) seems to have proved a blessing, for it was one case where doing nothing was the proper thing to do.

This episode is narrated at length, because it is thought that this account may be enlightening to any future monetary stabilizer or economic developer, as revealing the kind of crisis one is apt to face on such a mission. What might have happened if the Ambassador had been a political appointee, with direct communication to the President of the United States, had best be left to the imagination.

It must be borne in mind that the American Ambassador and staff in Bolivia were not amateurs or political appointees, but highly trained and competent career officers of the American Foreign Service, at least as intelligent as their counterparts in the foreign service of any other nation — in short, members of a corps of international experts of whom the American public may well be proud.

But to expect the expertise of the Foreign Service to extend to such matters as commercial and central banking, finance, investment, industry, commerce, public utility management, taxation, tax administration, fiscal budgeting and organization — from the practical and not merely the theoretical point of view — in short, to expect a comprehension of all the various aspects of a monetary stabilization or economic development program would be to ask the impossible. It is thus the duty of an economic or monetary adviser to keep the Ambassador so informed of his plans and program that he can count upon full support at all times, assuming, as was the case in Bolivia, that the U.S. government would be expected to foot the bill. This, again, points up the need for the adviser to have an adequate and competent staff of his own choosing, so that he will have time to keep the Ambassador abreast of events. It also emphasizes above all the importance of direct personal contact between the adviser and the Secretary of State (or, at the least, an Under Secretary), to prevent the lines of communication with Washington from getting fouled up in the red tape of State Department committees. *No top economic or monetary adviser should ever leave Washington without having first established such connection.*

Within the course of the next few weeks, however, I had the satisfaction of having each of the conferees at the Embassy meeting come in turn to express their confidence and pleasure in the way the stabilization program was working out. From then on, I received at all times the most gratifying support and assistance of the American Ambassador and the Embassy and USOM staff — this despite the fact that on several occasions the Embassy expressed considerable concern when my duties as an adviser took me into that nebulous field where fiscal policy is inseparable from politics and corruption.

Rumblings of discontent

That same day, President Siles summoned me to a private conference, not so much to ask advice, for the President stated that he was firmly committed to the stabilization program and intended to carry it through, come what may, but to tell me something of the troubles that were brewing behind the scene.

Lechín, and others of the opposition within the MNR party, had signed a declaration of the National Political Committee of the MNR on the preceding day, giving their full and unqualified support to the stabilization program,[28] but their agreement was reluctant and brought about largely through the forceful pressure of one of the President's loyal supporters, José Cuadros-Quiroga, Minister of Agriculture and Secretary General of the committee, a self-effacing but courageous man and one of the true heroes of the stabilization. Since then, however, there had been word that some of the left-wing mine leaders — Trotskyites, according to the President — and their counterparts in other unions, had been stirring up discontent among the *bases*, the Indian and cholo rank and file, which in turn would be reflected in the attitude of the "cell" leaders and the delegates to the forthcoming national soviet of the COB.

As has been iterated, Bolivia's labor leaders invariably wait to see which direction their followers are going before they start to lead them, and Lechín, it appears, was maneuvering to see where the majority would stand, in order not to be left out on a limb at the December 27 *ampliado* (soviet) — a leader with no followers.

The President stated that the House of Deputies had drawn up a list of twenty-nine loaded questions on the stabilization program which would have to be answered by the council, and he asked me to draft a memorandum to serve as a basis for the council's reply. Again the President spoke of going out on strike if the MNR and the COB failed to back him, and again I failed to grasp the significance of the President's words as, in all my experience in Latin America, I had never before run into a hunger strike. Going hungry never seemed an appropriate method of giving vent to one's feelings in Argentina or Colombia, or any other country where I had previously lived and worked.

Again, I urged the President to embark on a program of public information, with radio speeches and newspaper releases by him and members of his Cabinet, and pointed out that opposition was just beginning to develop at this point — that it would become far worse when the political leaders, whose influence had theretofore depended on their ability to hand out import and distribution quotas and other privileges, discovered that the stabilization measures had deprived them of a means of political livelihood.

In this connection, I recounted how, in the United States, after prohibition had built up crime as big business on a national scale, repeal had left the bootleggers with their huge gangster organizations, but with no business. The result was that they turned their criminal proclivities to horse racing, gambling, "protection," labor racketeering, and the corruption of state and municipal governments.

Unless steps were taken to prevent it, the same unholy alliance between politics and crime was bound to take place in Bolivia although in different directions. The *cuperos,* black marketeers, smugglers, labor leaders, and *políticos* would find themselves with their well-armed, well-organized national partnerships — and no business. As no private business was big enough to make it worth while moving in on, I prophesied that they would turn to the purchasing departments of COMIBOL and other government enterprises and, for that purpose, they would find it necessary to repeal the stabilization program with its rigorously controlled budgets and unitary rate of exchange. The only way for the President to prevent that would be for him to act first, *and immediately.* He should inaugurate a well-organized public relations program to get the great masses of the people so solidly behind him that no one would dare oppose him.

The President seemed to appreciate the enthusiasm, but nothing — or very little — came of the suggestion. Even later, when the perfidy of his enemies had become evident and the President had won a crushing victory over his adversaries, he refused to take advantage of their defeat to discredit them — as he could have done — by revealing that they had given their approval in advance to the stabilization program which they later attempted to repudiate. Nevertheless, he was determined not to let street riots and disturbances, fomented by his opponents, strike down the program before it had even had a chance to develop, and that afternoon he had his Minister of Government, Arturo Fortún-Sanjinés, announce a continuation of the state of siege which had been in effect since the September riots. A state of siege, common in Latin America, means the suspension of the constitutional guaranties of freedom of speech, press, assembly, etc., falling short of the rigors of martial law.[29]

The council carries on

Meanwhile, the Stabilization Council had a heavy legislative drafting schedule ahead of it in order to complete the many tax and other measures that were needed in the stabilization program but that could not be drafted and enacted by the December 15 deadline. There were a number of loose ends to be tied up in connection with certain aspects of fiscal policy and the finances of the various government enterprises, as well as in such troublesome matters as the unused *remanentes* and *re-vertibles* — the heritage of a controlled economy that had to be abandoned with the change to a free market economy. At the same time, the council could not ignore the political problems that beset it from the outset and that could only be tackled by a policy of public information.

To handle the work load, the council met six days a week throughout December (except for Christmas day), tapering off to an average of 3.3 meetings a week during the first three months of 1957.

Political problems. In the political and public relations field, Gisbert and the Ministers of Mines and Economy reported, at the first poststabilization meeting, numerous complaints and suggestions from labor and from business. The former complaints bore chiefly on the alleged inadequacy of the wage increases in the face of the high prices prevailing during the first two days of a free market, while the latter related to the "immovability" of labor — the fact that employers were not permitted to dismiss excess workers in the face of declining business.

In order to lessen the burden of replying to the flow of correspondence, I suggested it might be wise to announce that the council would be glad to entertain suggestions from all sections of the public; that it could not undertake to acknowledge any communications but that all suggestions would receive the consideration they deserved.*

The Bolivian members of the council promptly vetoed this suggestion on the ground that there was no use asking for trouble. They were unmoved by the thought that, with the new higher postage rates, the incoming mail would help balance the budget. I then launched into the same plea for an intensive campaign of public information that I had broached to President Siles the day before. As the President was not present at the meeting, it was suggested that they should all implant the idea that Siles was not only a hero in the April 9 Revolution and in the Chaco War, but the "Hero of the Stabilization" — that the campaign must make an emotional appeal to patriotic pride as well as a factual appeal to men's minds. The council was wholly in

---

*Hjalmar Schacht, under similar conditions in Germany, gave a like assurance, and promptly consigned all incoming mail to the wastebasket (*The Stabilization of the Mark*, p. 97). For the first time, it proved an advantage that the majority of the population in Bolivia were illiterates.

agreement with this suggestion, but, aside from the opening gun in the campaign, referred to below, and an occasional speech, we never succeeded in persuading the President of the necessity of a consistent and continuing program of public information.

As requested by President Siles, I did write a long memorandum in answer to the following five questions posed by the President and the Minister of Mines:

1. Can wages or additional compensation be raised at this time?
2. Can the exchange rate be reduced, say to Bs. 6,000, in order to bring prices down?
3. Can prices of articles of prime necessity be reduced or controlled?
4. Would it be possible to increase the stabilization fund to $30 million in order to reduce the rate from Bs. 7,700 to Bs. 6,000?
5. Would it be possible to promise the workers an increase in wages or a reduction in the exchange rate in the near future, or any other change in the stabilization decrees that would improve the lot of the working man?

The answers, of course, were in the nature of an explanation in simple terms of the background of inflation, the meaning of the stabilization process, and the hopes for the future that rested on a return to a free market economy, stressing the fact that prosperity was simply another word for abundance; that neither higher wages, nor price controls, nor any other government action could create abundance; that abundance could only come from increased production; that increased production could only result from hard work by labor in the farms, mines, and factories; and that increased production would automatically bring about lower prices, higher real wages, and real prosperity.[30]

The letter was released to *La Nación*, the government paper, as background material with instructions not to attribute it to its author. It was shortly thereafter published under the guise of supposed interviews with unnamed members of the council.[31] The substance of the letter was then completely rewritten by the Ministers of Mines and Economy, with supplementary data furnished by the president of the Central Bank on the causes of inflation, and a final draft was issued as an answer to the twenty-nine questions raised by the House of Deputies.

Wages and labor. The Minister of Labor appeared before the council to report that the Bs. 1,300 wage increase given to all sectors of the economy was too low and should be increased to Bs. 1,670 and, further, that the Bs. 450 compensation for loss of commissary privileges given to the factory employees should be extended to all workers, whether or not they had formerly enjoyed the privilege of subsidized company stores. He also stated that the railway workers were dissatisfied with the Bs. 1,350 that they were allowed for loss of commissary privileges, which compared unfavorably with the Bs. 3,950 given to the miners in the government mining corporation. He added that the petitions for wage increases presented by employees of the Bolivian Development Corporation, as well as by workers in two private factories, should be attended to, as they had been filed prior to stabilization.[32]

The President expressed the unanimous view of the council that no such increases could be allowed. The head of the Planning Commission pointed out, however, that a number of factories which, prior to stabilization, were required by law to maintain subsidized company stores had failed to do so, and that it would be unfair to the companies which had complied with the law to be compelled to grant the Bs. 450 compensation, while the violators were exempt. The stabilization decree provided that "manufacturing and other companies that maintained company stores at subsidized prices" must grant the Bs. 450 increase.[33] He suggested, and the council unanimously concurred, that the Labor Ministry should interpret that provision as meaning that all companies which had, *or by law should have had,* subsidized commissaries would be required to pay that additional compensation.

The Minister of Public Works then said that this interpretation should apply to all government employees, as the civil servants should also have enjoyed cheap commissary privileges. The Finance Minister rejected this construction on the ground that the budget simply could not stand the increase. He might have added that the stabilization decree left no room for interpretation, as it expressly provided that civil servants, "and others not included in the foregoing articles," would receive only the general increase of Bs. 1,300.[34] The Minister of Mines, who was aware of the Labor Minister's intentions and knew that the Federation of Butchers had become affiliated with the railway workers' union, stressed that the benefits for the railway workers must be confined to actual workers on the railways and

that the decree covered only those workers *who actually had,
or by law should have had,* cheap commissary privileges. (As
will be seen later, the Minister of Labor insisted on stretching
the decree to include not only the butchers but many others,
in direct violation of Bolivia's commitments to the lending
agencies.)

After the visiting ministers had left, I expressed the fear
that the railway workers' claim for higher compensation which
had appeared in the newspapers, *signed by the Minister of
Labor,* would give all labor groups the impression that wage increases were supported by the Cabinet. I added that I had been
equally disturbed by newspaper reports that the government
railways had placed a substantial order for locomotives to be
manufactured in Japan, despite the fact that the council had expressly excluded all such equipment orders from the railroad
budget, and that the foreign exchange budget would not permit
any further strain. The President replied with a smile that
these reports were on paper only and would go no further. This
did not prove to be the case (see p. 411).

The Mining Bank and the private mines. The Minister of
Mines brought up a problem that had arisen in connection with
imports of equipment, supplies, and other merchandise by the
government Mining Bank. Apparently, a good part of such goods
had been bought at high prices which included exorbitant profits
and flagrant graft. So long as the merchandise entered the
country at the official rates of exchange, the prices charged by
the Mining Bank to the private mines were still well below
world market prices, but the private mines now refused to take
the goods at prices which, at the new rate of exchange, were
greatly in excess of world prices. The Mining Bank was thus
stuck with a number of pending orders placed with foreign suppliers — in some cases with the merchandise en route to Bolivia
— which it would be unable to sell.

There was no problem there, I replied — if the government
could prove fraud, it could annul the contracts on the interna-
tionally acceptable legal basis that a contract grounded in fraud
is void *ab initio* — *ex dolo malo non oritur acto,* as Lord Mansfield had said in *Holman* vs *Johnson,* 1 Cowp. 343 [1775].

I suggested that the Mining Bank should give the council a
statement with the full facts on all such orders, and that it could
then be decided whether the order should be cancelled, or the
goods returned to the shipper or sold by the government at
competitive prices. As was to be expected, nothing further

came of this suggestion, as the Mining Bank operations involved the leading figures in the previous regime, and the change in the administration was at the top only — it was still the National Revolutionary Movement government. It was agreed, however, that orders not already placed with foreign suppliers should be withdrawn, and that, on the orders that had been placed, the Mining Bank should confer with the private mines to determine which orders they wished cancelled.

The private miners did have certain justifiable, or at least plausible, further grounds for complaint, which the president of the National Mining Association voiced in a newspaper interview that was, in those busy days, as good a way as any of getting the matter before the council, and took less of our time than would a formal hearing. The complaint centered on three points:[35]

1. They contended that the small mining enterprises should be given the same freedom as the medium-sized ones, to deal with the Mining Bank or not, at their option.*

2. They insisted that royalties be charged on the basis of net profits and not on gross revenues from exports. In this, they were supported by the Ford, Bacon & Davis report, but with all deference to the expertise of FBD in mining matters, the members of the Stabilization Council knew that, if the tax were levied on net profits, there would be no visible net profits to tax — in our opinion, it would take at least six months to determine whether the tax on gross was too high or not, and what mines would be compelled to shut down as a matter of economic necessity under the free market economy imposed by the stabilization measures.

3. They insisted that the *remanentes* to which the mine operators were entitled on their prestabilization exports "were a part of the price paid by the Mining Bank for their ores," that is, that they had been sending their ore shipments through the Mining Bank and had been paid partly in cash, in bolivianos, and were permitted to use the remainder (the *remanentes*) to purchase merchandise from abroad at the rate of Bs. 190 to the dollar.

*Publication of this book may perhaps show the private mine operators how strenuously the principle of a free market economy was advocated, and they will have no difficulty in placing the onus for this continued injustice to the smaller operators.

> This was the real incentive for exporting, and it permitted a number of noneconomic mines to continue in operation, in many cases disposing of their *remanente* rights to third parties.

The association insisted that the mineowners be permitted to use up their pending *remanentes* at the Bs. 190 rate. To this quite plausible complaint, the only answer possible was that there was no longer any such thing as a Bs. 190 rate and that the mine operators had known for the past six months that such privileges would be done away with when stabilization — which, it had been announced, would come — actually came; they should have stopped relying on a subsidy which they knew was artificial, but instead they had accelerated their shipments to take advantage of the subsidy while the going was good.

One other mining matter was brought before the council by the Minister of Mines — a proposed concession to Bolivian American Minerals, Inc., that had been negotiated prior to the stabilization decrees but which had not yet been signed. I stated that the only interest of the council would be that no concession contract should be executed that would be contrary to the stabilization program, but the Ministers of Mines, Economy, and Finance pointed out that the concession provided for rates of royalties and other conditions that were clearly contrary to the stabilization decrees, and the contract would therefore have to be approved by the council. Manifestly, no special privileges in violation of the stabilization measures could be approved, but the matter was left for later investigation and discussion (p. 361).

Government petroleum corporation. In the matter of government finances, one matter which we had intentionally let slide was how to meet expenses between December 15 and 31. It was impossible to make plans in advance for this period, as there was no certainty as to when the stabilization measures would be enacted, and meanwhile we had been authorizing increased currency issues to meet urgent expenses, while using Fabian tactics to keep such issues to a minimum. Fortunately, the Minister of Economy reported that he had sufficient unused funds to meet all government accounts for the last fortnight of 1956.

One problem which could not be met so easily, however, occupied the council for a good part of three sessions — what to do about some $1,889,000 of YPFB's foreign suppliers' accounts, of which $600,000 had been overdue since October and had to be paid immediately. It was at first proposed that the money could be advanced from the 1957 foreign exchange budget, but the YPFB representatives pointed out that the 1957 budget had been drastically scaled down and that any further cut would be reflected in an even greater loss of foreign exchange revenues. It was then proposed that, for the last two weeks of 1956, YPFB might be allowed an amount equivalent to one twenty-fourth of the 1957 foreign exchange budget, i.e., $500,000. This was accepted, and the problem then was for YPFB to find bolivianos to purchase that exchange, as the company had, of course, budgeted its 1956 foreign imports at Bs. 190 to the dollar and, all in all, there was a shortage of Bs. 17 billion, for which they demanded an overdraft at the Central Bank. That was out of the question, but, after long discussion, it developed that YPFB had budgeted repayment of a Bs. 3,250 million loan from the Central Bank. So the council decided that it should defer that repayment, which would take care of the most urgent 1956 needs, and that the bank, as an exception, could lend YPFB a further Bs. 1 billion, repayable in twelve monthly instalments, on condition that YPFB raise domestic prices for its products sufficiently to ensure repayment of that loan and to cover all 1957 expenditures.

That raised another question, that YPFB had been instructed by the President (without consultation with the council) that it would be permissible to raise gasoline prices, but not prices for kerosene or fuel oil. YPFB was consequently trying to work out new price scales and estimates in the hope that it could balance its budget under those conditions. Later, President Siles gave orders that kerosene prices must actually be cut Bs. 50 a litre.

In the request for a stabilization loan, Bolivia had agreed to set a price of Bs. 120 per litre (1.7 cents a quart) for kerosene in order to balance its budget, so that this was a clear violation of Bolivia's commitments in a matter on which the council had not been informed. The YPFB General Manager stated that he could not possibly reduce the price, as this would mean a deficit of some Bs. 1,890 million in 1957, and the Minister of Economy asserted that, if the council gave way in this one case, there would be no limit to the number of concessions to political expediency that would have to be made, with the consequence that the stabilization program would collapse. The council unanimously decided that no concession could be made, and that kerosene prices must not be reduced. This meeting, however, was not attended by the President, and the matter came up to plague the council again in 1957.*

The private banks and reserve requirements. Another matter that came before the council in the immediate poststabilization period was a request by the *Banco Nacional* — a private banking institution — for permission to erect a new bank building with its own dollar and boliviano funds. Under a free economy, there was no need for council authorization, but, in view of the regulations governing the ratio between the capital of the bank and its investment in a building, the council had to advise that this project must await passage of a decree permitting revaluation of bank assets, which was one of the many urgent matters pending before the council.

Dr. Sologuren, the council's legal adviser, in cooperation with the Finance Ministry, had drafted a decree in preliminary form, for consideration by the council, which provided for the revaluation of business assets, other than bank assets, which were recognized to be in a special category. This proposed decree was discussed in council, and agreement was reached in principle, but it was not until after the turn of the year that the decree was drafted in legislative form. Its enactment was delayed until well into 1957 because of political opposition.

The question of establishment of new ratios of bank reserves against deposits, and of limitations on deposits with relation to bank capital, was one of the most urgent, inasmuch as the wild inflation of the past four years and the stabilization of the currency at its new level had made all previous regulations obsolete. Control of bank credit ranked second only to control of the bank note issue in the monetary stabilization schema, as it was manifest that unrestricted credits by the commercial banks to the private sector could, and probably would, lead to

---

*During the long period of artificially subsidized prices, kerosene had been sold far below cost (at Bs. 30 a litre, in November 1956, then equivalent to 30 cents per 100 quarts). The farmers were no longer willing to use the conventional llama dung and other native fuels, yet rebelled at paying the actual minimal cost of kerosene. That is the main problem of stabilization in a welfare state — when the government, through its welfare measures, well-intentioned or demagogic, has finally so impoverished a nation that the majority of the population are paupers, it is hard to convince this majority that they are no longer entitled to get something for nothing.

speculation that might fritter away the stabilization reserves.* The content of the necessary decree and regulations was left in the hands of Ernest Moore of the U.S. Financial Advisory Mission, with the advice of John Woodley of the IMF mission. These experts, with the assistance of the Superintendent of Banks and the president of the Central Bank, together with our legal draftsman, Dr. Sologuren, whipped these measures into shape and Moore presented them to the council on December 31, when they were approved without change.

In brief, the decree and regulations provided for a double reserve ratio for all private commercial banks and for the banking department of the Central Bank. One reserve, set at the pre-existing legal rate of 40 per cent, was to be maintained against average deposits in the period from December 12 to 26, 1956, and was to consist of the bank's deposits in the monetary department of the Central Bank plus certain other assets expressly set forth in the regulations. The second reserve was to be computed by the Superintendent of Banks, on a weekly basis, against subsequent increases in deposits in excess of seven times capital liabilities (capital, reserves, undivided profits); this reserve ratio was 50 per cent and was to consist of demand deposits in the monetary department of the Central Bank plus bank notes. The government Mining Bank and Agricultural Bank were to be subject solely to the second reserve requirement. The commercial banks and banking department of the Central Bank were permitted to accept deposits up to seven times their paid-in capital and reserves, and were required to deposit any excess in the monetary department of the Central Bank.

The system was necessarily complex, by reason of the peculiar situation existing in Bolivia. There would be no point in outlining its provisions at length, as they were transitory and would scarcely be applicable to any other situation. The restrictions on credit were purely quantitative. The question of qualitative restrictions on credit — distinguishing between credits which would tend to increase production immediately, and those which would favor speculation or long-term projects — was left for later, until a sufficient basis of experience under

---

*The differences in theory between the "currency school" of thought, and the "banking school," and the fact that a country's demand deposits do not necessarily represent pure savings, but are largely a consequence of the creation of bank credit, will be discussed in a sequel to the present study.

stabilization conditions had been accumulated to relax the quantitative controls without endangering the stabilization fund. The immediate need in Bolivia was to shut off the credit faucet; it could later be determined how far the tap could be reopened without creating a flood.

Tax measures. To temper the initial poststabilization rise in prices for essential commodities, the council decided that all customs duties on foodstuff imports should be suspended until such time in 1957 as new local crops of the same or substitute foodstuffs came on the market. This was a matter that should have been determined at the time the new customs duties were approved by the council, but the four-day delay proved of no consequence, as the deferment did not require enactment of a decree-law, and was made effective immediately.

Four tax measures had been drafted in preliminary form by Dr. Sologuren in cooperation with the Finance Ministry, and these came before the council for discussion in the first week following stabilization: (1) a tax on the revaluation of assets; (2) a documentary stamp tax, levied in the form of excise stamps and stamped paper, common in all Civil Law countries; (3) a tax on alcohol and alcoholic beverages; and (4) a general sales tax.

The revaluation tax, together with the norms governing revaluations, had to be postponed until mid-1957 for political reasons. The stamp and liquor taxes, as well as the general sales tax, were enacted in February, 1957.

The first draft of the sales tax failed to meet with the approval of the council and, following a discussion of the various theories of taxation on sales and services and their applicability to the Bolivian environment, it was decided to place the matter in the hands of a subcommittee composed of the Director General of Revenues, Dr. Sologuren, and Roger Freeman, the tax expert of the U.S. Financial Advisory Mission. A draft soon came back from the subcommittee, providing for a general tax of 5 per cent on sales and services, and 15 per cent on luxuries, to be collected on the retail level. Freeman pointed out, however, that it would be impossible to raise the budgeted Bs. 30 billion in revenues if sales of virtually all major articles of commerce were tax-exempt, as was provided in the draft. In particular, he contended that there should be a 5 per cent tax on gasoline in addition to the long list of existing taxes on that product, as the present taxes were all earmarked for some special purpose or entity.

For my part, I urged that the council use the occasion for tax reform as well as for revenue by abolishing all earmarked taxes on sales and services. Freeman agreed with the desirability of that end, if it could be achieved, provided that the rate of tax and the limitation of exemptions were such as to ensure collection of the needed revenues.

The Minister of Finance pointed out the difficulties of collecting a tax at the retail level, under Bolivian conditions. He advocated a tax imposed at all levels — the importer or producer, wholesalers, and retailers — so as to increase the likelihood that the tax would be collected at least at one level. The disadvantages of "cascading" — the cumulative imposition of tax on tax — were emphasized by Freeman, but of course Freeman and I were not in so good a position as our Bolivian colleagues to appraise the difficulties of tax administration in Bolivia, so the bill was returned to the subcommittee to be redrafted on an all-level basis, but at a reduced rate of tax. (A value-added tax, on the French model, would have been absolutely impossible under Bolivian conditions but was mentioned by us as a matter of theoretical interest.)

On the following day, the decree was returned to the council in final form and approved. It provided for (1) a tax of 10 per cent on all sales of luxury goods (which were expressly specified); professional services; sales and charges made by restaurants, barbers, beauty parlors, etc.; telephone and telegraph bills; and so forth; and (2) a 3 per cent tax on all other merchandise sales; on electric light and power bills; on insurance, undertakers' bills, and all other charges for services not included under the 10 per cent tax and not expressly exempted. The tax was to be charged at all levels, no matter how many times the article might be sold and resold, or processed in the course of manufacture (on services the tax would normally be charged at only one level). The theory behind the multilevel tax, as expressed by the Bolivian members of the council, was that there was an undue multiplicity of middlemen and that the cumulative tax would in reality tend to lower prices by eliminating unnecessary stages in distribution. It would be hard to prove or disprove the validity of this thesis on the basis of the results achieved, as stabilization itself, and the elimination of multiple rates of exchange, did away with so many intermediate and illegitimate profits and middlemen that the influence of the tax cannot be segregated from other factors.

There followed a list of exemptions from tax so extensive that, in Freeman's judgment, they completely nullified the purpose of the tax. Some exemptions, such as those covering tobacco and liquor (which were separately taxed), foreign exchange (which could not be taxed under Article VIII of the IMF regulations), and postage and excise stamps (which were themselves in the nature of taxes), were logical and economically justifiable. The other exemptions may have been justifiable on humanitarian, social, or political grounds. As to that, no opinion is expressed, but, from a fiscal viewpoint, the decree fully justified Freeman's gloomiest prognosis.

The bill did, however, mark one advance of tremendous importance. It repealed 119 nuisance taxes, some of which were specially earmarked in favor of municipalities, universities, football clubs, political parties, or other entities, while others were merely additional sales taxes that went into the general Treasury. In lieu of the earmarked taxes, the beneficiaries were allotted subsidies for 1957 from the Treasury's general funds, equal to the amounts they had received from the earmarked taxes in 1955, plus 30 per cent. The expected saving in paper work and administration, to business as well as to government, would be enormous, and the amount represented by the new subsidies was less than would have been paid out if the earmarking provisions had remained in effect. With stabilization, the old earmarked percentages would have meant a windfall for the recipients at the expense of the taxpayers. (But see p. 316n for the strange dénouement of this measure.)

To guard against a return to the system of multiple taxes on a single transaction, the decree provided that, if it should ever become necessary in the future to increase taxes on sales and services, this would be accomplished by changing the rate of tax and not by imposing new taxes.* The provision was no more than hortatory, of course, as there was no way in which a decree-law could restrict a future act of the legislature, but it was felt that it would provide guide lines which might perhaps be followed more often than not.

Utility rates. One urgent matter that should have been attended to simultaneously with enactment of the stabilization

---

*At the end of 1954 there were over 1,000 different national taxes in force (Bloch report). Revenues from most of these taxes were negligible, in many cases less than the cost of collection, but their nuisance value (and consequent incentive to corruption) was tremendous.

decrees — and that had been placed in the hands of the Minister of Public Works with that intention — was the revision of public utility rates to meet the new conditions imposed by stabilization, and to enable the companies to operate at a profit and to attract the new capital necessary for the expansion of their services. The only private utility of any major significance (aside from the international communications companies) was the Bolivian Power Company, and the Minister reported to the council, ten days after enactment of the stabilization decrees, that the results of a study made by his staff showed that the company's rates would have to be increased 900 per cent, and that such an increase would be "unfair and unreasonable."

In reply, I pointed out that if the investigation showed that the rates had to be increased tenfold in order to give the company a fair return on its investment under the terms of its concession-contract it would be unfair and unreasonable to compel it to provide service to the public at any lesser rates. However, if it proved impossible to reach an agreement with the company prior to the next billing date, it might be acceptable to fix temporary rates at, say, five times the current rates if that were adequate to cover operating expenses, *provided* that permanent rates sufficient to yield a fair return and to attract new investment were established within six months, and *provided* that such rates included compensation for any inadequacy in the return during the interim period. The Minister replied that to increase the rates even five times would be politically disastrous, and that the concession-contract should be changed. President Siles intervened at this point to say that the rates, and not the contract, would have to be changed.

In the course of the discussion, it became clear that the Minister of Public Works was under the impression — which appears to be virtually universal in Latin America — that depreciation charges are not in reality an expense.* Under the

* From well over twenty years' experience in rate and concession negotiation, I can testify that, with extremely rare exceptions, public officials and economists in Latin America have no comprehension of the principles of depreciation accounting. Furthermore, they confuse the Spanish meaning of *amortización*, which means to repay a debt, with depreciation, so that they believe that the amounts charged by the company in its books for depreciation actually represent a repayment of capital investment. Thus, they believe that, at the end of the estimated service life of the property, the entire investment has been repaid and the company's investment is nil, so that it is not entitled to any further return. To make matters worse, they feel that the investments from current revenues in the expansion of

circumstances, further discussion of rates by the Council would have been futile and the President appointed a six-man committee to settle the problem, which was thus necessarily postponed until 1957. [36]

The Minister of Public Works reported that his staff was likewise investigating utility rates in Potosí, Sucre, and Cochabamba, as well as the passenger and freight rates charged by the government airline. He promised that an agreement would be reached on those rates in the near future.

The turn in the tide

Even in the first confusing week of stabilization, the changing swirls and eddies of public opinion gave promise of a turn in the tide. An evening paper reported that public confidence was returning, that housewives could now bring meat and bread home to their families. Prices are still high, it stated, but the important fact is that there *is* something to buy, that bread and meat can be seen in shop windows for the first time in years, that housewives are no longer forced to return home reciting the usual litany: "I couldn't buy a thing today." [37]

A morning paper, still shaken by the shock of stabilization, found reassurance in the fact that the Central Bank was meeting all demands for foreign exchange, that foreign exchange dealers were competing with the banks for the business, particularly in the trade for Argentine pesos, and that the boliviano remained firm. [38] Another paper reported that the council felt the stabilization program was proceeding satisfactorily and that no emergency measures were needed, that the banks were remaining open and transacting foreign exchange business without a hitch. [39]

Most notable of all, *El Pueblo,* a paper of the extreme left, carried flaming editorials five days apart, supporting President Siles and the stabilization program, and vehemently attacking

---

telephone plant, as well as in its maintenance and replacement, must have come from depreciation accruals (ignoring the fact that the shareholders may have sacrificed dividends in order to "plough back" earnings into plant). Hence, they hold that the investment has been paid for by the public, so that, at the end of 20 to 25 years, the company no longer has *any* investment either in the original plant or in the expanded plant. If it be pointed out that the stockholders have never received any repayment of their investment, and only modest dividends, they are sceptical enough to believe that the repayments are concealed somewhere in the accounts, and the government accountants are either too ill-informed or too politically motivated to apprise them of their error.

ex-President Paz-Estenssoro and the COB for not giving the program their full support. The editorials placed the blame on the Paz-Estenssoro administration for the crookedness, immorality, speculation, smugglers, *cuperos,* and *coleros,* which had created a new caste of *nouveaux riches* who were now receiving their just punishment as a consequence of the stabilization measures.[40]

On December 24 a morning paper printed a table showing bread prices the first day of stabilization at Bs. 300 a loaf, the second day Bs. 250, the third day Bs. 200, and the current price at the end of the week between Bs. 180 and Bs. 200.* Meat prices had fallen successively from Bs. 7,500 per kilo to Bs. 6,000, Bs. 5,000, and from Bs. 4,500 to Bs. 5,000 in the same period. The dollar, which had been quoted at Bs. 13,000 three weeks prior to stabilization, had slumped to Bs. 9,600-Bs. 10,500 the week before, to Bs. 7,700-Bs. 7,750 the day of stabilization, to Bs. 7,590-Bs. 7,650 by the end of the week.[41]

La Paz's evening paper on Christmas eve hailed Bolivia's "first Christmas with free prices" — it would have been a sad Christmas for everyone, the editor stated, had it not been for stabilization, but now, with free competition and the forces of supply and demand, the stores and peddlers have ample stocks of holiday merchandise to sell.[42]

The religious overtones supplied by the Christmas season to the first fortnight of stabilization seemed to strengthen the conviction that stabilization meant a "return to morality," a phrase that was echoed again and again in the press, pulpit, and in daily discussions. The tide of public opinion had by that time definitely turned, from scepticism, despondency, and panic to a "rebirth of faith" for Bolivia, as one paper put it.[43] Had that tide been taken at the flood, which it was not, it could have led on to victory, not only in the stabilization of the currency but in basic economic development as well. Instead, vacillation and a disinclination to effect a break with the forces of corruption within the Revolutionary party, led on to Armageddon.

Nearly two weeks had elapsed since the issuance of the stabilization decrees, and not a word had been uttered by Juan

---

*I had pointed out to the council that, with flour at current prices, the housewife could make her own bread for Bs. 130 a loaf, including the cost of yeast and fuel, so that the price of bread could not remain much above that price for very long. This proved to be the case, and bread prices stabilized at around Bs. 180 (2.4 cents) a loaf. (Letter to President Siles, December 21, 1956.)

Lechín since December 18, when he was forced to subscribe to an MNR statement supporting the program (see Rumblings of Discontent, p. 282 above). The silence was ominous, and it was evident that Bolivia's "maximum leader" was waiting for the outcome of the national convention of the COB to determine in which direction his followers wanted to be led.

Revolt of the COB

Finally, on December 27, the day arrived, Delegates and "cell" leaders from all over the country met together in the La Paz Municipal Library for their national convention.

There could be no doubt of the outcome. As *El Pueblo* had said, corruption, immorality, and speculation had been blasted by stabilization. The smugglers, black marketeers, and traders in quotas, permits, and privileges had been deprived of their livelihood; the politicians and labor leaders were no longer able to pass out political favors — and these gentlemen were not disposed to give up their prerogatives without a struggle. In one fiery speech after another, the leaders of the railway workers, miners, artisans, civil servants, construction workers, and communications employees, denounced the stabilization program in every way and from every angle, demanding the resignation of the labor ministers (the Ministers of Mines, Labor, Peasant Affairs, appointed to the Cabinet by the COB to represent the interests of labor in the "Co-Government"). One lone delegate, representing the millers, spoke out in favor of the stabilization program, citing Hegel, Lenin, and Franz Tamayo at great length in support of his views, and soaring far above the heads of most of his listeners.

The Minister of Mines (a member of the Stabilization Council) courageously and loyally came to the defense of the program "speaking as a labor minister — at least, up to this moment." (This reservation was prophetic as, shortly thereafter, Lechín's alter ego, Torres, was appointed Minister.)

But the prostabilization speakers were shouted down, and the chairman of the convention rose to address the audience — Juan Lechín-Oquendo, Executive Secretary of the COB and President of the Senate, a fine figure of a man and an orator without a peer. The COB had not been consulted, he stated, and had no prior knowledge of the stabilization plan. He personally had been acquainted with only a few details, but had not been informed of the plan in its entirety.

Latin Americans have a delightfully urbane way of charac-
terizing mendacity: "It is not historical," they say, and readers
may judge for themselves the dubious historicity of Lechín's
statement in the light of the conferences with Lechín prior to
creation of the Stabilization Council, and of his active participation with the council both in the early and final stages of the
drafting of the stabilization measures.

The orator still hedged his position, however, and coun-
selled the convention not to attack President Siles' plan until
the COB had time to prepare its own stabilization plan, at which
time he, Lechín, would announce his views. In a newspaper interview, he then stated that the COB had not yet defined its position and that it would be premature to comment.[44]

The hunger strike

There then occurred one of those phenonema which, despite
long acquaintance with Latin America — a quarter-century in
the case of Bolivia — I have never been able to comprehend:
the President declared a hunger strike.[45] Why self-imposed
starvation, as practiced in Bolivia or India, or self-immolation,
as in Vietnam or the United States, should prove the righteous-
ness of one's cause, passes all understanding; but, on this occasion at least, it proved remarkably effective.*

Expressions of adherence to the President's cause came
from all parts of Bolivia and all sectors of society. Newspaper
interviews with the man in the street and resolutions and declarations by oil workers, newspaper employees, chauffeurs,
printers, factory workers, youth movements, Chaco War veterans, gold mining cooperatives, miners in numerous individual
mines, MNR "cells," small-town councils, cattle growers,
farmers, and others, filled the columns of the daily press.[46]

---

*There appears to be no authoritative guide to the etiquette of hunger
strikes — how long they must be maintained to convince the public that the
self-victim is a martyr in a righteous cause. Apparently, in Bolivia,
moderation is the rule. Starvation is not carried to the point of inanition.
In this case, the hunger strike accomplished its purpose within two days
but, even when not successful, forty-eight hours appears to be the limit,
as Siles and Lechín joined together in a hunger strike in 1964 to block the
re-election of Paz-Estenssoro and abandoned it on the third day without
having accomplished their purpose (New York Times, May 30, 1964, June
1, 1964, articles by Juan de Onís).

The evening of December 28, the first day of the hunger strike, huge crowds milled around in the square between the presidential palace and the Congress from 7:00 p.m. to well after midnight, screaming for guns to kill those responsible for the hunger strike and meanwhile throwing stones at the Congress where Lechín, as President of the Senate, was presumably hiding — "a powerful and spontaneous manifestation of the entire public," as La Paz's leading independent paper phrased it.[47]

The hunger strike ended the following day. Siles' victory over his enemies was complete, not merely over Lechín but over all the corrupt *políticos,* labor leaders, smugglers, black marketeers, and others whose means of livelihood and of political influence had ended with the advent of stabilization.*

The "miracle" achieved

That day marked the absolute apex of President Siles' power. The Battle of Armageddon had been won by the forces of light over the forces of darkness. The press on January 1, 1957, hailed Siles as the man of the year, and stabilization as his great accomplishment. Even *El Pueblo* editorialized: "We are not supporting the Eder plan but we do not see any alternative," adding that "it is a lie that stabilization is opposed by the Communists — it is opposed by the black marketeers and crooks in the MNR party because stabilization means the end of their privileges."[48]

Had President Siles chosen to, he could have seized the opportunity to obliterate his enemies from the political scene for

---

*The Economic Commission for Latin America reports that the elimination of the old foreign exchange and quota systems put an immediate end to black-marketing and labor-union and political graft. Being an intergovernmental agency, it was unable to use so crude a term as graft, and referred to it as prebendalism. In Spanish, the term carries the connotation of an unearned emolument, yet is sufficiently recondite so that few of the erstwhile beneficiaries of the system would understand the meaning. ECLA likewise reports that, as a consequence of the stabilization measures, there was "an immediate disappearance of the vices that had originated in the system of controls and multiple exchange rates" and of "the illicit profits derived from the distribution of foreign exchange (and) quotas. . . . Even more important, . . . the reason for export smuggling to neighboring countries was eliminated. This fact, plus an increased availability of U.S. aid commodities, meant an increased supply of goods in the domestic market and the virtual disappearance of scarcity." (ECLA report, pp. 88, 83.)

all time; given his country for the first time in this century an
era of honest government from top to bottom; brought back to
Bolivia its citizens in exile whose intelligence, skills, and
money were so desperately needed; and started the nation
squarely on the course of a free market economy that, within a
decade, would have attracted foreign as well as flight capital
and enabled the country to achieve a degree of prosperity and
economic development limited only by its natural resources,
human and material.

Siles' loyal friends, within and without the National Monetary Stabilization Council, strongly urged him to that course.
Instead, he could not bring himself, as he told me in private, to
break with his comrades, Víctor Paz-Estenssoro, Juan Lechín-
Oquendo, and Ñuflo Chávez-Ortiz, who had brought him to
power. He gave Lechín asylum until the passions of the mob
had cooled, called for an end of partisan strife, and, within a
fortnight, Lechín was back solidly in the saddle and conspiring
with his comrades to wreck the stabilization program, or at
least to do away with what he considered its less attractive
features, as will be related in the concluding chapters.

Meanwhile, the Bolivian Institute of Public Opinion Polls
had been making investigations of public opinion.* Nine days
after the riots in the market place that marked the commencement of the stabilization era, the preliminary unpublished returns from the survey showed that 75 per cent of the public (in
La Paz) supported the stabilization measures. That was two
days before the hunger strike. The survey was exploratory, to
determine and perfect the methods of enquiry, and the margin
of error in the results was no doubt correspondingly wide.

The first *complete* urban survey was made during the first
fortnight of 1957, covering a sample that included housewives,
unskilled laborers, employees, students, and professionals,
weighted to give a fair cross section of public opinion in La
Paz, which was presumably fairly representative of urban opinion in the country as a whole, although sectional differences did

*The Institute was a small but competent organization, headed by Dr.
Juan Jáuregui-Oroza, a young man who had studied in the United States
and Mexico. Its methods were modeled on those developed in the Gallup,
Roper, and similar polls, with modifications that had been found necessary
in similar surveys in Mexico. Although subsidized by the U.S. Operations
Mission, its activities were completely independent, and there is no reason to believe that the results shown by its surveys were colored by that
fact.

TABLE 9

Public Opinion Poll, January, 1957*

Question	Response (Percentage)		
	Favorable or Affirmative	Unfavorable or Negative	No Opinion
What do you think of the stabilization measures?	92	4	3
Do you think there will be no more scarcities of prime necessities?	81	12	7
Do you think that a single rate of exchange and freedom of commerce are good for the country?	90	8	1
Do you think the Siles Government has the support of the people in its new economic program?	90	2	7
What are the principal advantages of the new system?	No more scarcities of essentials — 26 Higher value of the boliviano and freedom of exchange — 17 No more smugglers, black marketeers, etc. — 16 Freedom of trade — 12 Lower prices for some articles — 4 Other advantages — 19 No advantages — 12 No opinion — 7		
What are the principal disadvantages?	Increased cost of living; wages not high enough to meet exorbitant rise in prices — 17 Other disadvantages — 13 No disadvantages — 48 No opinion — 21		

*Instituto Boliviano de Encuestas de Opinión Pública, January 17, 1957; *La Nación,* January 20, 1957.

show up in certain phases of later polls. A survey of rural opinion, among the Aymara and Quechua Indian populations, was out of the question.

The results of this initial survey, coming as it did immediately following President Siles' successful hunger strike, are enlightening. (See Table 9.)

Public acceptance, then, was a fact. Prices had already commenced to retreat from the outrageous levels of the first day's rioting, although they were still far higher than they would be when imports started arriving and the local sources of production got under way. Stabilization had been achieved!

And here it might be well to quote a commentary on the German stabilization of 1948 by one of Europe's most prolific and respected writers on economics, Professor Wilhelm Roepke of the Graduate Institute of International Studies in Geneva, which shows that, despite the antipodal differences between the German and Bolivian economies, the essential processes of monetary stabilization, following a period of *monetary inflation*, are, after all, very much alike in any part of the world.*

> ...the German accomplishment was nonetheless — in economic terms — no miracle at all, if the essence of the reform of 1948 is clearly understood. Its success was on the contrary precisely what its architects had expected. The real miracle lay in the fact that, in this particular country and in a world still under the spell of inflationism and collectivism, it proved possible politically and socially to return to the economic reason of the market economy and to monetary discipline.... It was, to be sure, a long time before the inflationists and collectivists of every kind and degree bowed to the irrefutable evidence of the facts and abandoned their attempts, as numerous as they were scientifically untenable, to minimize or even deny the unexampled and historically unique success of the German economic reform of 1948. Outside Germany there still appear to be some diehards who — either out of ignorance of the facts and interrelationships, or against their better judgment — resist admitting that here is to be found the most

Monetary inflation is italicized, as it is recognized that increased general price levels are not in all cases the *consequence* of increases in the money supply. Hyperinflation, however, so far as can be recalled, has always been the result of monetary debasement, whether in Latin America, or in the two German inflationary experiences, or elsewhere in the world. And in such cases, the remedial measures must necessarily be monetary, and the results are inevitably immediate and amazing; cf. the "miracle of the Rentenmark" following Hjalmar Schacht's stabilization of the German currency in 1923-24 (Constantino Bresciani-Turroni, *The Economics of Inflation: A Study of Currency Depreciation in Post-War Germany*, trans. Millicent E. Sayers [London: Allen & Unwin, 1937], pp. 336-37).

convincing case in all history against collectivism and inflationism and for market economy and monetary discipline. . . . The essence of the German economic reform corresponds to the sickness which it was intended to cure. If the sickness was that combination of collectivism and inflation which we have designated as repressed inflation (meaning the attempt to curb inflation by price controls, rationing, and other interferences with a free market), the therapy for it had to consist, on the one hand, in the elimination of inflationary pressure and, on the other hand, in the elimination of the apparatus of repression and the restoration of market freedom, free prices, competition, and entrepreneurial incentives. Freedom in the realm of goods, discipline in the realm of money — these were the two principles on which rested the German economic revival from 1948 onwards. . . . It was not always easy to maintain, uninterrupted, the course of such a noninflationary market economy. The temptation was strong to give in to an anachronistic Keynesianism and to fight the persistently high level of unemployment, due to the continuing stream of refugees from the East, with a program of inflationary investments. The American occupation authorities exerted, over a considerable period, strong pressure on the German government and the German central bank in this direction.*

*Dr. Erhard himself confirms this pressure. Germany was forbidden by regulations laid down by the British and American occupation authorities to *alter* the price controls in force, but the "Allies never seem to have thought it possible that someone could have the idea, not to alter price controls, but simply to remove them." When this was precisely what Erhard did, General Clay backed him up, but "in the coming months and years the Allies [continued to try] to influence German reconstruction according to their ideas," which did not fit in with Erhard's insistence on a free economy. (Ludwig Erhard, *Prosperity through Competition*, pp. 14-15. Cf. Frederick G. Reuss, *Fiscal Policy for Growth Without Inflation: The German Experiment* [Baltimore: Johns Hopkins Press, 1963], p. 285; and Helmut Arntz [ed.], *Germany Reports* [2d ed., Bonn: Press and Information Office, 1955], p. 363.)

I have been given, by a responsible source, the following account of a discussion between General Lucius Clay, head of the American mission, and Dr. Ludwig Erhard, the German Minister of Economy. It appears that Clay had summoned Erhard to his office to question him as to the truth of reports that Erhard intended to balance the budget, abandon all price and other controls and restrictions, and return Germany to a free market economy subject only to the untrammeled forces of supply and demand. Dr. Erhard admitted that this was true. "My advisers tell me," General Clay commented, "that, if you do that, prices will rise sky high, unemployment will increase, and there will be chaos in Germany." "That's all

Fortunately, the Germans withstood both the pressure and the temptation, so that Germany was preserved from a relapse into the National Socialist [Nazi] policy of repressed inflation.[49]

---

right, General," Erhard is reported to have replied, "Don't worry. My advisers tell me the same thing, but I'm going right ahead." Which he did, with the result that Germany, on a free market basis and with a balanced budget, achieved one of the most remarkable eras of economic recovery that the world has ever seen. This anecdote is confirmed by William Henry Chamberlin (*The German Phoenix* [New York: Duell, Sloan, and Pearce, 1963], p. 72); and, more than a year after the June, 1948, currency reform and a return to a free market economy, Dr. Erhard writes that the American head of the allied Joint Export and Import Agency was still insisting on government controls (*Germany's Comeback in the World Market*, trans. W. H. Johnston [London: Allen & Unwin, 1954], p. 86. Cf. Lucius Clay, *Decision in Germany* [Garden City, N.Y.: Doubleday, 1950], p. 220).

V

SUBSEQUENT MEASURES

15

COMPLETION OF THE PROGRAM

There remained, at the beginning of 1957, a number of loose
ends to be tied together, chiefly legislative or quasi-legislative
measures that the council simply had had no time to attend to in
the last harried weeks of 1956. For the sake of clarity they are
grouped here under the heads of tax measures, banking and
credit regulations, and so forth, in logical rather than chrono-
logical order, although the work of the council was by no means
so neatly compartmentalized and all problems had to be tackled
concurrently, interspersed with fact finding, crises, and reports
to the nation.

Shortly before the close of the year, Congress renewed the
emergency powers of the President for a further twelve months,
which enabled him to continue enacting decrees with the force
of law, *on the advice of the Stabilization Council,* in all matters
affecting the stability of the currency.[1]

Tax Measures

From the viewpoint of the Stabilization Council, or at least
from that of its technical advisers, the sole legitimate objective
of tax reform was to procure the maximum revenues for the
government with the minimum detriment to the economy. Bolivia's economic position was too desperate, and the monetary
stability which had been achieved too precarious, for long-range
social objectives to be placed ahead of immediate revenues and
short term recovery in agriculture, mining, and business.

Congress, however, and the *Co-Gobierno* cabinet and *políticos* had different ideas. In the Revolutionary ideology, social
reform came first. This was distorted by the *políticos*, not so
much into a soak-the-rich philosophy — there were no rich remaining in Bolivia outside of the racketeering politicians and
labor leaders themselves — as into a posture which would deceive the masses into believing that their leaders were soaking
the rich. In the spirit of the Revolution, revenge for the evils
of the past took primacy over revenues for the present. This
conflict of aims will be apparent in the discussion of the various

tax measures proposed by the council and enacted, ignored, or emasculated by the Cabinet.

One measure entailing a tax was not basically a tax measure, at least in its intent, namely, a procedure for revaluation of assets. This measure is therefore covered in Chapter 16 rather than under the present head.

The income tax

Up to the time of stabilization, the personal income tax had been levied on a sliding scale of from 1 to 22 per cent, with exclusions and personal and family allowances that, at the time the law was enacted, excluded the vast majority of laborers and white-collar workers from tax.[2] Subsequent multiple wage increases as a consequence of the inflation, however, had brought virtually all wage earners within the ambit of the tax, which, needless to say, was never collected from those at the bottom of the economic and social structure nor, on the other hand, from the black marketeers, smugglers, and crooked *políticos* and labor leaders at the top — the new aristocracy.

Revenues from this tax, levied almost exclusively on the defenseless middle class and on the more highly paid officials in government, were negligible. Nevertheless, the law as it stood on the statute books, if enforced, contained what was needed to make it a fairly good revenue measure. It contained allowances, exclusions, and exemptions moderate enough to bring within the scope of the tax a sufficiently large number of taxpayers to make the tax worth while from a revenue standpoint, and to create a better climate for law enforcement, in that the masses of the population would know that they too were contributing their share to the support of the government and therefore had a right to demand that no one be allowed to escape.

On this foundation, and with certain improvements in the direction of better enforcement, it would have been possible to draft a well-planned income tax bill, retaining the existing provisions for withholding tax at source. Instead, the Stabilization Council was forced to bow to political expediency, and on January 24, 1957, a new income tax was enacted by the President and Cabinet as a decree with the force of law.

"Inasmuch as the present scales of tax would unfavorably affect the recently enacted wage increases (under the stabilization law)," the decree recited, the existing schedules have been amended. And the amendment was such that a married man with three children would have to earn Bs. 12,800 a day for 360 days a year to pay any tax. Bear in mind that, under the stabilization measures, even the miners — the best paid of all workers — received a base pay of only Bs. 7,500 a day, and that the new decree provided that incentive and other bonuses, family subsidies, social benefits, etc., were all to be excluded from income. Even a bachelor miner with no dependents — and no mine worker would admit this happy taxable state to a tax collector — would be barely touched by the tax: 51 cents a year! The provision for withholding went by the board, so that any possibility of collecting tax from *any* workman or white-collar employee was simply nil.

To make this demagogic approach to tax reform more shocking, the law, as amended in the Cabinet, provided for a surtax on incomes over Bs. 36 million a year ($4,650) at rates from 13 to 36 per cent. This was clearly nothing but a soak-the-rich camouflage to deceive the masses, as there were not over a handful of Bolivians remaining in Bolivia who could report an income in that bracket, aside from the political new aristocracy who would certainly not file returns on their illegal gains. On the advice of the tax expert of the U.S. Financial Advisory Mission, Roger Freeman, this was reported to the council, with the comment that tax revenues under the new bill would be virtually zero, while increased revenues were urgently needed to balance the budget and meet Bolivia's commitments under the stabilization fund agreements.

The council members agreed, but confessed that there was nothing they could do about it, as the law had been enacted under pressure from Lechín and Ñuflo Chávez, who were already complaining that the stabilization measures favored the rich, and that something had to be done to show that the government favored the working man. The incompetence of the Cabinet and its political advisers to draft or amend a tax measure was evidenced by the fact that their amendments to the income tax decree had to be corrected a week after publication, and that even after this correction the decree still contained an error in the surtax columns that, strictly construed, made the law meaningless.[3]

Shortly thereafter, the managements of COMIBOL and YPFB, the government mining and petroleum corporations, appeared before the council to say that their foreign *técnicos* (meaning anyone from a skilled mechanic to an engineer or manager) had served notice that they were quitting because of the new income tax, and that it would be impossible to operate the mines or oilfields in their absence. For a foreigner with a wife and three children and an income of $10,000, the tax and surtax would take over 27 per cent of his gross salary before deductions. By contrast, an oil worker in Venezuela was virtually tax-free, as Venezuela then received such huge revenues from oil royalties and taxes that personal income tax rates were negligible.

The Finance Minister proposed a 50 per cent tax cut for foreign *técnicos*. I contended that there should be no discrimination in favor of foreigners nor in favor of *técnicos;* that the 50 per cent cut should be for everyone or, preferably, that the surtax should be eliminated. All agreed in principle, but the soak-the-rich philosophy prevailed, and the minister's proposal was approved. In the end, however, Bolivian as well as foreign *técnicos* were allowed the tax cut, as otherwise YPFB would have lost its staff of trained Bolivian engineers and the discrimination in favor of foreigners would have proved impossible from a political as well as from a managerial point of view.[4]

The corporate income tax remained unchanged at 25 per cent,[5] but with this difference, that whereas, prior to stabilization the tax was based on fictitious profits that represented little more than the depreciation of the boliviano and was therefore in reality a tax on capital and not on income, it would now become a tax on real earnings measured in a stable currency, that is, once the proposed revaluation of assets measure was enacted.

Estate tax

Allied to the income tax, at least in its soak-the-rich motivations, was the subject of estate tax reform. The majority of the council members urged that the current $33\frac{1}{3}$ per cent estate tax be reduced on the ground that it discouraged saving and encouraged the flight of capital, and furthermore that a scale of lower rates should be established in the case of direct descendants and collateral relations, according to the degree of kinship to the deceased. This is customary in Latin American countries, where a comparatively low tax on the entire estate is supplemented by an inheritance tax at varying rates on each class of beneficiary.

The Finance Minister opposed any change in the existing tax, on the theory that it was the Bolivian nation, society as a

whole, that made it possible for any individual to build up a fortune, and that the estate tax represented a partial repayment of
the deceased's debt to society. This was a view with which one
might agree in theory, although recognizing that the wealthy
man's "debt" to Bolivia was a minus quantity, and that inflation
had virtually eliminated the basic nontaxable allowance, so that
the tax was imposed on ridiculously small estates.

The question came to a head when the President asked the
council's advice on the estate of a well-to-do decedent, José
Bach. Should the tax be divided 80 per cent for the municipality
and 20 per cent for the national government, as provided in the
existing law? This was certainly getting down to specific cases,
rather than the general legislation which was the proper concern of the council, and left me groping for a Spanish translation of "bill of attainder," when the council unanimously resolved that the best thing to do was to do nothing. This was
undoubtedly a wise decision. There were practically no sizable
fortunes left in Bolivia. From the point of view of revenue, and
hence of stabilization, the estate tax was of negligible importance, and to tamper with that tax at that particular time would
have stirred up a hornet's nest among the demigods and dema-
gogues of the Revolution.

Later, however, it proved feasible to take up the matter
again. Since the tax on individual inheritances, with variable
rates, was considered unwieldy from an administrative point of
view in Bolivia, a sliding scale of tax on the total estate was
proposed by the council, varying from 5 per cent on estates of
over Bs. 12 million to 30 per cent on estates of Bs. 500 million
or over. Because estates of any magnitude were so infrequent
in Bolivia, revenues from the estate tax could not be counted
upon as a steady source of revenue. The council therefore provided that 50 per cent of the tax go to general budgetary purposes, and the remainder to special projects which, of course,
left them free for political disposal. I proposed that the tax be
doubled to the extent that distribution was made to persons outside Bolivia, and the council agreed instead to a 50 per cent increase in tax in such cases. I also proposed, and the council
agreed, that bequests to universities, schools, and charitable
institutions be deducted from the gross estate.

Sales taxes

The tax on sales of goods and services approved by the
council in the closing days of 1956 was finally enacted on

February 27, 1957, but with so many additional exemptions that its revenue-producing objectives were defeated. The great accomplishment of that act, however, as has been stated, was the repeal of 119 laws, decrees, and ordinances that imposed multiple taxes of the nuisance variety on a long list of transactions. Most of these taxes had been earmarked for sports clubs, labor unions, municipalities, universities, and other agencies of various kinds, and, in the 1957 budget, these earmarked taxes were replaced by a direct subsidy equal to 30 per cent more than the 1955 revenues from those sources.[6] *

The delay in enacting this tax was motivated in this case not by political opposition but by the intervention of the U.N. tax expert in the Ministry of Finance, who drafted a sarcastic letter for the signature of the Director of Revenues, pointing out that the tax measure supposedly drafted by Roger Freeman would have cascading effects, i.e., that the tax would be levied again and again, tax on tax, from producer to consumer.[7] † This, of course, Freeman had already explained to the council. Instead, the U.N. expert proposed, and was in the process of preparing, a value-added tax on the French model, under which

---

*Months later, the government petroleum company representatives appeared before the council to state that they could not sell their products at the extremely low prices fixed by the government, and yet continue to absorb all the earmarked taxes that had not been repealed by the February decree, and they therefore asked that the sales tax (which would go to the government) be suspended. I replied that the earmarked taxes had all been repealed, but the Finance Minister then explained that the Cabinet had cut out the repeal section of the decree as the earmarkings were largely for various labor unions, and the labor members of the Cabinet had objected — this after the decree had already been enacted and published! The council had never been advised of this development nor had it been informed that for over three months the government had failed to collect sales tax revenues from the YPFB and other taxpayers because the earmarked taxes had consumed all the available revenues. I urged that the council reiterate its recommendation that the earmarked taxes be repealed, but the council evaded that issue and confined itself to replying to YPFB that it could not recommend postponement of the sales tax.

†This was not the first clash between the U.S. Mission and the U.N. tax expert. When Roger Freeman first arrived in Bolivia, the Secretary General of the council introduced him to the U.N. adviser, Jean Peset, remarking that Peset spoke English, to which the latter retorted: "Not since August 4" (the date of the decree creating the Stabilization Council which replaced the U.N. financial adviser). Peset refused to have any communication with Freeman (who unfortunately spoke no Spanish), except through an interpreter.

each seller in the chain of distribution from manufacturer to jobber, to wholesaler, to retailer would be responsible for payment of his share of the aggregate tax to be collected — in other words, each tax would be solely on the value added to the product (in distribution or further manufacture) by each vendor. The working of the value-added tax was explained to the council, and all agreed that it would be naive to expect so complex a system — ideal in theory — to work satisfactorily in the Bolivian administrative environment.*

In addition to the national 3 per cent tax on electric light and power services, imposed under the new decree, there remained in effect the old Municipality of La Paz tax of 10.6 per cent, of which 5.75 per cent was for the municipality and 4.85 per cent for the railway workers' union. With the expectation that electric light rates would probably be multiplied sixfold, there could be no justification for continuing these high tax rates, and the Finance Minister suggested to the mayor of La Paz that the tax for the railway union be changed to a subsidy based on their 1955 revenue from the tax, plus 30 per cent, following our adopted practice. Unfortunately, the Minister of Economy made the mistake of suggesting that the mayor *negotiate* with the railway workers, with the result that at the following meeting the mayor reported that the union insisted on a $4\frac{1}{2}$ per cent tax on the new electric rates, while the municipality would need $11\frac{1}{2}$ per cent for itself in order to enable it to pay for street lighting at the anticipated higher rates.[8] The council turned down that proposal in order to keep electric costs within reason, and authorized the Finance Minister, who was a tough and able negotiator, to bargain with the mayor on the best (lowest) basis possible.

This example is illustrative of the lack of comprehension on the part of even the most capable public officials of the necessity of reducing expenses. Everywhere it was the same story — they all agreed that expenses must be cut, but in some other department or agency, and they all demanded higher earmarked tax revenues.

*The French *valeur ajoutée* tax, theoretically 20 per cent, actually works out at 25 per cent, i.e., the actual rate of tax = rate ÷ (100 - rate). Its collection is only feasible in a country where business accounting is reasonably complete and reasonably simple to verify. In such cases, it is acknowledged to be one of the most effective taxes in the taxmaker's arsenal. See Martin Norr and Pierre Kerlan, *Taxation in France*, Harvard Law School World Tax Series (Chicago: Commerce Clearing House, 1966), pp. 975-1044, for a comprehensive description of the value-added tax.

A week before the new sales tax was published, the attention of the council was called to two related matters on which council action was urged: (1) the fact that the Cabinet, without consultation with the council, had reduced the tax on sports events and other public spectacles and had earmarked the proceeds of that tax for the construction of athletic fields; and (2) a new tax on gasoline, likewise enacted without consultation with the council, the proceeds to be earmarked to pay for social security benefits for veterans of the Chaco War. Taxes such as these, I objected, would exhaust the tax-paying capacity of the nation. On the other hand, the government was urgently in need of revenues, and the Cabinet had not yet passed the sales tax submitted two months earlier. Nothing could be done about the two unauthorized earmarked taxes; they were a *fait accompli,* as was the case with so many other improvised and ill-considered measures enacted by the Cabinet, but, at least, this objection did result in the early passage of the much-needed sales tax.

Liquor and tobacco taxes

A revised tax on alcoholic beverages, drafted in the Finance Ministry, was amended and approved in the council on January 24, but it was not until a month later that it was finally enacted, and again the delay contributed to the shortage in government revenues in the first half of 1957. [9]

Tax rates on cigarettes and tobacco approved by the Stabilization Council were cut by the Cabinet, without consultation with the council, under pressure from the labor ministers who insisted on keeping prices down for the working man regardless of revenue needs.* The Finance Minister maintained, however, that new calculations, based on higher cigarette prices, indicated that revenues would be double the budgeted amount, despite the tax cut.

---

*It is a nice question of constitutional law, and certainly one that will never be decided, whether this and similar legislation enacted by the President and Cabinet contrary to the recommendation of the council was in fact law. It was never intended to make the council a supragovernmental body. It counted on the prestige of the President, as president of the council, to carry its advisory resolutions into law. The emergency decree, however, only authorized the President and Cabinet to enact as decrees with the force of law such measures as were recommended by the council (Art. 1d, Appendix 2).

Stamp taxes

Politics was not the only obstacle to new taxes. New stamp tax rates, and new charges for official stamped paper, were held up through the influence of the Bar Association for over five months, despite the fact that it was obvious that the stamped paper, which was intended as a source of revenue, was being sold at less than the cost of the paper. Finally, after discussion at three council meetings, a new stamp tax bill was approved by the council, providing among other things that stamped paper would be sold at Bs. 100 a sheet ($1\frac{1}{3}$ cents U.S.) which was alleged to cover the cost — which seemed highly doubtful considering the size and quality of the paper, the printing of the documentary stamp, and the cost of distribution.

Mineral export royalties

Two months after enactment of the stabilization decrees, which included the export royalties on tin and other metals, the newly appointed Minister of Mines came to the council breathing fire and denouncing whoever it was who had drawn up the scale of taxes as having been motivated by "an evil purpose."

That was the first time at any council session that any of the members had questioned the good faith of any of the other members. It was apparent that, with the direct representative of Lechín now on the council, it would not be easy to keep demagoguery and worse out of our discussions, which had invariably, up to that time, approached the country's problems from the broad viewpoint of the national interest, or at least with due courtesy for opposing viewpoints.

The former Minister of Mines, who had been reappointed as Minister of Economy in replacement of the former minister of that department, quietly stated that it was he who was responsible for drafting the law with the help of a director of COMIBOL but that their original rate schedule had contemplated revenues of $5.4 million whereas, under the government's commitments to the IMF and other lenders, $7.3 million was required, and the Finance Minister had upped the rates accordingly. The head of the Planning Commission explained that the council realized that the schedule was far from perfect, but that they had consulted representatives of the small miners, the Minister of Mines, the U.N. mining expert, and Ford, Bacon & Davis, and were unable to get any suggestions for the

improvement of the rate schedules but only flat opposition to
any export taxes of any kind whatsoever.

With this explanation, the Minister moderated his tone, as
it was apparent that he had assumed that the tax measure had
been drafted by the IMF Mission or by me, and Lechín and his
associates could never get over the impression that my intention from the start had been the "evil purpose" of forcing the
government to turn COMIBOL back to private ownership.

A revised tax schedule was subsequently presented by the
new Minister of Mines but proved to be a hit-or-miss improvi-
sation, with inexplicable gaps and jumps in the two sliding
scales based on metal prices and metal content of the ores and
concentrates. I suggested that the simplest way to plot a smooth
curve would be to draw a straight line on logarithmic graph paper. This brought the discussion beyond the Minister's grasp,
and he had no further comment when it was resolved that the
schedule should be amplified to cover ores of extremely low
metal content on which the tax rates would have to be considerably lower or nil, as well as the high-content concentrates
which could support a higher rate of tax. [10]

This supplementary schedule had been expressly provided
for in the original decree, so that on the following day the Minister of Mines brought in a schedule that had been drawn up for
him, covering the high- and low-content exports, which was immediately approved by the council, and promptly enacted as a
regulatory decree. [11]

Not long after, a member of the House of Deputies asked
the council for its opinion on a bill he had drafted providing that
3 per cent of the royalties collected on minerals produced in the
Potosı area be earmarked for creation of an Industrial Credit
and Development Fund in Potosí. [12] That was the only occasion
on which any member of the legislature had ever asked the
council for its opinion on prospective legislation, and the council resolved that the Deputy should be advised informally why
his proposal was incompatible with the stabilization program.

Other export taxes

Reports were received by the council that smuggling of Bolivian products across the border to Brazil, and of imports in
the reverse direction, had practically ceased since stabilization, which would seem to indicate that the new export taxes on
Bolivia's forest products were not so high as to encourage

contraband shipments.[13] That proved not to be true, however, in the case of coca leaves which were being shipped in quantity, ostensibly for the commissaries of mines near the Bolivian frontier, but which never reached their destination and, instead, were smuggled across the border to Chile and Peru to escape the 10 per cent export duty. There were also complaints from the coca exporters that taxes were collected in La Paz instead of at border points, but the Finance Minister explained that border guards alone could never adequately patrol Bolivia's frontier and that taxes had to be paid in La Paz. This had been true since colonial days when La Paz was little more than a market place for the coca trade. After discussion, it was agreed that, although exports should be encouraged, the tax revenue was indispensable, and the council thereupon resolved to recommend reducing the export tax on coca to 5 per cent, to continue collections in La Paz, and to check border traffic in so far as possible.[14] As it turned out, revenues increased with the lower rates, which would indicate that smuggling had been curbed to some extent.*

Import duties

As was to have been expected, the U.N.-drafted customs tariff virtually paralyzed large segments of Bolivia's import trade. Of course, a large part of that trade — the imports at the official rate of Bs. 190 to the dollar or under other artificial stimuli — was bound to disappear with stabilization. But, with complete freedom of commerce — no import permits or licenses required, no foreign exchange restrictions — merchants were eager to replenish their stocks of merchandise, spare parts, raw materials, and other much-needed goods, and were even willing to risk using their dollar assets abroad to earn a legitimate profit under the new free market economy. This

---

*Apparently, though, even the lower duty made the contraband trade attractive to the larger exporters, as some years later the courts petitioned Congress to impeach Vice-President Juan Lechín (at the time, doubling as Ambassador to Italy) on charges of participating in the production and illegal export of coca leaves. Congress, dominated by the COB, rejected the petition and resolved that there was a "complete lack of evidence of guilt," notwithstanding which it was reported that Lechín "suffered some loss of prestige" and resigned his ambassadorship (*Hispanic-American Report*, XVI [September, 1963], 899; *ibid*. [November, 1963], 1085).

development proved to be the first evidence of a return of flight capital, as confidence in the stability of the currency was restored.

The knowledge in the market place that the Stabilization Council intended to make radical changes in the new tariff schedules as soon as it could get around to doing so was, of course, an added deterrent to imports. No merchant, obviously, would want to risk importing goods at a high tariff if his competitor might later be able to import similar goods at a lower rate of duty. It might perhaps be argued that the council should have kept its plans under wraps, prepared a new tariff schedule in secret, and refrained from announcing a proposed revision until the revised tariff was actually enacted. There were at least three reasons why this would have been impossible: (1) that, in Bolivia, nothing can be kept secret and that an attempt at secrecy means merely that those with the best connections are the first to learn of the matter; (2) that no one on the council wished to be held publicly responsible for a "tariff of abominations"; and, (3) most important of all, that, on my recommendation, the council had decided that the new tariff schedules should not be drawn up arbitrarily by government or U.N. experts but that every sector of mining, agriculture, industry, and trade that wanted to be heard should be given an opportunity of a hearing, with no obligation, of course, that their demands would be met, but with the promise that all views would be considered.

So far as can be recalled, this was the first and only time that a new customs schedule has ever been prepared in a Latin American country with anything approaching the public hearings that we are accustomed to in the United States.[15] The usual procedure is for the rates to be prepared by the Finance Ministry, with only the most influential lobbyists given an opportunity, in private, to mould the rates in their own interest.

The first complaint on the U.N. tariffs came from the COMIBOL management, which pointed out the folly of burdening an already hard-pressed industry with heavy import duties on essential equipment and supplies. They were promptly told to draw up a complete schedule of the changes they wished to propose, with the assurance that their needs would be taken into consideration, with due regard to the needs of the general economy. There followed similar complaints from other sectors of the economy, and the same procedure was adopted. The council then called upon the various chambers of commerce and industry, and other entities, to present their recommendations by February 10 at the latest.[16]

General criteria for new tariffs. Meanwhile, it had become clear that the Minister of Finance, who would have the major responsibility in drawing up the new customs tariffs as well as in administering them, was resolved to increase duty rates to the maximum — to 300 per cent and even 500 per cent in some cases — with the laudable but incompatible objectives of maximizing revenues and cutting down on imports of luxury goods in order to economize foreign exchange.

Rates of this magnitude, however — in fact any rates of over 50 per cent — were nothing but an invitation to smuggling. Or, if they served as a protective measure, excessive rates would lead to the encouragement of uneconomic industries to the detriment of the country at large. I therefore laid my plans carefully and, at the February 12 meeting of the council, announced that I wished to present for the consideration of the council certain general criteria or norms drafted as a guide to consideration of the rates to be applied to the twelve hundred or so import categories.

First, however, I asked the Finance Minister if he could let us know how many watches had been imported into Bolivia in the past year, before the council considered whether or not to increase the duty from 200 per cent to 300 per cent in the case of gold watches, and from 130 to 200 per cent for other watches, as the Minister had suggested. In a few minutes, the information was available: 378 watches had been imported in 1955; the 1956 figures would not be ready for several months. I pulled from my pocket a letter from the Swiss Consul General. In the year 1955, Switzerland alone had exported 102,523 watches to Bolivia.[17]

Manifestly, I would never have dared to use this tactic had my relationship with the Minister been other than the most cordial, or if I had not known that the Minister had a keen sense of humor as well as a deep devotion to the task of collecting the nation's revenues. Then, too, it was not the present Minister, but his predecessor, who could be charged with having permitted the smuggling that had obviously taken place, so all joined heartily in the laughter that followed this revelation.

It was then pointed out that, at least in other countries in Latin America, smuggling was only possible through the payment of graft, and that if the rate of duty were lower than the cost of graft there would be no smuggling. It was added that the council members were far better able than a foreign adviser to judge how low the duty rate would have to be to eliminate smuggling or, rather, what was the maximum rate we could safely impose *and actually collect.* This was not flattery. We could hardly have assembled a more knowledgeable panel to pass judgment on the practical aspects of customs collection and evasion than the Minister of Finance and his Bolivian colleagues on the council.

It would be better, for example, to collect $2 million in revenues with a 20 per cent duty on 100,000 watches, worth $100 each, than to collect $90,000 in revenues with a 300 per cent duty on 300 watches, aside from the encouragement that the lower rate would give to legitimate trade instead of to smugglers. They all concurred with this argument, and decided that, with a 15 or 20 per cent duty, there could not possibly be any room for graft or contraband, and they likewise agreed that it would be foolish to continue charging a higher rate on gold watches than on other watches, inasmuch as the higher-priced watches would automatically pay a higher duty, and there was no point in encouraging graft by adding a further differential between a gold watch and a gold-plated one.

With this preliminary spadework over, the list of norms was submitted and approved, with some changes made at that and subsequent meetings. At the suggestion of the Finance Minister, a tariff committee was then formed, headed by a representative of his department, and including representatives of the Ministries of Mines, Economy, and Agriculture, with Roger Freeman of the U.S. Mission, Jean Peset of the U.N. Mission, and a representative of the Ford, Bacon & Davis Mining Mission, acting as technical advisers. The committee was charged with reviewing the tariff schedule in the light of the norms approved by the council, and consulting with all sectors of trade and industry, reviewing their petitions, recommendations, etc., following which they would present their proposed rate revisions for final review by the Stabilization Council.

These norms proved invaluable in facilitating the final rate review, although they were not, of course, adhered to nor intended to be adhered to with doctrinaire rigidity. Since they may be equally useful as a guide in any similar tariff revision elsewhere in Latin America, with such modifications as may seem expedient in each particular case, they are presented below. The comments are based on the experience of the council in the course of the eleven sessions in February and March,

1956, which it spent in reviewing every one of the 1,197 customs categories, item by item.[18]

General Criteria for Determining Import Duties

1. *The national interest.* (Each item of the tariff should be studied and determined from the viewpoint of the national interest, and not from the point of view of any particular industry or sector of the economy.)

   This meant that protective tariffs should not be so high that the higher prices paid by the nation as a whole exceed the benefits to the employers and employees in the particular protected industry. Obviously, this criterion was to establish a general attitude or state of mind, rather than a measurable norm. It did, however, rule out differential tariffs for different regions of the country, which were demanded by certain local interests.

2. *Protection of established industries.* (A maximum protective duty of 50 per cent should be established, on the theory that any industry which requires a higher rate of protection, in addition to the natural protection of high mountains and higher freight rates, is prima facie uneconomic, and must cost the nation more than the benefits received.)

   The council members considered that the maximum must be raised to 70 per cent. It was pointed out that many industries had existed solely by grace of raw material imports at the Bs. 190 rate and that to eliminate these overnight would cause unnecessary hardship; also that Bolivian industry was handicapped by high social security charges, lack of labor discipline, and low productivity. A sliding scale was then suggested, starting at a maximum of 75 per cent the first year and reaching a 50 per cent maximum by the fifth year. It was agreed, instead, not to establish a fixed percentage maximum, and a number of protective rates even higher than 70 per cent were granted, leading, in the end, to complaints by the protected industries that they were being forced out of business by smuggling.*

*As an example of the difficulties under which Bolivian industry operated, a local bottle manufacturer had purchased and installed modern bottle-making machinery, and labor refused to allow it to be operated more than a certain number of hours a day, insisting that a certain percentage of bottles be manufactured by antiquated blowing methods. Hence,

3. *Maximum revenues.* (On merchandise where the duty is
not protective — i.e., intended to prevent or curtail imports — the objective should be to maximize revenues,
which means to minimize smuggling.)

Here I introduced what may have been a new criterion in
customs classification: bulky articles should be charged
high rates of duty, small articles low rates, the theory
being that it is easier to smuggle small articles, so the
duty simply has to be low. On automobiles, the Finance
Minister proposed a tax by weight or horsepower, to
which I objected that this would appear to discriminate
against American automobiles, and a uniform percentage
rate of less than 50 per cent on cost was proposed, with
the main revenue to come from annual license fees based
on weight. Automobile import duties were evaded everywhere in South America, but the license plate would provide an easy means of verifying that the tax had been
paid. The council members said that a duty rate as low
as 50 per cent would mean that the cars would be imported into Bolivia and smuggled across the border to
Argentina or Brazil, where cars sold for three to five
times their U.S. list price. To this I replied that if
neighboring countries, because of high duties and low
morals, facilitated smuggling, this would bring money to
Bolivia and revenues to the exchequer, and it was not up
to Bolivia to put a stop to the trade; that Bolivia could
become a low-tariff, high-revenue area in South America, as Curaçao is in the Caribbean. The council members expressed their approval of these concepts, but the
Minister of Finance decided that it would be political
suicide to propose reducing the automobile tariffs below
the current high levels as, in Bolivia, the motor car is
the conspicuous luxury of the ultrarich. In the end, the
council placed a 300 per cent duty on automobiles of
$3,000 CIF value or higher, 150 per cent on cheaper
cars, 40 per cent on station wagons, and 20 per cent on
jeeps. The $3,000 borderline was changed to $2,500 by
the Cabinet. The idea of substituting a fairly high annual
license fee for an excessively high import duty, however,
is a valid one, and could be applied profitably in most of
the Latin American countries.

---

enterprising smugglers imported peroxide in various sizes of bottles, including beer bottles, dumped the contents in the river, and sold the bottles
in competition with those of domestic manufacture. The cost of peroxide
and the rate of duty on pharmaceuticals were negligible. Probably, too, a
great deal of H_2O was imported under the guise of H_2O_2.

To forestall criticism, the Minister of Finance announced that, inasmuch as maximum revenues were a *sine qua non* for stabilization, the council had agreed to the necessity of charging duties at reasonable rates on articles of relatively popular consumption, as adequate revenues could not be obtained merely by placing high duties on luxury imports which are imported only to a limited extent.*

4. *Conservation of foreign exchange.* In some cases, duties should be imposed at rates high enough to discourage imports, not so much for the protection of local industry as to conserve foreign exchange, bearing in mind that Bolivia was importing some $20 million of goods a year which could and should be produced in the country. This should be a temporary expedient.

5. *Simplification.* (There should be a general simplification of customs procedures, reduction of consular fees to nominal amounts, elimination of multiple charges for alleged "services," etc.; also a reduction in the number of different rates charged, from an infinite number of rates, with surcharges, etc., to 12 categories.)

It was agreed that customs simplification would have to be covered in a later general reform of customs charges and procedures, rather than in the tariff bill. The major simplification, of course, came with the December 15, 1956, stabilization measures, which eliminated the special surcharges, etc.

6. *Minimum rate scales.* (Customs duties should be eliminated entirely on machinery, tools, equipment, and raw materials used in agriculture, mining, or industry.)

By the time we got around to studying tariff revision, I had changed my views in the light of revenue needs, and

---

*It may be pointed out, for the benefit of readers not familiar with the Bolivian economy, that import duties in Bolivia are *not* regressive; they do not burden the great masses of the population who do not normally have the wherewithal to buy imported products in quantities sufficient to affect the family budget. When I first visited Bolivia, in 1940, the Indians would buy one sardine or one teaspoonful of canned salmon in the Indian markets, as an occasional luxury, and a modest duty would hardly have affected the price to the consumer, compared with the profit made by the Indian or chola entrepreneur in the market place. The sardines and similar products that formed a part of the staple diet of the poor in 1953-56 were brought in at official exchange rates of Bs. 60 or Bs. 190 to the dollar, an artificial situation that could not be perpetuated in any normal economy.

I urged that all imports pay a minimum tariff of at least
5 or 10 per cent, contending that a tariff of that magnitude would not discourage industry, and would be a good
way of raising revenues. The head of the Planning Commission pointed out, however, that consular fees were 6
per cent and service charges 2 per cent, so that probably
an additional 2 per cent would be all that the traffic could
bear. In connection with the minimum tariff scales, the
council unanimously agreed that the government and government enterprises should pay the same rates of duty
as private enterprises, both as a matter of sound accounting for the true costs of government industries and
to prevent the flagrant "losses" of government property.*

With these criteria as guides, the tariff committee appointed at the suggestion of the Finance Minister commenced
its work of revision of the schedule of import duties, conferring
with groups representative of all sectors of the economy which
would be affected by the new tariffs. As each section of the
tariff schedule was completed, the committee's proposals, together with the petitions and memoranda addressed to the council or Finance Ministry, were presented to the council, which
devoted twelve meetings to an item-by-item analysis, accepting
the committee's recommendations in some cases and rejecting
them in others where, in the judgment of the council members,
the committee had failed to give proper weight to the revenue
needs of the government, or to the economic necessities of the
industry affected, or, in some cases, to political factors which,

*The head of the Planning Commission pointed out in this connection,
that the Bolivian Development Corporation had in the past imported large
quantities of merchandise free of duty, and at the Bs. 190 rate; that the
goods had then been "lost" by a trucker, warehouseman, or intermediary,
who was compelled to reimburse only the official "cost," and that this was
the source of a large part of the goods that had entered the black market
or been smuggled out of the country; also that it was a principal reason
for the unhappiness of the corporation at post-stabilization developments.
The high-priced cameras, wrist watches, and binoculars conspicuously
flaunted by members of the previous administration had all been purchased
by the Development Corporation or Army, and "lost," and the political
personage to whose care they had been entrusted merely repaid the
boliviano value which may have been one-fiftieth of the true value. These
acquisitions formed a not inconsiderable addition to the revenues of the
truck-of-the-month club members of that regime (see p. 30). The council
decision to apply uniform tariffs to government and private industry was,
however, soon breached in practice.

in the opinion of the ministers on the council, could not be ignored.[19]

The only technical innovation in the preparation of the rate schedules was one suggested to cover sugar tariffs. The council accepted my argument that, if the world market price of sugar were to exceed a certain level, the local sugar industry, including the government mill at Guabirá, would need no protection, and it would be unfair to the consuming public to let the Bolivian producers take advantage of the tariff to charge more than the world price; also that, regardless of the world price, the duty should not rise above a certain maximum rate as, if the local mills required more than say a 50 or 60 per cent rate for protection, it was manifestly an uneconomic industry under the second criterion, and the public should not be compelled to support it. With agreement reached on those points, I scribbled a pencilled chart to give a sliding scale of duty rates, diminishing with rising world prices. After consultation with the principal private producer and with the management of the government mill as to the two extremes of the scale, the tariff schedule was enacted on that basis (see Fig. 7).[20]

On the whole, the council adhered to its established norms, but there were some politically motivated exceptions which generally proved to be unwise. For example, the duty on caviar, and on precious and semiprecious gems, was placed at 200 per cent, on jewelry 75 per cent, on costume jewelry 20 per cent, and on fighting bulls 150 per cent, while all other cattle imports were free of duty. Manifestly, with proper pecuniary persuasion, even the most pugnacious fighting bull could be passed off in the customs as a peace-loving sire — perhaps even as a steer or cow — while Tiffany's finest jewels could pass for Woolworth's cheapest, aside from the incongruity of charging a higher rate on gems than on mounted jewelry. These duties encouraged smuggling and were all in violation of the principles established in the third criterion. Possibly, however, the relatively low rate on jewels may have stimulated a lucrative export contraband trade with Argentina and Brazil, to the profit of the Bolivian economy.

Planed lumber was placed at 200 per cent, but smuggling was probably minimal in view of its bulk; heavy imports of finished lumber prior to stabilization had resulted from importations at the Bs. 190 official rate of exchange, and this was no longer possible. Certain articles, such as shoes, gloves, textiles, and glass, were subjected to specific duties per pair or per kilo, in addition to ad valorem rates.

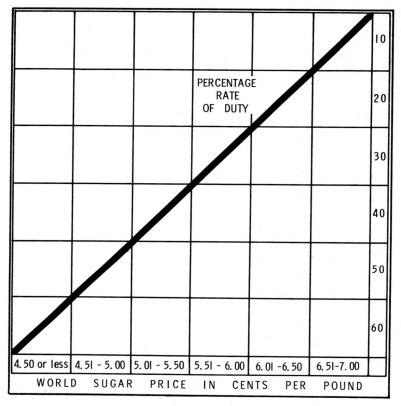

Fig. 7. Sugar tariff projection — maximum rate 60 per cent; duty-free if price exceeds 7 cents.

One low rate of duty — 2 to 4 per cent on wool — calls for explanation, as it might be thought that a somewhat higher rate should be charged in order to protect local wool production. A visit to one of the principal woolen textile plants in La Paz clearly demonstrated that it was more important at the time to protect the local textile industry than the local wool producers. Piled in one corner of the warehouse was the most incredibly filthy wool that I had ever seen, and I had been engaged in the wool import trade some thirty years before. Stones, mud, and straw were intermingled with a hopelessly tangled mass of greasy wool of varied classes and lengths. Some of the wool was being boiled in vats with various detergents to remove the lanolin and filth, but the expense was so high and the quality of the resultant product so low and unsuited for weaving in a power loom, that the management soon decided it would be more economical to dispose of the wool in the Indian market for what it would fetch. The wool had been purchased under government requirements in the prestabilization era, when textile mills were compelled to buy a certain percentage of local wool to get permits for the importation of foreign wool at the official rate of Bs. 190.

The council members were aware of this situation, as well as of the fact that the textile manufacturers (cotton and rayon as well as woolens) had survived the prestabilization period solely on the basis of Bs. 190 imports of raw materials and would be hit harder than any other industry under the new free market economy. Thus, they voted unanimously for the low rates. The head of the Planning Commission abstained from voting in view of his personal interest in a textile mill.*

The council completed its work on March 29 and sent the new tariff to the Cabinet on April 1 for immediate enactment, as the government was urgently in need of the revenues to meet its payrolls and other obligations. The Vice-President, however, was enraged at not having been consulted in so important a matter and threatened to withdraw his support from the *Co-Gobierno,* although constitutionally he had no power or right to intervene. The President therefore asked me to help pull the chestnuts from the fire, by accompanying the Finance Minister and explaining the proposed tariff schedule to the satisfaction of the Vice-President. Most of that meeting was taken up with explaining to the Vice-President the meaning of certain minor customs classifications until finally the Vice-President exploded that all those commodities put together did not amount to a row of beans — his choice of words was rather more scatological — and that there was no use wasting time putting a tariff on them. The Minister and I explained that we had followed the Brussels uniform classification and that, if we failed to enumerate some commodity, it might come in duty free or be placed in a class with some other commodity and pay a lower rate than it should.

* The Planning Commission head said he knew he would be criticized for favoring his own industry with low rates, but the plight of the textile industry was so obvious that this criticism never materialized. The Indian wool producers continued to have the women spin their wool, or sold it to others, as they had done for centuries, and were apparently not affected by the low duty on imported wool.

It was when we came to the category of watches, however, that the Vice-President really hit the ceiling. A 20 per cent duty on watches was outrageous — it should be 300 per cent, at least. The Minister patiently explained that a high tariff would encourage smuggling, an opinion based on the revelation of the disparity between actual imports and duty-paying imports, but the Vice-President insisted that, at the very least, the duty on gold watches should be double that on other watches — a poor man ought to be able to buy a cheap watch without paying the same duty as a rich man who buys a gold watch. It was explained that the duty on a $5 watch would only be 75 cents, compared with $75 on a $500 watch, but the Vice-President demanded that the rates should be 10 per cent and 20 per cent respectively, and the Minister and I tacitly agreed that he was probably right from the viewpoint of popular opinion and should certainly be allowed this meagre triumph in the long debate.* That concluded the discussion, and the Vice-President, still angry, said he would give the matter his further consideration.[21]

A week later, it was reported that government revenues were falling dangerously behind the budget schedule, largely because of the failure to enact the new tariffs (Appendix VI). Finally, on May 7, 1957, the new tariff was at last enacted, with half a dozen insignificant changes from the draft originally approved by the Stabilization Council.[22] The Vice-President's intervention had cost the government six billion bolivianos in uncollected revenues at a crucial moment, and had cost the business community many billions more with the paralyzation of trade as a result of uncertainty as to the new tariff rates.

Consequences of the new tariffs. The new rates were favorably received by business and the press, as well as they might have been, considering that for the first time in Bolivian history, and perhaps in the history of Latin America, a hearing had been given to every sector of the economy that had expressed a desire to be heard. A few minor complaints came to the council, such as the demand by the Forest Industries

---

*The council had itself been guided to some extent by political considerations. For example, while proposing a 60 per cent duty on clocks (more difficult to smuggle than watches), it made exceptions for alarm clocks (an article of necessity for the working classes) and for clocks to go on the outside of buildings (the poor man's wrist watch), and placed a 10 per cent rate on those items. The high duties on automobiles were, of course, politically motivated, and it would be unrealistic for a tariff-making body to insist on immunity from public opinion.

Chamber of Commerce asking for a 75 per cent duty on unfinished lumber (the lumber, including mine timber, was used chiefly by COMIBOL and the mining industry, and the council refused to raise the duty); and the demand of the Soap Manufacturers Association for a duty of 60 per cent on laundry soap and 75 per cent on toilet soap (this petition, too, was turned down).[23]

In the course of the ensuing months, as was to have been expected, other complaints materialized, probably most of them justified from the viewpoint of the industry concerned, but not necessarily so from the viewpoint of the national economy. COMIBOL, always a troublemaker for the Stabilization Council, announced to the press early in June that it was unable to make ends meet under the new tariffs, thus seeking to shift the blame to the council for losses attributable to its own shortcomings, despite the fact that the council had carefully followed COMIBOL's advice on every tariff affecting the mining operations, being overruled only in a few instances by the Cabinet. The council therefore announced that the public should submit all complaints and suggestions on the tariff rates to the council and that, after a further three months' experience, it would take a new look at the whole problem. Meanwhile, the President ordered COMIBOL not to air its troubles in the press but to take them up with the Minister of Mines or with the Council.

The smugglers protest. By far the most significant complaint, however, came from another source. On one occasion, shortly after enactment of the new tariff, as the Stabilization Council members were waiting in the anteroom outside the President's office, the President came out following a troop of as villainous-looking cutthroats as had ever been assembled in one place. The President put his arm around my shoulder and asked with a smile if I knew who his visitors were. No one on the council, with the exception of the Finance Minister, had the faintest idea. They were, the President explained, the leaders of the various units of the smugglers' league or union — friends of the most powerful politicians in the country — and their mission to the presidential palace was to complain that the "damned Eder tariff" was making it impossible for them to continue in business, and that the duty rates would simply have to be increased.

We all laughed, and I remarked that we now knew exactly what had to be done to prevent smuggling and increase government revenues, that there were still a number of duty rates that experience would show were too high, and that these should be reduced wherever smuggling became a problem. It never occurred to me that this lesson, so convincingly learned, would not be followed, or that rates would actually be increased to meet political pressures in support of the contraband trade.

But at council meetings in May and June the Finance Minister reported that, because of the intervention and pressures of "certain groups," the government had taken measures that made it impossible to prevent smuggling, and he hoped the council would take the matter up with the President. He stated that he could practically rid the country of smuggling in thirty days if he were given a free hand. The Minister of Mines objected that, if any drastic measures were taken, there would be a general uprising, as the smugglers' prices were lower than those charged in the stores, to which I replied that this was only natural as they paid no duties.

Two days before I left, at a farewell luncheon given by the board of directors of the Central Bank, the Finance Minister pointed out, from the roof of the Copacabana Hotel, the "smugglers' market," going full blast again and amply protected by friends in the *Co-Gobierno*. And two months later, the Stabilization Council vainly begged the President to permit the Finance Minister to take the measures that he said were needed to wipe out the smuggling that was ruining the textile industry, among others. [24]

Real property tax

According to the U.N. (Keenleyside) report, the inadequacy of real property taxation "is one of the weakest points in the Bolivian revenue system." [25] At the time that study was made (in 1950, prior to the Revolution), rural property was subject to a departmental tax of 0.4 per cent of assessed value and to a national tax of 0.18 per cent (called an income tax but actually on an imputed income based on the assessment). As a result of inflation, however, and "outmoded and incomplete self-assessments," with understaffed, poorly paid, and incompetent assessment offices, assessed values were "only a small fraction of actual current values" — probably less than one-third on the average. Urban real estate was subject to municipal taxes of 0.2 to 0.8 per cent of assessed value and to the national tax on the imputed income, equal in all to 0.32 per cent on the assessment. Keenleyside estimates, however, that, because of assessment deficiencies, the aggregate tax on urban property was only

0.1 to 0.4 per cent of actual current values, while some city property had never been assessed *and paid no tax.*

By 1956, when inflation had reached the galloping stage, the rural tax had been raised to 0.64 per cent of assessed value, and the urban taxes to about 6.5 per cent,[26] but the latter figure included charges for municipal services. Assessed values, however, were completely meaningless with the drop in the value of the boliviano from Bs. 60 to the dollar, at the time the Keenleyside report was written, to Bs. 14,000 to the dollar at the peak of the inflation. What "real values" may have been under such conditions would have been impossible to say, as rent controls were such that, on rented property, the income was in many cases less than the current charges for municipal services, and certainly far below minimum maintenance costs. A few fortunate landlords were able to rent to foreign diplomatic personnel, charging dollar rentals. In such cases, even though the owner's purpose in renting may háve been merely to avoid confiscation by the Revolutionary Government, and he may have charged rentals that were extremely low by any reasonable standard, there was at least some income of tangible value.

Under such circumstances, it would have been difficult to devise a sound system of land assessment for tax purposes that would place a fair value on three substantially identical properties, one rent-controlled in bolivianos, another subject to dollar-rentals, and the third owner-occupied. Rural land appraisal was in an even more disordered state as a consequence of inflation, "land reform," and squatter invasions.

Basis for self-assessment. With this situation in mind, I proposed, at a prestabilization council meeting, a single tax on real property to take the place of the existing multiple taxes on assessments, on imputed income, and on rentals, plus taxes disguised as charges for municipal services, etc., not to speak of a proposed tithe on farm production.

The difficulty in a single-tax proposal, the Finance Minister stated, was that it would take two to five years to make a cadastral survey of real property in Bolivia that could serve as a basis for a single tax (that is, a chorographic study, delineating property boundaries and placing an assessed valuation on each property); that, meanwhile, it was better to continue with the current system of multiple taxes in order to obtain maximum revenues; and that tax rates should be raised to produce a total of Bs. 60 billion a year in revenues in lieu of the Bs. 20 billion alleged to be collected at that time. The Minister further stated that the average cost of collection of the real property taxes throughout the republic was 25 per cent of the amount collected, but that it ran from as high as 115 per cent in the smaller towns to as low as 15 per cent in La Paz. He hoped to reduce the average cost to 20 per cent by increasing the compensation paid to the tax collectors and improving collection methods.*

These figures and percentages, in the confusion induced by the inflation peak, may all be taken with a grain of salt, but it was evident that there could be no real reform of the land tax system without adequate appraisals and that a cadastral survey could not be completed in time to be of any use in the stabilization program. This was borne out by the Keenleyside report, which held that it would take two to three years for such a survey, even under the better organized administration before the Revolution.[27]

With that in mind, I drew up an outline for a plan of self-assessment, which it was believed would be self-enforcing, and presented it to the council in March, 1957. The Finance Minister expressed his agreement with the proposal. The president of the Central Bank added the indispensable concomitant that controlled rents must be increased over a three-year period until they bore a rational relationship to property values. President Siles agreed that self-assessment under the proposed plan would be feasible, and that the distribution of rural lands under the "agrarian reform" should be completed by 1958, when it should be possible to commence taxing the peasants.

And yet, despite the agreement of the council on the proposal, and the urgent necessity of increased revenues and real property tax reform of one kind or another, nothing was done; and, in mid-1957, tax appraisals, even in the most advanced city of all, La Paz, were seventeen years out of date.[28] Seven years later, a proposed rural land tax drafted under the pressure of U.S., U.N., and IMF advisers, was postponed for "further study," and farm land, at this writing, pays no taxes whatsoever.[29]

Since one may hear and read *ad nauseum* statements by U.S. tax "experts," unfamiliar with the environment, that real property tax reform in Latin America is blocked by the wealthy

---

*Tax officials receive a 4 per cent commission on collections above specified target levels (Zondag, p. 28), so that presumably the Minister hoped, by raising their compensation, to minimize the temptations that might be offered to them by taxpayers.

landowners or by the "oligarchs," this example of inertia under a proletarian government may be enlightening. Perhaps it may be concluded that, so long as it is easier for Latin American governments to get their revenues from U.S. taxpayers, local taxes will never be increased.

Because the suggestions for self-appraisals may be valid as a temporary expedient in any country recovering from a galloping inflation, and because they contain certain self-policing provisions which it is believed have not been applied in other self-assessment schemes, an outline of the main provisions, taken from a memorandum left with the Stabilization Council in June, 1957, is given below:

Basis for Self-Assessment and Taxation of Real Property

1. Property owners should be required to file with the tax office a description of their property and boundaries, by parcels where appropriate, placing a separate value on land and buildings. Any property not declared within a specified time would be *bono vacante* and revert to the state. These descriptions and self-assessments would be kept readily available for public inspection, and the newspapers would be free to publish them at any time.

2. The owner would be free to revalue his property (or correct the description of its boundaries) at any time; but, to prevent undervaluation and subsequent revaluation immediately prior to sale or expropriation, and at the same time to impose a moderate tax on capital appreciation, there would be a 10 per cent tax on any declared *increase* in value. The tax could be on a sliding scale, diminishing according to the length of time the property is held following the latest self-assessment, and there could be a double penalty tax on any reassessment made within six months prior to an expropriation procedure.

3. The government would have the right to expropriate — for cash, and not for bonds of dubious value — any property or parcel, at any time, at 110 per cent of the self-assessed value (on later consideration, I would place this at 120 per cent), either for a public use declared by law or, in the alternative, being required to dispose of the property at public auction within three months, the owner meanwhile to retain title and possession. If the auction fails to bring a price at least equal to 110 (or 120) per cent of the assessed value, this will be considered evidence of the reasonableness of the owner's assessment, and he will be allowed to retain title and possession, and

be reimbursed for all costs, including legal fees. As a possible additional policing measure, it might be provided that anyone else (other than the government) would have the right to make a cash tender in the appropriate local court for, say, 150 per cent of the assessed value, and acquire the property at that price. Note that expropriation, or forced sale, under these conditions, where the owner is placed on notice by law at the time of self-assessment that the property may be expropriated or purchased at his own evaluation plus x per cent, is by no means the same as expropriation based on the tax assessment — whether self-assessed or not — where there is no such prior notice. Expropriation under such conditions would be clearly confiscatory.*

4. The national real property tax on that assessment would be at the rate of 1 per cent per annum, and this tax would be in lieu of all other national taxes on real estate or on income from real estate (rentals, farm products, etc.), other than on income from the subsoil (in Latin America, in general, petroleum and other mineral rights are taxed by royalties, surface taxes, etc., frequently under concession contracts). Municipal taxes would take the form of a surcharge on the national tax, collected simultaneously by the national tax collectors, and would not be greater than double the national tax, so that the total tax on urban real property would not exceed 3 per cent. This municipal tax would be in lieu of all other municipal taxes on real property, including charges for water, sewers, garbage collections, and other municipal services, the cost of collection of which is disproportionate to the revenue obtained. (This paragraph would be applicable solely to conditions in Bolivia; in other countries, it might be preferable to tax income from real

---

*The idea of self-assessment, of course, was not original, although it is believed that these safeguards are. Some years later, Werner Baer proposed a similar but less detailed plan which merits consideration, and Nicholas Kaldor suggested an amendment whereby an owner could refuse to sell his property at 120 per cent of the self-assessment but would be forced to reappraise at the highest bid, whereupon the frustrated bidder would be entitled to a reward equal to the amount of the additional tax. This points up the necessity of having tax measures conform to the local mores, as in the Latin American tax environment, certainly in Bolivia, Kaldor's scheme would be an open invitation to blackmail and graft (Werner Baer and Isaac Kerstenetsky [eds.], *Inflation and Growth in Latin America* [Homewood, Ill.: Richard D. Irwin, 1964], p. 503).

property under the income tax, and certainly to charge separately for water and other services.)

5. So long as rent controls are maintained, and on all existing leases, the landlord should be permitted immediately to add to the rent the difference between the new tax and the former tax. The controlled rent should thereafter be determined on the basis of a 6 per cent net return on the self-assessed value of the property, including among the deductible expenses the property tax, maintenance, and such other expenses as the rent control board may determine; the increase in rental determined in that manner should be applied at the rate of 25 per cent per annum for four years, following which rent controls should be abandoned.

6. There should be a 3 per cent transfer tax on all real property transfers, by sale, inheritance, or otherwise, except by expropriation. To police this tax, the claimed purchase price should prima facie be the purchaser's assessed value, subject to the 10 per cent tax on subsequent reassessments provided under paragraph 2.

Ultimately, of course, it would be expected that a self-assessment plan would be replaced by a proper official assessment system, but it is by no means necessary that such a system be based on the detailed military topographical surveys that are customary in Latin America. The only essential is that the maps and property descriptions, with the respective property evaluations, be sufficiently clear and readily accessible to any member of the public, so that property owners themselves will police possible curtailments of their property lines, or overassessments of their properties, in comparison with the boundaries and assessments of their neighbors. It would be hard to improve on the appraisal system instituted by William the Conquerer in 1085 A.D., with twelve-man local landowner juries to determine bounds and values under the supervision of the representatives of the crown.

Fiscal or Budgetary Measures

It will be recalled that among the data submitted by the Bolivian government and Central Bank to the IMF in applying for a stabilization fund loan was a complete budget of government receipts and expenditures, including among the latter the anticipated deficits of the various government enterprises (Table 6,

p. 203). The budget, however, was a legislative matter and, under the emergency decree, the President and Cabinet, "with the approval of the National Monetary Stabilization Council" (Appendix II), were empowered to enact the budget by decree with the force of law.[30]

In mid-February of 1957, that decree appeared in the press, having been enacted *without consultation with the Stabilization Council,* and revealing an increase in expenditures of Bs. 36 billion above the figures submitted to the IMF and other lending agencies.

The revenues to meet these additional expenditures were a result of the arrangements made by the head of the Planning Board with the Export-Import Bank of Washington. These arrangements deferred payments of $2 million due in 1957, $2.3 million in 1958, and $2.5 million in 1959, amounting in effect to a new $6.8 million loan from the Eximbank, but the arrangements were only made possible by Bolivia's budgetary commitments under its application for a stabilization loan. Furthermore, how a $4.8 million saving in 1958-59 could possibly be applied to balancing a 1957 budget was beyond comprehension. When the matter was brought up at the council meeting, the Finance Minister reported that it had been necessary to increase the government budget because, in the original figures, certain expenditures for foodstuffs, etc. had been miscalculated at the Bs. 190 rate![31]

This incident is but one of many that show how lightheartedly the Bolivian government entered into — and subsequently ignored — its commitments. Although Bolivia, as a sovereign nation, could not be held to its obligations by any foreign power, and much less by the Stabilization Council, on the other hand, neither could the U.S. government nor the IMF be compelled to continue financing Bolivia if it violated them.

To avoid future incidents of this kind, which might prove disastrous to the stabilization program, I informed the council that the mission headed by General Lawton Collins which had just visited Bolivia had been favorably impressed by the stabilization program as a whole. But I pointed out that they had remarked on certain "cracks appearing in the structure," in particular, that budgeted estimates of revenues were not being met because the Cabinet had failed to pass certain tax measures recommended by the council and had made changes in other measures which largely vitiated their revenue objectives.[32] The council was informed that the U.S. adviser on taxation, Roger

Freeman, had estimated that, as a consequence, actual tax revenues in 1957 would not exceed Bs. 130-Bs. 140 billion, compared with a budget estimate of Bs. 174 billion. It was emphasized that Bolivia should live up to its obligations under the stabilization program in order not to jeopardize the U.S. aid program which the Washington visitors had emphasized would soon be up for study by Congress.

Ross Moore, head of the U.S. Operations Mission in Bolivia, hammered away on the same theme in a strongly worded letter to the Minister of Finance, in which he pointed out that net receipts by the monetary department of the Central Bank from the Mining Corporation (COMIBOL) for the first quarter of 1957 were only $5,181,000, or at the rate of $20,724,000 a year, compared with estimated net receipts from that source of $30,859,850 in the foreign exchange budget which was presented to Washington as the basis for the stabilization fund financing. The letter went on to state that the deficit was all the more serious in that the budget had been computed on the basis of 90-cent tin whereas prices for the last three months of 1956 (on which receipts for the first quarter would be based) had been substantially above that figure. The letter closed with the statement that the contributions of the U.S. government to the stabilization fund presupposed the full and prompt sale of U.S. dollar receipts by the Mining Corporation to the Central Bank.[33]

Ostensibly, these repeated warnings had no effect whatsoever on COMIBOL or on the Bolivian government but, as a matter of fact, they were regarded seriously by the President and his colleagues on the Stabilization Council. What extremes Bolivian profligacy might have reached had it not been for such warnings may be imagined.

The foreign exchange budget was another measure that had to be enacted by decree. This, too, was done without consultation with the Stabilization Council despite the shifting of some $5 million on the expenditure side (as a result of the Eximbank debt postponement), as compared with the budget presented in connection with Bolivia's loan application.[34]

Banking and Credit Regulation

It is obvious that in any constructive program of economic development based even in part upon a free enterprise system, one of the first prerequisites is to remove all unnecessary restrictions on the nation's banking system so as to make it possible for the banks to finance the productive sectors of the economy — agriculture, mining, and industry.

Bolivia's banking system was in desperate straits after three years of galloping inflation, and many of the private banks were on the verge of bankruptcy.[35] The government banks were all in a state of insolvency, concealed in the accounting wonderland of multiple exchange rates, and were kept from bankruptcy by the government at the expense of the general economy.

Bank credits were further limited — that is, in addition to their lack of financial resources — by four principal legal restrictions: (1) the requirement, dating from October 27, 1955, that the private banks and the banking department of the Central Bank maintain reserves equal to 40 per cent of their deposits (the government Mining Bank and Agricultural Bank were exempt from reserve requirements); (2) a limitation, dating from May, 1955, on the deposits they were allowed to receive, equal to ten times their paid-in capital and surplus; (3) a qualitative credit restriction, dating from July, 1954, under which the banks' credits to commerce were limited to an amount equal to 10 per cent of their deposits, the remainder of their credit facilities being available for industry; and (4) various interest rates established by law for each type of loan, and a tax of 2 to 8 per cent per annum on all credits, dating from March, 1956, which further increased the rate of interest paid by the borrower.

For example, agricultural credits for the purchase of machinery paid 8 per cent interest, plus a 2 per cent tax, or 10 per cent in all; industrial credits paid 15 per cent plus 4 per cent tax; and commercial and private credits, 21 per cent plus 8 per cent.[36] Even this rate of 29 per cent per annum was, of course, a negative interest rate, in view of the galloping inflation — the borrower paid back much less than he had received in terms of actual purchasing power, and the lending banks found themselves increasingly impoverished year after year despite glowing reports of paper profits. Even the paper profits disappeared in 1956.*

*As an example of the plight of the nation's commercial banks, the following figures show the position of the largest private bank, the Banco Nacional de Bolivia, in 1956, prior to stabilization. Under the law at that time, the bank was permitted to receive deposits of Bs. 2.55 billion, or ten times its capital and surplus. Against this amount, it was required to maintain legal reserves of slightly over Bs. 1 billion (40 per cent), and

Credit controls

Supposedly, we on the council should have opened wide the floodgates of credit in order to restore life to a moribund economy, and this is what we were urged to do by the banks and by the press. But we were forced to build a dike against the sea of troubles that confronted Bolivia as a consequence of the inflationary tide.[37]

Industry was faced with a dearth of working capital, and the owners would have borrowed hand over fist if they had been allowed to, but industry's basic problems were lack of labor discipline, excess workers, high social security charges, and, above all, the importation by most Bolivian industries of raw materials at the fundamentally uneconomical rate of Bs. 190 to the dollar. To lend industry money under such circumstances would ruin the banks and perpetuate a situation that could only be remedied by a thorough process of reorganization, perhaps by bankruptcy.

Agriculture's problem was chiefly a matter of competition with subsidized imports, and that problem we had solved with the stabilization measures. Credit was not the immediate need, although we on the council were prepared to see that sufficient agricultural credits to promote increased production were made available as soon as feasible.

Mining was beset with many of the same problems as industry — excess labor, lack of discipline, and excessive social security costs, but most mining was basically not antieconomic and could contribute to the economy, so that the council was anxious to relax restrictions on mining credits for productive purposes as soon as that could be done safely.

Commerce faced the same three basic problems as mining and industry, but there was no such urgency in releasing credits

---

cash of Bs. 255 million (10 per cent of deposits). That left approximately Bs. 1.3 billion available for loans (including liquid assets available from the bank's capital and surplus). Assuming that this were all loaned at the highest permissible interest rate ($16\frac{1}{2}$ per cent), this would give gross revenues of Bs. 215 million. Actually, the bank's estimated gross revenues for 1956, including income from investments, amounted to Bs. 296 million. Its payroll, however, was Bs. 500 million and, with all other expenses, its estimated expenses for 1956 added up to Bs. 709 million, leaving a deficit of Bs. 413 million, or nearly double its capital and surplus *at the end of October, 1955*. In other words, throughout 1956, the capital and surplus shown on the books was a minus quantity. (Based on figures published in *El Diario*, April 26, 1956; Zondag report, pp. 39-40.)

for commerce as there was in the case of mining and agriculture. Credit to any sector of the economy would, of course, entail inflationary potentialities, by increasing the demand potential without immediately increasing the supply of goods. But, at
least, credits to agriculture and mining, and in a few cases to
industry, could, if wisely directed, increase the supply of goods
within a relatively short period — within a single crop year in
the case of farm products — while credit to commerce could
only, in the short run, be purely inflationary with no offsetting
advantages of increasing production.*

Above all, however, it was essential to take every possible
precaution against a flight of capital; and, if even a small percentage of the credits granted were to be diverted to the purchase of foreign exchange not needed for absolutely essential
goods or services, the stabilization fund would soon be depleted.
It was safer to err on the side of conservatism, even at the risk
of slowing economic recovery for a month or two, rather than
on the side of liberality at the risk of imperiling the whole
stabilization program. The government Mining Bank and the
Agricultural Bank, however, had proved incapable of operating
under the December 31, 1956, restrictions; so, with political as
well as financial considerations in mind, the council approved,
virtually without change, the revised reserve requirements and
credit restrictions drafted principally by the U.S. Financial
Mission expert, Ernest Moore, on January 22, 1957.

The old 40 per cent reserve requirement was kept in force
on the amount of deposits in the banks' books as of December
31, 1956, and an additional 10 per cent reserve (instead of the
December 50 per cent requirement) was placed on any deposits
in excess of those amounts. As the 40 per cent reserve ratio
did not apply to the Mining and Agricultural Banks, those banks
were subject only to a 10 per cent reserve limitation that applied solely to post-1956 deposits. In effect, they were free of
all restrictions. Deposit limitations were cut down from ten
times capital and surplus to seven times, with the requirement
that any excess over that amount must be deposited in the monetary department of the Central Bank.[38]

*There was no point, in a moment of such dire need, in contemplating
the essential economic contribution of marketing in all its aspects —
Bolivia was not suffering from a lack of distribution facilities so much as
from a lack of tangible goods; and, if we wished to avoid further inflation,
we could not allow the banks to create more money to chase the limited
supply of goods. Production, not distribution, had to be the primary purpose of credit.

Less than a fortnight after publication of these regulations, a delegation of bankers appeared before the council to plead for their revocation and for a return to the pre-inflation maximum reserve ratio of 20 per cent. There is no doubt that the situation of the banks was desperate, but at the same time it was equally clear that the bankers failed to grasp how essential it was to prevent a misuse of credit facilities.[39] Nevertheless, the council did allow a return to the former deposit limitation of ten times capital and surplus, although it refused to relax the reserve requirements. Moore suggested, however, doing away with any rigid ratio between commercial and industrial loans, chiefly because of the practical futility of most qualitative credit restrictions. For political reasons — the deep-rooted prejudice against merchants — the council compromised on that point by changing the ratio between industrial and commercial credits from 80/20 per cent to 60/40 per cent.*

As a further means of relieving the plight of the private banks, I suggested that the government be authorized to carry deposit accounts in those banks, and that the banks be permitted to pay interest on credit balances to attract such deposits, a suggestion which Moore quite properly amended by proposing a ceiling on interest rates on all deposits. It was pointed out, however, that the government was required by law to keep its deposits in the Central Bank (this could, of course, have been changed), so it was suggested that at least the various social security funds, including that of the CNSS, should be allowed to carry their deposits in the private banks and could reduce social security charges if they received interest in such accounts. Nothing came of this proposal.

*Some three months later, Moore presented a completely revised draft of regulations which, in general, froze reserves as of that time, but increased the reserve ratio on deposits after that date to 75 per cent, at the same time permitting the banks to receive deposits up to 15 times their paid-in capital and surplus. The Finance Minister complained that this was the third time since stabilization that changes in the reserve ratios had been proposed, but I pointed out that the regulations would have to be amended frequently during the early stages of the stabilization program, and suggested that future changes be made by the Superintendent of Banks, with the advice of the President of the Central Bank and of Moore and Woodley, rather than referred to the council, so as to avoid the popular impression that the council could not make up its mind. This was agreed. (Decree 4647, May 14, 1957; *La Nación*, May 16, 1957; 29th *Annual Report*, 1957, Central Bank, p. 133; revised regulations issued October 30, 1957, Resolution 75322, *ibid.*, pp. 22, 149.)

Shortly thereafter, the council did away with the tax on bank credits, which gave some relief both to the banks and to borrowers, and, a few days later, qualitative credit regulations were enacted with a view to giving priority in loans to those credits most likely to result in increased production over the near or medium term. Later, in April, 1957, other regulations were enacted, following consultation with the U.S. Operations Mission in Bolivia, which made it possible for the banks to extend credit for the procurement of imported equipment and supplies under the Point IV arrangements.[40] This not only provided some relief to the banks and to industry, agriculture, and mining, but served to cut the U.S. aid red tape which had impeded the supply of counterpart funds, desperately needed to make up the deficiency in current government revenues resulting from the Cabinet's failure to enact the tax legislation proposed by the Stabilization Council.[41]

Interest rates

In the discussions in council prior to enactment of these credit regulations, the question of interest rates arose. In conversations with Ross Moore I had advocated that the Central Bank should fix its interest rates as low as possible and do everything feasible to induce the private banks to follow suit, on the ground that low interest rates provide one of the strongest possible incentives to increased investment in agriculture and industry, and hence to economic recovery.

It was not a question of removing credit restrictions. I did not differ in the slightest from my more conservative colleagues as to the necessity, under then prevailing conditions, of restricting credits to productive uses in order to prevent a flight of capital. It was merely that, *where a credit proved justified and was granted,* it made sense that it be granted at the lowest possible rate. In Bolivia, this might have been in the neighborhood of 6 per cent per annum, now that we were banking on permanent currency stability. I was willing to concede, however, that the private banks were in such a precarious position that they could scarcely afford to engage in lending operations at that rate of interest, and that probably an 8 per cent rate for loans to the public for productive purposes would be appropriate for the time being.

I was not then and am not now persuaded that the conventional view that high interest rates tend to restrain inflation is applicable in a country such as Bolivia, recovering from an inflationary spree and desperately attempting to increase production. Even in a more stable economy, high interest rates are the most dangerous weapon in the monetary arsenal for combating inflation and may well prove to be a two-edged sword. In general, only the most reckless and improvident speculators will borrow money for investment at rates of 12 per cent or higher, and what we urgently required in Bolivia was to encourage sound investment for productive purposes by farmers, miners, and businessmen who might risk borrowing at 6 or 8 per cent, but not at 12 per cent or higher.

The Bolivian members of the council agreed that a 6 per cent rate would be desirable, although recognizing that the banks might require 8 per cent; but more conservative counsel prevailed and, in the event, a variable scale of rates was adopted, of 8, 10, and 12 per cent for U.S. aid import financing, depending on the nature and prospective use of the product. The 8, 15, and 21 per cent rates for agriculture, industry, and mining, respectively, were left in force, as well as an $11\frac{1}{2}$ per cent rate on interbank credits, but the council did obtain the repeal of the 2 to 8 per cent tax.[42] *

Revaluation of gold

One more step remained to be taken, both in justice to the banking community and to enable the private banks to utilize to the full their meagre resources in financing the recovery of the Bolivian economy. The matter affected only two banks, the Banco Nacional de Bolivia and the Banco Mercantil, S. A., but those two banks were the most important private banking institutions in Bolivia and the treatment accorded those institutions would have repercussions in banking circles both within Bolivia and abroad. †

*In 1959 the rediscount rate for U.S. aid imports was cut to the unrealistic level of 3 per cent, but a high interest philosophy continued to prevail with respect to commercial and industrial credits which were cut to 19 per cent and 13 per cent respectively (31st *Annual Report* [1959], Central Bank, p. 46).

†The Banco Nacional is Bolivia's oldest extant banking institution, established in 1871 in the capital city of Sucre, and successor to Bolivia's first bank, the Banco Boliviano, founded in 1869 by Henry Meiggs, whose name will be familiar to Latin Americanists as that of one of the American pioneer families whose spirit of enterprise contributed so largely to the

The Nacional had over one million dollars in gold bars and in sterling, while the Mercantil had a substantial but lesser sum in gold, sterling, and dollars. The problem was the revaluation of those assets, which would correct the picture of insolvency shown on their books, and multiply by many times the volume of credit that the banks could extend to the business community. In the case of the Nacional, it would permit the bank to erect a new bank building to replace its temporary decrepit structure as, under the banking laws, not over 10 per cent of the bank's capital and surplus could be invested in building.

A decree approving a revaluation of business assets in general, subject to a 3 per cent tax payable over two years, had been approved by the council on December 17, 1956, and after considerable political opposition was enacted on January 22, 1957; but that decree had provided that revaluation of bank assets, including gold and foreign exchange, would be covered by a separate act. Early in January, 1957, therefore, Ernest Moore had proposed that any gold or foreign exchange held by the banks should be revalued at the boliviano equivalent of $35 an ounce, subject to a 50 per cent tax on the increased value.

The subject was so delicate politically, however, with strong pressure from the *Co-Gobierno* members of the Cabinet to confiscate such holdings outright, that it was not until a month later that the council could turn its attention to the subject. On that occasion, I asked the Superintendent of Banks whether the gold and foreign exchange held by the banks, and in particular the million dollars, chiefly in gold bars, held by the National Bank, was actually and legally the property of that bank, or whether, in strict law, it was held by the bank as an agent for the government or for the Central Bank. The Superintendent replied that the question had been raised before and that there was no doubt that those assets were in fact the property of the banks. The president of the Central Bank confirmed

---

development of the Latin American nations from the time of their independence. (See *El Exportador Americano,* **CXXXI** [August, 1942], pp. 23-148, for history of American pioneers in Latin America.) Both these banks were banks of issue, their charters empowering them to issue bank notes. In 1914, however, the Banco de la Nación Boliviana (est. 1911) was given a monopoly on the note issue until, after scandalous mismanagement, its place was taken by the present Central Bank. The Banco Mercantil, S.A., was founded in 1906 by Simón Patiño. (Data on banks from *Polk's Bank Directory* [Nashville, Tenn.: R. L. Polk and Co., 1964] and Zondag, pp. 35-38.)

that this was true, adding that the proof of the fact that the government recognized the banks' title to their gold and *devisen* holdings was that, at the time of the prior revaluation in April, 1953, the banks had been required to pay a 50 per cent tax on the increased value of their gold and 12 per cent on revaluation of their other assets.*

If that were true, I stated, the banks might be required to pay a further tax on revaluation at the present time, but the question of title to the foreign exchange *since 1953*, and particularly to the gold, was so fundamental that the council needed to satisfy itself beyond any reasonable doubt that those assets were not in fact held for account of the Central Bank and, furthermore, whether, under Bolivia's Constitution and laws, any private individual or institution could lawfully possess gold in Bolivia or abroad. Moore added that the April, 1953, decree would appear to imply that the *devisen*, at least, were held by the banks as agents for the Central Bank. The council thereupon resolved that the Superintendent of Banks should confer with Dr. Sologuren, who had been acting as legal adviser to the council, in order to settle that question beyond peradventure.

By the end of February, Moore presented a draft decree to the council, accompanied by an opinion from Dr. Sologuren upholding the banks' title to their gold and *devisen* holdings. The question then arose as to the rate at which the revaluation of such assets should be effected, and I suggested a simple arithmetical conversion from Bs. 190 to the dollar to Bs. 7,500, with the gold valued at $35 a troy ounce. (Note that the usual rule in such cases is to use the lowest value for the local currency that can reasonably be anticipated at the time.) Dr. Antezana, the president of the Central Bank, however, suggested a rate of Bs. 7,000, partly on the ground that this would increase public confidence in the value of the boliviano, and partly because it would be unfair to tax the banks on a revaluation at the Bs. 7,500 rate if ultimately the boliviano were to be stabilized at Bs. 7,000 or less.

As to the rate of tax, for which Moore had suggested 50 per cent, I demurred that actually any tax at all would be confiscatory, as there was certainly no profit in revaluation — merely a

---

*Decree of May 14, 1953. There was a further revaluation (of real property only) in July, 1956, and on this revaluation the banks were forced to pay a tax of 7 per cent (Decree 4445, July 5, 1956; Zondag report, pp. 40, 172).

book entry showing the value in depreciated bolivianos of exactly the same asset that had previously been carried in the accounts, in bolivianos of higher purchasing power. Nevertheless, I admitted that an American was hardly in a position to argue the point, as the United States had confiscated private gold holdings, paying for them in dollars worth 59 per cent of the former gold value, and that other governments had done practically the same thing in one way or another, generally involving an even greater degree of confiscation. Thus, considering the previous revaluation taxes, perhaps a tax of 30 per cent on the paper profit should be the permissible ceiling. Dr. Antezana suggested, however — and this is a sound principle to bear in mind — that the rate of tax should be in inverse ratio to the degree of depreciation of the currency. He therefore recommended a 12 per cent tax. On further consideration, the council agreed with his reasoning, and Dr. Antezana's proposal of a Bs. 7,000 rate for revaluation, and a 12 per cent tax, were resolved unanimously.

The pressure for confiscation, however, was so strong in the Cabinet that it was not until May 14, 1957, three months after the council resolution, that the decree authorizing revaluation of bank assets was finally enacted.[43] Meanwhile, of course, economic recovery remained hampered by the lack of available credit resources that might otherwise have been provided without danger to the stabilization program.*

Governmental development banks

One other banking matter occupied the attention of the council, namely, the insolvency and inefficacy of the government's commercial and development banking agencies, represented by the banking departments of the Central Bank, the Agricultural Bank, the mining Bank, and the Bolivian Development Corporation.

The Central Bank had been established in 1928, on the recommendation of the Kemmerer Mission, and was intended to function solely as a central bank (see p. 44 for its background

---

*It was not until much later that political pressure had relaxed sufficiently to permit the government to authorize the banks to export this gold and thus provide much-needed foreign exchange to the economy (Decree 4723, September 5, 1957; *El Diario,* September 6, 1957; 29th *Annual Report* [1957], Central Bank, p. 129).

and history.) Following the Chaco War, however, it had been taken over by the government and, in 1956, was reorganized into two departments: (1) a monetary department which soon debased its central banking function into that of a currency printing press for financing the government's expenditures; and (2) a banking department which was intended to operate as a commercial and development bank but was soon diverted from its purpose by political interference, so that, at the time of stabilization, it had been reduced to a state of lingering insolvency, with its assets composed largely of uncollectible political loans.   The Agricultural Bank had been founded in 1942 as an agricultural development institution and, despite political interference and mismanagement, was performing a useful function in handling supervised credits to farmers in cooperation with the experienced farm credit staff of Point IV.   The Mining Bank (established 1936) was likewise a development bank. Its problems of political intervention, mismanagement, and apparent corruption, have been outlined at page 57.[44]   The problems of the Bolivian Development Corporation have been set forth at page 197.

Impressed by the United Nation's criticism of the development financing activities of the Mining and Agricultural Banks, and the Bolivian Development Corporation, as well as by its advocacy of a single Bank of Economic Development,[45] I sought to kill four birds with one stone by suggesting the separation of the banking department of the Central Bank from the monetary department and merging the former with the three other development finance agencies.   There was a sufficient nucleus of trained personnel in the Agricultural Bank and in the new top management of the Mining Bank to staff a single development bank, whereas it would be impossible to find in Bolivia — even if all Bolivians in exile were encouraged to return — sufficient qualified banking personnel to staff four such institutions. The surplus personnel — incompetent, corrupt, or both — could be dismissed, with profit to the budget, while one could hope that the four deficitary agencies would be replaced by one institution that might at least break even.   Then, too, it might be possible to persuade the Bolivian government to employ one experienced and hardheaded foreign banker, or banking mission, to get the new development bank started, but it would be impossible to procure four such experts or missions to head four separate institutions, and it was obvious that there was no one in Bolivia capable of managing any one of these agencies.

Ernest Moore, of the U.S. Financial Mission, was fully in accord with the view that the banking department should be removed from the Central Bank and had expressed that view soon after his arrival.   Thus, when representatives of the private banks presented a petition to the Stabilization Council late in January, 1957, asking that the United Nations be requested to appoint an expert or experts to assist the private banks in solving their postinflationary problems, and to help the government form an industrial development bank, the council was informed that Moore was already exploring the separation of the Central Bank banking activities from its monetary operations, and the merger of the former with the mining and agricultural banks to form a single development bank on the Chilean model, that would handle all governmental financing of economic development.*

The council expressed its approval of an investigation by Moore. As to the proposed assistance from the United Nations, the Bolivian council members asserted that they had had their fill of U.N. banking experts. They agreed that John Woodley of the IMF Mission and Ernest Moore of the U.S. Mission were fully competent to advise both the government and private banking institutions for the present and that their work might be hindered rather than helped by the employment of another expert who might lack their practical approach.

By May, 1957, Moore had completed his first draft of a decree-law reorganizing the Central Bank, together with a separate statute creating a development bank with which the banking department of the Central Bank would be merged. The president of the Central Bank was in complete agreement with Moore's proposals, but the latter stated that he would like to discuss the bills further with certain members of the Cabinet and others. This he did, and kept working on the project steadily, but political inertia was such that it was not until September, 1957, shortly before his return to the United States that Moore was able to present a full report to the council. In this report he recommended a number of much-needed reforms in Bolivia's banking system, including the proposal that the two

*The Chilean Development Bank is one of the two most successful such institutions in Latin America, although its operations have been completely distorted by persistent monetary depreciation. It has remained free from politics and corruption, and is, or should be, a model for development institutions elsewhere in Latin America.

departments of the Central Bank, "with divergent and conflicting aims," be segregated at the earliest possible date, by converting the monetary department into "a true central bank," and the banking department into "a true development bank," the latter to take over the Agricultural and Mining Banks and refrain from competing with the private commercial banks in the short-term credit field.[46]

This proposal, like so many others suggested to and approved by the Stabilization Council, came to naught, and eight years and some $300 million later, the United States is still helping to finance those four incompetent and improvident development institutions in Bolivia, and has even organized and helped to finance a fifth — the Industrial Credit Bank — as well as a new Savings and Loan Association, Bolivia's first (see p. 597).

16

CLEANING UP THE MESS

Finally, in addition to the tax measures, fiscal measures, and banking and credit measures recommended by the Stabilization Council as the final steps in the stabilization program, there were a number of other measures that can perhaps best be grouped under the head of cleaning up the mess — remedial measures to rid the country of the remaining distortions and disparities of the inflationary period.

Pending Prestabilization Accounts

The stabilization decree had abolished the old system of *remanentes, revertibles,* and *bonos de sobreproducción* — various expedients to increase the incentive to produce and export, by permitting the importation of other merchandise, in some cases at the market rate of exchange and in others at the rate of Bs. 190 to the dollar.* Obviously, when stabilization struck on December 15, 1956, many of these peculiar rights or privileges were still outstanding — the metal concentrates or agricultural products exported prior to that date, the import merchandise ordered or en route to Bolivia, foreign exchange bought or contracted for, etc. The problem was how to clean up

*There is no point in explaining the nature of these devices at length. They were peculiar to Bolivia, although other Latin American countries had and still have equally or even more complicated provisions made necessary chiefly by reason of the maintenance of multiple exchange rates and highly artificial rates of exchange (see Zondag report, Annex to Chap. 3, pp. 5-7, and Annex 1 to Chap. 4, for a brief description). The best description of the system is contained in a Planning Commission report, dated January-June, 1956, prepared by Humberto Fossati and D. A. Rangel, but this would not be generally available. Briefly, a *remanente* is the remainder due to the miner in foreign exchange on mineral exports for which he was paid only an advance in bolivianos. A *revertible* is a surcharge on foreign exchange that reverted to the government to offset what would otherwise be a windfall profit (p. 37). A *bono de sobreproducción* is a bonus for producing products that it might otherwise not have been profitable to produce, in theory, on *excess* production, that is, on production greater than in some prior period.

the last of these prestabilization accounts in fairness to the importers and exporters concerned, yet without detriment to other merchants or too great a strain on the stabilization fund or the national economy.

It was not a simple question of saying that the claim to these privileged imports constituted a vested right that had to be met by the government or the Central Bank, come what may. In the state of corruption preceding stabilization, many of these special import privileges had been obtained through questionable means, and to recognize those privileges as vested rights would have been to favor the most corrupt elements in the economy to the detriment of legitimate importers. In many, probably in most, cases the import rights had been transferred to others. My point of view was that those middlemen had bought the import permits with their eyes open, knowing for months in advance that stabilization was coming and that when it came the special privileges were bound to vanish. They nevertheless chose to take the risk, hoping to slip in under the wire.*

The President took the view that where the import permit provided for imports at the rate of Bs. 190 to the dollar, the holders of the permits should be allowed to stew in their own juice — it would be unfair to current importers to allow certain privileged competitors to bring in imports at that rate. On the other hand, where an importer had procured an unprivileged import permit, and had bought foreign exchange on the free market at Bs. 12,000-Bs. 14,000 to the dollar, it would be unfair to insist on charging the current, very much higher import duties, as this would put him in a position where he could not compete with those who were now importing freely at around Bs. 7,500 to the dollar.

---

*At one council meeting I reported that I had conferred with a number of the leading importers of German nationality, and that they had agreed that those who had engaged in import operations since August 4, 1956 (when the Stabilization Council was established), were fully aware of the risks they were running and should suffer the consequences. This was the more noteworthy, as the German business community stood to lose as much as anyone from the cancellation of prestabilization import privileges, but they were, for the most part, old enough to have lived through the German trillionfold inflation of 1923 and were willing to make any sacrifice for a "return to morality." The moral crisis, the corruption engendered and multiplied by inflation, was their chief problem, more serious, they said, than the inflation itself.

Much was to be said, and much was said, on all sides of the argument, and the council discussed the problem at meeting after meeting, from late January to the end of April, with petitions and pressures from every source, including the inexorable pressure of the *Co-Gobierno* leaders exercised through the Minister of Mines as Juan Lechín's representative on the Stabilization Council.[47]

Again and again during the discussions, it was necessary to insist that we needed to know the amounts involved in any proposed decision before an opinion could be ventured "on principle," and again and again the council members would embark on lengthy discussions of this or that solution of a problem with only the faintest idea of how much such a solution would cost the government or the Central Bank. This was in an area where valid arguments could be adduced as a matter of principle in favor of any one of a number of conflicting solutions, and where the one overriding principle should have been the preservation of the national economy. So far as could be judged from the alleged facts presented at the various council meetings, the total amount involved in *remanentes, revertibles,* and *bonos de sobreproducción,* may have aggregated some $5 million, but there were many other at least equally plausible claims for foreign exchange at the prestabilization official rate, from foreign consulates, the railways, and others.[48]

As an indication of the multiplicity of these claims for the recognition of prestabilization privileges, the agenda for one council meeting contained fifty-three separate questions for discussion and resolution by the council — proposed decree-laws; railway and public utility rates; prices for petroleum products sold by the government petroleum corporation; claims for foreign exchange at the official Bs. 190 rate by cable, radio, railroad, and airline companies, and by the Chilean, Brazilian, Peruvian, and Panamanian embassies; half a dozen complex problems presented by the Central Bank; labor dismissal and wage problems; petitions for tax exemptions; demands for credit submitted by the Development Corporation, the Mining Bank, and the Mining Corporation for funds; tax questions; problems relating to imports and exports under the Brazilian and Argentine trade agreements in fictitious trade-agreement dollars; and other problems — none of them simple. Nineteen of the items on the agenda involved demands for foreign exchange at the Bs. 190 rate, and no single solution was appropriate for them all.[49]

To have allowed all such claims would have been to give away $5 million — perhaps more — for less than 3 per cent of its value, and whereas this might be possible and even justifiable in a country with substantial foreign exchange resources of its own, it was certainly not appropriate in the case of a country whose foreign exchange balance was a negative figure and whose stabilization fund had been provided chiefly through the unwitting generosity of the American taxpayer.

If these claims were in fact a valid obligation of the Central Bank and of the government, as the president of the Central Bank contended, then, I argued, they were no more valid than the $40 million of claims of American and other exporters who were stuck with unpaid bills of exchange guaranteed by the Central Bank, and, in fact, no more valid than the $166 million owed to the bondholders. At the most, therefore, the claimants on *revertibles, bonos de sobreproducción,* and other prestabilization accounts, should get no better treatment than the five-year payment plan proposed for the foreign exporters. But the bondholders and foreign exporters were far away, and the miners and Bolivian exporters were close at hand. Uncle Sam proved to be a Santa Claus rather than a Shylock, and the conscientious head of U.S. aid in Bolivia was a much less menacing figure than Juan Lechín, so that, in the end, the American taxpayer and the stabilization fund did in fact contribute to paying off these privileged claims under the following conditions:

> Importers who had merchandise en route to Bolivia, in port, or in customs, imported under *bonos de sobreproducción,* derived from mineral, agricultural, or forest production exports and issued between November 3, 1955, and December 14, 1956, were given dollars to pay for the imports, at the prestabilization, official exchange rate, and were allowed to pay customs duties at the prestabilization tariffs which were equal to about one-fifth of the current tariffs. On the other hand, they were required to pay a 12 per cent "export royalty" but, as the importer was not usually the same person as the exporter of the minerals or other products, the export tax was computed on the value of the imported merchandise. Those who had already withdrawn their merchandise from customs were allowed to claim a refund under similar conditions. [50]

As the Mining Bank lacked available funds with which to make these payments, it was permitted to use for this purpose the funds it had in the Central Bank, which had been frozen in accordance with the stabilization fund agreements, and the government was expected to make good this withdrawal out of its 1958 budget — sufficiently far in the future so that, so far as is known, it was an obligation honored in the breach. [51]

Mining companies that had balances due them as of December 15, 1956, for *remanentes* (amounts usable for imports or other foreign exchange payments out of the proceeds of their mineral exports), were permitted to obtain dollars at the rate of Bs. 190 for the payment of salaries and commissions, and for imports of mining equipment, machinery, and spare parts; on imports of supplies, tools, vehicles, and parts they would have to pay the current rate of exchange, on the theory that such goods could be sold in the market at current prices. However, to prevent an immediate drain on the stabilization fund, the *remanente* balances could only be used in the form of, and to the extent of, a 10 per cent discount from the export royalties payable on future mineral exports.*

Imports under this decree, whether at the Bs. 190 rate or at the current rate, were required to pay customs duties at the tariff rates in force at the time of clearing through customs. The same decree ordered the Mining Bank to transfer to the Central Bank, in part payment of its debt to that bank, 755 kilos of gold bars (worth approximately $850,000) which the Mining Bank had acquired from various mining companies prior to stabilization. The value of this gold would be credited against the Mining Bank's overdraft in bolivianos at the current rate of exchange and at the current world price of gold, and the Central Bank was required to lend the government the boliviano equivalent, repayable without interest on May 15, 1962, to enable the government to cover the difference between the Bs. 190 rate and the current Bs. 7,500 rate on imports under this decree. [52] In theory, delivery of the gold avoided a direct, immediate drain on the stabilization fund, although in fact, as Bolivia's aggregate gold and foreign exchange resources were a minus figure, any drain anywhere lowered the general level and, in the end, it was always the American taxpayer who replenished the reservoir through the stabilization fund or through ICA grants.

*This limitation later brought a complaint from the National Mining Association that wolfram (tungsten) exporters were thereby barred from collecting their *remanentes*, as world wolfram prices were so low at the time that no export royalty was collectible. The same petition included a request that the small mining companies be released from the obligation of selling their output exclusively through the Mining Bank (*La Nación*, May 23, 1957).

An extreme example

Early in April, the Minister of Economy, supported by the president of the Central Bank, accompanied by the assistant manager of the monetary department presented a claim to the council for $319,000 at the Bs. 190 rate, principally on behalf of a cooperative company in Cochabamba that had been engaged in transporting Brazil nuts by plane from the forests of the Beni and Pando, cracking the outer pod and exporting the nuts in their shells. The $319,000 represented the balance supposedly due to that company and other exporters of agricultural and forest products, which, prior to stabilization, would have been used for such imports but, of course, could no longer be employed for that purpose. The Central Bank president contended that this constituted a debt of the bank and a legal and moral commitment of the government. In that event, I argued, the nut crackers should stand in line and wait their turn with the bond-holders and other creditors, who also held legal and moral claims against the government.

In the course of the discussion the Minister of Economy stated that current high freight rates, and the stabilization measures which prohibited the dealers in agricultural and commercial products from importing at the Bs. 190 rate, had ruined the Brazil nut industry; that the law of November 3, 1955, which had made possible that trade, had been beneficial to the country, "and the export statistics proved it"; and that it might well be said that the policy of the Paz-Estenssoro government had been to promote agricultural exports, while the policy of the Siles-Zuazo regime was to kill them.

The air transportation of Brazil nuts in their outer shells, as large as coconuts and much heavier, had only been possible because the government airline, which purchased equipment and aviation gas at the Bs. 190 rate for a fraction of the true value, charged freight rates so low that the airline's actual losses were many times greater than any possible profit to the exporter. The import privilege granted to the nut-cracking company, which was the real basis of the business, was costing the national economy 98 cents on every dollar of imports (the difference between the Bs. 190 rate and a typical prestabilization free rate of Bs. 10,000). How a person as intelligent and loyal as the then Minister of Economy could make such a claim, three months after the successful stabilization of the currency, can only be explained in the light of his later expression of pride in the fact that he had never been two-faced — had never voted one way in the council, from an objective economic viewpoint, and then taken an opposite stand in the Cabinet where his actions would have to be based on his political loyalties as a labor minister (see p. 451n).

In the end, the claimants were given the benefit of the Bs. 190 rate but were theoretically required to pay the export royalty, as set forth above at p. 357.   However, three weeks later, against my recommendation, the Brazil nut merchants were given $298,000 in cash, plus an advance of $37,000 for their *remanentes*, and in June, 1957, the Minister of Economy again appeared before the council to ask that the export tax on Brazil nuts be lowered from 10 per cent to 2 per cent, which was done. A few days later the Minister requested that the council authorize a Bs. 360 million, two-year loan from the Central Bank to the Brazil nut cooperative.   My viewpoint was that, if the business were sound from an economic standpoint, the cooperative should be able to borrow from a private commercial bank, and that, if it were not sound, the Central Bank should certainly not lend the money.[53]   It was resolved, however, that the Central Bank should look into the matter; and, as this was close to the time of my departure from Bolivia, and political influences in the Beni and Cochabamba were powerful, it seems likely that the credit was granted.

Other pending accounts

In addition to these claims between the government sector and the private sector, other claims were presented to the Stabilization Council for dollars at the prestabilization rate that involved the government sector alone.

A number of government departments, as well as the Development Corporation, COMIBOL, YPFB, and other government agencies, demanded dollars at the Bs. 190 rate for payment of goods that they had ordered prior to stabilization.   All of these orders had been placed in clear violation of the August 4, 1956, decree establishing the Stabilization Council which provided that "from the date of this decree, no government department or government agency may enter into new obligations without the express authorization of the council under penalty of nullity" (Appendix I, Art. 6).   The council was adamant against granting any exchange at Bs. 190 to the dollar, which would have meant depleting the Stabilization Fund to pay for overpriced merchandise; each case was handled on its merits, and in some cases a reasonable length of time for payment at the current rate of exchange was authorized.

The Chilean, Peruvian, Brazilian, and Panamanian consulates also presented claims for dollars at the Bs. 190 rate, on the ground that they had been charging that rate for consular fees and other services. Other consulates had been charging the free rate of exchange. The council decided that there was no vested right to foreign exchange at the Bs. 190 rate and ruled that it was up to the Ministry of Foreign Affairs to decide whether it wished to provide the funds at its own expense, which in the end it did.

Pending Concession Contracts

Much against its wishes, the council was drawn into a discussion of four concession contract negotiations that had been pending since before enactment of the stabilization decrees. The reason for the council intervention is that these pending contracts contained provisions for export taxes, or freedom from export taxes, or for duty-free imports or other privileges, which were contrary to the general rules laid down in the stabilization measures.

A mining concession and its aftermath

The most troublesome of these was a proposed mining concession that the Minister of Mines said had been pending for eight months prior to stabilization. The interested party was reported to have already invested $150,000; and, if the concession were not granted immediately, he would leave Bolivia, and the country would be deprived of an investment that would reach many millions of dollars. Offhand, it appeared that the only objection the council might have would be to the export royalties proposed in the concession, but a review of the draft contract would determine whether there were any other conditions that might run counter to the stabilization measures. If not, it would be up to the Ministry of Mines to approve or disapprove the contract. The council, however, asked me to obtain credit information in the United States on the party in interest, despite my expressed reluctance to get into that phase of the negotiation.

Thus, a month later, at the end of February, I was able to announce favorable reports received through the ICA from Dun & Bradstreet and from various banks with respect to the individual who was negotiating for the concession. However, the person in question was engaged in the textile business in New York with a modest capital and apparently had had no experience in mining. I further stated that the party had visited me at my hotel, where he confirmed those reports, and had insisted on showing me a statement of expenditures totaling $96,800 out of a paid-in capital of $150,000, with pending obligations of $75,000, not including $8,000 which he stated he had spent personally to cover traveling expenses to and in the United States for a certain high official in the Bolivian government, and for certain minor legal expenses. The listed expenses also included $3,000 to a Bolivian lawyer who was one of Juan Lechín's close advisers.

In view of these circumstances, I advised that it would be desirable for one of the Bolivian members of the council to suggest to the Minister of Mines (who was not present at the meeting) that, to avoid possible criticism, the matter might be left in the hands of the Planning Commission, although I emphasized that I had in fact been favorably impressed with the frankness and sincerity of the prospective concessionaire, and that I was not accusing the Minister or anyone else of any impropriety.[54]

It was suggested that the Planning Commission give the matter its immediate attention, making certain changes in the proposed concession contract which the concessionaire had said he would be willing to accept. I added that neither I nor the council should express an opinion as to whether the concession should be granted, as that was not a function of the Stabilization Council. I recommended, however, that the Planning Commission might wish to lay down as a general rule that no long-term mining concessions should be granted without fixing a reasonably short term for the exploration period during which the concessionaire should show some signs of real activity, inasmuch as Bolivia had over 14,000 mining concessions outstanding and not being worked, which stood as a potential threat of litigation to future legitimate concessionaires. Ernest Moore added that the Planning Commission should investigate the "moral solvency" of prospective concessionaires as well as their financial solvency, but I stated that it would be preferable not to include that in the recommendation, as it might be taken as a reflection on the integrity of the proposed concessionaire or other gentlemen involved in this particular concession.

Apparently, neither the President nor the other members of the council had been aware, at least not officially, of the fact that the trip to the United States of the official in question had been financed by a prospective concessionaire, and the Minister was so incensed at this revelation that he refused to attend the next twenty-one meetings of the council.*

Finally, on April 1, 1957 — the "Day of the Innocents" (see p. 422n) — a formal "reconciliation" was staged in the office of the Finance Minister. The Minister of Mines stated that the trip to the United States was in the interest of Bolivia and that payment of expenses by the prospective concessionaire meant an economy for the Bolivian government. For my part, I repeated before the Minister of Mines and other council members what I had previously stated at the February meeting, that neither then nor at any other time had I impugned the integrity of any official of the Bolivian government, but had merely reported to the council the statements which had been made and shown to me as Executive Director, and which I had a duty to report.

That ended the problem of personal conflict, but the President was so upset by the revelation, and so chary of all concessions as a consequence, that, over a month later, nothing had been done on this concession and I reported to the council a visit from the lawyer for the party in question, who was still interested in getting the concession in order to recoup what he had invested. On the suggestion of the Minister of Economy, the council recommended that the Minister of Mines study the matter, but that no privileges contrary to the stabilization decrees should be granted, and that the scale of royalties should be that provided in the present law or in any future amendment of that law.

It was further resolved: (1) that thenceforth the council would not intervene in any concession matter, and that all negotiations should be handled by the appropriate Ministry in conjunction with the Planning Commission; (2) that it should be put on record that this particular concession contract had been amended by the Executive Director, with the agreement of the

*This was the alleged reason for his absence, but it seems probable that his abstention from the council was due to a more serious revelation four meetings earlier, as he was likewise absent for those intervening meetings (see pp. 392-93).

prospective concessionaire, solely with respect to its conformity to the stabilization decrees; (3) that the council recommended that the draft contract be amended to conform to those
decrees, with no special privileges for royalties, taxes, or exemptions; (4) that existing vested rights in the region should be
respected and that the contract should include a provision for
its expiration if the area is not actively explored and developed
within a reasonable fixed period; and (5) that, in future, before
approaching the council, the Ministry and Planning Commission
should make a thorough investigation of the background, solvency, and experience of the proponent in the particular field of
activity involved.

Vegetable fibre and bag factory

Probably the first concession to come to the council's
attention was one for the cultivation of *kenaf* (a vegetable fibre
used as a substitute for jute) on an experimental scale, construction of a processing plant and bag factory, and technical
and other assistance to farmers who would grow the *kenaf* under
contract with the mill.   USOM/Bolivia had spoken highly of the
promoters; they had made an excellent impression on all concerned; they seemed to be adequately financed; the project,
which would have meant the immediate employment of some
1,000 workers, chiefly in agriculture, should have been one of
high priority from the viewpoint of economic development and
employment. Within eighteen to twenty-four months, the project
could save the foreign exchange needed by the government mining corporation, the independent miners, and the Ministry of
Economy for imported ore bags and gunny sacks. Yet negotiations were delayed month after month until the principals in the
United States had just about reached the conclusion that there
was no use in waiting any longer. There is good reason to believe that the only thing that was holding up this concession was
the influence of Bolivia's most powerful political leaders, who
were engaged in the lucrative sale of imported jute bags to
COMIBOL and the Mining Bank at well over world market
prices (see p. 392).
Whatever the cause of the delay, the proposed concession
contract was amended by the council to conform to the stabilization decrees (chiefly that the company would buy foreign exchange on the free market; that its purchases abroad would not
be guaranteed by the Central Bank; and that it would have full

freedom to import, export, and fix prices in a free market). The council then sent the contract back to the Planning Commission with the recommendation that the matter be given its earliest attention. The problem was now out of the council's hand, but, as economic adviser to the President, I had a further legitimate interest in economic development and attempted to speed a decision, favorable or otherwise, so that the negotiator could either go ahead with the proposed development or else abandon it. Finally, a thoroughly reliable source reported that the Planning Commission had given its immediate approval and that the matter remained unresolved in the President's hands because of powerful political pressures on the one hand and the President's wariness in approving any concessions on the other.*

Thus, Bolivia, clamoring for more U.S. aid for "economic development," forfeited what might have been an opportunity for real economic development by private enterprise which, had it failed, would not have cost the Bolivian government or the U.S. government one penny. The investors, however, could not go ahead without a concession, which in this case would have been merely a permission by the Ministry of Agriculture, a moderate protective tariff thereafter available to everyone, and at least reasonable assurance that COMIBOL and the Mining Bank would purchase their product if it proved competitive with imported bags in quality and price. The free market economy in Bolivia was still largely in the paper stage.

Gas plant concession

The only other concession proposal that came before the council was presented by the former head of Tippetts, Abbett, McCarthy & Stratton, the engineering firm that had worked on the Cochabamba-Santa Cruz highway and other projects. This gentleman was enthusiastic about the possibilities of

---

*I had been informed by the proposed concessionary, and earlier by his attorney, Luis Adolfo Siles, a lawyer of the highest reputation, that the contract was delayed because of insistence on the part of one government official for payment of $10,000, which was flatly refused. This was reported to the President, including the name of the official; the truth of this report was later confirmed by a person high in the President's confidence. Nevertheless, I am of the opinion that the high profit on imported bags, rather than the comparatively minor payment for "expediting" the concession contract, was the crux of the matter.

commercializing natural gas, which was largely a waste product of the YPFB. He was frank to admit that he had only $20,000 to $25,000 of his own to invest but that, if he could obtain a concession, he felt sure he could raise the needed funds in the United States. His reputation for integrity and competence was such that this seemed at least a possibility. YPFB was anxious to go ahead with the project, which they estimated would require an investment of about $1.5 million, and the head of the Planning Commission and I suggested that, in lieu of a concession, a simple, nonexclusive contract for the sale of gas for a reasonable period of years would suffice to give the proponent a *de facto* monopoly that would enable him to finance the operation without requiring the political approval that would be needed for a concession. YPFB had full authority to enter into such an agreement as a simple sales contract, but its board of directors believed it would be politically inadvisable to do so without calling for bids, and the other council members agreed. In the end, so far as could be learned, this requirement, because of the fear of political intervention, marked the end of the project, to the disappointment of the general manager of YPFB as well as of the proponent, and perhaps to the detriment of the country's economy.

Revaluation of Business Assets

One final major step remained to be taken to clean up the mess left in the wake of the four years of galloping inflation, namely the revaluation of business assets. It will be recalled that, while I was in Washington working on the financial arrangements for the stabilization fund, a decree had been submitted for my approval which would have provided for a flat Bs. 190 to Bs. 6,000 revaluation of physical assets, and a 3 per cent tax on the paper "profit" (p. 261).

Following my return, and an explanation of my objections to the original proposal, the council approved a revaluation decree on December 17, 1956, but, because of political pressures, it was not until late in January, 1957, that the measure was finally enacted by the President and Cabinet. The decree provided for an optional revaluation of fixed assets, not at an arbitrary ratio based on the depreciation of the boliviano in terms of dollars or general internal purchasing power, but at their "true present value." Revaluation could be made optional because business firms had a threefold incentive to revalue: (1) to revise their accounting, which had become meaningless not only because of the depreciation but because some assets had been bought at Bs. 190 to the dollar and others at free market rates of exchange up to Bs. 14,000; (2) to show their true net worth as a basis for future bank credit; and (3) to increase their depreciation charges on the basis of real values, which would, of course, reduce their income taxes. However, to deter exaggerated reappraisals, the revaluation accounts would have to be approved by the Finance Ministry (not an impossible task in Bolivia's limited economy), and, as a further deterrent, there was a 3 per cent tax on the amount of the write-up. The tax, however, would be payable, one-fourth at the time of presenting the reappraisal accounts, with a deadline at December 31, 1957, and the remainder in three equal instalments at six-month intervals.[55]

It may be asked why a voluntary system of true present value reappraisal was adopted, and why so modest a rate of tax was imposed. There is a long record of business experience with arbitrary revaluations in other countries of Latin America, with confiscatory taxation of supposed "profits" from revaluation, and it was hoped to avoid wrecking the Bolivian economy by imposing any such system.*

The fact is that, in a country where the currency has depreciated to one-fortieth of its previous value within a three-year period, as was true in Bolivia, a company which had fixed assets of say Bs. 10 million in 1953 would have had to write those assets up to Bs. 400 million in 1956, if a uniform

*In the French revaluations following World War I, and again under the law of December 28, 1959, assets were revalued on the basis of annual coefficients or indices of purchasing power, based on the date of acquisition of each individual asset. Such a system had much to recommend it, from the viewpoint of simplicity as well as to guard against exaggerated depreciation allowances in future income tax returns. A 3 per cent tax was imposed on the write-up under the 1959 law, and it may be presumed that this tax — a capital levy, as there was no profit merely in rewriting book values to correspond to the depreciation in the purchasing power of the franc — was not unduly burdensome *under conditions as they existed in France at the time*. The French example was emulated in a number of other countries, where the depreciation had been more extreme, and where the tax on the write-up was substantially higher. The consequences were not felicitous. (See Arthur Andersen & Co., *Tax and Trade Guide: France* [New York: Arthur Andersen & Co., 1961], p. 39, for a resumé of the French system of *réévaluation* reserves and tax; and Martin Norr and Pierre Kerlan, *Taxation in France,* pp. 322-33, for a comprehensive description.)

revaluation rate were imposed, and even a 3 per cent tax on the write-up would amount to Bs. 11.7 million. Now, in any country that has undergone a severe inflation, the invariable consequence is a diminution of working capital, with current indebtedness stretched to the bursting point; appreciation of inventories limited by price controls; and wage and other current cash demands, including taxes, inflated beyond any reasonably foreseeable working capital requirements. "Decapitalization" is the term commonly applied to this situation and, while decapitalization is the most serious business ill in every country of Latin America that has suffered from inflation, in Bolivia the decapitalization of commerce, industry, and mining was absolute. A tax of over 100 per cent of the preinflation fixed investment, and in many cases far more than 100 per cent of the preinflation capital stock, would have thrown every business enterprise in the country into bankruptcy. My arguments on this point were ably supported by the Finance Minister, the President of the Central Bank, and the head of the Planning Commission.

Privately owned public utilities were required by the decree to revalue their assets under the supervision of the appropriate authorities, as such reappraisals would affect rates as well as taxes. Government-owned enterprises were allowed to revalue over a five-year period, free of tax. Although this was wrong from any sensible accounting or economic viewpoint, it was clear that if COMIBOL and the other government companies revalued their assets — all purchased at Bs. 190 or Bs. 60 to the dollar — on any proper basis, and took annual depreciation on those values at any reasonable rate, their state of absolute bankruptcy would be too glaringly revealed for this to be politically possible.

This decree-law was enacted and published on January 22, 1957, but a month later, to the astonishment of the members of the American Financial Advisory Mission, the President informed us that, although the Cabinet had approved the decree drafted by the council, a group of labor leaders headed by Lechín demanded that the tax be increased to a sliding scale of 15 to 60 per cent, and the government — a *Co-Gobierno* split between the constitutional authorities and Lechín's COB — was faced with an impasse.*

*According to a speech made by Juan Lechín to the COB, the COB's demand was for a sliding scale of tax from 5 per cent to 50 per cent (*La Nación*, June 6, 1957). Such a tax, imposed on an obligatory revaluation of forty to one, as was proposed, would have meant the end of private enterprise in Bolivia.

Later, the Finance Minister reported that the labor ministers insisted on a 45 per cent tax but that the government ministers were holding out for a 5 per cent tax (3 per cent for mining), payable in a lump sum, and that the Cabinet as a whole — labor ministers and government ministers — demanded an additional 6 per cent capital levy on all business (the "patrimony" tax common in Latin America). I protested that inflation and taxes had squeezed the lemon dry and that, if those taxes were passed, Bolivia might as well give up any hope of economic recovery or permanent monetary stability.

On August 14, 1957, the government, which had expressly provided in the January 22 decree that the tax imposed by that decree would be the only tax levied on revaluation, reversed itself by imposing a 6 per cent levy on an obligatory and arbitrary forty-to-one revaluation. And taxpayers were not permitted to use the new valuation in computing depreciation accruals, nor could they charge the tax as an expense for income tax purposes! The sole saving feature of the decree was that the tax was payable in instalments over a five-year period. That decree marked the beginning of the end of any faith that business may have had in the ability of the *Co-Gobierno* to keep its promises. [56]

VI

THE FIRST YEAR

17

THE GOVERNMENT ENTERPRISES

The first year of stabilization, as might have been expected, brought its share of problems, as is evidenced by the fact that during the first three months of 1957 the National Monetary Stabilization Council sessions were held on an average of three times a week. There were crises, disasters, and triumphs, but the triumphs must have outweighed the disasters for, at the end of the year, despite an authorized increase in wages, the boliviano was firm, living costs were lower than at the end of 1956, and the stabilization fund was substantially intact. The members of the council could well look upon their work and see that it was good.

Moreover, in all the crises faced by the council during the first troubled year of stabilization, it may be said without exaggeration that there was not a single serious problem of an economic nature, not a single legitimate complaint from private industry, trade, agriculture, or mining that could not be solved by minor, necessary adjustments here and there within the basic framework of the stabilization program. The sole insoluble problems and crises came from within the government itself — and from the *políticos* and labor leaders who ran the government.

The Mining Corporation

The rate of exchange

Difficulties with COMIBOL, the government-owned mining corporation, continued to occupy the center of the stage throughout the 1957 year. Early in January, the head of the Ford, Bacon & Davis mining mission reported that COMIBOL would need an exchange rate of between Bs. 11,000 and Bs. 12,000 to the dollar, instead of the prevailing Bs. 7,500 rate, in order to operate successfully.

FBD was not, of course, in a position to judge the foreign exchange situation from the viewpoint of the general economy. It later turned out that neither FBD nor the COMIBOL management had sufficiently accurate information, even with respect to the COMIBOL accounts, to express a balanced judgment on the subject. Nevertheless, on the basis of statements emanating from FBD and from the COMIBOL economic staff, indiscreetly repeated in various circles, rumors were rife that the boliviano would be devalued, and the pressure was soon felt in the demand for dollars at the Central Bank.

The council had no authority to control the indiscretions of the FBD representative, so Ross Moore, the chief of USOM/ Bolivia was asked to help. A meeting was called, and Moore attempted to impress upon the FBD mission head that it was of the utmost importance that no further statements be made with respect to foreign exchange rates or COMIBOL's financial position, except to him personally or to me, as Executive Director of the council. I requested that he submit a pencilled statement of the accounting facts, as a typed statement could not possibly be kept confidential.

Despite that warning, the FBD representative and the chief economist of COMIBOL had a hectographed report prepared (February, 1957) purporting to show the rate of exchange that COMIBOL would require in order to operate without loss under various hypotheses, both mine by mine and in the aggregate, and gave this statement to the Minister of Mines — a direct channel to the opponents of the stabilization program. At the same time, they discussed its contents with at least two private mine owners. As a consequence, the gossip in financial circles was that the rate would be increased to Bs. 10,000 per dollar, and the stabilization fund lost two million dollars in cash in two weeks. This was flight capital, as investigation showed that there was no basic sudden need for dollars. [1]

At my request, President Siles arranged for a meeting with the COMIBOL top management, the FBD representative, and the Minister of Economy. Under questioning, the COMIBOL economist admitted that the figure shown in the hectographed computations for debt service was $750,000 in excess of a figure previously submitted to the council by COMIBOL. After half an hour of cross-examination, he conceded that the statement made no allowance for the budgeted 10 per cent profit on sales by the company's commissaries (a difference of Bs. 3 billion), or for dismissing the surplus miners in accordance with COMIBOL's promise to the government and the government's commitment to the lending agencies. Nor did it allow for the savings in customs duties under the new tariffs which, it was estimated, would further reduce expenses by some $2 million.

The Minister of Economy pointed out that the statement exaggerated the payments to the Social Security Administration by about $1 million (Bs. 8 billion), by failing to deduct for the medical services which would be rendered by COMIBOL itself, as had previously been arranged. In short, the hectographed statement was on its face completely unreliable, and was moreover tendentious in that it claimed specifically that COMIBOL could manage at the current rate of exchange, provided it were not compelled to pay export taxes or compensation to the former owners of the confiscated mines, or the contributions to the buffer tin stock. The report thus implied that those payments were improper, and that they were imposed, as the report expressly stated, by higher authority. In other words, if the mines were operated solely for the benefit of the COMIBOL management and workers, in disregard of the interest of the nation as a whole, there would be no problem.

It was finally agreed that COMIBOL would prepare a revised statement for 1957, following the same breakdown of accounts that they had used in the December, 1956, statement presented by the government in its application for a stabilization fund, which showed that COMIBOL could operate at a Bs. 7,000 rate. This rate was later revised to Bs. 7,500, based on a 40 per cent increase in costs in lieu of the 25 per cent increase originally calculated.

It was further agreed that COMIBOL would prepare a similar statement for the first six months of 1957. The latter would be almost entirely computed on known facts rather than on estimates, as the company's first semester receipts would come largely from tin already shipped and sold at an average price of 98.8 cents a pound, while the projected estimates were computed, with a margin for market fluctuations, at 90 cents. From the viewpoint of stabilization in the immediate future and the strain on our monetary resources, a cash flow budget was the important consideration, not an earnings statement.

Again (March, 1957), COMIBOL prepared a statement of its anticipated 1957 accounts, this time claiming that the company would need a rate of exchange of Bs. 10,026 to the dollar. And again, this statement proved as unreliable as its predecessor, with a simple arithmetical error staring one in the face, which, if corrected, would bring the rate down to Bs. 9,160. It also entered as a cash expenditure over Bs. 9 billion which, in reality, was a bookkeeping accrual to a reserve; and made a $200,000 overestimate in custom duties. With these corrections, and using COMIBOL's own figures, a rate of Bs. 8,720 would have been indicated. Furthermore, for the first six months of 1957 — and this was the crucial period for the stabilization program — a rate of Bs. 7,710 was shown to be ample to carry COMIBOL through; this figure was based almost entirely on known results, with a minimum of estimated projections. That rate, it is true, could only be maintained in the second semester either by reducing export royalties, which was inadmissible, or by reducing social security charges. If the latter charges were cut from 30 per cent to 8 per cent, but with medical services paid by COMIBOL, and if COMIBOL made an arrangement with its creditors to pay only 20 per cent on its dollar debts in 1957, as it was instructed to do, then a Bs. 7,300 rate would suffice for the entire 1957 year.

The accounts thus showed clearly that, at the prevailing Bs. 7,500 rate, COMIBOL could pay the full export taxes, plus indemnity to the former mine owners as well as the contribution to the buffer stock and that the only reason for COMIBOL's shortage was that it had paid and was continuing to pay a number of outstanding debts not allowed for in its budget. This was on a cash basis.*

On an earnings basis, and on the same premises with respect to taxes and social security charges, COMIBOL could — according to its own figures — have managed through 1957 with a foreign exchange rate of Bs. 7,560, assuming no increase in wages.[2] This last assumption was not entirely realistic, however, as the President had admitted that he could not resist further wage demands after July 1, 1957. These facts and conclusions were reported to the council, and the President agreed that there must be no more statements made by COMIBOL

---

*None of the accountants in the government or government enterprises had the faintest concept of the distinction between a cash flow statement (statement of the source and application of funds) and an income account. The so-called income or profit-and-loss statements received from the government enterprises were neither one nor the other, but combined features of both — no allowance for depletion or depreciation (or a fantastically low figure for the latter), but, on the other hand, treating cash flow as though it were income and therefore available for paying increased wages, even where the cash represented windfall payments for past years or future years. In this connection, to those readers for whom modern corporation accounting is a mystery and Perry Mason merely the protagonist in a series of mysteries, the author would recommend Perry Mason, *"Cash Flow" Analysis and the Funds Statement* (New York: American Institute of Certified Public Accountants, Accounting Research Study No. 2, 1961).

except to the Stabilization Council. He added that, despite these disclosures, he had confidence in the COMIBOL management — that they had achieved a miracle in doing away with the below-cost commissaries, which seemed impossible at the time, and they must now learn to live within their means and pay their taxes.

Thus, that crisis passed. The Bs. 12,392 exchange rate insisted upon by COMIBOL's advisers and accountants had been recklessly calculated, and as recklessly publicized, purely from the viewpoint of determining what rate of exchange would be most convenient to COMIBOL, with no regard for the economic well-being of the nation as a whole or for the preservation of the $25 million stabilization fund. They had proposed a value for the boliviano at the figure that would be most acceptable to the miners, with minimal reorganization of the company in the interests of efficiency, and on the assumption that the mines had been confiscated for the sole benefit of those who worked in them.* If sabotage of the stabilization program had been the deliberate intention, it could hardly have been more effective, but, that crisis over, the exchange rate and the demand for dollars once again settled down to normal.

None of the members of the Stabilization Council had any illusions as to the possibility of keeping the exchange rate at between Bs. 7,000 and Bs. 7,800 indefinitely, but, if we could only hold the line until the threatened wage increases in July, or preferably until 1958, it would suffice to demonstrate conclusively that stabilization had not only been successfully achieved but that it could be maintained. But the rate would have to be a consequence of supply and demand, and not held arbitrarily at some desired figure by government fiat. If the government continued to deviate from the stabilization program,

---

*This was, in fact, the position taken by the miners. They refused to permit the dismissal of excess workers, and claimed that, since the Revolution, "The mines belong to us, just as the land belongs to the peasants" (El Diario, June 5, 1957). This is a good illustration of what happens when the government itself engages in robbery under color of law, as in the seizure of land and of the mines without payment. The mines, whose taxes under private ownership had paid most of the expenses of government, had been confiscated for the supposed benefit of some three million Bolivians, but had become the private preserve of some 35,000 COMIBOL miners, and a drain upon the rest of the country. President Siles exhorted the labor leaders to remember that the nationalized mines constituted a part of the national wealth and must be used for the collective good (La Nación and El Diario, July 27, 1957). His words fell on únreceptive ears.

as political pressures dictated, yet insisted on holding the boliviano stable, the stabilization fund would dribble away like
water from a leaky tub.

If, however — and this was our hope — the President waited
until July or January for the general wage increases, it would
make no essential difference to the stabilization program if the
exchange rate were allowed to rise to Bs. 10,000 or Bs. 12,000,
or more. In fact, the rise would have exemplary value, as it
would show dramatically that any increase in wages not accompanied by an increase in production (or higher world tin prices)
was bound to be reflected in the foreign exchange rate and hence
in domestic price levels. Stabilization could proceed as before,
but at a less favorable level, and ultimately, perhaps, a government might come to power strong enough to act in the interests
of agriculture and of the majority of the people, instead of in
the sole interest of the miners' militia.

My own goal for the eventual wage-adjustment date was to
have increases limited to 20 per cent for the best-paid sector
(the miners), and up to perhaps 50 per cent for the worst-paid
sectors (teachers, government employees, etc.), with a reduction in employer-paid social security charges to 2 per cent for
the mines and oil companies (plus complete company medical
and hospital services) and $7\frac{1}{2}$ per cent for all other employers,
including the government. This was on the assumption, always,
that labor itself would contribute $1\frac{1}{2}$ per cent and $2\frac{1}{2}$ per cent
respectively, in order to put an end to the constant pressure for
higher social benefits that is bound to ensue when the cost is
paid exclusively by the employer. If labor refused to pay more
than 1 per cent, then the employers' contribution should be reduced proportionately. In either event, the National Social Security Administration should limit its services to what it — and
the nation — could afford.

Under those conditions, with a 20 per cent wage increase,
COMIBOL would need a rate of exchange of approximately Bs.
9,500. A 25 per cent wage increase for COMIBOL would call
for a rate of Bs. 10,000. Both rates were predicated on the dismissal of 5,000 excess miners, which COMIBOL and the Minister of Mines had agreed to but had not carried out. In the government sector, even a 60 per cent increase in wages could be
taken care of with the cut in social security to $7\frac{1}{2}$ per cent and
the dismissal of some 30 per cent of the personnel who were
clearly superfluous.

All employers, public and private, would have to be free to

dismiss excess workers, who could be taken care of by a three-point program already worked out with the head of USOM/Bolivia (Appendix VI).

Further accounting difficulties

Examination of the COMIBOL accounts in connection with these foreign exchange problems revealed a further shortcoming in the company's accounting controls that I had long suspected but had never been permitted to investigate.

Revelations of unsuspected bank deposits in the United States that came to my attention during the negotiations for the stabilization fund (p. 385), coupled with a certain vagueness as to the control over payments received for metal exports, aroused the suspicion that COMIBOL might have substantial concealed accounts receivable, due from the British smelters. I raised the question in the Stabilization Council, but the Minister of Mines replied, with the absolute assurance of good faith born of ignorance, that this would be impossible — Williams, Harvey & Co., Ltd., always credited the Central Bank immediately for all ore shipments. This was just three days before stabilization, and there was no time to push the inquiry.

Going over the COMIBOL accounts, however, I discovered that the smelters owed COMIBOL between fifteen and sixteen million dollars. Comparison with accounts for prior years revealed that the average amount outstanding, pending the settlement of accounts on current shipments, used to run around $10 million. Apparently, it had never occurred to anyone in COMIBOL or in the government to make this comparison. Even the latter figure appeared high, representing tin shipments for approximately two and one-half months. With proper controls in England, at the mines, and at the points of shipment, it would seem that the lag could certainly be cut substantially. But even the difference of $5-$6 million which, quite evidently, COMIBOL should have collected but failed to collect, would have enabled the company to pay all its overdue royalties as well as all contributions to the ex-owners and buffer stock, and yet not be perpetually short of working capital.

This situation was pointed out to Raul Gutiérrez-Granier, the president of COMIBOL, and to Goosen Broesma, the general manager. At the end of the meeting, Gutiérrez confessed privately, in despair and with considerable emotion, that he was absolutely unable to get any information from the COMIBOL accounting department. The accounts were hopelessly behind and utterly unreliable, but, with the control of the company by the workers' commissars, he was unable to enforce any discipline or replace the present accountants.

Gutiérrez asked whether Point IV could get a comptroller from the United States to help put the company's accounts in order and reorganize the accounting department. He recalled one accountant, whom he had known from his days as manager of the W. R. Grace & Company mining interests, who would be competent for the task if Point IV could get him to come for a year or preferably two years. He believed that the accountant in question was presently treasurer of W. R. Grace & Company. I pointed out the difficulty of getting a first-class comptroller, not only because of salary but because of the reluctance of a competent and rising corporate officer to take a protracted leave of absence in mid-career. Nevertheless, Gutiérrez was assured that every effort would be made, as this was a matter of the utmost importance not only to the stabilization program but to all U.S. aid to Bolivia.[3]

Later, when Gutiérrez informed the Stabilization Council that he had asked help in this matter, President Siles expressed amazement that COMIBOL had been unable to get competent accounting assistance in Bolivia. I backed up Gutiérrez' statement and added that the situation was not peculiar to COMIBOL and, in fact, not confined to Bolivia — that, in Latin America in general, there was little recognition of the difference between a bookkeeper and an accountant and, with few exceptions, no realization of the function of a corporation comptroller. No university gave practical, intensive training in accountancy of a calibre comparable to the instruction given in the United States.

To avoid injustice, I added that there were a number of competent Argentine accountants, many of them trained in firms such as Price Waterhouse & Company, or Deloitte, Plender, Griffiths & Company, or in American or British banks or companies. But the Price Waterhouse representative in La Paz had stated that it would take a staff of ten chartered accountants at least a year to put the COMIBOL accounts in order. Furthermore, even if outside auditors were employed, the company should have its own comptroller to reorganize the staff and ensure continuity.

Nothing ever came of the proposal to employ an American comptroller. COMIBOL could pay up to $500 a month for such a person, and presumably ICA was unable to pay more than the going rate for government accountants. But what was needed was not a run-of-the-mill accountant but a person with the imagination, competence, toughness, and experience called for in a comptroller or financial vice-president of a large U.S. corporation, and ICA had no way to pay a salary of perhaps $25,000-$50,000 to safeguard the $25 million stabilization fund, plus the $25 million or so of annual U.S. aid.

The incident did, however, result in COMIBOL's reducing its outstanding accounts receivable from the smelters from about $16 million to around $12 million, notwithstanding which it continued Bs. 9 billion in arrears on its taxes and Bs. 15 billion on its social security payments and was forced to come to the council again and again for authority to obtain short-term advances up to Bs. 10 billion from the Central Bank. This borrowing proved to be a perpetual revolving credit to supply working capital which was needed solely because of the lack of effective financial controls and a failure to live within budgetary limits.[4]

The Stabilization Council was warned that, largely because of COMIBOL's borrowing from the Central Bank and failure to meet its obligations to the government, the note issue had risen Bs. 45 billion in the first three months of 1957 and that, if that rate of increase were maintained, the note issue would double by the year end. It was recommended: (1) that the rate of exchange be allowed to rise to Bs. 7,700 or Bs. 7,800 (Bs. 8,000 being politically and psychologically inadvisable); (2) that the council insist upon COMIBOL's taking the economy measures previously agreed upon; and (3) that the Central Bank be authorized to advance COMIBOL temporarily the Bs. 8 billion it then asked to meet its tax arrears.

The President objected to increasing the foreign exchange rate, insisting that the council's technical advisers must be "flexible" in their attitude — this notwithstanding that the government was already spending far beyond its means because of its own flexibility in acquiescing in the impossible demands of the labor leaders, the *politicos,* and the National Social Security Administration.* He suggested that living costs could be

---

* "Flexibility" is the byword that can mark the epitaph of any stabilization program. To be sure, there can be flexibility: If the government insists on higher wages, it can reduce social security costs or dismiss workers; if it insists on spending more in one place, it can cut expenditures in another or increase its tax revenues. But if flexibility is in one direction only, stabilization is doomed.

reduced by having YPFB reduce its prices for kerosene and other petroleum products, and he could not grasp the fact that YPFB was already unable to make ends meet and that greater deficits would further increase the note issue and the pressure on the boliviano.

Accounting chaos reaches a climax

The revelations concerning COMIBOL's undisclosed receivables in England, and its general accounting ineptitude, prompted a further investigation into COMIBOL's bank accounts in the United States, and early in June I made the following oral report to the council:

> I have here two communications received from COMIBOL, one dated May 2, the other May 6. The first states that on April 30, 1957, COMIBOL had a credit balance in the Chemical Corn Exchange Bank of $210,388; the second, that its balance in that bank on that same date was $172,096. The difference is insignificant, but the discrepancy is symptomatic of the disorder that we on the council have been witnessing for the past year.

> However, I also have an official letter from COMIBOL to the Central Bank, dated May 17, 1957, stating that the COMIBOL balance in the Chemical Corn Exchange Bank on that same April 30 date was $2,936,819.89. If that figure is true — and unfortunately our experience in the council shows that we cannot rely on *any* figures presented by *any* government entity — COMIBOL could have paid the Bs. 3 billion it owed to W. R. Grace & Co. for U.S. aid products, plus the Bs. 15 billion it owes in taxes, and still have a dollar deposit larger than the maximum it is authorized to hold.

> In any event, whether or not the figure is correct, it shows that COMIBOL's accounting controls are just as deficient as those of the Central Bank, so that we can no longer justify letting COMIBOL retain 40 per cent of the proceeds of its exports. In its agreement with the lending agencies, the government promised that 100 per cent of the foreign exchange received from exports of government entities would be turned over to the Central Bank, and I recommend

that the council and Finance Minister investigate to see what action must be taken.*

But that is not all. I have here a report made to the Central Bank by the Mining Bank, showing balances in the First National City Bank, the Chase Manhattan Bank, and the Chemical Corn Exchange Bank, totaling $861,000; a report from YPFB showing balances in the Chemical Corn Exchange and American Security & Trust Co. totaling $79,360; a report from the National Social Security Administration showing a balance in the Chemical Corn Exchange Bank of $50,900; and a report from the Bolivian Development Corporation showing balances in the Chemical Corn Exchange Bank and the Liberty National Bank totaling $114,554. In all, these government entities, not including LAB or the

---

*One of the most important provisions of the stabilization program was that the government-owned enterprises must deposit *all* foreign exchange receipts with the Central Bank, but scarcely a month after stabilization the top management of COMIBOL appeared before the Stabilization Council, and Raul Gutiérrez announced that they would all resign in a body if COMIBOL were not permitted to manage its own foreign exchange without interference or control by the Central Bank, citing in support of his demand a series of flagrant errors committed by the bank in past operations. To persons unaccustomed to dealing with Latin Americans, this attitude must seem childish — "If I can't play the game my way, I won't play it at all." But it can better be characterized as extreme individualism, carried to the point where compromise, teamwork, give-and-take, and mutual sacrifice become impossible. In this case, the council was faced with the fact that the Central Bank was undeniably incompetent (through no fault of its president); that most of Bolivia's best brains were in exile or in disfavor with the Revolutionary Government; and that Gutiérrez and his two associates in the ultimatum were unquestionably the most competent (and honest) men who could be found in or out of Bolivia to manage COMIBOL. Any alternative would have been unthinkably worse, and COMIBOL simply had to be kept going, or the country's whole economy would fall apart. After long discussion, during the course of which I pointed out the imminent danger of attachment of COMIBOL bank accounts in the United States, it was finally agreed that a special account would be kept in the Chemical Corn Exchange Bank in the name of the Central Bank as agent for the Bolivian government, but for account of COMIBOL, and that 40 per cent of the proceeds of COMIBOL's sales would go directly to that account, with COMIBOL's officers alone authorized to sign checks against such deposits, subject to a monthly control to ensure that exactly one-twelfth of COMIBOL's annual budget of receipts and expenditures was handled through the account, with the additional proviso that the account would not run over $500,000 nor under $200,000. The limitations, of course, proved completely ineffective.

government railways, for which I have no data, had deposits of over $4,040,000 in the United States at a time when the government was desperately in need of foreign funds.

Under Decree 3403 of May 14, 1953, government development banks and official, quasi-official, and independent entities are prohibited from maintaining foreign currency balances without permission from the Ministry of Finance on the recommendation of the Central Bank. Aside from COMIBOL, I do not know whether the agencies I have mentioned are authorized to maintain balances abroad, but I do know that it is contrary to the interests of the government for them to do so. At the present time, with the danger of attachment of Bolivian funds that I have been pointing out to the council for many months past, all these accounts should be carried in the name of the Central Bank, not as its own funds, but in its capacity as agent for the government of Bolivia.

I also wish to inform the council that, according to the Federal Reserve Bank of New York, Bolivian private and government banks and the Bolivian government had $8.2 million on deposit in the United States on March 31. Subtracting the accounts of the private and government banks, and the other sums I have mentioned, there is a discrepancy of some $3 million. In other words, some government entity or department has $3 million on deposit in the United States of which we have no record. It may be that these figures are wrong, but I suggest that the Minister of Finance make an investigation and find out the correct and complete facts on that date as well as at the present time.

I have heard rumors, for example, that the Bolivian government has some $5 million in the United States for construction of an oil pipe line. I may point out that the information submitted by the government of Bolivia, to support its request (to Washington) for financial assistance, does not tally with the figures I have cited, although I do not have the complete December, 1956, accounts.*

*The head of the Planning Commission explained that the $5 million belonged to Gulf Oil Corporation and not to the Bolivian government, but of course that was merely one more instance of the Bolivian government's evading its commitments to the agencies that provided the stabilization fund. The money from Gulf was for advance royalties for oil concession rights, and Bolivia had no right to use that money, or to have Gulf use that money, for new government enterprises without consultation with the Stabilization Council (under Decree of August 4, 1956) and had at least an implied obligation to consult with the agencies that had financed the stabilization fund.

I may add that, on December 31, 1956, the banking department of the Central Bank, according to its own figures, had
a credit balance with Manufacturers Trust Company of
$2,832,410. A statement received from Manufacturers
Trust Company, however, shows that the Central Bank
banking department had a $614,806 overdraft on that date.
The $3.4 million discrepancy is not due to items in transit,
but to the fact that when Manufacturers Trust Company
opens a confirmed, irrevocable letter of credit by order of
the Central Bank, it quite properly debits the Central Bank
the full amount of that credit. The Central Bank should, of
course, show a corresponding liability on its books. Instead, the Central Bank has been issuing these credits with
no cash or other debit entry, and with no credit entry in the
account of its correspondent bank.

But, in my opinion, neither the balance shown in the accounts of the Manufacturers Trust Company nor that shown
in the accounts of the Central Bank is the correct one. As
I reported to the council last December, it often happens
that a credit is opened, say for $10,000. The merchandise
is shipped, and the invoice turns out to be say $9,237.42.
Manufacturers Trust Company naturally pays only the
amount of the invoice, but the Central Bank apparently
takes no step to cancel the remainder of the credit, and I
am virtually certain that it has some $500,000 or more on
deposit in the United States from these operations of which
it has no record. The Bolivian government could use these
funds if the bank accounts were kept in proper form, but
apparently nothing has been done to correct this situation
since I first reported it last December.*

I must add too, and I would like it to appear in the minutes,
that what I have stated with respect to COMIBOL — its constant requests for working capital, its failure to pay its
obligations to Point IV and to the Treasury because of lack
of funds, while all the time it seems to have had nearly $3
million in New York and more in London, does not affect in
the slightest the confidence I have in the integrity and
ability of Raul Gutiérrez and Goosen Broesma. On the
contrary, it merely serves to confirm what both those gentlemen have told me, that they can have no confidence what-

---

*Not only did the Central Bank have no record of partially used
credits; its record of letters of credit opened on its order, and of drafts
which it had guaranteed by endorsement *(aval)*, were incomplete and un-
derstated its liabilities by some $20 million.

soever in their accountants and that, as a consequence, Gutiérrez stated he did not know what the true position of the company was, its revenues, expenses, debts, or credits, ending by begging me to get a capable accountant for him through Point IV. Nor do I wish to give the impression that it is only COMIBOL whose accounts are in such disorder. To the contrary, as I have stated before, every government enterprise, with the possible exception of YPFB,* is in as bad or worse condition, owing to the lack of discipline and utter incompetence of their accounting staffs and the fact that they cannot be dismissed. Franklin Antezana (the president of the Central Bank) told the President the other day that 80 per cent of the bank employees were incompetent and should be fired.

Two days later, the council received a letter from COMIBOL to the effect that its balance in the Chemical Corn Exchange Bank on the April 30, 1957, date was not $2,936,819.89, as previously advised, but $718,509.68. I pointed out that we now had four different figures for the same account on the same date and, furthermore, that the last figure given was in excess of the amount that COMIBOL was authorized to keep in its foreign balances.

Political and management problems

But untrustworthy accounting was not the only problem that beset COMIBOL in the first year of stabilization. Political pressures continued to make effective management impossible. Within the council, the new Minister of Mines, Mario Torres-Calleja, acceded to all the council decisions and promised to

---

*Even this exception proved optimistic, as the following day Price Waterhouse & Co. reported that their examination of the YPFB books disclosed irregularities in the distribution and sale of products, although the books of account had been kept in accordance with usual accounting methods (*La Nación*, June 7, 1957). "Usual accounting methods" are, of course, predicated on the assumption of a reasonably stable currency, so that when YPFB had purchased its equipment and supplies at official rates of exchange for anywhere from one-fortieth to one two-hundredth of the true value, depreciation charges at conventional percentages were ridiculous. The Price Waterhouse representative in La Paz informed me, however, that their authority to audit the books of YPFB and certain other government entities did not extend to a critical examination of economic factors of that nature and that depreciation was computed on cost, in the currency of the country, in accordance with usual accounting practices.

see that they were carried out. But as soon as he left the council precincts and conferred with his chief, Lechín, his views suffered a complete reversal, with the result that the Stabilization Council decisions on COMIBOL's finances, which, under the Decree of August 4, 1956, had almost the force of law, were nothing more than a prayer to a hostile higher power.

The new Mines Minister proclaimed to the council with great emphasis that the mine workers must be disciplined, that no new workers must be hired, that from February 1 on accounts must be available on a daily basis and general balance sheets and income statements rendered monthly and on time, that COMIBOL must be run as a business enterprise without political interference, and that he would have a regulation drafted within ninety days to that effect. He agreed, too, that COMIBOL must live up to its promises by dismissing 5,000 unneeded workers, and he stated that the San José mine force could and would be cut to 350 miners and that the Quechisla mine should and would be worked *a maquípuras,* i.e., abandoned as a company operation and worked by individual miners and their families on a scavenger basis.*

Some four months went by, however, and the Minister of Mines had done nothing to carry out his promises. At a series of meetings, the COMIBOL management appeared before the

---

*The Ford, Bacon & Davis report placed the number of miners at San José in 1956 at 3,290 and reported that the output per man shift was 0.08 tons compared with 0.57 at Catavi; also that San José was by far the heaviest loser in the COMIBOL operations. They recommended that San José be operated by *pirquiñeros,* meaning by independent contractors under contract with COMIBOL, but hiring their own crews and depending on superior ability and hard work for their profits, a system prohibited by law under the Revolutionary regime. FBD considered that San José could support 1,000 workers on that basis. As to Quechisla, which Torres proposed to abandon, FBD showed that two of the Quechisla mines were among the four most profitable COMIBOL operations (FBD report, Vol. III, pp. 29, 31, 96, A-28, 9, 106). At a later meeting, the manager of the San José mine, Engineer Lucio Vega, testified that the mine employed 3,600 workers, and that he could get the same output with 1,200. Thus, it is clear that the minister's conclusions as to San José and Quechisla were the result either of a poor memory or a good imagination. Vega further testified that 30 to 40 per cent of the miners were out on sick report; that San José was being run as a charitable organization; its reserves were petering out, and it would soon have to be shut down; that its present debt was Bs. 658 million, and the workers were demanding Bs. 400 million in free enamelware cooking utensils! President Siles later used Vega's figures as an example of labor abuses (*La Nación,* June 4, 1957).

council with the managers of the most important mine centers, and, on one occasion, with the labor boss of one of the mines, with a view to finding a solution to COMIBOL's problems. Raul Gutiérrez, the COMIBOL president, announced: (1) that gross revenues for the first four months of 1957 were down $3,525,000 compared with 1956; (2) that COMIBOL could not pay export taxes and that the tax scale was unrealistic; (3) that the incentive bonuses under the stabilization decrees were inadequate and gave no incentive for higher production; (4) that social security charges must be reduced; (5) that he must be permitted to have *trabajo a pirquín* in some mines, but that it was illegal to employ *pirquiñeros* (p. 387 n); (6) that he wanted a negotiated moratorium on payments to the ex-owners of the mines, as COMIBOL could not continue to permit deductions by the smelters on that account; (7) that COMIBOL must similarly have a moratorium on its foreign debt, chiefly purchases under credit or trade agreements; and (8) that he must be authorized to clamp down on sudden work stoppages and not be forced to pay wages during unauthorized strikes or stoppages.

In a written memorial presented by Gutiérrez, the stabilization measures, and in particular the high duties on COMIBOL imports, were stressed as the chief causes of COMIBOL's troubles. The written petition would, of course, be used by the enemies of stabilization to discredit the program, so Gutiérrez was pressed for an answer on certain points:

Was it the new (May, 1957) tariff that was causing trouble? No, it was the old tariff; the present tariff was fine, except for the high duty on rice which COMIBOL purchased for its commissaries. It was pointed out that the council had recommended a lower rate, but that Vice-President Ñuflo Chávez had increased the rate to help the farmers and that the long delay in enactment of the new tariff had also been caused by that intervention. President Siles complained that COMIBOL was looking only at its own interests, and the Minister of Mines remarked that this was a [political] matter that should be discussed elsewhere (meaning in the Cabinet or in COB-MNR conclave).

As to incentive bonuses, it was pointed out that Article 17 of the stabilization decree gave COMIBOL carte blanche to arrange its production incentives, so long as the basic wage was not increased. President Siles recommended that production bonuses be tied in with the family subsidies and made dependent on the number of persons in the miner's family, but fortunately the head of the Planning Commission interposed an objection to that procedure. To sum up for the record, Gutiérrez was asked: "The drop in production, and the lack of incentive to produce more, are not then due to the stabilization decrees?" to which he replied: "Manifestly not! It is just that the miners are unwilling to work."

The council, with the exception of the President, then adjourned to the COMIBOL office with the COMIBOL management. There the council agreed with all of COMIBOL's recommendations with the exception of the elimination of export taxes, which it decided must remain in effect until COMIBOL was in a position to make a thorough analysis of costs and until alternative sources of government revenue could be found. It decided (subject to discussion with the President) that: (1) COMIBOL must provide its own medical and hospital services and that other social security charges must be eliminated (perhaps cut to 2 per cent as had been recommended); (2) the Pulacayo operations must be closed down (or turned over to scavenger *maquípura* operation); (3) the other submarginal mines must be placed on a contract *pirquiñero* basis.

These conclusions were duly reported to the President at the next full council meeting, where it was pointed out that COMIBOL production for the first four months had dropped 22 per cent in physical volume compared with the like period of 1956, while prices had dropped 14 per cent, so that the chief cause of COMIBOL's problems was not stabilization, not tariffs, but low output, thus emphasizing the need for incentives and for the increased production that would be assured by independent profit-seeking *pirquiñero* contractors.

The President remarked with some asperity that the Minister of Mines had raised no objection to the proposed reduction in social security contributions when, as a labor minister, he knew very well that labor's rank and file insisted on even higher social security charges and benefits. The head of the National Social Security Administration, who was then called in, stated that there would be no objection to exempting the incentive bonuses from the social security charges, so that point at least was gained.

In the course of the discussion, the Foreign Minister, who had been the first president of COMIBOL under the Revolutionary regime, stated that every "solution" now suggested had been proposed four years ago and that it was outrageous to go on talking about the San José mines, which should have been closed down at that time; that every alleged "solution" would founder on the opposition of labor. There was general agreement with this statement, and the President summed up by placing the blame directly on the labor commissars within the COMIBOL organization. [5]

A meeting the following day, after political clearance with *Co-Gobierno* leaders, confirmed the agreement that social security charges would not be applied to the miners' bonuses. The Finance Minister, however, insisted that income tax must be payable by the miners on their entire income, including bonuses, and it developed that 20 to 30 per cent of the miners worked not as employees but as individual contractors and earned from Bs. 400,000 to Bs. 450,000 a month, thus revealing a further area of evasion of the wage scales fixed under the stabilization decrees. The production bonuses would add some Bs. 70,000 to that figure, making the equivalent of about $70 a month in all. [6] Considering that the miners worked some 130 days a year (p. 15 n) in all, this was more than the $2.61 a day paid by Patiño *et al* before the Revolution, or than the $2.04 that the average mine worker was authorized to get under the stabilization decrees, and very much higher than the 83 cents a day (including the value of commissary privileges) that the miners received on the eve of stabilization (see p. 223).

The political problems faced by the COMIBOL management were not confined to those arising within the Cabinet. Soon after the beginning of the year, Congress passed a law requiring all company commissaries to sell merchandise at cost. This would, of course, chiefly affect COMIBOL and was a violation of Bolivia's commitment that goods would be sold at cost plus 10 per cent. The council resolved to inform COMIBOL that it must live up to its budget obligations and recommended that the President veto the act of Congress. So far as is known, the act was not vetoed but was apparently forgotten, and subsequent attempts to compel COMIBOL to sell at cost or below cost came from direct labor pressure rather than from law.

Because of labor's influence in government, and the constant fear on the part of the labor "leaders" of opposing the wishes of the rank and file, any attempt to impose discipline was impossible. Ford, Bacon & Davis reported that every payday and every *fiesta* was followed by a 20 to 50 per cent drop in the labor force, lasting for two to three days, and that the absentee rate after each week end ran between 20 and 30 per cent, resulting in serious work stoppages in mine and mill operations. The majority of the COMIBOL mines were being operated for the sole purpose of creating employment, thus wearing out equipment and calling for dollar replacement costs in excess of the value of their output, aside from the demoralization and human waste of maintaining in drunken idleness thousands of persons who could otherwise be put to work in productive areas. According to FBD, within five years (from December, 1956) some 45,000 relatively idle miners would be employed at these exhausted nonprofit mines. [7]

It would be natural, under such circumstances, to place the blame for these conditions on management. The FBD report points to many administrative shortcomings, such as neglect of proper replacement and maintenance of equipment and facilities, the lack of qualified maintenance personnel, a disregard of preventive maintenance and failure to shut down operations in time to prevent abuse to equipment, the old age and obsolescence of equipment in general, the exhaustion of existing veins and failure to explore and block out new ore reserves, etc. [8] On the other hand, under the conditions imposed by the Revolution, it is probable that no mine management, Bolivian or foreign, could have done any better than the top management in charge of COMIBOL throughout 1956 and 1957. Raul Gutiérrez summed up the situation when he stated in a note to the Minister of Finance that he was unable to provide a quarterly report of the company's operations "because of the constant interference by the labor leaders and worker commissars in the normal and timely accounting operations of the company, which makes it impossible even to prepare semiannual statements or to determine our costs.... The problem has been aggravated by the constant turnover of personnel and their replacement by persons who lack the necessary knowledge of accounting, whom we are forced to employ on the recommendation of the government itself, and of political committees and commands."[9]

Direct corruption. The most sinister kind of political interference, however, took the form of barely disguised graft on COMIBOL purchases. Prior to stabilization, when the government's supplies were purchased on credit, this meant that purchase orders were given to suppliers of inferior or inadequate equipment in Europe or neighboring countries who were able, with the assistance of their governments, to extend three- to five-year credits that came due largely in the latter part of 1956 and early 1957, precisely during the most crucial stages of the stabilization program.[10] Because of political pressure in favor of the two or three privileged intermediaries in this trade, COMIBOL was forced to pay these credits at the very time that the Stabilization Council was endeavoring to put all debt payments on a five-year basis.

During a visit to Buenos Aires at the end of 1956, I was informed by the Bolivian Ambassador that COMIBOL had been making its purchases of commissary supplies at two to three times the market price, from a firm whose dubious reputation was confirmed at the American Embassy. At the official exchange rates of Bs. 60 or Bs. 190 to the dollar prevailing prior to stabilization, these overpayments could be readily disguised. This was reported to President Siles, who stated that he would speak with Raul Gutiérrez, but that presumably such overpayments would be barred with the advent of stabilization.[11]

A month later, however, it was learned that COMIBOL (and the Mining Bank) had been purchasing "Lobenite" bags (a British trademarked ore bag lined with asphalt paper, made in Calcutta) through Hamburg at $850 to $859 a ton, while the market price for the same bags bought in Calcutta or England was $550 to $600 a ton. At the same time, the Ministry of Economy was buying gunny sacks (100 lb. content) at $1,150 a ton, when the world market price was $450. This was reported to the president of COMIBOL, in accordance with President Siles' instructions. Gutiérrez acknowledged the truth of the statement and confirmed the prior reports with respect to the Argentine shipments. He went on to say that the former head of the purchasing department was both honest and able — one of the few people in the organization in whom he had complete confidence, but that, prior to stabilization, the *políticos* had circumvented the purchasing department by arranging credits through the Finance Ministry and other ministries.*

Shortly after the stabilization measures made it possible for the head of the purchasing department to put a stop to such practices, Gutiérrez was visited by one of the highest representatives of labor in the Bolivian government, who told him with unmistakable emphasis that he would have to get rid of the purchasing department manager and appoint another person whom he named. Gutiérrez, much disturbed, reported this to

---

*Over $30 million of such credit contracts had been signed by COMIBOL from the end of 1954 to November, 1956 (COMIBOL report to the Chamber of Deputies, *Última Hora*, January 26, 1957). See Zondag report, p. 101, for reference to the poor quality and unsuitability of the merchandise purchased under these credits.

the President, who informed him that he would have to acquiesce in appointing the new purchasing manager but that he could transfer the former manager to another department. This was done, and the ex-manager was put to work reading the nine-volume Ford, Bacon & Davis report and preparing a report of his own with suggestions for carrying out the FBD recommendations.[12] This was a more dignified form of employment than cutting out paper dolls, and less insulting to the American ICA authorities (who had paid FBD), than if the FBD report had been consigned directly to the wastebasket.

This too I reported to the President and council that same day, as "political interference," but without mentioning the name of the person who had banged out his peremptory command on Gutiérrez' desk, a detail that I communicated to the President following the meeting. The information was no surprise to the President, and it later developed that the facts "revealed" were common knowledge among most of the council members. This was not remarkable, considering the rapidity of nonelectronic communication in Bolivia.

I stressed the gravity of the situation, pointing out that COMIBOL's purchases alone amounted to some $25 million a year and that even a 20 per cent markup — which the council members thought ridiculously conservative — would mean a serious drain on the national economy. The President, perhaps for the benefit of the Minister of Mines, who was present at the meeting, stated that the Minister and the Comptroller General had intervened in the COMIBOL purchases precisely for the purpose of avoiding irregularities. The Minister made no comment, but refrained from attending the next twenty-five meetings of the Stabilization Council, until a formal "reconciliation" had been effected with respect to a less serious revelation (see p. 363).

The Mining Bank

In January, 1957, scarcely a month after enactment of the stabilization measures, the acting president of the Mining Bank appeared before the council, together with the three top bank officers, to announce that the employees were out on strike and threatened to remain out unless they got a 52 per cent wage increase. He added that the bank's prospective deficit for 1957 was Bs. 1.4 billion and that, if the increase were granted, it would be Bs. 3.4 billion. What the employees asked was not labeled an increase, but a balancing or leveling (*nivelación*) of salaries to bring their wages into line. This could mean either a readjustment of wage scales within the bank itself or a readjustment to bring the bank's wage scale to a level with that in other enterprises. In either event, it would represent an increase in wages, which was forbidden under the stabilization decree. The acting president of the bank stated that the workers' petition was based on false premises, as they had already received a *nivelación* under a resolution of the Ministry of Labor of August 4, 1956, when a general leveling of wages was decreed. He added that it was his intention to support President Siles' stabilization program by refusing to grant any increases and by dismissing 30 per cent of the personnel, as had been agreed. The general manager added that 50 per cent of the bank's personnel was superfluous but that the union refused to permit the dismissal of even a single employee.

Since the council members agreed that the matter was too important to decide in the absence of President Siles, the meeting adjourned to the presidential palace. There the new Minister of Mines, disregarding what had just been said, reported to the President that the Mining Bank employees' demands were justified, as they had not received the increases given to employees in other banks. The Mining Bank head retorted that this simply was not true — that they had received a 40 per cent readjustment (*reajuste*) in wages, plus a later revision of job classifications (*recategorización*) that amounted to a 22 per cent increase, retroactive to June, 1956. I added that Bolivia had a "solemn moral obligation" to comply with its agreement with the lending agencies to dismiss 30 per cent of the bank personnel and to freeze wages. Wage increases, regardless of whether they were called *nivelación* or *reajuste* or *recategorización* or whether they took the shape of the illegal Bs. 450 additional compensation decreed by the Minister of Labor for all employees (and not just for those who had or who were entitled to have cheap commissary privileges), were all in violation of that obligation and might result in termination of the stabilization financing.[13]

The discussion was postponed to the following day, when the Minister of Mines again demanded the balancing of wages, to which the Finance Minister retorted that what was needed was a balancing of the government budget. I suggested that the workers' demand was a trial balloon, and that if the council failed to insist on holding the line, there would be demands for balancing wages from every other bank and industry. President Siles commented that it was not just a trial balloon, but trickery. With that, the Minister of Mines veered from his original position and stated that the strike must be discredited and the bank reorganized, a position that he reaffirmed in a statement to the press that evening.[14]

Two months later, however, the strike was still going on, and no step had been taken to declare the strike illegal. Three months later, the bank management again appeared before the council to state that they had been forced to meet the wage demands of the employees in full and retroactively. They also reported that they had not been permitted to reduce the staff, although 50 per cent of the employees were superfluous. The bank would have to borrow $3,163,000 from the Central Bank, as its funds were tied up in imports bought under trade agreements at exorbitant prices — for example, 103 compressors at Bs. 80 million each ($11,000). When ordered, at official exchange rates, these compressors would have cost only Bs. 2 million ($270) each, and the high original price, margin for graft, and poor quality could have been overlooked. With all sympathy for the predicament of the management, I stated that there was no point in deceiving ourselves. There was no money to be had from the Central Bank. Point IV and Ford, Bacon & Davis were agreed that the bank served no useful purpose and that if it went into bankruptcy its function of purchasing ore from the small miners could be taken over by the Mining Corporation. The only alternative was for the bank to live within its means. The Minister of Mines agreed with this conclusion and added that the miners should be permitted to sell their ores wherever they pleased, with no restrictions.[15]

A month later, the bank's general manager and the newly appointed president appeared before the council to state that the bank owed Bs. 215 billion for production bonuses and had only Bs. 1.2 billion available; furthermore, that it required Bs. 1 billion as a revolving fund to purchase gold from the miners in Tipuani, and £300,000 sterling (Bs. 6.3 billion) to pay its debt to the Antofagasta railway. In other words, the bank was more than $1 million short, and they asked that the Central Bank advance somewhat more than that amount as working capital, emphasizing that they, personally, had no interest in the matter as they had both tendered their resignations.

I asked why, under the circumstances, the bank had

increased its dollar deposits in the United States from $107,000 on December 31, 1956, to $848,000 on April 30, 1957, and requested a full statement of dollar accounts to date, plus a complete reorganization plan for the bank which would embrace the dismissal of at least 30 per cent and preferably 50 per cent of the surplus employees. It would have been pointless to provide credit for working capital, as it would disappear immediately if the bank continued to operate as it had been doing.

The president of the Central Bank then brought out that the Mining Bank was holding 750 kilos of gold which it had already been ordered to sell to the Central Bank, plus 150 kilos more (worth approximately $1 million in all). After discussion, it was resolved: (1) that the Central Bank be authorized to advance bolivianos to the Mining Bank against deliveries of gold which it would then sell by public auction for account of the Mining Bank; (2) that the Finance Minister repay the Mining Bank for the 10 per cent buffer stock deduction made by the British smelters, inasmuch as the tin in the buffer stock would be held for account of the government and not of the Mining Bank; (3) that the Stabilization Council would negotiate with the railway for postponement of the debt, with payments placed on an instalment basis; and (4) that the Minister of Mines reorganize the Mining Bank, dismissing surplus personnel without delay.[16]

The last resolution proved to be no more than a pious hope. The president and the general manager of the Mining Bank were both kicked bodily out of the bank by the employees when they attempted to enforce their orders. The administrative manager of the bank, who had already resigned, charged grave irregularities in the administration of the employees' retirement fund by the representatives of the employees, including loans to those representatives, sales of imported merchandise to the same representatives at the official Bs. 190 rate, and particularly certain sales of cement that had taken place subsequent to stabilization. The union officers were unable to deny the allegations, but they denied that there was anything improper in them and claimed that the bank had been unable to sell the cement, which was in danger of deteriorating. It is true that, at the realistic exchange rate of Bs. 7,500 to the dollar, and at the exorbitant graft-laden prices paid by the bank under Bolivia's trade agreements, the cement was unsaleable, but at the Bs. 190 price paid by the labor leaders there was ample margin for private gain.[17]

Bolivian Development Corporation

The Bolivian Development Corporation management appeared before the council again and again in quest of funds, and always with the same problem of figures fished out of the air and no trustworthy accounts to show where the corporation stood or where it was going. To cite one example of how necessary it is in Bolivia to go behind the figures and get the facts, so experienced an observer as Professor Alexander reports:

> A fundamental part of the Economic Development Program of the M.N.R. government has been the construction and improvement of the country's highway network. Some idea of the increase in this activity under Paz Estenssoro can be gathered from the fact that expenditures of the General Directorate of Highways increased from 60,000,000 *bolivianos* in 1951 to 988,000,000 *bolivianos* in 19F3.[18]

He quotes the figures from ECLA, which should be a reliable source. But Bs. 60 million in 1951 was worth $600,000 at the free rate of exchange, while Bs. 988 million in 1956 was worth $120,000 (using the average of the quarterly figures reported in *International Financial Statistics*). And those figures may be equally misleading for in 1956 Bs. 988 million may have been equivalent to anywhere up to $5.2 million, depending upon how much of the expenditure was for equipment imported at the official rate of exchange — probably less than 25 per cent in the case of highways, but a substantial proportion of the total in the case of Bolivian Development Corporation projects as a whole.

In sum, unless one is in a position to delve behind the figures and get the facts, and dig behind the facts to arrive at the truth — and no casual observer or official agency is in a position to do either — it may be better to forget the statistics and the accounts altogether and rely on general impressions. At least, in such case, one may make allowance for the degree of accounting experience and possible bias of the reporter and not be misled by the numerical symbols of certainty.

But, for the purposes of the Stabilization Council, it was desirable to arrive at the closest possible approach to an accurate accounting, and so I urged that Price Waterhouse & Co., which was engaged in a routine audit of accounts, be entrusted with the broader mission of determining the cost in actual dollars of each of the Development Corporation projects and the actual profit and loss accounts, past and budgeted, of those projects, with depreciation charged on true dollar costs. The most that the council would authorize, however, was that the corporation accounts be "audited" by the U.N. adviser to the Finance Ministry. Against my recommendation, the corporation was relieved of payment of interest on its indebtedness to the Central Bank, even at the modest authorized rate of $2\frac{1}{2}$ per cent, although, unless government-operated enterprises paid interest and taxes, there was no way of determining their contribution to or burden upon the national economy.

Among other demands for funds, the Development Corporation asked that the Central Bank pay $315,000 on its guarantees covering overdue accounts to the French Société Fives-Lille-Cail for the sugar mill at Guabirá, and a $75,000 draft payable to the German MIAG Mill Machinery Company (MIAG Muhlenbau und Industrie A. G.), for the cement plant in Sucre.[19] The Development Corporation had no boliviano funds to purchase the dollars, because they had computed their 1957 post-stabilization budget on the basis of Bs. 190 to the dollar! It was pointed out that, regardless of threats of attachment of Central Bank funds which were advanced as a reason for paying the MIAG drafts, the bank had placed its guaranty on at least $32 million of drafts that the council knew of, and the government owed at least $200 million in other debts, and it would be unthinkable to give preference to the Development Corporation creditors.

Later, the president of the Central Bank reported that he had received an offer from the Banco Alemán Transatlántico (Deutsche Ueberseeische Bank, Hamburg) to settle all outstanding commercial debts on a five-year basis, provided that the MIAG draft for cement plant machinery was paid immediately. Again it was objected that the council should not authorize piecemeal settlements with no knowledge of the total amount owed by the government or guaranteed by the Central Bank. After discussion, the council ordered the Central Bank to submit a full statement of its guaranteed debts.

Shortly thereafter, the Development Corporation president informed the council that he had arranged a six-month extension with Fives-Lille, which only served to confirm his lack of understanding of Bolivia's difficulties, a six-month delay being utterly worthless. The head of the Planning Commission recommended that the Development Corporation president, who was scheduled to go to Europe, be instructed to arrange ten-year payments with both Fives-Lille and MIAG, it being our hope that, with that instruction, he might at least obtain five-year extensions. It was so resolved.[20] A month later, the president of the Central Bank reported that arrangements had been made with the Banco Alemán Transatlántico for a five-year credit, but no report was made as to whether or not preferential treatment had been given to MIAG. As to Fives-Lille, it later turned out that the president of the Development Corporation had consented to pay an overdue draft for $221,000 and agreed that the $866,000 balance would be paid in the form of ore exports. The Development Corporation had no funds for payment and no authority to pledge any of Bolivia's exports, and certainly no right to give preference to any single creditor. Nevertheless, the sugar mill was so desperately in need of an engineer, whom Fives-Lille had agreed to furnish, that the council recommended payment of the matured draft and settlement of the balance over a five-year period. The stated amount of the indebtedness did not coincide with any figures previously submitted to the council by the Development Corporation.

Guabirá sugar mill

The new Development Corporation president reported that the sugar mill at Guabirá, contrary to the earlier claims of the former head of the corporation, would show a further deficit in 1957. The corporation had tried, without success, to interest W. R. Grace & Co. in taking over operation of the mill for at least a year. I suggested that the Bolivian government might attempt to get a competent manager and staff in Puerto Rico or Cuba, or perhaps arrange with some Cuban or Puerto Rican sugar mill to provide management, inasmuch as the harvest and grinding season in those islands was precisely the reverse of that in Bolivia and it should be possible to take advantage of that circumstance to get experienced management at a reasonable cost. Nothing came of that suggestion.

Villa Montes irrigation project

The mayor of Villa Montes appeared before the council, accompanied by the president of the Chamber of Deputies, to ask that the Development Corporation be given funds to proceed with its irrigation project which, according to him, was 75 per cent completed and would, when finished, serve to irrigate some 5,000 hectares of land. The highway from Tarija to Villa

Montes had been completed and was being maintained purely to service this undertaking which he stated had been constructed on the recommendation of the 1940 Bohan Mission and "had a tremendous political impact, as its success constituted a national necessity."*

In reply, I outlined Bolivia's critical financial position at length and stated that there simply were no funds available to complete the project. The TAMS (Tippetts-Abbett-McCarthy-Stratton) engineers and the head of Point IV had reported that the project had already cost many times more than the original estimate, and the latter had added that the soil in the vicinity was so eroded that the project was wholly uneconomical. At best, even if many more millions of dollars were invested, it would be ten years before the project could hope to bring a return. The president of the Chamber of Deputies admitted that the cost of the undertaking had been greatly inflated because of "political and legal reasons," but he could see no connection whatsoever between completing the project and monetary inflation. The head of the Planning Commission and Minister of Economy were reluctant to see the project scrapped after all

---

*This is typical of the half-truths that pass current for fact in Bolivia. Merwin Bohan, one of the most competent and experienced advisers who have ever gone from the United States to Latin America, headed a ten-man mission to Bolivia in 1941 and 1942 and recommended a number of highway projects, among others the Villa Montes-Tarija spur, together with certain agricultural, irrigation, and petroleum projects, *to be constructed by stages, according to Bolivia's capacity to finance the program, to repay foreign capital, and to provide available man power*. As to the irrigation project, without which there would be no need for the highway, the Bohan Mission reported that a survey by Mexican engineers showed that the total cost of a dam and ditches would be $1,510,870 and would suffice to irrigate 40,000 hectares, the dam to be a simple diversion dam with no need for a reservoir or flooding and no thought of pumping or conduits, but merely open irrigation ditches which was all that could be economically justified. The report went on to state that the area was practically unpopulated, that the soil was preponderantly silt and silt loam, and that, before the project could be recommended, further study was needed on these points: (1) international water rights, in view of Argentina's objection that the Pilcomayo River forms the boundary between Argentina and Paraguay; (2) transportation; (3) available population and labor; (4) soil and crop studies, with experimental plantings to determine economic possibilities; and (5) a careful study of land titles with the recommendation that the government purchase the land on the basis of its then value, without irrigation, and that it later resell the land at its value after irrigation (Bohan report, Part I, pp. 11-18; Part II, pp. 55-60).

that had been invested in it, and it was agreed that the former would talk the matter over with the head of Point IV to see if there were any solution.[21]

After the Planning Commission head and I had conferred with Ross Moore, the head of the U.S. Operations Mission in Bolivia, the council was informed, according to Moore and the agricultural experts in Point IV: (1) that only a small part of the region accessible to the irrigation project had desirable soil qualities (which probably accounts for the disparity between the original 40,000 hectares project and the current 5,000 hectare plan); (2) that the rest was so badly overgrazed and eroded that it would be generations before it could be used for economical agriculture (the gulleys looked like an imaginary photograph of the surface of the moon); (3) that, with the pumping installation located at 17 kilometers from the land to be irrigated (to satisfy, or at least to get around, Argentina's protests), it would be necessary to install cement conduits to bring the water to the land, as the intervening area was mostly porous soil; (4) that, under the circumstances, the work and investment could be considered only 5 per cent completed; and (5) that, quite aside from the fact that the region lacked the population to utilize the land, it would be far more economical to abandon the project entirely than to sink any more funds into what was nothing more than a pet political project. The head of the Planning Commission added that the region was plagued by locusts.*

President Siles replied that the political importance of the project could not be underestimated; that the nation had been forced to wage the Chaco War on the last occasion it had had to defend its frontiers; and that completion of the project was a question of national sovereignty, which effectually removed the discussion beyond the ambit of the executive director's expertise. It was also a pet project of former President Paz-Estenssoro for his home town (see Appendix IV).

---

*Anyone who has witnessed the damage done by recurrent locust plagues in neighboring Argentina, where thousands of workers and many thousands of dollars can be mobilized to combat the invasion, can realize what locusts can do in a comparatively uninhabited region. Suffice it to say that, following a locust invasion of the land, a billiard table would appear more luxuriant in vegetation, and certainly greener.

Social Security

The management of the National Social Security Administration appeared before the council again and again to demand additional loans from the Central Bank. Against my advice and the judgment of the council members, political pressure compelled the council to authorize credits of Bs. 18 billion in January and Bs. 6 billion early in February. By the end of February, the general manager of the CNSS demanded another Bs. 9 billion, alleging that, for the housing tax and family subsidy alone, the mining corporation owed the CNSS Bs. 6,283 million; the government Bs. 4,988 million; the YPFB (petroleum corporation) Bs. 801 million; the Development Corporation Bs. 485 million; and the private sector Bs. 1,927 million. The figures may have been extemporized, as the manager contended that the total of these debts amounted to Bs. 18,445 million (which is an overstatement of nearly Bs. 4 billion), and the YPFB president later presented figures for his corporation showing less than half the amount claimed by the CNSS.[22]

Again and again, I asked the CNSS to submit figures for its 1956 receipts and expenditures and for its 1957 budget, in compliance with the Decree of August 4, 1956, which established the Stabilization Council. On February 1, 1957, the council itself made a formal demand for this information; on March 8, the Minister of Finance repeated the demand; and on May 16, on the express authorization of the President, I again requested detailed information on the 1957 budget and actual receipts for 1956 and for the first four months of 1957, but to no avail.[23]

In June, 1957, the Social Security Administration published a pamphlet in bitter denunciation of my suggestion that social security and related costs must be cut drastically if the stabilization program were to be saved and the national economy to prosper. And in that pamphlet, which purported to "refute" my April 17 report to the President and Cabinet, the latest data that the CNSS could muster were for the year 1955! Even at that, the pamphlet contained within itself evidence of what was wrong with the management of the Social Security Administration, viz., figures that failed to add up to the totals shown, and, for the year 1955, the receipts and expenditures set forth in Table 10.

It is impossible to determine, for the accounts have never been made available, what proportion of the "surplus" shown in Table 10 was spent on imported supplies for the CNSS and for

TABLE 10

Social Security Receipts and Expenditures*

Item	Thousands of Bolivianos	Percentage
Total ordinary receipts	4,013,878	
Receipts taken from prior year reserves	1,040	
Total revenues	4,014,918	100.0
Paid for professional risk injuries	266,821	
Paid for maternity costs	57,400	
Family subsidies	859,457	
Professional risk payments from prior reserves	1,040	
Paid to doctors for professional services	50,299	
Total assistance received by workers	1,235,017	30.8
CNSS administrative expenses	446,628	
CNSS hospital administrative expenses	598,697	
Total administrative expenses	1,045,325	26.0
Surplus (spent chiefly for government buildings and supplies)	1,734,576	43.2
	4,014,918	100.0

*Figures taken from pamphlet published by the Social Security Administration containing the report of Germán Butrón-Márquez to the Second Workers' Congress of Bolivia (COB), June 7, 1957 (*Observaciones de la CNSS a los Planeamientos de Mr. Eder* [La Paz: *Caja Nacional de Segunidad Social*, 1957], pp. 21-23). Percentages computed by me.

imported hardware and equipment for the construction of government buildings, but all such imports would have been entered in the accounts at the Bs. 190 rate instead of at the actual average rate of exchange of Bs. 4,260,[24] so that, even if only one-third of the amount had been expended on imports, it would add over Bs. 12 billion to the cost of the CNSS, paid for not directly out of the workers' payrolls but as a subtraction from the nation's gold and dollar reserves. On that basis — which is admittedly nebulous — the workers would have received, directly or in doctors' fees, only $7\frac{1}{2}$ per cent of the total amount collected by the CNSS, instead of the 30.8 per cent shown in the table.

While it might be argued that the administrative costs of the CNSS, as well as of the CNSS hospitals, inure to the benefit of the workers, this argument is largely negated by the quality of the services rendered. The CNSS pamphlet reported that in the first four months of 1957 its two clinics had completed 128,630 laboratory analyses. With not over 130 working days in the year (p. 15 n), and, assuming an eight-hour day, this would be at the rate of over two analyses a minute, which would represent quite a load for the few laboratory assistants whom I saw taking their ease in the larger of the two laboratories. Later, following a newspaper article which pointed out that there must be some fallacy in this figure, the CNSS published a revised figure of 15,050 analyses but at the same time reported that in one clinic they had attended to 65,126 patients, which works out at more than one a minute, and in the other, 50,004 patients, or nearly one a minute.[25]

There may be some truth in the figure for the number of patients, as the complaints that patients were treated "unwillingly, tactlessly, contemptuously... and worse" were widespread.[26] In fact, in Argentina's largest packing plant, I have witnessed cattle being driven to the slaughter with more tender loving care than was meted out to the workers huddled miserably in line, waiting to be attended to in the chief CNSS clinic. If the workers managed to survive the clinics, it can only be explained by the fact that Bolivian workers are tougher than Argentine shorthorns.

The CNSS pamphlet included the report of the president of the CNSS Administrative Council, Germán Butrón-Márquez who, with Lechín and Chávez, was a leader of the Vanguardia Obrera Movimientista, the left-wing faction of the MNR. His report concluded with a reference to "Mister Eder... a fit representative of economic imperialism" who had completely overlooked the double purpose of the CNSS, viz.: (1) social security, and (2) "the redistribution of the national wealth."*[27]

Bolivians may judge for themselves to whom the CNSS had redistributed the national wealth, considering the percentage received by the workers, and the opportunities for private gain entailed by imports at the Bs. 190 rate. Clues are to be found

---

*This was the same term ("a representative of economic imperialism") used on a previous occasion by the head of the U.N. Mission in La Paz in referring collectively to the author, the American Ambassador, the chief of the ICA Mission, and a State Department representative. While the U.N. Mission chief intended the term as a jest, it was not without venom.

in the Bs. 100 million "loaned" by the CNSS to twenty-five workers in Cochabamba (Bs. 4 million each), "thanks to the cooperation of high labor leaders," and in a Bs. 13 million gift by the CNSS for the purchase of alcoholic beverages for a *fiesta* in connection with the COB meeting in June, 1957. This gift aroused such a scandal that it was repudiated, but not annulled, by the president of the CNSS Administrative Council. On the same occasion, the Bolivian government made a Bs. 300 million gift to the thousand labor leaders who attended the meeting (Bs. 300,000 each). [28]

Early in 1957 the head of the Planning Commission had reported that the International Labor Office actuary, serving as social security adviser on the U.N. Mission, was a "menace to the stabilization program," and was agitating behind the scenes for an increase in the housing tax from 2 per cent of payrolls to 14 per cent. [29] The success of this activity was demonstrated six weeks later, when it was proposed that the CNSS budget and its social security charges should be cut 25 per cent. President Siles commented that the proposal was indeed sensible, but that COB was considering increasing the housing tax to 14 per cent and that we must realize that the problem was a political one, not a financial one.

Guillermo Alborta-Velasco, no admirer of the stabilization program, attributes the "gigantesque" growth of the social security taxes to "Revolutionary euphoria which either overestimated the economic capacity of the nation or had preferred not to recognize economic reality." He quotes the Minister of Labor as estimating the total employer contribution to social security at 48.2 per cent of wages and salaries, but adds that, in practice, it is inoperative, as none of the taxpayers can meet this burden. [30]

The rates were already high — 30 per cent payable by the employers and, theoretically, $7\frac{1}{2}$ per cent payable by the workers, according to the general manager of the CNSS. However, the workers had always refused to allow even the old 5 per cent deduction from their pay, and the employers had been charged with the workers' share. In March, 1957, the president of the mining corporation reported that the Minister of Mines had instructed the miners not to pay the additional $2\frac{1}{2}$ per cent, and President Siles stated that the CNSS was considering a tax of a cent a pound on tin exports to take the place of the workers' $2\frac{1}{2}$ per cent. [31] Six weeks later, this tax was a *fait accompli* announced by the Minister of Mines, although never authorized by

the Stabilization Council, and hence illegal, as well as a violation of Bolivia's obligations to the lending agencies. Similarly,
a 2 per cent tax was imposed on gasoline sales without council
authorization in order to cover social security charges for the
veterans of the Chaco War.[32] The "menace" of the U.N. Mission
to the stabilization program, foreseen by the Planning Commission head, had been demonstrated, and so had the effectiveness
of the U.N.'s behind-the-scenes operators.

Bolivia's experience — and experience elsewhere in Latin
America — has shown that unless it is firmly established that
social security charges must be paid by employees as well as
by employers, preferably on a fifty-fifty basis, there is no limit
to the rise in rates, imposing a burden on payrolls and on the
nation that cannot be borne even by the most vigorous economy.

In view of my strong objections against a Central Bank loan
to the National Social Security Administration — it could hardly
be called a loan as there was not the remotest likelihood of its
being repaid — the council, at the insistence of President Siles,
resolved to have the Central Bank lend the government Bs. 2.5
billion to pay its debt to the CNSS, although the fact that the
government, COMIBOL, YPFB, and the Development Corporation were unable to pay their quotas to the CNSS made it apparent that the social security charges exceeded the economic
capacity of the nation.

The Petroleum Corporation

In comparison with other government enterprises, YPFB
appeared to be so competently administered, from the general
manager down through the accounting and engineering staff, that
the council and its advisers were disposed to take at face value
the assurances of the management that its proposed capital expenditures were economically justified, provided that they were
kept within the limits of the nation's financial resources.

Thus, when the YPFB chiefs appeared before the council
early in 1957 to ask for a further $5,000 a month in foreign ex-
change for railway freight on exports which had erroneously
been budgeted at the prestabilization rate of exchange, it was
readily granted. Later, the council even agreed to permit the
Central Bank to sell $422,000 in dollars to the YPFB at Bs.
1,500 per dollar to cover an outstanding debt to Brazil. This
was a $2,011,000 account under the Brazilian trade agreement,

on which YPFB had paid $1,589,000 prior to stabilization at the rate of Bs. 1,690, which was the special rate in force for YPFB transactions at the time. On the remainder still outstanding, YPFB had already paid the Central Bank in full, at the official exchange rate of Bs. 190. Hence, the council was inclined to regard the debt as a contractual obligation of the Central Bank, and took the stand that this warranted a departure from the rule that there was only one valid rate in force under stabilization — the rate determined by supply and demand. [33]

But when, a few weeks later, the YPFB general manager appeared before the council with his staff to complain that the company was running a Bs. 1.5 billion tax deficit, it was clear that there was something wrong. The complaint, in substance, was that the council had agreed to a single 3 per cent tax on all gasoline and fuel oil sales, eliminating the prior myriad taxes earmarked for political cells, labor unions, and other purposes. In point of fact, the YPFB people stated, the earmarked taxes had *not* been abolished, and YPFB's taxes were running at the rate of Bs. 2,591 million per annum instead of the Bs. 1,080 million budgeted. The government would not permit YPFB to pass the taxes on to the consumer. The Finance Minister then explained that the earmarked taxes which the council had voted to abolish had all been reinstated by the Cabinet, which was certainly news to the nonpolitical members of the council and to its advisers, who commented that it was hard to understand how YPFB could cut prices for kerosene, gasoline, and other products and pay more than double the taxes budgeted, when it was already on a deficitary basis. The YPFB general manager agreed wholeheartedly, but stated that President Siles himself had insisted on the price cut. [34]

And that was that! Not a single agency or enterprise of government was to be allowed to operate in the black, and U.S. aid of $20-$25 million a year would continue to pour down the drain of fiscal profligacy with no hope of economic recovery despite the stabilization of the currency.

18

FINANCE

The Central Bank and the Dollar Debts

Early in 1957 I received a letter from a former business associate, writing as director of the Peruvian Corporation, Ltd., and president of the American Overseas Finance Corporation (AOFC).* The purpose of the letter was to enquire what steps would be taken to pay Bolivia's debts to those two companies. As to the latter, a debt of some $1.5 million for freight charges, I was able to reply that the government was negotiating with the railway representative in La Paz for payment over a period of years.

The other debt consisted of a series of promissory notes from the Bolivian Civil Aeronautics Bureau to the order of the Pittsburgh Plate Glass Export Corporation for a total of $68,800, bearing the unconditional *aval* (guaranty) of the Central Bank. The notes had been purchased without recourse by the AOFC. With respect to this debt, I was only able to respond that the Central Bank had given its guaranty on $32 million of notes and that its available resources were zero, so that creditors would have to be patient.[35]

Some three months later, a letter was received from another old friend and business associate, a vice-president of one of New York's leading banks, enclosing a photostat of one of the Civil Aeronautics notes which it had received for collection and advising that the bank had some $500,000 of defaulted Bolivian government-sector notes or drafts, some with the *aval* of the Central Bank, which it held for various clients. Any one of these might lead to legal action and the possible attachment of Central Bank funds in the United States. By that time, with a fuller knowledge of the facts at my disposal, I was able to reply that, according to the Finance Minister, the total governmental

---

*This was an Edge Act Corporation founded in 1955 by five of the leading commercial banks in the United States. It numbered among its directors such well-known persons as John J. McCloy (chairman), Clarence Randall, David Rockefeller, William Batt, etc. The president was Norbert A. Bogdan, formerly vice-president of J. Henry Schroder Banking Corporation.

foreign debt outstanding amounted to over $50 million and that the Central Bank had endorsed or accepted some $33 million of drafts or notes; that I hoped to have the full facts available shortly, at which time it should be possible to negotiate an arrangement with creditors for a uniform policy of partial payment in 1957, with the balance payable over a period of years.[36]

As early as January, 1957, the president of the Central Bank had pointed out that the credit of the bank was gravely affected by its failure to honor its guaranty on the drafts and notes of various government enterprises which had incurred the obligation on the understanding that they could purchase dollars at the official exchange rate of Bs. 190, but they simply did not have sufficient bolivianos to buy dollars at the Bs. 7,500 rate.

He admitted that many of these obligations were tainted with impropriety and cited, as a typical example of the contracts entered into by one of the more notorious government suppliers, a shipment of trucks under a contract that had specifically called for delivery of trucks of English manufacture but which was filled by shipment of Swedish war surplus trucks which the supplier had bought for $4,000 each, charging the government $15,000 each. The purchase had been approved by one of Bolivia's top political personalities and the Central Bank had been instructed to place its *aval* on the notes under orders emanating from President Paz himself. Despite the apparent impropriety of this transaction, the bank president insisted that the Central Bank must not be placed in the position of failing to honor its obligations.

To meet the problem, I suggested that the bank should first prepare a complete list of all outstanding obligations, and that if it then proposed payment to creditors over a period of two to three years, it would create a favorable impression rather than the reverse, as it would mean that Bolivia was prepared to put its financial house in order. It was so resolved.

Two months later, however, the supplier in question had applied such political pressure that a delegation of seven directors of the Central Bank appeared before the council to say that the bank would be forced to honor the drafts held by that supplier, as otherwise he would hold the bank responsible and attach its funds. I commented that, if the bank were to pay the creditors who took legal action in preference to those who were willing to wait, it would be favoring those unfriendly to Bolivia's interests. Instead, I suggested that the government should either declare a moratorium or, preferably, propose and negotiate with *all* its commercial creditors a uniform arrangement for payment of say 10 per cent on account, with the remainder payable over four or five years. One of the bank directors then read Article XII of the supplier's contract to show that the nonpayment would be subject to arbitration by the International Chamber of Commerce in Paris, but I replied that no tribunal in the world could compel payment if the government were to declare a moratorium, notwithstanding which I strongly recommended a negotiated arrangement with creditors.[37]

The problem of the commercial debt of the Bolivian government was not confined to prestabilization accounts, however, for in June, 1957, the Brazilian Embassy presented a peremptory demand that the Central Bank give its guarantee on a contract dated November 23, 1956, entered into by the municipality of Santa Cruz, for $867,900 of water pipes ordered from the Companhía Ferro Brasileiro. I informed the council that I had received a visit at home from the Brazilian Commercial Attaché and an officer of the Companhía Ferro Brasileiro, which, I was given to understand, represented Companhía Siderúrgica Mannesmann, Belo Horizonte, a subsidiary of Mannesmann, A. G. of Duesseldorf. I had informed the visitors with all courtesy that there was nothing I could do toward getting the Central Bank to guarantee the contract, regardless of any possible commitment of the municipality or others to that effect, as they were aware that any contract entered into after August 4, 1956, without the prior approval of the Stabilization Council was illegal and void.

It was suggested to the council that if Santa Cruz wished to install a new water system it should get bids from all over the world, not just from a single Brazilian supplier, and obtain reliable estimates of the *total* cost of the proposed water works, not merely of a shipment of pipes. The total cost involved might be closer to $5 million than to $1 million, and certainly neither the government nor the Central Bank was in a position to finance the project at the present time. There followed a long discussion of the delicate problem of a separatist movement in Santa Cruz, the question of diplomatic relations with the Brazilian government, and again Bolivia's difficult position vis-à-vis her powerful and allegedly imperialistic neighbor (see pp. 68 n and 421 n), but it was finally resolved that the Secretary General of the Bolivian government should be informed that Bolivia was not in a position to consider financing except on at least ten-year terms, dating from 1958.*

Another post-stabilization operation illegally entered into without the prior approval of the Stabilization Council was for the purchase by the Government Railways Administration of twelve Mikado locomotives from Japan on a five-year credit basis. News of this contract leaked out to the press, and I brought the matter up at a council meeting in March, 1957, with the advice that it would be a mistake to purchase railway equipment under a short-term credit when it was obvious that the government would have no funds to meet the obligation when due. It was precisely that form of improvident financing which had brought the government to its present plight, and, if the purchase were economically justifiable, a detailed project should be presented to the World Bank for long-term financing, with bids received from all potential suppliers. The head of the Planning Commission agreed and stated that the prices tendered by German suppliers were lower than those received from Japan and that the only reason for accepting the Japanese proposal was the five-year credit. It was unanimously agreed that the council would not recommend this purchase.

Two months later, however, it was learned that the deal had actually been consummated and that, apparently as a down payment, the government had used one million dollars which it had received as a dividend from its share in the Bolivia Railway Company, a subsidiary of The Antofagasta (Chili) & Bolivia Railway Company, Ltd. This was a source of income that the Bolivian government had never revealed to the Washington lending agencies and that, up to that time, was unknown to the council advisers.† Considering the illegal and surreptitious manner in which this deal was concluded and the constant pressure for its approval, there is no reason to suspect that it was free from graft (see p. 157, item 2, and p. 288).

---

*My recommendation was more Draconian: Waterworks cannot be financed on less than a 20-year basis, and Bolivia's financial position was too precarious to undertake this additional commitment on any terms. Construction of these facilities simply could not be justified economically.

†The government owned 27 per cent of the stock in the Bolivia Railway Company (see ECLA report, p. 214, for background of its ownership of these shares).

The debt totals

It was not until June, 1957, that the council received from the Minister of Finance and from the president of the Central Bank statements of the commercial dollar debt of the Bolivian government and government enterprises that, taken together, appeared to be reasonably complete despite the inevitable mistakes in arithmetic (in this case, less than $80,000). According to the Ministry tabulation, shown in condensed and corrected form in Table 11, the total commercial debt amounted to $75,868,531.26. This amount included $45,847,777.99 purportedly owing to the Export-Import Bank of Washington, but, as a matter of fact, including only the Cochabamba-Santa Cruz highway debt which the Finance Ministry placed at $34,506.975, plus interest *due from 1957 through 1974*, which could hardly be considered as a debt until due. Subsequent examination of the Eximbank *Report to the Congress* for June 30, 1957 (not then available), showed that the actual total amount borrowed from

TABLE 11

Bolivian Government External Commercial Debt, May 15, 1957*

Debtor		U.S. Dollars
COMIBOL (Government Mining Corporation)		$ 9,619,991
Bolivian Development Corporation	$47,238,440	
Less debt to Eximbank	45,847,778	1,390,662
CNSS (National Social Security Administration)		287,892
Government Railways Social Security Fund		111,612
Government, municipal, and university debt guaranteed by Central Bank:		
Adalberto Markus (English)	$ 4,301,628	
Arpic Engineering (Belgian)	751,190	
Titeux Export (French)	2,019,212	7,072,030
YPFB (Government Petroleum Corporation)		4,143,892
Ministry of Economy (for motor vehicle purchases)		329,418
Johansson & Co., S.A. (for L. M. Ericsson telephone equipment)		774,423
Banco Minero de Bolivia (Government Mining Bank)		5,957,262
Miscellaneous government debts		253,817
Other debts guaranteed by Central Bank (approximate)		20,928,000
		$50,868,999

*Exclusive of debt to the Export-Import Bank. Figures supplied by Finance Ministry and Central Bank.

the Eximbank for the highway was $33,420,000, part of which had been repaid, and that the total debt outstanding on that date was $34,678,000 out of $42,148,000 borrowed.* The Ministry's compilation likewise erred in that it failed to include some $20,928,000 of obligations which had apparently been guaranteed by the Central Bank.† In neither case was the error attributable to the Finance Ministry, but to the erroneous information submitted by the Development Corporation and the Central Bank. Thus, the unsettled commercial debt on which creditors were pressing for payment appears to have been in the neighborhood of some $50 million.

The Finance Minister later, in a four-year report on the accomplishments of the Ministry, stated: "The estimate of the commercial debts was at first calculated at $120 million, but, as the investigations proceeded, it became evident that they exceeded $200 million." He added that it was difficult to obtain statistical and accounting data, particularly from COMIBOL and the Development Corporation.[38] These figures undoubtedly

*Export-Import Bank of Washington, *Report to Congress* (Washington, D.C.: Eximbank, 1957).

†This figure is derived by subtracting from the $28 million reported by the president of the Central Bank (letter to President Siles, May 31, 1957), the three debts to Markus, Arpic, and Titeux, listed separately in the table. The names of those three suppliers will be familiar to students of the Bolivian scene, as, whether justly or not, they were cited repeatedly in the press, and by the Bolivian members of the Stabilization Council, as the most notorious of the politically linked operators of the pre-Siles period. In an exchange of correspondence between the British Embassy in La Paz and the Central Bank, the latter stated that the merchandise supplied under the Markus contract failed to meet specifications either in quality or price, and had been "overinvoiced," as a consequence of which the matter was being aired in court. They invited the British Commercial Attaché to inspect the factual proof of allegedly improper invoicing at the bank's office. The British Ambassador emphasized that Adalberto Markus was not a British subject; that the transactions were between British exporters and the Bolivian government departments and agencies; and that the British government, through its Export Credits Guarantee Department, had insured the operations in reliance on the good faith of the Bolivian government and of the Bolivian Central Bank. The amount due to the British exporters was placed at £ 1,188,800 ($3,328,640), while the amount guaranteed by the Central Bank under the Markus agreement was $4,301,628. The "overinvoicing," if this is the source of the discrepancy, was slightly less than 30 per cent, which is understood to have been modest in the prestabilization era. The total debts guaranteed by the Central Bank (and hence the total shown in Table 11) are probably understated by some $800,000 (see Appendix V).

include the debt to the Export-Import Bank and other indebtedness listed in Table 4 (p. 145). They are significant chiefly in that they constitute an official admission of the Bolivian government's ignorance of some $80 million in indebtedness incurred by the government and government agencies during the financial chaos of the first MNR regime, and the consequent understatement of obligations in the government's petition for stabilization loan financing. The amount of the discrepancy is substantially greater than the figures shown elsewhere in this volume, which is neither to impugn nor to substantiate the accuracy of the figures but merely to confirm the impossibility of obtaining trustworthy figures of 1952-56 government expenditures and obligations.

Attachment of Bolivian bank accounts

What with this large sum of suppliers' accounts outstanding, many of them overdue, and preferential payments being made to some creditors and not to others, it was inevitable that eventually the chickens would come home to roost. As early as December, 1956, immediately prior to stabilization, I had warned the President and council that various suppliers had attempted to attach the funds of the Central Bank in New York; and I urged that all deposits of the government, and of all government enterprises and agencies, be carried in the account of the monetary department of the Central Bank as the agent of the Bolivian government, until such time as an arrangement could be made with creditors to spread out payments over a reasonable period of years.

The matter was again brought up in January, 1957, and it was emphasized that the COMIBOL accounts in particular should be transferred to the Central Bank, inasmuch as it was fairly well settled under New York law that freedom from attachment applied solely to government accounts and not to government-owned business enterprises. Bolivia should have known from experience that the law distinguishes between government acts *jure imperii* and acts *jure gestionis,* as they had previously had an attachment levied against the funds of the government Mining Bank as a business *(gestionis)* and not a governmental *(imperii)* agency.*

---

*The distinction had been recognized as far back as 1824 when Chief Justice Marshall ruled: "When a government becomes a partner in any

The council agreed with this suggestion, but still nothing was done to solve the problem of the various government enterprise accounts in New York banks or, more important, to enter into an agreement with creditors that would demonstrate Bolivia's intention to honor her obligations as soon as possible.

In April, the council was told of the friendly letter received from a New York bank warning of threatened attachments and pointing out that Bolivia, by failing to make some arrangement for payment of its commercial debts, was jeopardizing the excellent impression made by the stabilization measures. After discussion, it was agreed that Bolivia should immediately propose a 5 per cent payment to be made June 30, 1957, to all creditors, without discrimination, on all 1956 and 1957 maturities, with further 5 per cent payments to be made on June 30 and December 31, 1958, and the balance to be paid in equal installments over a five-year period.

Still nothing was done, and a month later I advised the council that the State Department had confirmed that there was little danger of an attachment of Bolivian government funds being sustained by the New York courts, provided that the funds were held in the name of the Central Bank and that the bank was actually acting as an agent of the government. But this did not apply to funds held by government enterprises, or for account of such enterprises. The council was also advised that a Treasury Department official, then in La Paz, strongly recommended that Bolivia enter into a negotiated arrangement with its creditors (rather than declare a unilateral moratorium). It was emphasized that the council still did not know the amount of Bolivia's indebtedness to suppliers, with or without the Central Bank *aval*, and that we simply had to have the figures. And it was proposed that the government, through the Embassy in Washington or through the Central Bank, should immediately arrange a meeting with creditors and with all the banks in the United States that had discounted Bolivian government or

---

trading company, it divests itself, so far as concerns the transactions of that company, of its sovereign character, and takes that of a private citizen." (*Bank of U.S. v. Planters' Bank of Georgia*, 9 Wheat. 904, 907.) The State Department decided to follow this "restrictive theory of sovereign immunity" in 1952 in view of "the widespread and increasing practice on the part of governments of engaging in commercial activities" ("Changed Policy Concerning the Granting of Sovereign Immunity to Foreign Governments," *Department of State Bulletin*, Vol. XXVI, No. 678 [1952], pp. 984-85), but this new policy has been breached on numerous occasions.

government enterprise drafts or notes, or were holding them for collection. They could then attempt to arrange for payment over a five-year period.[39]

Still, the Bolivian government procrastinated. Finally, the axe fell. Attachments were levied simultaneously on the Central Bank accounts in Chemical Corn Exchange Bank, the Chase Manhattan Bank, Manufacturers Trust Company, and the New York Agency of the Bank of London and South America, Ltd., all on behalf of COMIBOL creditors. The President, in desperation, summoned me to an unofficial (and unrecorded) council meeting at the presidential palace for my advice. At my suggestion, a telegram was sent by the Central Bank to the New York law firm of Anderson & Roberts asking that they represent the Central Bank and communicate with the New York banks named with a view to having the attachments lifted.* At the same time I agreed to draft a statement in English to be presented by the Bolivian Ambassador in Washington to the banks and principal creditors, which would explain the Bolivian situation and offer to make payment of the suppliers' credits that were due in 1956, or that would become due in 1957, payment to be made over a five-year period at the rate of 20 per cent per annum.[40]

On the following day, however, it was learned that the outstanding obligations guaranteed by the Central Bank were some $5 million less than had previously been reported, inasmuch as certain orders were reported to have been cancelled, although the drafts had apparently not been recovered by the Central Bank and were still in circulation. My confidence had already been badly shaken by previously discovered revelations that the government would turn over to YPFB for further expansion the money that it was receiving from certain oil concession rights; that the unexpected and unsuspected $1 million dividend from the Bolivia Railway Company would be used for the purchase of Japanese locomotives against the advice of the council; and that the $2 million available in 1957 from postponement of obligations

---

*By coincidence, this telegram was sent on the very day that the appointment of Robert B. Anderson as Secretary of the Treasury, subject to confirmation by the Senate, was announced in the *New York Times*, May 30, 1957. Under the circumstances, of course, Anderson could take no part in the matter, but his partner shortly thereafter succeeded in having the attachments lifted. At the time, thanks to my insistence, COMIBOL had no bank accounts in New York, and the New York funds were held for account of the Central Bank, presumably as agent for the Bolivian government.

to the Eximbank as a result of negotiations by the head of the Planning Commission would be dissipated in further government expenditures.* Manifestly, these four windfall sources of funds alone — some $17.5 million — plus the amounts already contained in the foreign exchange budget, would have sufficed for Bolivia to pay all its matured or maturing credits from suppliers, particularly if pains had been taken to eliminate all transactions tainted with fraud which, as I had explained to my colleagues on the council, were legally void *ab initio* and could properly have been settled over the course of time on a *quantum meruit* basis.

Despite the revelation of these hidden assets, I drafted what, in effect, amounted to an informal moratorium declaration, as I had agreed to do, but our ignorance as to the actual amount of the indebtedness of the government and government enterprises, even at this late date, was so great that it took over two weeks to prepare the draft. †

*I first heard of the payment to YPFB through the indiscretion of José Paz-Estenssoro, president of YPFB and brother of the former President, who told me gleefully at a cocktail party that YPFB would be receiving $3.5 million from Gulf Oil Corporation for concession rights in the Madrejones region and that this would be used to make good the council's cut in the YPFB budget from $15 million to $12 million. When I suggested to President Siles that this windfall be used to reduce the Central Bank's drawings on the stabilization fund, the President expressed chagrin that the secret was out, and said that for political reasons the money would have to be turned over to YPFB. Later, I learned that Gulf had agreed to pay $5 million in cash, and $3.5 million in equipment, both payments to be considered as advance royalties. There was a further windfall of $2.5 million for the transfer of the so-called McCarthy concession of which I was unaware until my return to the United States. (Data furnished July 25, 1957, by one of the bidders on the Madrejones concession.)

†My former associates in law and business may wonder why, with this cumulative evidence of continuing duplicity on the part of the Bolivian government, I continued to assist the government in its plans for a moratorium, particularly in view of the government's lack of candor in its dealings with me. As a matter of fact, I did draft a letter to the President on May 31, 1957, explaining that it would be impossible to continue serving the Bolivian government under the circumstances and presenting my immediate resignation. It was only after consultation with the American Ambassador and my closest associates on the council (the Central Bank president, the Ministers of Finance and Economy, and the head of the Planning Commission), that I came to the conclusion that it would be improper to add to the President's burdens at this critical juncture. President Siles was not a free agent but a minority voice in the Co-Government, and he refused to assume the powers of a dictator. There was no question of Siles' personal integrity, and my mission was "to control inflation...

At that, a number of the figures had to be entered with question marks in parenthesis, to be corroborated later by the Finance Minister or the president of the Central Bank. The document was presented to the council on June 21, 1957, and was accepted with only minor changes. It may be noted that I inserted, and the council accepted, a specific acknowledgment of the government's indebtedness for the confiscation of the mines and of the urban and rural properties seized under the "land reform" programs.

It was not until the end of July, however, that the Bolivian Ambassador in Washington reported that he had received the draft from La Paz and would like to confer with me on certain points of language and procedure.[41] On August 15, the document was presented by the Bolivian Embassy to the bankers so that they in turn might communicate with their clients.

This declaration of insolvency, showing only minor changes from the original draft, constitutes: (1) an official acknowledgment by the government of Bolivia of its past profligacy and of the efficacy of the stabilization program as well as (2) the twofold commitment to freeze wages unless compensated by reduced social security costs, and to incur no new obligations without the authorization of the Stabilization Council (text in Appendix V). Thus ended what must have been one of the most humiliating episodes to which a sovereign nation and a central bank have ever been exposed, reaching the point where dozens, perhaps hundreds, of checks drawn by the Central Bank were refused payment, many of them for sums of as little as $80 to $100.[42]

The Trade Agreement Dollars

In Chapter 11 a description is given of the system of trade agreement dollars whereby Bolivia would ship its products to neighboring countries, chiefly Brazil and Argentina, and receive payment not in actual currency but in *dollars of account* which could be used only for the purpose of purchasing goods in those countries, generally at prices several times higher than those

---

and...personally serve as adviser...to the President" — not to act as a self-appointed judge. So the letter was never sent, and I drafted the declaration of insolvency as agreed, insisting, however, that it contain "in all candor" a specific reference to the windfall funds (see Appendix V).

prevailing in world markets. The insistence of those countries, and of the Bolivian Ministry of Foreign Affairs, that Bolivia's debit balances in these accounts be paid off in actual dollars is also set forth, as well as my stand that a debt in fictitious dollars ought not to be paid in real dollars at the expense of those who were expected to provide the money for the stabilization fund. As this was a month before the International Monetary Fund and the U.S. government had agreed to finance the stabilization program, and the Bolivian government was counting on me to obtain the money, my arguments were unanswerable.*

With stabilization, however, it was another story. Less than a month after enactment of the stabilization decrees, I was forced to remind the council that the country was still giving away its products by selling them for trade agreement dollars. This led to a formal meeting in the Foreign Office between the Stabilization Council and the commission appointed to study the forthcoming negotiations with Brazil, which would discuss the railway debt to Brazil as well as the matter of the trade agreement dollars.†

*The late Frank Graham used to refer to such trade agreement currencies as "sham money," and pinpointed the problem when he stated that: "The practice of valuing goods in factitious money, as if it were real, leads to the presumably crazy policy ... of buying and selling in other than what, on the face of things, seem to be the best markets." In the "economics of Cloud-Cuckoo-Land ... the countries with overall credit balances, largely composed of sham-money, cannot buy the goods that they desire because they have wasted their resources on the acquisition of this so-called money, available, if at all, only for goods that they do not want" (Frank D. Graham, *The Cause and Cure of "Dollar Shortage "* [Princeton, N.J.: Princeton University Press, 1949], p. 11). In the case of Bolivia, importers with the proper political connections were able to buy trade agreement dollars at the "crazy" rate of Bs. 190 to the dollar so that the Bolivian market was supplied with expensive Brazilian and Argentine goods; Bolivia had a large debit balance to those countries; some exporters such as YPFB showed handsome paper profits; the nation showed a favorable balance of trade in "sham money"; and Bolivia had traded its birthright for a mess of pottage.

†The Mixed Bolivian-Brazilian Commission was headed by Alvaro Teixeira-Soares, Brazil's able Ambassador in La Paz, and Jorge Escobari-Cusicanqui, Bolivia's Under Secretary of Foreign Affairs. Negotiations took place in April-June, 1957, following President Siles' return to La Paz from a preliminary meeting with Brazilian President Juscelino Kubitschek at the Bolivian-Brazilian border. Siles was utterly charmed by Dr. Kubitschek, as well he might have been. President Kubitschek, Dr. Siles confided to me, was the greatest man he had ever met, greater than Roosevelt or Eisenhower, and with a complete solution to all Latin

One of the Bolivian Commission officials brought out at the meeting that Brazil was charging exorbitant prices on its exports, and I reported that tile importers in La Paz were paying three to five times higher prices for tiles purchased in Brazil than for German imports. At a later meeting I substantiated this report, as well as the fact that a shipment of electric heaters had been imported from Argentina at seven to eight times the price of comparable heaters from West Germany. A YPFB representative stated that his company would have to depend on the Brazilian market to take the output of its Santa Cruz refinery, to be completed in 1958, until such time as the pipe line to the Pacific was completed. YPFB could, however, purchase pipe and other supplies from Brazil for up to 60 per cent of the value of its exports. One of the Bolivian Commission members reported that Brazil was paying Bolivia 20 per cent more than world market prices for tin, and 30 per cent more for lead (in treaty dollars of course), but he admitted that Brazil made up the difference by charging excessive prices for its exports. I then asked, "Who's fooling whom?" — a sally that won the approval of all the Stabilization Council members present, and I recommended that Bolivia should demand real dollars for its exports, and should buy its imports wherever it could buy them most economically.

It was finally agreed, with respect to the treaty dollars, that the debt to Brazil must not be increased and that future imports must be on a strictly competitive basis, except that the Bolivian lead and tin smelters and YPFB would be permitted to use their exports to Brazil for the purchase of imports under the treaty arrangements, using any excess of exports to pay off the trade agreement dollar debt over a period of years. This

---

America's problems. The solution was a Keynesian one, with prosperity to be built on ever-increasing "planned deficits," that ended by bringing even so rich a nation as Brazil to the verge of bankruptcy and beyond. As Latin America's deficits alone would clearly not suffice to spend that area into prosperity, local deficits were to be supplemented by Kubitschek's "Operation Panamerica," to be financed by the United States. As it turned out, much to Dr. Kubitschek's chagrin, as expressed by him in private conversation, and in public at the Fogg Museum in Cambridge on March 7, 1962, President Kennedy ran away with the idea and changed its name to "Alliance for Progress." Some tone-deaf assistant in Washington translated this as La Alianza Para el Progreso, giving rise to the canard that the "Alliance Stops Progress" (para can mean either stops or for). And there the matter rests.

proved to be an unwise arrangement which resulted in a still further increase in trade agreement exports and debts.

Another Bolivian Commission member then brought out that the current expenses of the hopelessly deficitary Corumbá-Santa Cruz railway (see p. 66) were being charged to the cost of construction and added to the Bolivian indebtedness to Brazil, and a Foreign Office official stated that the Brazilian and Bolivian negotiators were proposing a frontier treaty with preferential tariff rates between the two countries, to be followed by a similar tariff arrangement between Bolivia and Argentina. When I suggested that this would violate Bolivia's most-favored nation arrangement with the United States, we were told that preferential tariffs were common in frontier agreements. To this I retorted that the U.S. Congress might consider it unfair for Bolivia to take the stand that all nations are most-favored but that some nations are more most-favored than others, particularly when the United States was subsidizing the Bolivian government with U.S. aid and was paying real dollars for its imports, not phony dollars.*

Subsequently I suggested that a free market be established for the treaty dollars so that importers and exporters could decide whether it suited them to sell or buy under the treaty arrangements, and at what price. It was finally resolved that the Central Bank would be authorized to advance up to 60 per cent of the value of mineral exports under the treaty arrangements, with no commitment for payment of the balance. Later, the bank was authorized to advance 50 per cent for agricultural exports, again without agreeing on a definitive exchange rate. Those arrangements, in effect, provided a moderate discount for the "sham money," but still left a solution up in the air.

Not long before, the National Chamber of Commerce had petitioned the council for lower import duties on goods that had

---

*It was at this meeting, attended by Foreign Office as well as Stabilization Council officers, and by members of the Bolivia-Brazil Treaty Commission, that I heard from all sides the most sweeping denunciation of Brazilian "economic imperialism" — an actual fact, I was told, which no one dared mention in public, while the alleged "Yankee imperialism" was nothing but a political slogan. The danger of Brazilian penetration in the entire frontier region was stressed, and it was stated that Brazil was stirring up trouble in the Beni, Pando, and Santa Cruz areas to soften Bolivia up for the treaty negotiations. Whether or not there was substance in these allegations I cannot say, but there was no doubt of the intensity of Bolivian sentiment in the matter.[43]

been ordered under the trade agreements prior to enactment of the stabilization decrees. The council asked the Chamber to draw up a complete list of treaty imports, with dates and prices, and later resolved that the Assistant Comptroller General of the nation should head a committee to make a full investigation of all such imports, listing the suppliers and purchasers and reporting on qualities and prices, as well as competitive world prices, on the various shipments.

As such an investigation would have trodden on many political toes, nothing came of the matter. But none of the Stabilization Council advisers was willing to see Bolivia continue to squander its resources and those of the stabilization fund, and on April 1, 1957 — "Day of the Innocents"* — the council was informed that YPFB, the government petroleum corporation, was continuing to sell its products for treaty dollars and had built up a balance of $4 million in that currency, for which the Central Bank was giving them real dollars. Previously, the council had learned that the Central Bank had increased its holdings of treaty dollars by $700,000 and was led to believe that the local tin smelters were responsible; but, with this new information, there was no doubt that YPFB was the major culprit.

Despite the possibility implicit in the situation that further contributions to the stabilization fund might be cut off, it was not until June, 1957, that a showdown took place, with representatives of the Foreign Office, YPFB, the Mining Bank, and the Central Bank summoned to the council meeting. Meanwhile, one of the most knowledgeable members of the import fraternity had informed the press that one U.S. dollar was equal in value to 6.7 trade agreement dollars, as was proved by the fact that the Argentine Central Bank was giving Argentine exporters 3.5 million Argentine pesos for $100,000 U.S. currency or for $670,950 in trade agreement dollars.[44]

This disparity probably exaggerated the overall relationship between the value, at world market prices, of the merchandise exported by Bolivia under treaty arrangements and that which was received in exchange, but it served to point up my insistence that the Central Bank should open up a free market for Brazilian and Argentine trade agreement dollars, precisely as it had done for U.S. dollars, sterling, and other currencies. It seemed to be the consensus at the council that, if such a

*April Fools' Day is *Día de los Inocentes*, not, of course, to be confused with Childermas, December 28, "Day of the Holy Innocents."

market were opened, supply and demand would place the value of the trade agreement dollars at somewhere between 40 cents and 60 cents U.S., despite substantiated reports of imports from Brazil and Argentina which, if they had been paid for in real dollars, would have cost from two to eight times the world market price.

At the showdown meeting, the president of the Central Bank announced that Bolivia's debt to Argentina in treaty dollars amounted to $5 million, and to Brazil $3 million. Earlier in the year, the head of the Planning Commission had stated that the debt to Brazil was $4 million, and it was known that the debt had increased since then, so that little reliance can be placed on any of these figures. When the subject was first raised, in November, 1956, the council was informed that the total treaty dollar debt to both countries was only $6 million.

The Central Bank president contended that YPFB and other exporters must be allowed to continue offsetting this debt with exports, as otherwise Bolivia would have to make payment in real dollars. He added that current imports from Brazil were practically nil inasmuch as, at current rates of exchange, Brazilian goods were priced at up to three times world market prices. This proposal overlooked the gist of the objections to the sham money arrangements, namely, that if the Central Bank continued to give YPFB and others real dollars for its exports in treaty dollars, as it was doing, it would mean an $8 million loss to the stabilization fund — again, a failure to face reality in "Cloud-Cuckoo-Land."

A three-way solution was therefore proposed: (1) Those merchants who were willing and able to balance their exports under the trade agreements with imports under the agreements should be permitted to do so, with no restrictions — it would be up to them to see that they did not lose money on the deal, and there would be no problem; (2) YPFB, which alleged that it had no market for part of its production except in Brazil or Argentina, should see to it that the admittedly high prices which it was compelled to pay on treaty imports were compensated by comparably high prices for its exports and that, under no circumstances, should it be allowed to export for treaty dollars more than it was willing to import for treaty dollars — in which event there would be no further problem there; and (3) the Central Bank should establish, and let other banks and foreign exchange dealers establish, a free market for the purchase and sale of Brazilian and Argentine treaty dollars which could be used for all other imports and exports — if that were done, there would be no problem there, and the whole question would be solved.

The representative of the Ministry of Foreign Affairs objected, however, and he read the pertinent section of the Argentine treaty: "The monetary authorities of both countries shall take the necessary steps so that the Argentine-Bolivian treaty dollars shall receive the same treatment as U.S. free market dollars, in the official market as well as in the free exchange market, for the same operations and in accordance with the exchange system in each country."

In reply, I maintained that they *would* be receiving the same treatment — the U.S. dollar and the treaty dollar would both be quoted according to supply and demand, and under Bolivia's present exchange system there was no official rate of exchange for any currency. The retired Central Bank officer who had handled the treaty negotiations contended, however, that it was the intention that one treaty dollar should be equal to one U.S. dollar, and the Finance Minister added that the Argentine Ambassador insisted on that point. To this I replied that if the treaty negotiators had intended to say that treaty dollars (*dólares convenio*) were equal to U.S. dollars they would have said so, instead of saying that the two should receive the same treatment, but that it was impossible to assume that intelligent negotiators had intended to say that phony dollars (*dólares engaño*) were worth the same as real dollars, which was to say that black was white. I contended that, if the matter were taken to the Hague Court, it would be decided on the basis of equal treatment and not equal value. The Finance Minister strongly supported my argument which was certainly in Bolivia's interest.*

---

*Later, I checked the wording of the treaty for myself, and found that Article 23 provided merely that the Argentine and Bolivian Central Banks were required to take such steps as might be necessary to ensure that the treaty dollars would be quoted at the same rate of exchange as free exchange dollars for operations effected under "identical conditions and circumstances" (*en igualdad de condiciones y circunstancias*). Inasmuch as the Argentine Central Bank was quoting treaty dollars at 6.7 to the free dollar, it may be wondered what impelled the Bolivian foreign office officials to insist that the Bolivian Central Bank pay one real dollar for one sham dollar.

The YPFB representative then said that it would be a serious matter indeed for his company if it could not get real dollars in exchange for the trade dollars in which it was forced to sell its exports, especially if the trade dollars proved to be worth only 60 cents on the free market. To this, I replied that it was a serious matter for the entire nation for YPFB to accept phony dollars for real dollars. I added that I had conversed with Brazilian Embassy officials and they had spoken of Bolivia as though it were a colony, or as Japan in the past might have spoken of Manchuria (see p. 68 n). In my opinion, the treaties with Argentine and Brazil were legally nonexistent and should be denounced, as they had been executed after August 4, 1956, without consultation with the Stabilization Council. Argentina and Brazil should therefore take their place in line as creditors, along with the bondholders and the Eximbank. I stated that I had fought 100 per cent for Bolivia's interests and had already sacrificed any friendships I might have had in Brazil or Argentina and could only hope that the Brazilians and Argentines would in time realize that I owed my present loyalties to Bolivia — that I would fight as loyally for Argentine or Brazilian interests if I were employed as their counsellor. Meanwhile, it was certainly up to the Bolivian officials and representatives to battle as strenuously for Bolivia's rights and interests as I had done.

Following this spate of eloquence, the council resolved unanimously to advise the Ministry of Foreign Affairs that the Stabilization Council believed that the Argentine treaty did not bar it from establishing a free market in Argentine-Bolivian trade agreement dollars, and that it would like to have the Ministry's views with respect to the provisions of other similar treaties.[45]

At the following council meeting, the Central Bank was authorized to suspend the advances that it had been making against exports under treaty arrangements, thus putting an end to any official encouragement of the sale of merchandise for treaty dollars. It will be recalled that, up until that time, the Central Bank had been advancing 60 per cent of the value of mineral export invoices under treaty dollar arrangements, and 50 per cent for agricultural exports, leaving up in the air the question of whether or when the exporters could collect the balance or whether the amount of the advance would be regarded as payment in full.

Government Finance

Early in 1957 the President asked the council for its advice on a bill passed by Congress which, unless vetoed, would impose a royalty on petroleum production for the benefit of the Department of Santa Cruz.   The Planning Commission head commented that petroleum was a national not a departmental resource and should be developed for the benefit of the nation. The Minister of Economy added that if Santa Cruz were permitted to tax oil production then every department where petroleum or other minerals were produced would demand a similar royalty, and the national budget could not stand this diversion of revenues. With these arguments, the council returned the bill to the President, recommending a veto on the ground that it was contrary to the stabilization program and to the national interest. The new Minister of Mines, however, in whose field the matter lay and who should have taken the lead in opposing the bill, abstained from voting, stating that he would have to consult with Juan Lechín and with the author of the bill and try to convince them of the necessity of a veto.*

A newspaper editorial of the time commented that it was unfortunate that Congress, after having given the President power to legislate by decree on matters affecting stabilization, should attempt to interfere with that power by passing financial bills not approved by the Stabilization Council.[46] This measure was defeated, but political pressures within and without the *Co-Gobierno* cabinet put through a reduction in the tax on cigarettes without council authorization, and other tax reductions and earmarkings were enacted — all of them illegal in the light of the limitations imposed on the President's emergency powers contained in the enabling act of November 22, 1956.[47]

These deviations from the program largely accounted for the fact that internal revenue collections for the first forty days in 1957 were only Bs. 6 billion as against Bs. 16 billion budgeted. The tax expert of the U.S. Financial Mission estimated that total collections for 1957 would reach Bs. 130 billion to Bs. 140 billion instead of the Bs. 174 billion budgeted.

---

*The author of the bill was Senator Omar Chávez-Ortiz whose relationship to Vice-President Ñuflo Chávez-Ortiz gave the bill its political importance.

Counterpart funds

Counterpart funds generated by Bolivian government payments in bolivianos for U.S. aid commodities could endanger the program in two ways: A scarcity of funds would unbalance the budget, as we were counting on counterpart for nearly 40 per cent of total revenues; on the other hand, a plethora of funds would mean that the "printing press" machinery of the Central Bank had started rolling again to furnish Point IV with the bolivianos that had proved so important a factor in the inflationary processes of prior years.

It was the latter threat that first confronted the council in the shape of a letter from the acting director of the U.S. Operations Mission to Bolivia, requesting Bs. 22 billion for the operation of their various *Servicios* (Agriculture, Highways, Public Health, and Education). Funds carried over from 1956, according to the letter, would barely suffice to keep the services in operation through the middle of February.[48]

A program of this magnitude was clearly beyond Bolivia's capacity to absorb and pay for without inflation. We had budgeted total counterpart receipts at Bs. 105 billion. In other words, it was hoped to sell enough U.S. aid commodities to the public at realistic prices to net that amount of bolivianos which could then be used to meet miscellaneous government expenditures without inflation. But, to prevent inflation, we planned to "sterilize" part of the funds, and had only budgeted Bs. 15 billion to be turned over in counterpart to USOM, of which only Bs. 5 billion — not Bs. 22 billion — was for technical assistance, and the remainder for various other projects (see budget Table 6, p. 203). Although it would have been preferable to slash the budgets of the various government departments and enterprises, rather than the Point IV services, the only politically feasible solution was to hold down payments to Point IV within the limits actually received, month by month, from the sale of U.S. aid commodities, and to keep as close to the Bs. 5 billion total as possible.

ICA had in effect approved the Bs. 5 billion figure by agreeing to finance the stabilization fund with the budget (Table 6) in front of them, so it was up to ICA and their Bolivian Operations Mission to finance the *Servicios* in part in dollars from the dollar aid funds at their disposal. In the end, this was what USOM agreed to do, Bolivia and USOM paying for the *Servicios* on a fifty-fifty basis, *with the Bolivian share donated by the*

United States. As a matter of tact and tactics, however, it was necessary to postpone a decision until the return of the head of USOM from abroad, rather than debate the problem with the acting director.

The other problem, that of a shortage of counterpart funds, was not long in materializing. U.S. aid commodities proved to be some 15 per cent higher in price than similar commodities from Argentina and other countries, and while this had made no difference so long as the imports were sold at Bs. 190 to the dollar, or some other equally arbitrary rate, it was difficult to find a buyer willing to take overpriced goods at a realistic rate of exchange. Certain Bolivian Cabinet members were indignant that Bolivia was "forced" to take high-priced U.S. commodities, instead of the United States giving Bolivia the cash so that it could purchase the goods wherever it wished. One newspaper complained that U.S. aid wheat cost $118.85 a ton in Bolivia, whereas Argentine wheat could be purchased at the border at $69.15 a ton.[49] This ignored the fact that the U.S. turned the full proceeds of sale over to the Bolivian government and that there was no evidence that Argentina intended competing on a give-away basis.

U.S. law, we were told, would not permit selling the commodities at a loss, but there was a possibility that freight charges might be absorbed by USOM or that the sales could be confined largely to machinery shipments rather than grain or other commodities on which U.S. Commodity Credit Corporation prices were higher than world prices. One difficulty in the way of Bolivian machinery imports on a counterpart basis, however, was that the United States could not at that time extend credit or grant aid to COMIBOL, as that would be subsidizing an enterprise founded on the confiscation of private property.*

---

*There was something inherently comic, of course, in the United States' insisting on "selling" the U. S. aid commodities at "cost" in order not to reveal a loss in its domestic agricultural aid program, when it would immediately give away the money it received in payment and when, for the previous four years, it had been "selling" the goods for phony money worth only a fraction of the selling price. It was equally absurd for Bolivia to be haggling over the price of the commodities it was going to get for nothing. No less ridiculous was the U. S. refusal (up to 1961) to help COMIBOL on the ground that it represented the confiscation of private property — straining at a gnat yet swallowing a camel by giving U. S. aid to a revolutionary government dedicated to the principle of confiscation of private wealth and the substitution of government enterprise for

Nevertheless, the Bolivian authorities constantly overlooked opportunities for developing counterpart. For example, it was reported that the Minister of Economy had given the chauffeurs' union a Bs. 500 million credit for the purchase of parts and replacements. This merchandise could just as easily have been purchased through Point IV (although it would have cramped the style of the union leaders on the price arrangements), and the money would then have been available to Bolivia as counterpart. * The Finance Minister stated that he had no control over Ministry of Economy finances, so I recommended that all government financial transactions should be handled by the Finance Ministry — one budget, one unified system of control.

Although the shortage of counterpart funds to balance the budget was one of our major problems, and although there were constant negotiations between Point IV, the Ministry of Economy, the head of the Planning Commission, and other members of the Stabilization Council, with the best of good will on both sides in the endeavor to find a viable solution, the question continued to plague the Stabilization Council in the following years. [50]

One incidental problem that arose in connection with the counterpart funds was the attempt of the Minister of Economy, the head of the Planning Commission, and the president of the Central Bank to compel the flour manufacturers to turn over to the Ministry the difference between the price of wheat at the Bs. 190 rate and at the current realistic rate of exchange, covering all stocks of wheat or flour that they had acquired under the U.S. aid program and had on hand on December 15, 1956. The Association of Flour Millers addressed a petition to the council refusing payment on "legal and economic grounds," alleging that they had purchased the flour prior to that date, that the purchase and sale transaction had been legally completed and closed, and that their cost computations had been made on the prestabilization basis. To the credit of U.S. business, let it be

---

private enterprise. But that was the way it was, and we had to play the game according to the rules, on a cloth untrue, with a twisted cue and elliptical billiard balls.

*The principal cause of the shortage, however, was that the Ministry of Economy failed to demand payment of Bs. 40-Bs. 50 *billion* due from 24 politically powerful individuals for U. S. aid commodities (American Embassy, *Annual Report* [La Paz, 1957]; *Hanson's Latin American Letter*, No. 628, April 12, 1958).

said that the only U.S. firm that handled wheat shipments under the U.S. aid program in Bolivia, W. R. Grace & Co., refused to subscribe to the petition of the Association of Flour Millers.

The Planning Commission head argued that if the government, on December 15, had called upon the millers to turn the flour over to the Ministry of Economy at a price based on the Bs. 190 rate of exchange, the millers would have had no "legal or economic" cause of complaint, and they were compelled to admit that this was true. I then remarked that, if this were the case, it looked like a consignment rather than a sale, and suggested that the legal form of the transaction should be investigated carefully. If it proved to be a consignment for processing and sale, then the government should demand delivery of the flour on the basis of a wheat price computed at the Bs. 190 rate; if it proved to be a sale, then we should impose a tax of say 95 per cent on the unearned increment, as it was evident that the millers had sold or would be selling the flour at realistic post-stabilization prices, and retroactivity in taxes within reason was a universal practice. The council agreed that either the tax or the payment should be collected by summary procedure, subject to consultation with Point IV and with the council's legal adviser, Dr. Santiago Sologuren. From later reports, however, it seems doubtful that the millers ever were forced to turn over these funds (or windfall gains), inasmuch as the distribution of U.S. aid had largely been handled by persons of considerable political influence.

University finances

Three months after enactment of the stabilization measures, the Finance Minister reported to the council that Congress had passed two laws creating new taxes and earmarking others as a subsidy to various universities. The President wished to veto them but, for political reasons, preferred to pass the buck by having me draft a memorandum to the effect that a veto was essential from the viewpoint of monetary stabilization.

As is true in many countries of Latin America, the Bolivian universities prior to stabilization had been supported by special taxes that had been enacted over the course of years in the thought that if their finances were subject to annual appropriations by the legislature it would be impossible to maintain any decent measure of academic freedom or financial autonomy.

By "autonomy," the universities meant absolute freedom from all legislative, executive, or other controls over budgets, receipts, expenditures, or other aspects of university life — the freedom of a medieval free university whose precincts can only be entered by the chief of state with the permission of the rector.

Bolivia had seven universities for less than eight thousand students, and each university had between seven and thirteen schools or colleges — certainly an excessive number of institutions of supposedly higher learning for an impoverished country of three and a half million inhabitants. As is pointed out in the two U.N. studies, the quality of their faculties — almost exclusively on a part-time basis — suffered accordingly. Even as far back as 1910, when the standards of Bolivia's universities were far higher than in 1957, Bolivia's greatest poet and educator, Franz Tamayo, characterized them as places "where one teaches everything and learns nothing." [51]

With monetary depreciation, faculty salaries which had at one time been adequate to support a professor in reasonable affluence had dropped almost beyond belief, as has been true in every Latin American country afflicted by that scourge. In bolivianos, salaries had been raised a hundredfold, within my memory, to Bs. 60,000 a month — equal to eight dollars in real money! [52]

Prior to stabilization, the universities had been financed by a 20 per cent share in all municipal revenues, plus innumerable earmarked taxes, including various percentages of the import and export duties. With the new customs duties and taxes enacted as a part of the initial stabilization measure, this would have meant an increase in revenues, in some cases running as high as forty times the old rates. The December 15, 1956, decrees had therefore substituted a flat subsidy at the 1955 level, plus 30 per cent. [53] This was the same arrangement that had been made for scores of other subsidized entities, but the rectors of four universities appealed to the President for restoration of their previous privileges. This he refused, whereupon the rectors turned to Congress and obtained passage of three bills, one of which would have created a new school of mining engineering to be subsidized by the government Mining Bank (which did not even have enough income to pay its own salaries and social charges), while the other bills would have established over thirty new earmarked taxes and placed a 5 per cent surcharge on some 260 customs classifications to be allocated for the benefit of one or another of the various institutions.

My memorandum on the subject was in the form of a letter addressed to the Minister of Finance in reply to "the consultation made on behalf of the President of the Republic." It was couched in the most diplomatic language I could summon to the occasion in order to avoid wounding the tender sensibilities of the rectors and legislators but, to avoid any possibility of misunderstanding, it opened with an unequivocal recommendation of a veto, followed by: (1) a careful analysis of Bolivia's worse than precarious financial situation; (2) a statement of the havoc that the legislation in question would wreak upon the stabilization program; and (3) the recommendation that the President form a committee to meet with representatives of all Bolivia's universities to find an immediate solution to their financial problems, consonant with complete intellectual independence and the economic limitations of the nation. The immediacy of a solution was stressed in order to avoid any implication that the commission would seek only to postpone a decision.

Suaviter in modo, fortiter in re, the letter stated:

> In that study it must be recognized as a first, basic, and inflexible principle that no institution whatsoever should receive a subsidy at the expense of the consumers, taxpayers, and inhabitants of the country, whether as a direct subvention or in the form of earmarked taxes, without adequate control by the state over its revenues and expenditures. University autonomy must not be distorted into financial anarchy, and the state must not turn over the funds of its citizens to be used in the free discretion of the recipients, without restriction and without control.... The universities, in their financial straits, must be careful not to force the state to print bank notes to balance the budget, which would mean bringing the currency to uncontrolled depreciation, and the nation to bankruptcy. I recognize, of course, the necessity of maintaining the intellectual and cultural independence of the universities, their autonomy in all matters related to their academic freedom, but that autonomy must not reach to the point of allocating to them earmarked taxes and revenues without a rigorous examination by the state of their income and expenditures, which must be kept within the economic possibilities of the country.

As Bolivia simply could not afford to maintain seven universities, each attempting to give a full curriculum of arts and sciences, law, engineering, and medicine, I added — as a possibility and expressly disclaiming possession of the knowledge that would be required to reach a conclusion on the subject — that it might be preferable for Bolivia to have a single confederated national university, maintaining the present existing "historical and prestigious institutions of learning," but allocating to each some particular branch of instruction, without duplication.*

At the council meeting, the head of the Planning Commission and the Minister of Economy suggested that the latter aspect of the letter be omitted and that it be confined to the question of financial and economic limitations, as the problem of university autonomy was one of the hottest of the hot potatoes on the Bolivian gridiron. Student rioting, egged on by the professors, could mean the overturn of the government. The head

*There are now eight government-supported institutions of "higher education" in Bolivia, including the Bolivian Technological Institute, founded in 1962 and financed chiefly with a $325,000 "loan" made by the Inter-American Development Bank from the U.S. Social Progress Trust Fund. The institute has five schools — Petroleum, Geology, Metallurgy, Mines, and Petrochemistry — and it proposes to invest a further $185,000 in classrooms and eighteen laboratories. (Inter-American Development Bank, *Annual Report* [Washington, D.C., 1964], p. 111.) One may well wonder whether the institute is not destined to show the same results witnessed by University of Michigan President Harlan Hatcher in a far richer country, Venezuela, where he was shown a nuclear reactor built largely with U.S. aid: "Architecturally the building is stunning. But it stands idle because there is not in the whole country of Venezuela a single person who has the knowledge necessary to make proper use of this facility.... Yet somehow this building symbolized for the people of this underdeveloped country the 'leap forward' which they so much want." He spoke also of equipment for an astronomical observatory: "But the significant realization which overcame the visitors was that in all of Venezuela there was not a single astronomer, nor a physicist, nor a mathematician, prepared to use these instruments..." (*Revolutions of Aspiration* [Detroit, Mich.: Wayne State University Press, 1963], pp. 12-13).

The deplorable fact is not so much the waste of money but the waste of human resources — hundreds of earnest Bolivian students who are destined to see their aspirations frustrated, their hopes turned to bitterness, when they are treated by foreign investors as inferior engineers, inferior agronomists, inferior scholars, because of the inadequate training that they can expect to receive in inferior institutions with pretensions to "higher education."

of the Planning Commission reported that several of the university rectors had agreed with him in private conversation that the system of earmarked taxes and revenues had to go, but they confessed that they did not dare to face the faculty councils or the students' federations with any such proposal.

President Siles, however, contended that the letter should cover both aspects of the problems. He did not have the figures available, but there was no doubt whatsoever that the government was spending more money on the universities than on elementary and secondary education combined, and "the base of the pyramid should be greater than its apex."[54] The council members thereupon unanimously resolved that: (1) The Comptroller General should assemble all necessary budget data, (2) the Finance Minister should confer at once with the rectors for an immediate definition of current subsidies, and (3) the President would appoint a committee to study the whole problem.

With this demonstration of courage in facing the facts, the problem was brought into proper perspective, the bills were allowed to die (apparently without a veto), and university revenues were kept within reasonable bounds, not only in 1957 but for the two following years. (An increase in 1957 revenues over 1956 was recognized as essential in view of the drop in the boliviano.) Their revenues continued to be tied to earmarked taxes, which was a possibility suggested in my letter, in the interest of university autonomy, provided the system were kept within reasonable bounds. With post-stabilization recovery and additional improvident earmarkings, however, their income from taxes shot up inordinately in 1960 and later years, as is shown by Table 12.

Although my letter was enthusiastically approved by the President and council, it was decided not to risk student and faculty reactions by publishing it, provided that the Finance Minister could reach a viable solution with the rectors, which is what was done.

Resumption of Debt Service on Dollar Bonds

During the course of the November-December, 1956, negotiations for the financing of the stabilization fund, the head of the Planning Commission, Miguel Gisbert-Nogué, and I had conferred with officials of the Foreign Bondholders Protective Council, Inc., in New York, and reached an agreement for

TABLE 12

University Income from Taxes*
(In Millions of Bolivianos)

1956	309
1957	765
1958	1,126
1959	1,236
1960	4,445
1961	5,670
1962	6,462
1963 (est.)	6,564

*From Central Bank, 34th *Annual Report*, 1962, p. 135. The 1963 estimate is based on two months' figures from Central Bank, 162d *Statistical Supplement*, March, 1963 (Banco Central de Bolivia, *Suplemento Estadístico Mensual* [La Paz: Central Bank, 1963].

resumption of debt service, on a greatly reduced scale of interest, commencing September 1, 1957. [55]

Final arrangements for an announcement by the Bondholders Council and execution of a formal agreement by the Bolivian Ambassador in Washington were completed by the end of January and should have gotten under way immediately, inasmuch as an agreement on resumption of interest on the funded debt was a part of Bolivia's commitment to the lending agencies. On February 11, however, the Stabilization Council was informed of a cable to the Foreign Minister from the Bolivian Ambassador in Washington to the effect that Vice-President Ñuflo Chávez had been negotiating with a New York brokerage firm and intended to propose another form of settlement which, the Ambassador feared, would seriously injure Bolivia's credit in view of the agreement already reached with the Bondholders Council. It was agreed that nothing could be done until receipt of the Ambassador's letter with a fuller explanation of the Vice-President's proposal.

A month later, the Stabilization Council was still without word of the nature of the Vice-President's intervention, but on March 11, to the dismay of most of the members, the President advised that Vice-President Ñuflo Chávez had proposed an arrangement whereby Bolivia, by not resuming payment immediately on its debt, could purchase a number of the bonds at a substantial discount and thus save money over the long run. The President expressed the opinion that this proposition would not necessarily conflict with the arrangements made by Gisbert. I disagreed with this view and stated that it was repugnant to all concepts of fair dealing for a nation to default upon its bonds and then take advantage of the low prices for those bonds, resulting from the default, to buy up the bonds at depreciated prices. If Bolivia did this, after its authorized agent, Gisbert, had already made a fair arrangement with the Bondholders Protective Council, it would ruin whatever remained of Bolivia's credit in the world, preclude any possibility of help from the World Bank, and wreck the stabilization program. The President stated that he intended to speak with Dr. Ñuflo Chávez to get more complete details as to his proposed plans and would meanwhile postpone comment.

Not long after, the President gave an audience to the labor leaders of the nationalized mines and told them that, within another month, the government would resume payment on its foreign debt "in order to win international confidence and thus be able to get a loan for hydroelectric, irrigation, transportation, and other projects."*

Meanwhile, I had managed to piece together the facts from the Ambassador's communications, from conversations with the Finance Minister, Gisbert, and the President, and from my own investigations. Thus, on April 17, 1957, when the President asked me to make a full report to him and the high command of the government and MNR respecting the progress of the stabilization program and its problems, I was able to give the following account of the matter.

"This brings me to a matter of the utmost gravity," I stated, and went on to relate that Gisbert had reached an agreement with the Bondholders Council — the most favorable ever arrived at — and had then spoken with the top officials of the World Bank who had promised to send a mission to Bolivia to

*This was the only reason that ever motivated the Revolutionary Government to pay interest on its bonds — the hope of borrowing more money. In fact, when interest payments were finally resumed, it was all I could do to deter the government from including a recital in the decree: "Whereas, by agreeing to pay less than $200,000 interest on the bonds in 1957, the government can expect to borrow one hundred times that amount from the World Bank, etc., etc." The argument was that the recitals (considerandos) were only for internal consumption in Bolivia. Abetted by Gisbert and other knowledgeable members of the council, I was finally able to convince our more politically minded colleagues that such a recital would be fatal to Bolivia's credit (President's talk reported in La Nación, March 22, 1957).

study projects that might be financed by that institution. At that juncture, the Vice-President had cabled to suspend the agreement despite the suggestion of the Bolivian Ambassador that this would jeopardize Bolivia's credit. It turned out that the Vice-President had had discussions with a broker or dealer in New York and proposed the purchase of $7 million par value of Bolivian bonds for $2 million, i.e., at approximately 30 per cent of par. I went on to state that the bonds could be purchased freely in the New York market at 18 per cent of par and that $7 million of bonds could easily be obtained somewhere between that price and a maximum of 25 per cent of par, so that the operation would mean "an enormous profit for those who took part in the deal, to the prejudice of the interests of the state."* I added that the bonds had risen from 13 per cent of par to 18 per cent in the past four months, so that it might be interesting to verify whether the price had been pushed up as a result of purchases already made by the dealer with whom the Vice-President had spoken. Furthermore, as a consequence of the Vice-President's action, any possible assistance to Bolivia from the World Bank would be delayed, perhaps for many months. (See Appendix VI.)†

Vice-President Chávez forced to resign

While I had been careful not to insinuate that the Vice-President's intromission had been motivated by the hope of personal gain — whatever profit there might be in the deal might very well have been a legitimate profit for the account of the bond dealer — the Bolivians were not so charitable. My sole

*Much later, I was able to confirm this statement in conversation with the leading New York dealer in defaulted securities, Carl Marks of Carl Marks & Co., Inc. (August 22, 1957). That quantity of bonds could have been purchased at the time at an average price of 20-22, meaning a profit of $460,000 to $600,000 for the intermediary.

†The interest of the International Bank for Reconstruction and Development in assisting Bolivia was confirmed in a report by the head of the Planning Commission to the Stabilization Council to the effect that Federico Consolo and Sune Carlson, during their attendance at the ECLA conferences in La Paz as representatives of the bank, stated that they would like to have full information on the following projects, although the bank could take no official action until Bolivia had resumed payment on its foreign debt: (1) rehabilitation of the government railways, (2) the Corani electric power project, (3) rehabilitation of the Colquiri mine, (4) the Carabuco electric power project.

interest was to get on with the stabilization program, to restore Bolivia's shattered credit standing, and thus to aid in eventual economic recovery. For that purpose, it was essential to prevent the Vice-President from interfering in negotiations that the President had entrusted to the head of the Planning Commission, the Ambassador, and the Minister of Foreign Affairs, who was then in Washington attempting to repair the damage that had been done by Ñuflo Chávez.

My oral report to the President, Cabinet, and inner circle of government was made at the express request of the President in order to bring the governing group up to date on the progress and problems of the stabilization program, and to get them to throw their full weight behind the reforms that were still needed to ensure the success of that program. The written version of the three-hour talk that was given out to the press, and published *in extenso* by the newspapers over six successive days, contained no mention of this incident, nor of another equally delicate and compromising interference with the stabilization program (see below at p. 441-43).

On June 22, 1957, however, just three days prior to my scheduled departure from La Paz, a communistic (PIR) newspaper published almost verbatim that part of my complete talk which had been delivered solely to the President (and to the American Ambassador), and which contained the reference to the intervention of the Vice-President in the matter of the Bolivian bonds.[56] Other papers picked up the story two days later amid much speculation as to who had let the cat out of the bag.[57] The Vice-President immediately placed the blame on President Siles, who replied indignantly that he did not play dirty ball, that he had corrected the Eder report with his own hand, and had cut out precisely that part which referred to the Vice-President. (This was true, but I had already marked with a cross the reference by name to the Vice-President, although leaving intact the matter of the delay in resuming debt service.) Later, the first issue of a paper published by Ñuflo Chávez' National Confederation of Peasants, to defend the interests of their leader, charged that Marcial Tamayo, the Secretary General of the Presidency and a loyal supporter of Dr. Siles, had leaked the item to the press.[58] My own guess, after having talked with Tamayo and the President, is that one of the eight Cabinet members or one of the three members of the National Political Committee of the MNR, present when I made my report, borrowed the draft from Tamayo and released it to

Orientación in order to discredit the Vice-President, who was one of the two bitterest opponents of the President and of the stabilization program. It seems unlikely that Tamayo himself would have leaked the story to an opposition PIR organ.

Be that as it may, the Vice-President told his intimates that he would shoot Mr. Eder on sight and immediately denied the truth of my statement, although admitting that he had cabled to Bolivia to suspend the arrangements made with the Foreign Bondholders Protective Council, Inc. He stated that the only private deal he had learned of in New York was one with Karl Marx (*sic*), an "unscrupulous" dealer who owned 50 per cent of the outstanding Bolivian bonds, "and that proposition was made through Mr. George Eder!"[59]*

Simultaneously, the Vice-President presented his "irrevocable" resignation to the Senate accompanied by a letter to Juan Lechín-Oquendo, as acting president of that body. In that letter, Nuflo Chávez charged that "imperialism has moved out of the shadows to achieve its objectives in Bolivia through its agent, Eder," a "Colombian-born adventurer, naturalized in the United States."[60]†

---

*It is interesting that the Vice-President should have known of the late Carl Marks who, although practically the sole dealer in Russian, Bolivian, and similar defaulted securities, was relatively unknown outside of Wall Street, where his reputation was of the highest. Although I had, of course, known him by name and reputation since 1933-37, when I was Manager of the Foreign Securities Division of Standard Statistics Company (now Standard & Poor's), I met him for the first time on August 22, 1957. I was then informed that Carl Marks & Co., Inc., held for their own account some $5 million of the $56 million of Bolivian bonds outstanding, perhaps purchased at prices of from 5 on up to 19, and that they controlled options, at that particular time, on over $19 million and had located the whereabouts of some $5 million-$6 million more. The remaining $26 million, Marks believed, were widely held, mostly in lots of one to ten bonds, and largely in the hands of the original purchasers — individuals and banks scattered throughout the United States who had bought the bonds at prices of $97\frac{1}{2}$ to 101 in reliance on the good faith of the Bolivian government. Contrary to the French maxim, *Qui s'excuse s'accuse*, Bolivians are inclined to believe that a failure to deny is equivalent to a confession, so I specifically deny having had any dealings with Carl Marks & Co., Inc., or having received any proposition made by that or any other dealer or broker.

†This was the first time I had learned of having been born in Colombia, which must have been difficult to arrange, as my mother was living in New York City at the time. I cheerfully admit that my grandfather sailed from California to Colombia in 1861, and there established a sugar planta-

There followed, as was to be expected, a series of scurrilous attacks on Ñuflo Chávez and equally impassioned defenses, as the Vice-President battled for his political existence in what turned out to be a *cause célèbre*. A special session of Congress was called to accept or reject the resignation. Juan Lechín and Minister of Mines Torres lined up on the side of Chávez and brought the mine union leaders and COB into the fray, while, on the other hand, the majority of the MNR party stalwarts backed the President, for it was clear that it was not and never had been a personal squabble between Ñuflo Chávez and Eder (who by that time was no longer in Bolivia) but a fight to the death between President Siles, in support of the stabilization program, and Lechín and Chávez, in support of the "good old days."

As it became increasingly clear that Siles would command a majority in Congress, Chávez withdrew his "irrevocable" resignation, and Lechín and Chávez cabled to Paz-Estenssoro, then enjoying an ambassadorship at the Court of St. James's, for him to throw his weight into the balance. This he did, with a telegram to Chávez and to the press requesting that Chávez withdraw his resignation. To this, Siles replied with a telegram to Paz, likewise given out to the press, demanding to know whether the Paz telegram meant that Paz was supporting the "stupid" manifesto of Chávez attacking the stabilization program. Paz-Estenssoro replied, also publicly, that his purpose was to unify the party in furtherance of the Revolution and that he would express his views with respect to stabilization on his return to Bolivia. Meanwhile, the Senate had taken the matter into its own hands and elected Federico Álvarez-Plata to replace Lechín as president of the Senate. Finally, on August 3, 1957, the Senate formally rejected Ñuflo Chavez' attempt to

---

tion and mill which recently celebrated its centennial anniversary. Many of the Eder descendants can take pride in being native-born citizens of that republic, as I am pleased to be a native-born American citizen of American ancestry.

This incident illustrates a phenomenon that is frequently observed in Latin America, although by no means universal — an unwillingness to accept as an expert anyone from another underdeveloped country, anyone whose accent fails to mark him as a foreign expert, even including, in one instance, resentment at the appointment of a distinguished Puerto Rican because he was not sufficiently non-Latin. Dr. Siles reported some months earlier that Ñuflo Chávez had angrily challenged my qualifications as an "expert" on the ground that I was not a *norteamericano* but a *colombiano!*

withdraw the resignation, and it became a *fait accompli.* Thus ended an episode in which I had played a reluctant part through a report made in good faith and which President Siles and I had in good faith attempted to maintain in confidence.[61]

Bond payments postponed, resumed, and again defaulted

As a consequence of the Vice-President's untimely intervention, it was not until June, 1957, that the decree providing for resumption of interest payments on the bonded debt was finally announced simultaneously in Bolivia and the United States, winning encomiums from most of the press and the definitive accolade from the COB which voted it "another example of submitting to Yankee imperialism."[62] The delay, however, did not signify a default in the arrangements that Gisbert had made with the Foreign Bondholders Protective Council, Inc., inasmuch as the first interest payment would not be due until July 1, 1957.

The July, September, October, and November coupon dates all passed, however, and there was still no move to resume payment. On December 17, the *New York Times,* always friendly to the Revolutionary Government, headlined regretfully that "A Vow Remains Unfulfilled" and reported that not only the bonds, but the settlement as well, were in default.

Finally, on June 17, 1958, Ambassador Victor Andrade for Bolivia and Kenneth M. Spang for the Bondholders executed the agreement in the offices of the Empire Trust Company in New York that meant that the holder of a $1,000 bond, with anywhere from $1,680 to $2,195.40 interest overdue and in default, could have his bond stamped $1,100 and later exchanged for new bonds of that denomination. The extra $100 would be in lieu of all defaulted interest, and the bondholder could thereafter hope to receive $5.50 per coupon, rising eventually to $11 a coupon, in lieu of the $30 to $40 per coupon promised on the bond.[63]*

---

*The 6 per cent bonds had been in default after the April 1, 1931, coupon, while the 8 per cent bonds had paid $4.60 (in lieu of $40) on the November 1, 1931, coupon, the last payment made. The two 7 per cent series were in default from January 1 and March 1, 1931 (Albert W. Kimber, *Foreign Dollar Bonds* [New York: White Weld & Co., 1951]; Announcement, Chase Manhattan Bank, June 17, 1958).

The $5.50-$11.00 interest may not have been such a bad return to those who had bought their bonds at prices of from $50 to $190 per $1,000 bond, but the promise written on the face of the bonds was an unqualified

Such hopes were soon shattered, however, for the July 1, 1934, coupons payable July 1, 1960, were late in payment, and the September, 1934, October, 1934, and November, 1935, coupons, payable in those months in 1960, were defaulted before the year was up, and not paid until 1962. Later payments and delays are noted in Chapter 22.

The Debt for Confiscation of the Mines

One of the essential moves toward economic recovery, as set forth in the Fifty-Step Plan for monetary stabilization (Step 23, Appendix III), was a negotiated agreement with Patiño, Aramayo, and Hochschild to compensate for the seizure of their properties. Washington had made this a *sine qua non* for a stabilization loan, at least with respect to the Patiño properties, which were the only ones in which there was an American interest and hence the only ones on which the State Department could properly lodge a claim.*

A bipartisan committee had been set up in April, 1954, to adjudicate the value of the properties, but the government representatives refused to negotiate in any true sense of the word, and in December, 1956, President Siles appointed another committee to carry out Bolivia's commitment under the stabilization program. This committee, exceptionally well qualified, was headed by Raúl Gutiérrez-Granier (president of COMIBOL), Mario Vernaza (a director of COMIBOL), and José Baldivieso (an attorney). Representing Patiño was an equally strong delegation, headed by Alberto Mariaca-Pando. The committee held two preliminary meetings, the second in March, 1957, and agreed to a *modus operandi*, with a third meeting scheduled for April 2, 1957, at which time they hoped to get down to facts and figures. [64]

---

one to all holders. Bolivia had received cash on the barrelhead from the banks and investors throughout the United States who had purchased the bonds in good faith when they were originally issued — the holders of perhaps $26 million of bonds, according to Carl Marks (p. 439n).

*National Lead Company had acquired a minority interest in the Patiño enterprises as early as 1922, and in 1924 Patiño Mines & Enterprises Consolidated was incorporated in Delaware with an authorized capital of $50 million (issued $30 million), of which about 4 per cent was taken by National Lead. In December, 1926, a block of 200,000 shares of $20 par value was sold to the public on the New York market (Cf. Margaret A. Marsh, *The Bankers in Bolivia* [New York: Vanguard Press, 1928], pp. 46-47).

In March, 1957, Gutiérrez reported in confidence that he was sure he could reach a negotiated agreement with the Patiño group for as little as $6 million, perhaps even less, provided he were in a position to offer a cash payment in dollars. In that event, he believed a settlement could be made with all three companies for not over $8 million. I had previously sounded out several bankers in New York with just such a possibility in mind and had been informed that, while it would be difficult to raise the money in the United States, it should be possible for Bolivia to borrow the necessary amount in England or on the Continent against a lien on the buffer stock of tin, provided that: (1) Bolivia carried out its agreement with the bondholders, (2) it demonstrated its ability to maintain a stable currency, and (3) it showed that the government and not the COB or the labor leaders was in control. This was communicated to President Siles in private, and, at his suggestion, to the council, with the recommendation that it was in Bolivia's interest to reach a definitive settlement as soon as possible rather than to go on paying $3 million a year to the Big Three (according to the 1957 foreign exchange budget) and yet not determining, or even necessarily diminishing, the amount of the debt.*

Matters were thus proceeding hopefully when Mario Torres, the Minister of Mines and Lechín's alter ego, came out with a terrific blast to the effect that negotiations must be in conformity with the nationalization decree that had been signed by President Paz-Estenssoro and Juan Lechín on October 31, 1952.[65] This meant that any settlement must be based on the figures shown in the companies' books as of December 31, 1951, plus or minus the movement in the accounts to the date of nationalization, less any amount due to the state, and less severance pay owed to the workers by reason of the companies' going out of business.

Considering that the boliviano had been worth Bs. 101 to

---

*This was reported to the Cabinet and MNR leaders orally at the April 17, 1957, meeting, together with a comment on the gravity of the situation in the light of the position taken by the State Department that a negotiated settlement with Patiño was a *sine qua non* of U.S. government assistance in the stabilization financing. To prevent any possible leak, however, that might strengthen the hand of the negotiators for the former mine owners had they been aware of Washington's attitude, I obliterated this section of my report from the written draft later submitted to the President, replacing the excision with asterisks which were clear to all who had been present at the meeting.

the dollar on December 31, 1951, and around Bs. 7,500 to the dollar when Minister Torres made his statement, any such settlement would be manifestly confiscatory ($40,000 for the entire Big Three properties, at current exchange rates). To require the companies to give severance pay, when the workers would have the same jobs with COMIBOL that they had had with the private companies that were forced out of business by the government, would be adding insult to injury.*

The decree had provided expressly for expropriation, which constitutionally implies prompt, adequate, and effective compensation, but the Revolutionary Government was callous enough to explain publicly that the mines were being expropriated rather than confiscated, as otherwise the government would be labeled as communist and could receive no aid from the United States.

The only authoritative appraisal of the value of the Big Three enterprises that had ever been made was that conducted in 1926 by the Permanent Fiscal Commission for Bolivia, which placed the value at over $135 million (Bs. 370,808,000).† This would not have been far from the valuation of Bs. 304 million, plus $16.8 million in foreign exchange assets, placed on the properties by the Revolutionary Government in the expropriation decree, had it not been for the 97 per cent depreciation of the boliviano between 1926 and 1952. What the true value of the properties was on the eve of seizure, which would be the proper

---

*This idea that a change in the corporate organization warrants payment of the legal separations pay is not peculiar to Bolivia. Ten years earlier, when I drew up the contract for the sale to the Argentine government of the ITT interest in the United River Plate Telephone Company, I incorporated in the contract a clause that the government would be liable for severance pay, if any. My colleagues chaffed me for being overcautious, as it was ridiculous to suppose that the employees would be entitled to a separations allowance merely because of a change in the form and ownership of the enterprise. As it turned out, that clause was all that saved ITT from heavy charges, even though the operation ultimately took the form merely of a sale of stock. The government later formed a new operating company and, of course, refused to entertain any claims for severance pay.

† Margaret Marsh's book, *The Bankers in Bolivia* (one of a series of "Studies in American Imperialism," which certainly cannot be charged with a capitalistic bias), states that "the Permanent Fiscal Commissioners in La Paz, representing the New York bankers, are in general welcomed and accepted as a beneficial force in the financial administration of the country." Thus, their valuation would seem to carry the weight of impartiality.

basis for expropriation, could only be determined by qualified and impartial appraisal engineers on the basis of ore reserves and physical assets, disregarding such politically engendered factors as the threat of confiscation and the depreciation of the currency.

In any event, an *ad referendum* agreement signed in Santiago, Chile, on April 2, 1953, between representatives of the Patiño group and COMIBOL, ratified in La Paz on June 10, 1953, and approved by the government on October 20, 1953, provided for the retention of certain agreed percentages (see p. 51) on the gross value of tin concentrates, shipped to the British smelters, Williams, Harvey & Co., Ltd., and for the retention of $10 per short ton of wolfram shipped to the General Services Administration, in the United States. The agreement provided that these "retentions shall be computed as payments on account, on the value of the nationalized properties, as well as interest on that value, the amount of which will be determined in the final arrangement." The retentions were to be free of Bolivian taxes and free "from any charge or obligation whatsoever arising in Bolivia."[66]

This last provision would seem to bar Minister Torres' claim for the deduction of severance pay to the workers or for amounts alleged to be due to the state, but the main problem was to determine what part of the annual retentions should be computed as interest, and what part as the amortization of principal. This could only be decided by a definitive agreement on the value of the properties. Manifestly, if the properties were worth even a quarter of the $135 million appraisal, then most of the $3 million budgeted for retentions would have to be considered as interest, and only a small part viewed as a payment on principal. To the contrary, if the original unilateral government valuation of around $10 million were taken as a base, the government would have more than repaid the debt and interest in full, certainly by the end of 1962.

Minister of Mines Torres, as has been stated, brought the government valuation down to $40,000. It was not until August, 1961, however, that confiscation of the private mines received what amounted in effect to a blessing by the government of the United States, when it was provided, as a condition for a "triangular" $37,750,000 million loan plan to COMIBOL, that COMIBOL must suspend all further retentions in favor of Patiño, Aramayo, and Hochschild, until the total amount of the indemnity had been defined.[67] This is set forth at greater length in Chapter 22.

19

POLITICAL PROBLEMS

Concessions to Reality

The whole monolithic structure of the stabilization program which we had erected depended for its strength upon the concrete cohesiveness of its constituent parts. It was planned that this would be assured by having the President of the Republic attend all meetings of the Monetary Stabilization Council as its president, so that the full weight of his prestige and power would be behind the council action. The strength or weakness of the program thus depended upon the strength or weakness of the Chief Executive. It was not long before the cracks appeared in the concrete.

Immediately following the hunger strike, when the President was for the first and last time strong enough to have crushed his enemies, he deferred to his foes in the *Co-Gobierno,* and agreed to a series of "concessions to reality," yielding in one place after another to political pressures that, with each succeeding victory, grew steadily stronger. As a consequence, the monetary structure became progressively weaker, and was shored up only by drawing on the stabilization fund. This fund, it will be remembered, was intended to be used as a safeguard against temporary exchange movements — not to counteract fundamental distortions in the economy. It could not be exhausted by the actions of the private sector, which did not have enough bolivianos to make more than a dent in the fund. It could only be exhausted by government profligacy and printing more bank notes.

Official price reductions

The first concession was in the matter of prices to be charged by the government petroleum company for gasoline and kerosene. The chauffeurs' union (which embraced truck and bus drivers and was one of the most powerful in the COB) had supported President Siles during the December, 1956, hunger strike crisis, so the President rewarded it by immediately giving in to the union demands for a Bs. 50 per liter cut in gasoline prices, despite the fact that the YPFB management complained that this would mean selling below cost, and a loss of Bs. 300 million to the company. At the same time, yielding to popular pressure — for the working classes had become accustomed to using kerosene instead of cheaper fuels — the President insisted on cutting kerosene prices Bs. 150 a liter, meaning a further loss of Bs. 3.8 billion to the petroleum company.

As a consequence, the YPFB budget, which we had balanced with such difficulty as part of Bolivia's obligations under the stabilization fund agreement, was thrown into complete disequilibrium within a fortnight after stabilization. The YPFB was forced to borrow Bs. 3,520 million from the Central Bank and was unable to repay its Bs. 500 million debt to the Ministry of Economy. The U.S. banking adviser, Ernest Moore, read to the council two memoranda I had left with him during a fortnight's absence in Argentina, in anticipation of just such an eventuality, urging that no action be taken that would unpeg the YPFB budget. To this, the Minister of Mines replied that the President had taken these measures because of the "political situation," while the Finance Minister courageously asked that it be made a matter of record that the action had been taken without consultation with the council.[68]

Wage increases

The next concession to reality, as was to be expected, was in the matter of wages. Early in January, a communiqué was issued by the Director General of Labor to the effect that the Bs. 450 daily wage increase for loss of low-price commissary privileges must be given to all employees of industry and commerce, and not merely to those who had formerly had such privileges.[69] This was done, not only without consultation with the Stabilization Council, but in direct defiance of the unanimous vote of the council, including the President, as well as of the specific instructions given to the Minister of Labor. The communiqué also announced that the year-end bonus must be based on payrolls for the last quarter (which would include fifteen days at the greatly increased post-stabilization wage), instead of on the full year's payrolls as the law required, and that 1956 social security payments by employers must be reckoned on the basis of the December wages.

The next day, the Bs. 450 increase was made expressly applicable to the milling and baking industries, despite editorial comments that these increases were in violation of law, and despite the objections of the director of the U.S. Operations Mission, who made his opposition the more pointed by stating, in a letter to the president of the Central Bank, that he was authorizing a $500,000 payment to the Stabilization Fund but would expect some assurance from the government of Bolivia that it intended to take steps to re-establish the basis requisite for such continued support.[70]

But all in vain. The wage increase was a *fait accompli* and the President would not repudiate the action of the Minister or Director General of Labor. And so it was throughout the next six months, with the Stabilization Council (or at least the original members and the technical advisers) attempting desperately to hold the line, at one meeting after another. In fact, the President was indignant that Ross Moore, the USOM director, should threaten to hold up a $500,000 payment unless COMIBOL paid its taxes and repaid its loan from the Central Bank, particularly when the government was supporting the USOM in refusing to give wage increases to the highway workers. The "support" did not materialize (see "April" below). His indignation was intensified by reason of the "formal promises" made by Moore, the American Ambassador, and General Lawton Collins to increase U.S. aid to Bolivia to help the country through its difficult situation. Investigation showed that there had been no promises, formal or otherwise, but merely a courteous affirmation of the deepest interest in Bolivia's plight and the assurance that the situation would be reported to the State Department and to President Eisenhower. It would have been impossible, however, to convince President Siles of that fact, which corroborates what has been previously said as to the necessity of emissaries from Washington learning to say "no" in an unmistakable fashion if they wish to avoid charges — that are heard repeatedly in Bolivia and elsewhere — of hypocrisy and broken promises (see pp. 158-62).

January through June, 1957

January. Throughout January, the complaints from USOM continued. The Finance Minister expressed the fear that government employees would demand the same Bs. 450 raise that was being given to everyone else, and this would cost the government Bs. 2,160 million a month. The Minister of Labor refused to allow excess workers to be dismissed — for example, in the case of the Mining Bank. A new Labor Minister was then appointed, who appeared before the council, but said he could not reverse the orders given by his predecessor. He did, however, accompany the Finance Minister in the latter's attempt to persuade the President to take action, but nothing was accomplished.[71]

February. In February, the Minister of Labor twice attempted to pass the buck to the council on a demand by the employees of the brewery (Cervecería Boliviana Nacional) first for free cases of beer, which they could, of course, sell, and second for a wage increase. The council, which certainly did not intend to rule on individual cases (of beer or wages) passed the buck back to the Minister on both occasions, with a note that all wages were frozen by law, and that it was up to the Minister to act accordingly. In the course of five council meetings, it was reported that wage pressures were becoming serious; that 60 to 65 per cent of the country's 170,000 wage earners (see p. 718, n *17*) were on the government payroll and the government had no funds for wage increases; that the director of USOM and a Treasury representative visiting La Paz had said there was no longer any basis for U.S. support of the stabilization fund; that the new Labor Minister had been instructed to reverse the orders of his predecessor but had failed to do so and was now on the point of letting the meat packers and gas station attendants merge with the railway workers' union, so that they could get the Bs. 1,350 increase allotted exclusively to railway workers.

My advice was that the government should declare illegal a threatened strike by the communications workers and that it would be better to repeal the stabilization decrees outright than to tolerate their piecemeal violation. The President replied that if the wage demands were not granted and strikes ensued the decrees would in any event be repealed *de facto;* that he could not hold the line beyond June 30; and that the railway workers' union was attempting to build up its strength by bringing in other trades, and even planned to bring in the cowboys along with the meat packers. The Finance Minister reported that he would need a Bs. 9 billion loan from the Central Bank to cover wage increases for school teachers and others whose wages had not previously been adjusted.

March. In March, the bank employees' union threatened to strike if they were not allowed a Bs. 1,750 daily wage increase, to be labeled a "leveling-off" or "equalization" *(nivelación)*, as *increases* were forbidden by the stabilization decrees. When this was denied by the council, they struck.[72] The head of the Planning Commission reported that the brewers had been given their beer, the textile workers so many yards of worsted, and the employees of moving picture houses were demanding one day a month for benefit performances for their union. He joined me in maintaining that these measures were all subterfuges amounting to wage increases; that anything which increased the cost of production was inflationary; and that the Administration should be firm in declaring that all strikes for increased wages or *nivelación* should be declared illegal and penalized by stopping wages.

April. In April, it was reported that the Ministers of Labor and of Public Works had supported the demand of the road repair gangs that they be reclassified as construction workers, which would automatically give them a 40 per cent wage increase. These laborers were paid by the Point IV Highways Service, so that this would unbalance the Point IV budget and break Bolivia's agreement with USOM. The head of the *Servicio* and the director of USOM emphatically opposed reclassification, but to no avail. I opposed allowing the municipality of Cochabamba to give its employees Bs. 450 additional compensation for commissary privileges which they had never had, and stated that, if that increase were allowed, the municipal workers of La Paz and other cities would demand the same (which proved to be the case). I recommended that the strikes declared by the Cochabamba municipal employees and the Development Corporation workers be declared illegal.

The Ministers of Mines and of Economy, on the other hand, held that the Cochabamba strike was justified, as the workers had been paid the Bs. 450 for one month on the basis of an *illegal* order of the Minister of Labor. Hence, if the city had the money, it had the legal power to pay the increase, and a decision was up to the Minister of Labor and not the Stabilization Council. To this, the Finance Minister retorted that all the municipalities were in a deficitary position and that the city of La Paz, which wanted to increase its wages, had a Bs. 13 billion deficit and was only able to pay 80 per cent of its current wages. The council members were reminded that there were three basic conditions contained in the stabilization loan agreement: (1) that the combined budget of the government and of all government agencies must be in balance, (2) that there must be a wage freeze for one year, and (3) that the exchange rate must be kept free and allowed to fluctuate — and the Bolivian government had failed to keep any of these obligations.

The three Ministers (of Mines, Economy, and Finance — the only voting members of the council present) nevertheless voted to authorize Cochabamba to pay the Bs. 450, if the city had the money, and then voted to grant the same increase to *all persons* having a family identification card *(libreta familiar)*. At that moment, the head of the Planning Commission entered the room and vigorously supported my opposition stand, saying that if everyone who had a card were given the raise, and not merely those who formerly had cheap commissary privileges as provided in the stabilization decree, it would mean that every wage earner in Bolivia would get the increase. The Minister of Economy calmly replied that this was quite evident.*

With the intervention of the Planning Commission head, the Finance Minister withdrew his previous vote, and it was finally agreed that he would report to President Siles that there was an impasse, with the Ministers of Mines and Economy lined up against the head of the Planning Commission and me.

May. In May, the Minister of Mines, who was also Secretary-General of Lechín's mine workers' federation, announced publicly that wages must be increased, that the employers' contribution for the housing tax must be raised from 2 per cent to 14 per cent, and that a tax of 1 cent U.S. a pound must be imposed on tin exports to cover maternity and sickness benefits. The Minister of Public Works declared, likewise publicly, that there must be a general wage rise in June and that the government was studying the matter. At this, the leading independent paper editorialized that such an increase would

---

*At this juncture, the Minister of Economy, Jorge Tamayo-Ramos, again spoke of the inherent conflict between his position on the Stabilization Council as an expert (a *técnico*), and his position in the Cabinet as a politician (a *político*), and said that he would never stoop to voting one way in the council and another way in the Cabinet. He had raised this same question at the first council meeting which I attended, and the Finance Minister and the chief of the Planning Commission had replied that the council members should without question vote for what they knew to be economically sound. But Tamayo, at the time Minister of Mines, had taken his oath as a labor minister in the Co-Government, and remained unconvinced. There could be no doubt of his sincerity — that he was doing his duty according to his lights. It was unfortunate, however, that a man of such ability and integrity should not have realized that his duty in both deliberative bodies was to do what he knew to be best for Bolivia, regardless of his political affiliations.

bring about the chaos, disorder, corruption, and poverty that
existed prior to stabilization, unless the government could obtain a substantial increase in foreign aid. The Finance Minister
announced that he, personally, had no knowledge of any wage
studies being made by the government, and the railway workers
declared a general strike to begin June 30.[73]

June. In June, the union of bank employees demanded that
retired employees be given the additional compensation of Bs.
1,750 (Bs. 450 plus Bs. 1,300, being an illegal increase that had
been given to the bank employees against the advice of the
council). Thereupon, the council passed a resolution against
this increase on the ground that the increases authorized in the
stabilization decrees were confined to wages, not pensions. The
Mining Bank was compelled to grant the wage increase demanded under the guise of "leveling-off," despite the fact that
the bank was insolvent; that the council expressly opposed the
raise; and that it was plainly illegal. Lechín demanded an increase in all wages but insisted that there must be no change in
the foreign exchange rate and stated that the wage increase
should be covered by a 12 per cent capital tax on all assets plus
higher import duties. He also demanded increased expenditures
for public works. At the end of the month, the President announced a plan: (1) to reduce the price of gasoline, fuel oil, and
diesel oil, which he stated would reduce transportation costs;
(2) to lower social security contributions; (3) to cut the price
charged to the public for U.S. food shipments; and (4) to increase the family subsidy; all of which, he stated, had been
carefully studied (certainly not by the council) and could be accomplished without affecting the stabilization plan.[74]

In sum, the record of the first six months of 1957, thus
summarized, would seem to indicate a losing battle for wage
and monetary stability, as, in every instance, the considered
recommendations of the technical advisers to the council were
overridden by the Co-Government Cabinet. Yet there can be
little doubt that, had it not been for our stubborn resistance,
abetted by the director of the U.S. Operations Mission and the
head of the Planning Commission, wage increases would have
got completely out of hand. All in all, then, measured by the
final results, the increases up to that time were held within
manageable dimensions, and the struggle must be adjudged successful. At least, our delaying action made it possible for
President Siles to score another victory over his enemies in
July (pp. 471-73).

Utility and railway rates

The council could not attempt to fix specific rates for each of the various railways and public utilities and, at its suggestion, the government appointed commissions to deal with the matter. The stabilization decree had laid down the general principle of a reasonable return on present fair value, with a provision for temporary rate increases until that value could be determined. No basis other than fair value was feasible, as the depreciation of the boliviano was such that the companies' books were meaningless, both on the asset side (capital investment) and the liability side (invested capital). At the same time, a good part of the equipment had been brought into the country at privileged, official rates of exchange, far below true values, so that it would be unfair to the public to equate "fair value" with replacement cost. Rate-fixing thus became largely a matter of stubborn negotiation between the private utility companies and the municipal authorities, with the appointed commissions and the Director General of Railways acting as intermediaries, or, in the case of the railways, between the companies and the Director General.

A number of cases came up before the council during the first quarter of 1957 for a specific ruling on one point or another — the electric power rates for La Paz, Oruro, Sucre, and Potosí, and the rates for the railways to Chile and Peru. Meanwhile, rates for the government railways had been fixed by the Director General of Railways at a level which, presumably and overoptimistically, should have sufficed for those lines to operate without a deficit. In general, in those cases which came before the council, provisional utility rate increases of 250 to 600 per cent were allowed, which would not appear to be excessive in the face of a fortyfold rise in the foreign exchange rate. But the municipalities were loathe to allow even these temporary increases and, so far as is known, there was never any recognition that permanent rates, substantially higher than the provisional rates, must be established to provide a fair return on capital and to attract the additional investment needed to expand and improve the existing rail and utility services.

Concurrently with the problem of rates, there arose the questions of government indebtedness to the railways, and the provision of foreign exchange for imported supplies ordered under prestabilization contracts. The rail officials, in particular, were taken aback at the tough stand adopted by the council on my recommendation in the matter of prestabilization contracts, in contrast to my liberal views in the matter of rates. In the matter of contracts, my stand, which was adopted by the council, may be summed up as providing: (1) that, even where there was a definite obligation to provide exchange at the official Bs. 190 rate, this would not be allowed, inasmuch as the imported supplies would be used to render services under the new railway and utility tariffs which were to be based on the current Bs. 7,500 rate; (2) that the three- or four-year precedent of exchange provided at the Bs. 190 rate for remittances abroad could not be taken as a binding obligation to provide exchange currently at that rate, even for past due obligations of the government itself; and (3) that any government indebtedness would be payable over a five-year period, and then only in the event that it was incontestably legal, or if the government had clearly received a commensurate service or benefit. In the latter event, recognition of the debt would be on a *quantum meruit* basis rather than on the basis of the alleged contract. In other words, neither side would be permitted "unjust enrichment," which is a Civil Law concept, but any alleged contractual obligation would be strictly construed, which is a basic principle of administrative law in Latin America as well as in the United States (cf. Chief Justice Marshall in *Providence Bank* v. *Billings*, 4 Pet. 514 [1830] and Chief Justice Taney in *Charles River Bridge* v. *Warren Bridge*, 11 Pet. 420 [1837]).

On the other hand, I was rather more disposed to recommend rate increases, believing that it was more important to establish a favorable climate for investment than to negotiate down to the last penny, and, further, that the demands of the companies were in fact more modest than they were led to believe. Above all, it was clearly not desirable, in Bolivia's situation, to stimulate an excessive demand for utility or transportation services based on below-cost rates. Political resistance, however, made even minimal rate increases difficult. In fact, the legislature passed a bill calling for substantial cuts in the freight rates and passenger fares charged by the government airline (LAB) to isolated regions of the country, to be compensated by a subsidy to the line from export royalties on products shipped from such regions. The council promptly recommended a veto of this measure, but, soon after, the Minister of Public Works decreed a radical cut in railway rates notwithstanding the President's warning that the railroads were operating at a loss.[75]

In the course of the rate discussions, many irregularities

were brought to light, as in the case of the Potosí light and power company, where the mayor opposed any rate increase whatsoever. He planned to seize the company's properties and turn them over to a cooperative, which would have solved nothing and merely brought a demand for earmarked taxes to meet the inevitable deficits. It developed that the mayor had previously permitted the company employees to remove the company's materials and supplies and store them in a municipal warehouse, whence they had promptly disappeared, probably looted by the same employees.[76]

Political changes in the council

The courageous stand taken by Minister of Mines Jorge Tamayo-Ramos at the COB congress in January, 1957, lost him the support of the miners' union, and he was replaced by Lechín's man, Mario Torres-Calleja. However, the President promptly reappointed Tamayo as Minister of Economy to replace Carlos Morales-Guillén, who was asked to resign for reasons that there is no point in examining.

In June, 1957, a second workers' congress demanded the scalp of Central Bank President Franklin Antezana-Paz, and he was replaced by Luis Peñaloza, an ex-Trotskyite and co-director of the MNR newspaper, En Marcha. This meant that, with Torres and Peñaloza, the council membership took on a political coloration from which it had fortunately been largely free up to that time.[77]

Government spending as a permanent policy

One "concession to reality" that was particularly disturbing was the President's attempt to conceal from me, lest it come to the attention of the lending agencies in Washington, a number of windfalls received by the Bolivian government — substantial new funds not anticipated in the government budgets. These funds — some $17.5 million in all (p. 417) — were expended without consultation with the National Monetary Stabilization Council on unbudgeted and improvised projects that would certainly not have passed muster had they been included in the government's application to the IMF and U.S. government for financial assistance.

In fact, it became clear that the government's sole solution for all Bolivia's troubles was to beg or borrow more and more money to be spent on more and more hastily improvised government projects, despite the clear evidence that it was precisely such profligacy that had brought Bolivia to its present plight. Any increase in government spending would only plunge the country further into debt, and into ill-conceived and worse-managed undertakings that each year would demand ever-increasing expenditures for their maintenance or survival.

Soon after the successful launching of the stabilization program, Bolivian Ambassador Víctor Andrade, in an address at Pennsylvania State University, declared that U.S. aid had sufficed to keep Bolivia alive, but not to make any real progress, and he suggested it was high time for the United States to re-examine its aid program and help Bolivia proceed with its development projects. The President followed this up with a public statement to the effect that he intended to ask for increased U.S. aid for the triple purpose of strengthening the boliviano, bringing prices and wages into equilibrium, and going ahead with the government program for economic diversification.[78]

In June, 1957, without consulting the Monetary Stabilization Council, the President announced to the COB, at their Second National Congress, that he was asking the U.S. government for $40 million to $60 million in aid, and he simultaneously presented the American Ambassador with a pitifully superficial memorandum outlining Bolivia's immediate needs — supervised credits of $10.5 million for COMIBOL, $5 million for the small and medium mines (to be disbursed through the notorious Mining Bank), $3 million for agriculture, and $1.5 million for industry, plus $10 million additional for roads and minor irrigation projects. With the current $20 million aid to cover budgetary deficits, this would add up to $50 million. At the same time, he approached the World Bank for financial assistance, but, as he had no specific projects to present and as Bolivia had not yet agreed to resume payment on its foreign bonded debt, nothing came of that approach.[79]

The hundred-million-dollar promise. In August, 1957, the President returned to the attack and presented the Assistant Secretary of State for Latin American Affairs with a request for an additional $80 million in foreign aid which, plus the $20 million currently in force, would add up to the $100 million that the Bolivian government was convinced had been "promised" them by the U.S. Embassy in La Paz (p. 160).

Twenty million dollars was wanted for budgetary support. This would have gone directly down the drain, as it was clearly nonproductive. Instead, the government might have reduced social security charges to a maximum of 10 per cent ($2\frac{1}{2}$ per cent to be paid by the employees), dismissed 20 per cent of their personnel, and increased the effectiveness of their tax laws and tax collections.

Twenty million dollars was alleged to be needed to capitalize a new National Institute of Supervised Credit. The figure was snatched out of the air by someone who had not the slightest concept of the meaning of bank credit or how to administer it. It is clear from the precedent of mismanagement at the Mining Bank and elsewhere that, even if such an institution had been needed, there was no one in Bolivia qualified to manage it.

Ten million dollars was allegedly needed to take care of "unemployment." According to USOM/Bolivia, there was no unemployment, but an actual shortage of workers in many areas, and a superabundance of persons maintained in idleness on both government and private payrolls. USOM/Bolivia had worked out a plan which would have taken care of 6,000 excess workers in the mines, government, and industry, at a cost of less than $500,000 *in bolivianos,* with no additional U.S. aid.

Fifty million dollars was demanded for "economic diversification," meaning resuming and expanding the Bolivian Development Corporation projects, which would have been fatal to any hope of eventual Bolivian economic recovery. And yet, in 1963, the United States succumbed to Bolivian threats of communism, and provided $83 million for its Ten-Year Plan, in addition to other aid (Chapter 24).

Moreover, Bolivia demanded greater freedom to use the remaining money in the stabilization fund, oblivious to the fact that the fund was to be used solely to tide over short-term fluctuations in supply and demand for foreign exchange. The use of the fund up to that time was proof positive that Bolivia had not been living up to its stabilization commitments. Up to August 21, 1957, $6,615,000 of the fund had been used, i.e., $9,153,000 drawn down, less $2,538,000 reserves. The government further wanted U.S. government assistance in procuring money from the International Bank for Reconstruction and Development, when the fact was that Bolivia had not presented a single project that could conceivably warrant bank financing. The Bolivian authorities — and this has been generally true in Latin American government financing — took the position that a mere statement that they wanted so many millions of dollars for a development project was all the proof needed to show that they ought to have it and would put it to good use, whereas actually the very vagueness of their "projects" was as clear proof as could be had that they were completely incapable of managing the project if the money were given them. To cap their demand, they wanted the U.S. government to persuade the IMF to take a more "flexible" attitude which would permit the Central Bank to give YPFB the bolivianos it needed to buy dollars for allegedly essential expenditures. Manifestly, if YPFB were short of bolivianos, it should not have reduced its prices for gasoline and kerosene below production costs, and Central Bank credit to the government and government agencies was precisely what had caused the printing-press-currency and monetary-debasement cycle of the preceding four years.

Political Crises

Thus far, in this discussion of the problems and crises of the first year under the stabilization program, the accent has been on the financial and economic aspects of the picture, but actually the most serious crises were political in origin and motivation. During the first six months of 1957, the papers were filled with violent speeches and policy declarations attacking the stabilization program or me personally, or at times the President himself. More hypocritically, when it became clear that the public overwhelmingly supported both the stabilization program and President Siles, the program in general would be praised, but changes were demanded that would have made stabilization an impossibility.

These attacks reached a crescendo of violence in January, 1957, at the national convention of the COB; in April, during the celebration of the fifth anniversary of the Revolution; and in June, at the time of the Second National Congress of the COB. On those occasions, the personal vituperation, hypocrisy, and mendacity of the orators reached extremes that would simply be beyond the comprehension of anyone unaccustomed to the Latin American scene.*

*Perhaps the viciousness of Latin American political action can best be illustrated by one of the few occasions on which it was brought home to the American public, namely, at the time of the unprovoked attack on Vice-President Nixon and his wife in Venezuela, which left them covered with saliva and dazed with shock. The attacks on me were, fortunately, purely oratorical or in print, never face to face, and never reaching the stage of personal violence, so that I was free to walk through the streets and

The January crisis

In anticipation of the forthcoming national workers' convention, the Party of the Revolutionary Left (PIR), communist but not Stalinist, and powerful in the ranks of the COB, led off the attack with a ten-point program which would raise wages, control prices, establish a "realistic" foreign exchange rate, and embark on a national development program.[80] Their manifesto ended with the solemn warning that the government of the United States had "assumed the material and moral responsibility for stabilization under the Eder Plan" and therefore carried the full weight of responsibility for Bolivia's economic development "before the nations of the hemisphere."*

Juan Lechín-Oquendo followed up at the convention with an attack on Eder, the "miracle man whose magic wand made the rich richer and the poor poorer ... an interventionist in wages but an advocate of a free economy in prices." (This sarcasm had the ring of plausibility but, of course, a free economy in wages would have meant complete freedom to dismiss excess workers, curtailment of the overwhelming power of the labor unions and labor militia, and lower wages for the miners. Moreover, the free economy in prices was not a one-way street — competition could, and did, drive prices down as well as up, and the net movement was downward.)

In the end, the COB convention, following speeches by Lechín, President Siles, Minister of Mines Tamayo (who immediately thereafter lost his status as a Labor member of the Cabinet), accepted the stabilization plan, but demanded five fundamental changes which would have completely vitiated the program and brought matters back to where they were in

---

marketplaces unaccompanied, and greeted everywhere by friends and strangers who were grateful for my having brought monetary stabilization to Bolivia — this despite the fact that two of Bolivia's leading *políticos* had sworn to shoot me on sight (p. 197n; p. 439).

*This attitude that an underdeveloped country can demand foreign aid as a right, and not ask it as a favor, is not confined to Latin America, e.g.: "Any American who expects to purchase Asian friendship with dollars is courting disillusionment. The average Asian who thinks of foreign aid at all is inclined to regard gifts from the West as a long-overdue return, in small measure, for the resources drained from Asia by Western countries in the colonial past. The Asian's invariable reaction is that he should have more." (Robert Trumbull, *The Scrutable East* [New York: David McKay, 1965], p. iii).

1953-56. Thereupon, Siles threatened to resign the presidency, Lechín capitulated and, together with the other leaders of the COB and MNR, signed a declaration reaffirming the "monolithic unity" of the MNR. This declaration was followed by a list of fifty questions, most of them captious, which could be boiled down to the single question: "Why cannot prices be lowered, wages raised, the boliviano stabilized at a more favorable rate, the rich taxed more and the poor less, and the Bolivian economy developed so that the miners, farmers, and industrial workers will all be more prosperous?"[81]

The daily press took no discernable stand, pro or con. The program was too new to warrant criticism. *Presencia*, the Christian Socialist weekly, supported me, as it did consistently, and hailed the stabilization program on grounds of morality as well as of economics. *El Pueblo*, the communist paper, also supported me, as it did sporadically, and stated that the Bolivian masses now know that "Mr. Eder's baby is a male and will live long and save the Bolivian economy." However, the Communist Party came out two days later for higher wages, price controls, and restoration of the subsidized commissaries.[82]

When the tumult and the shouting died, Lechín, on behalf of the COB convention, presented a memorandum to President Siles containing a nine-point critique of the stabilization program and suggestions for its improvement, all of them as improvised, counterproductive, and politically motivated as any of the measures that had led the country to its 1956 crisis. Nevertheless, the memorandum had been released to the press, and the President and the Stabilization Council asked me to draft a reply for the President's signature, conciliatory in tone, but emphatic in substance. This was done, and a draft was presented to the council which approved it almost without change. Weeks went by, however, during which the President wavered between attempting to support the stabilization program and, on the other hand, appeasing Lechín and keeping his *Co-Gobierno* Cabinet of COB and MNR pacified and intact.[83] In the end, nothing was done, thus paving the way for the second crisis of the stabilization program. This is not said in criticism. The President's choice had to be either to eliminate the opposition and assume control as a dictator, which he refused to do, or to strive for unity among the revolutionary factors. The latter choice made vacillation inevitable. The council members regretted the choice, but his was the sole responsibility.

A blunder. Early in the course of the January crisis, I committed what was doubtless the least excusable *gaffe* of my Bolivian career, thus adding to the burdens of President Siles and of the American Ambassador, although both those gentlemen were too understanding of the circumstances to hold me at fault.

Returning to La Paz from a fortnight's vacation in Argentina, I was stopped on the street by one of the ablest and most *simpático* of Bolivia's young reporters and asked to comment on the criticism of the stabilization program at the COB convention. Unthinkingly, I replied that the only persons injured by the stabilization measures were those political or labor leaders who had formerly profited from U.S. aid and foreign exchange quotas and permits, but that stabilization would benefit the nation at large, and all that was needed to set Bolivia on its feet again was hard work and greater productivity. I concluded: "If I could speak as eloquently as Juan Lechín, I am sure I could convince the workers of that fact."[84]

To this, Lechín quite rightly retorted: "If I spoke the way Eder does, I would long ago have ceased to be a labor leader!" I have previously commented on Lechín's intelligence, ability, and wit. It is only regrettable that his other qualities were not so helpful to the stabilization program. The mining and peasant leaders in Congress immediately denounced me as having wounded the dignity of the Bolivian people, sullied the national sovereignty, and committed the crime of intervening in Bolivian politics under the cover of the Monroe Doctrine!

It was worse than a crime; it was a blunder. The Minister of Foreign Affairs was forced to tell the Chamber of Deputies that he had protested to the American Ambassador. The Ambassador expressed his regret that I had been misquoted, and said that I had not meant to imply any criticism of Lechín. And I kept my mouth so tightly shut from that time on that the newspapers later complained of my silence.[85]

The April crises

The months of February and March gave some respite from open political attacks on the program, although not from undercover agitation against the council's legislative activities. But events soon shaped up for a second all-out assault in connection with the celebration of the fifth anniversary of the Revolution on

April 9. Touched off by Lechín's speech to the railway workers' union, the battle began again, and this time there was no attempt to use me as a scapegoat. It was a direct attack on President Siles himself and on the stabilization program.[86]

In a ringing address to a huge crowd in the Plaza Murillo, the President undertook the defense of the stabilization program and paid tribute to U.S. aid and to me personally. At the mention of "Doctor Jackson Eder," I am pleased to say, there was vociferous applause from the crowd, and there was no doubt that the President had carried the day. But Lechín delivered an effective counterattack in an address before the factory workers' union on April 16 and was scheduled to preside over a miners' congress in Pulacayo and Uyuni later that month.[87]

The "Report to the Cabinet." In those mining regions Lechín ruled supreme, and there was the danger that he might call out the miners' militia, the most powerful armed body in the country, in support of his position. In the face of this threat, the President decided to consolidate his position, following Lechín's disturbing speech to the factory workers, by asking me to make a full oral report on the stabilization program to the loyal members of his Cabinet and of the national political committee of the MNR. Included among the former were the Minister of National Defense, General Julio Prado, and the Minister of Government, Roberto Méndez-Tejada, whose position gave him command of the Carabineers, a sort of national police force.[88]

The conferees, and particularly the national political committee, were representative of the full power of the National Revolutionary Movement, the MNR. If they aligned themselves behind the President, he could risk defying Lechín and the miners' union, and could exert a fair measure of control over the nonaligned forces in the COB; if not, and if Ñuflo Chávez and the peasants' confederation joined Lechín in opposition, Siles would be forced either to abandon his stabilization program or to resign.

As it happened, I was not unprepared. At a council meeting two weeks earlier, the President and Foreign Minister had complained that Ross Moore, head of USOM/Bolivia, lacked "flexibility" in his judgments — Bolivia needed more aid, and Moore insisted that she first adhere to the stabilization program. I had countered by saying that Moore was a reasonable man, but that the facts themselves were "inflexible"; it was impossible to raise wages without affecting the exchange rate. I thereupon launched into an itemized exposition of the departures from the stabilization program and their consequences, with the result that, three days later, the President and council asked me to prepare a full report on the status of stabilization. With that in mind, I had drawn a number of large charts on various aspects of the stabilization program, which I had expected to show the President and council at the next council meeting. With these charts and a hastily prepared outline, I was thus able to give the assembled conferees at the Cabinet meeting a thorough exposition of the status of the program — its achievements, its shortcomings, and its problems — and the exposition doubtless gained in effectiveness from the fact that it was extemporaneous.

The content of my presentation was financial and economic, so that it will be discussed later in Chapter 20. The political effect, however, was immediate and salutory. For many of the conferees, including the ministers of government and national defense and the members of the national political committee of the MNR, this was the first time that they had ever listened to a complete report on the nature and problems of the stabilization process. Even for those on the Stabilization Council, the summation was a revelation, and a sobering one at that, for it showed in sharp relief how much remained to be done and why it would be impossible to accede to the demagogic demands of Lechín, the COB, Ñuflo Chávez, and the Trotskyites. There were many questions from the group, and the discussion extended for over three hours, but when it was through there was no doubt that the President could count upon the wholehearted support of the leaders of the MNR, including the Army and Carabineers. The fact that there were three Labor representatives present — the Minister of Labor and two of the members of the national political committee, who must certainly have listened to my presentation with mixed emotions — served to bring back to Lechín, the COB, and Ñuflo Chávez the determination and unanimity of the party leaders.

Thus, the April Congress of Pulacayo — the mineworkers' conference — opened with a reasonably mild speech by Lechín, in which he continued to attack the "Eder Plan," claiming that "Sr. Eder has not fulfilled his promises to the people ... the workers are receiving starvation wages." He did not, however, attack Siles directly, and admitted that "we still do not have a workers' plan" for stabilization.[89]

Even the May 1 festivities passed without major incident a

few days later.* Lechín, of course, was the central figure of
the day, and addressed the mob with a demand for "equality of
sacrifices." Only the poor, and not the rich, have suffered
from stabilization. The crooks (picaros) should be named and
brought to justice. These were his themes, but he neglected to
mention in which categories he considered himself included.
His speech was violent, but so mild by Bolivian standards that
the press complimented the various May Day orators for their
"objectivity."[90]

The June crisis

The next political crisis was scheduled to come in June,
coincident with the Second National Congress of the COB. In
anticipation of that event, President Siles returned to the
defense of his program on May 13 — the "Day of the Factory
Worker," commemorating the "Massacre" of Villa Victoria. In
his speech to the factory workers he stated that, had it not been
for the stabilization measures, the boliviano would have dropped
to Bs. 30,000 to the dollar and the plight of the working man
would be infinitely worse than it was. "No one," he declared,
"dare call me a reactionary face to face" — a direct allusion to
Lechín's May Day speech. Pulling no punches, he added: "It is
a *lie* to say that sacrifices are demanded only of the poor."[91]

---

*May Day is celebrated in the USSR and other socialist countries as
Labor Day, dating from the first Congress of the Second Socialist International in Paris in 1889. In the Latin American countries, it is generally
the signal for more or less riotous demonstrations by the proletariat, depending upon the strength of the socialist (Second International), communist (Third International), and Trotskyite (Fourth International) forces.
(The First International was that founded by Karl Marx in London in 1864;
the Second International included such outstanding socialists as Bernard
Shaw, Ramsay MacDonald, Pilsudski, Lenin, Mussolini, and Laval. In
Bolivia, all sectors of the MNR drew their inspiration from the Founder.)
One consequence of the political truce that extended from the Congress of Pulacayo until after May Day was that, in order not to provoke a
resumption of the crisis, it was announced that President Siles was not
well, and hence confined to his residence. Thus, when the new American
Ambassador, Philip Bonsal, arrived in La Paz on April 26, the President
was unable to receive him at the palace for him to present his credentials.
The following day, both the President and the Ambassador advised me in
private of their desire to meet, so I arranged a meeting at home for May
2, perhaps the first time an Ambassador has ever been presented without
speeches or protocol — a diplomatic disaster but the beginning of a warm
mutual friendship.

Publication of the "Report to the Nation." Two days after Lechin's speech, President Siles asked me to prepare my oral report of April 17 for publication. The timing could not have been better, not only because of the forthcoming COB congress, but because of the presence in La Paz of outstanding economists and government representatives from all over Latin America, who were assembled in a major conference of the highly influential Economic Commission for Latin America (Comisión Económica para América Latina — hence known as CEPAL or ECLA). An ill-timed remark by any one of these distinguished visitors, based on an inadequate knowledge of the Bolivian stabilization measures, could do irreparable harm to the program, while conversely, their approval could prove an unanswerable defense. Thus, it was in every sense desirable to have the report available during the course of the ECLA meeting.

To avoid giving undue prominence to my position as Executive Director of the Stabilization Council, I had suggested that the report be edited and issued as a council study, rather than have it attributed to me. The President overruled this suggestion, doubtless because he felt that the report's frank criticism would be helpful at the time and that it would be accepted as more objective if it came from a foreign "expert" than if it emanated from the council. Nevertheless, I took it upon myself to expunge all references to the disrupted negotiations with Patiño, Aramayo, and Hochschild, as it was absolutely essential to prevent a leak that might strengthen the hand of those companies by letting them know that the U.S. government had made a negotiated settlement a *sine qua non* for stabilization aid. With that exception, marked by asterisks, the complete report was placed in the President's hands (and, with his consent, copies were delivered to the American Embassy) on May 8.

But the complete version would hardly have been suitable for publication at the time, in view of the reference to Vice-President Ñuflo Chávez' untimely intervention in the bond negotiations. Moreover, the report constituted a factual indictment of practically everything the MNR had done over the previous four years, and it was scarcely to be expected that the government would wish its ineptitude proclaimed to the ECLA representatives in so frank a manner. Again with the President's consent, I asked the American Ambassador to excise from the report any paragraphs that might conceivably be detrimental to Bolivian-American relationships, leaving it to the President to censor those parts that might be politically prejudicial from the

Bolivian point of view. The President, the Ambassador, and I thus worked simultaneously on editing the document for the press, with the final word up to the President himself.

At last the report was ready for distribution. At the request of the President, it was given to the press piecemeal in five instalments, to be published from May 26 to 30. This was both for wider publicity, as it was too large a mouthful to be digested all at once, and because the council's small staff was physically not equipped to retype the minutely corrected version in a single day. The original version was too loaded with dynamite to permit its being typed elsewhere — even in the President's office.[92]

The result of publication was electric, far exceeding the council's expectations. Each day, every major newspaper carried the daily instalment in full with excellent reproductions of the charts, and each day, in the streets and market places of La Paz, little groups of Indians and mestizos congregated around a central figure who read the report out loud, or translated it into Quechua.

From that time on, until I left La Paz some four weeks later, there could be no doubt as to the popular success of the stabilization program. Attacked by the communist paper, as the liberal import of the plan became clear, it was supported by editorials in the majority of the country's press.[93]*

The COB congress. The opposing forces were not long, however, in returning to the fray. The Trotskyite Workers' Revolutionary Party delivered a manifesto to the Second National Congress of the COB, declaring that there had been a definite rupture between the COB and the MNR regime headed

---

*The term "liberal" is here used in its pristine sense, as it is used practically everywhere outside the United States, and as it was originally used in this country, meaning a policy based on individual liberty as opposed to an economy planned and directed by the government. The communists and Trotskyites in Bolivia expressly attacked the "Eder program" for its "liberal" viewpoint.

The translator of Roepke's *Economics of the Free Society* points out this distinction, as Roepke uses the term throughout the book in its original sense. Roepke and his disciple, Erhard, are not advocates of "old-style liberalism ... which is identified with economic laissez-faire," but of "neo-liberalism in which the positive role of the state in establishing the juridical, competitive, and monetary framework necessary to a viable market economy is recognized and supported." (Wilhelm Roepke, *Economics of the Free Society*, trans. Patrick M. Boarman [Chicago: Regnery, 1963], p. 69.)

by Siles with the support of the oligarchs, the imperialists, and the army. It called on the workers, in the name of the Fourth International, to go forward resolutely with the worldwide Marxist Revolution.[94]

Because of a "sudden illness," which was understood to be tactical, Juan Lechín failed to attend the opening session of the congress on June 4, and the meeting commenced with an address by President Siles, calling for the unification of all sectors of the revolutionary movement. On the following day, Lechín loosed an impassioned attack on me personally, on the report, the stabilization program, and President Siles, filling thirty solid columns of type in the local press.[95] It was a well-written speech, magnificently delivered, and evoked ovation after ovation from his auditors who had been provided with travel expenses and an abundance of liquor by the National Social Security Administration. By the time the orator delivered his closing peroration, there were shouts of *"Muera Eder!"* (Death to Eder!) from the crowd, and there is no doubt that he could have led that particular audience to a gala lynching party with me as the central figure.*

---

*The communist paper headlined: "Lechín vents his wrath on Mr. Eder," while the Christian Socialist paper had a wonderfully witty pro-Eder column with me protesting in pidgin Spanish that my death would not help the Bolivian economy (*El Pueblo,* June 8, 1957; *Presencia,* June 13, column by Alfonso Prudencio). Early the following morning, in response to the reporters, I stated that I had not read Lechín's speech, "not that it does not interest me, but that I have not had time to read it"; this was regarded as Machiavellian in its cleverness although it was a simple statement of fact. I also stated: "But, in any event, I have no intention of commenting on it." The press severely criticized my silence, notwithstanding that, only a few months earlier, I had been attacked for entering into politics merely for lamenting that I could not equal Lechín's eloquence (see *El Diario, Última Hora,* June 7, 1957). Contrary to Professor Alexander's statement, based on his talk with an "ex-Trotskyite leader" of the COB, that "Mr. Eder frequently felt called upon to defend his recommendations to the press and public," I never once defended my recommendations or the program to the press or public. I gave a single press interview and made a number of speeches, *before* enactment of the program, explaining what we intended to do, at the express request of President Siles and of the council, and on April 17, 1957, I made a full report to the President and Cabinet on the operation of the program. President Siles saw fit to release that report to the public in five instalments. That was all, but that one report was too "frequent" for Professor Alexander's informant and his fellow "ex-Trotskyites," Trotskyites, and communists (Alexander, *The Bolivian National Revolution,* pp. 207-8).

Aside from personal defamation and oratory, however, there was nothing of substance in the speech that had not been said over and over again — the demand for higher wages, lower prices, taxation of the rich, punishment of evildoers, and expansion of Bolivia's development program. Nevertheless, President Siles asked me to draft a reply. This I did, but in the form of a memorandum to be used as the basis of a reply for the President's signature and not my own. It would have been foolhardy for a foreigner to engage in a personal polemic with so doughty an opponent as Lechín. Among the twenty-one misrepresentations of fact in Lechín's speech, only three items merit comment at this point, as the remainder were either purely polemical or are covered at length in the "Report to the Cabinet" of April 17:

1. In his speech Lechín attempted to wash his hands of any responsibility for the stabilization plan, despite the fact that he had taken part in its final formulation and had agreed to the wage increases and other measures incorporated in the December 15, 1956, decrees. He reverted to this theme in the later discussions at the COB Congress, with a direct misrepresentation to the effect that he had not been informed of the plan or of the content of the stabilization decrees. The President set the record straight by replying that it was President Paz-Estenssoro who had created the Stabilization Council with the unanimous approval of *all* the leaders of the Revolutionary Government; that it was President Paz who had appointed "Dr. Jackson Eder" director of the council; that President Paz had approved the plan in its general outlines and declared that there was no possible alternative course of action; and that the Vice-President (Ñuflo Chávez), the President of the Senate (Juan Lechín), the President of the Chamber of Deputies (Renán Castrillo), and the Executive Secretary of the Central Political Committee of the MNR (José Cuadros-Quiroga), *had all been consulted in the preparation of the plan,* and "their suggestions incorporated in the final program, thanks to Dr. Eder's understanding and willingness to compromise." Because of Lechín's persistent misrepresentation on this point, the President was forced to reiterate, in a speech to Congress two months later, that the top leaders in government and labor had all taken part in the preparation of the plan and had *all* agreed on putting it into immediate effect.[96]

2. Lechín referred in his speech to my improper pressure
    on COMIBOL for a settlement with Patiño and stated
    that "Mister Eder should explain whether he is exerting
    this pressure as the agent of Patiño Mines and under
    what kind of instructions." For the record and because,
    as has previously been explained, Bolivians regard a
    failure to deny an allegation as an admission of its
    truth, I must state that I was not acting as an agent of
    Patiño, Aramayo, or Hochschild, had never met any of
    those gentlemen, had had no connection or correspon-
    dence or understanding with any of those firms or their
    representatives, and that, to the contrary, I was acting
    solely for and in the interests of the government of
    Bolivia.

3. Lechín claimed that the "miracles wrought by Mister
    Eder" — and applauded by Assistant Secretary Henry
    Holland — were not in fact miracles, "but merely the
    natural consequence of a free market policy" *(una
    orientación librecambista)*. This was, of course, all
    that I had ever claimed. But it was a remarkable ad-
    mission for one so closely identified with a government-
    planned and government-controlled economy to confess
    that a free market economy could produce so many
    miracles in so short a time.

Lechín's clarion call to the COB was followed by an equally
dangerous, although less inflammatory speech from a source
that would hardly have been suspected capable of such an attack,
Luis Bedregal-Rodo, the mild-mannered and *simpático* director
of the National Social Security Administration. Bedregal characterized the "Eder plan" as "fallacious and infantile," and
proposed instead that the government embark on a new inflation,
but this time directed and controlled by the government so as to
maintain a just parity between wages and prices, with a general
increase in wages prior to July 1. Failing this, he advocated a
general strike.*

*It can only be surmised that this intelligent and likable young man,
like so many young economists in Latin America, had imbibed too deeply
from the Pierian spring of John Maynard Keynes without having had the
practical financial experience to avoid becoming intoxicated by some of
that beguiling teacher's wilder theories. This would go a long way toward
explaining why Bedregal could never comprehend that Bolivia's social
security charges far exceeded the country's economic capacity. Keynes,
it will be remembered, believed that a government can spend the way to
prosperity by borrowing, or by taking money from one group of citizens

Called sharply to account by the President for his disloyalty to the stabilization program, Bedregal issued a confused and partial retraction, stating that either the nation must follow the present stabilization plan, with no increase in wages, or it must face a new inflationary process with all its consequences, and that the compromise solutions proposed at the COB congress would, in his opinion, all be inflationary. But to this he added that economic realities in the nation compel it to embark on a new inflationary process and that it is essential that the inflation be an inflation controlled by the government.

This is common neo-Keynesian theory as propounded throughout Latin America (see definition at pp. 474 n, 475): If inflation just happens, it is bad; if it is intentional, it is good. However, Bedregal claimed that, with the elimination of multiple exchange rates, the outlook under a new, planned inflationary movement was more favorable than in 1956, provided the Central Bank had ample dollars to meet the demand, which presupposed the continuation of U.S. aid.[97]

Bedregal's comment is significant, not only because the exorbitant social security charges were, and remain, one of Bolivia's gravest economic problems and threats to monetary stability — as is true everywhere in Latin America — but because this peculiar circularity of reasoning is illustrative of what the monetary stabilizer or economic adviser must expect to meet with in any country that has undergone a galloping inflation. The argument comes not from corrupt or demagogic politicians but from exceptionally intelligent and well-educated young men whose abundance of theoretical knowledge is untempered by practical experience.

The COB congress closed with a wordy manifesto embodying sections from the Fourth International Trotskyite program previously referred to, interspersed with passages presented by Ñuflo Chávez-Ortiz on behalf of the peasants' confederation.

---

and spending it on government enterprises instead of letting the citizens spend it on private enterprises, even going so far as to write that pyramid-building, earthquakes, and wars may serve to increase wealth — that if the government were to fill old bottles with bank notes, bury them in abandoned coal mines, and cover them with rubbish, leaving it to private enterprise to dig them out again, unemployment could be solved, and the real income and capital wealth of the community would probably be increased. Keynes also wrote that "it is astonishing what foolish things one can believe if one thinks too long alone, *particularly in economics.*" (John Maynard Keynes, *The General Theory of Employment, Interest, and Money* [New York: Harcourt Brace, 1936], pp. vii, 129.)

On the whole, as the press pointed out, it was a "90 per cent Trotskyite" document, which is not surprising considering that Trotsky's *Permanent Revolution* is said on good authority to be the Bible of the Revolution, as it is in other similar movements elsewhere in Latin America.*

To keep the record straight, however, as the official Trotskyite Party (the POR) and the official Communist Party (the PCB) and its predecessor in Bolivia (the PIR) were out of favor with one or another of the leaders of the COB, the manifesto paid tribute to Lenin and managed to comment extensively on Stalin and Khrushchev without taking sides, while calling for a "United Anti-Imperialist Front for the unification of Latin America." The latter was straight out of Trotsky's primer. In the matter of stabilization, opinion was so divided in the congress that the only comment the COB could agree upon in the fourteen-column, closely worded manifesto was that the "Eder plan" was blocking Bolivia's "economic emancipation" and adding to unemployment and the general poverty of the country.[98]

The showdown. All during the ten-day COB congress, and for weeks thereafter, declarations of support for the stabilization program, together with contributions of gold or money, flowed into the presidential palace, from labor unions, gold miners, veterans' organizations, political "cells," and, in fact, from every sector of the Bolivian economy.[99]

Even among the delegates to the COB congress, representing that part of the population most opposed to President Siles and most solidly behind Lechín, 65 per cent of the delegates thought that Siles had the support of the workers for his stabilization plan, 26 per cent believed the contrary, and 9 per cent would express no opinion, according to a poll of the delegates. This was in spite of the fact that 54 per cent of the delegates thought the plan detrimental to the working class, against 37 per cent to the contrary (although 60 per cent confided in its ultimate success, against 27 per cent who foresaw its failure).

---

*Lev Davidovich Bronshtein ("Leon Trotsky"), *La Revolución Permanente* (Buenos Aires: Mar Dulce, n.d. See *The Permanent Revolution*, trans. Max Schachtman [New York: Pioneer, 1931]) is probably the most influential of a series of books and pamphlets published during Trotsky's Mexican exile in furtherance of his Fourth International. Other writings of Trotsky in the series, widely circulated throughout Latin America, include: *Por los Estados Unidos Socialistas de América Latina* (Buenos Aires: Coyoacan, 1961); *El Proceso de Moscú* (Mexico: Neuva Era, 1937); and *La Revolución Traicionada* (Buenos Aires: Claridad, 1938).

Significantly, 87 per cent believed that the workers could increase their production and thus aid stabilization (10 per cent to the contrary), while 59 per cent thought that any increase in wages should be dependent on increased productivity and 9 per cent favored lowering social security charges in order to increase wages. Only 2 per cent wanted higher wages regardless of inflation.[100]

Finally, at the closing evening session of the COB congress, Siles delivered a dramatic defense of the stabilization program, with Lechín photographed sitting glumly at his side, the delegates interrupting again and again during the talk with thunderous applause.

Outside, in the Plaza Murillo, the crowd filled the square carrying placards: "The people are for Siles," "*Viva la Estabilización Monetaria,*" "No communism for Bolivia," and so forth. As Siles' speech came over the loud speakers, the crowd went wild with enthusiasm, and when Siles appeared, he was carried on the shoulders of the mob and forced to deliver another speech extempore, with the crowd in delirium, shouting over and over again: "*Viva Siles-Zuazo,*" "*Muera Lechín,*" and "*Muera COB.*" Stones were thrown at a huge portrait of Lechín over the congress building, and later the mob was about to set fire to the automobile of one of Lechín's henchmen, when Siles appeared on the balcony and begged the demonstrators to return to their homes and cease their violence.

Later that night, as Lechín and his bodyguards attempted to withdraw without being seen, they were attacked by the mob with stones and yells. Lechín managed to escape in the dark while his bodyguards continued to battle the crowd. On the following morning, Lechín and a group of his followers were surrounded by a threatening mob on the far side of the Plaza in front of the cathedral. Again Lechín escaped, and he later denied that he had been assaulted personally, but, according to good authority, he was set upon by a crowd of Indian and chola women in the marketplace behind the cathedral, and would have been murdered had it not been for the prompt action of the *Carabineros* whom Siles dispatched to restore order.[101]

Thus ended the June crisis, with Siles once again triumphant over his enemies — at least for the time being — exactly six months after the initiation of the stabilization program. But Lechín's speech and his attempt to destroy the program — or, as he put it, to amend the program — had its repercussions. Public confidence in Bolivia's political stability, and in Siles' ability to hold the line on wages, was badly undermined, and the boliviano, which had been maintained stable at Bs. 7,700 to the dollar, suffered its first serious reverse, and dropped to Bs. 8,100. It was not reassuring to Siles' backers, and to those who believed in the program, to read a telegram from Paz-Estenssoro to *La Nación* announcing that he would be returning from London to work for party unity,[102] which would seem to foreshadow a Gresham's Law of politics, with the bad *políticos* driving out the good.

The Experts

Mention has been made of the presence in La Paz of the delegates to the ECLA conference precisely at a time of great political commotion and of the possibility that any one of these distinguished visitors, through an untimely or ill-considered remark, might endanger public confidence in the program or give aid and comfort to its enemies. Long before that, however, once at the very inception of my task in Bolivia and again in January, 1957, at a time when the program had barely got under way, the plan appeared to be similarly threatened by a superabundance of experts.

Admittedly, no one expert can be so wise, so knowledgeable, that he might not stand to benefit from the advice of others, even from the advice of others less experienced than he — perhaps even particularly in that case, as such persons might bring a fresh outlook to the solution of a problem, being less encumbered with preconceived ideas. Full, free, and frank discussion among opposing experts is splendid in an institution of higher learning, or in the market place of ideas, books, pamphlets, and meetings of learned societies. But where a task is to be performed, whether in business or war or monetary stabilization, the discussion and the reconciliation of opposing opinions must take place within the group or council charged with responsibility for achieving results. Some one person must make the final decision, and once that decision has been made someone must have both the authority and the courage to carry it out, and the others in the group must support that decision.

During the immediate, critical stage of monetary stabilization, the *post factum* opinion of outside experts and non-experts that takes the form of second-guessing or back-seat driving can be particularly hazardous to the person whose hand is on the wheel, and who must be given full responsibility for a safe arrival at destination. In a free society, such outside criticism cannot and should not be denied, but it can seriously endanger the program of those who have been entrusted with the responsibility of decision, and a responsible critic must weigh carefully whether he wishes to risk wrecking a program before giving it fair time to prove itself.

It is not generally a case of reaching a compromise between two opposing points of view, for in most cases the middle way would be less desirable than either extreme. The person who prides himself on being middle of the road is precisely the one most likely to collide with vehicles going in both directions. The safest posture, in economics as in driving, is to keep well to the right, yet not be afraid of going to the middle, or even to the far left, when it is necessary to overtake a slower-moving economy or vehicle. (In England for traffic, and presumably in the USSR in economics, keeping well to the left might be the wiser course.)

It is seldom that a middle-way compromise between opposing expert opinions will work. In a dispute between engineers who favor building a bridge and those who favor a tunnel, it would hardly do for the town council to compromise by building an under-water bridge or an aerial tunnel. Similarly, in monetary policy, there is no viable middle road between the Keynesian economists who believe that a government can blaze the way to prosperity through spending and borrowing and those who believe that the only way to stop a galloping inflation is for the government, and the nation at large, to live within its means. This is why I was so dismayed to learn that the International Monetary Fund proposed sending a mission down to Bolivia while my own ideas and plans were still in embryonic form, and why I was so delighted to have the expert assistance of the IMF mission, once I had gone over those plans with the IMF staff in Washington and found that they and I spoke the same language.*

---

*Some of the IMF experts had studied under Professor Keynes, but most of them were sufficiently experienced to distinguish between the valid economic principles taught by that extraordinary teacher and some of his more fanciful propositions which were either uttered with tongue in cheek or with a political aim, and were certainly never intended to be applied in an underdeveloped economy. Keynes himself wrote:

> Lenin is said to have declared that the best way to destroy the Capitalist System was to debauch the currency. By a continuing process of inflation,

In the following pages, I deal at some length with the influence of Keynesian economics, of the London School of Economics and Political Science, and of the various U.N. agencies, because of their relevance not only to Bolivia but to Latin America as a whole. The U.N. Economic Commission for Latin America, with its headquarters in Chile, for many years under the able direction of Raúl Prebisch, Latin America's foremost Keynesian, has served as a training center for some of the most brilliant South American economists, many of them graduates of the London School of Economics and Political Science, and all steeped in the theories of John Maynard Keynes. A number of them, together with other graduates of the London School, have returned to their native countries to assume positions of high responsibility as ministers of finance or economic development. And in every country of Latin America where inflation has been rampant, the political philosophy of the London School and neo-Keynesian economics, the theory that government spending can promote economic development, have been at the root of the problem — "neo-Keynesian" because Keynes, at least in his less exuberant writing, advocated government borrowing, taxing, and spending as a temporary and not as a perpetual spur to the economy, and believed with Hayek that socialism is the "road to serfdom."* But, in the Latin

---

governments can confiscate, secretly and unobserved, an important part of the wealth of their citizens. By this method they not only confiscate, but they confiscate *arbitrarily;* and, while the process impoverishes many, it arbitrarily enriches some.... As the inflation proceeds and the real value of the currency fluctuates wildly from month to month, all permanent relations between debtors and creditors, which form the ultimate foundation of capitalism, become so utterly disordered as to be almost meaningless; and the process of wealth-getting degenerates into a gamble and a lottery.

Lenin was certainly right. There is no subtler, no surer means of overturning the existing basis of society than to debauch the currency. The process engages all the hidden forces of economic law on the side of destruction, and does it in a manner which not one man in a million is able to diagnose (John Maynard Keynes, *Economic Consequences of the Peace* [New York: Harcourt Brace and Howe, 1920], pp. 235-36).

*The neo-Keynesian postulate, as developed in Latin America, appears to be based on a triune mystique: (1) Economic development is only possible through government action; (2) deficits, if planned, are not inflationary, because of the multiplier effect of government spending (which presumably does not work with private spending); and (3) government spending of revenues obtained through taxation is more productive than

American context, the easy way to unlimited government spending by borrowing from the central bank and printing currency proved so attractive that, once a policy of "controlled inflation" and proliferating governmental enterprises was embarked upon, it became a permanent way of life, and controlled inflation turned out to be uncontrollable.

Even outside of Latin America, the great monetary stabilizers — Schacht and Erhard in Germany, Ikeda in Japan, Costanzo in Greece, Rueff in France, and Kemmerer in five Latin American countries — have all been anti-Keynesians or pre-Keynesians; nowhere have the Keynesian theories served to control a rampant inflation. This subject will be dealt with at greater length in a companion volume which will be a general survey of the facts and fallacies of inflation and development in Latin America. But, as the present study is intended as a case history and guide for prospective monetary stabilizers, the impact of U.N.-sponsored neo-Keynesian theories in Bolivia is discussed in detail, as they are bound to encounter the same problem in every hemisphere country that is faced with the scourge of monetary debasement.

The U.N. mission

In previous chapters reference has been made to the grave problems that arose on precisely that point, viz., the impossibility of reconciling opposing points of view with experts having other ideas and perhaps other ideologies — Louis de Battista, the U.N. adviser in social security matters (pp. 173, 405); Jean Peset, the U.N. adviser in the Finance Ministry (p. 316 n); and Arthur Karasz, the U.N. adviser to the Central Bank (pp. 104-107, 114). Some background on the U.N. mission would seem relevant at this point.

The United Nations Technical Mission in Bolivia had been formed on the recommendation of a three-man Preparatory Mission in 1949, headed by Carter Goodrich of Columbia University, and of a fifteen-man Mission of Technical Assistance

---

private spending, both because of the multiplier effect and the supposedly permanent gap between private savings and investment. See, for example, the statement by former Colombian Finance Minister, Carlos Sanz-de Santamaría, one of Latin America's outstanding Keynesians and a graduate of the London School, that the "planned deficit" for 1963, unlike previous unplanned deficits, would enhance Colombia's economic prospects.[103]

to Bolivia in 1950, under the leadership of Hugh L. Keenleyside, who had headed up U.N. technical assistance for many years and later was given charge of its activities in the field of public administration. At the time of my arrival in Bolivia, the U.N. mission consisted of over fifty technical advisers distributed throughout the principal government departments, agencies and enterprises, including COMIBOL, the Development Corporation, the National Planning and Coordination Commission, the Central Bank, the National Social Security Administration, and the Ministries of Finance, Economy, Agriculture, Rural Affairs, etc. Its annual budget in 1956 was $640,000. [104]

Their plan of operation was radically different from that of the U.S. advisers. Point IV worked outside the ministries, and through the independent *Servicios* described at pp. 115-19. The U.N. experts worked inside the various ministries and government enterprises, and by their skills, natural abilities, and ideological viewpoint, were able to consolidate their positions in the good graces of the Revolutionary Government, at the top as well as at working levels. All of them were fluent in Spanish.

In briefings at the American Embassy, and later in the office of the American delegation to the United Nations in New York, I had been forewarned of the unfriendly political orientation of the head of the U.N. mission in La Paz and of some of his subordinates, as well as of certain members of the U.N. secretariat in New York. Herbert Feis, former Economic Adviser of the Department of State, writes that the chief obstacle in the technical assistance programs of the United Nations "has been the conflict with Communism which has divided two sets of its members, inside and outside the United Nations conference rooms. . . . This rift has hampered the benevolent activities of the United Nations in still other ways. The capitalist nations have usually been well disposed toward plans and projects that might bring about an expansion of private capital and enterprise; the Communist members have tried to persuade the poorer countries to debar private capital and extend government ownership and control." [105]

Considering that the majority of the governments represented at the United Nations embrace a socialistic viewpoint of one degree or another, it is not surprising that the U.N. economic, political, and social missions and agencies should be to a large extent socialistically inclined. This is not to equate the extreme socialism of the USSR with the Fabian socialism of

England's Labour Party.* From the viewpoint of the domestic economies and social philosophies within those countries, from the viewpoint of the foreign policy and internal security of the United States, they are as different as day is from night. But from the viewpoint of monetary stability — in a country such as Bolivia, which had undergone a rampant inflation attributable to government intervention in the economy, government control of the major forces of production, and government incompetence and corruption — any political and economic philosophy predicated on socialism of any degree, whether on "statism," "interventionism,""*dirigisme,*" or government planning and control, was a menace. And the U.N. mission in Bolivia was composed, for the most part, as was inevitable, of men who believed in the efficacy of government intervention in the economy.

Throughout most of 1955 and early 1956, there is no doubt that it was the opposition of the U.N. mission and the close rapport between President Paz-Estenssoro and the U.N. adviser to the Central Bank, both ardent Keynesians, that were responsible for Bolivia's long hesitation in inviting a U.S.

---

*Although, in theory, England's Fabian socialism broke with Marxism because the Fabians hold that utility — not labor, as Marx believed — is the origin and measure of "value," the essential difference, as the Fabian economist G. D. H. Cole points out, is that the Fabians believe in achieving socialism by evolution as a continuing gradual development while Marx taught that socialism could only be attained by revolution. The ultimate goal is the same: control by the state of the land and natural resources and of the means of production. This is not the place to debate the relative virtues of individual freedom and a free market economy versus a system in which the government plans and controls man's labor for the common, social welfare, in an ideal society. But, in Bolivia with monetary stabilization as the goal, the violent partisans of the Third and Fourth Internationals were scarcely more dangerous to my ends than were the couth and cultivated disciples of the London School of Economics and Political Science, founded by members of the Fabian Society, and so brilliantly successful — from George Bernard Shaw, Beatrice and Sidney Webb, Annie Besant and Graham Wallas down to Harold Laski and G. D. H. Cole — in indoctrinating two generations of political economists all over the world in the Fabian approach to socialism whose goals are outlined in Graham Wallas' book, *The Great Society* (London: Macmillan, 1914). Nowhere have these theories gained greater currency than in Latin America, but the Latin American temperament is so little disposed to accept the dilatory tactics of Fabius Cunctator that Latin American economists, while generally accepting the "utility" theory of the Fabians, and the Keynesian rather than the Marxian dialectic, are inclined to insist on government planning and government control, now and immediately, or else.

financial and stabilization team to help Bolivia put its house in order. It is true that I was "invited" to Bolivia by President Paz, but it was an invitation extended virtually under duress and with repeated hints of the curtailment of U.S. aid.[106]

U.N. opposition to the monetary stabilization program was evident from the outset, which was natural, as the success of that program was predicated on a return to a free market economy (to the extent possible), and this meant the reversal of most of the measures that had been carried out on the advice of the U.N. experts over the preceding four years.

Arthur Karasz had been the principal architect of the ill-fated "stabilization" measures enacted by the government of Dr. Paz-Estenssoro on May 14, 1953.[107] These were based on the theoretical concepts of Keynes and Samuelson as to the beneficent multiplying effects of spending for "investment."* These concepts, as applied in Bolivia, were wholly divorced from the practical consideration of whether or not a given investment by the government would in fact be productive within the foreseeable future or whether it would merely be more money down an endless drain.

There was one point in Karasz's economic philosophy, nevertheless, which was unquestionably valid: "There can be no economic improvement without greater productivity and hard work."[108] It apparently did not occur to Karasz that the system of multiple exchange rates, exchange controls, price controls, and other aspects of "interventionism" by the government enacted by the decrees of May 14, 1953, and the seizure of the private mines which he advocated,[109] would prove to be the worst blows to increased productivity that Bolivia has ever

---

*Karasz's philosophy, expressly based on the writings of those economists, as stated in a series of lectures in May, 1953, at the University of San Andrés, La Paz, was that "... a government should be empowered and able to direct the economic destinies of its people" (Revista de Derecho, XVIII [March, 1954], p. 157). He was in no sense a communist. His whole career had been spent in combatting, or fleeing from, communism. He was, however, a fervent disciple of Keynes and an advocate of government "interventionism" in the economy, including price and foreign exchange controls. His financial background was as president of the Hungarian Central Bank during a brief period which terminated just before the pengo reached its record low of 1.4 nonillion (10 to the 30th power) to one (ibid., pp. 117-21, 124-32). That experience was scarcely suitable to putting a stop to inflation in Bolivia, aside from the fact that his economic theories did not look on government spending and borrowing as a cause of inflation, nor inflation as an evil in itself.

suffered and would leave in their wake the conditions of chaos and corruption that have been described in Chapter 2.[110]

Three years after enactment of Karasz's stabilization measures, when the bolivian peso had bid fair to follow in the course of his native pengo, he gave a farewell address at the University, still tenaciously clinging to the idea that the solution of Bolivia's problems could be found in more and more controls, despite the disillusioning experience of the past. This was on July 24, 1956, after I had given the President and his advisers (including Karasz) a draft of a decree establishing the National Monetary Stabilization Council, plus a complete agenda and time schedule of a stabilization program, and an oral outline of the basic concepts of the program itself, with stabilization to be based on the complete abandonment of government controls and a return to a free market economy.*

In his July, 1956, lecture, Karasz had reaffirmed unequivocally that the 1953 "stabilization" theories and decrees were a "success" but that their beneficial effects had been frustrated: (1) by a drop in the price of tin from its all-time peak of $1.21 a pound during the Korean War; (2) by the lowered productivity of labor, lack of mining machinery and spare parts; and (3) by the anomaly of a "mixed system" (i.e., part socialist, part free, inasmuch as only some, but not all, of the mines had been taken over by the government, and the government mining corporation was not free to dismiss its excess workers, as it would be in the case of a 100 per cent socialist society such as the USSR). As to the impact of printing press currency, he maintained that: "The increase in note circulation, and the increase in the free

---

*On my first meeting with President Paz-Estenssoro, and as I left the President's office with the American Ambassador, Karasz was waiting in the vestibule. Later, it was learned from a U. N. officer that he had presented President Paz with a complete monetary stabilization plan in July, 1956, which would certainly have stymied my program had it not been for my strenuous opposition, backed by the threat of suspension of U. S. aid. In June, 1957, it was learned that a certain high U.N. official, reputedly a communist (which may or may not be true), had suggested the appointment of a member of the U.N. Bolivian mission, shockingly unqualified for the task, to replace Arthur Karasz as adviser to the Central Bank. The proposed replacement was likewise considered by some to be a communist (Alexander, *The Bolivian National Revolution*, p. 191). Backed by the American Embassy, which had warned me that the U.N. mission would attempt to sabotage the program, I managed to oppose President Paz' attempts to make Karasz's successor a permanent member of the Stabilization Council.

market rate of exchange, are the consequences and not the causes of inflation. They are merely statistical data and nothing more."*

Karasz expounded these views to me at some length, as a matter of Keynesian revealed truth not open to argument, at our first meeting the week of my arrival in Bolivia, adding that the only possible solution for the drop in the value of the boliviano would be to give the miners additional incentive pay to increase their output, and that the only way for the government mining corporation to operate in the black would be with a price of $5 or $6 a pound for tin. The current world market price was around $1 a pound, and if the Bolivian economy could only be sustained with five-dollar tin, it might be wondered why any adviser should waste his time in La Paz. He also suggested naming Juan Lechín as a member of the proposed monetary stabilization council, as a *sine qua non* for its success. [111]

Fortunately for the success of the program, Karasz' views made less impression on President Siles and his advisers than they had on his fellow-Keynesian, President Paz, and, with his departure, this problem was of short duration. The difficulties

*At my first meeting with Karasz, June 7, 1956, I requested figures for note circulation, deposits, the free market rate of exchange, and commodity prices or indices, on the assumption that the Technical Consultant to the Central Bank would have such data at his fingertips. To my amazement, but in consonance with Karasz's monetary theories, he had never assembled such data, but he said that I could compile the material if I thought it of any interest. In contrast to this cavalier attitude toward statistical data, Dr. Franklin Antezana-Paz, the president of the Central Bank, who had been trained in economics at the Sorbonne, showed me a chart, which he had kept up to date personally each week, projecting the future course of note circulation, based on expected credit demands from COMIBOL and the Mining Bank, together with his own estimated projection of foreign exchange rates. He also kept a commodity price index, using an unweighted (but actually falsely weighted because of the disproportionate quantities of the commodities selected), aggregative formula, based on retail prices for various foodstuffs, which he had his assistants compile at the two principal markets patronized by the poorer classes. The index was crude, but I had no time to compile a properly weighted index, using a Laspeyres or similar formula, and it was the only index then compiled by anyone in Bolivia that used actual, prevailing prices in lieu of the unrepresentative official prices. Furthermore, so far as is known, Antezana was the only Bolivian who was sufficiently aware of the relationship between note issue and monetary depreciation to keep a current chart, although Humberto Fossati did recognize the existence of the vicious sequence of government borrowing, note issue, prices, and exchange (*El Diario*, July 26, 1956).

with the U.N. advisers to the CNSS and Finance Ministry, particularly the former, were more prolonged, as is described in previous chapters. Again and again it was learned through Bolivian sources that the contingent of U.N. advisers, working within the various ministries and government enterprises, were responsible for blocking or emasculating the measures approved by the Stabilization Council by their advice to the labor ministers and other enemies of the program.*

The ILO special mission

On January 15, 1957, there arrived in La Paz a mission from the International Labor Office which had been invited by the Bolivian government, at the suggestion of the U.N. mission, for the purpose of studying wage-price relationships in Bolivia. The stabilization plans had barely gotten under way a month previously. The wage increases under that program were necessarily arbitrary, and prices had not yet declined appreciably, so that any third-party investigation at that time would be bound to reveal inequalities, and an adverse report might well wreck the program. The mission was headed by Sir Arthur Tyndall, an engineer by profession, and Judge of the Court of Labor Arbitration in New Zealand since 1940 — one of the pioneers in New Zealand's highly advanced labor legislation, and a world-renowned authority on the subject. He was accompanied

---

*This persistent sabotage led me to suggest to former Assistant Secretary Henry F. Holland that he use his influence to recommend the abandonment of the United Nation's world-wide activities in the social and economic field. Otherwise, the time would come when Congress would learn that the United Nations was engaged in socialist or Marxist indoctrination throughout the world, and would be so incensed at the thought that the United States was subsidizing this activity that they would succumb to the baby-bathwater syndrome, and endanger the irreplaceable functions of the United Nations in the field of international conciliation, together with the constructive activities of the IBRD and IMF. Holland expressed his concurrence as to the danger, but stated that, even when he was in the State Department, the forces favoring the United Nations were too powerful to combat, and that time alone could bring the remedy. A similar written suggestion was sent to John B. Hollister, Director of ICA, but the routines in Washington were such that the reports on the stabilization program in Bolivia never reached the persons to whom they were addressed. In any event, Hollister was summarily relieved of his duties when he announced that, as a matter of policy, the United States would not give aid to government-owned industries, so that it is unlikely that his intervention could have been of help.[112]

by Hubertus Zoeteweij, a highly qualified labor expert from the Netherlands.

Despite the high calibre of these experts, labor problems in New Zealand and old Zeeland were so vastly different from those in Bolivia that I regarded with considerable apprehension the potentialities for damage entailed in the visit of those gentlemen. My qualms were not allayed by the warnings from the British and American Ambassadors that Sir Arthur was loaded with misinformation on Bolivia and unreceptive to any extraneous ideas.

Following an introduction by the British Ambassador, the two experts visited me at home where, in the company of the American Ambassador, an Embassy officer, and Ernest Moore, I outlined at length the Bolivian background, and the plans and problems of the stabilization program, in a conference that lasted from three in the afternoon to seven in the evening, interrupted only by the clink of the ice.

The apprehensions with respect to the ILO mission turned out to be groundless, and the British and American Ambassadors later completely reversed their first impressions. When these visitors departed a month later, following their exhaustive analysis of the Bolivian situation, President Siles informed me that they had left with him, in strict confidence, a most interesting report which he did not intend to release, as no action was needed — the ILO mission had given its unqualified support to the stabilization program, a fact that Sir Arthur confirmed to me in person years later in Cambridge.[113] Thus passed the second threat to the program from the intervention of outside experts.

The ECLA mission

A more serious potential menace to the progress of the stabilization program was the Seventh Plenary Conference of the Economic Commission for Latin America held in La Paz in May and June, 1957. To this conference there came delegates from all countries of the hemisphere, many of them economists of distinction and, above all, Raúl Prebisch, the Secretary General of ECLA, and formerly Director General of the Argentine Central Bank. Prebisch was one of Latin America's most ardent Keynesians, but he was a man of too great experience and wisdom for any direct attack on the stabilization program

to be feared from him. In fact, in his first statement to the
press in Bolivia, he declared:

> Despite all experience to the contrary, the idea continues
> to prevail that a massive increase in wages, beyond the
> limits of national productivity or of reasonable profits, is
> the way to raise the living standards of the masses....
> There is no point in deceiving oneself. Inflation is never
> an instrument of distributive justice, but it can be an in-
> strument to other ends. If the aim is to destroy the eco-
> nomic system, to dislocate its dynamic forces, and to bring
> about contraction and stagnation, then inflation is indeed a
> most effective instrument of social regression.... The
> struggle against inflation calls for enormous moral cour-
> age, a profound and unbreakable conviction, and the spirit
> of self-sacrifice which will discard dangerous and easy
> remedies in favor of the authentic and enduring interests of
> the people. To those brave and farsighted men who have
> undertaken to conquer inflation in Bolivia, I therefore pay
> the spontaneous homage of my admiration and proffer my
> fervent hopes that their action will be understood, and that
> it will in the end prevail and triumph as an illuminating ex-
> ample in which those in other distressed countries may
> find inspiration to proceed, with the same abnegation, along
> the hard road of the struggle against inflation.[114]

The danger lay in Prebisch's dedication to the idea that industrial development must have primacy over agriculture in the
process of economic development; in the fact that his experience had been almost wholly in relatively developed economies
such as that of Argentina; and that he could hardly be expected
to realize how terribly Bolivian agriculture had suffered, and
how artificially industry had been stimulated, during the past
four years of Bolivia's rampant inflation. In fact, in that same
press conference, he did advert to the necessity of developing
Bolivia's industries to absorb the excess employment in the
mines. But the great danger was not so much in Prebisch's
statements, but in those statements that might be made thought-
lessly or inopportunely by any one of the score of younger, less
experienced delegates to the conference, who might lack his
widsom and discretion.

The Finance Minister had had me prepare facts for a
statement to be presented to the ECLA delegates by President
Siles which, in effect, would have constituted a warning that
Bolivia would regard as "an intolerable intervention in its internal affairs" any discussion of the stabilization program by

any international body other than the IMF. With this statement (which happily was never issued), plus the urging of the head of the Planning Commission and of Dr. Siles' other advisers, the President finally authorized publication of my report of April 17, which filled the front pages of the press for five days and more, and thus effectively took the limelight off the ECLA discussions.

It was just as well. Three months earlier, in preparation for the conference, the head of the Planning Commission had brought around to my office two young economists on the ECLA staff who were engaged in writing a preliminary report on the Bolivian economic situation for the use of the delegates. One of those economists, José Antonio Mayobre, a graduate of the London School of Economics and Political Science, proved to be a man of outstanding ability, who later won distinction as Finance Minister of Venezuela.* I made it my business to provide them both with all the material I could assemble as to the background, aims, and progress of the stabilization program. That part of their published report which quite evidently bears the traces of Dr. Mayobre's guiding hand gives a decidedly favorable enumeration of the strides made under the program:

> ...the immediate disappearance of the evils that had their origin in the old system of controls and multiple exchange rates...the illegitimate profits from the distribution of foreign exchange and quotas...the elimination of smuggling ...the virtual disappearance of scarcity...the maintenance of the position of the boliviano with only minor use made of the stabilization fund...the psychological climate created by the disappearance of unjustified privileges, and the honesty and energy with which the program was being applied ...the foreseeable increase in agricultural production as a consequence of the anti-inflationary measures...the disappearance of the queues *(colas)* and of black-marketing, and the return of the peasants to work in the fields.... Basically, stabilization means that the country will have to live within its means, plus U. S. aid...consequently, a diminution in national income which, needless to say, was bound to occur in any event, to the same or even greater extent, with the exhaustion of all the extraordinary resources on which the country had been living during the inflation and which were on the point of exhaustion...[115]

*See biographical sketch, *New York Times,* May 17, 1965, p. 14.

Unfortunately, the report had been completed in April, 1957, when prices and living costs had only begun to fall (8.8 per cent), so that it concluded that the real income of factory workers in La Paz had dropped as a result of the elimination of subsidized prices.[116] Such a statement, had it reached the general public, could have been damaging in the extreme to the stabilization program, and there were other parts of the report — in fact, the greater part of the published volume — that were so theoretical and divorced from reality, with projections based upon statistics of worse than dubious value, that its publication at the time would have been disastrous. Luckily, it was circulated only among the delegates, and in mimeograph (the printed ECLA report was not published until February, 1958, still with the same April, 1957, conclusions and misinformation). It was so voluminous in that preliminary form, and so illegible, that it was easier for the delegates to read the more up-to-date figures in my "Report to the Cabinet" which were appearing daily in the local press.

Consequently, try as they might, the enemies of the stabilization program, and the opposition press, were unable to get a single unfavorable statement from the ECLA conference delegates; and even the Hungarian observer, as the only representative from behind the Iron Curtain, when asked by Prebisch what he thought of communism as it was working out in Bolivia, snorted: "Communism...bah! It's not communism. It's chaos!"

To the contrary, following publication of the final instalment of the report, the press was full of the laudatory remarks of such distinguished conferees as Roberto Oliveira Campos of Brazil, José Antonio Mayobre of Venezuela, Ricardo Tórrez-Gaitán of Mexico, and Raúl Prebisch himself, on the nature and progress of the stabilization program, and particularly with respect to the courage and determination shown by President Siles in inaugurating the program and in having successfully maintained it in the face of all opposition.[117]

20

PROGRESS: THE FIRST YEAR

With this resumé of the perils that confronted the stabilization program during the first year of its enactment in mind, we may turn to an analysis of the material progress witnessed under the new monetary regime.

The Report to the Cabinet — A Summation

My report of April 17 to the President, his Cabinet, and the political leaders of the Revolution, is reproduced in full in Appendix VI, as it constitutes the only complete analysis that had ever been made — up to publication of this volume — of the Bolivian stabilization program, its background, achievements, and problems. Many parts of that report (shown in italics) have never before been published. They are significant in that they reveal precisely what comments were regarded as unsuitable for publication at that time, either because they were too damning of the acts of the Revolutionary Government from 1953 through 1956 or too compromising with respect to the activities of politicians then holding high positions in government.

In reading this report, it should be borne in mind that it must be regarded not merely as a self-serving account of the achievements of the stabilization program by one who was closely associated with its authorship. The talk had been originally prepared for the Stabilization Council and was delivered before an audience of fourteen of Bolivia's leading political figures, all of them thoroughly aware of conditions in Bolivia both before and after stabilization, and three of them politically aligned with the opponents of the program.

It was my task to win the wholehearted support of this group for the program, or at least of the eleven who were not already committed in opposition. If there had been the slightest exaggeration of the program's accomplishments, or slurring over of its shortcomings and of the complaints from various sources, it would have been counterproductive, and the support of the MNR would not have been forthcoming. The questions raised during the course of the address (the answers to which have been incorporated into the published transcript) showed that the audience was following closely the thread of the dissertation. The fact that they thereafter gave their full support to the program proves that the report must be regarded as a frank and true survey of conditions as they appeared in mid-April, 1957, four months after enactment of the stabilization measures, and that it was accepted as such by a highly qualified group of observers, who were right there on the spot — in more ways than one.

Achievements of stabilization

I began by listing the immediate achievements of the program — the "miracles," as Henry Holland had called them a few days previously:

1. The disappearance, "between sunset and sunrise," of the queues of people waiting endlessly in line for bread and other necessities
2. The complete elimination of export smuggling, including that of U.S. aid commodities
3. The elimination of black-marketing
4. The abundance of commodities and merchandise of every kind
5. The continuing drop in commodity prices to 26 per cent below prestabilization levels, *with no price controls*
6. The immediate brake on the downward course of the boliviano, which had remained virtually stable since December 15, 1956, *with no restrictions on the purchase or sale of foreign exchange*
7. The fact that Bolivia, with zero reserves and zero credit, was able to borrow $25 million from the U.S. Treasury and other agencies, with no guaranty other than its solemn promise that it would carry out the stabilization program *which the Bolivian government itself had approved and presented*

Complaints

From achievements, I turned to complaints:

1. The complaints of labor that wages were too low, which I countered by showing that low wages were the result

of extremely low output, caused, chiefly, not by lack of
capital investment in machinery but by the absence of
labor discipline, and strikes, absenteeism, surplus and
idle workers, etc., none of which was the result of stabilization

2. Complaints of declining business, from manufacturers
   and business in general, which I pointed out was chiefly
   attributable to the fact that prestabilization industry and
   commerce had depended largely on raw material imports at absurdly low official exchange rates and that
   industry was finding it difficult to readjust to reality

3. Complaints of credit restrictions, made necessary as a
   temporary measure

4. Justifiable complaints from various sources, which I
   stated would be largely met by measures under consideration or already approved by the Stabilization Council
   but not yet enacted into law by the Cabinet*

Summing up, I made it clear that the majority of the complaints related to transitory problems. To attribute those
difficulties to the stabilization program was much like complaining when the dentist extracts an infected tooth — the extraction may hurt, but the pain should be blamed on the infection
and not on the dentist. The current problems, similarly, were
not because of stabilization but because of the "economic
anarchy" of prior years.

Background and causes of inflation

With that, I embarked on an outline of the background and
causes of Bolivia's inflation, which have been fully set forth in
Chapter 6 except that, by April, 1957, I was able to add later
data on government finance and could outline the obligations
assumed by the Bolivian government in its negotiations with the
lending agencies. To illustrate the fact that Bolivia's troubles
were not attributable to the drop in the price of tin since the
Korean War, I used a chart showing that tin prices for the
years 1952-56 averaged higher than during any other five-year
period in Bolivia's history (a replica of this chart, brought
down through 1965, is given in Figure 13, p. 535).

---

*These complaints were analyzed in detail; see Appendix VI. They
are skimmed over here to avoid repetition.

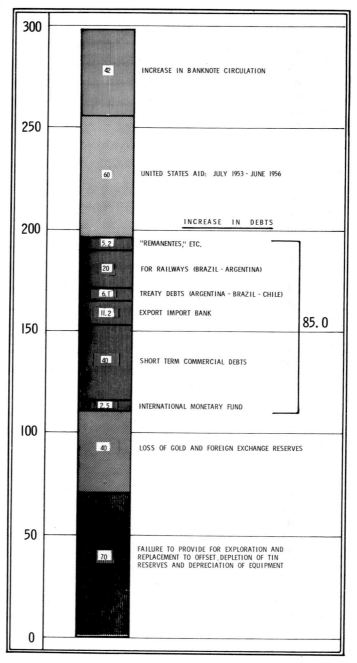

Fig. 8. Consumption of capital: July, 1951 - June, 1956. In millions of dollars. (Source: Central Bank Statistical Department and other sources.)[118]

I then showed Figure 8 to emphasize that Bolivia would have to pull in its belt, not by reason of stabilization, but because the country had been living on its fat over the previous five years, by consuming nearly $300 million in capital assets in excess of its current resources, through: (1) the exhaustion of mines and deterioration of mining machinery with no provision for exploration, blocking out new veins, and depreciation to take care of replacements; (2) the dissipation of Bolivia's entire gold and foreign exchange reserves; (3) the increase of the government's foreign debt; (4) the use of U.S. aid — largely wasted through black-marketing and export smuggling; (5) the increase in bank note issue which, in effect, through the resultant monetary depreciation, represented a capital tax on corporations and citizens largely, squandered by the government. This is what the U.N. report had in mind when it stated that, as a consequence of stabilization, Bolivia would have to live within its means (plus U.S. aid), having exhausted the "extraordinary resources" on which it had lived during the inflationary years.

Deviations from the program

Here I referred to the illegal wage increases and other "concessions to reality" mentioned at pp. 446-58; to the inopportune intervention of the Vice-President in the matter of the foreign bonds, and of the Minister of Mines in the matter of a settlement with the former mineowners (pp. 435, 443); as well as to the continued inflationary pressures since stabilization. These pressures, as set forth in Figure 9, could be calculated at Bs. 47.2 billion, of which Bs. 41.7 billion was attributable to government credits and Bs. 5.7 billion to the private sector. These pressures resulted in a Bs. 25.4 billion expansion in the note issue, plus $2.7 million sales of foreign exchange from the stabilization fund that should have been reflected in a Bs. 20.9 billion reduction in the note issue inasmuch as every sale of foreign exchange had to be paid for by turning over to the Central Bank an equivalent amount of boliviano bank notes. The aggregate inflation was therefore Bs. 46.3 billion, corresponding almost exactly to the inflationary pressures shown in Figure 9.*

*Figure 9 shows inflationary pressures from December 18, 1956 (the first business day following stabilization), to April 13, 1957. The chart used for my oral report also showed the increase in bank note issue from November 17 (when the Bolivian government prepéred the data it pre-

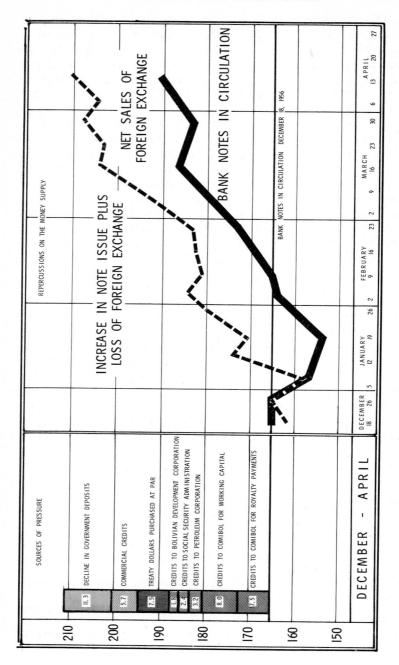

Fig. 9. Inflationary pressures. In millions of bolivianos. (Source: Central Bank.)[119]

I likewise warned of the dangers to the stabilization program, and to the country at large, arising from the failure of the Cabinet to enact the legislative decrees approved by the Stabilization Council — or the emasculation of those measures so that they failed of their purpose — mentioning specifically the new customs tariffs and stamp taxes and the decree providing for the revaluation of assets.

In this portion of the talk, I painted a sombre picture of the progress of the program — far too sombre considering how little remained to be done in comparison with how much had been accomplished. But the council members all felt that the real danger lay not in a radical abandonment of objectives, but in scores of minor deviations, each leading to a further divergence that, in all, might add up to a complete departure from the ultimate goal. Here then was the opportunity to impress the leaders of government with the necessity of adhering strictly to the program, and I took advantage of the occasion.

Solutions

In referring to Bolivia's most pressing problems, I spoke of the necessity of higher wages, and particularly of the need to increase the wages of those, such as the teachers, who had suffered most from inflation.* But any wage increase, I pointed out, would have to be dependent upon increased productivity per worker, freedom of employers to hire and fire, a substantial cut in the excessive social security charges — on this last point, I blazed away with both barrels — and adoption of a three-point program worked out by Point IV to take care of excess miners and others dismissed from their jobs, viz.: (1) lengthening the period of army service to a year and a half; (2) construction

---

sented to the IMF and other lending agencies in support of its request for a stabilization loan) to December 18, 1956, in order to explain to the conferees why the boliviano-dollar crossrate had to be set at Bs. 7,750 on the latter date, instead of at Bs. 7,000 as originally contemplated. Between those two dates, bank note circulation increased $21\frac{1}{2}$ per cent, from Bs. 136 billion to Bs. 165.3 billion.

*In the published version, the President cut out all reference to the teachers whom he regarded as "enemies of the Revolution." The bitterness with which the MNR leaders looked on the teaching profession was shown in June, 1957, when a number of teachers were sent into exile because, in utter desperation, they protested that their salaries were at starvation levels (*Orientación*, June 22, 1957).

work on roads and schools under army supervision, the army
being the only effectively run branch of the government; and (3)
creation of medium-sized farms in vacant valley areas near
the larger cities, but calling a halt to the seizures of private
property under the agrarian reform program. The President
cut out the references to the army in the published speech, but
left in the suggestion that the agrarian reform be brought to a
close, revealing that he did not mind antagonizing Ñuflo Chávez,
the champion of the peasants, but that he was chary of opposing
Juan Lechín, whose armed militia was violently opposed to any
support for the army.

The three-hour dissertation closed with a peroration that
met with the enthusiastic approbation of the audience:

> The future lies in the hands of the Bolivians them-
> selves; and, with the greater productivity resulting from
> human effort, private capital, and the enormous wealth of
> the soil and subsoil, Bolivia can look forward to an era of
> prosperity such as it has never had in its history. This
> does not mean sacrificing the enduring conquests of the
> Revolution — namely, universal suffrage, the distribution of
> the large estates, elimination of a mining empire more
> powerful than the State itself and, now, monetary stabiliza-
> tion — but rather preserving those conquests under a re-
> gime of monetary and financial integrity.*

*I was criticized by one of the most intelligent observers of the
Bolivian scene, a Bolivian newspaper editor, for my laudatory remarks on
the three major "conquests of the Revolution." I neither praised nor
criticized those "conquests," but referred to them as "enduring" (per-
durables), and I would contend that that is the mot juste, as it would be
absurd to think that they could have been reversed in April, 1957 — or
in April, 1967. As a matter of fact, I confess a considerable degree of
sympathy with the objectives of all three conquests, but object to their
methods. Universal suffrage could have been achieved over a generation
through primary education; agrarian reform could have been attained
through suitable tax policies, the distribution of vacant lands, education,
roadbuilding, and Point IV help; and the mines could have been purchased
through negotiation for comparatively little; or, better still, an honest and
capable government could have left the mines to be run by private enterprise without the mines running the government. In any event, the peroration achieved its purpose, evoking the enthusiastic applause and
gratitude of all members of the audience — Revolutionaries all — and the
assurance of their support. Eight years later, the leader of the counter-
Revolutionary coup d'etat, General René Barrientos, referred to these
three achievements as "irreversible conquests of the national reality"
which he promised to "respect and consolidate" (Bolivia [La Paz: Dirección de Informaciones de la Presidencia de la Republica], p. 5).

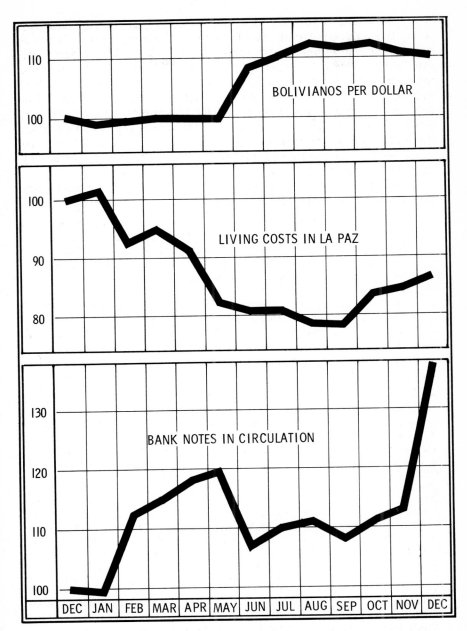

Fig. 10. Foreign exchange rates, living costs, and bank note circulation. December 31, 1956=100. (Source: *International Financial Statistics*.)[120]

Exchange Rates, Prices, and Bank Note Circulation

The proof of the success or failure of the stabilization program, of course, was whether or not it had achieved what it had set out to accomplish. Had it put an end to the precipitous drop in the dollar value of the boliviano and the equally calamitous rise in domestic prices; and had it effectively braked the engine of inflation — bank note circulation — fueled by unrestricted government expenditures?

Judged by these criteria, the program, in its first year, had been a resounding success. In the accompanying chart (Fig. 10) the course of foreign exchange rates, the "cost of living," and bank note circulation, in 1957, is plotted on a uniform scale, using December 31, 1956, as a base.

Exchange rates

For the first five months of stabilization, the foreign exchange rate remained remarkably stable *at below the initial stabilization rate,* with comparatively little use being made of the stabilization fund (less than $3 million net at any time in that period), and subject, for the most part, to the untrammeled forces of supply and demand. In June, however, demagogic attacks on the stabilization program, coincident with the COB congress, and demands for broad wage increases not warranted by increased productivity, caused alarm in business circles as to whether the government would have courage enough to hold the line. Within a week the stabilization fund had lost over a million dollars of its resources, plainly as the result of the withdrawal of public confidence, as there were no basic reasons in the economic situation for any drain of capital. [121]

The Foreign Exchange Committee, which included Dr. Antezana-Paz, President of the Central Bank, and Ernest Moore of the U.S. Financial Mission, was compelled, in order to preserve the stabilization fund, to let the boliviano exchange rate drop from Bs. 7,740 to the dollar to Bs. 8,100 and then to Bs. 8,340, closing the month of June at Bs. 8,375, and continuing to drop through November to Bs. 8,625. By that time, however, the President was convinced, thanks to the firm attitude taken by the council's technical advisers, that the foreign exchange rate was not something that could be manipulated at will. Increased credit restrictions were imposed on the private sector — for, from June through November, the private sector as well as the public sector was responsible for the inflationary pressures.* The exchange rate closed the year at Bs. 8,565.

The government sector had been kept under control by a substantial increase in the availability and use of counterpart funds resulting from a more realistic exchange rate for those transactions, by rigid economies, more rigorous methods of tax collection, and higher prices for the products of the government petroleum corporation. Thus, by the end of November, 1957, the government had increased its net borrowing from the banking system by only 1.7 per cent (Bs. 19.5 billion) over June 30, while the private sector could be blamed for a 13.1 per cent increase (Bs. 11.7 billion).[122] This picture changed radically in December (see pp. 501-502, under "Bank note circulation").

It has been hinted above that the exchange rate was not at all times governed solely by the forces of demand and supply. Each morning the Foreign Exchange Committee would meet in the Central Bank to determine, on the basis of receipts of foreign exchange from the country's exports and demands for exchange from importers and others, the rates at which the Central Bank should be willing to buy and sell dollars and other currencies, always bearing in mind the overriding necessity of protecting the assets of the stabilization fund. In other words, they might allow the fund to be used to smooth over temporary fluctuations in supply and demand, but they could not permit it to be dissipated in an attempt to maintain the boliviano at an artificially high level; nor, on the other hand, would they wish to deter essential imports and restrict economic development by unduly adding to the fund through keeping the boliviano low when basic supply-demand forces tended to push it higher.

During the first weeks of stabilization, as we had expected, there was a strong demand for dollars and, by February 2, the net drawings on the stabilization fund (i.e., Central Bank drawings, less remaining reserves on deposit in the Federal Reserve Bank of New York) amounted to $2.7 million, the high point up to that time, and certainly no cause for alarm. During

*It is probable that the increase in the use of private credit, and in bank loans to the private sector, was attributable to desperate attempts by industry to resuscitate businesses that were basically uneconomical, to equally desperate attempts to raise money for taxes, particularly the social security taxes, and to even more desperate attempts to salvage what remained of their business by getting money out of the country in anticipation of a further debasement of the boliviano as a consequence of political pressures.

the next few weeks the demand for dollars slackened. The public simply had no more bolivianos with which to buy dollars, and we had purposely clamped down on bank credits. The supply of dollars from exports proved adequate, public confidence in the success of the stabilization program rose, and by February 23 the net drawings on the stabilization fund had dropped to $1.4 billion. The boliviano was quoted at Bs. 7,500, compared with our initial stabilization rate of between Bs. 7,745 and Bs. 7,750, and Dr. Siles and the public at large regarded the Bs. 7,500 rate as a triumph. This was the proof of the program, and, if there had been no subsequent deviations, we would never have had to use more than perhaps $2 million of the stabilization fund.

And then one morning I arrived at the Central Bank from my second office in the Embassy to find my colleague, Ernest Moore, the picture of gloom. The foreign exchange demand logically called for a slight dropping of the rate. Then, too, Moore, an old hand in such matters, wished to keep the speculators in exchange in a constant state of uncertainty so that they could never bank with any assurance on continuity in the upward or downward trends. However, Dr. Antezana, the president of the bank, had informed the Foreign Exchange Committee that they would not be allowed to move the rate to Bs. 7,525, inasmuch as President Siles had given categorical instructions that the rate must not again go above Bs. 7,500. I marched into Dr. Antezana's office with Moore and stated that there must be no political interference with the free movement of exchange rates. That was one of the postulates of the stabilization program; and, if the rate were not permitted to fluctuate, I would so cable the ICA, and that would probably be the end of the stabilization fund. Dr. Antezana, in our presence, phoned President Siles, and the rate was set at Bs. 7,525.

But a month later, with steady pressure on the boliviano, owing chiefly to rumors put in motion by a joint COMIBOL and Ford, Bacon & Davis report that the dollar rate would have to be increased (see pp. 373-77), one of the Foreign Exchange Committee members reported that the rate would have to be changed to Bs. 7,800, to prevent a further drain on the stabilization fund. President Siles was firm — the rate must not be allowed to rise, because it would have adverse political repercussions. Dr. Antezana proposed a compromise at Bs. 7,750, and I suggested a maximum of Bs. 7,780, anything below the Bs. 7,800 level in order not to add fuel to the FBD-COMIBOL rumors of further devaluation. But the President was adamant, and the rate was kept artificially at an unrealistic Bs. 7,725 for two months while the stabilization fund's resources continued to dwindle. By April 13, net drawings had again reached $2.7 million.

With reiterated warnings by the council's technical advisers, and publication of my report in May, the Foreign Exchange Committee was once again given a short-lived freedom to let the exchange rate fluctuate with supply and demand. It is fortunate that this was the case, even though it proved a transient victory, as this permitted the rate to rise in June, 1957, when the demand for dollars motivated by Lechín's attack on the stabilization program again threatened the program. Otherwise, the stabilization fund would have been immediately depleted, with a "bargain" rate of Bs. 7,740 available for speculation and the flight of capital.

Freedom, however, proved a tender plant, not easily nurtured on Bolivian soil. In the single month of December, 1957, when the Bolivian government started the monetary printing press rolling again (see Fig. 10) and President Siles refused to allow the exchange rate to rise above Bs. 8,600 to the dollar, the fund lost a further $6 million. At the year-end, drawings on the $25 million fund amounted to $4 million of IMF funds (of which $3 million had been drawn in 1956) and $8,440,000 of ICA funds — more money down the drain simply because no one in Washington or La Paz chose to say no.[123]

If this drain on the stabilization fund had been caused by the private sector, it would have meant a commensurate drop in bank note circulation, as credits to the private sector were strictly circumscribed. Thus, the loss would have been almost immediately corrected. But it was caused exclusively by government borrowing from the Central Bank and was hence reflected by an increase in bank note circulation instead of a decrease (see Fig. 10 and comment at p. 501).

Prices

As may be seen from Figure 10, following a temporary rise in living costs in January, 1957, immediately after stabilization,* the competitive forces under the new free market

*As early as the last week in January, however, the press began to comment on the drop in prices, e.g., *La Nación*, January 22, 1947. By April, and certainly by June, there was no doubt of the downward trend, e.g., *La Nación*, April 12; June 4, 7, 14, 16, 17, 30; July 3, 1957.

economy carried prices and living costs down steadily through
the third quarter of the year, to a low of 78 in August and September. They rose in the final quarter as a consequence of
disguised wage increases and higher quotations for foreign exchange, beginning in June (the December wage increases were
not reflected in living costs until the following year).

The living cost index finished 1957 at nearly 14 per cent
below the December 31, 1956, base. Commodity prices for
articles of prime necessity dropped even more sharply than living costs, to an estimated index of 70 at the end of May when the
aggregate living cost index stood at 82.1.[124] Prices for meat,
corn, potatoes, rice, sugar, wheat, and flour in La Paz and in
eight other principal market centers all declined, the drop being
attributed by the Ministry of Agriculture to increased domestic
production as a consequence of the stabilization measures.[125]

It will be recalled that, at the time of computing the necessary allowances for the loss of subsidized commissary privileges and other increased living costs expected to result from
enactment of the stabilization program, a table had been prepared based on estimated expenditures of factory workers in
La Paz, divided between their purchases in the commissaries
and in the free or black market (Table 5, p. 189). The assumption naturally was that the post-stabilization free market prices
would be substantially higher than the subsidized prices, but
lower than the black-market prices. In all, it was estimated
that stabilization would mean an increase in daily expenditures,
based on a list of nine major commodities, of Bs. 1,768 per
diem. On that basis, rounded off, factory workers were granted
an increase in pay of Bs. 1,750. In June, 1957, a recomputation
was prepared on the basis of actual current prices in the free
markets of La Paz, using the same quantities of commodities
used in the original computation, and arriving at the conclusion
that the actual increase in costs was only Bs. 1,349 per diem.
Furthermore, taking not just the nine major commodities, but a
list of the eighteen major commodities and services that went
into the workingman's family budget, it was found that the actual
increase in living costs was only Bs. 1,226 per diem, meaning
a clear gain of over Bs. 500 a day for the factory workers
following stabilization, and disregarding the wage increases
in 1957.[126]

Later, official index numbers were published for living
costs and for wages on a nationwide basis, comparing the full
year 1956 with the full year 1957. These showed that living

costs had dropped 13.8 per cent, while wages had increased 97.5 per cent, a gain in terms of real wages of nearly 130 per cent as a consequence of the stabilization measures. The Central Bank reported that "after twenty five years of continuous price rises . . . the cost of living index in La Paz dropped from 470 in January, 1957 to 401 in December." The bank attributed the drop to greater quantities of merchandise available to the public as a consequence of the stabilization program.[127]

None of the index series referred to in the three preceding paragraphs can be accepted without some reservations, but they are sufficiently indicative of general trends to give the lie to the politicians and labor leaders who claimed that the lot of the workingmen had deteriorated as a result of stabilization.

Bank note circulation

The rise in bank note circulation from the end of December, 1956, (Bs. 160.0 billion) to the end of May, 1957, (Bs. 191.9 billion) was a consequence of the credits extended to COMIBOL, the National Social Security Fund, and other government agencies (p. 738, n *120*). The sharp drop from that peak to Bs. 170.4 billion at the end of June is explained by the flight of capital as a result of fears as to the future course of stabilization, engendered by Lechín's inflammatory speech at the COB congress (p. 467).*

*Occasionally, as in this instance, it is possible to trace capital flight to some specific cause, and even to assign a figure to the amount of flight, in this case, possibly, some Bs. 21.5 billion ($2.5 million), if one may judge by the drop in circulation. What total capital flight at any time may amount to, however, whether in Bolivia or elsewhere, is a will-of-the-wisp that has eluded the most dedicated search by economists, central bank and government officials, and others. For what it may be worth, Sr. Forgués, Assistant Manager of the Banco Industrial y Commercial, in testimony before the council in February, 1957, placed the capital flight of Bolivians in exile (presumably since 1953) at $10 million, and of Bolivians still resident in the country at $5 million. On the other hand, *Orientación* June 22, 1957, states that the Central Bank, during the Paz-Estenssoro regime, loaned Bs. 1.6 billion to political and labor leaders of the MNR and COB (which appears to be true), and that those leaders had $80 million on deposit outside of Bolivia (which can only be a guess). President Siles stated that one party member alone got Bs. 80 million from the Central Bank (*Última Hora*, June 26, 1957). The $80 million capital flight by political leaders would appear exaggerated, as this is approximately equal to the total of U. S. cash and commodity grants up to that time. Conservatively, up to 30 per cent of this, plus an equal percentage of govern-

Note issue kept fairly constant from then until December, when deficits in the public sector gave rise to increased borrowing from the Central Bank, in part because of wage adjustments and in part because of renewed spending and borrowing by COMIBOL and other government enterprises and agencies.[128] In all, the increases during the course of 1957 raised wages by 27.5 per cent above the level at the beginning of the stabilization program. The government sector was by far the largest employer in the nation, so that any wage increase immediately put into motion the Central Bank inflationary machinery which ground out a further Bs. 39.7 billion of bank notes — an increase of 22 per cent in the course of a single month during which government debt increased by Bs. 98.8 billion (33 per cent).*

---

mental purchases, may have passed into political hands, which would mean some $50 million from 1951 through 1956. It is doubtful whether more than a fraction of this amount would have been deposited abroad, but all such figures are, of course, purely conjectural. The president of the Central Bank placed capital flight immediately prior to stabilization at $28 million, and this must be accepted as the most informed estimate that was reported to the council.

*Bank note circulation is used in Figure 10, rather than total money supply, in order to be consistent with Figures 3, 4, and 5 in Chapter 6, where, as explained in that chapter, the addition of demand deposits to note issue proved to be a source of confusion (p. 110). Over the short term, the trend is practically identical. For the longer trend, as in Figures 1 and 15 (pp. 42, 588), the total money supply is shown.

Perhaps, however, in a simple economy such as that of Bolivia, the bank note issue alone may be the best guide, just as in a more complex economy one may well question whether note issue plus demand deposits is a sufficient index of the money supply, or whether one should add savings bank and savings and loan deposits, certificates of deposit, brokers' accounts, discounted commercial paper, Treasury bills, and other forms of quasi-money to the money formula. It may be noted that Friedman and Schwartz, in their monumental study (Milton Friedman and Anna Jacobson Schwartz, *A Monetary History of the United States, 1867-1960* [Princeton, N.J.: Princeton University Press, 1963]), lump savings and checking deposits in commercial banks in their figure for money supply, yet omit deposits in savings banks and savings and loan associations, for the simple reason that the commercial bank deposits were not segregated prior to 1914. Notwithstanding this omission, they conclude that this inconsistency does not impair the utility or relevance of their money supply series. If that is true, then certainly there can be no objection to using a single consistent series of bank note circulation to represent the trend of the money supply in Bolivia.

Economic Development — The First Year

Figures for national income, GNP, etc. are perhaps the least reliable of all statistics in the less developed countries. Nevertheless, where marked changes do occur between one year and the next, they may give an indication of basic trends; so, for what they may be worth, figures for gross domestic product for 1956 and 1957, before and after stabilization, are shown in Table 13, and, as a basis of comparison with pre-Revolutionary days, for 1952. The figures are in millions of U.S. 1958 dollars.

TABLE 13

Gross Domestic Product*
(In Millions of 1958 U.S. Dollars)

Sector	1952	1956	1957
Agriculture	113.1	104.2	110.7
Mining	58.3	46.1	47.4
Petroleum	2.1	13.1	14.7
Manufacturing	49.0	51.4	36.0
Commerce	45.1	43.7	45.3
Transportation	23.9	29.7	27.1
Government	55.0	26.0	20.7
Other services	34.3	35.9	36.2
Miscellaneous	7.0	4.7	4.8
Total	387.8	354.8	342.9

*Taken from Table 1, "Bolivian 10-Year Development Plan: 1962-71," published in *Planeamiento* (La Paz: Junta Nacional de Planeamiento, September, 1961), the organ of the National Planning Board, Juan Lechín-Oquendo, President (this was formerly the National Planning and Coordination Commission, which was under the presidency of President Siles but administered by Miguel Gisbert-Nogué, Executive Vice-President). The "10-Year Plan" is a 288-page pamphlet, prepared with the assistance of the U.N. Advisory Mission, including advisers from ECLA and FAO. The increase in agricultural production registered in 1957 is undoubtedly underestimated (see p. 509n). If farm consumption could have been more closely estimated the aggregate GDP would undoubtedly show a substantial rise in 1957 compared with 1956.

The only sectors of the economy unmistakably operating on a lower level in 1957, as a consequence of the 1956 stabilization measures, were manufacturing and government, the latter because the balanced budget, insisted upon as one of the postulates

of stabilization, forced the government to pull in its belt as it
had never before been compelled to do. The comparison with
pre-Revolutionary days is particularly worthy of note. Despite
the fact that the government had greatly expanded its purely
governmental activities since 1953, the expansion was chiefly
in government-owned enterprises and in the disastrous attempts
at economic development. The civil service itself had approximately doubled in the number of personnel (despite the practical
elimination of the army), but the debasement of the boliviano
under the MNR regime had cut salaries to starvation levels
(this is not hyperbole), and the total payroll was less than half
that of 1952, *in terms of dollars of stable purchasing power.**

In all, gross domestic product dropped $11.9 million (3.35
per cent) from 1956 to 1957, according to Table 13, the difference being in reality too small to be statistically measurable.
The insignificance of the decline is the more noteworthy when it
is recalled that the "Report to the Cabinet" pointed out that
Bolivia had been living in excess of its own resources over the
preceding five years, at the rate of some $60 million a year
(see Appendix VI), meaning that — allowing for $20 million a
year in continuing U.S. aid — the nation's expenditures would
have to be reduced by some $40 million a year. The report
concluded, however, that the effect on the general economy
would not be as grave as might be gathered from that figure, as
the bulk of the capital expenditures had consisted of foreign
purchases (almost entirely by the government), and the elimination of such expenditures would not greatly affect local wages
or the domestic economy. This prediction, fortunately, proved
to be true, as there is no doubt that the consumption of capital
in excess of resources, shown in Figure 8 (p. 490), ceased with
stabilization, yet GDP dropped less than $12 million, if that.

Mining

The volume of mineral production was maintained in 1957
at practically the same levels as in 1956, in spite of continuing

---

*There is, of course, a fallacy in measuring the value of one country's
production in terms of the "stabilized" currency of another country. But
at least this approach removed changes in the purchasing power of the
dollar (although for U.S. production, not Bolivian) and was probably better
than any other available yardstick. Volume figures are even more misleading, as tin ore (production down) and gold (production up) can scarcely
be weighed in the same scale.

labor agitation and the increasing interference with production
by the labor commissars in COMIBOL. But production and exports were maintained only by milling current stocks of ore,
and exhausting easily assessible veins, in a desperate effort to
keep up production in the face of labor difficulties, thus continuing the process of depletion of Bolivia's mineral resources
that, under government management, has left the confiscated
mines only an empty shell compared to what they were under
private management.[129] The consequences were seen in the
production figures for the following year — $32.7 million com-
pared with $47.4 million in 1957, and with $58.3 million in 1952,
all in constant dollars.[130]

At midyear, President Siles attempted to bolster declining
production by an appeal to the conscience and patriotism of the
miners and labor leaders, pointing out that total mineral production for the first six months of the year had reached only
24,925 tons, compared with 31,235 tons in the first half of 1956,
and that, if the miners had done their share, the boliviano could
have been maintained at Bs. 7,000-Bs. 7,500 to the dollar and
the stabilization fund could have been kept intact.[131] The appeal
was in vain.

On my return to the United States, I got into touch with ten
of the leading mining corporations in the United States in the
attempt to interest them in investigating mining possibilities in
Bolivia in the light of the strides made under the stabilization
program. They were interested in the progress of stabilization,
but had no interest in capital investment in Bolivia for the time
being, because of labor anarchy, political instability, and the
predominating influence of Juan Lechín, of whose activities they
were all well aware.[132] So that appeal too was in vain.

USOM/Bolivia attempted to persuade the government to
publish the Ford, Bacon & Davis report, in the thought that the
force of public opinion might compel COMIBOL and the government to carry out the FBD recommendations and thus bolster
declining production. But the report was too damning of mining
operations under the MNR regime for labor to permit its release, despite considerable pressure from more responsible
quarters.[133] So there again, the appeal was in vain.

Petroleum

Petroleum production was the only area in which any substantial gains were made over the pre-Revolutionary period,

and both production and prospects looked brighter in 1957 than they had at any previous time. Production of crude rose from 508,080 cubic meters in 1956 to 568,426 in 1957, while exports of crude and derivatives rose from 121,867 to 197,637 cubic meters.[134] The exports, however, were almost entirely to Argentina, and hence payable in treaty dollars, so that this trade must be looked upon as a subtraction from the nation's wealth rather than as a source of income.

On the other hand, in the private sector, world-wide interest in Bolivian petroleum was encouraging, thanks to enactment of the Petroleum Code and prospects for economic progress under the stabilization program. This interest may be gauged by the fact that, in January, 1957, the representatives of nine major oil companies and suppliers, and of five lesser companies, were present in La Paz, including Gulf Oil Corporation, Texas Company, Richfield Oil Corporation, Socony Mobil Oil Company, Shell Oil Company, Andes Oil Company (a subsidiary of Pure Oil Company), Teikoku Oil Company, and Williams Bros. Company.[135]

Manufacturing and trade

The one section of the economy that bore the full brunt of the readjustments inevitable under stabilization was manufacturing. Production in the manufacturing industries dropped, according to the GDP figures, from $51.4 million in 1956 to $36 million in 1957 (both figures in terms of 1958 dollars), and there could be no prospect of early recovery. In January, a delegation from the National Manufacturers Association conferred with me at length to discuss their problems, and later, at my request, embodied their remarks in a formal memorandum. Sales in the cotton textile industry had fallen off some 90 to 96 per cent, and in the wool textile field around 80 per cent, compared with the period immediately preceding stabilization.

As a solution to their problems, the manufacturers proposed that the government let down the bars on bank credits, impose higher protective tariffs, and grant financial facilities for obtaining new machinery and "rationalizing" production. As the conferees expounded their views, however, the true reason for their distress became only too glaringly apparent. One of the leading textile firms, for example, had formerly imported $615,000 of raw materials each quarter, which cost it Bs. 612

million, say $60,000 (this included all tariffs and other charges).
Under stabilization, and the December 15, 1956, tariffs, the
same dollar value of raw materials would cost Bs. 4,734 million, say $630,000. Two other firms were even worse off, so
far as increased costs were concerned.

What could the Stabilization Council — or any workable stabilization program — do to remedy a situation like that? The
large volume of Bolivia's prestabilization textile sales was attributable to raw material purchases (U.S. aid and other) at Bs.
190 to the dollar, when the real rate of exchange in 1956 averaged some Bs. 4,000 to the dollar and ran as high as Bs. 14,000.
Thus, prior to stabilization, despite the difficulties of operation
under chaotic labor conditions and constantly changing government controls, the Bolivian mills were able to export at a profit
to Peru and Chile, in competition with the much larger and
more efficient Peruvian and Chilean mills. It was estimated
that at least 50 per cent of the Bolivian output was smuggled
into those countries.[136]

The manufacturers recognized that as a fact but, so far as
domestic sales were concerned, they were convinced that the
drop in sales was due to the diminished purchasing power of the
laboring classes. As has been seen, however, the purchasing
power of wage earners had actually been increased by stabilization. What had occurred, quite simply, was that, when textiles were practically given away as a result of raw material
imports at a fraction of their real value, Bolivian workers had
been able to buy in practically unlimited quantities, and when,
as a result of stabilization and a return to reality, textiles had
to be sold at their true cost, the workers could no longer afford to buy in such quantity and refused to pay the market
price.

For the council to authorize bank credit to finance industries that had expanded beyond the needs of the market, and
were clearly uneconomic, would have been to act against the
true interests of the manufacturers themselves and would have
drained the stabilization fund dry through the inevitable diversion of part of these credits to the flight of capital.

The manufacturers did, however, have real cause for complaint in the matter of the December, 1956, customs duties, and
the Stabilization Council did all it could to accelerate enactment
of a new tariff schedule. The industrialists could also justly
complain of excessive social security costs and of the fact that
they were not permitted to dismiss excess and idle personnel

(they did not dare mention such touchy subjects in their formal memorandum although they expatiated on them at length in discussion).*

But, on the whole, there was little that could be done to succor the textile industry, and some industries were in even worse condition (such as the bottle factory referred to at p. 325n). In all justice, it must be said that the manufacturers, although the hardest hit of any part of the private sector, loyally supported the stabilization program from its inception, preferring, as they said again and again, to suffer the immediate hardship, in the hope of an eventual return to reality and, above all, to morality. To skeptics who refuse to believe that morality plays a significant part in business thinking, let it be said that businessmen in Bolivia were fed up to the teeth with the graft and extortion of the preceding four years, which exceeded anything in prior Bolivian experience.

Domestic retail trade fell for the same reasons that affected domestic manufacturing, as well as because consumer products could no longer be brought into the country at fictitious rates of exchange. Trade in foodstuffs shifted from the black market to the free market, and undoubtedly expanded with the revival of agriculture (see below). Imports fell from $84 million in 1956 to $70 million in 1957 — a healthy sign, as this represented largely the elimination of imports of manufactured goods and raw materials at artificial prices that had done so much to wreck the Bolivian economy. Exports, other than minerals (minerals are referred to above at pp. 504-505), fell from $81.3 million to $66 million, as a consequence of the elimination of such artificial exports as textiles, and operations such as that of the Brazil nut industry described at pp. 359-60.[137]

Agriculture

As manufacturing was the hardest hit sector of the economy, following stabilization, so agriculture was undoubtedly that sector most immediately benefited, as I had predicted when I

_____

*These views as to the uneconomic nature of most of Bolivia's inflation-built industries were shared by one of the left-wing MNR labor ministers; but, of course, the minister did not go into labor's responsibility for the plight of industry (see Alfredo Franco-Guachalla, *En Torno a la Cuestión Social* [La Paz: Ministry of Labor, n.d.], pp. 74 ff, cited by Guillermo Alborta-Velasco, *El Flágelo de la Inflación Monetaria en Bolivia, País Monoproductor* [Madrid: Ed. Románica, 1963], pp. 384-88).

first outlined the basic principles proposed for the stabilization program. The GDP figures in Table 13 show a 6.2 per cent gain in agricultural production, from $104.2 million in 1956 to $110.7 million in 1957, and this figure was destined to grow steadily in the succeeding years (see p. 529).*

To ensure an abundance of farm crops in the spring and summer of 1957, Ross Moore, head of USOM/Bolivia, had enlisted the cooperation of the Point IV experts in the agricultural *Servicio,* as early as September, 1956, to spread the good word: Stabilization would be coming before the end of the year, and when it came there would be no more subsidized imports of farm products, under U.S. aid or otherwise, to compete with the Bolivian farmer. To the contrary, the farmers could count on selling all they could possibly produce, and at fair and remunerative prices. So strong was the confidence of the Bolivian peasants in these expert and hard-working "county agents" that, by the year-end, the *Servicio* was able to report that ploughing, planting, and fertilizer use were on a greater scale than at any time since the Revolution.

In January, 1957, President Siles reported to the Council that the advent of stabilization and the end of the sinecure of earning a living by waiting in line or smuggling, coupled with the decline in manufacturing and trade, had sent many peasants back to earning a living on the farms. This report was confirmed by the Point IV experts, as well as by the published report of the U.N. Economic Commission for Latin America, which likewise attributes increased agricultural planting and production to the stabilization measures.[138] By the following spring, from La Paz to Cochabamba, the arid areas of the altiplano, with the help of good growing weather, took on a look of verdure such as had not been seen in years.†

---

*The gain was grossly underestimated, probably owing to the difficulty of estimating production consumed on the farms. According to President Siles, 1957 crops were 58 per cent above the 1956 level (*La Nación* June 14, 1957), and this was borne out by reports from the Point IV agents (*El Diario,* June 5, 1957).

†The fulfillment of the prognostications as to the favorable effect of stabilization on farm prices and sales, relayed to the peasants by the Point IV agents, had its useful repercussions the following spring when the head of the agricultural *Servicio* stated that farmers were asking him whether or not to plant increased acreage of sugar cane to supply the needs of the government mill at Guabirá. Our favorable reply resulted in nearly doubling plantings in May-June, 1957, with a corresponding increase in the 1958 cane crop (Letter from Ross Moore, April 8, 1957, relaying inquiry from Elton Smith, head of the *Servicio*).

Progress and Poverty — A Consensus

From the foregoing outline, it is clear that much financial and economic progress was made during the first year under the stabilization program. It is equally clear that in Bolivia, more than in most countries, the poor always ye have with you, and that, in any country, no mumbo-jumbo of government proclamations, laws, and decrees can add one scrap of meat to the poor man's pot — poverty can only be alleviated by hard work, thrift, and investment, by greater productivity and increased abundance for all to share.

Monetary stabilization had done its part — less than might have been hoped, more, perhaps, than might have been expected. Whether or not, over the long run, it could and would be maintained depended largely upon public opinion — what did the public at large think of the stabilization program? Had stabilization made enough of an impression for the public to support it through years of adversity, rather than be inveigled by demagogic promises of higher wages and government handouts?

The polls

Despite their shortcomings, the polls taken by the Bolivian Institute of Public Opinion Polls throughout the first half of 1957 give perhaps as close an approximation as any to the shifts in public opinion on the stabilization program (see p. 303n for background of the institute). The initial poll, taken principally to test techniques, covered 274 persons. A second poll, the largest taken, covered 5,000 persons. As a result of comparisons of results by classes, occupations, and so forth, it was decided that future polls could safely be held down to between 100 and 300 people, depending upon whether a general survey was made, or merely a survey of one particular occupational group. The composition of the "universe" polled varied from poll to poll, as did also the questions asked, depending upon the judgment of the institute as to the public interest at the particular time. Hence, it is impossible to chart the trend of replies by question, or by economic classes. The line graph shown in Figure 11 does, however, show the changing consensus of public opinion in general with respect to the program as a whole.

It will be noted that the shifts in public opinion follow closely the tide of political events catalogued at pages 458-73,

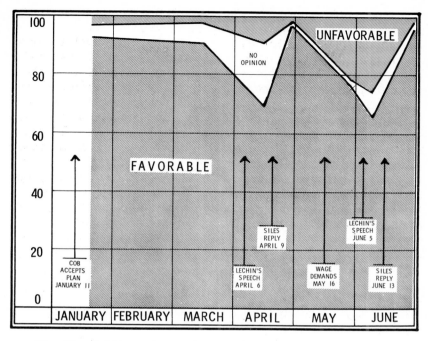

Fig. 11. Public opinion on the stabilization program. In percentages. (Source: Instituto Boliviano de Encuestas de Opinión
Pública.)[139]

each crisis and each speech attacking or supporting the program being reflected in public sentiment pro or con. This was
natural, as the polls gave greatest weight, as was proper, to the
working classes at the lowest level, and the sentiments of Bolivia's workers are volatile in the extreme, varying from the
shouts of *"Muera Eder!"* to those of *"Viva la Estabilización!"*
and *"Muera Lechín!"* as the passions of the mob were swayed
from day to day in one direction or the other.*

*No poll was taken following publication of the "Report to the Cabinet"
(May 25-30), until after the violent attacks by Lechín and the COB. The
director of the institute stated, however, that reports from his poll-takers
showed a decided reversal in favor of the program as a consequence of
that report. Before the poll could be completed, Lechín's attack sent the
program's popularity down to its lowest ebb, as shown on the chart. However, this shift is exaggerated, as that particular poll was taken exclusively among the delegates to the COB congress and not from the country
at large. Thus, the 65 per cent support for the program, in that group,
may be regarded as a favorable omen rather than otherwise.

The polls represent, in general, urban opinion among laborers, white-collar workers, government employees, businessmen, etc., weighted according to their proportions in the population. In only one poll is peasant opinion registered (78 per cent in favor), and this poll was taken among delegates to the COB congress in June, 1957, so that it represents the opinions of peasant leaders under the banner of Ñuflo Chávez, rather than the opinion of the peasants themselves. Probably peasant opinion must be gauged, if it can be measured at all, by the indisputable fact that the peasants returned to the land as a consequence of the stabilization program and that, in the course of time, they produced more than they ever had produced before and received a higher return for their efforts, in terms of stable dollars, than they had ever before attained, at least back to the time of the Inca Empire.

The press

The communist press was the first to note "a return to morality" as a consequence of the stabilization program, after "four years of immorality in the public administration," but it was not long before the two communist papers attacked me personally as "an unrealistic theorist," and the plan as one "imposed by Yankee imperialism." In the end, I was castigated for failing to divulge the names of the culprits among the politicians and labor leaders responsible for the immorality and profligacy in government.[140]

Of the three papers that might perhaps be referred to as representing the serious element of the press, *El Diario* characterized the stabilization program as "the only road"; *Última Hora* eulogized the "Report to the Nation" and called the stabilization program a "return to reality," the "only route in sight"; while *La Nación* editorialized:[141]

Every problem of the supply of articles of prime necessity has thus far been solved almost immediately and without interruption, while prices have maintained a downward trend as a consequence of free competition. The currency has kept a constant value which makes it possible to prepare budgets and long-term economic plans of every kind. Commercial credit has been fully re-established, with obvious benefits for the entire population. Confidence has been restored in every sector of the economy, and Bolivia has become one of the most attractive countries in the world for private investment, not only by reason of its natural resources but because of the seriousness with which the government has undertaken its program of economic rehabilitation. All these factors, of which the working classes are fully aware, have meant that, in this difficult hour that the country is passing through, the nation has maintained a firm and hopeful faith in a better future, even at the cost of the inevitable immediate sacrifice.

Other comments

In the President's address to Congress, as reported in *Time* magazine and the *New York Times,* he stated that the "economic stabilization program adopted by his government and based on the recommendations of a United States economist, George J. Eder, had saved the country from disaster."[142]

Outside of government circles, business opinion is expressed by the following excerpts from a letter from the Bolivian National Chamber of Commerce:[143]

At the conclusion of your mission to Bolivia, the National Chamber of Commerce wishes to express the feeling of special sympathy with which it has followed the course of your difficult task in the National Monetary Stabilization Council...

Bolivian business congratulates you on your inflexible and honest advice to the council, and thanks you for all you have been able to accomplish in that body in initiating measures that will contribute to the stabilization of the currency and the strengthening of the national economy...

On the other hand, Professor Robert Alexander, who has made a number of trips to Bolivia, and who attended a meeting of the COB in July, 1957, as "a temporary employee" of ICA, reports considerable criticism of the stabilization program by the "ex-Trotskyites" and Trotskyites whom he interviewed at that meeting, as well as by the manager of the Bolivian Development Corporation and others whose operations were curtailed as a result of stabilization. He reports that the program "put an end to some of the worst forms of corruption in the MNR regime," and comments that "Eder did not make himself popular," but adds:

It is doubtful, however, if even a more tactful man could have defended the stabilization program without incurring some enmity from groups which felt their interests harmed

by it. The measures taken in December, 1956, were Draconian and could not help but cause discontent in some
quarters.[144]

And this about sums it up. There was certainly an important and well-organized sector of Bolivian public opinion
violently opposed to the stabilization measures and probably an
even larger sector that would have liked to see the measures
modified in one respect or another, in some cases without com-
prehending why no fundamental change could be made without
wrecking the program. It is to that sector, largely, that this
book is addressed. But perhaps Dr. Walter Guevara-Arze, the
first Foreign Minister of the Revolutionary Government and one
of the ablest members of the MNR, best expressed the general
feeling at the close of 1957 when he stated: "It would be idle to
refer to the desirability of stabilization since not only does
there appear to be complete unanimity of opinion with respect
to it, but there is no alternative to it."[145]

Foreign opinion

Foreign financial opinion as to the success of the stabilization program was uniformly favorable. Reference has already been made to the commentaries of the ECLA conferees.
The reviews of the First National City Bank of New York and of
the Guaranty Trust Company carried laudatory comments, the
former being reprinted at length in the Bolivian press and the
latter giving the following summation of the results of the
year:[146]

> Before the stabilization program, Bolivia suffered from the
> worst inflation in Latin America. . . . A National Monetary
> Stabilization Council headed by a United States economist
> was appointed, and its recommendations became the Na-
> tional Stabilization Program in December, 1956. . . . Most
> important of all, the root cause of Bolivia's inflation,
> namely, government borrowing from the central bank, was
> resolutely attacked with a policy of balancing the budget at
> whatever political cost.
>
> The program has been a resounding success. . . . No longer
> discouraged by price controls which made production unre-
> munerative, and by competing food imported at unrealistic
> exchange rates, farmers have been increasing their pro-
> duction dramatically. With the elimination of price con-
> trols, the incentive to smuggle food out of the country also

disappeared, and the greater supply of food on the home market has meant a big import saving...

At the end of last year the Bolivian Congress expressed its faith in the government's difficult reform program by approving a one-year extension of the President's emergency economy powers for carrying out the stabilization plan.

Summation

In short, public opinion at home and abroad testified to the success of the stabilization program. And yet, more realistically, it should have been evident to anyone in full possession of the facts that the program had failed of its purpose. The government still refused to recognize that monetary stabilization cannot, over the long run, be artificially maintained; that currency stability without progress is meaningless; and that, in Bolivia at least, economic progress cannot be achieved through government planning and control. The premonitions of ultimate disaster, as the year 1957 drew to a close, have been reinforced by the events of succeeding years as related in the final section of this volume. This is true even though the Bolivian currency has remained stable for close to a decade and, by that standard alone, the stabilization program has proved to be an unqualified success.*

---

*The original title of this study was to have been: *Mission Accomplished: A Study in Failure*. This about sums up the situation at the close of my assignment in Bolivia and emphasizes the futility of undergoing the agony of monetary stabilization if it is not to be used as the basis for enduring economic advancement.

VII

AFTERMATH

21

POLITICAL DEVELOPMENTS

Nearly ten years have passed since the creation of the Bolivian National Monetary Stabilization Council, time enough to see in retrospect that it has performed its allotted task — it succeeded in bringing stability to Bolivia's currency. But it failed to bring stability to Bolivia's politics, and, without political stability, there can be little hope for substantial economic and social progress and little prospect of permanent monetary stability.

The year 1958 brought uprisings in Santa Cruz in May, and in La Paz and the Beni in October and November, all reportedly led by right-wing forces. In January, there was an alleged plot to assassinate President Siles, and in July the head of Bolivia's only surviving "rightist" party, Oswaldo Unzaga-de la Vega, was placed under arrest for his alleged links to the murders in the bloodstained Congressional elections of 1958.* Lechín returned to the attack on the stabilization program in September, and President Siles informed Vice-President Nixon that Bolivia was threatened with economic collapse and must have $20 million more U.S. aid (in addition to the regular $20-$25 million a year) to forestall a communist takeover.[1]

The year 1959 brought mob attacks on the U.S. Embassy in La Paz and on the U.S. Information Service offices in Cochabamba and Oruro, triggered by the indiscreet remark of a U.S. aide that there was no justification for Bolivia's existence.†

---

*Actually, Unzaga's Falange Socialista Boliviana was a Socialist party, modelled in name only on the Spanish *falangistas*, and labelled by its opponents as fascist. It was rightist only in the sense that it was well to the right of the MNR. The only truly conservative party in Bolivia was the Liberal Party, founded in 1880 and espousing the doctrine of individual liberty, but that party had long been moribund.

†According to *Time*, the United States had at that time spent $129 million in aid to Bolivia, and the Embassy officer was quoted as saying: "We don't have a damn thing to show for it. We're wasting money," adding that the only solution would be to "abolish Bolivia and let its neighbors divide the country and its problems among themselves." The State Department, carefully choosing its words to assuage Bolivia's feelings, without actual prevarication, denied that it had any proof that the statement had

The mob action brought a demand from Senator Styles Bridges (Republican, New Hampshire) that Washington send troops to protect American lives and that it discontinue U.S. aid. But U.S. aid was more seriously jeopardized by widespread strikes and the miners' demands for restoration of below-cost sales at the company commissaries. The situation reached the point where Under Secretary Dillon characterized U.S. aid to Bolivia as a failure, with the consequence that aid commitments in 1960 shrank to $14.9 million, the lowest since 1954 (see Fig. 16, p. 596). The *Falangistas* were completely crushed in April, following an alleged uprising in the course of which Unzaga-de la Vega was reported to have "accomplished the difficult feat of suicide by two mortal gunshots to the head." The original government autopsy had shown that he had died of pistol and rifle shots fired from different directions. His death was followed by further revolts in the Santa Cruz area.[2]

The most important event in 1960, according to the annual report of the Central Bank, was a change in the Constitution permitting President Víctor Paz-Estenssoro to return to the presidency for a second term. But that event, the bank stated, "has not affected the monetary stabilization program, enacted December 15, 1956. In fact, the government in 1960 (following Paz' re-election) has reaffirmed the anti-inflationary policy... and maintains the firm decision that the budgets of the national government and of all its agencies shall be balanced, and that no government agency shall resort to Central Bank credit."[3]

The re-election did, however, affect the internal tranquility. Paz was named the official 1960 candidate of the MNR, following a bitter intraparty contest between Paz and Walter Guevara-Arze in which the latter established his own Authentic Revolutionary Party (PRA). Shortly thereafter, the police in La Paz broke out in a revolt which was quelled by the army. In the end, Paz won the support of the Communist Party by throwing his weight in favor of Juan Lechín for the vice-presidency. The Paz-Lechín ticket won the elections by an official count of 735,619 to 231,030, in one of the bloodiest contests ever held in Bolivia, during the course of which several U.S. flags were burned in appropriate ceremonies, to the accompaniment of

---

been made by an Embassy official, but the editor and publisher of *Time* reported, after investigation, that its account was factually correct. *Time,* March 2, 1959; *New York Times,* March 3, p. 8; March 4, p. 11; March 5, p. 1.

inflammatory speeches and incendiary cries. Later in the year, the American Ambassador's car was stoned, and his residence bombed.

As the year closed, the USSR sent a mission to La Paz and offered $150 million in aid, with no strings attached. The chief attraction in the Russian proposal was the offer to build a tin smelter in Bolivia, which for years had been Bolivia's cherished ambition, although every economic study had demonstrated that it would be an irretrievable waste of money. Ñuflo Chávez-Ortiz who, despite his quasi-impeachment as Vice-President, had returned to the government as Minister of Mines and Petroleum, presented the USSR mission with a list of Bolivia's minimum needs: $72,735,000 for COMIBOL, $4,173,512 for the Mining Bank, $77,565,000 for YPFB, and $103,400,000 for the government railways — a total of $257,873,512. The American, British, and West German embassies were reported to be alarmed and to be exploring the possibility of a counteroffer to the Soviet bid. This materialized in the following year in the shape of a Triangular Plan for COMIBOL and, in 1964, culminated in plans for a tin smelter![4]

The year 1961 began with a bang and ended with a whimper, the latter being Lechín's resignation as a result of charges linking him with the smuggling of coca leaves, or cocaine, into Argentina. His resignation was rejected by Congress, and, two years later, the legislature absolved Lechín of guilt. Notwithstanding Congressional absolution, the *Hispanic American Report* states that the incident left his reputation "somewhat tarnished as a result." The bang, a bomb thrown into the automobile of the American Ambassador, plus the promise of Soviet aid, had its reverberations a fortnight later in an announcement by the Foreign Minister that the United States had promised to increase its aid to $30 million. This was followed by reports of a $10 million loan by the Inter-American Development Bank, and $20 million "emergency aid" from the United States, later trimmed to $10 million but with the assurance that the total would be over $50 million — a first instalment against the USSR offer of $150 million. In the end, U.S. aid commitments in 1961 turned out to be $33.7 million, or more than double the 1960 figure, plus $11.2 million from the IDB. To this must be added the $38 million-$130 million Triangular Plan loan, approved in August, 1961, for the rehabilitation of COMIBOL (see Chapter 22).

Guevara-Arze, who had been the opponent of President Paz

in the 1960 elections, was forced to seek asylum in the residence of the Papal Nuncio; later he escaped to Chile.* From there, he issued a statement that Paz was shielding the pro-communist activities of Juan Lechín and, some months later, Guillermo Bedregal-Gutiérrez resigned the presidency of COMIBOL on the ground that the government failed to back him up in his efforts to curb strikes and communism. What happened was that the COMIBOL management had had eight mine leaders jailed on charges of robbing the Siglo Veinte mine, and the labor commissar and his cohorts, armed with guns and dynamite, had set them free with no attempt made by the government to restore law and order. In the end, Bedregal was persuaded to continue with COMIBOL in order to help carry out the commitments under the Triangular Plan.[5]

In 1962 President Paz, who had demonstrated remarkable powers of survival in his political divagations from Nazism to Marxism to capitalism, apparently decided, after two reportedly communist attempts on his life in 1962, to throw in his lot definitely with the United States. In July he resumed payment on Bolivia's bonds, which he had allowed to go into default almost immediately after assuming office in 1960.[6] As a result of his support of U.S. policies, U.S. aid in 1962 was further increased, the 1961-62 commitments being five times as great as in 1960, prior to the $150 million Soviet offer (Fig. 16, p. 596).

In 1963 President Paz widened the breach with Lechín by abolishing the workers' veto in COMIBOL management, following a bitter struggle between COMIBOL president Bedregal and Lechín's Miners' Federation. The action was reportedly taken under U.S. pressure, but the government continued to carry water on both shoulders as, in April, 1963, traveling Ambassador de Lesseps Morrison saw posters plastered all over La Paz celebrating the second anniversary of the U.S. defeat at the Bay of Pigs. These posters were printed in the Bolivian government printing office. By the close of the year, it was evident that President Paz-Estenssoro intended to run for a third term,

---

*Walter Guevara-Arze, reputedly a former communist, was one of the most talented members of the MNR and a thorn in the flesh of the party, repeatedly saying things that everyone knew to be true but that no one else dared say. Some years earlier, he had charged openly that Lechín was the *agent provocateur* of the so-called "Catavi massacre" which was the MNR and communist symbol of oppression by the "oligarchs" and "tin barons." Letter from former President Enrique Hertzog, *El Diario*, September 2, 1958.

and open warfare broke out in Cochabamba between the supposedly procommunist peasant forces and those loyal to the President. Peace was restored by Air Force General René Barrientos-Ortuño, reputedly a candidate for the vice-presidency. Later, Barrientos' car was sprayed with machine-gun bullets, but accounts differ as to whether the bullets came from the communist or the Paz faction. In September, President Paz received a $5 million commercial credit from President Josip Broz Tito of Yugoslavia and bestowed the Grand Collar of the Order of the Condor on his guest in order to dissipate "any suspicion that the United States has a hand in shaping our foreign policy."[7] In October, Paz visited the United States, where he was cordially greeted by President Kennedy, paving the way for the massive ($117.6 million) U.S. aid of 1963-64, which got rather less publicity in Bolivia than Tito's $5 million.*

Two communist leaders in the miners' federation were jailed on murder and sabotage charges and, in retaliation, Lechín's supporters seized seventeen hostages, including three U.S. Embassy officials and one Peace Corps worker at the Siglo Veinte mines.[8] This time, the hostages were neither raped nor murdered as on a previous occasion, and ultimately the prisoners as well as the hostages were released. With the backing of the Minister of Labor, some two hundred anticommunist labor leaders formed a new COB (Bolivian Workers' Federation) which denounced the old COB headed by Lechín, who had meanwhile formed his own political party, the Leftist National Revolutionary Party (PRIN). According to the U.S. Embassy, the new COB represented two-thirds of the urban workers and all the peasants, but not the miners. Meanwhile, the Central Bank reported that the government "continued the stabilization program enacted six years ago, again achieving an unvarying rate of exchange, complete freedom in foreign exchange and commerce, and marked stability in domestic prices."[9]

The year 1964 was an eventful one for the destinies of the MNR party — and for Bolivia. It opened, as was expected, with the nomination of Víctor Paz-Estenssoro as the third-term MNR candidate, but what was not expected was that Paz would

---

*Senator Barry Goldwater (Republican, Arizona) demanded that the U.S. cease its aid to Bolivia, claiming that the Paz regime was a despotic dictatorship, but his voice was unheeded (*New York Times,* October 25, 1963).

throw his weight against General Barrientos for the vice-presidency, and in favor of Federico Fortún-Sanjines, president of the Senate and minister of government during Paz' first administration. Barrientos withdrew his candidacy in anger but stated that he would respect the vote of the party convention for Fortún. Later, however, Paz was forced to reconsider, and Barrientos was placed on the MNR ticket. The Minister of Labor then broke with the new COB and confessed that his control of that organization had been financed by the U.S. Labor Attaché, who had provided the funds to bribe recalcitrant labor leaders.[10] Lechín, as leader of the militant left, denounced the Paz dictatorship and, on the eve of the elections, staged a hunger strike in Oruro, the heart of the mining district, in a strange political and dietary *mésalliance* with Hernán Siles-Zuazo, in which they jointly called for a boycott of the elections. According to Juan de Onís of the *New York Times:* "The United States, which has poured $300 million in aid into Bolivia since the 1952 revolution, is clearly behind Mr. Paz. Douglas Henderson, the United States Ambassador, has appeared with the President at a number of political rallies." More important, probably, the army took up strong positions around Oruro to prevent any possible march of the miners' militia on La Paz. Despite violent demonstrations at the Catavi, Machacamarca, and Colquiri mines in the Oruro and Potosí districts, and student demonstrations in La Paz and elsewhere, Dr. Paz won without opposition, although with some 30 per cent abstentions in defiance of the fact that voting is compulsory. The hunger strikes of Lechín and Siles, in which they had been joined by the students, were called off. Lechín announced that he would "keep on fighting against the tyranny of Paz-Estenssoro," while Siles called for "peaceful coexistence," and the students declared that they would continue the fight for "democratization," by violence if necessary.[11]

On August 6, 1964, as Paz took office for his third term, Lechín "was seized in the street by about twenty plainclothes men. He was kicked, beaten with revolver butts, and abandoned in a pool of blood on the sidewalk." A month later, with Lechín in hiding, former President Siles was arrested and unceremoniously exiled along with thirty-three other leaders of the MNR party. Many others were under arrest, students as well as *políticos.* Barrientos was hospitalized after a terrorist bombing attack on his house — the fifth assault on the General in a year — and five COMIBOL officials were held as hostages by the miners to back up their demand for higher wages. Later, government troops occupied Oruro, the first open clash between the army and the miners' militia. La Paz and Oruro were turned into battlefields as the militia attempted to recapture Oruro, while communists and others rioted at the university in La Paz and sacked the municipal library as well as the government newspaper *La Nación*. Five thousand troops of the peasant militia were brought to La Paz from Cochabamba and joined with the MNR militia to back the President and the army against the miners' militia.

For four days, from October 30 to November 3, it seemed that peace had been restored. And then, suddenly, the army garrisons in Cochabamba, La Paz, and at least half a dozen other centers revolted in unison. President Paz fled in a military plane to Peru, where he is reported to be living "in luxury." A week later Air Force General René Barrientos-Ortuño was installed as President of the Republic by a military junta (under General Alfredo Obando-Candia) that had taken command upon the departure of Paz. [12]

In January, 1965, an attempted counter *coup d'état* was reported, and one hundred persons described as adherents of Paz-Estenssoro were exiled. Elections were scheduled for September, then postponed to October, and later scheduled for 1966, with General Barrientos announcing that he did not intend to be a candidate. In February a labor truce was declared, meaning that, until after elections, no employees could be dismissed and all wages would be frozen. Lechín, in exile in Paraguay, was accused of having received $25,000 from Luigi Longo, the Italian communist, to finance subversion in Bolivia, and in May the government published the Lechín-Longo correspondence. This was followed by a strike in the mines, a threat of revolt by the COB, and a bloody week of conflict between workers and the army, in the course of which General Barrientos "narrowly escaped a fusillade of bullets when his motorcade was attacked by terrorists." General Obando-Candia, the leader of the 1964 coup, joined General Barrientos in a two-man presidency, the wage freeze was decongealed, and an uneasy truce ensued with both sides — miners and army — reported "to be living in mortal fear of each other." [13]

In January, 1966, General Barrientos resigned as co-President and announced his intention of running for the presidency under the banner of the Frente de la Revolución Boliviana (the Bolivian Revolutionary Front, composed of four parties united in their opposition to the MNR). Elections were scheduled for July 3, 1966, and the inauguration of General Barrientos for August 6. Meanwhile, the General engaged in "a desperate search" for candidates to oppose him at the polls, having assured the press that neither violence nor "anything or anybody will postpone the elections," adding that "the junta is dedicated to a return to civilian government; Bolivia's credit and economy depend on it."

Even before the elections were held, Juan Lechín declared, from the secret hiding place in Bolivia to which he had returned from exile in Paraguay, that the elections were "rigged." He joined with former President Paz-Estenssoro and other dissidents in asking the electorate to cast their ballots in blank. Notwithstanding this opposition, General Barrientos succeeded in finding two opposition candidates, one being Victor Andrade, the former Bolivian Ambassador to Washington, who headed a moderate wing of the MNR, and the other General Bernardino Bilbao-Rioja, a conservative hero of the Chaco War, heading the Christian Democratic Community. The Barrientos slate, with Dr. Luis Adolfo Siles (see pp. 365n and 748, n 54) running for the vice-presidency, won handily with 62 per cent of the 850,000 votes counted.[14]

In sum, nearly ten years of bloody political strife have put the stabilization program to the acid test. Through it all, as will be seen in the following pages, the measures adopted under that program have proved their efficacy. After a preliminary shakedown, the currency has been stabilized *de facto* and *de jure* and has remained unchanged in terms of dollars for the past eight years. In Bolivia it has been proved again — as it has been proved in nine other countries of Latin America — that monetary stability can be maintained despite political instability, and despite structural stress or economic strain, provided the government refrains from borrowing and spending more than its income. And in this proviso is the whole of the Law and the Prophets — the rest is commentary.

22

ECONOMIC DEVELOPMENTS

The economy has continued to improve steadily since stabilization, as measured by the statistics for gross domestic product (in constant 1958 dollars). From 1956, the last pre-stabilization year, to 1964, GDP has increased by 26 per cent, chiefly by reason of a spectacular advance in agriculture. This was a consequence of the elimination of price controls and of imports at subsidized exchange rates, together with the return of the peasants to the land, all directly attributable to the stabilization measures. Even manufacturing production, hard hit by stabilization when raw materials could no longer be imported at artificial exchange rates, has recovered to well over its pre-stabilization or pre-Revolutionary levels, and in 1964 stood 51 per cent above the 1957 low, as may be seen in Figure 12 and its supporting data.

Expenditures by the government, however, curtailed at first by stabilization, have risen even more rapidly than manufacturing — up 82 per cent from the 1957 low. Furthermore, the growth of population has seemingly outstripped the advance in production — certainly compared with pre-Revolutionary years — so that, after ten years and over $400 million of U.S. aid, the people are even more impoverished than they were in 1952.*

Agriculture

The GDP figures represented in Figure 12 show a 48 per cent increase in agricultural and livestock production, from

*Neither population nor GDP figures are to be taken too seriously in Bolivia. The latter are the product of highly refined mathematical methods applied to wholly unreliable raw statistics, while population figures reveal such wide variances as, for example, a 1960 population of 3,824,500 shown in the Planning Board's official Ten-Year Development Plan (*Bolivia: 10 Años de Revolución* [La Paz: *Dirección Nacional de Informaciones,* 1962], p. 42a) and a 3,400,000 population shown for the same year by IMF, from equally authoritative official sources (International Monetary Fund, *International Financial Statistics* [Washington, D.C.: IMF], March, 1962). The per capita GDP figures (from USAID/Bolivia, *Economic and Program Statistics* [La Paz: USAID/Bolivia, 1965], based on official Bolivian sources) show a drop from $123.8 in 1952 to $104.5 in 1956 and to $110.1 in 1964.

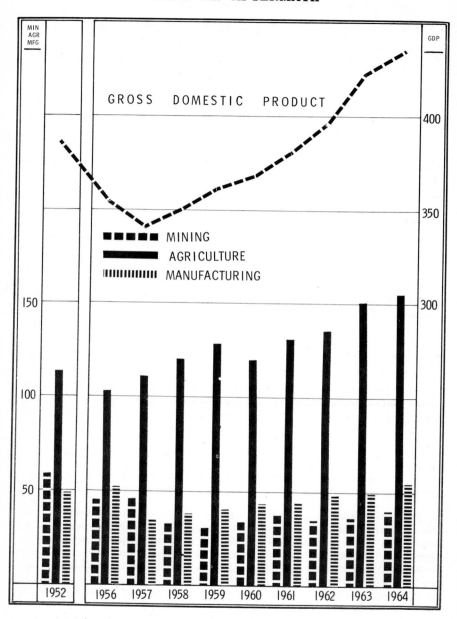

Fig. 12. Gross domestic product. In millions of 1958 constant dollars. (Source: USAID, *Economic and Program Statistics* and other sources.) [15]

$104.2 million in 1956 to $154.3 million in 1964 (both figures in constant 1958 dollars). On a tonnage basis, agricultural production is reported to have increased 140 per cent, from 10,000 metric tons in 1956 to 24,000 metric tons in 1962 (later figures not available). The same source indicates that imports of agricultural products, after rising from 5,000 metric tons in 1956 to 12,000 in 1957 (chiefly U.S. aid), have since dropped to "virtually nil" in 1961 and 1962.[16]*

In short, there has been a spectacular rise in agricultural production as a direct consequence of the stabilization measures, which ensured free market prices for farm products, eliminated the subsidized imports at the Bs. 190 rate, and brought the peasants streaming back to the farms when they could no longer earn a living as smugglers or *coleros* (selling their places in the bread lines). The contention, in my July 12, 1956, exposition of the proposed stabilization plans, that Bolivia had been "importing some $20-$25 million of farm products that she could, and should, produce herself" had been borne out, and the country is now producing $50 million more in agricultural products than in 1956.†

---

*The statement about 1962 imports seems open to doubt. See dollar figures in Table 19, p.556.

†Those economists who contend that inflation in underdeveloped countries is incurably linked to structural causes, those who argue for economic development through industrialization and high taxes on agriculture, and those who favor greatly expanded shipments of agricultural products under U.S. aid (P. L. 480) argue that farmers do not respond to economic incentives and that increased prices will not cause them to increase production — e.g., Joseph Grunwald, "The Structuralist School on Price Stability and Development," in Hirschman, Albert O. (ed.), *Latin American Issues: Essays and Comments* (New York: Twentieth Century Fund, 1961) and R. O. Olson, "Impact and Implications of Foreign Surplus Disposal on Underdeveloped Economies," *Journal of Farm Economics,* LI (December, 1960), 1042-45.

Walter P. Falcon, in "Farmer Response to Price in a Subsistence Economy: The Case of West Pakistan" (*American Economic Review,* LIV [May, 1964], 580-81), however, attributes that belief to the preconceived notions of certain theoretical economists as to "peasant behavior and institutional limitations." He shows that, in actual practice, at least in West Pakistan, "the farmers, when given the opportunity, *do* respond to price and income incentives." (See also Raj Krishna, "Farm Supply Response in India-Pakistan," *Economic Journal,* LXXXIII [September, 1963], 477-87 and Rex Daly, *Appraisal of Pakistan's Second Five-Year Plan* [Karachi: USAID monograph, 1960].) This has certainly proved to be just as true in Bolivia as in Asia.

Production of sugar cane, rice, and cotton reached all-time records in 1964, with an estimated aggregate increase in agricultural production of 5 per cent over the previous record for 1963. The increases in production, as is pointed out by a Rutgers economist, have occurred in areas and crops not affected by agrarian reform.[17] Provided the government refrains from further agricultural imports and price controls, Bolivia can remain virtually self-sufficient in agricultural production. All that agriculture needs is the encouragement of a free market economy, plus Point IV technical assistance and adequate protection of life and property in the rural areas. *There is no other way in which Bolivia can so quickly foster economic diversification and development.*

Sugar

In one area of agricultural production, in fact, Bolivia threatens to become more than self-sufficient, according to a survey made for AID by Booz, Allen & Hamilton. Unfortunately, it is an area in which Bolivia is ill equipped to compete in the world market — sugar. The Booz, Allen & Hamilton report was prepared in connection with a Development Loan Fund (AID) loan that had gone sour — a $1,750,000 loan made in June, 1961, to a private sugar mill, La Esperanza, with the stipulation that a further $750,000 would be raised from private sources. The investment fell short of that goal, and AID ordered suspension of DLF disbursements pending an inquiry. BAH, after making projections of Bolivian demand and production capacity, reached the conclusion that the mill originally planned would be marginal and that to be profitable its capacity would have to be nearly doubled, with consequent total financial requirements of some $4.1 million to $4.2 million, of which DLF would have to provide $3.4 million. On that basis, projected combined productive capacity of Guabirá (the ill-fated and costly government mill*), La Esperanza, La Bélgica (a tightly managed private mill that had obtained a previous $2 million DLF loan), a small private mill, San Aurelio (that had obtained a $174,000 DLF

---

*The most authoritative estimate of the total cost of the Guabirá mill was one of $10 million made by the Economic Commission for Latin America, with the assistance of the Bolivian National Coordination and Planning Commission. To that must be added a $2 million loan made by the Inter-American Development Bank in 1961 (IDB news release, August 14, 1964).

loan), and Bermejo (a government mill financed with a $3.4 million Japanese credit)[18] would be as shown in Table 14.

TABLE 14

Sugar Production and Projections
(In Metric Tons)

Sugar Mill	PRODUCTION*						PROJECTIONS†	
	1959	1960	1961	1962	1963	1964	1965	1969
Guabirá	12,000	14,800	18,700	19,800	25,800	31,000	27,750	27,750
La Bélgica	4,200	7,500	17,300	21,000	28,200	39,000	27,750	27,750
La Esperanza	700	2,100	2,400	3,400	4,500	4,700	9,113	20,400
San Aurelio	600	...	2,800	5,100	10,100	18,900	10,838	12,750
Bermejo	...	...	...	...	...	...	...	11,500
Totals	17,500	24,400	41,200	49,300	68,600	93,600	75,451	100,150

*USAID, *Economic and Program Statistics*, 1965, p. 10.
†Booz, Allen & Hamilton, Inc., *Report to AID on the Feasibility of Expanding Sociedad Industrial Azucarera La Esperanza, S. A.* (La Paz: BAH, 1963), p. 24.

Total Bolivian consumption for 1965 was projected by BAH at 71,400 to 76,400 metric tons, and at 80,900 to 100,100 metric tons for 1969 (the latter figure being based on the assumption of a constant 7 per cent compounded annual increase). Both estimates were perilously close to the projected capacities of the mills, as may be seen from Table 14.

In a practically closed market, such as that of Bolivia — where high tariffs, high mountains, and high costs combine to impose an effective barrier to either import or export trade — the proper formula to apply is Micawber's law: Annual consumption 150 million pounds, annual production 149 million pounds, result happiness. Annual consumption 150 million pounds, annual production 151 million pounds, result misery. The danger point has been reached. Sugar production was 15,500 tons in 1958 and, as Table 14 shows, did not change radically until 1961. In 1963, and again in 1964, production surged upward, with a record 93,600-ton output reported for the latter year. Five hundred tractors were imported for the canefields in 1965 on five-year credit terms, and the 1965 harvest was expected to be the largest on record.[19] The BAH report contained the warning that, if the Bolivian government were to build another government owned and operated mill at Alto Beni or Chaparé (and it appears to have every intention of building both), "then the Bolivian sugar capacity would far surpass projected demand." [20]

In other words, not only will the new government "investment," financed by the United States, go down the drain as has been the case in the past, but competition from subsidized government mills may drive the private producers into insolvency, to the detriment of the DLF loans. Not only that, but the earnings projections in the BAH report are based on the assumption of a continued tax exemption on operations, an exemption that is fiscally and economically untenable, and would not be needed were it not for government competition and for uneconomic conditions imposed by the government in the operation of private industry. [21]

Other crops

Crops other than cane have shown little improvement since 1958, owing apparently to continued shipments of U.S. surplus commodities under the so-called P.L. 480 aid program. Table 15 shows the latest available figures. It may be noted that corn and cane are now being consumed chiefly by the kilo rather than by the quart, which was definitely not the case prior to stabilization.

TABLE 15

Agricultural Production*
(In Thousands of Metric Tons)

Product	1958	1959	1960	1961	1962	1963	1964
Hulled rice	26.0	26.6	27.2	28.0	28.5	29.7	28.4
Sugar cane	220.0	243.4	307.8	551.8	532.5	822.5	936.4
Potatoes	592.0	602.0	580.3	617.2	566.6	621.5	621.5
Corn	262.6	260.2	247.8	260.1	234.1	260.0	261.0
Wheat	64.3	71.5	68.1	67.2	60.5	55.2	58.0
Cotton	0.3	0.1	0.7	0.4	1.0	1.1	1.3

*From USAID, *Economic and Program Statistics*, 1965, p. 10. The same source for 1964, based on equally authoritative official data, shows production figures that are radically different for every item with the exception of rice. For example, the 1964 publication shows cane production of 440,000 tons in 1958, exactly double the output shown in the 1965 publication, in which the figures appear to have been doctored in order to show a more reasonable relationship to the sugar production shown in Table 14.

Agrarian reform

Agrarian reform, which severely curtailed agricultural production during the first four years of the Revolution, has about petered out for the time being, for the simple reason that there are very few remaining accessible and arable lands left to distribute. In the first ten years of the Revolution, according to one official report, 3,117 properties (2,988,730 hectares in all) were confiscated and deeds given to 74,137 individual proprietors and to 59,696 collective farms; while a further 356,428 hectares had been seized and distributed, with 44,551 deeds remaining to be processed.[22]* Another official report claims 5,500,000 hectares distributed to 140,000 families or cooperatives. In all, that would make the average farm, resulting from the agrarian reform, somewhere between 46 and 96 acres in size. This would include the collective farms and, with that figure as the average, the majority of the individual holdings would be submarginal under Bolivian conditions, meaning the perpetuation rather than the alleviation of human misery as a consequence. Eventually, according to the same source, the government expects to distribute a further 14 million hectares.[23]

Those figures, however, tell only part of the story, as thousands of properties were invaded by squatters who continue to occupy these lands, mostly submarginal, without the formality of a title deed. Each new access road that has been opened up into the valleys surrounding the larger cities has meant a similar "gold rush" of squatters onto private as well as public lands.[24] Squatters in Bolivia, as elsewhere in Latin America, are almost invariably too ignorant and indolent to thrive as farmers. Having acquired their properties by theft, they have little regard for property rights, conservation, or thrift, and once they have depleted the soil by "agricultural mining" rather than husbandry, they tend to move on to new areas as new roads are opened, leaving desolation in their wake.

---

*Since then, the attempt to pass title by legal process has been abandoned and the occupants of seized lands have been given "full and absolute title of ownership" by decree instead of by due process of law (*El Diario*, August 3, 1965; International Monetary Fund, *International Financial News Survey*, XVII [September, 1965], 320).

Agricultural credit

On the other hand, supervised agricultural credits have made continued progress, although on a limited scale, as only 9,000 such loans were granted from 1954 to 1962.[25] But the peasants who obtained these credits, granted and supervised with the assistance of the Point IV advisers, represent the cream of Bolivia's new farmers. Almost certainly a large proportion of these farmers will be among the comparatively few who will continue to be self-supporting over the coming years.

Recently there has been a new look at the agricultural credit program. The Agricultural Bank of Bolivia, with 41 branch offices, was completely reorganized with the help of Point IV in 1963. In the first year of operation it granted 250 loans for a total of 5.7 million pesos. Of the farms that received these loans, 59 per cent were classed as small, 19 per cent as medium-sized, and 22 per cent as large agricultural enterprises. The latter took the lion's share of the funds loaned, and it was apparent that increased agricultural production, rather than social reform, was the motive behind the loans. In 1964, the total reached 33.4 million pesos, and, for the first 7 months of 1965, 18.3 million pesos.[26]

Mining

The most important development for the Bolivian mining industry in recent years has been the phenomenal rise in the price of tin. It will be recalled that when Bolivia first embarked on its stabilization program many Bolivians — especially in government — blamed the difficulties of the government Mining Corporation (COMIBOL) on the fall in the price of tin and were chagrined rather than pleased to be informed that tin prices for the five-year period from 1952 through 1956 (covering the five years under the Revolution) were higher than in any previous five-year period in the present century. It is true that prices had slumped from the record high of $1.28 a pound (New York market average for 1951), reached during the Korean troubles, to an average of $1.008 a pound in 1952-56; but, as may be seen from Figure 13 and the supporting figures, even this price was more than double the average ($0.493) prevailing over the preceding thirty-year period. [27]

But, of course, it is true of every Latin American economist

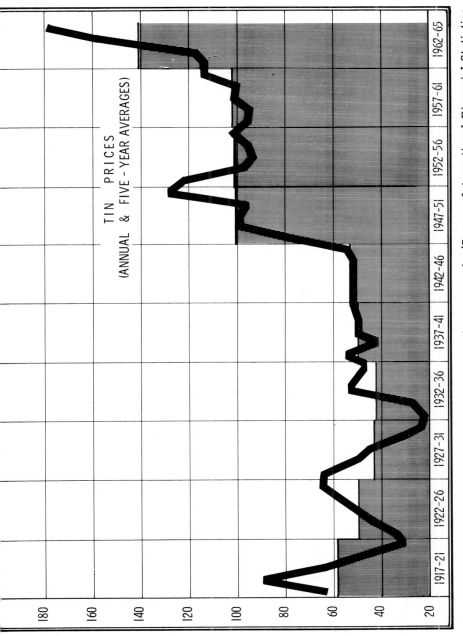

Fig. 13. Tin prices. New York market — cents per pound. (Source: *International Financial Statistics* and other sources.)[28]

who bemoans the unfavorable "terms of trade" — as it is of
every golfer — that one's best round is always regarded as
average for the course. Bolivia had grown accustomed to $1.28
tin and could not easily make the adjustment to a price of only
double the normal level. In fact, when tin slumped to $86\frac{1}{2}$ cents
a pound in September, 1958, there were bitter recriminations
against the USSR — by the Bolivian representative to the U.N.,
by Under-Secretary Dillon at GATT, by the Central Bank, and in
the press — for "dumping" Chinese tin in the world markets.[29]*

But the effect of Soviet dumping was short-lived, as may be
seen from the chart (Fig. 13). Disturbances in Malaysia, and
the sharp drop in Bolivian tin production under government
management, enabled the International Tin Council in London to
take advantage of the threat to the world's tin supply and raise
prices to the record levels shown in the chart. In fact, on October 29, 1964, tin prices reached the unprecedented high of $2.18\frac{1}{2}$
a pound, topping the $1.83 peak attained during the Korean
crisis. Prices have remained firm ever since, closing the 1965
year at $1.75\frac{1}{4}$. As a consequence, COMIBOL has signed an
agreement with a U.S. company, International Metal Processing
Corporation, for processing the tailings that wasteful mining
methods of previous years had left as residue, for at those
prices even the low-metal-content ores and tailings can be
processed at a profit.[30]

The production record is less reassuring. Gross Domestic
Product of the mining industry (Fig. 12, p. 528) has shown little
improvement in recent years and was down to $40,300,000 in

---

*Since September, 1962, Congress has authorized the General Services
Administration to dispose of 148,000 long tons of its (approximately)
350,000-ton stockpile (GSA Press Releases: 1,772, August 24, 1962; 1,953,
March 22, 1963; 2,025, June 21, 1963; 2,059, July 19, 1963; 2,262, March
20, 1964; 2,498, October 23, 1964; 2,672, February 26, 1965; and 2,689,
March 12, 1965). There has never been any complaint of dumping, however, as the sales price on the 57,343 tons of tin sold through June 30,
1965, has averaged close to $1.50 a pound. (Some 3,930 tons in a separate
inventory transferred from Federal Facilities Corporation were sold at an
average of over $1.30 a pound.) Note that the total U.S. stockpile was
equal to more than thirteen years of Bolivian tin exports (p. 745, n. *31*), so
that the stockpiling may be regarded in part as a concealed form of U.S.
aid which, thanks to the Malaysian crisis, has turned out to be a profitable
investment in addition to its national defense objectives (see U.S. Congress,
Senate, 87th Cong., 2d Sess., 1961, pp. 1722-49; *Inquiry into the Strategic
and Critical Material Stockpiles of the United States*, data from GSA, July
8, 1965).

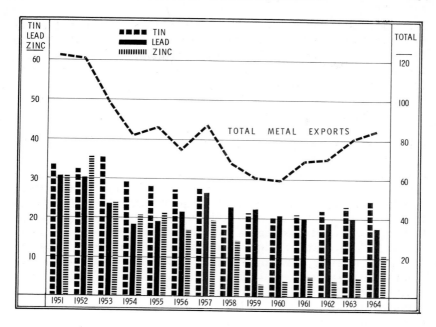

Fig. 14. Metal exports. In thousands of metric tons. (Source: Central Bank and other sources.)[31]

1964 (the latest year available), compared with $58,300,000 prior to nationalization of the mines (both figures in constant 1958 dollars). The volume of metal exports reveals the same trend, as may be seen from Figure 14.

Volume figures, of course, have the defect that gold and silver can scarcely be weighed in the same scale as lead or zinc, and even tin is worth ten times as much per pound as either of the two baser metals. Tonnage does, however, reveal the quantitative production or exportation — virtually identical in Bolivia — better than value, as it is free from the distorting effect of such extraordinary price fluctuations as are reported above in the case of tin.

The virtual disappearance of zinc production in 1959-63, as shown in Figure 14, is explained by the fact that in Bolivia zinc is a by-product of lead and silver mining and that there are only three mines which have produced or could produce silver-lead-zinc ores on a large scale — Matilde, Pulacayo, and Animas, all of which were nationalized.[32]

Matilde had been fairly well developed and prepared by the

former owners, up to the stage of construction and operation, and its geological potentialities were reported to be favorable. To put the property into profitable production, however, called for more capital and greater know-how than COMIBOL was able to muster. Ford, Bacon & Davis had strongly advised in 1956 that it be turned over to private operation, necessarily foreign, but it was not until 1962 that the government authorized COMIBOL to call for bids. Meanwhile, the Matilde mine remained nothing more than a nonproducing, maintenance operation.

Shortly before the November, 1964, *coup d'état*, COMIBOL announced that it had reached a preliminary agreement with a Japanese company, Overseas Mineral Resources Development Co., Ltd., for an investment of $11 million and operation of the mine on a joint venture basis with the government. [33]

With the change in government, this arrangement was repudiated, and the new president of COMIBOL, Colonel Juan Lechín-Suarez,* entered into an agreement with a German firm, Stolberger Zinc Company of Aachen, to operate the property, likewise on a joint venture basis, with COMIBOL retaining a 51 per cent interest while Stolberger, with the assistance of the West German government, agreed to raise $8 million as its share. It had been announced that the Bolivian negotiators would also attempt to find employment in West Germany for some 5,000 of COMIBOL's excess mine workers, but nothing further has been heard of that phase of the project. [34]

Pulacayo was one of Bolivia's greatest mines prior to the 1952 Revolution, but, as FBD pointed out in 1956, it had about reached the end of its economic life. It has been practically out of production since 1957 and was shut down in 1959 because of the total exhaustion of its ore reserves. [35] This is the principal reason for the decline in zinc exports. The other reason is that Animas, the second producer of zinc, had only about two years' reserves available in 1956. FBD recommended certain construction and exploration operations at the time, but since nothing was done that mine too has virtually ceased production.

The reason for the drop in overall exports of ore is clear

---

*Colonel Lechín-Suarez is a half-brother of Juan Lechín-Oquendo, but, according to AID officials, his appointment as head of COMIBOL was apolitical. (Conversation with Alex Firfer, director of USOM/Bolivia, November 18, 1964, in the office of Allen Gordon, Bolivian desk, AID/Washington.)

TABLE 16

Mining Production*
(In Thousands of Metric Tons)

Year	TIN		LEAD		ZINC		TOTAL	
	Private	Comibol	Private	Comibol	Private	Comibol	Private	Comibol
1950	29.3	...	29.6	...	19.6	...	96.2	...
1958	3.2	17.4	13.6	7.5	.4	8.4	23.8	36.5
1959	3.7	15.8	13.2	6.3	.6	2.2	24.4	26.6
1960	3.9	15.2	13.5	7.2	.7	3.4	26.4	28.1
1961	6.3	14.8	12.8	6.8	.7	4.2	29.5	27.9
1962	6.8	15.3	12.2	6.4	.2	3.4	31.6	27.3
1963	7.0	15.4	11.5	7.7	.9	3.4	44.2	28.6
1964	7.0	17.7	9.9	7.3	6.0	3.4	47.4	30.7

*From USAID, *Economic and Program Statistics*, 1965, p. 11.

from the production figures in Table 16. Under private ownership, in 1950, Bolivia produced 96,200 tons (metal content). After nationalization of the major mines, total production dropped
to 60,300 tons. Since then, production in the government-
operated mines has fallen from 36,500 tons to 30,700 tons, while
production in the privately operated mines has climbed from
23,800 tons to 47,400 tons.

The private mines

Government management of the mines confiscated from the
Patiño, Aramayo, and Hochschild enterprises has proved to be
a disaster to the government and to the nation. Meanwhile, the
remaining private mines, despite every obstacle of tax and
social security discrimination and other privileges accorded to
their government-owned competitor, have nearly doubled their
output.

The year 1961 brought a modicum of relief to the private
operators in that the monopoly of the Mining Bank on the sale
and marketing of certain ores was abolished, leaving the mines,
in theory, free to sell their output to the highest bidder.[36] But
this was in theory only, and it was not until the MNR regime
was overthrown and a new Mining Code enacted in July, 1965,
that the monopoly of the Mining Bank, corrupt and discredited
though it was, was finally broken, and the private mines were
free to sell where they chose.[37] The 1961 legislation also
brought a change in tin export royalties, eliminating the tax
when prices were less than 80 cents a pound — scarcely grounds
for elation in a year when prices averaged $1.13 and gave no

sign of diminishing — but imposing royalties on low metal content concentrates that had previously been tax-free and drastically increasing the rates when world tin prices exceeded $1.40 a pound, which was the case throughout 1964 and 1965. Here again, it was not until enactment of the new Mining Code that the export royalty rates were simplified and private mining given the encouragement that had been lacking since 1952.[38]

Unfortunately for the private mines, another decree had been enacted in 1961 as part and parcel of the Triangular Plan whereby all mineral export royalties were earmarked for COMIBOL,[39] following a similar practice of taxing the private oil operators for the benefit of YPFB (see p. 551).*

*Discouraging as it may be for a private enterprise to be subjected to special taxes for the specific benefit of a tax-free, subsidized, government-owned competitor, this is not uncommon, even in the United States. For example, the Porto Rico Telephone Company was forced to pay a 2 per cent tax on gross revenues for the exclusive benefit of a small telephone company owned and operated by the Communications Authority. Because of the disparity in the size of the two companies, the revenues from this tax amounted to a subsidy of $160 for each telephone added by the CA to its system; which had also received direct subsidies from the government of over $14 million (nearly $1,900 for each telephone in service). These facts were brought out in my brief before the Public Service Commission of Puerto Rico, January 23, 1952.

An even more extraordinary case of a private enterprise being called upon to subsidize a government-owned competitor occurred in Argentina, where the province of Buenos Aires, in the early part of the century, imposed a tax of one peso per telephone pole on the United River Plate Telephone Company, Ltd., for the purpose of subsidizing a Provincial Government telephone system (which was never built). Nearly forty years later, no one associated with the URPT company had ever heard of the tax and, so far as the company records showed, it had never been paid. Then, without warning, the former Director of Taxes of the province, who had just retired after 25 years' service, "denounced" the company as a tax delinquent, and the province commenced a series of annual lawsuits against the URPT for back taxes, year by year as each year's tax was on the verge of being barred by the statute of limitations *(prescripción)*. The total amounted to some 20 million pesos (about $5 million), on which the former director, no longer a civil servant, would be entitled to a 25 per cent finder's fee. Even after I discovered, after much digging in musty law books, that the provincial budget law, for the year following enactment of the tax, listed those taxes that would be in effect for the ensuing year, *and repealed all taxes not listed* (and the peso per pole tax was *not* listed), the courts continued to decide against the company in case after case. It was not until I drew up the contract for sale of the company to the government and expressly provided that the government would be liable for all the company's obligations, actual, contingent, and future, including claims, suits, legal actions, taxes, etc., that the provincial tribunals finally threw the cases out of court.

Table 16 does not reveal the full extent of the recovery in the private sector. One important advance has been in gold production that is not apparent in the gross tonnage figures. The only major producer is South American Placers, Incorporated, a subsidiary of South American Gold & Platinum Company (since merged with International Mining Corporation) that obtained a 25-year gold-dredging concession in 1956, covering some 37,000 acres in the Beni region 80 miles north of La Paz. The concession was ratified in December, 1957, and the company commenced dredging operations in October, 1959. Its gold production increased from 41,970 ounces in 1962 to 67,612 ounces in 1964 but dropped to 33,861 ounces in 1965 as a consequence of difficult dredging conditions and a drop in the grade of ore. In all, the company has produced close to $9 million of gold, sold in world markets at around $35 an ounce, and has paid the Bolivian government some 20 per cent of its gross revenues in taxes. [40]

The Bolivian Minister of Mines has announced that five foreign and domestic companies are seeking concessions in the area between the Beni and the Peruvian border to exploit what the Minister terms "an inexhaustible supply of gold in the area." The term "inexhaustible" is doubtless literally true, but what proportion of the reserves it may be economically feasible to develop is unknown, and it would be hard to substantiate the Minister's further claim that gold deposits north of La Paz are valued at from one to three billion dollars and that by 1972 gold production in the area should reach $22 million per annum. [41]

What is known is that, by the end of 1965, Tidewater Oil Company was "preparing to end its gold exploration efforts in Bolivia after intensive testing of the [Bol-Inca Mining Corporation 65,000-acre concession]...failed to locate gold in economically attractive quantities." [42]

The futility of relying upon official statements for any information is confirmed by the official statistics of metal exports, showing a drop in gold exports from $5.3 million in 1963 to $1.7 million in 1964, when the data previously cited show that International Mining Corporation production alone, all of it exported, amounted to nearly $2.4 million in 1964, compared with less than $1.4 million in 1963. The discrepancy is too great to be explained by year-end lag, although it may be attributable to gold transactions by the Central Bank. The total value of metal exports, which must be accepted in the absence of other data, is stated to have risen from $80.2 million in 1963 to $108.2 million in 1964. Of the total $28 million increase, $24 million is accounted for by tin exports, as a result, chiefly, of higher tin prices. [43]

COMIBOL

The COMIBOL picture is less encouraging. As a consequence of the drop in COMIBOL tin production, Bolivia was unable to fill its quotas under the International Tin Agreement, and the quota has been cut progressively, from 28 per cent of the world total (December 15, 1957), to 20.43 per cent (March 31, 1958), to 19.4 per cent (January 1, 1960), to 18.43 per cent (July 1, 1960), and to 16.389 per cent (July 1, 1962). The Bolivian government and Bolivian labor leaders have frequently ascribed the drop in exports to the cut in the quota, but the 1960 *Annual Report* of the Central Bank admitted that, to the contrary, the quota had been reduced because Bolivia had failed to fill its previous quotas for "reasons which were well known." [44]

The reasons are set forth frankly in a COMIBOL report published in March, 1964, viz.: (1) The mine labor leaders are the most belligerent and politically powerful labor sector in Bolivia; (2) by the time the Triangular Plan was initiated, labor-employer relations had reached an impasse; (3) COMIBOL's financial difficulties made it impossible to provide adequate stocks for the subsidized, below-cost commissaries;* (4) illegal strikes in 1961 meant a loss of 447,700 man-days and $1.9 million; in 1962, 172,500 man-days and $0.5 million; in 1963, 446,656 man-days and $2.4 million. Finally, in 1963, for the first time, under the financial pressure of the Triangular Plan, COMIBOL ceased to pay the miners during their illegal strikes. [45]

According to the COMIBOL report, in 1952, under private operation, the nationalized mines employed 28,973 miners. In 1956, the last year prior to stabilization, under COMIBOL operation, the mines employed 36,558 workers to produce one-half

---

*It will be recalled that elimination of the below-cost commissaries was a *sine qua non* of the agreements that made it possible for Bolivia to finance the stabilization fund. By this time, however, the stabilization fund had been exhausted, and U.S. aid was providing all the money necessary for Bolivia to balance its budget and keep the currency stable, so that there was no longer any obligation, other than a moral one, for Bolivia to live up to its commitments.

as many tons of ore. The 7,500 excess workers, according to the same report, were miners who had been dismissed by the private operators, allegedly in antiunion reprisals, but it was "indispensable" for COMIBOL to rehire them as they had played an important part in the 1952 Revolution. This was "the origin of the problem of the excess workers."

In any event, by 1958, COMIBOL had rid itself of most of these unemployable excess miners and reduced its payroll to 28,885. By 1963 the total had been cut to 25,524. But, instead of taking care of these workers at minimal cost through projects of the WPA type (road work, school construction, agricultural development, and colonization), under the relatively economical direction of the army, as the head of Point IV had suggested in 1957 (Appendix VI), they were given WPA-type work under the auspices of the Development Loan Fund, administered by the Inter-American Development Bank, the Bolivian Development Corporation, and the Bolivian Ministry of Peasant Affairs. *The cost was almost certainly greater than the previous cost to COMIBOL,* and the program was financed by the United States as a "soft" loan at $1\frac{1}{4}$ per cent interest, "payable" in 25-30 years. Furthermore, in accordance with the Triangular Plan, despite the fact that most of the miners were given other government sinecures, they were all given severance pay for leaving COMIBOL, and the cost of that pay was met with U.S. counterpart funds.[46]

The miners' pay, according to the same COMIBOL report, averaged $66 a month, exclusive of social benefits, which would bring the payroll cost to $92, or $1,104 per annum. With the exception of YPFB, which employs relatively little low-skilled labor, these were the highest pay rates in Bolivia, as the average monthly pay in the medium-sized private mines was $49, in the small mines $33, and in manufacturing industries $35. The miners were deserving of such pay rates, it was alleged, inasmuch as the per capita output of the mineworkers was around $2,000 U.S. a year, which was higher than the per capita production in any other Bolivian industry. The writer of this statement was apparently oblivious of any other costs entering into production, milling, smelting, and transportation. In point of fact, in 1963 for example, COMIBOL showed a labor cost of $25,075,000 and a deficit for the year of $14,861,000, so that the company was paying its workers $10,214,000 more than it could afford. If productivity is to be taken as the criterion, then a 40 per cent wage cut would have been indicated. This deficit, moreover, is exclusive of any allowance for depletion, depreciation, and capital costs.

The Triangular Plan. Bolivia's failure to fill its tin quota and the cessation of tungsten shipments to the United States, which had fulfilled its stockpile requirements, [47] coupled with Soviet dumping of tin, brought total Bolivian exports down to $50 million in 1958, compared with $106 million in 1952 prior to nationalization of the mines (see Table 19, p. 556). COMIBOL tin production had shrunk to levels where the company could not possibly continue to operate, and production fell even further in 1959 and 1960. Finally, in 1960, the Bolivian government contracted for the services of a German mining mission, Salzgitter Industriebau, G.m.b.H., which arrived in La Paz at the same time that the USSR was offering $150 million in aid "without strings." [48] Shortly thereafter, the Inter-American Development Bank contracted with C. C. Huston & Associates of Toronto; a financial and development plan was quickly devised and agreed to on June 9, 1961, by the governments of Bolivia, Germany, and the United States (hence "triangular"), as well as by the IDB.*

A formal contract was executed on August 31, 1961, by the government of the United States, the Federal Republic of Germany, and the Inter-American Development Bank, as lenders, and COMIBOL as the borrower, with the guaranty of the Central Bank. In it, the lenders agreed to advance $37,750,000 to COMIBOL, over a three-year period, for exploration, metallurgical research, repairs, supplies, and equipment, including transportation equipment. [49] Of this total, approximately $18 million was to be expended during 1962. Under the contract arrangements, German engineers and suppliers were to provide the engineering and other services, as well as the bulk of the supplies and equipment, on short-term credits or with funds provided by the U.S. or IDB. Argentine suppliers provided some $1.5 million in equipment on short-term credit. The IDB credit

---

*The Ford, Bacon & Davis, Inc., survey took over a year to prepare. Its existence may have made it possible for the Salzgitter and Huston reports to be prepared in such haste. The FBD report was politically unpalatable, as it was so damning of government mismanagement of the nationalized mines, as well as of labor. The Salzgitter and Huston reports were confined to preparing a financial plan for the rehabilitation of the mines on the assumption, which proved well-founded, that the United States would provide the major financing.

is repayable in fourteen semiannual instalments, beginning March 1, 1965, at the end of which term the United States will be the sole remaining creditor under the contract.

The contract contains a series of provisions prohibiting illegal strikes, limiting the role of the labor commissars, and laying down rules intended to improve labor discipline. These conditions, however, proved easier to write than to enforce.[50] The Triangular Plan further provided that COMIBOL be exempt from all import duties and export royalties and *that all export royalties paid by the private mines be turned over to COMIBOL* to replenish its working capital. This was the only way in which the capital investment contemplated in the Triangular Plan could be proved remunerative, even on paper. It meant, of course, that the COMIBOL deficits would be transferred to the government budget where they would be financed directly by U.S. aid (see the Solomon report* in Chapter 24), and that the entire mining industry — private as well as nationalized — would be operated almost exclusively for the benefit of the COMIBOL workers and management.

A USAID report published in December, 1965, shows a total U.S. commitment for the Triangular Plan of $8.5 million, from the inception of the plan through the end of 1965, by which time the loan operation was supposed to have been completed. On the other hand, data published by IDB, COMIBOL, and the Bolivian Central Bank reveal that expenditures and commitments through 1965 (for the "first three phases," with no assurance of completion) amount to $40,100,000 for the United States and a total of $56,730,000, compared with the original $37,750,000 budget for the entire operation (see Table 17).

But the table does not reveal the whole story, for COMIBOL reported that, "for reasons beyond its control," the operation would not be completed until the first quarter of 1966 and that meanwhile COMIBOL's cash deficits "have been financed exclusively by U.S. aid to the government of Bolivia."†

---

*Anthony Morton Solomon, Norman S. Fieleke, and Frank W. Krause, *The Finances of the Public Sector of Bolivia* (Washington, D.C.: USAID, 1963). (Mimeographed.)

†According to the editor of *Inter-American Economic Affairs*, U.S. government officials attempted to investigate the expenditure of the first $41 million of the Triangular Plan funds, but were informed by the Bolivian officials that such an investigation would be an intrusion on their independence (Simon G. Hanson, "The Alliance for Progress: The Third Year," *Inter-American Economic Affairs*, XVIII [Spring, 1965], 12).

TABLE 17

Financial Commitments under the Triangular Plan
(In Millions of Dollars)

	Original Contract		Actual Commitments		1964-65
	1962	1963-64	1962	1963	
Inter-American Development Bank	$ 4,500,000	$ 4,000,000	$ 4,500,000	$ ...	$ 2,500,000
United States	9,000,000	11,000,000	13,000,000	11,000,000	6,100,000
"Additional funds"	...	...	...	10,000,000	...
Germany	3,700,000	4,050,000	3,750,000	2,880,000	1,500,000
Argentina	1,500,000	...	...	...	...
	$18,700,000	$19,050,000	$22,750,000	$23,880,000	$10,100,000
Totals		$37,750,000			$56,730,000

Note: The data on contractual commitments for 1962 and on actual commitments for 1962, 1963, and 1964-65 are from Inter-American Development Bank, *Annual Report* (Washington, D.C.: IDB), 1961, p. 94; 1962, p. 79; 1963, p. 57; and from *International Financial News Survey*, XVII (October 22, 1965), 396. See also Bank of London and South America, Ltd., *Fortnightly Review* (London: The Bank), XXX (December 11, 1965), 1081, which would indicate that agreement on the $10 million for the "third stage" was not reached until October 11, 1965, with an admitted $44 million expended in the two prior stages. These figures cannot be reconciled with USAID *Economic and Program Statistics*, 1965, p. 34, which shows total U.S. commitments of $8.5 million through the end of 1965. The total original contractual commitment through 1964 is from 33d *Annual Report*, 1961, Central Bank of Bolivia, p. 203, while the breakdown between the German and U.S. commitments for 1963-64 is estimated on the basis of *Operación Triangular* (La Paz: COMIBOL, 1964) plus the "additional funds" figure shown in the IDB *Annual Report*, 1963. A further $2.5 million loan was announced by the IDB in a press release, February 14, 1966.

The report shows that these deficits were $9,556,000 in 1961, $16,155,000 in 1962, and $14,861,000 in 1963. A book by a Bolivian author on the nationalization of the mines, which he calls "a history of frustration," reveals the total chaos prevailing in COMIBOL and in the implementation of the Triangular Plan. While his polemics must be taken with a grain of salt, being based largely on material supplied by a former controversial Minister of Mines, Mario Torres, they are confirmed by a letter to President Paz from the former general manager of COMIBOL, Goosen Broesma, who reveals what he considers to be the scandalous incompetence of the IDB technical advisory mission supervising the plan. [51]

Were COMIBOL a normal business operation, the phenomenal current prices for tin would remove any possibility of deficits in 1964 through mid-1966, but, by virtue of a Bolivian version of Parkinson's law, expenditures may always be counted upon to expand to the limit of available resources, including U.S. aid. Thus, the latest reports show that COMIBOL's production costs in 1965 averaged $1.78 per pound of tin. Labor demands and managerial extravagance, fostered by U.S. deficit financing of the Bolivian budget, have increased production costs by over 30 per cent in a single year to the point that continued deficits in the government mining industry are practically guaranteed as a consequence of the Triangular Plan.*

This is despite the fact that royalties paid by the private mining industry are turned over to COMIBOL instead of to the Treasury, thus likewise guaranteeing continued government deficits which in turn are financed by U.S. aid. To cap the climax, the present government has established a profit-sharing system under which the miners receive 25 per cent of the profits of the mines in which they work, plus 25 per cent of COMIBOL's overall profits. Considering the way in which COMIBOL's "profits" are computed, it may be taken for granted that 25 per cent of the alleged profits will be well over 100 per cent of the actual net income, thus fulfilling the Marxist slogan of the miners' union that the profits of the mines are for those who work in them. This is borne out by a report of $800,000 alleged "profits" for June, July, and August, 1965, and by a presidential decree in May, 1965, increasing wages by percentages ranging from 10 to 60 per cent and granting added compensation of 5 pesos ($0.42 U.S.) to make up for the elimination of below-cost sales by the COMIBOL commissaries.[52]

Taking into consideration known and probable cash deficits, the Triangular Plan may be expected to cost upwards of $130 million, disregarding the loss of the customs duties and royalties no longer paid by COMIBOL and the royalties paid by the private sector to COMIBOL, all of which must be made up by U.S. aid to balance the government budget. To the extent that Development Loan Fund "soft loans" are used to take care of

---

*The 1964 report, Operación Triangular, placed COMIBOL's production costs at $1.34 per pound in 1962 and $1.33 in 1963, placed in the New York market. Similarly, Operación Triangular "prognosticates" that, after improvements are completed, COMIBOL may show "profits" for the 10-year period from 1966 to 1975 of $23 million with $1.12 tin, or $55 million with $1.30 tin. It must be pointed out, however, that COMIBOL counts its "profits" with no allowance for depletion, exploration, blocking out new areas, or research and development; and no allowance for royalties or a return on the capital investment which, in this case, should include indemnization to the former owners of the mines. They allow (in 1963, for example) only $644,000 for depreciation on depreciable assets of $21,368,000! Export royalty rates were cut approximately 30 per cent, beginning April 1, 1964. (Operación Triangular, pp. 11, 17, 20, 25; FBD report, Vol. 3, Appendix D-1.)

the excess workers dismissed by COMIBOL, these too must be charged to the cost of the Triangular Plan. This entire cost will be borne by the United States, inasmuch as the Argentine, German, and IDB credits are on a short-term basis and will have to be made good by U.S. deficit financing of the Bolivian budget as they come due (see Solomon report, Chapter 24).

   Confiscation endorsed by tripartite agreement. In Chapter 18 it was stated that confiscation of the private mines had received what amounted in effect to a blessing by the government of the United States when it was provided that Bolivia must suspend all payments to the former owners as a prerequisite for the Triangular Plan loan. That part of the agreement is "classified" in the United States, meaning that its terms are not available to Congress or to the general public. However, according to Article 5 (a) of the contract, published in Bolivia, no payments can be made to Patiño, Aramayo, and Hochschild as indemnity for confiscation of the mines, *until the total amount of the indemnity is fixed.*[53]

   Considering that the only impartial appraisal of the Big Three properties was that made in 1926 by the Permanent Fiscal Commission for Bolivia, which gave a value of $135 million, and that Minister of Mines Torres shattered any possibility of arriving at a reasonable settlement by refusing to countenance any payment of more than $40,000 (p. 444), it cannot be said that the Bolivian government has in good faith ever attempted to negotiate an acceptable arrangement under the agreement which was signed in Santiago, Chile, with the Big Three in 1953.* Thus, the insistence under the Triangular Plan that all further payments to the former mineowners must be suspended until the Bolivian government agrees to settle, or until the former owners in desperation accept the government's unilateral valuation, gave ostensible international legal sanction to the confiscation.

   *Two negotiating commissions had been set up following confiscation of the properties, but they failed to reach an agreement. A third commission was formed by President Siles on December 16, 1959 (Supreme Resolution 88688; Central Bank, 31st *Annual Report,* 1959, p. 62), and was scheduled to meet in Montreal early in 1960 with Antenor Patiño and representatives of the three companies. With the return to power of the Paz-Estenssoro regime on August 6, 1960, this commission, too, came to naught. The attitude of the government is evidenced by the public statement of the government negotiating commission, on the eve of the Second National Workers' Congress, that they would adhere to the conditions laid down by Minister Torres (*Última Hora,* June 5, 1957).

The total payments made to the former owners of the mines, from 1953 to December 31, 1962, were:[54]

Patiño Mines & Enterprises Consolidated, Inc.	$9,683,826
Compagnie Aramayo de Mines en Bolivie	3,257,272
Mauricio Hochschild, Sociedad Anónima	
Minera é Industrial	7,295,565
	$20,236,663

Whether or not the above sum represents payment in full for the properties seized or whether, as the former owners claim, it represents merely an inadequate interest return on the principal sum may perhaps be gauged by the amount of the investment contemplated under the Triangular Plan, which, under the most optimistic projections, will still fall short of returning the properties to the state of profitability they enjoyed under private management.

Financing of tin smelters in Bolivia. Before Bolivia could escape the necessity of making further payments to the owners of the confiscated mines, however, it was essential to establish alternative smelting facilities for its tin exports. So long as Bolivia was compelled to send the bulk of its concentrates to Williams, Harvey & Company, Ltd. (and the lower-grade ores to Capper Pass & Son, Ltd.), it was inevitable that deductions would continue to be made from the proceeds of sales for payments to the Big Three.

For decades prior to the Revolution, Bolivian nationalists had aspired to the establishment of a smelting plant in Bolivia even though it should have been clear that the investment could not be justified on economic grounds. With the Revolution, the construction of a smelter became a "Revolutionary imperative," the paramount objective of which was to escape the continued payments to Patiño *et al.* The U.N.'s Economic Commission for Latin America supported the idea as a means of augmenting Bolivia's foreign exchange resources and reported that "the Pyrometallurgical Laboratory of the Banco Minero is said to have discovered a new smelting method with great economies and technical advantages. Although the establishment of a smelter operation with this new process would cost about $20 million, foreign exchange savings would amount to $11.5 million annually."[55]

The following year, in 1955, a $60,000 survey was made by the German firm of Krupp-Lurgi on behalf of the Ministry of

Mines. The investigators reached the conclusion that construction of a tin smelter in Bolivia could not be justified on any conceivable economic grounds, particularly because the smelting of complex ores was a highly technical operation for which labor and management skills were totally lacking. The Krupp-Lurgi survey thus put the expertise of the Mining Bank and the gullibility of the U.N. economists in their proper light, and its conclusion was supported by an extensive survey made for the Ministry of Mines by Ford, Bacon & Davis, Incorporated, which stressed the lack of adequate ore reserves to warrant an investment of the magnitude of a smelting plant, plus the fact that Bolivia's mining regions are so far apart that a single smelter could handle only a small part of the total ores.[56] And when the USSR offered to build a tin smelter for Bolivia, the American economic adviser warned that it could prove to be a millstone around Bolivia's neck.[57] But, apparently working on the theory that if enough experts are hired one expert will ultimately come up with an opinion that does not run counter to one's desires, a Corporación Nacional de Fundiciones was created in 1963 to investigate plans and projects for a Bolivian smelter equipped to handle Bolivia's total output.[58]

There were already, it is true, 15 so-called smelters in the country, all privately owned, but only two of these were still in operation in 1956 at the inception of the stabilization program, and those two were only able to operate by virtue of exports to Brazil in exchange for "treaty dollars" which, until the advent of stabilization, enabled them to profit from the import of Brazilian merchandise at the official rate of exchange.[59]

Subsequently, with the diversion of funds made possible by U.S. aid for budgetary support and the financing of COMIBOL deficits, a government-owned refinery was set up in Oruro. It was reported that this refinery smelted about 25 per cent of the tin production in 1963 and was expected to handle some 50 per cent in 1964, allegedly at a cost of 3 cents U.S. a pound less than it could be refined for abroad.[60] This claim was presumably based on cash operating costs, disregarding depreciation and capital charges, and figuring the payments to the Big Three as part of the cost of foreign smelting. But the validity of that claim was in any event conclusively disposed of when the new Mining Code provided that the private mines would be required to use the local smelters only when they offered terms at least as good as were offered by the foreign smelters, thus revealing that the prior "preference" was in reality a choice made under duress.[61]

Pressure from the Bolivian government had continued to mount ever since the decision to reject the USSR offer to construct a tin smelter; and in July, 1964, the American Ambassador presented Washington with Bolivia's request for a $500,000 loan to cover the cost of a preliminary survey for a refining plant of 15,000-ton annual capacity. So highly "classified" was this information, so far as the U.S. public was concerned, that in November, 1964, although the proposed survey was a matter of public knowledge in Bolivia and in London, the head of USOM/Bolivia and the head of the Bolivian desk in AID/Washington stated that they knew *nothing* of any plans for construction of a smelter in Bolivia.[62]

In May, 1965, the British Ambassador to Bolivia announced a £1 million loan to help finance the construction of four smelting plants, while the Capper Pass company offered its technical assistance in the smelting of low-grade ores. A year later, however, Bolivia executed a contract with Klockner Industrienlagen, a West German firm, for construction of a smelter in Oruro with an annual capacity of 20,000 tons. Where the money is to come from is not reported.[63]

Petroleum

Petroleum production, which accounted for little more than $\frac{1}{2}$ of 1 per cent of the gross domestic product in 1952, reached 4.3 per cent in 1957 but has remained virtually stable since that year, both in terms of 1958 dollars, as shown in the supporting figures for the GDP chart (Fig. 12), and in volume of output. In fact, as will be seen from Table 18, oil production has never since reached the 1957 peak, nor have exports ever again equalled the high mark set in 1958.

YPFB

In comparison with other Bolivian government enterprises, the government petroleum company, YPFB, has operated successfully. However, it pays no income tax, and it receives 50 per cent of all royalties paid to the government by the private oil companies,* despite which the YPFB accounts showed a $2.3

---

*See comments under COMIBOL (p. 540n) on payment of taxes by private enterprise to a government owned and operated competitor, both from the point of view of unfair competition, and of the drain on government revenues.

TABLE 18

Petroleum Production and Exports
(In Thousands of Cubic Meters*)

Year	Production	Exports
1952	83.6	10.1
1953	95.5	10.6
1954	269.4	9.0
1955	428.1	75.7
1956	508.0	121.9
1957	568.4	147.6
1958	546.2	219.1
1959	504.0	152.2
1960	568.2	180.8
1961	475.2	111.3
1962	443.7	76.2
1963	522.2	107.9
1964	511.0	n.a.

Note: Production figures, 1952-62, and export figures, 1952-55 from 1962 and 1963 *Annual Reports,* Central Bank. Later data from *International Financial Statistics.*
*One barrel (U.S. measure) = 0.159 cubic meters.

million loss in 1961, and zero profit or loss in 1962. In 1963, 1964, and 1965, profits of $2.4 million, $7.9 million, and $7.4 million, respectively, were reported.[64]

These figures, however, are misleading in that depreciation and depletion are both inadequate, the former because a large part of the fixed YPFB investment in equipment was imported at Bs. 190 to the dollar and depreciation is charged on that fictitious cost basis (or the asset has been wholly written off), and the latter because depletion is computed as a percentage of operating profit, which, in the case of YPFB, is comparatively low. That depletion method is used in the United States, but solely for income tax purposes and by reason of the requirements and benefits of the U.S. Internal Revenue Code. In normal financial accounting, unit of production depletion is employed, computed on a per barrel basis. If that method were used by YPFB, which would be proper, it would show losses in all years. Furthermore, no allowance is made in the YPFB accounts for capital costs, the properties operated by YPFB having been confiscated from Standard Oil Company (New Jersey), which, after five years of negotiation, received only a fraction of the value of its property rights. This payment was made by the government and not charged to YPFB. An "operating surplus" of 28 million new pesos ($2.4 million) was officially reported in 1963, but what that term may include or exclude would be hazardous to guess.

The most authoritative report on YPFB, made by De Golyer & MacNaughton, Inc., a Dallas firm which investigated YPFB operations in 1960, 1962, and 1964 under contract with AID, states that although YPFB continued to generate substantial cash income it does not operate within that income, and its "excess expenditures must, in the long run, be a drain on the overall Bolivian economy."[65]

With careful planning, the report states, the company could live within its income and have adequate funds for modest exploration, but if it continues its exploration program at the current high level it must be in a position to borrow *with no obligation of repayment.* "YPFB has had little success in its exploratory efforts to date.... There are just not enough trained geologists in YPFB... this reflects on the efficiency of the wildcat drilling program, and... more exploratory wells are being drilled annually than can be properly justified."* This may have been true up to the time the report was written, in March, 1964, but economic projections in the oil industry are as hazardous as wildcatting. By drilling an old Standard Oil field at greater depths than were possible or customary in former times, YPFB claims to have brought in an area at Tatarenda with a current output of 800 barrels a day and a reported potential of 20,000 barrels. If this report is to be relied upon, it could completely change the prospects for the government oil company. On the other hand, Brazil is pressing Bolivia to construct a $200 million natural gas pipe line from Santa Cruz to Brazil which, if built, would renew the unprofitable barter arrangements and add to Bolivia's herd of white elephants.[66]

Deficiencies in YPFB's financial management, however, are visible not only in its disproportionate drilling expenditures, but in the low ratio of current assets to current liabilities

*The lack of geological expertise was borne out by YPFB's chief engineer, Eduardo Hinojosa, who stated that there was not a single producing area being exploited by YPFB that had not been drilled by Standard Oil and that the increase in production was attributable solely to the fact that modern drilling methods, in worldwide use, permit drilling at greater depths than when the properties were operated by SONJ. (Conversation at Camiri, July 1956.)

(1.85 to 1.00, compared with 2.19 to 1.00 for a comparable operation in the United States); the extremely low percentage of cash to current liabilities (5.3 per cent; U.S. average, 40.2 per cent); the excessive ratio of working capital to sales (76 per cent; U.S. average, 19.4 per cent); and its high ratio of fixed assets to net worth (149 per cent; U.S. average, 86.1 per cent), which means that its creditors are supplying an undue proportion of the fixed capital (as was true in 1956).

Private oil companies

Gulf Oil Corporation's subsidiary, Bolivian Gulf Oil Company, appears to be making substantial progress.[67] Gulf was the first private company to obtain concession rights in Bolivia, following enactment of a Petroleum Code, first by decree in 1955 and later by act of the legislature on October 25, 1956, enacted as a part of the monetary stabilization program. The Gulf concession covers some four million acres, strung out over about 550 miles in the eastern part of Bolivia. Since the inception of operations the company is reported to have invested some $50 million in exploration and has spent an additional $15 million on a recently completed 400-mile pipe line from Santa Cruz to Sica Sica, which connects with the 250-mile line from Sica Sica to the Pacific port of Arica (Peru) that Gulf will rent from YPFB. Gulf has already developed substantial reserves capable of a daily production of about 25,000 barrels, and it is expected that this will be raised to 50,000 barrels, which is the pipe line's capacity. This compares with YPFB's production of 8,360 barrels a day in 1963 (including its 50 per cent share in the privately operated Madrejones fields) and production of 610 barrels a day by all private operators in that year.[68] Of the 101 wells drilled by Gulf, 55 have proved productive, which is considered a high ratio for a new area.

The contrast between the effectiveness of private investment in six years of operation and government operation over a thirty-year period (since 1936) is thus as striking in petroleum development as it has proved to be in mining. As a consequence of the success of Gulf's operations and the failure of YPFB to make ends meet, the YPFB management and engineers waged a vitriolic press campaign against Gulf Oil Corporation, coupled with the demand that YPFB should look to the Soviet for its future financing.[69] This was prior to the 1964 *coup d'état*.

Ten other private companies, in addition to Gulf, have been

attracted to Bolivia since 1957 but have thus far failed to produce results.[70] Their expenditures, however, will be borne by
the foreign investors, as a normal business risk in the petroleum industry, and will not be a subtraction from the Bolivian
economy. Nor is it lack of capital that has impeded government
development; for, as has been shown in Figure 8, p. 490, the
government squandered $300 million of capital from July, 1951,
to June, 1956, and between then and December 31, 1965, has had
an additional $300 million in U.S. aid placed at its disposal
(p. 754, n *135*).

Manufacturing

The manufacturing industry had been built up to artificial
levels during the 1953-56 inflation by the stimulus of below-cost
raw material imports and the export smuggling of consequently
low-cost finished manufactures. It has been slowly and pain-
fully recovering from the shock administered by a return to
reality under the stabilization program, as is seen by the supporting figures for Figure 12 (p. 528), showing industry's contribution to gross domestic product. Since 1964, manufacturing
is once more playing a key role in Bolivia's economic recovery,
having increased its contribution to GDP by nearly 10 per cent
in 1964 and manifested continued progress in subsequent years.
Even the textile industry, the hardest hit of all Bolivia's manufactures, is showing new life. A new textile mill began operations in Cochabamba in 1964, and one of the largest mills in La
Paz is proceeding with plans that will double its capacity. Increased production of wool, cotton, and synthetic fibers, and of
wearing apparel, is reported.[71]

The Industrial Credit Bank, inaugurated early in 1963
with the objective of aiding small business, is getting under
way. By June 30, 1964, the bank had ended its first year of operations, with 12 million new pesos (a little over $1 million) in
loans granted and outstanding.[72] For the fiscal year ending July
31, 1965, an additional 30 million pesos of loans were granted.[73]

Foreign Trade

One basic improvement in the Bolivian economy directly
attributable to the stabilization measures is seen in the decline

in imports of livestock, food, and raw materials from 1956 through 1960. Even prior to the Revolution, such imports had long been subsidized to the detriment of Bolivia's farm population, in order to allay discontent among the less numerous but politically powerful workers in the mines and factories. Table 19 shows a drop in imports in these three categories, from $38,635,000 in 1952 to a low of $19,807,000 in 1960. (Raw materials include some nonagricultural as well as agricultural products, but wool and cotton are among the major items in that category.) But since 1960, with the return of Paz-Estenssoro to the presidency, foodstuff imports again increased as a result

TABLE 19

Imports by Major Categories and "Net" Exports
(In Thousands of Dollars)

| Year | Imports* | | | | Exports † ("Net" Value at Bolivian Ports) |
	Livestock	Food	Raw Materials	Total	
1952	3,357	24,450	10,828	92,620	106,500
1953	3,027	22,660	9,970	68,006	94,800
1954	1,466	21,559	9,810	65,483	80,400
1955	4,382	20,282	9,281	82,394	75,300
1956	5,046	16,503	7,198	84,058	75,900
1957	931	26,551	5,724	90,288	66,000
1958	193	15,273	4,742	79,592	50,100
1959	36	16,011	4,970	64,986	59,000
1960	44	13,871	5,892	71,477	51,300
1961	146	18,861	5,500	77,686	58,000
1962	2,623	17,913	5,855	97,726	58,900
1963	5,046	17,679	6,728	103,774	65,700
1964	3,000	15,300	15,500	102,700	85,600
1965	...	...	...	...	99,000

*Figures for 1952-63 from Central Bank, *Annual Reports*, 1962 and 1963. Figures for 1964 from USAID *Economic and Program Statistics*, 1965, p. 13. The data for raw material imports for 1964 are not comparable with those of prior years; i.e., the latter source shows 1962 and 1963 raw material imports as $15.1 million and $14.6 million, respectively, in lieu of the Central Bank figures shown in the table.

†Figures from *International Financial Statistics*, various issues. They represent estimates made by the Bolivian Bureau of Statistics of the f.o.b. value of exports, i.e., the "net" value at Bolivian point of export, after deducting freight, etc. and, in the case of ores and concentrates, after deducting smelting charges. (See *IFS*, June, 1958, p.261n.)

of renewed government-subsidized importation to satisfy the demands of the miners and factory workers, and Bolivia appears to have reverted to the practices that brought about the ruin of native agriculture.*

Exports, likewise shown in Table 19, dropped sharply, from 1952 to 1956 and from 1956 through 1963, in part because of lower tin prices, but chiefly as a consequence of lowered production at the nationalized mines. There was a marked improvement in 1964 as a result of unprecedented high prices for tin, but the value of total exports is still below the pre-Revolutionary level. †

Investment and Development

In Bolivia, as elsewhere in Latin America, economic development is thought of solely in terms of government action, of an increase in gross national product, planned, promoted, and implemented by the government.‡

*See, however, apparently contradictory figures at p. 529, indicating that agricultural imports had been cut to practically nil in 1961-62.

† Discussion of the over-all balance of payments is omitted in the first place because of the dubious accuracy of such figures, and secondly because of their doubtful relevance in view of the magnitude of U.S. aid, in commodities and otherwise. There can be no doubt, however, of the substantial improvement in Bolivia's balance of payments under the impact of higher tin prices and continued U.S. and international aid. This is evidenced by the rise in Central Bank holdings of gold and foreign exchange, from $10.4 million at the close of 1963 to $22.4 million at the end of 1964 and $36.4 million at the end of 1965. At the same time, the United States reported a rise in Bolivian government and Bolivian commercial bank assets in the United States, from $32.6 million at the end of 1963 to $43.2 million at the end of 1964 and $67.4 million at the close of 1965. (*International Financial Statistics,* May, 1966.)

‡ It is not in Bolivia alone that "economic development" is interpreted as excluding economic growth achieved by private enterprise and individual planning, saving, investment, and productive effort. With the exception of historical surveys, such as Jonathan Hughes's *The Vital Few* (Boston: Houghton Mifflin, 1966) and J. A. Schumpeter's trail-blazing *The Theory of Economic Development* (Cambridge, Mass.: Harvard University Press, 1934), none of the outstanding works on economic development published over the past three decades makes more than passing mention of the contribution of individual farmers, manufacturers, businessmen, and commercial and investment bankers to economic progress. Yet, if economic development is only to be regarded as such if planned and promoted by the government, then it would seem that the United States must be considered an underdeveloped country.

So true is this that when I insisted upon restricting the expenditures of the Bolivian Development Corporation and of other government enterprises as the *sine qua non* of initiating and maintaining the monetary stabilization program, President Siles exclaimed: "You have given us stabilization, but at the price of economic development." This was despite the fact that it should have been obvious that there was not a single enterprise fostered by the Development Corporation and not a single government industry or activity that had not left the country poorer as a consequence of its operations.

But the damage occasioned by the rampant inflation of 1953-56 was so manifest, the evidence that inflation had been caused by borrowing from the Central Bank so convincing, the limitations of increased taxation so apparent, and the success of the stabilization program so dramatic, that it was clear that if Bolivia's yearnings for an immediate Utopia were to be fulfilled by the government, it could only be through foreign aid. Thus, all Bolivia's development plans from 1958 on were necessarily geared to that solution. But, as no nation likes to acknowledge a state of permanent mendicancy, the Bolivians justified their *demands* for U.S. grants and "loans" by claiming that the United States had robbed them for decades by paying low prices for the tin that was needed to win the war and had imposed a stabilization plan which made it impossible for Bolivia to carry on with its economic development plans, so that it was the *obligation* of the United States to finance Bolivia's development.*

Government development

The old National Planning and Coordination Commission (Comisión Nacional de Coordinación y Planeamiento) was

---

*The international agencies were likewise considered to be duty-bound to help Bolivia: "In those fields where private capital is not interested at this moment, we consider that it is the *duty* of the [World Bank and IDA] to substitute momentarily for this lack of interest, in order to initiate productive activities in fields which up to now are almost virgin." So speaks the president of Bolivia's Central Bank, oblivious to the fact that lack of private interest is not necessarily a proof of public necessity. The fields may have remained untouched because it was not worth the time, effort, or money to cultivate them (Luis Peñaloza, in International Monetary Fund, *Summary Proceedings, 1959 Annual Meeting* [Washington, D.C.: IMF, 1959]).

changed to the National Planning Board (Junta Nacional de Planeamiento). This was more than a change of name. The president of the former commission was the President of the Republic. Víctor Paz-Estenssoro, himself an economist, had presided over its affairs in person. Under Hernán Siles-Zuazo, a lawyer, the day-to-day administration of the commission was left in the capable hands of the commission's executive vice-president, the engineer Miguel Gisbert-Nogué. In 1960, however, when Paz-Estenssoro had the Constitution amended to permit him to serve a second term and Juan Lechín was named Vice-President in return for his support and that of the Communist Party, Lechín demanded that he be permitted to rule the destinies of Bolivia's planning agency. Hence, the decree establishing the new Board provided that the Vice-President of the Republic would be the president of the Board.[74] At the same time, this arrangement automatically gave Lechín or his representative a second post on the National Monetary Stabilization Council.

The magnum opus of the new Board was a Ten-Year Development Plan, 1962-71, prepared with the assistance of ECLA, FAO, and of the U.N. advisory group working as the permanent technical staff within the Planning Board.[75] The plan was impressive in its bulk — 288 pages of statistics, projections, and text — as well as in its aims: to raise the per capita income 50 per cent, to $165 per annum; to increase gross national product at the rate of 8 per cent per annum; to improve the average diet from 1,800 calories per diem to 2,400; and to build and equip schools to take care of 70 per cent of the population of school age instead of 30 per cent.[76] Population projections forecast an increase from 3,824,500 in 1960 to 4,931,200 by 1970 and 6,445,500 in 1980, so that the proposed increases were too large to be predicated on any conceivable rise in domestic savings and investment, and the plan was frankly intended as a blueprint for U.S. aid.[77]*

However, since the macroeconomic generalities of the Ten-Year Plan were too vague to meet the requirements of AID and the Inter-American Development Bank, with the help of AID and

---

*One feature of the population projections which it will be interesting to check at some future date is that, whereas the 1960 population was placed at 49.46 per cent male and 50.54 per cent female (a sequela of the Chaco War), masculine preponderance is expected to be attained by 1970 with 50.22 per cent of the total population.

IDB officials and of various advisory groups paid for by AID, specific projects were devised that laid the basis for the massive injections of U.S. financial assistance discussed below.*

Bolivian Development Corporation. Despite this assistance, however, the annual deficit of the Bolivian Development Corporation was increased from 5 million pesos to 29 million pesos in a single year (from 1962 to 1963). A million-dollar-a-year contract was entered into with Deutsche Projekt Union, G.m.b.H., of Bonn, for engineering advice to be given to the Development Corporation by a syndicate of six German firms. This was financed, in the first year, 5 per cent by Bolivia, 15 per cent by the Inter-American Development Bank, 40 per cent by the United States, and 40 per cent by Germany which, of course, would get compensation in the form of salaries that ranged from $21,600 to $34,200 per annum for each of the engineers and experts, plus the profits on such future orders for equipment and supplies as might be expected to come to the six German backers from the advice of the German engineers.[78] The percentage contributions for subsequent years were left for future determination, but they have thus far remained without change.

The first National Cement Factory, a Development Corporation project that had commenced with the diversion of funds raised for earthquake relief and which, it will be recalled, had been located in Sucre against all engineering and Planning Commission advice, finally got into production in April, 1960, with an output of 14,500 tons, raised to 24,490 tons in 1963, compared with a planned capacity of 30,000 tons. Its cost on completion was reported at $1,349,352 in U.S. aid, Bs. 90 billion in counterpart funds, and Bs. 4 billion from the Development Corporation. The boliviano amounts could theoretically represent anywhere from $8 million to $500 million, depending upon the

---

*The first annual report of the Inter-American Development Bank refers to the fact that prospective borrowers are incapable of drawing up projects worthy of consideration as the basis of bank credits, and that "one of the bank's most important activities . . . will be to provide technical assistance in the preparation of loan projects and applications" (1960 *Annual Report,* p. 14). It does not seem to have occurred to the IDB or to AID that if the prospective borrower is incapable of drafting and substantiating an application for a loan, there might be grounds for questioning the borrower's ability to construct or to manage the proposed enterprise efficiently. As the Mexican economist, Javier Márquez, writes: "The very fact that prolonged and severe inflation has occurred would appear to be sufficient proof of a lack of administrative or fiscal ability." Baer and Kerstenetsky (eds.), *Inflation and Growth in Latin America,* p. 417.

proportion expended upon imported equipment, and the rate of exchange used, but probably $10 million at the most would be the aggregate cost. A second cement plant, better located at Viacha, near La Paz, was producing 31,754 tons by 1963, and a third plant of 100,000 tons capacity is to be built in the politically strategic city of Cochabamba by *Société Fives-Lille-Cail* at an estimated cost of $7 million.[79]

Another more costly Development Corporation project was revived — the ill-fated Villa Montes irrigation plan. This was hailed in the book, *Bolivia: 10 Years of Revolution,* as a scheme that "will permit" the irrigation of 7,000 to 9,000 hectares of land.[80] Twenty years earlier, the Bohan report had pointed out that the project had been condemned by a group of Mexican engineers for the very reasons which have continued to militate against its success to the present time — the area practically unpopulated, the soil unsuitable, the expense unwarranted.*

The Development Corporation also received a $6.5 million, $1\frac{1}{4}$ per cent long-term "loan" from the Social Progress Trust Fund (a fund created with monies donated by the United States and administered by the Inter-American Development Bank) for land settlement, i.e., for the establishment of fifty colonies of settlers throughout the country, the construction of sanitary and water facilities, carpenter shops, the supply of implements, seeds, etc. To this was added a $2.6 million colonization "loan" from the IDB, plus a $435,000 IDB "loan" to the government (to be administered by the Ministry of Rural Affairs and the government Agricultural Bank). By the end of 1965, the government hopes to settle 2,000 Indian families at Chaparé on the new Cochabamba-Santa Cruz highway, with an allotment of 50 acres per family, plus cacao, rubber, and citrus plant seedlings. Chaparé already has 3,135 settlers located, the other main resettlement projects being at Santa Cruz (3,727 Indian families remaining) and Caravani (2,751 families remaining).[81]

Unfortunately, the U.S. Embassy reports that a substantial number of families in the Okinawan colonies — one of the most promising of all the groups established in Bolivia — are planning

---

*In the report of the Committee on Government Operations (Sen. John L. McClellan, Democrat-Arkansas, chairman), it is called "a worthless project, poorly planned, and poorly administered." U.S. Congress, Senate, *Administration of United States Foreign Aid Programs in Bolivia*, 86th Cong., 2d Sess., 1960, p. 10.

to leave the country because of lack of educational facilities, water, and marketing possibilities, and high credit costs, as well as other unfavorable factors. The cost of this failure, in human tragedy even more than in dollars wasted, is beyond measure. Despite high hopes, foreign colonizaticn in Bolivia has not been a success, notwithstanding which the Bolivian government has agreed with Japan to spend some $300,000 over the next three years (1966-68) to take care of some 4,000 Japanese immigrants. Perhaps the most significant part of that agreement is that the immigrants will be permitted to import machinery and equipment free of customs duties. This means that the United States will be in the position of financing Japanese exports in privileged competition against U.S. exports, by reason of U.S. subsidies to meet Bolivian budgetary deficits that will be increased by the customs exemptions.[82]

The Social Progress Trust Fund also "loaned" $4 million to the Development Corporation for housing, plus a nonreimbursable $150,000 grant from the IDB for technical assistance in that field. The IDB "loaned" the Development Corporation $10 million for agricultural, industrial, mining, electrical power, irrigation, and drainage projects, plus a $250,000 nonreimbursable grant for technical assistance, and a $1 million joint U.S.-German-IDB grant for the same purpose.[83] The funds are reloaned by the Development Corporation, in part to private enterprise, but chiefly to so-called "parastatal" enterprises, which are government enterprises independent of the regular government budget.

Another IDB "loan" for $3.5 million to the National Electric Power Administration (Empresa Nacional de Electricidad), a subsidiary of the Bolivian Development Corporation, has been made in conjunction with a $15 million credit extended by the International Development Association for electric power development. It is misleading to describe these "soft" loans and credits other than as gifts, as there can be no expectation of repayment except out of the proceeds of further similar "loans" and grants. In this case, as in the case of other IDA financing, the funds are repayable over 50 years without interest; in the case of the IDB "trust fund," at $1\frac{1}{4}$ per cent over 25-30 years.

IDA is an affiliate of the International Bank for Reconstruction and Development, and this is the first (and only) World Bank financing for Bolivia since the intervention of former Vice-President Ñuflo Chávez blocked a settlement with the bondholders.* Five million dollars of the IDA credit will be reloaned by the government, at $5\frac{1}{2}$ per cent interest, to the Bolivian Power Company, Ltd., a subsidiary of the United States- and Canadian-owned International Power Company, Ltd., in order to expand its power facilities in La Paz and Oruro. The remainder will be used by the newly established National Electric Power Administration, which will be responsible for most of Bolivia's future power development outside of La Paz and Oruro.[84]

In all, the Inter-American Development Bank "loans" to Bolivia, up to December 31, 1964, totaled $37,820,000, of which $11,260,000 was in Social Progress Trust Funds provided by the United States, and the remainder from the bank's Special Operation Fund, provided largely by U.S. contributions. These "loans," however, entail aggregate commitments of $97,125,000, and the remaining funds will come almost entirely from U.S. sources.[85]†

Other government investments. For 1965 and 1966, "investments" by the government were estimated in the Ten-Year Development Plan at $52.7 million and $55.2 million respectively. The amounts were expected to be provided chiefly by U.S. aid. It is difficult, however, to determine the actual scope

*It is the practice of the World Bank to inform loan applicants who are in default on their publicly held foreign debt that the bank will be unable to assist them until they take appropriate steps toward an equitable settlement of those debts (International Bank for Reconstruction and Development, *Some Techniques of Development Lending* [Washington, D.C.: IBRD, 1960]).

† The IDB capital resources have been contributed as follows:

U.S. government:	
Paid-in capital	$ 150,000,000
Fund for Special Operations (paid)	150,000,000
Fund for Special Operations (committed)	750,000,000
Social Progress Trust Fund	525,000,000
U.S. banks and public (bonds)	225,000,000
	$1,800,000,000
Nineteen Latin American governments:	
Paid-in capital	$ 231,580,000
Fund for Special Operations (paid)	68,921,000
Fund for Special Operations (committed)	150,000,000
Italy, United Kingdom, Germany (bonds)	47,594,000
Canada (credits)	10,000,000
	$ 508,095,000
Total	$2,308,095,000

(Source: IDB, *Fifth Annual Report*, 1964, pp. 14-15, 62, 100.)

of future commitments from government planning figures as, despite the ostensible accuracy of the estimates down to decimals, they are nothing more than numbers drawn out of the air on the apparent assumption that, once a project is promised and commenced, USAID and the international agencies will be committed to conclude it even though the ultimate cost may be five or ten times the original estimates — as has been true in the case of practically every project undertaken by the Bolivian government.

For example, in April, 1965, IDB announced a $2.6 million loan to improve and expand the public water supply system in Oruro, but this "investment" is to finance only the *first stage* of a project prepared by a West German consulting firm.[86] Nothing was said of the ultimate cost of the project, or how it would be financed (presumably out of the $750 million that the United States has committed in advance for the Fund for Special Operations to be managed by the IDB). More important, no consideration seems to have been given to the possibility that this "infrastructure" expenditure may be top-heavy for a town in a mining area that is being operated by COMIBOL on a deficitary basis, or to the fact that a water supply system cannot be expected to provide a net income from which to meet even the below-cost $2\frac{3}{4}$ per cent interest charged by IDB, to say nothing of amortization of principal over a 25-year period.

To continue the tally of government enterprises — other than the Development Corporation, COMIBOL, and YPFB — LAB, the government airline, became completely insolvent and had to be reorganized, following which it leased a second-hand DC-6B from American Airlines, Incorporated, and expanded its domestic services, which again proved nonremunerative despite a management advisory contract with North Central Airlines, Incorporated, paid for by U.S. aid. The company has negotiated a USAID "loan" for working capital and equipment and is now operating international as well as domestic services, in competition with the commercial airlines and the deficitary "prestige" lines of other Latin American governments. LAB has taken steps to invalidate the concession contracts of the Braniff and Panagra airlines on the ground of "unfair competition"; i.e., the private company services to Bolivia were being increased and improved. There is no expectation of actual cancellation of the contracts, but their revision under threat of revocation may be expected to bring advantages and subsidies to LAB, in the same way that COMIBOL and YPFB are now being subsidized by their privately operated competitors. To meet the international competition, LAB is now considering the purchase of three super-Caravelle jets on liberal credit terms. The French Ambassador has gallantly "praised the high quality of the LAB personnel" as well as of the Caravelles, and Bolivia and France are evidently counting on the American government to continue meeting LAB deficits.[87]

Bolivia's landlocked position has somewhat inhibited the expansion of government enterprise into maritime transportation, but a 2,000-ton freighter purchased from Yugoslavia, following Tito's visit to La Paz, is being operated by the government on the Pilcomayo River, from an Argentine freeport at Barranqueras down to the Atlantic.[88] Another white elephant, still in the planning stage, is a steel mill, and the government has set up a General Bureau of Iron and Steel to determine principally where and how the money can be obtained.[89] One is reminded that an eminent European statesman, who had been approached for aid by the president of an underdeveloped country, later commented: "That country has a very sensible development program — no steel plant."[90]

Since the November, 1964, *coup d'état,* contemplation of a steel mill has been postponed for the second phase of the Ten-Year Plan, which has been broken down by ICAP (Inter-American Committee for the Alliance for Progress) into three stages: (1) increasing foreign exchange earnings through the promotion of mining and petroleum exports and the encouragement of agriculture; (2) import substitution through agricultural production and the manufacture of fertilizers, explosives, petrochemicals, paper, and canned foods; and (3) expansion of the domestic market by increasing the purchasing power of the Indian peasants. The present Bolivian government is aware of the fiasco of government enterprise, and is reportedly anxious to give greater emphasis to private enterprise.[91] Whether or not this will fit in with the objectives of ICAP, which will control the availability of foreign aid, remains to be seen.

National Railroad Administration. The development of Bolivia's electric power, highway, and railway systems is to proceed throughout all three stages of the Ten-Year Plan. The government now owns and operates all the railroads in the country with the exception of the 60-mile Guaqui-La Paz Railway, having acquired the principal privately operated line — the Bolivia Railway Company, Ltd. — as a consequence of the failure of the MNR regime to live up to its commitments.

Under the stabilization decree, it will be recalled, the government was required to grant immediate temporary rate increases. It was further committed, within the next six months, to establish permanent rates adequate to cover operating expenses, including depreciation, and a fair return on capital. Despite the repeated petitions of the local railway management, and of the parent company — The Antofagasta (Chili) & Bolivia Railway Company, Ltd. — and the formation of one government commission after another to study the matter, nothing was done. Meanwhile, the local company's financial position steadily deteriorated. With increased wages and social security charges, a 40 per cent loss in traffic, the indiscipline of the workers, and no way of dismissing excess personnel, the company's losses amounted to some £500,000 in 1958, and there was every indication that conditions would get worse, not better. In the light of the government's refusal to meet its promises on tariffs, the parent company finally offered to sell the railway to the government on a twenty-five-year payment plan, advising that it could no longer afford to finance the operation of the line. The government appointed another commission and decreed that if the company ceased operations the lines would be operated by the National Railroad Administration, *and that all losses would be chargeable to the company,* a condition that the company naturally refused to accept. On February 18, 1959, the company did cease operation, and the government took over, without, however, acquiring ownership.[92]

Under government operation, the condition of the track, installations, rolling stock, and, above all, the service deteriorated to such a point that the Bolivian government, in desperation, appealed to the company to resume the operating management under a decree whereby ownership of the properties passed to the government on March 30, 1962, on terms and conditions that were not settled until June, 1966. Under the agreement, the government is to pay the company £2,530,000 for its properties, one of the conditions being that the company is not liable for the losses incurred while under government operation or ownership. The management agreement has been extended, and the lines remain under the same management as prior to the government takeover.[93]

At the close of 1964, all railways, with the exception of the Guaqui line, were consolidated into the National Railroad Administration (Empresa Nacional de Ferrocarriles) which is attempting to modernize the system. A new, rapid service was inaugurated on the La Paz-Oruro-Cochabamba line; the La Paz-Beni line was discontinued; and 245 employees have been laid off. YPFB has reduced its charges for fuel oil, meaning that the visible railway deficits will be decreased and the concealed deficits of YPFB increased. USAID is financing the purchase of equipment, spare parts, and stores, as well as the cost of the British technical staff employed by the Railroad Administration; it is the general expectation, at least in Bolivia, that the money for the purchase of the Antofagasta line will in the long run be provided by the United States. Meanwhile, regardless of management, continued deficits are assured by the operation of the Brazilian and Argentine railroads referred to in Chapter 3. Over the past eight years the acknowledged deficit has never been below $2.1 million and has run as high as $3.1 million (1963).[94]

Private investment

"My country has opened its resources to private capital..." declared the president of the Central Bank of Bolivia in 1959, in justification of his demand for World Bank and IFC assistance.[95] And so it had — from the Bolivian perspective. Congress had enacted a Mining Code and a Petroleum Code, and investors had flocked to Bolivia in search of concessions. So when, in 1960, Congress enacted an Investment Law, it was hard for the Bolivians to understand why investors in other fields — manufacturers of machinery, tools, tractors, and other products, who were expected to give employment to thousands of workers at high wages — failed to heed the call. There were even suspicions of nefarious designs on the part of the industrial nations of the world to maintain their monopolies and thus compel Bolivia to continue in her role of economic serfdom as a producer of raw materials.

For approved, new foreign investments the provisions of the 1960 investment law were:[96]

Article 3 guaranteed that there would be no expropriation without prior payment of the amount invested, in terms of the currency in which the investment was made. *(But there was no guaranty of remittance, nor of recognition of earnings ploughed back into the business, and no guaranty that Bolivia would respect that guaranty any better than she had met her other commitments.)*

Article 5 provided for a 50 per cent reduction of income tax on reinvested earnings; the right to revalue assets from time to time at replacement value, free of tax; a five-year exemption from new direct taxes enacted after the registration of capital; and exemption from customs duties on the importation of machinery and equipment. *(But the equally solemn promise given in 1957 that there would be only one tax and no more taxes on the revaluation of assets had been broken seven months after the promise was made.)*

Article 6 provided a number of miscellaneous tax exemptions. *(But Bolivia's past record showed that where special privileges were granted they could later be offset by special taxes on those enjoying the privileges, as in the case of the revertibles.)*

Article 8 created a National Investment Committee to pass on and approve all new foreign investments, without which approval none of the law's guarantees would be applicable. *(But any system of prior approval meant at best interminable delay and red tape, and at worst was an open invitation to graft, not only on the initial investment but on all subsequent additions to that investment.)*

It was difficult for the government planners to understand that a reputation for fair treatment of existing investments, and of local as well as foreign investors, was more important than special privileges for new foreign capital; that fair enforcement of reasonable labor legislation, moderation in social security costs, and the assurance, based on past history, that the government would not enact and the courts would not tolerate expropriation without prompt and adequate compensation were the factors that would attract investment. Nor, on the other hand, did the planners grasp the fact that excessive nationalism, antagonism towards profits on foreign capital, burdensome taxation, red tape, and restrictions on the freedom of management were factors that would deter investment; that political, social, and monetary stability were an absolute *sine qua non* for investment (except perhaps in enterprises such as the petroleum industry, where the risk of finding or not finding oil in profitable quantities is so great that the political factor is just one more problem to be taken into account as a business risk); that, except for mining, petroleum, and public utility operation, a concession was neither necessary nor desirable; that, in sum, all those elements entering into the hackneyed phrase, "fair investment climate," were far more important than any investment law or guaranty; and, above all, that so long as the U.S. government and the international agencies continue to subsidize unprofitable and tax-consuming government enterprises, there can be no solid basis for the expansion of private enterprise.[97]

Thus the 1960 Investment Code failed to bring in the flow of new private investments that had been hoped for, and in 1963 another commission was set up to study a new Investment Code which was enacted on October 19, 1965, and provides equal incentives to foreign and Bolivian investors under the supervision of the new investment institute *(Instituto para la Promoción de las Inversiones en Bolivia).*[98]

The U.N. (Keenleyside) report states: "Capital... whether from foreign or domestic sources, will not now be invested in Bolivia in any significant measure unless the prospective investors can be satisfied that there exists a persuasive prospect of reasonable security and profit. But even if arrangements can be made for technical assistance and capital investment the results will still be meagre in the absence of economic and political stability."[99] The ECLA report emphasizes the lack of judicial safeguards, "the absence of basic law and order," and contains an enlightening discussion of the deficiencies of Bolivian labor, the lack of education, and the psychological, ethnical, and social factors which make for a disinclination to work, a tendency to violent indiscipline, and other qualities that make it difficult for the Bolivian Indian or mestizo to adapt to an industrial economy. These difficulties, the report points out, are aggravated by the shortcomings of higher education and of the government bureaucracy.[100]

In sum, with or without an investment law, private investment is bound to be a slow-growing plant, and Bolivian capital is more likely to be attracted than foreign capital, except in mining or petroleum investment, which will flow wherever the wealth of natural resources outweighs the dearth of other inducements. Thus, in the post-stabilization decade, such private investment and economic development as has taken place in Bolivia, other than in gold dredging and petroleum as reported above, has thus far been almost entirely a matter of the renaissance of agriculture and the slow but steady improvement in private mining and manufacturing, almost entirely achieved with Bolivian capital.

Nevertheless, a change may be in sight, and there are several important signs pointing in that direction. The new Mining Code, enacted May 7, 1965, has already begun to attract favorable attention from responsible mining interests. The new Investment Code is considered a decided improvement over its predecessor; and, although a code in itself is of little consequence, as has been stated above, the tenor of the legislation indicates a new attitude on the part of the government, which welcomes business and investment as essential to the economic and social advancement of Bolivia. Most significant of all, the First National City Bank, New York, opened a branch in La Paz in January, 1966; W. R. Grace & Company and three other U.S. companies have formed a $5.5 million tin-mining company under the name of ESTALSA; and the Bolivian Power Company, Ltd., a Canadian-American enterprise, has announced that its new power station will be completed shortly and that it is going ahead with further expansion plans.[101] My insistence, in the early days of the stabilization program, on a fair rate of return, despite political opposition (pp. 297-98, 453-55), had made it possible for the Bolivia Power Company, Ltd., to operate at a modest profit over the troubled years from 1957 through 1965, and this fact, plus monetary stabilization, is now beginning to pay off to Bolivia's benefit.

Government Finance

It is not easy to form a clear concept of the state of Bolivian government finances. The figures from the various official sources are so disparate that it is impossible to discern which are true — or reasonably true — and which are false. In some cases, receipts from borrowing are commingled with revenues from taxes or from budgeted appropriations so as to show a fictitious balance in the account. In other cases, expenditures that are properly current expenses are considered as capital investment, *and are excluded entirely from the official published expenditure accounts.* And in practically no instance is it possible to determine whether the accounts are on a cash basis or an accrual basis or, what is more likely, on a basis that is neither one nor the other. All that can be stated with any assurance is that the government revenues and expenditures were so out of balance in 1958 that they came close to wrecking the whole monetary stabilization program, as is set forth in Chapter 23, and that, in later years, there has been at least some semblance of order and balance in the accounts, thanks chiefly to a continuing injection of U.S. aid for budgetary support.

TABLE 20

Consolidated Accounts of the Government Sector
(In Millions of New Pesos)

	1962	1963	1964	1965
Income	1,756.3	1,834.8	2,313.6	2,366.4
Central government	487.6	552.8	691.8	734.0
COMIBOL	539.0	548.4	814.8	798.0
YPFB	212.5	225.6	238.3	238.2
Railroads	82.5	85.2	87.1	90.2
Other agencies	434.7	422.8	481.6	506.0
Expenditures	2,126.7	2,290.8	2,533.2	2,698.8
Central government	361.5	451.2	537.0	610.7
COMIBOL	779.0	780.0	915.6	906.0
YPFB	265.8	283.2	225.1	302.6
Railroads	107.3	114.0	123.4	115.5
Other agencies	613.1	662.4	732.1	764.0
Deficit	370.4	456.0	219.6	332.4

Source: USAID, *Economic and Program Statistics*, 1965, p. 28. Note that these figures do not include Social Security Administration taxes and expenditures. The former are given as 129.2 million pesos in 1964 and 134.0 million pesos in 1965. Another source, which may not be comparable, gives social security taxes (in millions of pesos) of 116.1 in 1962, 110.2 in 1963, and expenditures of 106.7 in 1962, 112.1 in 1963, and 96.1 (budgeted) in 1964 (*Bolivia: 10 Años de Revolución*, p. 195). One new peso = 1,000 bolivianos = 11.88 cents U.S.

It is with some misgivings, therefore, that the accompanying Table 20, purporting to show the financial operations of the government sector, is presented. The figures will agree only in part with those obtainable from other sources (or from the same sources). Note that the table is not complete with respect to capital expenditures, inasmuch as it omits those capital expenditures that are financed directly by U.S. grants. The deficits are covered by the United States in the form of counterpart funds or additional dollar aid.

Some of the items in the table call for comment.* The

*There is no way to reconcile these figures with those for any long-term series. However, the Central Bank reports an increase in government expenditures from 290,740,000 pesos in 1957 to 508,099,000 pesos in 1962. The figures mean little, but the percentage increase of 75 per cent is significant (Central Bank, *Annual Report*, 1960, p. 147; *Annual Report*, 1962, p. 133).

COMIBOL, YPFB, railway, and other government enterprise figures are shown almost entirely on a cash basis; that is, as has been pointed out, depreciation and depletion allowances are nonexistent or inadequate, and there is no allowance for any return on the capital investment, whether it represents a confiscated asset, or one entered in the books at an artificial official exchange rate, or one acquired since stabilization at a realistic rate of exchange but free of duty. There are no taxes shown in the expenditure columns of those enterprises (which are tax-free), and, per contra, there are presumably included in the YPFB and COMIBOL revenues those taxes paid by private enterprise and earmarked for those companies. In other words, Table 20 purports to show surpluses or deficits, not profits or losses. Furthermore, the government revenue figures include export royalties that should be, but are not, paid by COMIBOL; i.e., they are carried as though COMIBOL paid taxes, and the government loaned COMIBOL an equivalent amount.[102]

A breakdown of government tax revenues by sources is shown in Table 21 (the figures do not coincide with those in Table 20, or with duty revenues reported by an equally official source). Customs revenues from imports have increased notably since 1959, not because of any significant increase in duty

TABLE 21

Government Tax Revenues by Source
(In Millions of New Pesos)

Source of Revenue	1962	1963	1964	1965
Personal income tax	21.2	21.6	22.0	26.0
Corporate income tax	67.6	82.8	85.0	90.0
Social security taxes	116.1	110.2	129.2	134.0
Import duties	200.9	200.4	247.0	250.0
Export taxes and royalties	55.5	72.0	137.8	142.0
Foreign exchange tax	11.9	15.6	18.0	19.3
Consular fees and communications taxes	24.4	30.0	25.0	26.7
Sales taxes and other indirect taxes	92.7	110.4	137.7	156.8
Total	590.3	643.0	801.7	844.8

Source: USAID, *Economic and Program Statistics*, 1965, p. 26, except for 1962 and 1963 social security taxes, from *Bolivia: 10 Años de Revolución*, p. 195. These tax revenues include royalties from COMIBOL which were not in fact collected; they do not coincide with those shown in Table 20 or in the substantiating data for Figure 16. The latter figures are probably closest to the truth.

rates, but because of greater efficiency in deterring evasion.* Since 1959, on the advice of a staff of British customs experts, a number of reforms have been put into effect, and the following year the customs guards were reorganized and placed under the command of the Cuerpo Nacional de Policías y Carabineros (national police force), with the result that customs collections on imports jumped from 116.2 million new pesos in 1959 to 125.2 million in 1960, 180.2 million in 1961, and 226.5 million in 1962 (these figures are not reconcilable with those shown in Table 21).[103]

In justice to former Finance Minister Hugo Moreno-Córdova, it should be said that there is scarcely a single major measure put into effect on the advice of the British experts that had not been repeatedly advocated by the Minister in 1957, but he then lacked the power to enforce his recommendations against the powerful political forces in the government that opposed them. It was not until the near-collapse of the stabilization program in 1958 that the government bowed to the insistence of the USOM representatives and agreed that it would employ the British advisers and carry out their recommendations.

In 1963, however, the government enacted certain import licensing measures and sharp increases in customs duties on a long list of consumer imports, the increases running as high as 90 per cent in some instances. The higher duties were supposedly to counteract the rise in imports which was beginning to affect the foreign exchange position, but the measure overlooked the fact that by far the greater part of the import increase was attributable to duty-free imports by the government, COMIBOL, and other government enterprises. Less than a year later, the U.S. Embassy reported the inevitable consequence of the higher customs duties — smuggling was again rampant, and, despite that, businessmen were insisting on still higher tariffs on textiles, shoes, pharmaceuticals, paints, and other items. The lesson learned in 1957 — that smuggling could be virtually eliminated and government revenues increased by lower, not higher tariffs — was forgotten, as well as the conclusion that any local industry that requires a protection so high that it is unenforceable must be uneconomical, costing the

---

*The virtual elimination of smuggling as a result of the 1957 customs tariff was a short-lived triumph of the stabilization program, for reasons set forth at p. 333ff.

consuming public more than the benefits reaped by the local manufacturers and laborers. On September 5, 1965, a completely new customs tariff was enacted, giving still higher protection to local industry, but the new law is already shot through with duty-free import privileges.[104]

Deficits in the government sector

Information compiled by the Solomon mission (p. 734) makes it possible to present approximate information on the deficits of each of the major branches of the government sector for 1961-63 that is not available for earlier or later years. The figures are set forth in Table 22.

The deficits shown in the table were financed largely by U.S. aid. In other words, as is pointed out in the Solomon report, the impact of U.S. aid on Bolivian development is diminished to the extent of these deficitary operations in the government sector. It is money down the drain. Nor can the reported deficits or alleged surpluses be taken without reservations, for there is no telling to what extent the figures conceal a backlog of unpaid bills and additions to short-term debt. So far as the government enterprises are concerned, the accounts may mask a failure to allow for adequate depreciation, depletion, capital charges, and, in the case of the government banks, reserves for bad debts, such as the uncollectible loans to political persons and parties.

Earmarked revenues

Among the developments that have adversely affected the government financial picture have been the elimination of royalties paid by COMIBOL and YPFB; the earmarking of 50 per cent of private oil royalties in favor of YPFB and of the remainder for the department where the oil is produced;[105] the earmarking of 100 per cent of private mineral royalties in favor of COMIBOL (p. 540); and tax and customs exemptions for all government enterprises, which the Stabilization Council had successfully opposed in 1957. Earmarked taxes for the universities jumped from 765 million new pesos in 1957 to 6,462 million in 1962;[106] and seemingly any attempt to control or even audit the university receipts and expenditures continues to be the "hot potato" that it was in 1957.

Other earmarkings and tax exemptions granted in the

TABLE 22

Deficits and Surpluses (+) in the Government Sector — Calendar Years
(In Thousands of New Pesos)

	1961 (Actual)	1962 (Preliminary)	1963 (Estimate)
COMIBOL	118,460	116,853	79,487
YPFB	27,900	43,900	81,800
Development Corporation (exclusive of loans)	17,000	19,231	39,403
Antofagasta railway (nationalized)	29,000	29,230	25,940
National Railroad Administration	24,837	6,857	4,681
Social Security Administration	35,818	25,819	26,220
Agricultural Bank (exclusive of loans)	636	1,206	1,254
Mining Bank (exclusive of loans)	8,267	+13,352	...
Lloyd Aereo Boliviano (airline)	7,541	10,226	11,028
Central Bank (exclusive of loans)	+263	+1,797	+1,797
Public Health Service	10,718	+1,521	...
Highway Service	15,028	17,467	18,000
Education Service	2,783	3,218	...
Agriculture Service	16,740	8,652	14,272
Petroleum Social Security Administration	+817	+1,757	+475
Military Retirement Fund	3,671	3,114	3,276
Railway Social Security Administration	682	n.a.	n.a.
Miscellaneous enterprises and agencies	+2,310	+390	1,128
Total government enterprises and agencies	294,893	268,022	304,217
Central government (reported budget operations)	95,461	81,800	65,000
(Less subsidies to enterprises and agencies)	(71,811)	(45,979)	(34,958)
Total deficit in public sector	318,543	303,843	334,259
Total deficit (in U.S. dollars)	*$26,800,000*	*$25,600,000*	*$28,200,000*

Note: Certain agencies for which it was impossible to obtain data are omitted, as are also the deficits of the railways constructed by Argentina and Brazil which were currently financed by those countries. Data taken from Solomon report, Table III, and based on official sources, on USAID data, and on estimates made by the Solomon mission. The subsidies received by the various enterprises and agencies from the central government have been added to the deficits of those units.

post-stabilization decade include a 10-year tax exemption for all new hotels and a special 500-boliviano ($\frac{1}{2}$ new peso, or 6 cents U.S.) *Pro Vivienda* tax stamp that must be affixed to all documents (receipts, bills, contracts, etc.) except checks and savings accounts, the revenues being earmarked for the construction of housing for government employees.[107] Like all such privileges, these earmarkings and exemptions are the result of political pressures or humanitarian improvisations rather than of sound fiscal, social, or economic planning and are among the contributing causes of the heavy budgetary support demanded of U.S. aid.

The Solomon report strongly recommended the elimination of all earmarkings on revenues and at the same time urged the repeal of certain legislation that permits various government departments (and, it may be added, certain government enterprises and agencies) to collect special taxes and use the revenues free of budgetary controls.

Social security

The Social Security Administration (CNSS) shows total receipts of 116.1 million new pesos in 1962, 110.2 million in 1963, and 119.7 million (budgeted) for 1964. Benefits paid, according to the same source, were 106.7 million in 1962, 112.1 million in 1963, and 96.1 million (budgeted) in 1964. It would appear, however, that these figures refer to total expenditures of CNSS rather than to benefits paid to the workers.

The number of workers entitled to social security benefits under the CNSS has increased from 52,727 in 1956 to 111,529 in 1961. Including dependents, 345,639 persons were covered by CNSS. Adding the independent civil service and railway funds, the total number of workers enrolled under social security is reported at 123,517 in 1961 and at 122,104 in 1962, but the figures are apparently not reconcilable.[108]

In 1962 a law was enacted creating a commission to lay plans for extending social security benefits to the peasants.[109] If this comes to pass — and it is difficult to halt eleemosynary legislation once the prospective beneficiaries are encouraged to believe that it will be enacted — Bolivia's economy will be totally submerged beneath the weight of a social security structure quite beyond its economic capacity, with retirement at the age of fifty or under and benefits that cannot possibly be paid out of the income of the country's two million peasants. The legislation, if it advances beyond the commission, can only contemplate that Bolivia will remain a permanent ward of the United States.

Foreign bonds

In June, 1957, as has been narrated in Chapter 18, an agreement was announced for resumption of payment on Bolivia's foreign debt, following an eighteen-month delay caused by the untimely intervention of the then Vice-President, that ended with his resignation. That agreement was defaulted on, and a new agreement was executed on June 17, 1958; but on September 1, 1960, the bond coupon due on that date was defaulted, and it was not until July 30, 1962, that it was announced that payment would be resumed.[110] Table 23 shows the payments actually made on coupons that, under the agreement with the Bondholders' Council, were due in September, 1960, and subsequently.

TABLE 23

Coupon Payments on Defaulted Bonds

Bond Issue	Coupon Date	Agreed Payment Date	Actual Payment Date and Amount
6 per cent due 1940 ($30 coupon)	Oct. 1, 1934	Oct. 1, 1960	July 30, 1962 ($ 8.25)
	April 1, 1935	April 1, 1961	July 5, 1963 ($ 8.25)
	Oct. 1, 1935	Oct. 1, 1961	June 30, 1964 ($ 8.25)
	April 1, 1936	April 1, 1962	Dec. 31, 1964 ($11.00)
8 per cent due 1947 ($40 coupon)	Nov. 1, 1935	Nov. 1, 1960	Nov. 9, 1962 ($ 8.25)
	May 1, 1936	May 1, 1961	Nov. 15, 1963 ($ 8.25)
	Nov. 1, 1936	Nov. 1, 1961	June 30, 1964 ($ 8.25)
	May 1, 1937	May 1, 1962	Dec. 31, 1964 ($11.00)
7 per cent due 1958 ($35 coupon)	Jan. 1, 1935	Jan. 1, 1961	Jan. 2, 1963 ($ 8.25)
	July 1, 1935	July 1, 1961	Jan. 2, 1964 ($ 8.25)
	Jan. 1, 1936	Jan. 1, 1962	June 30, 1964 ($11.00)
	July 1, 1936	July 1, 1962	Nov. 30, 1964 ($11.00)
7 per cent due 1969 ($35 coupon)	Sept. 1, 1934	Sept. 1, 1960	July 30, 1962 ($ 8.25)
	March 1, 1935	March 1, 1961	June 4, 1963 ($ 8.25)
	Sept. 1, 1935	Sept. 1, 1961	June 30, 1964 ($ 8.25)
	March 1, 1936	March 1, 1962	Nov. 30, 1964 ($11.00)

Sources: Compiled from Foreign Bondholders Protective Council, Inc., press releases, June 17, 1958; January 2, 1963; May 22, 1964, and *Report 1962 through 1964* (New York: FBPC, 1964), pp. 10-11.

In May, 1964, the Council announced that it was discussing with the Bolivian government the problems connected with issuance of the new $1,100 bonds (per $1,000 face value of old bonds) that were supposed to have been issued not later than June 30, 1962, as well as the arrears of interest since the 1960 suspension of payments. The 1964 *coup d'état* delayed negotiations, but the military government made the December, 1964, remittances and has indicated its intention of complying with the obligations under the 1958 agreement.[111] There would appear to be a reasonable expectation that payments will be resumed and thereafter continued so long as Bolivia's receipts of U.S. aid substantially exceed the amounts payable under the agreement.*

*In March, 1966, the Bolivian government announced that the new bonds would be issued shortly, and on April 1, 1966, the Empire Trust Company, as paying agent, stated that it had funds on hand to pay the coupons in arrears on the old bonds. Standard & Poor's *Standard Corporation Descriptions*, A-B, June-July, 1966, p. 7832.

23

THE STABILIZATION PROGRAM

To the informed observer, it was clear by the second half of 1957 that the government was not carrying out its commitments under the stabilization program. The consequences could be seen in the weakening of the boliviano in terms of dollars beginning in May and the upward trend in living costs from September on, until finally, in December, 1957, the sharp increase in bank note circulation left no doubt whatsoever of the dangers beneath the surface (see Chapter 20, Fig. 10, and pp. 501ff). Superficially, however, all appeared serene. Living costs were still well below the prestabilization levels (although labor leaders would not admit it), and the boliviano had closed the year at Bs. 8,565 to the dollar, which compared favorably with the prestabilization peak of Bs. 14,000 and was certainly far better than the levels toward which the currency was indubitably headed before the Stabilization Council was created.

Digressions from the Stabilization Program

The very success of the program, however, led to its undoing. The digressions from the plan, which I had warned against in the April 17 Report to the Cabinet and later to the nation, gave little outward indication of perturbing the smooth course of events. And so, little by little, the President was apparently misled into believing that he could give way here and there — his urge for "flexibility" — without sacrificing the goal of monetary stability. Or perhaps it would be nearer the truth to say that political and labor pressures exceeded the President's power to cope with them without risking some more serious catastrophe.

Wage increases and government borrowing

In any event, although wages were ostensibly frozen in 1957 and early 1958, the President granted an increase in the family

subsidy that amounted in effect to a 10 per cent rise in wages.*
There were also readjustments in employment classifications
and promotions to higher wage brackets that added a further
undeterminable amount to government and private payrolls.
Together with other adjustments, general wage levels by mid-
1958 were 27.5 per cent above the average at the commencement of the stabilization program. In the second half of 1958,
teachers' salaries were raised 50 per cent above the December
15, 1956, stabilization levels. They comprised the most neglected sector of the economy, and apparently my arguments on
their behalf in the Stabilization Council had produced a belated
effect, although their wages are still at starvation levels. Bank
employees were given a 33 per cent increase, railway workers
27 per cent, and civil servants 27.5 per cent above the rates
fixed in the stabilization program. The government sector, as
the largest employer of labor, moved inevitably into a deficitary
position, and both the government and the private sector were
compelled to borrow to meet their payrolls.

Tin production and exports dropped because of illegal
strikes and work stoppages which were nothing more than paid
vacations. All together, Bolivian labor worked only 136 days in
1958, and the miners, as the least disciplined and politically
most powerful group, undoubtedly worked less than the national
average, encouraged by their union leaders.[112] Pressure on the
balance of payments and on the boliviano increased, but the
President, after permitting the exchange rate to rise to Bs.
8,855 in March, absolutely refused to allow any further change
and compelled the Central Bank to maintain the rate artificially
at that level for fear of accelerating the rise in prices and pro-
voking a demand for further wage increases.[113] This was, of
course, in direct violation of Bolivia's express commitments
under the stabilization program.

Table 24 shows a Bs. 9 billion increase in the money supply from the close of 1957 to the close of 1958. To this, however, must be added the Bs. 47 billion increase from November
30 to December 31, 1957, to get a clear picture of the consequences of the wage increases and other circumstances set

*The family subsidy, common in Latin America, is an additional wage
not corresponding to the worker's rank or productivity but to the number
of his dependents. The President, with his deep humanitarian instincts,
had pushed harder for increases in such payments than for any other form
of higher compensation.

TABLE 24

Monetary Survey
(In Billions of Bolivianos or Millions of New Pesos)

	Money Supply*	Net Claims on Government*	Claims on Private Sector*
1957 (November)	244.2	196.0	48.5
1957 (December)	291.2	360.1	61.4
1958 (December)	300.5	413.2	71.7
1959 (December)	385.5	507.3	78.4
1960 (December)	418.6	590.6	81.7
1961 (December)	495.7	635.1	116.0
1962 (December)	556.0	664.5	141.9
1963 (December)	665.0	686.2	194.2
1964 (December)	802.8	709.7	249.5
1965 (December)	1,011.1	842.2	269.9

*Figures as of the end of each period.
Source: *International Financial Statistics.* (Note: IFS classifies claims on the government development banks under claims in the private sector, which tends to minimize the loans to government agencies.)

forth above. Claims on government (meaning government borrowing from the Central Bank) increased Bs. 53 billion in 1958, plus Bs. 164 billion in December, 1957, while claims on the private sector rose Bs. 13 billion in December, 1957, and a further Bs. 10 billion in 1958.

In sum, therefore, from November 30, 1957, to December 31, 1958, government borrowing increased Bs. 217 billion while private borrowing increased Bs. 23 billion. The fact that the money supply increased by only Bs. 56 billion in that period is explained in part by lag, but chiefly by the fact that President Siles refused to permit the exchange rate to rise in accordance with supply and demand. This produced a loss in the stabilization fund of $6 million in the month of December, 1957, alone, and the drain continued through September, 1958, to a total loss of $9 million in ten months. Each dollar's loss in the foreign exchange resources had to be paid for with a corresponding number of bolivianos withdrawn from circulation — nearly 100 billion bolivianos. Had the President permitted the Foreign Exchange Committee to increase the dollar rate to its proper level, there would probably have been no loss in the fund.

The drain on the stabilization fund

In 1956, to commence the stabilization fund operations, the Central Bank had drawn $3 million against the IMF quota. In 1957 the bank drew a further $1 million from the IMF and $8,440,000 from ICA, most of it in the month of December alone. In 1958 $2 million was drawn against the IMF and $1,259,000 against ICA, almost entirely during the first nine months. That left in the $25 million stabilization fund only $1.5 million to be drawn against the IMF and $301,000 yet available with ICA, plus the $7.5 million U.S. Treasury *tranche,* which was still untouched but, in actual fact, *could not be drawn because the Bolivian government had flagrantly violated the provisions of its contract* (contract terms at p. 251).*

The New Stabilization Agreement

By September, 1958, Bolivia's deviations from the agreed plan were so substantial that there was no longer any justification for further contributions to the stabilization fund. While it was rather late to lock the stable door, the threat of a potential crisis was sufficient to bring Bolivia to its senses, both because there would have been a tremendous loss of face at home if the stabilization financing were to be publicly withdrawn and because an outright break might even jeopardize U.S. budgetary support, which, it was clear, would have to take the place of the stabilization fund.

The new U.S. Executive Director of the Stabilization Council, Victor R. Rose, insisted, as the price of continued support:

*Following a return to the provisions of the stabilization agreement, as set forth in the following pages, Bolivia was permitted to draw a further $250,000 against the IMF in 1959, $1,000,000 in 1960, and the remaining $250,000 in 1961. It drew $33,000 on the ICA in 1959, and the remaining $268,000 in 1961. The entire $7.5 million Treasury *tranche* was cancelled, ostensibly to save the annual stand-by fee.[114] In point of fact, it would not have been consistent with the contract with the Treasury for the credit to be continued where there was no apparent intention on the part of Bolivia to live up to its commitments. From the Bolivian viewpoint, there was no urgency to do so, as ICA (and later AID) more than made up the difference with direct budgetary support, and with no obligation of repayment. As the President of the Central Bank (Peñaloza) said, when criticized for having disposed of Bolivia's gold: "Why keep the gold when we have U.S. aid?" (*Última Hora,* January 22, 1960).

(1) that the budget of the government sector be balanced, (2) that the boliviano be left free to drop to its proper supply-demand level, (3) that private investment be encouraged in fact as well as in theory, and (4) that the stranglehold of the labor unions on employment be broken. C. David Finch, who had accompanied Dr. Costanzo on the IMF stabilization mission in 1956, arrived in La Paz and was reported by the press to be engaged in closely guarded negotiations with Rose, the council, and other government officials.[115] To prevent speculation, the Stabilization Council ordered the suspension of all foreign exchange transactions, amid well-founded rumors that devaluation of the boliviano was imminent.[116]

The Central Bank report for that year attributed the interruption of foreign exchange dealings and the depreciation of the boliviano to the suspension of world tin sales on September 18, 1958, as a consequence of Russian dumping of 18,300 tons of Chinese tin.[117] In actual fact, however, the USSR sales had only a transient effect on the tin market and little or no perceptible effect on Bolivia. The sole reason for the drop in the boliviano and the suspension of exchange operations was that the Bolivian government had deviated so far from the stabilization program that the stabilization fund was practically exhausted.

The new exchange rate

It was agreed that, so long as the exchange markets were closed and a new rate of exchange would have to be fixed, it would be well to make all necessary wage and other adjustments simultaneously, so as to avoid the need for further deviations from the program at a later date. The government announced that it would reduce its expenditures and increase its revenues sufficiently to cut the deficit in the overall public sector to Bs. 40 billion for the last quarter of 1958, and this deficit, it was reported, would be chiefly attributable to nonrecurrent year-end wage adjustments and to severance pay as a result of the dismissal of excess public employees.* COMIBOL was pledged to

*The year-end adjustment turned out to be a Christmas bonus for all government employees, equal to one month's salary per year, *payable retroactively from December, 1957* (Law of January 8, 1959; Central Bank, 31st *Annual Report*, 1959, p. 161). With this exception, the IMF reported in its 1959 *Annual Report* that "wages generally ceased to rise in 1959, public sector deficits financed by borrowing were eliminated, and the exchange rate and the cost of living were again stabilized. Mining production and exports, however, continued to be low." (p. 111).

close its submarginal mines and dismiss 3,200 excess employees. A 27 per cent wage increase was to be granted to all workers who had not benefited from the latest round of increases.

With those adjustments, the Central Bank resumed foreign exchange operations on October 1, setting an opening rate of Bs. 11,000. The year 1958 closed with the boliviano quoted at Bs. 11,935,[118] and it has continued at that rate or better to the present time.

As part of the agreement, the Central Bank was permitted to issue a further Bs. 43 billion in bank notes to cover the government's obligations. COMIBOL agreed to increase prices for goods sold in its commissaries, inasmuch as, despite the stabilization commitments, merchandise had been sold at below cost throughout 1958. A 27 per cent raise was granted to the miners, and that percentage was established as the minimum for all private as well as public employees.[119]

The stabilization program resumed

Aside from the new exchange rate, no change was made in the 1956-57 stabilization plan, with one exception. A new 2 per cent tax was imposed on all sales of foreign exchange. This tax had been advocated in the original Fifty-Step stabilization program (Appendix III, step 8, p. 632), except that, under that plan, the proceeds of the tax would have been used for the specific purpose of building up Bolivia's gold or foreign exchange reserve instead of blanketed in with general revenues (see p. 240).

The remaining 1956 and 1957 stabilization decrees continued in full force and effect, with such changes in tax and royalty rates as were enacted from time to time. The new rate, of course, meant a 35 per cent reduction in the value of the boliviano, but it had been provided in the stabilization measures from the very beginning that the rate of exchange would be left free to find its own level according to market pressures, and it was foreseen that if the government failed to hold the line on wages the dollar rate of exchange would have to rise. The departure from the original plan was not in the new value fixed for the boliviano, but in the unpublicized deviations over the preceding ten months, when the President had refused to permit the exchange rate to fluctuate and had thereby drained the stabilization fund of $15.7 million of its resources, with the Treasury

$7.5 million *tranche* withdrawn in 1960. The only other departure from the plan, not generally publicized, was that, from 1960 on, with the stabilization fund exhausted, AID has provided Bolivia with whatever amounts it needed to balance its budget, so that stabilization has since been maintained not by a return to reality — as the first twelve months of stabilization proved to be possible — but by a return to a new world of unreality in the shape of continuous U.S. subsidies for Bolivian deficits. This is shown in Figure 16 in Chapter 24.

The trade agreement dollars

One more hole in the program remained to be plugged, namely, the bilateral foreign exchange agreements under which Bolivia was losing good stabilization fund dollars in return for the «sham dollars" referred to in Chapter 18.

In March, 1958, a new treaty was signed with Brazil, covering foreign trade matters in general, including questions of frontier trade, the establishment of free ports for Bolivia in Corumbá and Santos (Brazil), railway credits (for the once-a-week railway referred to at p. 67), the establishment of an agency in La Paz of the Banco do Brazil, and an adjustment of the «treaty dollar" *(dólares convenio)* debts between the two countries. By December 31, 1958, Bolivia owed $4,470,000 in treaty dollars to Argentina, $1,751,000 to Brazil, and $85,000 to Uruguay. Per contra, Spain owed Bolivia $69,000 in treaty dollars, and Chile owed $91,000. These figures, however, did not include Argentine credits of $5 million in treaty dollars ($1.3 to COMIBOL, $1.2 to YPFB, and $2.5 million to the Ministry of Economy), for the importation of foodstuffs for sale at the COMIBOL and YPFB commissaries and at those maintained by the ministry. These credits were negotiated on October 30, 1958, *after the new stabilization agreement had been concluded.*[120] The credits made it possible for Bolivia to continue selling foodstuffs to the miners and others at less than world market costs, but with the losses disguised through the use of "sham money."

The IMF Increases Its Quotas

When the IMF in 1958 found itself running short of loanable funds, the only way it could increase its resources was to raise the quotas of all nations, meaning that the United States and other nations that were then solvent would contribute their quotas in dollars or other "hard" currency, while the insolvent countries would pay 25 per cent in dollars and the rest in their local currencies, which would be for all practical purposes sterilized and thus not add to local inflationary pressures. The member nations could then borrow *in hard currency* up to the total amount of their quota, hard or soft.

For Bolivia, this was a golden opportunity; and, in its urgency to get three dollars for one, it enacted a decree on January 10, 1959, in such haste that it had to be corrected and another decree enacted on April 15, 1959. Under that decree, Bolivia's quota in the IMF was raised from $10 million to $22.5 million.[121] Because of the haste in drafting this second decree, still another decree was needed in September to authorize the Central Bank to deposit the balances required under the quota in dollars and bolivianos. The latter were paid into IMF at the rate of Bs. 8,550 per dollar, although immediately thereafter the boliviano was devalued, for IMF transactions, to Bs. 11,500 per dollar.[122]

U.S. aid, which was interest-free and did not have to be repaid, made it unnecessary for Bolivia to take full immediate advantage of its new quota, but it drew $1 million in 1960 and signed a new stand-by agreement in 1961 with the IMF for $7.5 million, expiring July 26, 1962. By that time, or rather up to the end of the 1962 fiscal year (April 30), total IMF financial assistance to Bolivia, under stand-by arrangements or otherwise, amounted (in millions) to: 1954-$2.5; 1957-$7.5; 1960-$4.6; 1962-$7.5; *Total*-$22.1 million. The stand-by agreement was extended and increased to $10 million in 1962, reduced to $7.5 million in 1963, increased to $10 million and later to $12 million in 1964, and to $14 million in 1965 (expiring August 31, 1966).[123]

Another round of IMF quota increases was proposed in 1965, on this occasion for the purpose of providing funds for the United Kingdom and the United States, whose currencies were still hard but under strain, and Bolivia's quota was raised from $22.5 million to $29 million.[124]

Exchange Rates, Prices, and Money Supply

But, after all, the proof of monetary stabilization is in the record of foreign exchange rates and domestic prices, and in the money supply which, as has been stated before, provides the fuel for the engines of uncontrolled inflation.

Judging by the dollar-boliviano cross-rate alone, as represented graphically in Figure 15, the monetary stabilization program has been as completely successful from its inception in December, 1956, through 1965 as it was during the first year of its existence. This is to disregard, of course, the divagations from the plan that made it necessary to establish a new level of stabilization in 1958 and to disregard, too, the fact that the loss of foreign exchange during that period of apostasy had to be made good by U.S. aid. The new foreign exchange rate has been maintained without change from January, 1959, to date. Even including the 1958 hiatus, one can apply to Bolivia's currency stabilization the historic motto of the city of Paris: *Fluctuat nec mergitur* (It is tossed by the waves but does not sink).

Living costs have followed the same course as foreign exchange with remarkable fidelity, except for a lag during the early years, which is chiefly explained by the fact that rent controls were not removed until 1959 and after, and then only gradually, as will be seen from Table 25 below (p. 590).

The one index that goes counter to all expectations, and calls for explanation, is that of money supply (including note circulation in the hands of the public, shown on the chart, and demand deposits). The rise in the money supply has already been shown to be attributable almost entirely to an increase in government borrowing from the Central Bank (Table 24, p. 581; also Fig. 1, p. 42). How is it then that this rise of over 300 per cent since December, 1956, has not been more closely reflected in the foreign exchange rate and the cost of living, which went up 53 per cent and 52 per cent, respectively, in the same period?* In explanation, the nine-year span shown on the chart may conveniently be divided into two periods, the first extending from December 31, 1956, at the inception of the stabilization program, to December 31, 1958, when the Bolivian government was forced to permit the boliviano to "find its own level," and the second dating from that time to the present.

*Not even the most ardent "monetarist" would expect an exact correlation, and, at best, it may be said that an increase in the money supply *tends* to produce a commensurate increase in foreign exchange rates and domestic price levels, *ceteris paribus*. But other things seldom remain the same and, in Latin America at least, time lags, artificial controls, natural resistances, and extraneous circumstances (such as U.S. aid) are such that it is only by coincidence that the money, price, and exchange curves will ever be identical.

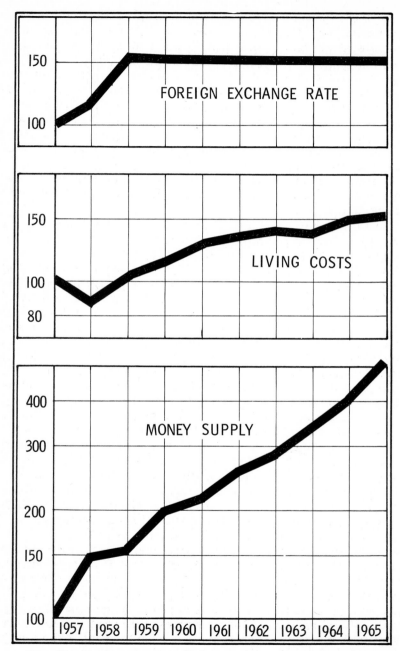

Fig. 15. Exchange rates, living costs, and money supply. December 31, 1956=100. (Source: *International Financial Statistics*.)[125]

In the first period, as has been seen (p. 579ff), the Bolivian government had attempted to hold the foreign exchange rate immobile at the same time that it was raising wages and borrowing hand over fist from the Central Bank. Over $15 million of the stabilization fund was frittered away in the course of that experiment, but when the U.S. government finally insisted that Bolivia adhere to its commitments under the stabilization program as the price of continuing U.S. aid, the boliviano was once again allowed to find its own level in the foreign exchange market. As a result, when the 1958 year drew to a close, it was found that the boliviano-dollar cross-rate had gone up 54 per cent since December, 1956, and that the money supply had increased 52 per cent in the same period (see Fig. 15 and supporting data at p. 753, n *125*).

In 1959 and 1960 U.S. aid was cut back to the lowest levels since 1954 (see Fig. 16, p. 596). Out of the total aid in those years, $8.7 million and $9.3 million were disbursed in the form of cash grants,[126] which enabled the government, through the Central Bank, to support the boliviano at its pegged rate of Bs. 11,885 to the dollar despite an increase in the money supply of Bs. 85 billion ($7.2 million) in 1959 and Bs. 33 billion ($2.8 million) in 1960. Beginning in 1961, and up to the present time, there has been a massive injection of U.S. aid that has been dissipated largely in budgetary support (see Solomon report), so that Bolivia was able to maintain its currency at an *artificially pegged* level throughout 1961 and 1962, in spite of continuing government borrowing and a rising money supply.

Since then, there has been no problem, since, in addition to the continued rise in U.S. aid, high tin prices made it possible for Bolivia to increase its net known dollar assets, reported by the U.S., from $17.4 million on December 31, 1962, to $67.4 million on December 31, 1965. The Central Bank gold and foreign exchange holdings rose from $3.9 million to $36.4 million in the same period.[127] The difference, in Central Bank holdings alone, is equivalent to over 386 million pesos (one new peso = 1,000 bolivianos), offsetting most of the 455 million-peso increase in the Bolivian money supply over that period. As the Bolivian currency is freely convertible into foreign exchange and vice versa, the increased monetary liabilities are more than balanced by the increased foreign assets, public and private, so that the trend has not been inflationary; to the contrary, such artificial pegging of the foreign exchange rate as has taken place over the past three years has usually been to offset a tendency for the Bolivian currency to rise above its official level.

Domestic prices, like foreign exchange rates, have been artificially controlled for many products and services — namely, rents, railway and public utility rates, and prices for petroleum products, wheat, bread, and sugar. This is what European economists refer to as "repressed inflation." There is no doubt that prices can be controlled for a limited time, and to a limited extent, particularly in a country as isolated from the world by high transportation costs as is Bolivia. If carried to too great extremes, repressed inflation can lead only to shortages and to export smuggling, as is undoubtedly occurring in Bolivia at the present time in the case of sugar, and perhaps wheat. And it must be pointed out that the deficiencies in railway and public utility services are in effect equivalent to what would be termed "shortages" in commodity or general merchandise trade.

The relative stability of prices for "articles of prime necessity" (chiefly food) and fuel (chiefly gasoline and kerosene), as shown in Table 25, would be amazing were it not that these

TABLE 25

Cost of Living, La Paz
(January 1956 = 100)

Year*	Articles of Prime Necessity	Fuel	Clothing	Services	Rent	General Index
1956	742	433	208	571	100	465
1957	577	537	191	669	484	401
1958	625	607	232	1,418	928	476
1959	667	564	284	1,012	1,669	524
1960	744	543	293	1,012	2,452	580
1961	781	497	314	1,015 †	3,151	623
1962	781	520	318	1,015 †	3,844	643
1963 †	749	497	329	1,075	3,844	633

*All figures shown are for December of the given year.

Sources: The 1963 figures and the earlier figures marked with daggers (†) are from Central Bank, 35th *Annual Report*, 1963, p. 39; all other figures are from *ibid.*, 1962, p. 124. The 1962 report showed the index for services at 1,075 in December, 1961 and 1962. The figure given in the above table is from the later volume, on the dubious presumption that it may represent a correction. The Central Bank figures shown above cannot be reconciled with the cost-of-living figures shown in *International Financial Statistics* which have been used in the graph in Figure 15 (p. 588).

are precisely the articles that have been most subject to price controls. Clothing is the index item that has most nearly followed monetary trends, advancing 58 per cent from December, 1956, to December, 1963, or almost precisely in the same ratio as the foreign exchange rates in that period (53 per cent). Services have gone up substantially more than general living costs, as is usually the case in a period of rising prices and rising wages. Rents, however, have shown the most striking advance, from the absurdly low, controlled levels prevailing before stabilization, to the higher, but still controlled and ridiculously low levels for 1957 authorized by the stabilization decree. Gradually, as controls were progressively removed, rents rose to levels more nearly commensurate with current wages and costs. As a result of these various factors, the living cost index as a whole advanced 36 per cent from December, 1956, to December, 1963. (Note, however, that the living cost index given in *International Financial Statistics* shows a 57 per cent rise in the same period; see Figure 15 and supporting data at p. 753, n *125*).

The New Bolivian Peso

The last stage of the Fifty-Step Plan, it will be recalled, called for stabilization *de jure,* following a sufficient period of *de facto* stabilization for the boliviano to reach its "proper" level (p. 155, and Appendix III). The plan proposed that a new

TABLE 26

Boliviano Quotations, 1956-62*

Date	Buying Rate	Selling Rate	Index
December, 1956	7,710	7,760	100.0
December, 1957	8,550	8,565	100.4
October, 1958	11,915	11,935	153.8
December, 1958	11,915	11,935	153.8
January 27, 1959	11,875	11,885	153.2
December, 1959	11,875	11,885	153.2
December, 1960	11,875	11,885	153.2
December, 1961	11,875	11,885	153.2
December, 1962	11,875	11,885	153.2

*Central Bank, 34th *Annual Report,* 1962, p. 31.

currency unit be established at that time, to be known as the "peso" or "condor," or by some other name, and with both denominations, e.g., "10,000 Bolivianos" and "10 Pesos," written on the face of the bill, so that the wage earner would not feel cheated at receiving the smaller denomination, and yet the public would gradually become accustomed to the new currency.

It was not until July, 1962, however, that stabilization appeared sufficiently assured to warrant doing away with the fluctuating rate of exchange that had served its purpose up to that time. At the year end, the Central Bank published a table (Table 26) showing the course of the boliviano over the six years following stabilization, in evidence that the time was ripe for a fixed rather than a fluctuating currency.

A July, 1962, decree established the new *Peso Boliviano,** equivalent to one thousand of the old bolivianos, and with both denominations engraved on the face of the bills, which were in denominations of one to one hundred pesos. Holders were given to January 1, 1965 (later extended to December 31, 1965), to exchange the old bills for new, after which the former would be null and void. The November, 1964, *coup d'état* failed to shake the determination of the government to maintain the peso at its official level.[128]

Stabilization *de jure* as well as *de facto* had arrived.

---

*The Finance Minister had proposed calling the new currency the "Potosí" after the city of that name where the Spaniards had established their principal mint in South America (Central Bank, 34th *Annual Report,* 1962, p. 159n).

24

UNITED STATES AID

U.S. aid to Bolivia, as has been seen, was one of the major factors in the Bolivian inflation that carried the currency down from Bs. 60 to Bs. 14,000 to the dollar between 1952 and 1956. At the same time, both during that period and subsequently, it has been a major deterrent to economic recovery in that it has relieved Bolivia of the necessity of readjusting to economic reality and has intensified the country's two major ills — indolence and political chicanery.

As one Bolivian paper put it, "Aid to Bolivia has reaggravated the country's chronic illness — loafing." To which another Bolivian newspaper added, "Everyone knows that U.S. aid, and its distribution in Bolivia, has been the most potent source of illegal enrichment that has ever been known in our history."[129]

As late as 1959, after 13 years' experience, Under Secretary Dillon publicly characterized aid to Bolivia as a failure; yet aid kept pouring in, always under the same pressure — the threat that if U.S. assistance were not forthcoming, Bolivia would turn to communism. This was the leitmotif of Paz-Estenssoro's appeal for large-scale aid in 1952-53. It was what President Siles told Vice-President Nixon in May, 1958, when he claimed that Bolivia must have $50 million a year for four years, or the communists would take over, and again when he asked for $20 million more in September, 1958, "to curb the Red drive."[130]

This last demand prompted *American Metal Market,* always a close although not too friendly observer of the Bolivian scene, to comment:

> In one respect, this forward-looking group of left wing "nationalizers" of industry has truly been eminently successful. It has shown how to get something for nothing — an unceasing flow of U.S. tax money via the U.S. Treasury, which just as unceasingly goes "down the drain" without producing anything. The Bolivian regime has, in fact, proved itself to be the master moocher.[131]

This was unfair, at least so far as President Siles was concerned. Siles truly believed that only U.S. aid on a massive scale could prevent a communist takeover, and this he was determined to prevent. In any event, the $21.7 million (average) aid that Siles was able to procure during his four-year regime was a mere trickle compared with what came afterwards. His successor and predecessor, Paz-Estenssoro, proved more expert in brandishing the threat of communism as an inducement to U.S. assistance. Elected in 1960 with the support of the communists, thanks to Lechín's influence, President Paz first attempted to increase the flow of aid by sending Lechín to the United States in December, 1960, with the plea that the miners were getting out of hand and that Lechín could only retain their loyalty to the MNR administration if the United States gave Bolivia $100 million. [132]

The $100 million failed to materialize during Lechín's visit, but the appeal coincided with the USSR mission to La Paz, and its offer of $150 million in aid, "without strings." This resulted in doubling U.S. commitments for the ensuing fiscal year, from $14.9 million to $33.7 million, with the promise of more to come (p. 521). In 1961 the bombing of the U.S. Ambassador's automobile and other acts of violence kept the communist threat alive. On the theory that "the axle that squeaks the loudest gets the most grease," as Herbert Feis puts it,[133] this procured a further increase of U.S. assistance, including an agreement to go ahead with the $37 million Triangular Plan. In 1962 President Paz broke with Lechín but, with the express purpose of showing that he was not subservient to the United States, he accepted a much publicized $5 million credit from Yugoslavia as a preliminary to a personal visit to President Kennedy in search of money (p. 523).

Massive and continuing U.S. aid dates from that visit, but President Paz still kept his trump card in reserve — a break with Cuba — throughout his second term and until after he commenced his third illegal term in August, 1964 (the Constitution had been amended in 1960 to give his second term the color of legality). In a prescient article in the *New York Times,* Juan de Onís wrote that relations between Bolivia and the United States, as Paz commenced his third term, were "just short of an open quarrel" because of Bolivia's failure to break off diplomatic relations with Cuba, despite U.S. pressure and financial aid. On this, de Onís comments: "This has been a highly political aid program, clearly designed to bolster the revolution that [resulted in] nationalization of the mines and a chaotic but sweeping agrarian reform that gave new political and social status to the Indian peasants." Two weeks after the *Times* article, Bolivia took the hint, received its *quid pro quo* in the assurance of continuing aid, and broke off relations with the Castro government.[134] Two months later, as communists, Trotskyites, and others of the extreme left braced themselves for a showdown, Paz was overthrown by an anticommunist army junta whose presidential appointee remains in control of the situation at the present writing (June, 1966).

Amount and Scope of U.S. Aid

The impact of U.S. financial assistance on inflation in Bolivia may be appraised by comparing the amount of U.S. aid with the amount that the Bolivian government has been willing and able to collect from its own citizens and corporations, and from foreign corporations and residents, by way of taxes. Figure 16 brings out this comparison graphically. In the eleven years from 1954 to 1964 Bolivian tax and customs revenues amounted to $287 million, while U.S. aid commitments totalled $343 million. In 1965, Bolivian tax and customs revenues rose to $71 million (up from $67.5 million in 1964), while U.S. aid commitments to the new anticommunist government dropped sharply to $16.5 million (down from $72.1 million in 1964). Total U.S. aid, to the end of 1965, aggregated $408.8 million, with a further $100 million under discussion.[135]

A similar chart, covering only the first four double bars (1954-57), was used in my April, 1957, address to the Cabinet, when I stated that the Bolivian taxpayer had paid, in taxes and customs duties, less than one-half as much as the American taxpayers had paid to support the Bolivian budget, warning that Congress could not be expected to go on indefinitely subsidizing Bolivia's mistakes. This underestimated Washington's generosity with what Justice Brandeis used to call other people's money.

But these figures and the chart reveal only a part of the picture.* They do not include American aid to Bolivia in the shape of an annual $6.2 million purchase of tungsten at higher than world market prices,[136] or U.S. government tin purchases

---

*AID authorizations for the 1963 fiscal year were $68.3 million and for 1964 $78.5 million (*Inter-American Economic Affairs*, XVIII [Spring, 1965], 66). This is $20 million more than the published AID figures shown in Figure 16.

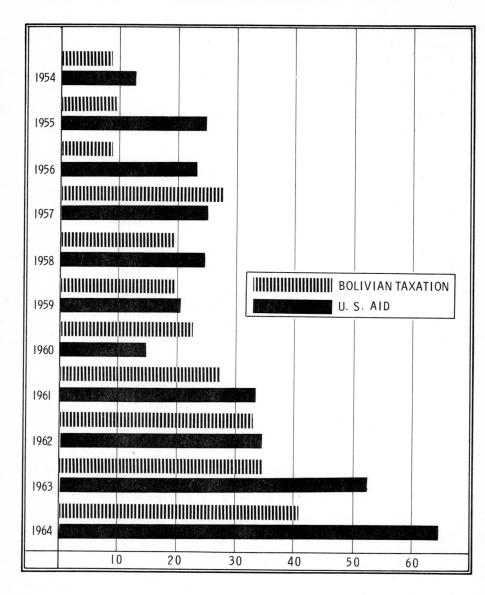

Fig. 16. U.S. aid and Bolivian tax revenues. In millions of dollars. (Source: U.N., *Statistical Yearbook, 1963, Economic and Program Statistics,* and other sources.) [137]

for a 350,000-ton stockpile. A tin stock of this magnitude, equal to some 13 to 14 years' normal exports from Bolivia, must be regarded as a disguised form of foreign aid.*

The figures also fail to disclose the full U.S. commitment to COMIBOL under the Triangular Plan, inasmuch as AID shows only a gross commitment of $8.5 million for that plan whereas the actual U.S. commitment at the inception of the plan was 40 per cent of $37.5 million (i.e. $15 million), and the total cost of the plan may well run as high as $130 million, all of which will eventually be borne by the United States (see pp. 544-48).

Nor do the AID figures fully reveal the extent of U.S. commitments under Bolivia's 10-Year Development Plan. These aggregate $83 million in immediate or near-term expenditures, which was alleged to be sufficient to permit Bolivia's *take-off* into the area of economic development (but see the Solomon report [p. 604] showing that 70-75 per cent of U.S. aid goes down the drain, to cover budget deficits, instead of being used for economic development).

The $83 million was supposed to be distributed as follows: $6 million for technical studies; $3 million as a subsidy for public works; $21.4 million for rural development and colonization, housing, drinking water, and the Mining Bank; plus an agreement to consider additional grants of $5.5 million to the Mining Bank; $3.5 million to the Agricultural Bank; $2.4 million to the newly formed Industrial Credit Bank; † and to furnish an

---

*Tin stockpiling has its origins in the testimony of Bernard Baruch before the House Foreign Affairs Committee in 1934 advocating that the United States accept tin in part payment of the war debts. His consistent advocacy of that measure culminated in enactment of the Strategic Raw Materials Act of 1939 (Carter Field, *Bernard Baruch* [New York: McGraw-Hill Book Co., 1944], p. 254; Morris Rosenbloom, *Peace through Strength* [New York: Farrar, Strauss & Young, 1953], pp. 199-200). But Baruch certainly never intended that tin stockpiling should continue indefinitely as a disguised form of foreign aid.

† In addition to the $2.4 million "loan," USAID contributed $600,000 to the capital of the Industrial Credit Bank and was later called on for a donation of $725,000 for a "crash rehabilitation program." The "crash" may be expected if or when the United States withdraws its financial support, as there are simply not enough persons in Bolivia qualified to direct and staff even one government bank, let alone the seven government banking and lending institutions that have been brought into existence. The Mining Bank, despite its past record (pp. 55-57), was given an $8 million "loan" by USAID and the Inter-American Development Bank (American Embassy, *Quarterly Economic Summaries* A-354 [October 31, 1963], pp. 10, 12; A-67 [August 13, 1964], pp. 4, 8).

unspecified amount of capital and technical advice for formation of a National Development Bank; plus an additional agreement to finance, following feasibility studies, up to $42.2 million in additional unspecified projects. The IDB was expected to provide $11.4 million of the initial immediate financing; the Social Progress Fund (all U.S. grant money, but administered by the IDB as a "soft" loan) would provide $10 million; and AID would provide the rest. The contract, which does not appear to have been published in the United States, was executed on July 20, 1962, between the government of Bolivia, the IDB, and AID.[138]

And even this does not complete the picture of the commitments made by AID, although the funds have not yet been authorized or appropriated by Congress. It omits, *inter alia,* the cost of the *second* Cochabamba-Santa Cruz highway which is already under construction and which even the most ardent proponents of the *first* Cochabamba-Santa Cruz highway admit will make the older route useless. The first highway cost an estimated $50 million, some five times more than the original estimates. Interest alone on the debt, plus highway maintenance, work out at some $200 per truck trip (see Appendix IV), so that its description as a "white elephant" is, if anything, an injustice to the potentates and pachyderms of ancient India.*

A cost estimate of $33.4 million has been reported for the second highway, but a former top-level AID official stated that it would cost around $60 million. This same official also stated that, until the highway project was presented, AID had found it impossible to get from Bolivia anything but the vaguest plans for the use of U.S. aid, whereas the highway was something they "could get their teeth into," so that, at last, the Bolivian aid program could really get under way. Significantly, the USAID press release which announced the financing of this northern route as "a dramatic road project designed to open the way to an economic revolution in Bolivia ... the most expensive single development project yet financed by the Agency for International Development under the Alliance for Progress," failed to mention the $50 million that had gone down the drain in building the first Cochabamba-Santa Cruz highway.[139]

---

*The McClellan Committee reported that many of the development projects "stand in Bolivia today as 'white elephants' symbolic of maladministration of the technical assistance phase of the U.S. aid program." (U.S. Congress, Senate, Committee on Government Operations, *Administration of United States Foreign Aid Programs in Bolivia,* 86th Cong., 2d Sess., 1960, p. 9).

The new highway will take a more northerly and circuitous route than the first highway but will have easier gradients over the Andes and traverse less arid land, going by way of Chipirirí in the Chaparé area to Guabirá, where it will connect with the present Guabirá-Santa Cruz highway that had been constructed solely for the benefit of the government sugar mill in that location. The original road was financed chiefly by a $33,420,000 series of loans from the Export-Import Bank of Washington. That loan, and other Eximbank loans for a total of $34 million outstanding, plus some $10 million in accrued interest, have been in default since 1958, although the default is not shown in the annual *Report to the Congress* which claims "a loss ratio of $\frac{1}{24}$ of 1 per cent" on loans "charged off as uncollectible."[140] It would appear that unless a loan is charged off as a bad debt it is not regarded as defaulted; but, whether the Bolivian loans remain in default or are later paid off with U.S. aid, this is an example of why it is considered misleading to characterize any loan to Bolivia by the U.S. government as anything other than an outright gift (p. 562).*

Nor do the duplicate Cochabamba-Santa Cruz highways represent the total of U.S. aid destined to go down the drain of transportation facilities to Bolivia's almost uninhabited expanses. An even more costly 4,000-mile superhighway is being sponsored by the Inter-American Development Bank to skirt the uninhabited eastern edge of the central Andean cordillera, linking Colombia, Peru, Ecuador, and Bolivia. The total cost was originally placed at $216 million, of which the Bolivian share would be $62 million, the figures later being raised to $500 million and $160 million, respectively. Judging by preconstruction estimates and ultimate costs for similar projects in the past, these figures may have to be multiplied many times, with the major share of the cost borne by the United States. Thus far, only preliminary surveys have been made, but local aspirations have already been aroused with promises that the highway

---

*Herbert Feis, former Economic Counsellor to the State Department, reports that the fine lending record of the World Bank has been achieved by having the U.S. government (and to a lesser degree, other governments) take over the burden: "Time and again, by coming to the rescue of the debtors, they spared the Bank the annoying necessity [of] demanding payments on its loans from governments in financial distress." (Herbert Feis, *Foreign Aid and Foreign Policy* [New York: St. Martin's Press, 1964], p. 226.)

"will encourage the economic development of the four countries by opening up vast areas," to quote from a U.S. Embassy report.[141]

The theory seems to be that any vacant spot on the map without highways (and with neither population nor production) needs only a highway conjured up by the magic wand of U.S. or IDB aid to convert a wilderness into a thriving community, and in Latin America there is no end to empty spaces.

Already under construction in Bolivia with U.S. aid are some $35 million (preconstruction estimates) of access roads, from Cochabamba to Puerto Villaroel on the Mamoré River, a tributary of the Amazon. Among other highways being built with U.S. aid is one to the Amazonian Beni region, which is being constructed, according to a U.S. Embassy report, to make possible "the systematic exploitation of the gold resources of that area." It may be noted that the International Mining Corporation has managed to transport a huge multimillion-dollar dredge and equipment to the gold mining area, and in 1964 shipped out some 2.3 tons of gold (67,612 ounces, worth $2,367,000), with no government-built highway or other assistance, and paid the government some 28 per cent of the gross value of its production in royalties and taxes.[142] Even the most optimistic, and wholly unsubstantiated, government estimates of $22 million gold production per annum from the Beni area by 1972 would scarcely seem to justify a modern highway to transport some twenty-two tons of gold a year.

In addition to the direct loans and grants, U.S. AID makes grants for technical assistance, generally known as Point IV, and including the *Servicios* which are administered jointly with the Bolivian authorities. During the first ten years (1942-51), the total cost of the technical cooperation program averaged a little over $300,000 a year. For the next ten years (1952-61), its total cost averaged some $2,500,000 a year, with a figure of $1,294,000 for 1961. Since then, technical assistance expenditures have been stepped up sharply, to $9,480,000 in 1962, $7,335,000 in 1963, $7,103,000 in 1964, and $4,070,000 in 1965.[143] Despite the harsh comments in the McClellan Committee Report on the shortcomings of the *Servicios*,[144] it may be said that, at least up to mid-1957, Point IV technical assistance, and particularly that rendered in the *Servicios*, was the one aspect of U.S. aid that merited encomiums. Whether or not this is true on its present scale is another matter.

Basic Causes of Failure of U.S. Aid in Bolivia

The basic problems of economic development in Latin America in general will be discussed at length in a companion volume on the facts and fallacies of inflation and development in Latin America, but the difficulties outlined in that volume, now in preparation, apply with particular force in the case of Bolivia.

Bolivia today, with many of her capable citizens in exile and a large part of her potential working capital in hiding abroad, is lacking in most of the essentials for economic development: (1) a generally literate population; (2) adequate elementary and technical education; (3) political stability; (4) law and order, and respect for life and property; (5) a government dedicated to ensuring that respect as its primary and imperative duty;* and (6) an environment that encourages both domestic and foreign capital, not through special privileges, but by giving free rein to private enterprise in a free economy. There must, above all, be a deep-rooted understanding of the fact that no one can hope to get something for nothing, that material advancement can come only through many years of hard work and productive saving.

We are entitled to question the motives of anyone who tells Bolivia's peasants and laborers the contrary, or who insists that Bolivia will not wait, that time has run out — for there is no shortcut to economic development, whether under socialism, communism, or free enterprise.

The "big push"

There is a theory advanced by proponents of financial aid to underdeveloped countries, eagerly embraced by Bolivia, that all that is needed is enough capital and technical assistance to push a country to Rostow's "take-off point," and that thereafter

---

*If a government collects taxes, yet fails to safeguard the rights of citizens, it is robbery pure and simple for, according to Thomas Aquinas: "It is not robbery if princes exact from their subjects that which is due to them for the safeguarding of the common good, even if they use violence in so doing; but if they extort something unduly by means of violence, it is robbery, even as burglary is. Hence St. Augustine says: 'If justice be disregarded, what is a king but a mighty robber, since what is a robber but a little king?'"

the country can fly off by itself into the wild blue yonder of its heart's desires. The M.I.T. Center for International Studies expresses that idea in the following terms:

> Launching a country into self-sustaining growth is a little like getting an airplane off the ground. There is a critical ground speed which must be passed before the craft can become airborne.... This, in a nutshell, is the contention of the theory of the big push.[145]

But it will do little good to push a country to the take-off point unless that country has an engine in its plane. No foreign handouts can provide that engine, nor can they take the place of a country's own initiative, hard work, thrift, and push. That is why Marshall plan aid in Europe, and similar *temporary* financial assistance in Japan, proved so helpful to the war-ravaged countries of Europe and Asia in getting them to a new take-off point, and, basically, why foreign aid has proved a failure in Bolivia. Japan, Germany, and other countries of Europe have their own engines in their planes; Bolivia, in the political state of its past decade, does not.

It may seem callous to argue that foreign aid should be given only to those who have no fundamental need for aid, much as bankers are often accused of granting credit only to those who do not need it. But a government official who disburses foreign aid should be like a wise banker — a fiduciary for the funds entrusted to his care. Bankers are schooled in the maxim that the three C's of Credit are Character, Capacity, and Capital, of which Character and Capacity are the indispensable ones. A banker knows that it would be of no help to the borrower, and would bankrupt the lender, were he to extend credit with no assurance of: (1) the borrower's integrity — *no background of confiscation and broken promises, such as Bolivia's;* (2) the borrower's demonstrated competence and ability to put the money to good use — *no record of mismanagement of the national resources, such as Bolivia's;* and (3) sufficient capital to show the borrower's financial capacity to carry on the business — *not a history of $700 million squandered in a dozen years, such as Bolivia's.*

If poverty and unfulfilled aspirations were justification enough for a loan, bankers would lend to spendthrifts, thieves, and ne'er-do-well's rather than to thrifty farmers and businessmen. This, however, would not be lending, but charity, and charity with "other people's money" is scarcely one of the cardinal virtues, either for a banker or for a government dispenser of the public funds.

This is not to say that there is neither honesty nor competence in Bolivia. The integrity of President Siles and of my friends and colleagues on the Stabilization Council, and the demonstrated competence of such Bolivians as Simón Patiño and José Avelino Aramayo, the founders of the tin industry, prove the contrary. But Bolivia's most capable managers of commercial, industrial, mining, and agricultural enterprises are to be found in the private sector — or in exile — not in the government sector. Clearly, the qualities that enable a person to rise to high political office in Bolivia, whether by revolution or election, are not necessarily those which would qualify him to manage a business enterprise, or to choose those best qualified to run one. The fact that a man may be trained as a lawyer, economist, or engineer — intelligent, dynamic, and loyal to the political party in power — does not in itself qualify him to manage a bank, a public utility, a sugar mill, or any other business enterprise, and much less to direct the entire economy of a country. Long experience in a position of high managerial and financial responsibility in a successful business, in addition to native intelligence and education, is needed before a man can be considered ready to assume the presidency of a railway, mine, or other business activity — and political appointments in Bolivia are not traditionally made on that basis.

The record is clear, and it is a record of almost invariable incompetence and corruption in government, if not at the top level — for Bolivia has had its statesmen as well as its *políticos* — then certainly at other levels. And the record shows that, regardless of the success or failure of government owned and operated enterprises in other countries, there is not now and never has been a successful government enterprise in Bolivia.

In sum, so long as foreign aid is routed through government channels in Bolivia, it should be clear from the record that it can lead only to further impoverishment of the nation through investment in ill conceived and worse managed government enterprises, and through infrastructure expenditures beyond the country's economic capacity to utilize or to maintain.

So scholarly a commentator as Herbert Feis writes the following (and he may well have had Bolivia specifically in mind, although his comments apply equally to some other Latin American countries):

The plight of some of the most pressing petitioners for aid... is due to their careless compounding of unpaid debts to private foreign vendors, resulting from excessive purchases either of dispensable consumer goods or of equipment wanted for overambitious plans for industrial expansion. It is likely to be made worse by flight of domestic capital to escape the impact of rapid inflation or mistreatment. The responsible authorities may refuse to recognize or admit that these are the real causes... Rejecting all critical analyses, they may maintain that their difficulties were unavoidable. Unrepentantly, they may confront the American government with a choice of bearing their ill will, or continuing to finance their laxity, or witnessing their default on debts to private or public lenders. [146]

The Solomon report

The foregoing observations on the failure of U.S. aid are corroborated by a landmark report, *The Finances of the Public Sector of Bolivia.** For the first time, a candid official examination of the subject has been published, bringing to light the total failure of U.S. aid in that country as well as the reasons for that failure — at least to the extent that they could be disclosed in the course of a comparatively brief investigation and an unclassified report.

With reference to the "eighty million dollar Memorandum of Understanding between the United States, the Inter-American Development Bank, and the Government of Bolivia," the Solomon report points out that "the Memorandum carries the clear implication that all other U.S. funds (aside from a reasonable level of budget support) are for development purposes." The fact is, however, as Solomon shows, that the Bolivian government and some forty government enterprises and agencies have incurred deficits in current account of over $20 million a year; that "such heavy net consumption by the public sector drains resources from possible investment uses and inhibits economic growth," so that savings within the private sector, together with

*The report, dated March 1, 1963, was prepared for AID by a special mission headed by Anthony Morton Solomon, at the time a Lecturer at the Harvard University Graduate School of Business Administration, following his retirement from a long and successful business career in Mexico and elsewhere. Since April 18, 1965, he has been Assistant Secretary of State for Economic Affairs. His associates on the mission were Frank W. Krause and Norman S. Fieleke, both from the U.S. Bureau of the Budget.

foreign aid, "can represent net investment only to the extent that they exceed these operating deficits."

The report calculates a total cash deficit of $27 million in 1961; in 1962, $25 million. Actual expenditures of U.S. aid in those years amounted to $26 million and $27 million, respectively. This would indicate that $52 million of U.S. aid went down the drain of recurring deficits. And for 1963 the deficit was estimated at $28 million.

"With the available data," however, the Solomon report goes on to say, "and given the accounting inadequacies in the state enterprises in Bolivia, it is impossible to determine the exact extent to which the U.S. is directly or indirectly financing Bolivian operating deficits," but it is estimated that, not counting $10.6 million of P.L. 480 supplies, some 70 per cent of the dollar aid was used in 1961-62 to cover deficits. A further 75 per cent of the $50 million in local currency aid disbursements was similarly used to finance operating deficits in the public sector.

In other words, at the most only 25 to 30 per cent of U.S. aid was used for "capital investment" or could conceivably have been helpful in economic development. The following comments from the report shed some light on the effectiveness of such "investment."

COMIBOL is variously estimated as having on its payroll a surplus of from 3,000 to 6,000 employees out of a labor force of some 25,000. But *two-thirds* of the supposedly active working force are employed above ground, "due to the large number of ill men, unfit for work below ground, and the large number of 'labor bureaucrats.'" The report concludes that any further U.S. local currency aid, until COMIBOL "puts its house in order ... will only have the harmful effect of permitting continued administrative and financial irresponsibility." If COMIBOL fails to make the "hard decision" to close the Catavi and Siglo Veinte mines, and to dismiss excess employees (finding jobs for them elsewhere), and if the United States continues to provide additional assistance to meet recurring alleged emergencies, "the probability of a real solution will continue dim."

Padded payrolls are likewise reported in the Development Corporation and in the Petroleum Corporation (YPFB), although on a lesser scale, with the added note that the presidents of those enterprises are either unaware of, or refuse to admit, the extent of the excess labor force.

"The various ministers with whom we spoke argue that the

only way to eliminate the operating deficits is through a massive injection of foreign capital to bring about development and employment opportunities," but they fail to "recognize the impracticability of immediate capital injections into the public mining sector (for example), which at this time is characterized by administrative disorganization and inadequate management."

The report strongly recommends that, in addition to the auditors working in COMIBOL, audit teams be sent into other major government enterprises (the Development Corporation, YPFB, the railways, the airline), and that standard accounting systems be introduced. Meanwhile, the United States "should not continue to finance capital investments for state enterprises which do not make progress in reducing their operating deficits," and steps should be taken to deter the managements of those enterprises from "irresponsibility utilizing outside borrowing and an increasing backlog of unpaid bills to break the ceiling established in the budget."

Turning to YPFB, the report points to the difficulty of analyzing its accounts, which are complicated by the practice "of periodically appreciating the book value of its assets, of indiscriminately capitalizing exploration expenditures, and of omitting foreign assistance from available financial data... with the result that surpluses reported by the Corporation in its own statements for 1961 and 1962, and the balance estimated for 1963" are in reality deficits which have been growing successively larger. The report goes on to state that YPFB has received $12.7 million in credits from U.S. aid, and is seeking a further $3 million, and recommends that unless the company succeeds in developing producing wells U.S. aid should be reduced "with the objective of inducing a curtailment of the present scale of operations of YPFB."

As to the Bolivian Development Corporation (Corporación Boliviana de Fomento), the report emphasizes "the confusion and unreliability of its financial data" and states "that an audit and reorganization of its accounting system is probably more critically needed than in any other public entity in Bolivia... that in fact the financial situation of CBF is... desperate [and] the Corporation makes no attempt to separate operating expenditures from new investments."

The nationalized Antofagasta railway, despite the economies effected by the British management team, is reported by the Solomon mission to be running a deficit of around $2 million a year, of which some $1.6 million is financed directly by AID.

The following recommendations are made, all of which "are feasible only with strong central government support": (1) dismissing excess employees; (2) raising railway rates on articles of prime necessity; (3) eliminating the payment of 13 per cent of gross traffic revenues to the government Railway Administration, which is used to conceal the deficits of the State Railways.

Two general conclusions reached by the report are particularly pertinent:

> The actual rate of net saving and investment for the economy as a whole, including foreign assistance, is very small due to the dissaving of the public sector. The more optimistic estimates of growth in the GNP are that it is about even with population increase...

> The monetary stabilization program in Bolivia continues to be a psychological "must"; its break-down would be regarded throughout the political spectrum as a conclusive failure of both the government and the Bolivian effort to mix state and private control of the economy.

In conclusion, the report gives a summary description of the financial management procedures employed by the Bolivian government, coupled with fifteen specific recommendations for their improvement. These recommendations include such matters as the establishment of "a realistic timetable for the preparation of budget estimates," "standing instructions for budget formulation to all government organizations," and so forth.

Regrettably, it must be pointed out that each new economic adviser, each new investigating mission, starts out with high hopes of accomplishment, makes its recommendations, sometimes even stubbornly insists upon them — and ends up in utter frustration, because of two factors: (1) the absolute incompetence (and in some cases corruption) of many key Bolivian officials; and (2) the fact that the U.S. government continues to pour out U.S. aid despite the recurring evidence of its misuse and futility.

The reason why each new adviser or investigator ignores the experience of the past is that, because of organizational shortcomings in Washington, no one in AID or in the State Department has a complete record of what has happened in the past, and why it happened. It is almost as though Washington were attempting, consciously or otherwise, to draw a veil over its past mistakes rather than bring them to light so that similar mistakes might be avoided in the future. That is one of the purposes of the present volume — to give Washington in general, and the heads of future economic or financial missions in particular, a clear picture of what has happened in Bolivia, and why.

For it is certain that so shrewd and knowledgeable an investigator as Solomon, *if he had had all the facts at his disposal,* including the background on the very officials he was dealing with in 1963, would have arrived at conclusions not too dissimilar from those reached in the present volume. He might then have questioned the competence of the Bolivian government to manage some 80 or 90 per cent of the economic activities of the country (aside from subsistence farming), as well as its ability or willingness to mend its ways. In that event, he might also have questioned the utility of further U.S. aid under present circumstances, rather than confining himself to suggestions for the improvement of budgetary methods that Bolivian government officials and staff have consistently shown themselves incompetent or unwilling to carry out.

25

CONCLUSIONS

To sum up, the outlook for Bolivia is mixed. On the one hand, there has been a definite and encouraging improvement in the economy, and the Central Bank gold and foreign exchange reserves have been built up from zero at the inception of the stabilization program to $36.4 million on December 31, 1965, thanks to phenomenal tin prices and U.S. aid, but thanks too to the fact that the government has kept its expenditures within manageable limits. The present military government has shown a constructive attitude towards private enterprise and has taken firm steps to remove communist and Trotskyite influences from labor union leadership. As a final accolade to the achievements of Bolivia since stabilization, the First National City Bank, New York, opened a branch in La Paz in January, 1966, and bank officials are frank to state that they would not have taken this step if they had not been confident of continuing monetary stability in Bolivia as the harbinger of further economic progress in the years to come.[147]

On the other hand, the country is racked by civil strife, corrupted and pauperized by fourteen years of U.S. aid which, far from promoting Bolivia's economic development and social progress, served only to maintain in power a government that proved unworthy either of American or Bolivian support and which, without American aid, would admittedly have fallen almost at the inception of the Revolution. It was a government, itself incompetent and corrupt, which has corrupted the great masses of the Bolivian people by permitting violence and robbery to go unpunished; by arming mobs under the euphemism of a "People's Militia"; by teaching labor that the rewards of loafing are greater than those of hard work; by discouraging thrift through the debasement of the currency; by inculcating the idea that prosperity and progress must depend upon government action (whereas, in Bolivia at least, nothing could be farther from the truth); and, above all, by reducing a once sovereign nation to the indignity of a truculent mendicancy, with the government claiming as rightful compensation for fancied wrongs what is patently nothing more than a gratuity motivated in part by blackmail and threats of communism, and in part by the compassion of the American people coupled with a feeling of guileless guilt for our prosperity in a world of poverty.

Subtract U.S. aid, and Bolivia is less prosperous today than it was before the Revolution — further from the "take-off point" to economic progress, both by reason of the depletion of wasted resources and because of the degradation that has come from idleness and dependency.

The outlook is not reassuring, but that is not to say that it is hopeless. Certainly it is no more discouraging now than when the Stabilization Council undertook the then apparently hopeless task of bringing stability to Bolivia's currency. But people's memories are short, and the troubles of the moment always appear more ominous than the greater catastrophes that have been successfully surmounted in the past.

The vast majority of Bolivians, regardless of party, realize that the monetary stabilization program has been a success, or at least they do not dare to abandon it, knowing that the masses would not put up with a return to the monetary chaos of the first Paz-Estenssoro regime. President Barrientos, as chief of the military junta that took office in December, 1964, announced that there will be no change whatsoever in monetary policy, and he repeated that assurance in July, 1966, in the course of a fund-raising expedition to Washington.[148]

Approval has not, of course, been unanimous. The leader of the Trotskyite Revolutionary Workers' Party (POR) attacked me personally as well as President Siles in two violent speeches in 1957 and proclaimed the stabilization program a failure. In 1962, the president of COMIBOL during President Paz' second term of office condemned the program because it had failed to solve Bolivia's infrastructure problems, and in the same year a left-wing MNR leader referred to the program as "a strange mechanism, improvised and transitory," adding that "the inflationary scourge of Bolivia still exists."[149] Aside from such extremists, it is realized that there are still some tenacious believers in what Wilhelm Roepke characterizes as "an anachronistic Keynesianism,"[150] both within and without Bolivia, who would contend that both the diagnosis and the therapy were wrong, and that what was needed was an even larger dose of government spending. But, in every case in Latin America where such Keynesian remedies have been applied, the most that can be said at the autopsy is that "the operation was a success but the patient died."

My own misgivings as to the stabilization program go

deeper. It *was* a success — for the first twelve months. The record since then proves little, inasmuch as well over a quarter of a billion dollars of U.S. aid has enabled the Bolivian government to continue spending beyond its means without taking the measures essential for progress. But it does prove that a balanced budget — whether balanced with taxes or with windfalls such as U.S. aid — can make possible a stable currency in spite of social, economic, and political instability.

For the future, monetary stability *can* be maintained, come what may, as is proved by the experience of other countries in the hemisphere under conditions of political and economic adversity far more extreme than Bolivia has ever encountered. Whether it *will* be maintained when tin prices fall from their present precarious peak, or if or when the United States ceases its policy of perpetual subsidy, will depend upon the strength and determination of the Bolivian government in power at the time.

Certainly it will be hard for the government to get used to balancing the budget and ridding itself of deficits in government enterprises when tin drops from $1.90 to $1.00 a pound, or perhaps to a more "normal" 70 cents, and when the COMIBOL reserves finally peter out under government mismanagement and lack of adequate exploration and development.*

Whether or not the YPFB petroleum discoveries, in the wake of Standard Oil's geological surveys, will suffice to make good the decline in tin production is hard to say, but if revenues from that source and from U.S. aid are used to permit the Bolivian government to continue its expansion of government owned and operated industrial enterprises and the proliferation of government development activities, then there would appear to be little prospect of material advancement or of permanent monetary stability. For — it cannot be reiterated too often — the record proves that there is not a single industrial, financial, or

---

*Abnormally high tin prices have brought the inevitable consequence of the development by American Can Company of an all-steel solderless can and the announcement by that company in August, 1965, that it would license other manufacturers to produce under its patents. Continental Can Company is also producing tinless cans (*Annual Report,* 1965). A drop in tin prices may safely be forecast, although when that will occur, and how serious the drop will be, lies within the province of the speculator rather than of the economist. Meanwhile, more than twelve years have passed, and COMIBOL has done nothing in the way of metallurgical research or in developing new uses and new markets for tin.

developmental enterprise of the Bolivian government that has
not left the country poorer as a result of its activities. Bolivians must ask themselves whether, in the light of their own
history, it is wise to entrust the government with the responsibility of planning, shaping, and even taking an active part in the
development of the economy, or whether it would be better for
Bolivia if government activities were restricted to the essential
functions of government, including above all the maintenance of
law, order, and justice.*

It is true that President Hernán Siles-Zuazo and his loyal
associates within and without the Monetary Stabilization Council — as well as many of his predecessors in the presidential
office — have shown that there have been and can be men of integrity in government. But does Bolivia's experience indicate
that the country can count upon a succession of honest governments to which it can safely entrust its economic destiny? Or,
if honest, have any of Bolivia's governments demonstrated a
capacity for economic wisdom and achievement comparable,
say, with that demonstrated by Aramayo and Patiño in the development of Bolivia's greatest industry, for their own benefit
and for the benefit of the nation? And if it be argued that private enterprise has not invariably been both competent and
honest, it may be answered that incompetence in private industry is soon weeded out through competition and bankruptcy.
With respect to dishonesty, if the government is incapable of
preventing or penalizing dishonesty in the private sector, then
certainly it is incapable of eliminating corruption within its
own ranks.

*See Appendix I, Articles 4 and 5, p. 619, for a definition of "govern-
mental" and "nongovernmental" functions. These definitions are in terms
of absolutes in an ideal, theoretical economy, but in every country there
are certain nongovernmental functions so deep-rooted and so generally
accepted that it would be folly to attempt to uproot them. In Bolivia, for
example, I never attempted to reverse the confiscation of the mines, oilfields, and farms, which were *faits accomplis* — unfortunate but irreversible. The economic adviser, in Bolivia or elsewhere, must determine
what he regards as the ideal *attainable* admixture of government *dirigisme*
and a free market economy and must advocate that aim with all the persuasiveness he can muster to the task. He must make no concessions in
his recommendations, knowing that concessions will inevitably be made by
those who have the political responsibility of carrying them out and that it
is not up to him to discard as unattainable everything that is politically
risky, even though, in the end, he must be content with achieving say 80
per cent of his goal, lest by attempting more he lose everything.

The present military government has come out strongly in favor of private enterprise and has not hesitated to arrest and deport the "anarcho-syndicalist" or Trotskyite labor leaders and to suppress violence in the mines with force.[151]   On the other hand, it has paid tribute to the masses by proclaiming that "the economic and social conquests achieved by the heroic struggle of the people" and the nationalization of the mines, agrarian reform, educational reforms, and universal suffrage will be respected and consolidated "as irreversible conquests of the national reality."[152]

Bolivia's hopes for future economic and social progress, and for permanent monetary stability, must rest upon the ability of the military junta to carry out its announced purpose of a return to a free market economy, and on the expectation that the junta will in due course be succeeded by a freely elected government equally imbued with that purpose.

A free market economy is one of untrammeled but not necessarily ruthless competition — of survival of the fittest, but not necessarily of oppression of the weakest.   Priestley's maxim, popularized by Bentham, of "the greatest happiness of the greatest number" is accepted as the goal by free enterprisers and socialists alike.[153]   Justification of the free market must hence be founded on these premises: (1) that the masses, and even those who are least fitted for the competitive struggle, will be better off if the nation is prosperous; and (2) that prosperity is more likely to be achieved in a climate of freedom than where the government plans the economy, regulates prices, determines what shall be produced and what shall not, and competes directly with private farmers, miners, businessmen, and manufacturers, whom it then burdens with taxes and restrictions, partly on the theory that by impoverishing the rich it can enrich the impoverished, and partly because government enterprise is unable to keep up with private enterprise on the basis of fair competition. The goal of twentieth-century advocates of the free market, as exemplified by Erhard and Roepke, is not *laissez-faire*, but an economy in which the government refrains from direct participation, while providing the "juridical, competitive, and monetary framework necessary to a viable market economy."[154]

But, just as in law the ideal is justice tempered by mercy, so in economics the ideal must be freedom tempered by compassion — and there is no country more in need of compassion than Bolivia.

APPENDIXES

I. Decree Establishing the National Monetary Stabilization Council • II. Emergency Powers Act • III. Fifty-Step Plan for Monetary Stabilization • IV. Analysis of Bolivian Development Corporation Projects • V. Bolivian Commercial Indebtedness — Proposed Amortization Plan • VI. Report on the Progress and Problems of the Stabilization Program.

APPENDIX I

DECREE ESTABLISHING THE NATIONAL MONETARY STABILIZATION COUNCIL

Decree 4469, August 4, 1956 — Ratified by Law of October 29, 1956*

VICTOR PAZ ESTENSSORO

Constitutional President of the Republic

WHEREAS: The inflationary process begun as a consequence of the world crisis of 1929, and which gathered momentum through the Chaco War, has become more acute in recent years;

WHEREAS: Inflation directly affects those sectors with fixed incomes, nullifying the increases in wages and salaries by the constant rise in prices;

WHEREAS: An inflationary situation destroys every incentive for saving and the formation of capital, at the same time making it impossible to accumulate funds for social security, inasmuch as the employers' and workers' contributions run the risk of continuous devaluation;

WHEREAS: The possibilities for investment of foreign private capital, necessary for economic development, are limited by monetary instability, other than in the field of extractive industry for export, which, in general, is dependent upon the international markets;

WHEREAS: The economic development and diversification plans, with which it is sought to increase the supply of marketable goods, are likewise obstructed in their fulfillment by the persistent monetary devaluation which makes any cost budgeting inapplicable;

WHEREAS: Up to the present, no brake on the velocity of the inflationary process from which the country is suffering has been achieved, because the measures taken by the government have been partial and isolated;

WHEREAS: Such experience makes clear the need to face the problem in its entirety, acting on all the factors which bear on the monetary situation;

*Translation by the author. The recitals were drafted by, or under the supervision of, Miguel Gisbert-Nogué, a member of the original organizing group.

IN COUNCIL OF MINISTERS

DECREES:

Formation and powers of the council

Article 1. There is hereby formed the National Monetary Stabilization Council, which shall have charge of studying, coordinating, reviewing, and recommending the appropriate measures to be taken by the national government, prefectures, and municipalities, as well as the independent, quasi-independent, and autonomous agencies, with respect to economic and financial policy, particularly in matters of budgets, taxes, the investment and expenditure of funds, credit and public service contracts, money, foreign exchange, price controls, and other matters that may affect the internal and external credit of the country or the stability of the currency.

Article 2. The President and Vice-President of the Council shall be the President of the Republic and the Minister of Finance, respectively. Together with these, the permanent members of the council are the Ministers of Foreign Affairs, of Mines, and of National Economy, the Executive Vice-President of the National Coordination and Planning Board, the President of the Central Bank of Bolivia, and the Executive Director. In matters concerning a specific department, the respective minister shall be admitted with the right to vote; and in matters which do not directly concern him, and on which he may be consulted, he shall have a voice but no vote.

Government officials who may be called by the President of the Council, as well as the Executive Director and the technical advisers thereof, shall attend meetings, with a voice but without a vote.

A Secretary General, named by the council upon proposal of the Executive Director, shall likewise be a member thereof, being charged with calling meetings, correspondence, the minute book, and other inherent functions.

Article 3. The members of the council, the Executive Director and the technical advisers whom the executive branch of the

Art. 2: The original draft had not included the Minister of Mines as a member of the council; see discussion at pp. 96-97.

Art. 3: The technical advisers referred to here and in Art. 10 were my associates on the U.S. financial mission. It was not intended that the President appoint advisers without limit, which could have been embarrassing, but that the U.S. operations mission designate the advisers by contract, as in the case of the Executive Director. The second paragraph gave the Executive Director the power of veto by bottle-neck which, from the government viewpoint, had the advantage of making him a scapegoat in event of delay.

government shall appoint by decree, shall propose concrete measures to halt and control inflation; to stabilize the currency; to modernize budgetary, tax, and fiscal control procedures; to improve government finances and those of the independent, quasi-independent, and autonomous government agencies; to strengthen and employ the nation's internal and external credit; and to promote the investment of private capital, domestic or foreign.

The council shall study the measures proposed, and those which are approved following a report by the Executive Director shall be submitted for the consideration and approval of the executive branch of the government.

Article 4. With respect to strictly political functions of the government such as the maintenance of public order, the conduct of foreign relations, the administration of justice, and analogous functions, the council shall limit itself to recommending those measures which are necessary to ensure the greatest possible economy in administrative expenses, without impairing the efficiency of the respective services.

With respect to social and economic functions such as public education, the construction and maintenance of roads and other means of transportation, bridges, dams, water supply, and public health and sanitary facilities, social security, the promotion of basic industries, etc., the council shall take care that the expenditures, financial commitments, and investments shall not exceed the resources of the government, and that there is no uneconomic duplication of services.

Article 5. With respect to electric power, transportation and communication services, and other industrial, commercial, or financial enterprises capable of being carried on by private capital or by governmental operation, the council shall make the respective studies and, where appropriate, shall charge the Executive Director with sounding out the possibilities of attracting private capital to establish or improve these services, and to enter into contact with potential investors, advising the council so that it may make the appropriate recommendations thereon.

Art. 4: The original draft had combined Arts. 4 and 5, prefacing them with the recital: "For the purpose of determining those activities of the government and of the government agencies which are of primary importance to the safety of the state and the welfare of the people, with a view to establishing essential priorities in expenses, projects, financial commitments, investments, and other outlays of cash or of property, and to limiting the budgets and commitments to such resources as the government has at its disposal, the council shall distinguish between the following categories of governmental functions and activities:"

Article 6. Within 30 days hereof, the ministries, government bureaus, and independent, quasi-independent, and autonomous government agencies shall send the President of the Council complete details of their financial receipts and expenditures in national and foreign currency, over the past four years as well as over the first six months of the current year, indicating in each case the rate of exchange used for the conversion of foreign currencies. They shall likewise submit a complete description, as of June 30, 1956, of all their obligations, commitments, agreements, and contracts which may imply the expenditure of funds or their equivalent. Meanwhile, and from the date of this decree, no government department or government agency may enter into new obligations without the express authorization of the council, under penalty of nullity.

From January 1, 1957, and within 60 days of the end of the preceeding period, the said departments and agencies shall submit to the council a complete annual report of their activities, investments, receipts, and expenditures, together with an annual balance sheet and profit and loss statement where they engage in commercial or industrial activities. The President of the Council or the Executive Director may request from them all the information which they deem necessary for the said purpose of assuring financial and monetary stability.

Article 7. The Executive Director and technical advisers of the council shall advise the House of Deputies and Senate Committees of

Art. 6: The original draft of the first paragraph of this article had provided: "After expiration of the periods referred to... and until all the said information has been submitted... none of the said entities shall enter into any discussion, negotiation, obligation, or debt, or make any contract, agreement, treaty, or commitment whatsoever entailing the expenditure of funds or delivery of materials or property... and any measure taken by the said entities without the prior decision of the council... shall be legally null and void." It is doubtful whether this language would have been any more effective unless the President were prepared to take civil or criminal measures to enforce the law.

Art. 7: The original draft had not provided for advice to the House of Deputies or Senate. It did provide, however, that the President of the Republic should turn over to the council for its opinion every bill passed by Congress entailing the expenditure of funds or thé delivery of property, and every bill or other legal measure (this would cover executive decrees, etc.) relating to the council's field of competence or to mining or other national industries. It provided, further, that the President should veto every such bill or measure not approved by the council. To avoid delay, either house of Congress was to be permitted to submit drafts of bills in advance to the council for its opinion and comments. Had these provisions been approved, they might have obviated much hasty and ill-advised legislation, and would have relieved the President of censure for vetoing popular but unsound measures.

Finance, Budget, and others of an economic nature, with respect to the preparation of laws relating to matters covered by the present decree. If bills passed by Congress are not in accordance with the provisions of Title Thirteen of the Constitution, the Monetary Stabilization Council may request the President of the Republic to make use of the power conferred upon him by Article 77 of the said Charter.

Article 8. The council shall meet regularly under the chairmanship of the President or Vice-President as the case may be, in accordance with regulations adopted by it. It may likewise meet when convened by the President or Vice-President.

At each meeting, minutes shall be kept of the matters taken up, and the President of the Republic, in conformity with constitutional principles, shall draft the legal measures which he deems desirable to carry out the recommendations of the council.

Article 9. The council shall draft its own internal regulations. The fees which the voting members shall receive for each complete meeting attended shall be fixed by Supreme Resolution in Cabinet Council.

A special budget shall be voted for the salaries and expenses of the council. The government shall provide adequate offices for the Executive Director, technical advisers, and other officials or employees.

Article 10. The executive function of the council shall be exercised by the Executive Director or, in his absence, by a temporary or permanent alternate appointed at his suggestion by the President of the Council. The Executive Director shall have charge of the general administration of the business of the council, being empowered to appoint or remove the personnel who will work with him.

For the purposes of this decree, he may submit appropriate measures for the consideration of the council, and he shall coordinate the work of the technical advisers, who shall at the same time be special advisers to the Ministries of Finance and Economy.

Article 11. The council may charge the Executive Director with undertaking exploratory discussions with foreign financial agencies, central or reserve banks, commercial banks, investors, and other enterprises and entities, including representatives of holders of government bonds, in order to attract foreign capital.

Article 12. The President of the Republic may call upon the Executive Director for technical advice in all matters which affect

---

Art. 9: The original draft had provided for fees for the voting members (i.e., the Bolivian members) of Bs. 100,000 for each full meeting attended, but not over Bs. 5 million per annum for any member (equivalent to a maximum of $660 a year at the stabilization rate).

or may affect the internal and external credit of the country or the stability of the currency.

General provisions

Article 13. Following the date of this decree, the Central Bank of Bolivia shall neither issue nor put into circulation any new bank notes except in substitution for and to retire used notes, nor shall it increase its portfolio by credits to the government, prefectures, municipalities, or independent, quasi-independent, or autonomous government agencies, in current account or by the acquisition of bonds, without the previous unanimous approval of the voting members of the council. The council shall not authorize such operations without having previously carefully studied the data and information submitted by the appropriate technical adviser. Until the said technical adviser is named by decree, and until he takes over his full assignment of duties, the President of the Central Bank of Bolivia shall carry out this function for the purpose of monetary stabilization.

Article 14. There are hereby revoked all measures in conflict with the present decree.

The Minister of State for Finance and Statistics shall be charged with carrying out and complying with the present decree.

Given in the Government House, in the city of La Paz, on the fourth day of August, nineteen hundred and fifty-six.

Note: The original draft included an article empowering the President, with the advice of the National Monetary Stabilization Council, to enact decrees with the force and effect of law, to enter into contracts, to suspend or modify existing laws, and to do other things necessary to carry out the objective of financial and monetary stabilization. These provisions were instead embodied in a separate Act of Congress (see Appendix II). The decree establishing the Stabilization Council was ratified by Congress as one of a number of decrees regularly presented to Congress for simultaneous ratification, in accordance with the author's original suggestion.

APPENDIX II

EMERGENCY POWERS ACT

Law of November 22, 1956*

Article 1. In order to give effect to the powers set forth in Decree-Law 4469, which was given the force of law under Act of October 29, 1956, the President of the Republic, as Chief Executive, and as President of the National Monetary Stabilization Council, shall carry out such specific measures as may be appropriate to deter the inflationary process, to which end he is granted the following extraordinary powers:

A. The President of the Republic, with the approval of the National Monetary Stabilization Council and of the Cabinet, may enter into contracts, on behalf of the state or of any state enterprise, with foreign governments, central reserve banks, commercial banks or other banking institutions, and representatives of the holders of government bonds, and may contract loans or other facilities conducive to the formation of a stabilization or reserve fund, or for any other purpose conducive to currency stabilization, to elimination of restrictions on foreign exchange, and the re-establishment of the internal and external credit of the country, providing in such contracts such conditions as may be necessary and appropriate; the terms and provisions of such contracts cannot be altered other than by agreement between the parties.†

B. The President of the Republic, with the approval of the National Monetary Stabilization Council and of the Cabinet, may grant franchises or concessions, and enter into contracts with national or foreign individuals or corporations *(personas naturales o juridicas)* for the investment of capital in industries and businesses of every kind, including public utilities, which may be helpful to the national economy, and he may stipulate in such contracts such terms as may be appropriate, notwithstanding any prior legal provision to the contrary. Within such power are included such provisions as may be established for participation by workers and employees in business profits, and which may guaranty a fair return on the investment, or

*Translation by the author.

†The wording of this entire Act follows almost verbatim the original draft presented on June 26, 1956, as part of the decree establishing the National Monetary Stabilization Council. This particular clause was included to make it clear that Congress would have no right to alter any contract entered into under this Act; the members of the council endorsed this unusual precautionary clause. The Act, in final form, was approved by the council at its meeting of November 1, 1956.

623

which may establish a percentage of revenues or profits to be paid to the Treasury in lieu of all other taxes or contributions; these contractual provisions cannot be altered other than by agreement between the parties.*

C. The President of the Republic may, by Supreme Decree in accordance with the formalities of the present Act, enact such measures as may be necessary, amending or revoking any provision of law which may threaten the financial stability or credit of the country or which may endanger monetary stability.†

D. The President of the Republic, with the approval of the Cabinet, shall enact all appropriate legal measures, which may revoke prior measures, and which carry out any provision recommended by the National Monetary Stabilization Council, in fiscal, tax, banking, monetary, or public utility matters, or which may affect the budgets, revenues, expenditures, subsidies, expropriations, obligations, commitments, or projects of any government department, including any legal provision relating to the control or fixing of maximum and minimum prices for any kind of articles, goods, or services. ‡

Article 2. The powers granted to the Executive Power in the preceding Article are of an emergency nature, and hence shall remain in force for one year from the date of promulgation of the present Act, at the end of which period the National Congress may in its discretion extend this period by further act of law. §

Article 3. All measures enacted by the executive power in accordance with the extraordinary powers hereby conferred shall have the force of law, in conformity with Article 58, paragraphs 5 and 7, and Article 94, paragraph 6, of the Constitution.

---

*The repetition here was intentional, based on experience with decisions in Administrative Law in Latin America which have held that provisions for tax exemptions must be specifically approved by Congress. The provision for possible employee participation in profits, *unalterable save by agreement,* was necessary for the protection of investors against excessive future inroads on profits.

†In the original draft, this paragraph likewise provided for the approval of the Stabilization Council. The council members, probably on the advice of Dr. Sologuren, considered that the phrase "formalities of the present Act" was sufficiently specific.

‡The original draft added, as sweetening for Congress, labor, and the peasants: "...but in no case shall maximum prices be established or maintained for wages or salaries, or for the primary products of domestic agriculture, forestry, mining, or fishing." It was the intent, of course, to have no price fixing, maximum or minimum. However, the council members quite rightly believed that the proposed clause would be asking for trouble.

§The Act was in fact extended for another year by Act of December 6, 1957.

Note: The original draft also included the following article, but the members of the council considered that it would be impossible to obtain the consent of Congress and that its inclusion might jeopardize passage of the remainder of the bill:

Likewise with a view to assuring financial and monetary stability, the council shall decide, in the case of any bill entailing expenditures on the part of the government, whether the funds provided by the legislature at the time are sufficient to cover them. (N.B. This is based on Article 117 of the Constitution, which provides that all expenditures must be covered by revenues specifically appropriated.) To this end, the President of the Republic shall turn over to the council, for its study and opinion thereon, every bill submitted to him by Congress entailing an outlay of funds or the delivery of property, and in the absence of a favorable opinion with respect to the provision of funds, an executive veto shall be obligatory. Similarly, with a view to promoting the investment of private capital, the President of the Republic shall submit to the council, for its study and decision, every bill and every other legal measure relating to investments in mining or other national industries, vetoing any bill or measure of such nature that fails to have the favorable opinion of the council.

In order to avoid delay in the legislative process, the council shall study and give its opinion on any draft of a bill of that nature which may be submitted to it by either chamber of Congress, and shall return the said draft to the respective chamber with its opinion or comments with respect to the sufficiency of the funds provided. In such case, the President of the Republic may promulgate the law, in the event that the bill is presented to him by Congress, provided he has received the favorable opinion of the council, being otherwise required to veto it.

APPENDIX III

FIFTY-STEP PLAN FOR MONETARY STABILIZATION

The Fifty-Step Plan is substantially identical with the original Forty Points (see pp. 141-42), except that the latter were drawn up by subject matter, while the Fifty-Step Plan was drafted in stages: (1) measures which the State Department and the International Cooperation Administration considered essential to be taken even before considering the possibility of stabilization assistance; (2) the initial stabilization measures themselves, leading to stabilization *de facto;* and (3) the final stabilization measures, or stabilization *de jure.*

Subsequently, Washington came to the realization that it would be impossible to expect Bolivia to take the preliminary measures without assurances of the financing that would make possible enactment of the stabilization program, and the Stabilization Council was permitted to telescope Stages I and II (p. 168).

The comments on the Fifty-Step Plan, attributed to Washington and shown below in italics to distinguish them from the text of the program as presented to the National Monetary Stabilization Council, were received by cable from the Department of State. They embody the joint views of the State and Treasury Departments and of ICA.

The remaining comments, not credited to Washington, are shown in parentheses. ·They represent the views of the author or the action taken by the Stabilization Council.

Stage I — Preliminary Measures

(*NOTE:* None of these preliminary measures, whether immediate or subsequent, is of a nature that would directly affect the cost of living of the working and middle classes and thus set in motion a further price-wage spiral.)

A. Immediate Steps

    1. Compliance with Article 6 of the Monetary Stabilization Decree; i.e., provision of complete figures of receipts and expenditures, in bolivianos and dollars, of government and of all governmental agencies and entities for 1952, 1953, 1954, 1955, and the first six months of 1956.

    Washington suggested concentrating on the 1956 and 1957 budget figures to speed up results.

626

a) Conversion of the above figures at the yearly average of official and auction market rate of exchange, audited by Comptroller General, showing results in terms of bolivianos and in terms of dollars.

2. Preparation by the Ministry of Finance of an analysis of the 1956 budget of government and all agencies and entities by separate major projects and activities; dollar figures for both income and expenditures to be converted into bolivianos at illustrative rates of Bs. 4,000, Bs. 5,000, and Bs. 6,000.

Washington suggested using a single rate to save time. This would have been unwise as a "preliminary measure," as it would have revealed our hand and led to speculation. The time saved would have been negligible. In view of the telescoping of Stages I and II, however, all computations were made on the assumption of a rate of Bs. 6,500-Bs. 7,000.

a) Statement of obligations and commitments (purchases on credit and other) by major projects and activities, showing maturity dates.

3. Study of revenue measures that can be put into effect immediately to assist in reaching a true balanced budget.

Washington suggested concentrating on those measures that would be immediately productive of increased revenues.

a) Revocation of all measures providing for *revertibles,* CIF surcharges, or other charges on imports, and their replacement by a simple system of ad valorem taxes payable on the full dollar, sterling, etc. invoice price, with criminal as well as civil penalties for false invoicing or smuggling. Certain imports, as determined by the government, might be admitted free of duty, such as agricultural, road-building, public utility, and industrial machinery and equipment, and government imports other than for the industrial or public utility activities of the government or government agencies. (I later changed my views on this point, and recommended minimum 5 per cent or 10 per cent duties.) Other imports might pay a basic ad valorem rate of from 25 per cent to as high as 100 per cent, the latter on luxury imports, care being taken not to make the duty so high as to make it impossible to control smuggling. The President would be free to place products under each schedule, or to change them from one category to another, on 60 days' advance notice.

Washington suggested postponement until arrival of IMF

*mission, by which time the council was so overwhelmed
with work that it was forced to leave the entire question
of import duties in the hands of the Finance Ministry.
The Ministry, equally overburdened, took the tariff schedules that had been worked out by the U.N. mission experts
which, because of the pressure of time, had to be enacted
on December 15, even though their shortcomings were
apparent to the council members. A wholly new tariff
schedule was enacted early in 1957 (see pp. 322-25).*

b) Subjection of all government owned or operated public
utility, mining, and industrial enterprises to the same
taxes, royalties, and regulations as private enterprises;
elimination of all subsidies, direct or indirect, to private
or governmental business enterprises; elimination of all
special benefits to governmental enterprises that are not
enjoyed by private enterprise; installation of sound accounting principles, including adequate depreciation allowances in governmental business enterprises; and other
measures required to make such enterprises stand on
their own feet on a par with private enterprise.

*Washington suggested postponement until arrival of IMF
mission.*

c) Enactment of as many of the following tax measures as
the government may consider appropriate and urgently
necessary at this time, for the purpose of increasing revenues and making it easier to arrive at a balanced budget.
The remaining measures should be postponed for discussion with the appropriate technical adviser, due to arrive
in October:

> A new cadastral valuation of all property based on
> actual values, and establishment of a single tax on
> real estate high enough to replace all taxes on rents
> and income from real property; to provide adequate
> revenues; and to encourage the productive use of ur-
> ban and rural property. (I later recommended short-
> cutting the cadastral survey. However, little headway
> was made in improving the real property tax struc-
> ture. See pp. 334ff.)

> Enactment of option, permitting substitution, instead
> of a corporate or other company income tax, of a tax
> on gross revenues in the case of public utilities, and
> of a 30 per cent income tax to be withheld on all do-
> mestic dividend payments and 40 per cent on dividend
> payments remitted abroad. (*Note:* Public utility ac-
> counting is so little understood in Latin America that

it is better to pay a tax on gross rather than net, provided the tax is not too high. Nothing was done in this direction, and I had no time to pursue the matter. The tax on dividends rather than on net income is administratively simpler and encourages the reinvestment of earnings.)

A revised income tax on all wages and other personal income derived from Bolivian sources, other than on rents or dividends from domestic companies, with reasonable minimum exemptions, and on a sliding scale of from 10 to 25 per cent; imposition of criminal as well as civil penalties, and perhaps a double-checked government estimate of income in the absence of a tax return. (*Note:* "Bolivian source income" would be defined in accordance with standard international usage, not U.S. usage. The income tax was enacted in 1957, but on a basis that was intended to be punitive rather than as a revenue measure. It failed in both respects. See pp. 312-15.)

Adequate excise and sales taxes. (Some action was taken in 1957, but fell far short of adequacy, either in concept or administration. See pp. 315-18.)

Elimination of all taxes that fail to produce revenues commensurate with the cost of collection and the nuisance to the taxpayer, perhaps including stamp taxes. (The Finance Minister made considerable progress in this direction. I dropped the proposal regarding stamp taxes, as the prime need was to boost revenues.)

Elimination of all special earmarking of taxes *(destinados)*, other than under Item 8 below. (Earmarked taxes had been cut from 70 per cent of national revenues (!) in 1953 to 30 per cent in 1956, the one beneficial consequence of monetary depreciation which diminished the revenues from old taxes and brought about many new, nonearmarked taxes. The major beneficiaries of earmarked taxes — the universities — remained a problem. See p. 430.)

4. Consideration by President and Cabinet — this involves a political decision — as to the expediency of increasing wages and salaries of governmental personnel by 40 per cent to coincide with increases which, it is understood, have been granted to all other branches of labor.

Washington agreed, but warned that this must not be allowed to start a new round of increases for the miners. This measure was carried out with no untoward consequences.

a) Elimination of governmental departments and agencies and reduction of governmental personnel, to the extent that this is made possible by elimination of governmental functions and activities as set forth in Item 5 below. (This was a lost cause.)

5. Preparation of a new twelve-month budget, based on analysis of the 1956 budget (Item 2, above); and estimated increase of revenues to be derived from tax measures deemed feasible at this time (Item 3, above, making allowance for increased true costs of governmental enterprises under Item 3a); and wage increases, if any, under Item 4, above. This budget would be based on enactment of all measures contemplated in Phase I, dollar figures to be converted into bolivianos at illustrative rates of 4,000, 5,000, and 6,000. The selection of which projects, public works, and governmental activities must be eliminated to arrive at a true balanced budget is a political decision, to be made by the President and Cabinet. The council can merely recommend that preference be given to (a) those activities that will provide an immediate (within twelve months) or early return in *devisen (Washington suggested: "or reduction in need for* devisen"); (b) those that will provide an immediate or early return in local currency. (These criteria were supported by the council.)

a) This budget must show elimination of any need for increasing the net indebtedness of the government and agencies to the Central Bank or to any other lender, on an annual basis. Before reaching Phase II, gross current government and agency borrowing from the Central Bank must have been restricted to amounts less than their deposits in the Central Bank, including the "sterilized" counterpart funds. This is based on the assumption that, during Phase I, to deter inflationary tendencies, counterpart funds will be expended on the basis of present counterpart conversion rates (averaging Bs. 1,000 to the dollar; actual rate to be fixed following report of IMF mission), and that the difference between that rate and the selling price to the public of U.S. aid commodities will be held by Central Bank for government account and sterilized to the extent recommended by the Stabilization Council.

Washington suggested limiting this paragraph to the first sentence, pending study by the IMF mission; meanwhile, the release of counterpart funds should be held to a minimum.

6. An agreement entered into between the Minister of Economy and ICA, whereby sales prices to the public shall be fixed monthly for agricultural products, whether imported under the U.S. aid program or otherwise imported by the government, at levels high enough to encourage domestic production in Bolivia and to discourage smuggling to neighboring countries *(Washington suggested ending this paragraph here, pending study by the IMF mission)*, but not higher than world market prices CIF Mollendo or Arica, converted during Phase I at the rate of Bs. 4,000 per dollar, and thereafter at such rates as shall be established. Counterpart funds resulting from the sale of U.S. aid commodities shall be used by the government for the public purposes set forth in previous agreements, at an average rate not exceeding Bs. 1,000 to the dollar (actual rate to be fixed after study by IMF mission), and the remaining counterpart funds, consisting of the difference between the said usable amounts and the full counterpart funds created at the Bs. 4,000 or later established rate, shall be held by the Central Bank for government account, and sterilized to the extent recommended by the Stabilization Council. (In view of the telescoping of Stages I and II, the Bs. 1,000 rate proposed here and in Step 5 was inappropriate.)

a) The prices for agricultural products fixed under the said agreement shall be made public and shall become effective on or prior to the date when the next local crop of such products, or of products competitive therewith, comes on the market, as determined by agreement between the Minister of Economy and the director of ICA operations in Bolivia, with due regard to the effect that such price announcements may have on hoarding and the creation of artificial scarcities.

Washington suggested that prices for such commodities be fixed on the responsibility of the Minister, who should consult with USOM. Washington failed to realize that my phrasing would relieve the Minister of political pressure. The mechanics were the same.

b) Arrangements must be made, with the assistance of ICA, to insure that adequate supplies of essential foodstuffs are available at all times. (This was stressed, and standby arrangements were made for food airlifts in case of need. The airlift proved unnecessary, as a return to a free market economy brought out quantities of food previously black-marketed or smuggled out of the country.)

c) These increased prices shall not become effective during Stage I, and, as shown under Stage II, will then be accompanied by appropriate wage increases.

7. Preparation by the Central Bank of an estimated twelve-month balance of payments, at illustrative Bs. 4,000, Bs. 5,000, and Bs. 6,000 rates, based on enactment of all measures contemplated in Stage I, showing necessary elimination of government importations of capital goods to the extent required to create a free excess of hard currency exports sufficient to create Central Bank free foreign exchange reserves at the rate of at least $4 million a year, with no increase in foreign debt or commitments of any nature, and allowing for payment of existing commitments (see Item 2a, above), and for payments called for under arrangements reached on foreign debt and nationalization of mines, as well as any payments that may be required on loans covering International Tin Agreement commitments. (If not otherwise agreed, allow 15 per cent on tin exports, as proposed by Messrs. Williams Harvey and Company, Ltd.) (*Note:* This estimate would allow for scheduled U.S. aid; the Central Bank took care of this step, using a Bs. 6,500-Bs. 7,000 rate, and using a foreign exchange budget format rather than attempting a complete balance of payments.)

8. Creation of tax of 2 per cent, payable to the Central Bank, on all foreign exchange transactions (both purchase and sale, and including the conversion of Bolivian currency into *devisen*), the tax being payable in *devisen*, for the purpose of building up a dollar reserve at the rate of approximately $4 million a year.

Washington cabled that this must await IMF approval, in view of their general opposition, under Article VIII of the IMF regulations, to any tax on foreign exchange. The $4 million reserve was a Treasury idea. As the Treasury dropped its insistence on building up a prestabilization reserve, the 2 per cent tax was likewise dropped, but was later enacted in somewhat different form (see p. 584).

9. Revocation of all measures establishing official exchange rates of Bs. 190 per dollar for imports or government or ICA accounting, or of Bs. 1,200 or Bs. 1,500 for exports, and all other controlled or artificial rates for imports, exports or any other purposes, except that during Phase I no change shall be made in the prices fixed for the sale of essential foodstuffs to the public by the government (see Item 6, above).

a) Establishment of a provisional, uniform rate of Bs. 3,500 for all exports and imports by the government and government entities effective until the commencement of Stage II, with peremptory requirement that no government branch, department, agency, or entity can resort to the Central Bank or to the Treasury for additional subsidies or assistance or the issuance of bank notes, except such subsidy as may be proved essential to cover losses on the below-cost company stores *(pulpería barata)*. (This was approved by the council, except that the telescoping of Stages I and II made it possible to cut out the *pulpería* exception.)

10. Revocation of all measures whereby the government imports, or purchases locally, or otherwise acquires commodities or goods of any nature whatsoever, other than for its own use or for the use of established governmental agencies, and except for foodstuffs during the duration of Stage I. (The Minister of Economy insisted on the need of rationing private imports by maintaining control of foreign exchange and issuing permits to importers on the basis of bids. The concept of a free market economy is a difficult one to grasp for persons who have been schooled in a government-controlled economy, and it was not until after enactment of the stabilization program, when it was manifest that a free market actually worked, that the opposition of the Minister could be overcome, or outvoted.)

11. A law, or decree authorized by law, eliminating all price and other controls on exports; repealing *inter alia* the decree of July, 1956, fixing prices for exports of rubber, forest products, vicuña wool, etc.; permitting exporters of minerals to use the services of the Mining Bank or not as they see fit; and eliminating all taxes on exports (as recommended by Kemmerer), but solely in the event that the proposed new mining code adopts a system of royalties on metal exports in lieu of export taxes — otherwise, imposing an export tax on all mineral exports other than petroleum, including COMIBOL exports, the tax perhaps varying according to world mineral prices, but averaging 10 per cent (there would also be the 2 per cent foreign exchange tax, which would bring the total up to the 12 per cent average prevailing before nationalization of the mines).

Washington cabled that Steps 11 and 12 should be postponed pending arrival of the IMF mission. This measure was substantially enacted, except for the 2 per cent tax and exceptions made for the Mining Bank and certain export taxes. (Approved by the council.)

12. A law, or decree authorized by law, eliminating all price and other controls on imports, except that the President may at any time, by emergency decree for a period of one year, to be extended if necessary, provide that imports of luxury and certain other goods be prohibited or subjected to an import permit obtained prior to shipment, against payment at the time of obtaining the permit, of the requisite foreign exchange to cover CIF plus customs duties. (Approved by the council. This restriction on luxury imports and requirement of prior exchange deposit was contrary to the free market philosophy. I had incorporated it into the original Forty Points on the insistence of my Bolivian colleagues in the organizing group.)

13. Immediate cessation of the expansion of government into fields that can be filled by private initiative, such as the proposed creation of a government import corporation, construction of further hydroelectric plants, rice mills, sugar mills, and other public utility, industrial, and business enterprises. (Approved by the council.)

14. Immediate cessation of all projects referred to in Article 5 of the Monetary Stabilization Decree and suspension of all projects referred to in the second clause of Article 4 that have not yet been substantially commenced, until such time as the Monetary Stabilization Council can investigate and present its recommendations with respect to such projects. (Approved by the council.)

15. Investigation of all pending long-term foreign credit or barter arrangements of the government or governmental entities, whether by treaty or contract, with a view to denouncing such treaties at the earliest possible date in order to restore all imports and exports to the normal channels of trade, and to eliminating unjust enrichment in those cases where long-term credits have meant higher than reasonable prices and where the contract has been obtained by improper means.

    Washington objected to this step on the ground that U.S. interests might be adversely affected.

    a) Adoption and announcement of the policy that all exports must henceforth be made in exchange for *devisen* completely free from restrictions; that no further barter arrangements will be made; and that no privileges or special concessions or arrangements will be made with any individuals, entities, or governments, for the importation or exportation of products, or for the exploitation of the country's natural resources, that are not open to everyone under established codes such as the Petroleum Code and the prospective Mining Code.

Washington suggested omitting "completely free from restrictions," pending study by IMF mission. President Siles (and the council) approved Step 15 as a statement of permanent policy, the Minister of Economy pointing out that it is unnecessary to denounce the treaties or annul the contracts, but merely to refrain from buying any more merchandise under them.

16. A law, or decree authorized by law, reducing the payments for social security and other benefits to not over $2\frac{1}{2}$ per cent for employers and $2\frac{1}{2}$ per cent for employees, establishing the retirement age at 65 for men and 62 for women, and providing further that the entire contributions be invested in U.S. dollar securities; that they be devoted exclusively to the benefit of employees; and that benefits be limited to those that can be justified on an actuarial basis.

    Washington was concerned that the dollar investment requirement might affect the balance of payments; I proposed it for only until such time as the currency was stabilized. The $2\frac{1}{2}$ per cent rates were purely for bargaining (see pp. 172-73).

17. Revision of labor laws and decrees to eliminate the "immovability" of labor and make possible the transfer of labor from one enterprise to another; to restore managerial functions to management, improve discipline, and increase production while at the same time preserving for labor its bargaining power in collective negotiations with management; and, in the event that disputes are not settled by direct negotiation, the right to arbitration under the auspices of the government, which will have as its criterion justice to the workers as well as to the shareholders or taxpayers whose investments have made possible the establishment of the enterprise, at the same time prohibiting any measure or activity on the part of employees or employers which diminishes production unless caused by curtailment in demand.

    Washington suggested postponing Steps 17 and 19 for later stages, as being too much for the government to tackle at one time. As a result, nothing was ever done.

18. A temporary freeze on all wage or salary increases during the period of Phase I, except such increase as may be considered under Item 4. (This step was approved by the council.)

19. A law, or decree authorized by law, empowering the President to transfer to private investors — preferably Bolivian — all government public utility (including transportation and communication), industrial, and business enterprises, under sale or management or lease or concession contracts, as and to the extent that private capital, domestic or foreign, can be induced to take over the ownership or management of such enterprises under rate and other conditions adequate to attract private investment. These provisions should form a part of the Investment Code (Item 31), notwithstanding which no increase in (utility) rates, however justifiable, should be put into effect during Stage I of the stabilization program, if such increase would directly affect the cost of living of the working and middle classes. In the event that any justified rate increase is postponed for that reason, it should be made effective at the commencement of Stage II, plus an additional increase to compensate the company for the delay in its application. (This step was agreed to by the council, and embodied in the emergency powers law. See Appendix II.)

20. A law, or decree authorized by law, authorizing real property rentals payable in foreign currencies, and mortgages and mortgage certificates on such properties, likewise payable in foreign currencies and in such form as to be readily negotiable abroad. This measure is not essential to stabilization, but can result in a certain amount of foreign investment even prior to stabilization.

   Washington objected to this, probably because IMF has natural objections to foreign currency contracts. Their usefulness in stimulating investment is, however, undeniable.

21. Establishment of a new cost of living index based on actual free market prices of commodities in current use. This measure is desirable, so that when the later stabilization measures are taken, they will not show an unreal increase in the cost of living.

   Washington considered this so important that they suggested postponement pending study of the IMF mission, with the result that nothing was ever done about it. The council did decide that the Finance Minister should have the General Bureau of Statistics compile a living cost index, with an October, 1956, base, with the cooperation of the Economic Commission for Latin America, and using actual market prices and appropriate weights, but by then we were too busy to press the matter.

22. Commencement of negotiations for resumption of payment

upon the foreign debt under bilateral agreement. (Authorized by the council. See pp. 254, 441).

23. Commencement of negotiations for settlement, by direct negotiation or by arbitration, on a mutually acceptable basis, of the debt arising from the nationalization of the mines and other properties.

Washington objected to "and other properties," as this might include properties owned by Bolivians. This is precisely what I intended, in the belief that private enterprise cannot be encouraged where there is confiscation of property, domestic or foreign.

24. Ratification by Congress of the Stabilization Council Decree of August 4, 1956, and of the Petroleum Code. (This was accomplished on October 25 [*El Diario,* La Paz, October 26, 1956].)

25. Passage of a law giving the President emergency powers for one year, empowering him, with the advice of the Stabilization Council, to take all measures necessary to implement the purposes of the Decree of August 4, 1956, as ratified by law, such measures to have the effect of law, and revoking all prior legal measures contrary thereto; passage of a law embodying all the measures in Phase I, and, in general terms and as far as can be defined, the measures in Phases II and III, and giving the President, with the advice of the Stabilization Council, full powers of regulation and enforcement of those measures and other measures necessary to implement that act and the act ratifying the Decree of August 4, 1956. (Substantially the first alternative was enacted, on November 20, 1956, this being, of course, my first choice. See Appendix II.)

26. Demonstration of Bolivia's capacity, over a reasonable period of time, to maintain a climate that will attract private investment.

Washington refrained from comment on this step, and on Steps 27-36, which were not for immediate action, and could hence be postponed until arrival of the IMF mission.

B. Subsequent Steps

27. Investigation, recommendations, and report of IMF mission in cooperation with the Executive Director and the appropriate Technical Director of the National Monetary Stabilization Council and associates.

   a) A review by IMF, Central Bank, and appropriate technical

adviser of the Stabilization Council, of reserve requirements against bank deposits, with a view to establishing
quantitative credit control, and initiation of credit restrictions appropriate to Stage I. (In my original Forty-
Point Draft, I had proposed a 100 per cent reserve against
circulation until such time as the Stabilization Council
recommended a lower ratio, and a 100 per cent reserve
against deposits to be reduced gradually to __ per cent,
pari passu, as the stabilization loan was paid off. This
was considered unduly restrictive by Washington [see p.
142]. In modern theory there is no reason to differentiate
between note circulation and deposits, but at this stage it
seemed wise to have a prohibitive ratio for any increase
in bank note circulation and a diminishing ratio for deposits. In 1927 Kemmerer had advocated a reserve of *at
least* 50 per cent against notes and deposits [Art. 60, proposed law, Kemmerer report, p. 190].)

b) An agreement entered into between the President of the
Republic and IMF, with advice of the Stabilization Council, on a practical credit restriction program, for implementation at the beginning of Stage II, involving special
reserve requirements for new deposits.

c) An agreement with IMF, as above, on a definitive program
for Stage II, with particular reference to prospective revisions of the exchange system and related controls.

28. Preparation of a revised budget, similar to Item 5, but based
on decisions reached as a result of IMF investigation and on
steps to be taken under Stage II.

29. Preparation of revised balance of payments, similar to Item
7, but based on decisions reached as a result of IMF investigation and on steps to be taken under Stage II. (Steps 27, 28,
29 were taken care of in cooperation with the Central Bank
and the Finance Minister.)

30. Passage of a fair mining code, to be reviewed by the National
Monetary Stabilization Council prior to enactment. (*Note:*
This was not enacted until after stabilization. I had put it
under "Preliminary Measures" only at the insistence of the
State Department.)

31. Passage of a fair investment code, to be reviewed by the National Monetary Stabilization Council prior to enactment.
(*Note:* I realized that this measure could not be improvised;

it was put under "Preliminary Measures" solely to satisfy the State Department.)*

32. A law, or decree authorized by law, providing that future takings of private property be subject to prior prompt, adequate, and effective compensation; and, in the case of foreign investments, in the money of the country of origin of the foreign capital. (Step 32 was inserted at the suggestion of Washington; it is covered in theory by the Bolivian Constitution.)

33. Conclusion of a satisfactory bilateral agreement for resumption of payment on foreign indebtedness. (Note that Step 22 is for "commencement of negotiations.")

34. Conclusion of a mutually acceptable arrangement on compensation for nationalization of mining and other properties (Step 23 refers to "commencement of negotiations.")

35. Effective implementation of the Ford, Bacon & Davis reorganization plan for COMIBOL, with satisfactory evidence that COMIBOL can and will operate without loss under the conditions of Stage II. (*Note:* This was not insisted upon by Washington, with the result that nothing was done, and nine years later COMIBOL is still in difficulties.)

36. Prior to initiation of Stage II, Bolivia must have increased its free foreign exchange reserves by $1 million, and the monthly rate of accumulation shall have reached $300,000 per month, with no increase of Bolivia's foreign debt or commitments of any kind. (*Note:* This was impossible; it was inserted solely at the insistence of Washington.)

Stage II — Initial Stabilization Measures

(*NOTE:* These measures must all be taken simultaneously, following the recommendations made by the Stabilization Council in collaboration with the IMF mission. The following draft is purely

---

*It had been my intention to draft an investment code for Bolivia before I left. Such a task would have fallen squarely within my field of competence, and I had as a starting point a fair practice code drafted for the National Association of Manufacturers by H. W. Balgooyen, Executive Vice-President of American & Foreign Power Co., Inc. However, I simply did not have the time to draft a code, nor was there any urgency for such a code up to the time of my departure, as political and labor conditions were such that no investments could be expected, outside of oil and mining, for which special codes were required.

tentative and subject to substantial modification based on the experience acquired during Stage I of the prógram and on the specific conditions set forth in the contract referred to under Step 37.)

37. A contract, authorized by law and by presidential decree, on recommendation of the Stabilization Council, entered into between the Central Bank and the International Monetary Fund, the U.S. Treasury Department, ICA, and a consortium of private bankers, the contract to provide *inter alia:*

a) A loan of $__ million to be made available on a stand-by basis or on deposit in the United States to the credit of the Central Bank, for stabilization purposes, and as a reserve against the entire note circulation and deposits of the Central Bank and private banks, the percentage of such reserves to be determined in the contract. (*Note:* Siles hoped that $30 million could be obtained instead of the $25 million advocated by the author. I explained that $25 million gave adequate security as, even if everyone lost confidence and tried to buy dollars, there were not enough bolivianos available to buy $25 million; also that it was expected that only $5 million would have to be used.)

b) The loan to carry a stand-by charge of __ per cent, plus interest at __ per cent on amounts actually used.

c) The loan to be reduced by deposit of the 2 per cent tax on foreign exchange transactions (which includes a 2 per cent charge on conversion of Bolivian currency into *devisen;* see Item 8), the bank being permitted to accelerate payment at its option.

d) That, to the extent the borrowed dollar reserve is replaced by Bolivian dollar funds, the dollar reserve against bank deposits is to be reduced *pari passu* from __ per cent to __ per cent and ultimately eliminated, with adequate reserve requirements established in Bolivian currency or in *devisen* at the option of the respective banks.

e) That no further bank notes be issued except against a __ per cent dollar reserve computed at Bs. __ to the dollar, or at such rate as shall later be established under Stage III.

f) That the agreements and arrangements as to reserve requirements, credit restrictions, the exchange system, and related controls, entered into with the IMF (see Item 27) be implemented in legal form.

g) That metallic currency to be issued under Stage III of the program be limited to 10 per cent of the note issue.

h) That the government promulgate all the measures listed as requisite for monetary stabilization and undertake not to repeal or amend those measures without the consent of the lending institutions.

i) That, for the duration of the loan agreement, the Central Bank employ a person recommended by the lending institutions as a technical adviser charged *inter alia* with supervising the implementation of the said measures. (*Note:* Items c, d, g, and i were not insisted upon by the lending agencies. In my opinion, this was unfortunate.)

38. Computation of a boliviano-dollar equivalent, for initial *de facto* stabilization purposes, at such rate as will enable the Mining Corporation (COMIBOL) to operate at a profit, despite the increase in wages referred to in Item 43, below, and assuming adequate accruals for depreciation, depletion, and research and exploration; competent organization and management of COMIBOL; cooperation on the part of labor; and allowing for the possibility of a drop in the price of tin to 80 cents a pound, with a corresponding decline in the price of other metals. (Initially, there was some objection to fixing the rate on the basis of the COMIBOL accounts. The Minister of Mines contended that YPFB would have to have a lower rate. The Minister of Economy insisted that the government and government enterprises be allowed to import at Bs. 190 on existing commitments. I insisted that there was no point in disguising deficits; they had to be eliminated. In the end, of course, that viewpoint was upheld, as it was the essence of the plan.)

39. Prices fixed for the importation by the government of agricultural products, whether under U.S. aid or otherwise, shall enter into effect, product by product, as set forth in Item 6. (Approved by the council.)

40. Elimination of the below-cost company store *(pulpería barata)*, in all enterprises, governmental or private, and of all subsidies connected therewith. (Approved by the council.)

41. Revocation of all measures establishing controls of any nature whatsoever over foreign exchange transactions or rates, or the importation, exportation, ownership, purchase or sale of national or foreign currency, other than as set forth herein:

a) Exporters of petroleum or other minerals, and public utilities and other enterprises operating under contracts or concessions granted by the state, shall be subject to the conditions of such contracts or concessions and to the terms of the Petroleum Code, the Mining Code, and other codes or laws governing their contractual position.

b) There shall be promulgated a law, or decree authorized by law, revoking the Law of May 19, 1932, and the Decree of May 25, 1932; and providing that all exporters of goods of any kind, and all persons or entities in Bolivia receiving payment in foreign exchange in transactions of any nature, shall dispose of the corresponding *devisen* by sale to a licensed banking institution or exchange agency in Bolivia in exchange for national currency, subject to payment of the 2 per cent tax set forth under Item 8. (*Note:* The 2 per cent tax referred to here and under c and d was abandoned. See Step 8.)

c) All purchases of foreign exchange, by importers or others, shall likewise be made through a licensed banking institution or exchange agency in Bolivia, and shall be subject to payment of the said 2 per cent tax.

d) All purchases and sales of gold (other than by mining enterprises), and of *valuta,* shall be handled by the Central Bank and by licensed banking institutions and exchange agencies, with no restrictions or controls, other than that all such dealers, including the foreign exchange department of the Central Bank, shall make a monthly report of all transactions in gold, *valuta* or *devisen*,[*] to the monetary department of the Central Bank and shall pay the tax of 2 per cent in dollars or other free *devisen* as the case may be, upon all such purchases and upon all sales of *devisen,* chargeable to the respective buyer or seller, the proceeds of such tax to be used to establish a Central Bank dollar reserve in the United States. This tax may later be reduced to 2 per cent solely on purchases of gold, *valuta* or *devisen,* once the loan referred to in Item 37 is repaid. (*Note:* The tax and reserve requirements were dropped as contrary to Article VIII of the IMF regulations. The Finance Minister suggested that the exchange agencies (*casas de cambio*) and the foreign exchange departments of the commercial banks should be prohibited from operating, as this would encourage speculation and the flight of capital. In the end, exchange was left free of controls, with reports for statistical purposes and information, but no penalties.)

[*]*Devisen* are checks, bills of exchange, etc.; *valuta* are foreign currencies.

42. Promulgation of such legal measures as may be requisite so that the President, on the advice of the Stabilization Council, may repeal, as necessary and appropriate, all measures providing for the control of rents and of prices for goods of any kind, or for government sales or dealings therein, or subsidies whereby goods are sold or properties rented at prices other than those fixed by untrammeled supply and demand, such revocation to be effective:

a) In the case of foodstuffs and other agricultural products, not earlier than the time fixed by the Minister of Economy as set forth under Item 6, it being essential that, at such time as these controls are removed, there be adequate supplies of such products available, either from local production, from U.S. aid, or from other sources. (*Note:* In order to insure adequate supplies, the head of the U.S. operations mission, Ross Moore, and his associate, William Ketner, were invited to the council meeting. Moore gave assurance that there would be ample supplies of wheat, flour, oil, powdered milk, and rice, and adequate transportation. The Minister of Economy stated that there would be a shortage of meat and sugar, and asked $4 million to cover imports of the latter. Moore held that there would be no shortage of meat if prices were not controlled, and I insisted that Bolivia would have to cut its sugar consumption back to 30,000 tons instead of the 60,000 tons it consumed, or smuggled out of the country, under the system of importing at artificial rates of exchange. Consumption in 1953 was only 23,000 tons, and there were no dollars available for greater imports. The whole problem solved itself with stabilization.)*

b) In the case of all other products, not later than two months following the commencement of Stage II, unless otherwise recommended by the Stabilization Council. (The Minister of Economy asked whether this meant the abandonment of controls over manufacturing costs, and I explained that, under a free market economy, there would be no cost or price controls, adding that the Minister

---

*The original foreign exchange budget of the Ministry of Economy was $37 million and the Minister informed the President that he considered it rash to reduce it to $4 million (which the council allowed him), as it meant that everything depended on the success of the stabilization program. The President was concerned that there would be scarcities of certain products, such as tires, but Gisbert and I tried to reassure him that if there were no price or import controls there would be no shortages of anything. This proved to be the case.

could balance his budget by eliminating all personnel presently engaged in those operations.)

c) In the case of rentals for new buildings or for property not presently rented, as soon after the commencement of Stage II as the Stabilization Council shall recommend.

d) In the case of existing rentals for buildings or property, not later than two years after the commencement of Stage III unless a further one-year emergency extension be proclaimed by the President of the Republic. (*Note:* The Finance Minister and Gisbert suggested that all rents be raised immediately to a fixed percentage of the new property assessments, to encourage building and in justice to property owners, as in many cases rents were not high enough to pay taxes. In the end, commercial rents were raised 400 per cent and residential rents, for 3 rooms or more, 200 per cent, which was absurdly inadequate with the boliviano worth one-fortieth of the previous official parity.)

43. A decree increasing wages of miners, railway workers, and others now enjoying cheap commissary privileges by a percentage sufficient to compensate for the loss of such privileges, commissary articles thenceforth to be sold at cost plus 10 per cent as provided in the July, 1956, Decree. (*Note:* COMIBOL and other enterprises proved to be powerless to insist on the latter provision.) The same decree should provide that no further increase in wages will be permitted for one year and that, thereafter, wages will not be regulated by government but by individual or collective bargaining, with provisions for impartial arbitration to settle differences. (*Note:* No progress was made in the direction of collective bargaining.)

44. A decree increasing all other salaries, wages, and compensation for services, other than those of government and government agency employees, by a percentage (or on a sliding scale) sufficient to compensate for the anticipated increase in the cost of living as a consequence of the other stabilization measures herein set forth, the decree to contain the same freezing and other provisions set forth above.

45. A decree increasing the salaries and wages paid to employees of the government and government agencies by the same percentage as set forth in the preceding paragraph, provided, however, that the number of employees is reduced sufficiently (as a consequence of eliminating governmental

controls and other government activities) so that the total governmental payroll will not be increased. (*Note:* The reduction of government personnel was "accepted in principle," which, translated from government language, means "nothing will be done.")

46. A law, or decree authorized by law, promulgating such of the revenue measures listed under Item 3c as may not have been passed under Stage I, and such other measures as may be proposed by the appropriate technical adviser of the council and approved by the council and President, including:

   a) Tax-free revaluation of company assets to give effect to changes in real values; in the case of public utilities and petroleum, mining, or other enterprises operating under contracts or concessions granted by the state, such revaluation shall be subject to supervision by the appropriate government agency. (See pp. 261, 366 for discussion of tax revaluations.)

47. A law, or decree authorized by law, providing for and encouraging the establishment of savings banks, savings departments in commercial banks, the establishment of foreign commercial banks, and sound domestic and foreign insurance companies. (*Note:* This was not accomplished during my term of service in Bolivia. This step and Step 48 should properly have gone under Stage III.)

48. Abandonment, within two years from the commencement of Stage II, of all enterprises referred to in Item 19 (other than COMIBOL or YPFB) that cannot be disposed of to private industry and that show a loss on the basis of sound commercial accounting, with adequate depreciation and other accruals, and without subsidies or other special favors. (*Note:* A consummation devoutly to be wished, but nothing more.)

Stage III — Final Stabilization Measures

(*NOTE:* These measures may be taken as soon as an agreement with the IMF can be reached as to a *de jure* stabilization rate, allowing a reasonable time for experience under the *de facto* rate set under Stage II and for the printing of the new currency contemplated in Stage III. See p. 591 for achievement of this stage.)

49. A law, or decree authorized by law, providing for a new currency unit (herein called the "peso," although "condor" or any other denomination might be appropriate) equivalent to __ grams, of gold __ fine.

a) Alternatively, the new unit might be made equivalent to one or more "Interamerican Monetary Units," which unit could be established by treaty creating an Interamerican Monetary Union, the unit to consist of .0987+ grams of gold 900 fine (equivalent to 10 cents U.S.; 10 centavos Cuban, Dominican, Guatemalan, Panamanian; Colón 0.25 Salvadorean; Lempira 0.20 Honduran; and Gourde 0.50 Haitian). (For the past thirty years, I had advocated an Interamerican Monetary Unit, with suitable arrangements for hemisphere monetary stability, and it occurred to me that Bolivia would be pleased to have credit for initiating such a plan. It was dropped because of Washington opposition to what might have been a rival monetary institution to the IMF, although there was precedent in the peaceful coexistence of the OAS and the United Nations.)

b) The same law or decree would provide that pesos shall be exchanged for dollars in the United States, and vice versa in Bolivia, without restriction, other than the 2 per cent charge on purchases of dollars as set forth in Item 41*d*. (*Note:* The 2 per cent tax referred to here and in Step 50 was not enacted.)

c) The same law or decree would provide that the new paper currency shall carry the double denomination (say, so many "Bolivianos" and "One Peso") for two years, after which time the boliviano denomination would be dropped, the interim currency to continue in circulation until exhausted. (See p. 135 for genesis of this idea.)

50. The loan and stand-by arrangements referred to under Item 37 would be paid off and cancelled by the deposit of the proceeds of the 2 per cent tax herein referred to, or by such additional deposits as the Central Bank may make for that purpose. Thenceforth, the currency will be backed by the reserve against bank notes, in dollars or in such other free and stable *devisen* as Bolivia may decide.

* * * * *

Following the final stabilization measures, it is recommended that a careful, impartial, and apolitical study be made of wages and living costs, preferably with the technical assistance of ICA or of the IMF, in order to determine what measures of relief can and should be given to persons on salaries or wages at all levels. It is the impression of the undersigned (Eder) that real wages and salaries in terms of purchasing power, particularly the latter, are far below those prevailing at any previous period within recent years. Once stabilization is achieved and maintained on the basis herein proposed, social security costs reduced to an appropriate level, and government expenditures cut to a minimum, wages and salaries can then be raised to adequate levels without resulting in international depreciation of the Bolivian currency. Even though such a step may result in some degree of internal inflation, this should be offset by the deflationary measures herein proposed; moreover, it is an act of elementary economic justice wholly consistent with and absolutely essential to the encouragement of free private enterprise. (*Note:* No such impartial study has ever been made; probably ILO rather than ICA or IMF should have made the study, particularly with a view to raising the salaries of the politically impotent — school teachers and others.)

APPENDIX IV

ANALYSIS OF BOLIVIAN DEVELOPMENT
CORPORATION PROJECTS*

Sugar mill at Guabirá

The site of the mill had been chosen by U.N. experts who plotted the exact center of sugar cane production in the Santa Cruz area and decided upon that spot as the location of the mill, with the result that the plant was built in the middle of a swamp, and the contractors were forced to sink 2,850 thirty-foot piles for the foundation (Víctor Paz-Estenssoro, *Mensaje del Presidente de la República* [La Paz: Ediciones S.P.I.C., 1956], p. 64). This meant an avoidable additional expense of some $250,000 or more. A soil survey would have shown that the optimum location for future cane production was not in that area but some twenty miles to the north, and one of the major problems of the mill in the early years was to procure enough cane to keep it in active operation during the five months a year for which it was planned. At the time of the Stabilization Council meeting I had been unable to obtain from the Development Corporation any information as to the total investment in Guabirá, in dollars and bolivianos, but the government newspaper, *La Nación,* had published a laudatory article based on information supplied by the Development Corporation, which boasted of an $8 million investment. The president of the corporation, however, claimed that the total cost was $5 million, apparently improvising the figure, as he was unable then, or at any later date, to provide substantiating data for his statement.

I pointed out that, on a visit to Guabirá, I had seen deliveries to the mill by neighboring farmers *(colonos)* of sugar cane that had been pulled up virtually by the roots and loaded with stones (it was to be paid for by weight), any one of which could have cracked the grinding rollers. Furthermore, the cane had been lying around for weeks and stank of fermentation, which did not speak well for management.

Following the council meeting, I visited the offices of the Development Corporation, where I was informed by General Manager, Joaquín Lemoine, that the total investment could be conservatively placed at $5 million in dollars plus five billion in bolivianos, say $6 million in all, but that no exact estimate could be given, as there

*Presented by the author to the National Monetary Stabilization Council in October, 1956, supplemented by later data.

648

was no way of ascertaining what bolivianos had actually been spent in Bolivia for local wages and expenses, and what bolivianos had been used for the payment of dollar expenditures through the Central Bank, at the official Bs. 190 rate. Hence, the books might show anywhere from a fifteenth to a seventieth of the true value for such outlays.

A subsequent investigation made by the Economic Commission for Latin America, with the assistance of the National Coordination and Planning Commission, put the total investment in the Guabirá mill at $10 million, which may be accepted as the most trustworthy estimate possible under the circumstances, and probably three times as high as a reasonable commercial investment would have been for a similar operation (see ECLA report, p. 147). The author, while far from claiming expertise in sugar mill management, was not unfamiliar with such operations, having a fairly substantial investment in a family sugar mill and plantation in Colombia which recently celebrated its centennial anniversary, and having visited sugar mill operations in Cuba, Puerto Rico, Argentina, and Hawaii.

Aside from the evidence of mismanagement and extravagance, further irregularities had developed from the Guabirá operations. The mill sold its raw sugar output (the plant produced raw sugar, not refined) to the government Agricultural Bank at Bs. 30,000 per quintal (101.5 lbs.), which enabled it to pay cane growers a price high enough to induce them to bring their cane to the mill. Any lower figure would have meant that the cane would have been converted into alcohol. In fact, the diversion of cane to illicit stills continued to be one of the principal problems of the mill (see ECLA report, pp. 147-48; data also based on testimony of the president of the Development Corporation before the Stabilization Council). The Agricultural Bank in turn sold the sugar to distributors ("with political connections," as Zondag writes) at Bs. 8,000 per quintal. This was the "controlled" price maintained for the purpose of keeping consumer prices down, as part of the government's futile efforts to "avoid inflation" prior to enactment of the 1956 monetary stabilization measures. The distributors, however, instead of selling the sugar to the public, smuggled it to Brazil where they could sell it for Bs. 60,000 a quintal, with the result that there was an acute sugar shortage in Santa Cruz in the heart of Bolivia's major cane-growing area (Zondag report, p. 92).

Note that, although Washington and La Paz continued to pay lip service to the idea of fostering private enterprise, the Guabirá mill was engaged in competition with two long-established private mills in the area, which found it difficult to obtain enough cane for active operation when Guabirá cane prices were based on Bs. 30,000 sugar and controlled sugar prices were Bs. 8,000. The government mill had other advantages: It paid no customs surcharges; it could always get foreign exchange at the official rate and European credits guarantied by the Central Bank; it had roads built at public expense from the mill to the Cochabamba highway and to the canefields; it could employ Argentine "technicians" (electricians, mechanics, etc.) for $200 a month, or Bs. 40,000 at the official rate of exchange, while the private mills had to pay Bs. 1.4 million a month at the free rate of exchange. Above all, Guabirá enjoyed the political advantages and tax-free status shared by all government enterprises (Zondag report, Annex to Chap. V, pp. 708; Luis Iturralde, *Consideraciones Sobre el Momento Actual de la Industria Azucarera Nacional* [La Paz: Editorial e Imprenta Artística, 1956], pp. 19 ff.).

Cochabamba-Santa Cruz highway

The route of the highway had originally been traced by engineers from the U.S. Bureau of Public Roads as a link in the Pan-American Highway, and its construction had been recommended in the Bohan report at a time when construction costs would have been less than a fifth as high as they ultimately turned out to be, and when Bolivia's economic position was such that the road could have been financed out of its own resources, without U.S. aid. Construction was commenced in 1942, and the Economic Commission for Latin America places its total cost at over $50 million, or $160,000 a mile for its 501 kilometers of length (ECLA report, pp. 232-37). The Central Bank *Annual Report* for 1961 (p. 57) places the cost at $42 million, plus Bs. 28 billion (see Zondag report, pp. 86-87, for Bolivia's position at the inception of the highway project). The high cost may be attributed in part to the easy gradients and wide curves called for by Pan-American Highway specifications, but chiefly to mismanagement and waste, as for example in the asphalting of one section in the rain forest just east of the Andean ridge after the engineers had reported that it would simply be throwing money away to asphalt the road until the land had settled and the danger of landslides had passed.

The amount due to the Export-Import Bank of Washington (chiefly for the highway), at the time of the October 17, 1956, meeting of the Stabilization Council, was stated to be $41,920,000 (this figure was provided by the Finance Ministry; the correct figure for the highway debt was $33.4 million, of which $29.4 million was outstanding). The Central Bank accounts showed the Development Corporation budget for interest and amortization on that loan at $5.5 million for 1955 and $8.7 million for 1956. Arrangements had been made, however, for a moratorium, suspending amortization, extending the maturity to 1980, and paying interest only, which was stated to be $3.6 million in 1955 and $3.8 million in 1956.

Maintenance costs are estimated by the Economic Commission

for Latin America at an absolute minimum of $500,000 per annum, but the U.S. engineers stated that at least double that figure would be conservative if the highway is to be kept in first class condition and landslides promptly repaired. A traffic count reported by ECLA revealed that the highway carried 16,442 trucks in 1955, with a 1956 estimate of 20,000, and total freight transported of 78,000 tons in both directions (ECLA report, pp. 232-37).

When I traversed the highway in 1956, over four out of five of the trucks passed en route carried either equipment or materials for the construction company to repair slides in the rain forest area, or carousing parties of Indians. Less than a fifth of the traffic was such as to warrant building a highway. Zondag cites an authoritative actual traffic count of 7,900 trucks in 1955 and an estimate of 1,200 trucks a month in 1956 (Zondag report, p. 145). The president of the Development Corporation told the council that the 1955 traffic was 9,000 trucks, apparently meaning in each direction. This was a guess, not a traffic count (see *Annual Economic and Financial Review*, American Embassy, April 6, 1956, p. 13).

Taking the figures for interest alone, for 1956, plus $500,000 as minimum maintenance, and disregarding boliviano construction costs, this would work out at $215 a truck trip, or $55 a ton. (Later figures place the traffic at some 25,200 vehicles of all kinds a year, but even this figure would work out at over $170 per vehicle.) These figures would seem to be sufficient reason for describing this $50 million project as one of the three largest white elephants donated to Bolivia by its neighbors. (The other two were the Brazilian and the Argentine railways.)

A herd of lesser elephants had been bred, however, by this major project, in the shape of a 207-kilometer network of feeder highways to the north of Santa Cruz. The president of the Development Corporation informed the council that the entire area traversed by the main highway itself was "practically a desert" and that the highway would be useless without feeder roads.

Colonization projects

This was the sole project handled by the Development Corporation for which I had nothing but praise at the October, 1956, council meetings. On a trip around the country with President Paz-Estenssoro, the American Ambassador, and the head of the U.S. Operations Mission, I had seen immigrant colonies of Japanese, Okinawans, Italians, Central European Mennonites, and, most significant of all, of Aymara Indians brought from the Andean highlands to the semitropical plains and valleys near Santa Cruz and other parts of eastern Bolivia. The Asiatics and Europeans, it is true, proved far better farmers than the Indians, but I refrained from mentioning that fact at the council meetings. There was in fact simply no comparison between the intelligence, initiative, energy, and manifest prosperity of the Japanese, Okinawans, and Mennonites and the equally obvious shortcomings of the Aymara colonizers. It was as though the latter had been transplanted bodily from a more primitive era, having little in common with modern man.

This offhand impression was later confirmed by recent production figures: $1,738 a year per family in the case of the Mennonites, $1,195 in the case of the Okinawans, and $1,025 in the case of the Japanese, as compared with $418 for the native families. The Mennonites were capable of cultivating three times as many acres per family as the Okinawans, five times as many as the Japanese, and nine times as many as the natives (Casto Ferragut, *The Progress of Land Reform in Bolivia, Discussion Paper No. 2* [Madison, Wis.: Land Tenure Center, University of Wisconsin, 1963], p. 7). Ross Moore, head of the U.S. operations mission, summed up the difference in two words: "Hard work."

Be that as it may, the condition of the Indians in the colonies was so manifestly superior to their life on the altiplano that no one in the presidential entourage could pronounce the migration as other than a success from the standpoint of the migrants, disregarding the millions of dollars that may have been spent to relocate a few hundred families. There was no way of assessing the costs from the Development Corporation accounts; but, regardless of the economic utility of the venture, the encouragement of internal migration was the only aspect of the Bolivian government development program that seemed to be handled with reasonable efficiency, thanks to the assistance of the U.N. mission and of the U.S. Point IV.

This may be rather optimistic, however, as the Okinawan colony, for example, after the colonists had worked for a year to clear and cultivate the land, was forced to move because the government was unable to give clear title to the property. This happened again the following year, but when I visited the Okinawans at their third site they were hard at work with oriental resignation, determined to succeed. Finally, however, nine years later, they seem to have given up hope and are preparing to leave Bolivia (p. 561). These immigrant colonies, of course, do nothing to solve Bolivia's problems; they merely form unassimilable foreign enclaves that may or may not prosper. Keenleyside points out that "most successful colonization of empty land has taken place from contiguous settled areas ... and from similar rather than dissimilar environments"; (Keenleyside report, p. 57). Furthermore, there was constant dissension between the mission of the United Nations' Andean Indian Programme and the Bolivian Development Corporation, and on one occasion the Bolivian Mining Corporation intervened to prevent the departure of a group of miners from the altiplano to a farm colony started by the mission (Lockwood, pp. 385, 387).

At one of the colonies visited, the government employed an ingenious and effective means of stimulating emigration from the Andean plateau, for, left to their own devices, the Indians would not voluntarily have abandoned their *pacha mama* (the earth goddess and, by extension, their native soil).* Army conscripts from the altiplano were formed into labor battalions and put to work clearing land for the new colonies, building comfortable two-room brick and stucco houses, and planting crops. Then, at the end of their term of service, the conscripts were told that if they wanted to own one of these houses and a 20-hectare (nearly 50 acres) farm, they could have it, paying only half the cost, and over a five-year period. Fewer than one in eight took advantage of the offer; these generally returned to the altiplano and came back to the colony with an Aymara bride. Of these, some went back home sick and discouraged, but enough remained so that the project could be termed a success, at least in comparison with the U.N. project where it is considered fortunate if one in twelve of the migrants remains (Dwight B. Heath, "Land Reform in Bolivia," *Inter-American Economic Affairs,* XII [1959], 3-27). According to Heath, the plots are 50 hectares each, but this was not the case in 1956 at the colony I visited.

Later, the Economic Commission for Latin America reported that the colonization program deserved the fullest encouragement and that as many as 15,000-20,000 families could well be relocated in that way, not only in Santa Cruz but in the valleys adjacent to La Paz and to Cochabamba (ECLA report, pp. 272-73; cf. Zondag, pp. 87, 177). Zondag states that 5 per cent to 10 per cent of the Indian migrants remain in the colonies. (For more recent studies of colonization in Bolivia, see Raymond E. Crist, "Bolivians Trek Eastward," *The Americas,* April, 1963, pp. 33-38; and James Lawrence Tigner, "The Ryukyans in Bolivia," *Hispanic-American Historical Review,* May, 1963, pp. 206-29; also John P. Powelson and Anatole A. Solow, "Urban and Rural Development in Latin America," *Annals of the American Academy of Political and Social Science,* CCCLX [July, 1965], 58.)

Probably no one, however, expects internal colonization to solve Bolivia's problems, as the number of migrants that can be persuaded to leave the altiplano is too limited to relieve the population

---

*McBride writes that "...to the Bolivian aborigine 'land is the very breath of life.' ... So dear is it to him that, in time of famine, he will sell his child rather than part with his diminutive parcel of ground.... He looks upon every traveler with a suspicious eye for fear the stranger may covet his tiny holdings.... The Indians not only love their land; they cling to it generation after generation. Most of the families have lived on their present holdings from time immemorial. Nothing will induce them to move." (George McCutcheon McBride, *The Agrarian Indian Communities of Highland Bolivia* [New York: Oxford University Press, 1921], p. 3.)

pressure there, while those who remain continue to breed up to the minimum subsistence level (cf. Zondag, p. 88).

Villa Montes irrigation project

This project, commenced in 1954, was originally planned to draw water directly from the Pilcomayo River by means of a diversionary sluice, but diplomatic protests that the Pilcomayo was an international, navigable stream, whose water level was of vital interest to both Argentina and Paraguay, compelled Bolivia to abandon the original location as well as the machinery and the construction work already begun at that site (information given to me by the president of the Development Corporation and the engineers at the Villa Montes project, July, 1956). The work was recommenced some miles away on a tributary stream, requiring a pumping station and far more costly construction, with the result that the water must be pumped nearly 11 miles (17 km.) to reach the lands to be irrigated. (Tapping the tributary, it would seem, would deprive Argentina of as much water as pumping the Pilcomayo, but this is one of the mysteries of diplomacy.)

According to the chief of the U.S. Operations Mission, it would be necessary to build concrete canals or conduits to carry any appreciable volume of water that distance, considering the character of the soil. This would increase the originally planned cost of the project at least tenfold. Furthermore, the soil in that area was so badly eroded from overgrazing, and the lack of population in the region was so manifest that it would take many generations before the irrigation works could be of any economic utility. In his opinion, it would have been better for Bolivia's economy to scrap the entire plan, even though an estimated $970,000 plus Bs. 650 million had been put into the installations, rather than pour more money into a useless project (cf. Zondag, p. 177).

Following an earlier council meeting in September, 1956, news of my comments on the Development Corporation leaked out, and I was summoned to confer with former President Paz-Estenssoro at his residence, where I was told that Bolivia must not abandon the Development Corporation projects, and especially could not cut down on the Villa Montes irrigation program in Paz's own home town. I parried the attempts of Paz to advise me on the essential measures that must be taken in a stabilization program (which came strangely from the man under whose administration the inflation had reached its extreme), stating that all measures taken would be up to the council and that I would not oppose any particular government project so long as the total government expenditures were balanced by revenues. The incident is indicative of the causes of inflation (and not merely in Bolivia) — each *político* is adamant against cutting down on his particular favored project, and the sum total of all projects adds up to more than the country can stand. In the case of Bolivia, it would have been butting one's head against a stone wall to suggest turning COMIBOL back to private ownership, even assuming that any private investor would have been willing to take it over after three years of mismanagement. There was not the slightest chance of persuading the government to dispose of YPFB, so that the only possibility of major economies consisted in radically paring the activities of the Development Corporation and of the Social Security Administration.

The U.N. (Keenleyside) report, while not actually recommending abandonment of the project, points out with specific reference to Villa Montes that "large and costly storage dams should not be undertaken in any specific area before some degree of agricultural development has taken place in that area," and that agricultural development is more hampered by lack of labor, drainage, transportation, and land clearing than "by lack of irrigation water from costly reservoirs." Both that report and the report of the Economic Commission for Latin American stress the value of small scale, minimum cost irrigation projects rather than the more impressive "prestige" undertakings such as Villa Montes (Keenleyside report, pp. 55-56, 53; ECLA report, pp. 274-75; Zondag, Annex to Chap. V, p. 11).

Reyes cattle breeding project

I reported to the council that I had seen a herd, reportedly of 610 head of Zebu cattle, at the Reyes project and that, while admittedly not an expert, I had seen considerable cattle of Zebu and mixed breeds in Texas and at my family plantation in Colombia, and that I had never seen a sorrier lot of cows and bulls than those in the Reyes corrals, diseased, malformed, and undernourished. On inquiry, the Point IV cattle expert who accompanied me said that the cattle had been purchased by the Development Corporation from someone in Brazil who had obviously picked out all the culls he could find from his own and perhaps other herds of Brazilian Zebus and crosses, and that in the entire lot there were only two bulls which were of passable quality, one of which he pointed out. As to the others, he stated that to breed this herd with the range cattle in the Beni area would set back the cattle industry in Bolivia by two generations.

A previous shipment of 150 cows and 20 supposedly purebred Zebu bulls had been imported in 1954, but I had no opportunity to see these. Foot and mouth disease *(aftosa)* and mismanagement had hampered the project, and, all together, some $470,000 had been invested in the Reyes program, current expenditures running around

$80,000 plus Bs. 250 million a year (Zondag report, pp. 175-76; Alexander, *The Bolivian National Revolution*, p. 179).

On the other hand, I reported having seen some splendid Brangus (i.e., Zebu, or "Brahman," crossbred with Angus) and Santa Gertrudis (Zebu and shorthorn) bulls brought to Bolivia by the U.S. Inter-American Agricultural Service. The same agency had imported some purebred Holsteins for La Tamborada dairy near Cochabamba, hoping to restore by artificial insemination both the beef and dairy industries that had been destroyed by the agrarian reform (cf. Zondag report, Annex to Chap. V, p. 12; ECLA report, p. 263).

Powdered milk plant at Cochabamba

This project was initiated by UNICEF for the purpose of providing free powdered milk to "underprivileged" children. Funds ran short, and U.S. aid made up the difference, the total investment being estimated at $280,000 plus Bs. 210 million. Unfortunately, at the time I visited the half-completed plant, the dairy industry around Cochabamba had been wiped out by the agrarian "reform" which eliminated the larger dairy herds and resulted in the indiscriminate slaughter of breeding stock, so that I suggested to the Stabilization Council that further expenditures might be suspended until there was some prospect of milk being available for processing. The McClellan committee reported waste and incompetence in planning and execution of the project, and three years later the U.S. Embassy stated that the plant was running at 25 per cent of capacity. There was little market for the powdered milk, which was being sold at the equivalent of $12\frac{1}{2}$ cents U.S. a quart, liquid basis. Constant large deficits were aggravated by a defalcation of Bs. 80 million by the plant accountant (U.S. Senate, *Administration of U.S. Foreign Aid Programs in Bolivia*, pp. 12-13; cf. Zondag, Annex to Chap. V, p. 12, also p. 177; ECLA report, p. 147; American Embassy, *Quarterly Economic Summary*, A-354 [October 31, 1963], p. 8).

Cement plant at Sucre

This project was commenced prior to the Revolution as a political pork barrel. The chief of the U.S. Operations Mission pointed out that if a 200-kilometer circle were traced around the site of the plant, it would take in less than 3 per cent of the country's population and that transportation costs would make it prohibitive to market the cement anywhere but in Sucre. The United Nations had recommended that the plant be constructed at Cochabamba rather than Sucre. The original cost estimate was $1.4 million plus Bs. 500 million. By 1962 the plant was still working at only 74 per cent capacity; i.e., 22,109 tons production out of 30,000 tons capacity (Zondag report, p. 175; interview with Ross Moore; Keenleyside report, p. 88). The head of the Planning Commission later confirmed that the plant had been built against the advice of all the experts and that funds had been diverted from earthquake relief to construction of the cement plant, under political pressure (Central Bank, *Annual Report,* 1960, p. 56; *Annual Report,* 1962, p. 45).

Electric power projects

Two major electric power projects were under way under the aegis of the Development Corporation: an enormous installation at Montepunco, including a highway to the plant; and a less ambitious project at Corani. The highway alone to Montepunco was estimated by the Development Corporation to call for some $7 million which, judging by other corporation estimates, was probably grossly understated. I traversed about half of the proposed route in a four-wheel-drive vehicle, across streams and rugged valleys, and was impressed with the fact that the road led from no place to nowhere. The power plant, located in a wilderness, was to have cost $14 million. The project was turned down by the Export-Import Bank of Washington, but the Development Corporation continued to divert funds and equipment to it from other projects (Zondag report, pp. 144, 176).

Diversion of funds and equipment has always been one of the constant complaints of the U.S. aid operations. Bulldozers and other equipment would be taken from one of the Point IV operations and sometimes discovered months later at some project that had been vetoed by USOM as economically inexpedient (cf. the P.L. 480 scandal in Austria, *New York Times,* January 2, 1964, p. 1).

The Corani project was adjudged a sounder proposition, its objective being to supply badly needed electric power to the city of Cochabamba at an estimated cost of $5.5 million. Nevertheless, I pointed out to the Stabilization Council that if the government were willing to authorize adequate rates the plant could be built and operated by private enterprise, undoubtedly more economically than if it were built and run by the Development Corporation, and that if the government were unwilling to authorize adequate rates it should abandon any plans for the construction as it would only add to the inflation (see Zondag report, pp. 176-77).

APPENDIX V

BOLIVIAN COMMERCIAL INDEBTEDNESS –
PROPOSED AMORTIZATION PLAN*

The government of Bolivia [as you know] is embarked on a program of monetary and financial stabilization that has already accomplished striking results despite difficulties which, only some six months earlier, might have seemed insurmountable.

Under the guidance of a National Monetary Stabilization Council, established by Decree of August 4, 1956, a complete plan of monetary and fiscal reform, and financial and economic recovery, has been worked out and the initial measures promulgated on December 15, 1956. The transition from an unbalanced to a balanced budget, from a controlled economy with multiple auction, official, and black-market rates of exchange to a free economy with a single exchange rate subject only to supply and demand and no restrictions on imports, exports, prices, or exchange, has been abrupt, after a quarter century of monetary and economic instability, and the consequent readjustments have been difficult and painful.

Nevertheless, the success of the measures taken is already evident. The scarcities of foodstuffs and merchandise, the long lines of people patiently waiting for the scanty available supplies, the black markets, the smuggling of goods from Bolivia to neighboring countries, have all disappeared, almost overnight. Prices of articles of prime necessity, which shot up suddenly in the first hectic days after December 15, have now dropped to some 30 per cent less than those prevailing prior to that date, and goods of all kinds are available in an abundance which has not been seen in Bolivia for many years. Agricultural production has revived with a free economy; the country for the first time in years is almost self-sufficing in meat, and crops now coming on the market and those which should reach market during the remainder of the year are larger than they have been in decades and should ensure the prosperity of the farmers who form the vast majority of the population.

Above all, the boliviano, which had fallen as low as 14,000 to the dollar, and would certainly have reached over 40,000 to the dollar by the present time, has remained comparatively stable since

*This statement, issued by the Bolivian Ambassador to Washington, the Honorable Victor Andrade, on August 15, 1957, is a verbatim reproduction (except for the changes indicated in brackets) of my draft of June 19, approved by the Stabilization Council on June 21.

December 15, 1956, fluctuating between 7,400 and 8,400 to the dollar according to the varying forces of supply and demand. On the other hand, approximately $5.5 million net of the $25 million stabilization fund at the disposal of the Central Bank of Bolivia has been utilized, largely as a result of lowered receipts from the government Mining Corporation and, in recent weeks, [as a consequence of] the demand for dollars as a result of strong agitation for a break in the wage freeze.

The most difficult readjustments have been in government finance, industry, and private mining and in the ranks of the white-collar workers and manual labor, approximately in that order.

Wages and salaries are undoubtedly low, but productivity per worker has declined so drastically that wages cannot be raised without again setting in motion the upward wage-price spiral, with consequent bank note inflation and monetary depreciation.

Private mining and industry have been largely decapitalized by currency depreciation over the past four years, and, with the present low output of labor and other conditions engendered by circumstances in recent years, the transition to an economy of free competition has been extremely difficult and, in some cases, has not yet been fully achieved.

It is in the field of government finance, however, that the adjustment has been most drastic. For many years* the government had become accustomed to balance its budget by the printing of currency, and to finance its ambitious program of economic diversification by heavy borrowing and the consumption of capital in the form of the exhaustion of a large part of the mineral reserves and of the entire gold and dollar holdings. Now, with a return to normality, it suddenly finds itself in a position where — with the exception of American aid — it must live within its means, with the consequence that virtually all its public works have had to be suspended and its expenditures reduced to the absolute minimum that can be achieved without creating social problems so grave that any hope of financial and economic stability would have to be abandoned.

[As evidence that the government is not squandering its resources, it may be stated that the President's salary is less than $90 (?) a month, a Cabinet Minister's $40 (?). The entire budget, of the government and of the various governmental agencies, has been carefully reviewed by representatives of the International Monetary Fund, and it seems evident that any further reduction at this time would be politically and socially impossible.] †

*My original draft had stated, "Since 1952." That put the onus too clearly where it belonged: on the MNR regime.

†This paragraph was omitted after discussion in the council, and I cannot explain what quirk of judgment prompted me to include it in the first place.

The government and the Central Bank, however, find themselves saddled with an indebtedness that is so clearly beyond any possibility of immediate repayment that a readjustment of payment arrangements has become inevitable. The government of Bolivia and the bank firmly intend to pay every penny of their legitimate obligations, but they urge their creditors to have patience, and to realize that payments must be deferred within the limits of the nation's capacity to pay, that too close a schedule of amortization of the debt might so strain the economic structure of the country as to threaten political and social disorders that could lead only to a renewed and permanent default.

The Export-Import Bank of Washington has already recognized the necessity of postponement and has agreed to a deferment of the 1957-59 maturities of the Bolivian Development Corporation to 1972-74. The Foreign Bondholders' Protective Council has similarly agreed to present to the holders of Bolivian government bonds a proposed schedule of payments which will result in converting some $110 million of unpaid interest into bonds of a par value of approximately $5.6 million, reducing interest payments on the total principal from an average of 7 per cent to adjusted rates which will not reach a maximum of 3 per cent until 1964.

Bolivia expects in due course to reach an agreed adjustment of its indebtedness with all creditors, but the magnitude of this task may be seen from the following approximate figures of its outstanding obligations:*

*The figures in this table had been given by the Minister of Finance and president of the Central Bank and I had included them in the original draft with interrogation marks, with the request that they be verified. As no changes were made in the three months between the date of my draft and the release of the statement by the Bolivian Ambassador, this fact would appear to corroborate their authenticity. Nevertheless, the debt to the Eximbank was overstated by nearly $13 million (see p. 412) and, with respect to the $28 million of debts guaranteed by the Central Bank, the monetary department of that bank had informed Cornelius Zondag that the correct figure on June 30, 1956, was "about $28.8 million" (Zondag report, p. 66), and there is no reason to believe that the figure would have been lower on August 15, 1957. See Table 11, p. 412, for a more detailed breakdown of the commercial debt. In my draft, I had unwisely included the railway construction debts to the governments of Brazil ($147 million) and Argentina ($12.7 million), based on statements submitted to the council on May 6 and 24, 1957, by Jorge Escobari-Cusicanqui, Under Secretary of Foreign Affairs. Those amounts, however, were purely hypothetical and have elsewhere been estimated at $46 million and $22 million, respectively; the ultimate amount of the indebtedness depended on the rate of exchange, so that it was largely wiped out by the depreciation of the Brazilian and Argentine currencies (Zondag report, p. 68). All mention of these debts was wisely eliminated in the Embassy statement, probably on the

To the bondholders (reduced from $167 million)	$ 61,906,000
Debts of the Mining Corporation of Bolivia	9,619,000
Debts of the Bolivian Development Corporation (mostly to the Export-Import Bank)	47,238,000
Debts of the Yacimientos Petrolíferos Fiscales Bolivianos (Government Petroleum Corporation)	4,144,000
Debts of the Banco Minero de Bolivia (Mining Bank)	5,957,000
Municipal debts guaranteed by the government	774,000
Miscellaneous debts of the government and government agencies	983,000
Debts under treaty agreements with Argentina, Brazil, Chile, and Paraguay	8,000,000
Debts guaranteed by the Central Bank (not included above)	28,000,000
Internal debt for expropriations under the rural and urban land reform laws	1,000,000
Other internal debt (conversions at Bs. 8,000 per dollar)	6,000,000
TOTAL	$173,621,000

The foregoing table does not include the indebtedness to the former owners of the nationalized mines, the amount of which is now under negotiation.

The government of Bolivia considers that one of its most urgent tasks at this time is to reach a workable agreement with respect to its entire foreign commercial debt, including all bills of exchange and notes bearing the guaranty or acceptance of the Central Bank. These debts, included in the above table, amount to around $104 million, of which roughly $15 million is already due but unpaid, and $17 million will become due during the remainder of 1957. This latter figure includes $5.4 million of bills of exchange guaranteed or accepted by the Central Bank of Bolivia with the maturity date in blank, and which may or may not be presented for payment in 1957.

Despite every effort made by the National Monetary Stabilization Council over the past twelve months, the government of Bolivia cannot be certain that these figures are accurate or that they embrace all the obligations of the national government and government agencies, but it is reasonably certain that they do represent a minimal figure both of total debt and of imminent maturities, subject to negotiation in the case of the indebtedness to Brazil and Argentina and in certain other cases. [This was left in, even though the debts were omitted from the table.]

In any event, the past due and unpaid indebtedness, plus

_____

advice of the Ministers of Foreign Relations and Finance, and doubtless in order to avoid any official recognition of the amounts, which were under continuing negotiation.

subsequent 1957 maturities, amounting to about $32 million in all, represents a figure far beyond Bolivia's present capacity to pay, and the government has no alternative but to request its creditors to demonstrate the same patience and understanding shown by the Export-Import Bank of Washington and the Foreign Bondholders' Protective Council, Inc., and to accept a scale of payments within the limits of its possibilities.

In November, 1956, at the time the government of Bolivia solicited the financial assistance of the International Monetary Fund and of certain U.S. government agencies for the creation of a Monetary Stabilization Fund, it budgeted the sum of $9,778,000 in its foreign exchange budget to take care of all scheduled commercial debt payments in 1957 in the government and private sectors combined, but at that time it was believed that the total commercial debt outstanding, governmental and private, was only $12.6 million. With the realization that this indebtedness is far beyond the budgeted amount, and the knowledge that the available foreign exchange will fall far short even of the $9.3 million [$9.8 million] budgeted for commercial debt payments, as a result of an unanticipated 25 per cent drop in the production of the Mining Corporation of Bolivia, the government of Bolivia has reached the conclusion that, in order to treat all creditors alike as nearly as possible, it cannot authorize payment of more than 20 per cent of the governmental indebtedness in the 1957 year.

With that in mind, it is endeavoring to reach agreements with its European and American creditors, either to make immediate payment of all such debts already matured, up to June 15, 1957, in which event no further payments can be made until 1958 or, alternatively, to pay in 1957 20 per cent of the indebtedness already due or maturing in 1957. In either event, the remaining indebtedness will have to be paid at the rate of 20 per cent per annum in the years 1958, 1959, and 1960, with full payment of such indebtedness in 1961.

This represents the studied judgment of the government of Bolivia as to its maximum potentialities of payment at the present time. If, however, new sources of foreign exchange revenues should develop, the government of Bolivia pledges its good faith to accelerate the proposed amortization of its indebtedness to the extent that this is feasible, as it is the desire of the government to re-establish its credit at the earliest possible date.

In all candor, it must be stated that the Bolivian government has received, in the first half of 1957, $1 million as a dividend from The Bolivian Railway Co. [sic], not budgeted in its statement to the IMF and U.S. government agencies. This sum, however, has been [expended] invested for the purchase of rolling stock for the government railways for reasons of extreme necessity which, in the opinion of the Bolivian government, could not be deferred.

Similarly, the Bolivian government expects to receive in 1957 some [$3.5 million] substantial sums in advance royalties for certain petroleum concessions to be transferred or granted in the course of the present year. This sum, however, will not be available for the repayment of past indebtedness, as it is the considered opinion of the Bolivian government that this sum must be used in its entirety for necessary capital investments of the government petroleum corporation.

The Executive Director of the National Monetary Stabilization Council, who is an American adviser loaned to the government of Bolivia, urges that creditors recognize that this use of these funds is proper and necessary, inasmuch as the petroleum corporation, according to the report of Price Waterhouse & Co., is now operating on a paying basis, and the only hope of increasing its contribution to the government's resources, according to the corporation's management, is by way of further capital investment, particularly in pipe lines which are expected to open up new markets for the sale of petroleum products, in free foreign exchange. This recommendation is based on the assumption that these funds will be used exclusively for additional capital investment above the amounts allocated in the budget and that they will not be dissipated in increased wages or in reduced petroleum prices not warranted by adequate cost studies.

The government of Bolivia is bound by its agreement with the International Monetary Fund to freeze all wages until the end of 1957 and has no intention of allowing any increase not warranted by increased production and tax revenues, unless compensated by reductions in indirect payroll costs. Furthermore, no new obligations can be legally incurred by the government or government agencies, nor additional bank notes issued, without the prior authorization of the National Monetary Stabilization Council, by virtue of the initial stabilization Decree-Law of August 4, 1956, so that creditors may be assured that all government expenditures will be carefully reviewed with a view to maintaining "the internal and external credit of the country and the stability of the currency."

The purpose of the meeting held by the Bolivian Ambassador with representatives of some New York banks* is to work out with the bankers who have discounted the notes and bills of exchange of the government and government agencies, as the only easily available representatives of the commercial creditors — meetings are being held simultaneously in La Paz with the representatives of the European creditors — a uniform plan for the payment of the foreign commercial debt and particularly to decide upon a workable mechanism, acceptable to the creditors, for taking care of the deferred payments on that indebtedness.

*The original draft stated: "The purpose of the present meeting, therefore..."

APPENDIX VI

REPORT ON THE PROGRESS AND PROBLEMS OF THE STABILIZATION PROGRAM*

In the present report I propose to outline the results to date of the stabilization measures taken last December, pointing out the problems we now face and solutions for them, as I am convinced that there is no problem without a solution.

I may begin by quoting Henry Holland, who stated, a few days ago, that the stabilization program had wrought miracles since the date of his last visit to Bolivia in August, 1956. What are the "miracles" to which Mr. Holland referred?

1. In the first place, between sunset and sunrise, there disappeared the long lines of waiting people, which was the sight that most struck the eye in the days prior to December, 1956.

2. In the second place, there disappeared simultaneously the smuggling of Bolivian products to neighboring countries, including the contraband of a third of the goods donated to Bolivia under American aid.

3. The black markets also vanished suddenly — where the unprivileged public was forced to buy the scanty available merchandise at exorbitant prices.

4. Similarly, within four days from promulgation of the first stabilization measures, the merchandise which had been hidden under the shelves of the black marketeers and merchants made its appearance. Where, a few days earlier, bread and meat were practically nonexistent in Bolivia's markets, these were available openly and in abundance, and markets and stores throughout the country now display an abundance of articles of prime necessity, and all kinds of merchandise, such as had not been seen in Bolivia for many years.

5. Another result of the stabilization program has been the drop in prices which is already occurring. Bread, which on the first day after the stabilization measures was sold at Bs. 600, can now be bought easily for Bs. 200 and at even lower prices, while meat, which had risen to Bs. 8,000 and even to Bs.

*This is a translation of an oral report to the President of the Republic, *et al.*, April 17, 1957, by George J. Eder, Executive Director of the Stabilization Council. The material in italics was included in the talk, but not in the draft given to the press. The material in parentheses was given to the press, having been added subsequent to the talk.

10,000 per kilo, can be purchased at Bs. 3,000 or less. *An index compiled by the Central Bank shows that prices for 45 articles of prime necessity in the Rodríguez market in La Paz rose to 122 on December 24.* Subsequently, prices have continued to fall as shown in Chart I, reaching an index of 74 on April 8, or 26 per cent below the level prior to stabilization. True, this is not a weighted index. The customary quantities in which each foodstuff or other article is bought have been taken without regard to the proportion that each item has in the family budget. Thus, the cost of a pound of salt and kilo of beef has been used, and it is clear that those items are not used in those proportions; nevertheless, a weighted index prepared on the bases used by the General Bureau of Statistics also shows a marked drop in prices since December 10, 1956, although not in the same proportion that is shown in the chart.*

Outside La Paz, the drop in prices has been even more remarkable. In the department of Beni, as a result of the stabilization measures, rice, corn, and fuel are sold for a fifth of the price prevailing prior to December 15. From Santa Cruz, Pando, Tarija, and all sections of the country come similar reports. Prices have dropped appreciably, are continuing to drop, and will drop still further as domestic agricultural products start coming on the market, *and when the new customs tariffs recommended by the National Monetary Stabilization Council are approved.*

6. Another miracle witnessed by Mr. Holland was the sudden and immediate cessation of monetary depreciation, as is shown by Chart II.* This chart commences with the year 1918, that being the last year in which the boliviano was quoted above par, that is, at Bs. 2.40 per dollar when par in that period was Bs. 2.57. The broken line represents a mathematical computation made by the president of the Central Bank, showing that if the stabilization policy had not commenced with the decree of

*The chart used to show this was based on an unweighted index of 45 articles of prime necessity, compiled personally by the president of the Central Bank. Using a base of 100 for December 10, 1956, it had dropped to 74 on April 8, and it subsequently dropped to 62 on June 24, and to 60 on July 1, 1957 (*La Nación,* July 3, 1957). For a weighted index, see Fig. 10, p. 496.

† The chart used was a double chart, showing on the left-hand side the drop in the boliviano from 1918 through 1956, almost entirely during the MNR regime from 1953-56, going as low as Bs. 14,000 to the dollar, and with a projected drop to Bs. 24,000 to the dollar in December, 1956, calculated by the president of the Central Bank as its probable level had it not been for creation of the Stabilization Council by decree of August 4, 1956. The movement from December 15, 1956 on was shown in the companion chart, on the right-hand side (see Fig. 10, p. 496, for trend through December, 1957).

August 4, 1956, the dollar would have reached at least Bs. 24,000 by December, 1956. What happened was that, with the decree of August 4, speculators did not dare take full advantage of the inflationary tendencies, and, with the measures of December 15, depreciation of the monetary unit was definitely arrested, the quotation dropping from Bs. 11,000 per dollar to about Bs. 7,700, being maintained since then around that level without major fluctuation.

7. Another result of the program — perhaps the only one that should be characterized as a "miracle," inasmuch as the others were merely the calculated and foreseeable result of the measures taken — is that Bolivia, absolutely lacking in either resources or credit, was able to obtain from the U.S. Treasury and other agencies the creation of a $25 million stabilization fund, with no guarantee other than the promise to carry out the program presented by the Bolivian government itself.

In short, the results of the stabilization measures taken since August 4, 1956 — and it must be noted that the program is still far from completed — demonstrate beyond a doubt that Bolivia can have a currency as stable as any in the world and that the measures sponsored by the Stabilization Council have been conducive to that end.

Complaints

Of course, as was inevitable, there have been complaints from various sections of the economy. Labor leaders, for instance, complain that the compensation for elimination of the subsidized commissaries, and for the effects of the new monetary regime, are inadequate, that wages are not high enough to cover the workers' needs. In many cases this is true, but it is not due to the stabilization measures but to the *extremely* low output of the Bolivian *workingman.*

In the United States, for example, the average miner produces $16,560 of ore a year, and with that production it is easy to pay an average annual salary of $4,500. In Bolivia, on the other hand, the net value of the COMIBOL miner's output amounts to only $1,500 a year, and in the private mines it is less than $500 a year. *

With such a low output as at present, it is obvious that the workers' remuneration must also be low, since in any enterprise, whether government or private, wages can only come out of gross

*Later figures show an output of $32,433 per miner per year in the United States (*Fortune*, LXX [July, 1964], 191). Bolivia has dropped still further behind in the race for survival.

revenues, and there are many expenses which must be met before there can be any revenues out of which to pay the workers' wages. Thus there is no remedy for inadequate compensation other than increased production by each individual and by the entire nation.

Chart III (see Fig. 14, p. 537) shows that exports of minerals in tons have declined over the past five years, whether by reason of the lack of discipline among the workers, or because of strikes and absenteeism, or because of the lack of foresight on the part of management in not having developed new ore reserves. But, in any case, if the output of the miners continues to decline it is inevitable that their real wages must also decline, and this has nothing whatsoever to do with the stabilization measures. It must also be noted that in the same five-year period the number of workers in the mines has increased approximately 20 per cent, judging by the government mining corporation figures, so that the export of minerals per worker is only half what it was five years ago. COMIBOL production in tons, for the first four months of 1957, is even lower than in 1956, and 22 per cent less than the budgeted output. To insist, under such circumstances, that the miners deserve higher compensation *is demagoguery or worse.*

The high output of the American worker is of course due to the capitalist, free enterprise system in the U.S., under which, for each worker in the manufacturing industries, for example, there is a capital investment of over $12,000 in machinery, etc. Every American worker has his strength multiplied more times, by more horsepower of energy and more production machinery, than the worker in any other country of the world, and this means that in the big industries the American worker can produce more than workers in other countries and hence earn the highest wages in the world — real wages in money with real purchasing power, that enables him to maintain living standards beyond compare.

Over the past fifty years, the proportion of gross national product in the United States that has been paid to the workers in the form of wages has scarcely varied; that is, salaries have run between 15.5 and 17.9 per cent of the total value of output over the entire period (16 per cent in the latest year available), showing that today's higher salaries and the higher standard of living have come from greater output per worker, as a consequence of a greater capital investment behind each workingman. Capital investment per worker has risen more than five times since 1900; the workers' productivity has increased four times and their compensation, in real values, more than three times.

The comparative lack of capital investment per worker is not the only reason behind the low output of the Bolivian laborer. For instance, a bricklayer in Bolivia lays an average of between 150 and 250 bricks a day, in comparison with a base of 800 *bricks a day in* *the United States, and an output of several times that figure when there is no labor union interference. In some European countries the base is* 1,000 bricks daily, and masons receive production bonuses for output in excess of that figure.*

Furthermore, the introduction of modern machinery does not necessarily mean increased output unless there is full cooperation on the part of the workers. A La Paz bottle factory, for instance, has installed automatic machinery which would enable Bolivia to compete in cost and quality with the production of any other country of the world, with only the natural protection afforded by high transportation costs on imported bottles. The factory, however, is forced to keep on producing bottles by old-fashioned blowing methods, *because of the workers' demands,* and what the company makes on its automatic production it loses on the uneconomic production by antiquated methods.

As a consequence, the cost of bottles is so high in Bolivia that the Stabilization Council has received a protest from local drug manufacturers that peroxide is being imported in bottles and that the cost of bottles is so high in Bolivia that the importers can dump the peroxide in the river and sell the bottles for other uses at a lower price than locally manufactured bottles, or sell the bottled peroxide at a price with which the local industry cannot compete. Labor union interference of this kind increases the cost of production and affects the family budget of everyone in the country.

Another cause of the low output of Bolivian laborers and employees, which makes it impossible to increase their wages, is the number of superfluous employees, which enormously increases the cost of production and makes it impossible to reduce prices. I shall take up this matter later when I come to the solutions for current problems.

It is clear, therefore, that low wages and salaries and the difficulties workers have in balancing their family budgets are not the result of the stabilization measures but of deeper causes in the Bolivian economy, and apparently the workers themselves recognize this fact. The latest poll on monetary stabilization, put out today by the Bolivian Institute of Public Opinion Polls, shows that 91 per cent of public and private employees, and 81 per cent of the laborers (100 per cent in the April 24 poll), believe that under present conditions an increase in wages would bring about a rise in prices, which reveals a more thorough understanding of economic science on the

*The figures for bricklaying in the United States and Europe were the best available at the time. According to *Richey's Reference Handbook for Builders, Architects, and Construction Engineers* (New York: Simmons-Boardman Publishing Co., 1951), p. 6-45, one man should lay 1,000 to 1,200 common bricks per day.

part of the workers than on the part of the labor leaders who continue to demand increased compensation without a proportionate increase in output.

The same poll shows that 50 per cent of the public believes that prices have dropped as a result of stabilization, against only 14 per cent who believe that the measures have brought about an increase in prices; the remainder polled find no difference in prices, or give no opinion. (According to the latest poll, May 3, 1957, 61 per cent believe prices have dropped; 20 per cent, that they have gone up.)

From manufacturers there have likewise come complaints of various kinds, despite the fact that industry almost unanimously supports the stabilization program as a necessary measure for the country's progress. The reason for many of the manufacturers' difficulties is found in the fact that in recent years many industries have been established which are completely uneconomic, *as in the case of a factory in Cochabamba which received Brazil nuts by air express from the Beni and then cracked and exported the nuts at low prices in order to make their profits on the imports which they could bring in under privileged conditions under the rules in force at that time. Manifestly, a product of such comparatively low value as Brazil nuts cannot support the high cost of air freight, and the country cannot continue to subsidize uneconomic industries to the detriment of the national interest by giving them privileges that have no relation to reality.**

The textile industry, for example, has lived to a large extent on the import of raw materials at artificial rates of exchange, and on smuggling its products to neighboring countries. There is a cotton textile factory in La Paz which, according to its own figures, has a production capacity of twelve million meters per annum, while the consuming capacity of the entire country is only seven million meters.† Under such conditions, and this is only one of many cotton textile plants, it is evident that the industry must suffer with a return to normalcy and, to do justice to the owners of the factory in question, they are quite willing to face the new situation of reality under a free enterprise system which would allow them to readjust their production costs to current conditions.

Manifestly, the government cannot satisfy the complaints of the manufacturers to the extent that these arise from causes of this nature. As to their justified complaints — and they are important — these should for the most part be met by the measures already proposed by the Stabilization Council.

*The fact that President Siles personally censored this paragraph confirms the power and corruption of the *políticos* in Cochabamba and the Beni who profited from this operation (see pp. 359-60).

†These figures, like all Bolivian statistics, are questionable, but they were given to me by a responsible source, and the conclusions are correct.

The same is true with respect to the complaints of importers and of the private mining companies, whose just complaints should be met by the decrees already sponsored by the council or by those which are now being studied.

There has likewise been some criticism in banking and industrial circles with respect to the so-called "inflexibility" of credit restrictions. Manifestly, neither the council nor the Superintendent of Banks can look into each credit application. "Flexibility" cannot come from those agencies or from the regulations; it must come from the bankers themselves who, in their good banking judgment, should give credit to those who deserve it, within the authorized limits. Of course, the reserve percentages are not immutable; they must be changed from time to time as the economic situation of the country warrants, and for that reason the decree provides that changes can be made by a simple executive resolution on the recommendation of the Stabilization Council. Critics, perhaps, may not realize that credits have been quite liberal since the stabilization date, that one local bank has tripled its credits since the middle of December, and that the commercial banks in general have doubled their loan portfolios. Nor do they realize, probably, that a large part of the credits was used for purposes not conducive to an increase in production and that when the credit restrictions were tightened the stabilization fund receipts were strengthened and its disbursements diminished. When the pending decree on revaluation of assets, other than gold and foreign exchange, is passed, the banks' lending capacity will be increased. Moreover, in cooperation with ICA, means are being studied of relaxing restrictions on certain credits for immediate productive use. But, of course, it would be absurd to grant credits to such industrial or other enterprises whose problems arise, not from a temporary lack of cash, but from the closing of the contraband market, an excess of personnel, social security costs beyond their capacity, a reluctance to bring back their own capital from abroad, or other causes which cannot be removed by relaxing credit restrictions.

In short, the majority of the complaints which have come from labor leaders and employers relate to transitory problems. To attribute these difficulties to the stabilization measures is more or less like complaining when the dentist pulls out an infected tooth. It is true that the extraction of the tooth may cause considerable pain, but the pain should be blamed on the infection and not on the dentist. In the same way, today's temporary difficulties do not arise from the stabilization measures, but from the *economic anarchy of* prior years.*

*I am indebted to Roger Freeman for this metaphor.

Background of stabilization

Among those who are complaining of the stabilization measures today there are very few who realize what the basic situation was in the country *in August 1956 when the present government took office* ("as a consequence of the inflationary process begun over a quarter century ago" — inserted by President Siles).

For example, many people think that the present hardships are due to the drop in the price of tin. True, current prices are lower than during the Korean War. On the other hand, during the five years ended June 30, 1956, the average price of tin was $1.035 per pound, which is higher than in any previous five-year period in the history of the Republic. The best previous five-year period showed an average price of $0.927 per pound and, as is shown in Chart IV (see Fig. 13, p. 535), tin prices over the past nine years have been far above those prevailing in any of the last forty years. The chart could be carried twenty years further back, to the year 1897, when the price of tin was only $.137 per pound, so that it is clear that the present difficulties of the country cannot be blamed on low tin prices.

The same is true with respect to the total amount of foreign exchange that Bolivia has received from its metal exports, inasmuch as, during the five years ended June 30, 1956, its total receipts from that source amounted to $559.5 million, or $71 million more than in any previous five-year period in history. Chart V (this is the metal export graph on Fig. 2, p. 105) shows this fact, and likewise shows the economic capacity of the country to have and maintain a stable currency. If, in 1918, with mineral exports of only $68.7 million, Bolivia could keep its currency above par, it is evident that in 1956, with exports of over $100 million there should be no major difficulty in maintaining the currency at par with the dollar. *Today, with the drop in labor output, the problem is more difficult, but not insurmountable.*

It is true that the purchasing power of the dollar is less today than in 1918, but the Stabilization Council is not attempting to give Bolivia a better currency than the dollar — it would suffice if the boliviano today were quoted at $.40 U.S., as it was in 1918, even if today's dollars are not worth as much as at that time. *Bolivia can then adjust its imports to correspond with the value of its exports, especially when, with the stabilization program, it can eliminate the importation of some $30 million of agricultural products which can be produced in the country, and which would have been produced had it not been for the importation of so many items at the artificial rate of exchange of Bs. 190 to the dollar, which has contributed to practically killing commercial agriculture in Bolivia in recent years.*

Similarly, most people fail to realize that over the past five years Bolivia has lived to a large extent on the consumption of capital in excess of its resources ("in an attempt to promote economic diversification" — inserted by President Siles). As is shown in Chart VI (see Fig. 8, p. 490), Bolivia has spent some $300 million of loaned or donated capital.

We arrive at this figure by taking, in the first place, the fact that in the five years ended June 30, 1956, gross mineral exports amounted to $559,473,000. Now, in any well-run mining enterprise, at least 15 per cent of gross production would be devoted to the renewal of equipment and to exploration, blocking out, and development. This ensures that what is happening now will be prevented — that the tailings of ores mined years ago show a higher percentage of metallic content than some of the ores which are now being mined — and that there will always be mineral reserves available for future exploitation. With the exhaustion of many of its mines, and the obsolescence of most of its equipment, Bolivia has been living on its own fat — meagre as that may be — consuming its capital, instead of using it in re-investment for the future. The chart assigns only $12\frac{1}{2}$ per cent of gross mineral exports as the amount of capital consumed in this way, that is, $70 million.

To this must be added the loss of Bolivia's gold and foreign exchange reserves of some $40 million; also $2.5 million loaned by the International Monetary Fund prior to July, 1956, and some $40 million increase in short-term debt, of which approximately $33 million bears the guarantee of the Central Bank, *which neither the bank nor the government is able to pay*. Perhaps the exact figure would be closer to $60 million than to $40 million, but I have not wished to exaggerate and we still do not have complete data.

The net debt to the Export-Import Bank of Washington has likewise been increased by some $11.2 million in the same five-year period; $50 million has been received in American aid; and a debt of $6.1 million has been incurred under the barter and payment agreements with Brazil, Argentina, Chile, and Uruguay.

Likewise the debt to Brazil and Argentina, for construction of railroads and the Río Bermejo-Tarija highway, increased by perhaps $20 million. The exact figure cannot be given, as the government accounts are not carried in dollars but in pesos and cruzeiros whose value has not yet been fixed.

The government likewise owes some $5.2 million for production bonuses and unpaid accounts to the miners, and on quotas for farm and forest exports, and, finally, it has spent the equivalent of some $42 million beyond its resources by printing approximately Bs. 156 billion of bank notes over the past five years, computed at the average free rate of exchange each year. These unbacked note issues, made necessary by government expenditures in excess of revenues, constitute a capital levy on every inhabitant of the country, confiscating the capital of the Indians who kept their savings in the form of bank notes as well as that of every industrial, mining, and commercial enterprise in the country.

In all, it is shown that the country has consumed, over the last five years, some $60 million a year beyond its resources. With the return to reality, the country will have to live within its own income, meaning that — if American aid continues at the rate of $20 million per annum — it will have to curtail its expenditures *by some $40 million a year* until such time as the recovery of agriculture as a result of the stabilization measures brings about an increase in national production, or until a propitious investment climate begins to attract new capital.

It is this *profligacy in* expenditures beyond the nation's true resources that has been partly responsible for the temporary difficulties of the present time. The effect on the general economy, however, will not be as grave as might be gathered from these figures, inasmuch as the bulk of the capital expenditures consisted of foreign purchases, and the elimination of such expenditures abroad will not affect the income of the public within the country in the shape of wages, salaries, and the sale of local products.

Unfortunately, however, we still do not have a complete picture of the economic situation of the country, either now or at the time when this government took office. One of the most serious problems which has faced the Stabilization Council has been the lack of adequate economic and financial data on which to base its recommendations.

For example, by September 4 every government department and agency should have given the council complete details of its receipts and expenditures, in bolivianos and dollars, for the four prior years and for the first six months of 1956, showing the rate of exchange for conversions from foreign currency in each case. They should likewise have submitted complete details of their outstanding obligations, commitments, and contracts, which might involve the eventual expenditure of money or the equivalent; and, meanwhile, as provided in the August 4, 1956, decree, no government agency or department is permitted to undertake new obligations without the express authorization of the council, under penalty of nullity.

Despite these categorical provisions, and our repeated demands, we have not been able, up to the present time, to get from the Development Corporation the simple detail, in dollars and bolivianos, of what that agency has spent for each of the projects which it has under way. What we do know is that the Development Corporation changed its accounting methods some four years ago so that its expenditures in dollars and bolivianos are hopelessly commingled and no one can know the true state of its accounts.

Similarly, the National Social Security Administration has never given the council the data we requested early in February. From the partial figures submitted by the administration, we do know that the expenditures of that agency for the benefit of the workers amounted to only Bs. 973 million for the year 1955, whereas the administration's total receipts during that year amounted to Bs. 4,305 million.

Nor do we know, as I have already stated, the actual amount of the debt to Argentina and Brazil in dollars, or how much that debt has increased over the past five years.

Throughout the deliberations of the Stabilization Council we have run across new revelations of obligations or debts that no one had any idea of when we began our work. For example, when the government made its presentation on November 29, 1956, to the International Monetary Fund, asking for a loan, it stated that the national short- or medium-term debt amounted to $12 million. Now we know that the debt amounts to at least $33 million with the guarantee of the Central Bank, not counting other unguaranteed debts which may amount to some $20 or $30 million more. So far, in spite of our insistence, we do not have a breakdown of that debt with respect to amounts, maturities, creditors, debtors, and nature, although I believe that finally we are about to get this information (up to May 20, the information has not yet come in).

I am referring to these matters, not with the intent of criticizing any particular government enterprise or agency, because in virtually all of these agencies the accounts are in utter disorder. There is an almost complete lack of the data that might give us an over-all idea of the financial and economic situation of the country, and this has tremendously hampered the task of the Stabilization Council.

In the case of the Mining Corporation, for example, that agency prepared certain statements last February which apparently demonstrated the need for an exchange rate of over Bs. 12,000 to the dollar in order to balance its budget, in spite of the fact that in December, 1956, it had given us a budget showing that a Bs. 7,000 rate would have sufficed for the purpose. Fixing the rate of exchange at around Bs. 7,700 helped the COMIBOL operations, of course, since the greater the amount COMIBOL received in bolivianos for its dollars, the easier it would be for it to meet its local currency costs.

On the other hand, there was a considerable increase in transportation costs and in the cost of the materials COMIBOL had to buy locally, and the management could not compute this in advance. After allowing for these costs and correcting certain omissions that COMIBOL had made in its February, 1957, computations, the company gave us another statement of account, purporting to show the need for an exchange rate of over Bs. 10,000 to the dollar. In this statement, we likewise found a mistake in arithmetic, this time making a difference of Bs. 1,000 in the exchange rate; and, after a number of conferences and a great deal of correspondence, it was found that COMIBOL's difficulties in the payment of royalties to the government, and its lack of working capital, were primarily due to two causes:

1. *That the company had spent some $1,225,000 for supplies in two months when, according to its approved budget, it should only have spent $1.7 million in the entire year.*

2. *That the foreign smelters owed COMIBOL over $15 million, whereas the normal indebtedness of the smelters during the period of transportation, smelting, and accounting, in previous years, never exceeded $10 million.*

When these facts were pointed out, COMIBOL made an exact computation of the revenues which it is going to receive in the first six months of this year, and of the expenditures it will have to make in the same period, and arrived at the conclusion that an exchange rate of Bs. 7,710 would be enough to cover all its needs. These figures are based on ore shipments in the last three months of 1956 and the first three months of the current year, so they should represent almost exact approximations, and not mere estimates of future results.

There are nevertheless certain basic difficulties in the Mining Corporation operations which must be corrected. I shall refer to these later when I take up the solutions for the country's fundamental economic problems.

At the same time, I wish to state that my remarks must not be interpreted as criticizing in any way the top management of the Mining Corporation. On the contrary, in November and December, 1956, no one but a prophet could have made an exact budget for COMIBOL's future operations, since it would be based on past accounts that had been carried at many different rates of exchange, particularly when COMIBOL had to work with local material and transportation cost estimates based on preliminary data submitted by YPFB and the Director General of Railways and other agencies — data that, under the pressure of time, proved to be underestimates.

The fact is that, in its cooperation with the work of the Stabilization Council, the COMIBOL top management has achieved a miracle in eliminating the subsidized commissaries and dismissing a number of superfluous miners, and I think it my duty to say that Bolivia has been very fortunate that the top management of COMIBOL as well as of YPFB — the two most important enterprises in the government's financial picture — has been of such high calibre. The only things that might be criticized are that COMIBOL's accounting is still carried in such a way that, up to the present time, we do not know exactly how it has spent its money during the first months of the year, and that it has let nearly four months go by without having paid a penny of the Bs. 10 billion in royalties that it owes to the government, when these royalties could have been paid with only a fraction of the amounts that COMIBOL should have collected from abroad.

Chiefly as a consequence of this nonpayment, the Finance Ministry has collected only Bs. 19.9 billion of taxes up to March 20, whereas it should have collected Bs. 36.3 billion according to its budget.* The Finance Minister has also accomplished miracles in managing to meet government payrolls in spite of the shortage in revenues, but in the Ministry too the accounting is carried in such a way that we still have not received the details of expenditures for the current year, and Point IV has received a letter from Washington pointing out that if they do not get details of revenues and expenditures for January, February, and March, the comptroller will not be able to authorize any further U.S. aid disbursements. This is categorical. Point IV aid will cease until the government puts its accounts in order, so that Washington can tell how the monetary stabilization plan is working out.

The accounting disorder in Bolivia is not limited to government agencies, since certain private companies have also complained of the lack of discipline, of the absolute absence of any sense of responsibility and of duty on the part of employees, with the result that, instead of the accounts being up to date at all times, they are three months or more behind.

There is another grave aspect of this matter, and that is the situation of the counterpart funds with which the national budget will have to be balanced. Point IV has placed these funds at the disposal of the government but, up to the present time, orders of merchandise from the government and government enterprises with the use of Point IV funds have been very scarce, and apparently — we do not yet know for sure — some counterpart funds have been used or wrongfully retained without proper controls. As a consequence, there has been a shortage of counterpart funds in bolivianos for budget purposes, still further hampering the task of the Finance Ministry.† It is to be hoped that this situation will be remedied in the course of the next few weeks, but this has been a very serious

---

*For the first four months of the year, collections amounted to only Bs. 34,810 million against budgeted receipts of Bs. 59,751 million. This entire paragraph, after having been deleted, was later reinserted elsewhere in the press release, somewhat out of context.

†For the first four months of the year, the government created only Bs. 7 billion of counterpart funds, against Bs. 37.5 billion budgeted. This entire paragraph was first deleted, and then reinserted elsewhere in the press release, somewhat out of context.

problem for the stabilization program inasmuch as, according to the budget, counterpart funds should provide 40 per cent of the total government revenues and will probably reach 50 per cent (because of lower than budgeted tax collections).

There is one matter which I must point out for the information of the ministers and others present who are not members of the Stabilization Council, namely, that neither the council, nor the technical advisers and representatives of the International Monetary Fund, made up the budgets of the government departments and agencies or the figures accompanying the program presented by the Bolivian government to the International Monetary Fund and to the U.S. government agencies. The technical advisers insisted merely that the budgets be in balance, but they had to work on the basis of the figures submitted by the government itself and by the agencies. The determination of compensation for elimination of the cheap commissaries, and as an adjustment to the new monetary system, as well as the determination of the initial rate of exchange at the beginning of the new regime, were made on the basis of those figures *by officials of the Bolivian government. Neither the technical advisers nor the monetary fund representatives had any vote whatsoever in the decisions of the council.*

Naturally, in fixing these compensations and the initial rate of exchange, the President and the voting members of the council took into account the fact that, out of over three million inhabitants in the country, only some 150,000 earn wages that would be affected by such measures, and that 65 per cent of such wage earners are government employees whose remuneration cannot be increased without directly affecting the budget, and, consequently, the exchange rate and commodity prices.

It must be emphasized that the lending agencies did not impose conditions of any kind on the loan which they made to Bolivia for the stabilization fund. The government of Bolivia presented various statistical data, together with certain or programmed measures, saying in effect: "This is our monetary and financial stabilization plan which we propose to follow, and, on the basis of that plan, we request financial assistance." The directors of the International Monetary Fund, representing some sixty nations of the world, studied the plan and decided to grant a loan of up to $7.5 million as and to the extent that Bolivia might require, provided that the borrower carried out the program which it presented. The U.S. Treasury and the ICA in Washington then agreed to grant, the Treasury as a loan and the ICA as a donation, up to $7.5 million and $10 million, respectively, likewise as and to the extent that the funds might be needed, and on the basis of the compliance by Bolivia with the measures which Bolivia itself had presented on requesting this aid. Bolivia, of course, only pays interest on the funds which it needs, and up to the present has only drawn $5.5 million, of which it still has some $3 million (now $1.9 million, May 20, 1957).

Thus it is not a matter of conditions imposed by any foreign government or international agency; rather, Bolivia has a solemn *moral* obligation to carry out, *to the letter,* the program which it presented as the basis for its request for funds. If it fails to follow that program — and unfortunately it has already deviated from the program in certain important respects — or if it attempts now, after only four months from the date of the loans, to make fundamental changes in the plan which would vitiate any possibility of monetary stabilization — such as increasing wages without a corresponding cut in social security or dismissing surplus employees — the world-wide credit of Bolivia, which was nil prior to December 15, would again become nonexistent, closing the door to any possibility of future financial aid and endangering even the availability of the remainder of the stabilization fund.

This does not mean that Bolivia, as a sovereign nation, cannot legislate or take any other measures it wishes. Its freedom of action is complete, but, naturally, if Bolivia wishes to draw against the stabilization fund or obtain any additional financial aid, she must refrain from taking measures that are diametrically opposed to those which she herself imposed, and which would be contrary to the only possible basis for a stable currency and a sound economy.

On the other hand, if Bolivia carries out faithfully its stabilization program, it will have demonstrated its determination and its capacity to maintain monetary and financial stability, and it may rest assured that the doors of the World Bank, of USOM, and of private investors will never be closed to the discussion of investments or loans of a strictly economic and productive nature.

Departures from the program

The lack of financial and economic data, and the inexactness of much of the data provided, however, have not been so serious in hampering the stabilization program as the failure to follow the program and comply strictly with the conditions which the Bolivian government itself imposed when it requested assistance from the International Monetary Fund and the cooperation of the U.S. government agencies.

During his visit in August, 1956, Henry Holland pointed out specifically, in conversations with the President of the Republic and the President of the Senate (Juan Lechín) that it would be extremely difficult to get the American Congress to continue U.S. aid unless Bolivia put its house in order, as Holland phrased it, by carrying out a monetary and financial stabilization program and re-establishing its world credit through bilateral agreements with the bondholders and the former mine owners. He concluded by saying, nevertheless, that Bolivia had more than eight months in which to fulfill these conditions.

Now, on his recent visit, Holland repeated this warning, with this difference — that Bolivia no longer has eight months to fulfill these conditions, since the U.S. Congress will be studying the question of foreign aid this month and in the month of May.

This brings me to an extremely serious matter. Early in December, 1956, Miguel Gisbert, with full powers to act on behalf of his government, made an arrangement with the representatives of the Foreign Bondholders' Protective Council in New York. The agreement reached was the most favorable that had ever been authorized by the Bondholder's Council and represented a resounding success for this government. After making the arrangement, Gisbert spoke with high officials in the World Bank in Washington (International Bank for Reconstruction and Development), and they expressed themselves as highly pleased that the Bolivian government had decided to resume its debt service — *on a very reduced scale, of course* — and they promised to send a special mission to Bolivia in February or March of this year to sound out the possibilities of financing certain appropriate projects with a view to relieving the difficult economic situation in the country.

The arrangement was concluded, when the Vice-President sent an urgent telegram from Washington to the Bolivian government asking that the arrangement be suspended until his return to Washington, notwithstanding the well-founded suggestion of the Bolivian Ambassador to Washington that such postponement would seriously injure the nation's credit. It now turns out that the reason for the Vice-President's intervention in the matter was that he had spoken with someone in the United States who had offered to retire $7 million par value of the Bolivian government bonds for a price of $2 million.

Some seven months ago, the President of the Republic had consulted me on another proposal of the same kind, and I replied that it is considered highly unethical for a government to buy back its obligations at bargain prices when the reason for the low prices is the government's failure to pay the interest due. It is considered that if a defaulting government has money enough to buy back its bonds it should use the money to meet its obligations to the bondholders and not to make a profit on its defaulted debts.

Now, another similar proposition is advanced, aggravated by the fact that the intermediary offers to buy back $7 million of bonds for $2 million,* when the bonds can be purchased freely in New

*An uncorrected draft stated that this meant an average price of 35 per cent of par, and this figure was later published. The correct figure would be 28.6 per cent. The profit would be approximately $460,000 (see p. 732, n 57).

York at 18 per cent of par, according to a cable which I received recently from the United States. It is evident that the $7 million of bonds could be purchased at a price which would run from the present price of 18 up to a maximum of 25, so that this transaction would mean an enormous profit to whoever intervened in the operation, to the prejudice of the interests of the state. It may also be noted that in December, 1956, the bonds were selling at between 13 per cent and 15 per cent of par, so that it would be interesting to find out whether those same intermediaries have been buying the bonds in the interim and causing the price to rise to 18 at the present time.

I am very much afraid that this intervention, and the consequent delay, may have irremediably injured Bolivia's credit, inasmuch as Gisbert acted with full powers to represent the government of Bolivia, a task which he performed with the greatest ability and success. Luckily, Bolivia has two excellent representatives to iron out the trouble — the Foreign Minister who will be leaving soon for the United States, and the Ambassador in Washington; and I am sure that those gentlemen will do everything possible to renew the negotiations with the Bondholders' Council, so inopportunely interrupted.

One consequence of this intervention which cannot be remedied is that the World Bank (which under its regulations cannot lend money to any country in default) did not send a mission of investigation to Bolivia in February or March, and we now know that they will not send anyone until May, and probably not a study mission before August. It is of interest to note that a representative of the World Bank was in La Paz recently, Torgier Finsass; however, he did not come for the purpose of looking into the Bolivian situation, but to study a loan to the Peruvian Corporation, for which reason he wished to confer with the representatives of the Guaqui Railway. Had it not been for the interference referred to, it is quite likely that he or some other representative would have also entered into discussions with Bolivian government officials. Now, any possible aid from the World Bank has been put off, perhaps for many months — something that could have aided greatly in the economic recovery of the country and in the definitive de jure stabilization of the currency.

In other matters too, Bolivia has departed from the stabilization program, for it must be noted that the program does not consist merely in the decrees of August 4 and December 15, but in the whole parcel of decrees enacted and to be enacted and in the obligations entered into between the Bolivian government and the representatives of the International Monetary Fund, Point IV, and the Treasury of the United States, as a condition for the cooperation of those agencies in creating a monetary stabilization fund.

(Here there is omitted my statement concerning Bolivia's obligation to enter into a negotiated agreement for repayment of the debt to the former mineowners, insisted upon by the government of the United States, and agreed to by the government of Bolivia as a condition for the creation of the stabilization fund. Any such agreement was, however, precluded by the untimely declaration by the Minister of Mines. For Bolivia's protection, I kept no written record of the text of this statement. The substance is, however, fully set forth at pp. 443-45.)

Another matter which, from the beginning of the prestabilization studies, was pointed out as indispensable for the financial recovery of the nation and of the government, and hence for monetary stabilization, was the need of carrying out the Ford, Bacon & Davis recommendations with respect to reorganization of the mining industry and particularly of the government mining corporation. So far, nothing has been done to implement the FBD report, one particularly urgent matter being to increase the powers of management in order to reinforce the principles of authority and autonomy, with the exception of the approval of the annual budget, and the accounting and financial control carried out through the Comptroller General and the Ministry of Finance.

In other matters, too, there has been a departure from the conditions of the monetary stabilization measures. In the matter of wages, the December 15 decree expressly required that wages and salaries, *by whatever name they may be known,* be frozen, it being evident, as the workers themselves recognize, that any increase not justified by a corresponding increase in production must inevitably result in a renewal of the vicious spiral of inflation. Notwithstanding this, additional daily compensation of Bs. 450 for elimination of the subsidized company stores was *extended by the Minister of Labor against the express order of the President of the Republic,* not only for those who had a right to such compensation but covering all industrial workers regardless of the number of workers. This was in itself a minor matter, so far as the amount involved was concerned; but, as the first departure from the clear provisions of the decree, it gave a precedent which endangers the entire monetary stabilization program.

Later an increase was authorized for the employees of the Mining Bank even though the bank itself is insolvent; subsequently, service station and garage employees were classified as railroad workers, with a consequent increase in compensation; and recently the classification of the Point IV highway workers as construction workers instead of as public servants resulted in a strike and demands for increased compensation.

Finally, the construction workers of the municipality of Cocha-bamba and other municipal employees are on strike, likewise demanding compensation for the elimination of the subsidized commissaries that they never had, and notwithstanding that the De-cember 15 decree expressly states that public employees will receive a Bs. 1,300 daily increase, and no other increase in compensation.

Inasmuch as, up to the present, no strike has been declared illegal even though clearly contravening the provisions of the December 15, 1956, decree-law, strikes have become a form of paid vacation, and there is no incentive whatsoever for workers to continue working when they know that at the end of their vacation they will not be penalized by reason of the strike.

If the demands of the construction workers are met, it is evident that the matter will not stop there, but will be extended to all other civil servants, which will cost the government some Bs. 8 billion and further unbalance the national budget. If that is so, it means more unbacked currency issues and the definite collapse of the stabilization program.

There has also been a deviation from the stabilization plan in the matter of credits, the effect of which cannot be other than inflationary. For example, the government has granted, without prior consultation with the Stabilization Council as required by the August 4 decree, loans for various amounts to the La Paz union of chauffeurs, to the municipality of La Paz, and to other entities (and has recently authorized Bs. 100 million for the ECLA conference and another unknown amount for the University of San Andrés, none of which was included in the budget).

Any credit or expense not compensated for by tax collections, no matter how small the amount, means the issuance of bank notes. Chart VII (see Fig. 9, p. 492) shows that, between the date when the Bolivian government prepared the data for its request for funds from the International Monetary Fund and the date on which the first stabilization decree was put into effect, the bank note issue in the hands of the public increased from Bs. 136 million to Bs. 165.3 billion, a rise of $21\frac{1}{2}$ per cent in one month. This fact, together with other matters, made it necessary to commence stabilization at an exchange rate of Bs. 7,750 per dollar, instead of at Bs. 7,000 as had been previously contemplated.

Since then, the bank note issue of the Central Bank in the hands of the public has increased from Bs. 165.3 billion to Bs. 190.7 billion in the course of four months, or an increase of nearly 15 per cent. In the same period, $2.7 million net has been sold from the stabilization fund, which should have reduced circulation by some Bs. 20 billion, inasmuch as sales of foreign exchange must be paid for directly or indirectly by delivery of bank notes.

Hence, the inflation from the date of promulgation of the stabilization decrees up to April 13, 1957, has reached Bs. 47 billion. The direct cause of this inflation is seen in the column on the left-hand side of Chart VII which shows that credits have been granted to the Mining Corporation for Bs. 7.5 billion by discounting drafts which were delivered in lieu of export royalties, and Bs. 8 billion for working capital; Bs. 3.2 billion to the Petroleum Corporation; Bs. 2.4 billion to the Social Security Administration; and Bs. 1.9 billion to the Development Corporation. The Central Bank has also purchased Bs. 7.5 billion of "treaty dollars" (under the Argentine and Brazilian agreements) at par, when it is obvious that the imports bought with treaty dollars cost from two to six times the proper prices. Government agencies, chiefly the Mining and Petroleum Corporations, have likewise used up Bs. 11.3 billion of their deposits. The inflation in the private sector has amounted to only Bs. 5.7 billion.

In order not to complicate the matter unduly, the chart does not show all the factors of inflation, since we should add the increase in bank deposits to the increase of bank notes in the hands of the public. But suffice it to say that if the inflationary tendencies continue at their present rate — and that includes not only the credits but any increase in salaries and wages, whether under the guise of "leveling," "regrouping," "readjustment," or any other name — the bank note circulation in December, 1957, will be double what it was at the beginning of the year, or else we shall lose an equivalent amount from the stabilization fund, which comes to the same thing. In other words, the monetary stabilization program will have collapsed because its provisions, and those contained in the government's proposal in its request for funds, have not been carried out.

The direct and inescapable relationship between the bank note issue and monetary depreciation is shown in Chart VIII (see Fig. 4, p. 111), which reveals a correlation between the two curves, from 1918 to July, 1956, that is so exact that it is almost impossible to distinguish one curve from the other.

This chart, or rather a similar chart which I prepared in June, 1956, formed the apodeictic argument that I presented to President Paz-Estenssoro and his financial advisers to convince them that monetary depreciation was indisputably due to the issuance of bank notes by the Central Bank; that the cause of this excess note issue was that the government and government agencies were spending money beyond their means; and that the way to put a stop to monetary depreciation, and to the vicious wage and price spiral, was to restrict governmental expenses within the limit of their cash resources — and that there was no other way in the world to achieve a stable currency.

This graphic demonstration, plus other data and charts which I prepared within a few weeks of my arrival in the country, paved the way for promulgation of the August 4, 1956, decree which created the National Monetary Stabilization Council. By the end of July, I had presented, for the consideration of President Paz-Estenssoro and of the present President and their respective advisers, a complete agenda of the stabilization program from its inception up to the definitive de jure stabilization and the creation of a new monetary unit, and we would have arrived at that result by the middle of this year had it not been for the *interferences I have mentioned, and for the departures from the plan not authorized by the Stabilization Council.*

In that event, I would have had the honor of continuing to cooperate with the government of Bolivia until the stabilization plan had been carried to a happy and successful conclusion, but my personal affairs will not allow me to remain in La Paz beyond June, and I shall have to leave to others the conclusion of the task in accordance with the program already presented.*

Again referring to Chart VII, I must state that the credits referred to in that chart were granted without the precautions called for in the August 4 decree. Article 13 of that decree provides that the Central Bank may not issue bank notes, or grant credits to the government or government agencies, without prior unanimous approval of the voting members of the council, and that the council shall not authorize such operations without careful study of the data submitted by the respective technical adviser, that is, by the expert in banking matters, Ernest Moore. Until the said adviser is named by decree — *and he has not yet been appointed up to this time* — it is provided that the president of the Central Bank shall carry out his functions but, unfortunately, each time that one of the government agencies has come to the council for money, it has been claimed that it was absolutely necessary to grant the funds that afternoon. At times we were given a period of as much as twenty-four hours but always with the threat that, if the loan were not granted, there would be a general strike or some other disaster which took the matter from an economic and financial plane to a political one. This supposed urgency, which demonstrates the lack of foresight and the financial disorder in the agency requesting the funds, made it impossible to carry out the proper functions of the technical advisers, and of the voting members of the Stabilization Council, all of whom did everything possible within their powers to comply at all times with the requirements of the monetary stabilization plan but were unable to resist the apparent urgency and the political pressure of the moment.

---

*This was the first announcement of my intended departure. President Siles asked me to remain and later asked the American Ambassador to attempt to persuade me to postpone my departure but, aside from my personal financial and business obligations, I was too exhausted physically and otherwise to continue even another month in La Paz.

All that I can do is to warn, with the utmost respect, the honor-able representatives of the Bolivian government that the best and most carefully laid financial plans are bound to fail if they are put aside because of political or labor union pressure, or because of other self-seeking demands of the moment, and that it is not pos-sible to give way here and there in matters which of themselves might not be of major importance, but which in sum must inevitably lead to the failure of the entire monetary and economic structure of the country.

In another matter too, the recommendations of the Stabilization Council have been ignored. Certain tax decrees have been so changed by the Cabinet that the income tax, for example, will not produce more than $50,000 in revenues, inasmuch as practically the entire population is exempt, at the same time that a minute fraction of the public is subjected to exorbitant and uncollectable tax rates. *Similarly, taxes on sporting events and on sales have been altered without taking into consideration the criteria which guided the Sta-bilization Council in its recommendations, and particularly without considering the effect that the changes would have on the government budget.*

Likewise, certain measures urgently required for the success of the stabilization program and for national economic recovery have not yet been promulgated in spite of having been sent to the Cabinet long ago, in some cases several months ago. Among the pending decrees is the customs tariff. The delay in this bill has paralyzed industry, commerce, and mining, and has made impossi-ble the success of the credit plan sponsored by USOM and already announced by the Central Bank. (Finally on May 7 the new tariff was approved by decree, but the delay has postponed for five weeks the collection of some $800,000 in revenues which the Treasury sorely needs; and, in the end, only a few insignificant percentage changes were made from the draft presented by the council.)

Likewise pending passage are two decrees for the revaluation of assets, the first referring to commerce and industry and the sec-ond to banks. Among those who are urgently calling for passage of the first decree is the government petroleum corporation, which must know what the regulations will be in order to complete a pend-ing study of costs and prices that may possibly permit of some price reductions. The lack of passage of the second decree deprives the government of needed revenues and curbs the reasonable extension of bank credit. (*Note:* The latter decree was finally passed, but so changed as to limit its application. Both measures were delayed because of objections raised in the Cabinet.)

I understand that there have been objections to the basis of the revaluation decree, which provides that the assets of any private or government enterprise may be reappraised at their true present value, private companies to pay a 3 per cent tax, over a year and a half, on any increased value. *The economy of the country cannot stand any higher tax under any conditions.*

On the other hand, I understand that the President of the Senate is sponsoring a compulsory revaluation, based on the change from the official Bs. 190 rate to the current rate, in other words, multiplying all company assets forty times.

In the first place, revaluation does not mean a profit to the company, but merely a recognition of the *debasement of the* currency. In the second place, properties have not increased uniformly in value; some properties may be worth one hundred times more than before, while others would be worth very little more, and still others might be worth less — for example, houses which are leased at controlled rents and which, by reason of the low rent, have not been maintained in good condition. In industry there is the example of excess capacity of certain factories as a consequence of the return to reality.

Finally, revaluation at an arbitrary percentage with a high tax would bankrupt every industrial, commercial, and mining enterprise in the country, meaning that all productive private property would disappear and be replaced by 100 per cent statism. For example, if the accounts of a given enterprise show assets of, say, Bs. 10 million, and if it must revalue its assets arbitrarily by forty times, that is, at Bs. 400 million, paying a 50 per cent tax, where would it find the nearly Bs. 200 million to pay the levy when its capital is only Bs. 10 million?

The decree on stamped paper and stamp taxes has likewise not been enacted, and even though this measure is not perfect, and will probably have to be amended after experience with the new rates, the failure to enact it has deprived the Treasury of much-needed revenues.

The decree on bonuses for excess mineral production and on cash balances due to the miners was likewise delayed, leaving private mining without working capital, so that it was unable to contribute to the increase of national production.

Another decree urgently called for by the government mining and petroleum corporations, and by every domestic and foreign company employing engineers and technical personnel on foreign currency salaries, is a measure which would eliminate the special taxes that fall only on such employees and which would put Bolivia in a position to compete with other countries in obtaining experts essential to increase production. For example, a technician employed by an oil company in Venezuela, at a salary of $300 a month, pays no tax whatsoever on his income. In Bolivia he would pay 12.7 per cent. An engineer who may now be employed in Venezuela, at a salary of $1,500 a month, which is not high for a first-class engineer in worldwide competition, would have to pay 38.6 per cent if he came to Bolivia, as compared to 2.3 per cent which he would now pay on the salary he received in Venezuela.

Under such conditions, who would come to work in Bolivia with the exception of those engineers and technical personnel who have been failures in other countries and cannot obtain any other work? Every government enterprise insists, as do the private companies, that without the cooperation of the best technical personnel, who must be paid in foreign currency, it will be impossible to increase national production. (This decree has now also been passed, but with an amendment that partly nullifies its purpose.)

Thus, as a consequence of the *interferences,* departures from the program, and the delays to which I have referred, not only the monetary stabilization program but the entire economic future of Bolivia has been jeopardized. *We cannot assume that the political and labor leaders who have interfered with, and who are continuing to attack the stabilization program, have no desire to understand it, or that they wish to sabotage it, or that they have any ulterior or subversive motives. Instead, I may say that the fault is ours for not having explained the program with the necessary clarity. But the fact remains that the attacks on the program, and the interferences with it, on the part of those who should cooperate, have in actual fact sabotaged President Siles' program, for I repeat and shall continue to repeat that the Stabilization Program is not an "Eder Plan," as it is called by those who do not dare to attack the Chief Executive in person, but the program of the government of Bolivia, presented by that government as the basis for its request for financial aid.*

Solutions

Luckily, it is not too late to save the situation, and I wish now to propose solutions for the basic problems that the country faces at the present time.

In the first place, I may say that a wage increase is less needed now than it was at the beginning of the year in view of the drop in prices, and it will continue to become less and less necessary as the cost of articles of prime necessity continues to drop when the new crops reach the market under a free economy, and when the customs tariff is passed in the form proposed by the council.

The purpose of the stabilization measures is to improve the standard of living of the entire population. They are already beginning to show results for the farmers, and they will show results for the workers and middle class as prices go down and production goes up. Thus, time will provide its own remedy, although I admit that nowhere are workers inclined to consider a drop in prices as the equivalent of an increase in wages, so that there will always be pressure, in part demagogic, for a general increase in wages notwithstanding the fact that, unless there is increased production, a wage increase can only be illusory and inflationary.

What is needed more than a general wage increase is a readjustment of the remunerations received by the various sectors of the economy and I recommend, as an urgent and unpostponable measure, that the government make — or that it request ILO experts affiliated with the U.N. office in La Paz to make — an immediate study of the discrepancies in compensations between the various groups. Such a study should not be politically inspired; that is, it should not recommend increases merely for those groups which are numerically or politically the most influential, but should recommend the higher rates of compensation for those whose knowledge and years of preparation — *whether doctors or mechanics, whether teachers or miners* — are most deserving of higher remuneration. *For example, to my way of thinking, it is paradoxical that the school teachers who have had to dedicate so many years of their lives to preparing themselves for their tasks, and in whose hands rests the destiny of the country, should receive less than those workers who require no special preparation.*

Of course, as a corollary of adequate wages and salaries, absolute dedication to the job should be demanded from the professional as well as from the laborer; that is, the school teacher must lay his eight hundred bricks or more of daily instruction just as the laborer should lay his eight hundred bricks of clay.

Inasmuch as, in readjusting wages and salaries between the various occupations, it will be impossible to reduce wages in any sector, this means, as a practical matter, that a readjustment process will result in an increase of the total wage bill. Probably no sector, no matter how well paid, can be left without some increase.

Now, inasmuch as any increase of wages and salaries without a prior increase in productivity inevitably means the issuance of bank notes and a renewal of the inflationary spiral, two other indispensable steps are necessary, namely, a simultaneous cut in the contributions to the National Social Security Administration and other similar funds, and the right of freedom to hire and fire.

As to the first measure, no country can support a contribution for social security which, according to law, is equivalent to $37\frac{1}{2}$ per cent of the payroll. It is true that the workers' contribution is theoretical since, although the new social security code promulgated late in 1956 calls for a workers' contribution of $7\frac{1}{2}$ per cent, this is not in fact being paid, and the major labor groups have demanded a cut to 1 per cent. A proportional cut in the employers' contributions, which would be equitable, would reduce their charge from 30 per cent to 4 per cent. (At the present time, unfortunately, certain labor leaders are advocating that the workers' contribution be replaced by a $.01 [U.S. currency] charge on every pound of tin — which would cost the government over $500,000 per annum — and that the employers' contribution for cheap housing be increased to 14 per cent, which would raise the employer tax to 42 per cent, bankrupting the government, and every government and private enterprise in the country.)

The problem of social security costs is so simple *that it is hard to comprehend why the labor leaders themselves do not understand it.* If in a given enterprise, whether government or private, the operation of the business makes it possible to pay a total compensation of $1 a day to the workers, it is clear that this compensation can be distributed either entirely in the form of wages, salaries, and direct payments to the workers or partly in direct form and partly in the form of a contribution to a social security fund. The accounts of the Mining Corporation, for example, show beyond dispute that it can pay its employees a total of some Bs. 160 billion per annum. The business cannot yield any more money. There is nothing that the corporation, or the government, or the labor unions can do to increase this amount, unless the miners increase their production or unless, by good fortune, there is an increase in the price of tin or of other metals. Now, at the present time, the Mining Corporation pays one-third of this total compensation in the form of social benefits or in medical services rendered directly by the company; that is, for every Bs. 10,000 that the workers receive, it pays Bs. 5,000 in "social benefits." If the company could eliminate these social security charges and services entirely, it could increase the direct payments to the workers and employees proportionately; the question is, which would the workers prefer — whether in the Mining Corporation or any other enterprise in the country — would they rather have the company pay them, say, Bs. 7,500 a day and pay Bs. 2,820 (37.5 per cent) to the social security fund, or would they rather receive Bs. 10,320 directly, and eliminate social security?

Of course, no one advocates either extreme, but, as a guide, I may say that in the United States we have learned that we are not sufficiently wealthy to support a social security charge exceeding $4\frac{1}{2}$ per cent of the payroll, the employees paying $2\frac{1}{4}$ per cent and the companies paying $2\frac{1}{4}$ per cent. An equal contribution by the employers and employees is essential inasmuch as the company receives no benefit whatsoever from social security, and if the employee received all the benefits, paying little or nothing of the tax, there would be no limit to the demands of the workers, who would not immediately realize that any contribution to social security must come from their own pockets, as the only source from which this contribution or their wages can come is from the company's gross revenues.

Now, as to the situation in Bolivia, I have conferred at length with the top officials of the Mining Corporation — the greatest enterprise in the country, on whose prosperity depends the welfare of the entire nation. As a result of these conferences, and of accounting studies, we have reached the inescapable conclusion that there are only two roads open for the corporation — unless it is wished to abandon the present monetary stabilization and let the boliviano drop to a point which would be incompatible with the welfare of the three million inhabitants of the country who do not live on wages and salaries. These two alternative roads are either to eliminate the payments to the social security fund and shut down certain mines or rent them out on a contract basis, or else to eliminate the payment of export royalties.

Manifestly, the royalties cannot be eliminated or reduced, inasmuch as a balanced budget depends upon collection of these royalties, which cannot be changed until at least a year's experience shows the true cost of mining production and the possibility of obtaining adequate income for the Treasury from other sources.

There remains then as the sole alternative a cut in the social security contributions. The company's accounts prove that even total elimination of social security charges will not entirely solve the problem, but at the same time it is recognized that from a practical point of view the company cannot replace its own medical services with the uncertain medical services that might be rendered by the Social Security Administration; the Mining Corporation management considers that a mining company cannot leave it to any other agency to render services so important in maintaining production. Following this criterion, the conclusion is that the mining industry, whether government or private, must be required to continue rendering medical services as it has done in the past, and that it must also be compelled to contribute to the National Social Security Administration for other services an amount not in excess of 2 per cent of the base pay of the workers and employees. Mining, and particularly private mining, cannot carry a heavier burden and still continue to produce.

With the same criterion, we are compelled to reach the conclusion that industry, commerce, and the railways, as well as the government and governmental agencies, cannot continue to carry the present burden, and I must recommend that employer contributions be reduced to a maximum of $7\frac{1}{2}$ per cent of the workers' base pay, provided that the workers' contribution is reduced from 7.5 per cent to 2.5 per cent. If the workers do not consider that social security benefits are worth more to them than 1 per cent, the employer contributions should not, under any circumstances, exceed 4 per cent and, in either case, the National Social Security Administration and other similar institutions should adjust their budgets within that framework, which defines the maximum limit of the economic possibilities of the nation.

Even by reducing the social security charges within those limits, commerce, industry, mining, and the government itself, are in no position to balance their respective budgets, and much less to increase wages, unless they are given the right to close uneconomic mines and enterprises, and to dismiss excess laborers and employees, the employer — whether government or private — being given complete liberty to hire and fire.

In the case of the government departments, for example, and of the non-profitmaking government agencies, I would suggest purely as a personal opinion — the figures are hypothetical and subject to the results of a study of interindustry leveling of wages — an increase of 30 per cent in basic wages, the dismissal of 30 per cent of the employees,* and the reduction of social security charges to 7.5 per cent or to 4 per cent on the base pay, according to the employees' contribution. This would permit balancing the national budget and consolidating the economy of the country.

Of course, under present circumstances, freedom to fire cannot be granted without a comprehensive program to avoid unemployment. Such a program is being drawn up in Point IV, following the suggestions of the President of the Republic and of the Planning Commission, and consists chiefly of two [three] measures:

1. *The army should be authorized to accept as recruits all persons who apply to fulfill their military duties and should extend the period of conscription to two years, or, at the least, to a year and a half.*

2. (1) Plans should be initiated without delay for the construction of schools and of access roads between the principal centers of population and the neighboring valleys and "yungas." *This construction program would have to be managed by the army, as only the army is equipped to maintain those workers on a reasonable budget. I understand that the army feeds its soldiers well, and cheaply, on a daily expenditure of Bs. 700, plus an allowance of Bs. 300. In all, the cost of maintaining the conscripts, including lodging and uniforms, amounts to less than Bs. 2,200 a day, which shows that the Ministry of Defense is one of the best-managed agencies in the country, and the only one capable of carrying out a construction program of the necessary magnitude.*

3. (2) As the [third] other feature of the program, following the recommendation of the President of the Republic, every suitable person who requests it would be given a plot of

---

*Note that dismissing 30 per cent of the employees, and increasing wages 30 per cent, would mean a 9 per cent cut in the payroll.

land in the valleys or "yungas," close to the centers of
population and of a size large enough not only for suste-
nance but to contribute to the commercial agricultural
production of the country.

Point IV is prepared to assist in this program with dollars and
with counterpart funds in bolivianos, providing not only seeds, tools,
equipment, and machinery, but also agricultural and other instruction necessary for the success of the program. As a matter of fact,
Ross Moore already has plans under way, looking toward taking care
of some 6,000 workers divided into teams of 600 persons each. A
period of active productive labor of, say, six hours a day is contemplated, some two hours daily being devoted to instruction in order
that those who participate in the program, whether in construction
or on the farms, may learn to be farmers, mechanics, carpenters,
electricians, etc., and, above all, to become good citizens with a
clear concept of their duties and obligations as citizens of this nation and with the literacy necessary to fulfill those duties. All the
instruction work would, of course, be in the charge of Bolivians, and
Point IV would confine its activities to giving the technical instructors the necessary technical training for them to carry out their
mission.

The representatives of the National Manufacturers' Association
who visited me a short time ago informed me that they are likewise
prepared to contribute to the cost of providing food for dismissed
workers, up to a maximum of one year, in addition to paying the
legal indemnization and compensation for the loss of their jobs.
They estimate that, all together, industry, commerce, and private
mining might have to dismiss a maximum of six thousand employees;
but this process would be spread out over the course of a year,
which would be easily within the capacity of the program to absorb.
The government might well consider passing a decree which would
give any concern complete freedom to hire and fire, but requiring
as a temporary condition that the employer pay the government Bs.
700 per diem for a period of one year for each person fired, in
order to cover the cost of feeding, with perhaps an additional Bs.
300 for pocket money.

Women, and those unable to participate in such a program,
would not present a major problem, inasmuch as the impetus given
to industry, commerce, and mining by these measures, and by the
reduction of social security charges, would suffice to revive the
national economy immediately, thus giving employment to anyone
willing to work who cannot be taken care of in the construction and
agricultural development program.

It should be remembered that amounts paid directly to the
workers in wages are spent almost entirely and immediately in

articles of consumption, thus contributing to the promotion of commerce and industry and giving employment to many more people in those fields. In Bolivia only a part of the contributions to social security goes directly to local industry and commerce, or else there is a long delay, so that social security taxes represent a diminution in national purchasing power and directly reduce the number of people that the country can employ.

These measures, that is, the reduction of social security taxes, the freedom to hire and fire, and the unemployment program, are essential and urgent. I can see no alternative which would permit Bolivia to maintain a sound currency since without these measures the stabilization program must inevitably fail in view of the departures from the original plan. In that event, the continuation of U.S. aid would be endangered, together with any possibility of interesting foreign or domestic capital in the development of the national economy.

As another equally essential and urgent point, *Ross Moore, Director of Point IV, points out* the necessity of putting a definitive and early end to the agricultural reform, since the large estates have already been eliminated and small and medium farmers are now afraid to sow crops or cultivate their lands, under the menace of possible or probable expropriation.

As Bolivia has millions of hectares of vacant land, it is hard to understand why it continues to expropriate private property, particularly as this does not increase production and on the contrary diminishes it to a marked extent, deterring new sowing and cultivation and transferring land from the middle-sized farms — which in any country are always the most efficient* — and converting it into holdings of submarginal size which cannot contribute to commercial production or even suffice to sustain the life of the farmers without continued subsidies which the government is not in a position to pay.

Pending plans

The monetary stabilization program has only recently begun, and many other measures are pending which should be studied as soon as some of the more urgent problems which I have outlined are remedied. Among these pending problems which the council will be studying shortly is the treatment that must be given to the "treaty dollars," and to the treaty and free dollars arising out of farm and forest exports (recommendations have already been made with

---

*This is sentimental rather than strictly factual. The medium-sized farm is generally more efficient than the old-fashioned hacienda, less efficient than the large, modern commercial farm. But the family farm, large or medium-sized, has tremendous social and political advantages.

respect to the latter). Likewise, the problems of the railroads must be taken care of in due course, as well as the problem of reorganizing the Mining Bank in order to take the burden off the national budget.

Similarly, among the problems which are now under study by the technical advisers of the council, is the proposed creation of an Agricultural and Industrial Development Bank which would have as its basis the present organization of the Agricultural Bank and which could, among other matters, handle the Point IV supervised credits. The capital would be provided principally by counterpart funds.

Likewise, we have in mind a tax on real property which should provide a more adequate return to the Treasury and to the municipalities, and which would have to be linked to the eventual unfreezing of rents.

Similarly, a tax on agricultural products has been suggested, to be collected upon entry of the produce to the centers of consumption, such as has been collected since early times in almost every country of Europe and which is still imposed in many places where the collection of direct imposts is simpler than that of an income tax.

Another extremely urgent matter is an arrangement with the creditors of the government and government agencies. For many months I have urged that such an arrangement be made, inasmuch as the government apparently has between $35 and $65 million of commercial debts and does not have a cent to pay them, but up to the present we have not been able to obtain the necessary data to make a recommendation in the council. Meanwhile, there is always the threat of an attachment of funds abroad which would bring about a very disagreeable situation, not to say a dangerous one.

Steps have likewise been taken to draft a Mining Code which should awaken interest on the part of local and foreign investors in mining operations, the same as has been true in the case of oil, following promulgation of the Petroleum Code and within the respective limitations of the two industries.

We must not expect miracles, however, and the drafting of such a code will take at least eight months, as I have been told by a law partner of the American lawyer who cooperated in the drafting of the Petroleum Code. It would scarcely be worthwhile to enact a code which might fail to attract investors, and it is not enough that the code be drafted by the most eminent jurisconsults and professors of law in Bolivia. Before any reputable mining enterprise will invest millions of dollars in a country *whose past history offers little inducement for the risk of capital,* it will insist that the legal background be carefully studied from its own point of view, and it in no wise reflects on the competence of the Bolivian experts to ask the services of a lawyer who might perhaps be better versed in the requirements of the investor. Meanwhile, it is better to allow reputable and experienced mining companies to come into the country under the present system of special contracts than to improvise a code which, because of some defect in detail that might appear to be insignificant, could scare away future investors for decades.

It would also be advisable to promulgate a general investment code, and I already have at hand all the data necessary to draft such a code on the basis of my experience as draftsman of a subcommittee appointed by the Committee on Banking and Currency of the U.S. Senate, which had as its purpose to ascertain what the government of the United States should do, and what other governments should do, to stimulate investment in Latin America by foreign investors.

Not long ago the Vice-President of the nation asked me to prepare a draft of such a code over Holy Week, but it is completely impossible to improvise in matters of this importance and, in spite of my experience as an adviser in international investment matters for over thirty years, I would not undertake to prepare an acceptable code in so short a period. Nor, under present circumstances, is there any urgency for enactment of an investment code, since, until Bolivia restores her credit abroad by arrangements with the bondholders and former mineowners, and by consolidation of the stabilization program, there is no likelihood of either foreign or Bolivian capital coming into the country, outside of the oil and mining industries, where the natural risks of the business are so great that the additional hazard of an unfavorable investment climate is just one more factor that must be taken into consideration as a business risk. For any other class of investment, whether public utility, or industry, or commerce, the government must offer a more favorable investment climate than exists at present, meaning a political environment of tranquility and stability, a sound and stable currency, and labor conditions under which an investor can be sure of being able to manage his own business without labor union or political interference.

Likewise, among the matters that the council must consider in order to consolidate the gains made under the stabilization program, are the economic problems of the universities and municipalities. The council has already presented a full report on the financial problems of the former, and it is to be hoped that the recommendations contained in that study will be published and carried out without further delay.

Prospects

The picture which I have just painted may seem to contain more shadow than light, but that is not the case, and some rays of light and hope are already in sight for the future.

This will depend on increased production, and agriculture

stands out above all as the industry which gives the most promise of achieving this goal within the coming months. In recent years, as a result of competition from imported products at the official rate of exchange and the immediate consequences of the agricultural reform, domestic agricultural production available for local trade has dropped to such an extent, as I have already pointed out, that imports of agricultural products amounted to $30 million per annum. Today, as a result of the stimulus given to agriculture by a free economy system, and of the assurances given to farmers by Point IV people, months before the actual date of the stabilization measures, we know that crops this year will surpass those of any year in recent times, and it is already evident that imports of agricultural products in 1957 will be considerably lower than in 1956. A $5 to $10 million drop in imports is equivalent, from the economic point of view, to the creation of a new export industry of that size. The drop in agricultural imports in 1957 and 1958, thanks to the stabilization program, will represent a higher figure than the entire exports of petroleum products.

The country is already almost self-sufficient in local meat products, and we no longer see the prestabilization spectacle of cattle purchased in Brazil and Argentina sold in Bolivia at an official price at the Bs. 190 rate and smuggled out again to the countries of origin, with enormous profits for the smugglers, the cattle then being again imported into Bolivia at the official exchange rate, thus forming an endless chain, with the steers following their own tails in their migrations across the frontiers. That indeed was a vicious circle which has been eliminated by the monetary reform.

Next among the factors which will mean increased national production is the development of the petroleum industry, and although there is a long step of perhaps five or six years between the initial concession contract and the eventual export of the product, there is meanwhile a continuous influx of funds into the country. I have been informed, for example, that for every $5 million of investment, approximately 80 per cent is represented by machinery and equipment from overseas, meaning that some $1 million is distributed within the country for royalties, wages, and local supplies, and in the shape of salaries paid to foreign technical personnel and expended within Bolivia. Thus, even in the preliminary stages, investments by reputable oil and mining enterprises have great importance for Bolivia, and the first favorable reports that come from the oil fields will arouse enormous interest on the part of investors of every kind and from every country.

Of more immediate interest to Bolivia would be the possible investment in productive enterprises on the part of the World Bank (IBRD). Negotiations with this agency were halted by *the intervention of the Vice-President in* the matter of the bonds, *but I trust that*

*the Foreign Minister can settle the matter on his visit to the United
States,* although we can never recover the time lost.

Another prospect is the continuation of American aid, but I must
point out that this aid cannot be taken for granted. I should like to
show you Chart IX (see Fig. 16, p. 596) from which you will see that,
over the past three years, the Bolivian taxpayer has paid, in taxes
and customs duties, less than one-half as much as the American
taxpayers — among which I include myself — have paid to support the
Bolivian budget. In the current year, according to the budget, the
government tax collections should be somewhat higher than the
American contributions, but this figure is solely an estimate, and
from the results thus far it seems almost inevitable that the American taxpayer will continue to carry the major portion of the load.

*The U.S. Congress does not have a copy of this chart, but it
should have the figures, and it does not seem likely that it will look
favorably on further U.S. aid to Bolivia unless Bolivia settles the
matters of the bondholders and ex-owners of the mines as soon as
possible, and thus* demonstrates, beyond all doubt, its determination
to carry out the full stabilization program which it presented when
it requested financial assistance.

*I also consider it quite unlikely that Congress will authorize
any form of aid that makes it possible for the government of Bolivia,
directly or indirectly, to go on expanding its activities in the industrial or economic sphere, in view of the disastrous consequences of
those activities in the past.* The bulk of the almost $300 million of
capital consumed in recent years, according to Chart VI (Fig. 8, p.
490), has been dissipated in projects, supposedly for economic diversification, but without having produced any increase whatsoever
in production and with not the slightest probability that these investments will prove to be profitable in the future.*

(At this point, I summarized briefly the way in which money had
been wasted in the sugar mill at Guabirá, the cement factory in
Sucre, the irrigation project in Villa Montes, the cattle project in
Reyes, as examples of the profligacy and uselessness of government "investment" in Bolivia. As this has been outlined in full
in Appendix IV, it is omitted here; it was not released to the
press.)

---

*The expression of opinion as to the expected action of Congress, here
and in the preceding paragraph, was admonitory rather than anticipatory,
as I was fully aware of the fact that Congress had only the vaguest concept of the true state of affairs and that ICA and the State Department
would do their best to keep that concept vague.

Conclusions

It may be that this report has given an impression that stabilization is at the point of collapse, and if so, I wish with all my heart and with all the vehemence of which I am capable to declare that any such impression is completely false.

The stabilization measures already taken have had a resounding success, as I showed at the beginning of my report, and when the program is completed with the promulgation of the measures already approved by the council and the others which I have just set forth, there is no doubt whatsoever that Bolivia can overcome the temporary difficulties of the present moment, and that it will go forward towards a future *of hope,* of abundance, and of prosperity.

Bolivia is at the crossroads, and it is not too late to take the right road which the President of the Republic has marked out for us with a program of monetary stabilization and sound government finance. The departures from the program thus far, although serious — and I would be remiss in my duty as an adviser if I were to deny it — need not be fatal, but it is essential to eliminate not only the errors which have been incurred but likewise the cause of these errors. In other words, the government should use every means of informing the public with respect to the significance of the stabilization program and with respect to the circumstances that brought the country to last year's crisis and which make the present measures essential.

Therein lies the great failure of the program up to the present — that the public has not been informed of the truth of the present situation and its causes in order that the people may know fully the reasons for the measures taken and the reason why it is impossible to depart from those measures or to take other steps that might seem plausible.

The attacks against the stabilization measures have been widely disseminated, including suggestions and demands that wages should be increased without affecting the rate of exchange, that the debts of the Central Bank should all be paid, and other suggestions, which might appear quite reasonable simply because the reasons why they are impossible under present circumstances have not been broadcast.

It has been forgotten that truth is the best weapon against honest error, and that the public has the right to know the truth; that the government cannot hope to have the support of the public for a program as heroic as that of stabilization unless the people know the facts demonstrated by the charts presented in the course of this report — in order that they may realize the enormous waste of capital over the past five years, the absolute lack of government resources at the present time for any projects whatsoever, and the fact that all the government development projects and all the government interventions in the national economy have accomplished nothing but to leave the country poorer than ever.

In that way, the people can decide whether *they wish to listen to the advice of those who brought the country to the utter ruination of 1956, and who continue to proffer advice that is incompatible with reality, or whether* they prefer to accept the new course laid out by the government of President Siles with the stabilization program, living within their resources and understanding that there can be no real increase in wages or salaries that does not correspond to an equivalent increase in production.

But if the truth with respect to the past is to be broadcast there should likewise be broadcast the truth regarding the future. There is no reason to speak of "austerity," "abnegation," or "sacrifice" unless austerity means not spending more than one earns, unless abnegation means not living on borrowed money or gifts, and unless sacrifice means to earn a living by the sweat of one's brow.

The truth in Bolivia, as in any other country, is that the people can only consume what they produce — except for some extraordinary and temporary circumstance such as American aid — and if they wish to eat better and live better, they will have to produce more. There is nothing this government or any other government can do to change this postulate, and no increase of wages or control of prices, or any other measure, can change it in the slightest.

What the government can do is to remove the obstacles in the path of prosperity, to offer a favorable climate for work, savings, and the investment of capital, without political or labor disturbances or interferences, thus permitting private initiative and free enterprise, great and small, to increase the economic development and diversification of the country and the prosperity of its inhabitants.

Bolivia is perhaps the richest country in the world in the value of its natural resources per capita. To profit from this wealth, nothing is needed but human labor and enterprise and the investment of capital. *Three hundred millions of dollars of capital have already been consumed under a regime of government development and operation, and the consequences are seen in the fact that national production has diminished and that the people remain submerged in poverty.*

Thus no other road remains for the development of the national economy but private investment, domestic and foreign, and conscientious and diligent labor on the part of the workers, without strikes and without interruptions.

The future lies in the hands of the Bolivians themselves; and, with the greater productivity resulting from human effort, private capital, and the enormous wealth of the soil and subsoil, Bolivia can look forward to an era of prosperity such as it has never had in its history. This does not mean sacrificing the enduring conquests of the Revolution — namely, universal suffrage, the distribution of the large estates, elimination of a mining empire more powerful than the state itself, and, now, monetary stabilization — but rather preserving those conquests under a regime of monetary and financial integrity.

NOTES

NOTES

These notes consist of citations, dates, or statistical or other material to substantiate statements made in the text, except that, for Bolivian readers and to complete the historical record of stabilization in Bolivia, the names of persons and other materials not of general interest are likewise included. Any notes believed to be of interest to the general reader are placed as footnotes in the text. All newspaper references are to La Paz papers unless otherwise indicated.

Preface

1. *Rebelión de las Masas,* p. 67.
2. *Presencia,* January 23, 1960.
3. Draft contract sent to me on May 2, 1956, in accordance with an understanding reached April 9-10 with Rollin S. Atwood, Harry Yoe, *et al.* of ICA. The contract was never executed, owing to objections of the government Accounting Office to a contractual arrangement for more than one year on a $75 per diem basis. Instead, I was employed on the basis of a standard "Application for Federal Employment" executed in Washington on May 15, 1956, and appointed with the title Monetary Stabilization Adviser in Foreign Service rank FSR-1. The terms of reference stipulated in the contract remained unchanged.
4. Editorial, *Última Hora,* October 3, 1958.

Part I

1. Harold Osborne, *Bolivia: A Land Divided* (3d ed., London: Oxford University Press, 1964), p. 1.
2. Bolivian areas and altitudes from Osborne, pp. 3, 6-7; Zondag report, pp. 20-21; Keenleyside report, pp. 51-52. Llanos population computed from tables in Zondag report, p. 216, and ECLA report, p. 252.
3. Osborne, pp. 2-3.
4. Conversation with Federico Ahlfeld, author of *Los Yacimientos Minerales de Bolivia* (La Paz: Privately printed, 1941) and *Mapa de los Yacimientos Minerales de Bolivia* (Buenos Aires:

Privately printed, 1946); Raymond M. Gilmore, "Fauna and Ethnozoology of South America," in *Handbook of South American Indians*, Bureau of American Ethnology Bulletins, No. 143, ed. Julian H. Steward (7 vols.; Washington, D.C., 1946-50), VI, 438-39.

5. Zondag report, pp. 98, 237. The percentages are for 1940-50; the importance of tin has declined in later years but varies according to relative prices as well as output. Petroleum is a recent addition to the export trade. Note that tungsten is sometimes classified in export figures as wolfram.

6. Percentages computed from table in ECLA report, p. 251. See p. 744, n*30*, for tin prices.

7. Keenleyside report, p. 53; ECLA report, p. 252; J. Alden Mason, "Languages of South American Indians," *Handbook of South American Indians*, VI, 224.

8. Gilmore, p. 440. See also Gilmore, pp. 435-54 for references on altiplano flora and fauna.

9. Carl O. Sauer, "Cultivated Plants of South and Central America," *Handbook of South American Indians*, VI, 496, 513; ECLA report, p. 255; Osborne, pp. 21-22.

10. Sauer, pp. 333-39, 538-41; Osborne, p. 22; ECLA report, p. 255; Zondag report, pp. 20-22.

11. Osborne, pp. 88-90.

12. One million, according to Keenleyside report, p. 54; over three million according to American Embassy, *Quarterly Economic Summary* (February 7, 1964, p. 4), which places present stock at two to three million, "less than before the 1952 revolution."

13. Zondag report, p. 151; ECLA report, p. 255. Julian Duguid, *Green Hell* (New York: Century, 1931).

14. Sauer, pp. 507-9; ECLA report, p. 255; Keenleyside report, pp. 53-54.

15. Osborne, p. 91.

16. This and the two following paragraphs are based almost entirely on Mason, pp. 196-275.

17. Luis Peñaloza, *Historia Económica de Bolivia* (La Paz: Imprenta El Progreso, 1953), Vol. I, pp. 143-52.

18. This and the preceding two paragraphs are based largely on Osborne, pp. 34, 93-94. Other population figures from Zondag, pp. 19-20, 26; and United Nations, *Report of the Commission of Enquiry on the Coca Leaf* (Lake Success, N.Y.: U.N. Economic and Social Council, 1950), p. 55. The Hosmann citation is from Elena Hosmann, *Ambiente de Altiplano* (Buenos Aires: Editorial Peuser, 1945), p. 48.

19. Keenleyside report, p. 94; Olen E. Leonard, *Santa Cruz: A Socioeconomic Study of an Area in Bolivia* (Washington, D.C.: U.S. Dept. of Agriculture, 1948), p. 15; ECLA report, p. 252;

Richard W. Patch, "Bolivia: U.S. Assistance in a Revolutionary Setting," in Council on Foreign Relations, *Social Change in Latin America Today* (New York: Harper & Bros., 1960), p. 113.

20. Ellsworth Huntington, "The Adaptability of the White Man to Tropical America," *Latin America*, ed. George H. Blakeslee (New York: G. E. Stechert, 1924), p. 368.

21. Zondag report, p. 78; Keenleyside report, p. 92.

22. Leonard, *Santa Cruz*, p. 54. Leonard, *Cantón Chullpas: A Socioeconomic Study in the Cochabamba Valley of Bolivia* (Washington, D.C.: U.S. Dept. of Agriculture, 1948), pp. 56-60, gives this percentage as well as a number of tables showing family expenditures for different items, by expenditure brackets, and averages, but the "all other" category (which may be chiefly *fiesta* expenses) is so large — as large as alcohol — that no aggregate expenditure for coca, alcohol, and *fiestas* is possible. In his *Santa Cruz* study, pp. 52-59, Leonard gives only percentages, by expenditure brackets, with no money amounts, so that no breakdown is possible. The conclusion as to coca, alcohol, and *fiesta* expenditures in the altiplano is that of knowledgeable Bolivians but is without substantiating data.

23. United Nations, *Report of the Commission of Enquiry on the Coca Leaf*, pp. 28-32.

24. William H. Prescott, *History of the Conquest of Peru,* Book II, chaps. iii, iv, pp. 275-81. Garcilaso-de la Vega, *Comentarios Reales de los Incas,* 2d ed. (Buenos Aires: Emecé Editores, 1945), pp. 34-37, 179-84, 237-38.

25. Osborne, p. 62. George McBride also states: "...the Bolivian people live in ill-concealed fear of a general uprising." (*The Agrarian Indian Communities of Highland Bolivia* [New York: Oxford University Press, 1921], p. 27).

26. Keenleyside report, p. 2.

27. Fonda, pp. 29-30.

28. Osborne, p. 61.

29. Cordell Hull, *The Memoirs of Cordell Hull* (New York: Macmillan Co., 1948), p. 1388. See also U.S. Army, *Area Handbook for Bolivia*, pp. 673-82.

30. Keenleyside report, pp. 95-96.

31. The preceding paragraphs on the background of the 1952 Revolution are based largely on Alberto Ostria-Gutiérrez, *Un Pueblo en la Cruz* (2d ed., Santiago, Chile: Editorial del Pacífico, 1956). The facts have been checked with Robert J. Alexander, *The Bolivian National Revolution* (New Brunswick, N.J.: Rutgers University Press, 1958) and in conversation with friends in the MNR, between January and June, 1957, in order to guard against partisan distortion. The May 3, 1951, pact

between José Fellman-Velarde (representing the MNR), Jorge Quiroga-Vargas (Communist Party), and Juan Lechín (Trotskyite and FSTMB) is confirmed by Jules Dubois, *Operation America* (New York: Walker & Co., 1963), pp. 212-13, on the basis of photostatic evidence. The content of the photostat was fully reported in the press at the time.

32. Alexander, *The Bolivian National Revolution*, pp. 230, 231.

33. Osborne, pp. 44, 61. Cf. Antezana-Paz, p. 18; Zondag report, pp. 26, 28, 33.

34. September 27, 1954, report by Henry S. Bloch to Sune Carlson.

35. Ostria-Gutiérrez, pp. 195-96 (*The Tragedy of Bolivia*, pp. 122-23). Information on MNR militia given by a high MNR official. See also the U.S. Army, *Area Handbook for Bolivia*, pp. 660, 673, 682-89, which places the militia at 50,000-70,000 in June, 1956.

36. This statement was relayed to me by a person of cabinet rank, close to the President, and was borne out by later statements at the time of Ñuflo Chávez' resignation.

37. Charles A. McQueen, *Bolivian Public Finance* (Washington, D.C.: Bureau of Foreign and Domestic Commerce, 1925), p. 63; *Pick's Currency Yearbook* (New York: Pick's Currency Report, 1955).

38. See *International Financial Statistics,* X (1957) for "free" rates. With respect to the "street rate," I personally cashed a $100 check at Bs. 13,800 at the Central Bank the first week in July, 1956, and was informed that in foreign exchange agencies the rate was Bs. 14,000. The Zondag report, chap. iii, annex, p. 11, cites "street rates" of Bs. 9,000 at the end of June, 1956, although the "free" auction rate was only Bs. 6,697 (*International Financial Statistics,* X [1957] shows Bs. 7,360). In Zondag's opinion, the "street rate" was of greater significance than the auction rate (*ibid.,* p. 41; cf. ECLA report, pp. 57 ff).

39. *Los Decretos del 14 de Mayo de 1953* (La Paz: Ediciones S.P.I.C., 1953), pp. 14-52; ECLA report, p. 78; Franklin Antezana-Paz, *La Política Monetaria de Bolivia* (La Paz: Banco Central de Bolivia, 1954), pp. 6, 7, 22-25, 37-43; Paz-Estenssoro, *Mensaje del Presidente,* from *Los Decretos...,* pp. 5-13. Free rates of exchange from *Pick's Currency Yearbook, 1955.* According to Dr. Antezana-Paz, there were eight or nine different rates in force prior to May, 1953 (pp. 5, 15) while, by the end of 1954, the Zondag report cites thirteen rates of exchange (chap. iii, annex, p. 5).

40. ECLA report, pp. 79-80.

41. Average counterpart rates computed from tables in Zondag,

pp. 270, 271. Free rates from *International Financial Statistics* [X], (January, 1957).

42. Zondag report, pp. 29, 32, 43.

43. Zondag report, pp. 24, 28, chap. iii, annex, pp. 5-10.

44. The Zondag report (chap. iv, annex 1, p. 2) refers to these higher rates as a "bonus." The ECLA report refers to them as a "subsidy" (p. 79). Actually, they represented neither bonuses nor subsidies but a partial compensation for the artificially low rates paid by the Central Bank for COMIBOL and other exports. See also Zondag report, p. 166.

45. Gesualdo A. Costanzo, *Programas de Estabilización Económica en América Latina* (Mexico City: Centro de Estudios Monetarios Latinamericanos, 1961), p. 80. Zondag report, p. 161, shows commissary prices of Bs. 23.90, Bs. 8.70, Bs. 16.90, and Bs. 11.20, respectively, per kilo. The conversions in the text are made at the rate of Bs. 7,360 per dollar, based on June, 1956, quotations in *International Financial Statistics*. The FBD report, Vol. III, p. 82, gives comparable figures: rice $\frac{1}{10}$ cent; sugar $\frac{1}{18}$ cent; can of sardines $\frac{1}{5}$ cent; can of corned beef ($\frac{1}{2}$ kilo) $\frac{1}{5}$ cent; etc.

46. The Zondag report cites beef prices at Bs. 500-Bs. 1,200 per kilo (pp. 219, 161), a figure based on the General Bureau of Statistics' figures; but Antezana-Paz considered those prices unreliable and had an unofficial index compiled by the Central Bank showing considerably higher prices even in the cheapest workers' market. The Bs. 8,000-Bs. 10,000 figure was used in my report to the President and Cabinet in April, 1957 (Appendix VI) and was accepted by that audience as accurate, but this applies only to purchases by the wealthiest classes. The Central Bank index, used by the National Monetary Stabilization Council in its basic computations, showed a price of Bs. 1,200 per kilo for "beef with bone" at the cheapest market place, where there were long waiting lines and little meat available (see also ECLA report, p. 269).

47. The estimate of 80,000 workers who benefitted from the cheap commissaries was given by President Siles in a speech to the COB congress, June 14, 1957. Siles placed the number of heads of family at 600,000 and the number of wage or salary earners at 150,000. On the other hand, the Zondag report (p. 217) and the ECLA report (p. 99) would indicate a total of some 300,000 wage earners, and elsewhere a figure of 170,000 is reported (p. 718, n*17*).

48. ECLA report, p. 82.

49. Figures in billions of bolivianos, as of December 31 of each year, except for mid-1956 figures as of June 30:

	1951	1952	1953	1954	1955	June 1956	Dec. 1956
Note circulation	4.16	6.48	12.39	21.12	42.36	75.11	160.02
Demand deposits	2.76	4.22	7.59	14.14	26.09	37.88	80.86
Total money supply	6.92	10.70	19.98	35.26	68.45	112.99	240.88
Net claims on government	2.73	5.70	16.91	23.75	51.21	90.45	183.66
Claims on private sector	2.19	2.84	2.87	4.42	8.37	12.00	23.32

Source: *International Financial Statistics.*

50. I.e., Zondag report, pp. 221-22 (circulation); 220, 224 (living costs); 224 (free market rate index); 249 (gold and foreign exchange reserves and current debt); 231 (internal debt); 67-69 (external debt). The figures for government borrowing and money supply, however, are those portrayed in Figure 1 and are from *International Financial Statistics* (see note 49).

51. The wording here is largely borrowed from Federal Reserve Bank of New York, *Monthly Review,* XLIV (April, 1964), p. 66, although it is likewise drawn from my recollections as a commercial banker from 1920-23.

52. Carl Snyder, Irving Fisher, J. W. Angell, Willford King, and other leading economists agree with Friedman and Schwartz (pp. 10, 11, 317-19, 410, 692) that the FRB could have attenuated the severity of the 1929-33 crisis by a timely increase in the money supply.

53. Mendoza-López, pp. 55-90, 133-44, 300; McQueen, *Bolivian Public Finance,* p. 59.

54. Mendoza-López, p. 144.

55. See Zondag report, p. 34; Keenleyside report, pp. 13, 15.

56. Antezana-Paz, pp. 34, 52, 57, 60. In November, 1956, at the time of applying for a stabilization loan, the Central Bank provided the council with figures showing a gold reserve of $1.0 million and foreign exchange of $2.7 million; less $6 million in bilateral account, $4.9 million in outstanding Central Bank letters of credit, and $7.7 million in collections outstanding against Bolivia — a net deficit position of $14.9 million. Several months later, it was learned that the Central Bank had given its guaranty on at least $10 million additional credits and drafts not shown in its accounting records.

57. Supreme Resolution 75434, November 13, 1957; Central Bank, 29th *Annual Report,* 1957, p. 152; Supreme Resolution 83198, March 23, 1959; Central Bank, 31st *Annual Report,* 1959, p. 168.

58. These percentages are from the Keenleyside report, p. 47. Other figures from Bolivian sources are cited in the ECLA report, pp. 10-11, showing decidedly lower percentages, at least for earlier years; but, from discussions with competent observers in Bolivia, it would seem that the mining industry's contribution to government revenues was certainly not lower than is indicated in the text. The 65-75 per cent figure is from the Fossati-Rangel reports.

59. ECLA report, p. 9. See also ECLA report, pp. 10, 30-33; Keenleyside report, pp. 47, 52; Zondag report, pp. 58, 98-99 for material in this and preceding paragraph. This was the $33 million "Nicolaus" loan, floated by Stifel-Nicolaus Investment Co., St. Louis, together with Equitable Trust Co. and Spencer Trask & Co., New York. For an informative report on the mining industry in Bolivia prior to the Revolution, see Aramayo, *Memorandum Sobre los Problemas de la Industria Minera de Bolivia* (Madrid: Imprenta Gráficas Reunidas, 1956). I have refrained from quoting from that report, as it may be considered biased, although Bolivia's problems appear to be discussed dispassionately, despite the source.

60. Keenleyside report, p. 47.

61. These computations are based on the statements of account published in *Moody's Manual of Investments, Industrials,* for 1953, pp. 1286-88. The material in this and the following paragraph of the text is based on *Moody's,* and on Zondag report, p. 61. The MNR Minister of Mines placed a $40.7 million valuation on the Big Three properties, as of December, 1951, which Zondag states is "probably far too low" (*ibid.,* p. 97).

62. The Longhorn Smelter referred to was subsequently purchased by Wah Chang Corporation and reactivated in April, 1958; *Metal Statistics, 1960* (New York: American Metal Market, 1960), p. 417. The material in this and the following paragraph is largely based on that publication, except that the amounts withheld and paid to the Big Three are taken from the FBD report, Vol. III, p. 4; see also Paz-Estenssoro, *Mensaje al Congreso, 1956,* p. 19.

63. Zondag report, pp. 2, 97-98, 102; FBD report, Vol. III, pp. 73-76, 115; statement to Stabilization Council by Goosen Broesma, COMIBOL general manager.

64. Breakdown of 1950 dollar wage computed from table in FBD report, Vol. III, p. 92. The official wage statistics published in the Keenleyside report, Appendix 6, p. 120, give a daily wage of $3.64 in 1948; but Keenleyside points out that this is unrealistic, as conversions were made at the official rate of exchange. He substitutes a figure of $2.55 (p. 47n), which is not far out of line with the FBD estimate. However, if the

percentages of the daily wage paid in the form of fringe benefits and commissary losses, shown in the ECLA report (p. 33),
are added to the $2.55 wage, a total payroll cost of $5.91 per
diem would be reached. Greater weight may be given to the
FBD figures, in view of the competence of the FBD staff and
the greater length of time at their disposal for the compilation
of facts. Nevertheless, the miners' payroll under private
operation may be placed at somewhere between $2.61 (FBD)
and $5.91 (U.N.) per diem. For a general survey of labor con-
ditions prior to the Revolution, including education, health,
social security, etc., see International Labor Office, *Labour
Problems in Bolivia* (Montreal: I.L.O., 1943).

65. Zondag report, p. 96; FBD report, Vol. II, p. 6.

66. FBD report, Vol. IV, pp. 84-85.

67. FBD report, Vol. IV, p. 86; Vol. II, pp. 2, 6, 37, 61; Vol. III,
pp. 5, 13.

68. FBD report, Vol. VII, p. 35; Zondag report, pp. 35, 106-7;
ECLA report, p. 36. The Mining Bank had originally been
chartered by Decree of July 24, 1936.

69. Zondag report, p. 106.

70. Data from ECLA report, pp. 191-92; Zondag report, pp. 29,
113-22.

71. These statements were made by the YPFB chief engineer,
Eduardo Hinojosa.

72. Zondag report, pp. 113-19; Alexander, *The Bolivian National
Revolution*, p. 159. Zondag waxes enthusiastic over the YPFB,
and Alexander refers to its "spectacular economic success,"
but neither of these authors was in a position to analyze the
YPFB accounts and finances, nor to appraise the shortcomings
of management in extending the company's short-term commitments far beyond its capacity, even after enactment of the
stabilization measures which made such credits illegal.

73. Zondag report, pp. 116-17.

74. ECLA report, pp. 191-205, p. 203 *(n)*.

75. ECLA report, p. 203 *n*; pp. 219-21. See Osborne, pp. 38-39.
Article VI of the treaty provided for development of Bolivian
oil resources by joint Brazilian-Bolivian efforts, "in compensation for the assistance given by the Brazilian government in
the preliminary studies, exploration, and drilling." *Última
Hora* (June 4, 1957) quite naturally points out that, as Brazilian assistance has been nil, there is no obligation on Bolivia
to respect the treaty.

76. Keenleyside report, p. 16. See U.S. Tariff Commission, *Economic Controls and Commercial Policy in Bolivia* (Washington, D.C.: U.S. Tariff Commission, 1946), p. 22, for background of Development Corporation.

77. See Zondag report, p. 26, for 1954 decree requiring segregation of dollar and boliviano accounts. In a letter of September 19, 1957, to *El Diario,* the president of the Development Corporation contends that the change in the corporation's accounting methods (i.e., the commingling of boliviano and dollar expenditures) was not for the purpose of concealing the facts, but at the suggestion of Price Waterhouse & Co. in 1951, and again in 1952 (at a time, of course, when the boliviano was comparatively stable). The change was made beginning January 1, 1953 (*La Nación,* September 20, 1957; *Última Hora,* September 20; *El Diario,* September 21). See also attack on George Eder by Carlos Salmón-Baldivieso, former General Manager of the corporation, for criticizing the corporation projects and accounting methods (*Última Hora,* November 5, 1957).

78. Nearly 83 per cent of ton miles of freight, and over 81 per cent of passenger miles; percentages computed from ECLA report, Tables 140, 142-50, pp. 211-20.

79. Cf. Osborne, pp. 31, 37-38; Zondag report, pp. 136-42; ECLA report, pp. 210-11, 216-19; Keenleyside report, pp. 74-76.

80. Budget analysis prepared by Ministry of Finance (see p. 118); also see Zondag report, pp. 138-40; ECLA report, p. 216. For explanation of rail freights, see ECLA report, pp. 219-20, 203*n;* Zondag, pp. 68, 61.

81. American Embassy, *Quarterly Economic Summary* A-67, August 13, 1964, p. 10.

82. ECLA report, pp. 220-21; Zondag report, p. 68.

83. Reception at Brazilian Embassy, June 8, 1957; conference with Ambassador Alvaro Texeira-Soares. Coronel Nunes, representative of PETROBRAS, and Messrs. Mario Pope de Figueredo and Haddock-Lobo, of the *Commisão Nacional de Petroleo,* were present, but I cannot recall which, if any, of these gentlemen were present at the time of the Ambassador's comment (see also p. 421n. Statement by Sen. Lourival Fontes from *Hanson's Latin American Letter,* August 24, 1957).

84. Zondag report, p. 148.

85. ECLA report, Table 170, p. 239; p. 241.

86. Keenleyside report, p. 98.

87. Cf. Zondag report, p. 17.

88. ECLA report, p. 249.

89. Zondag report, pp. 83-86; cf. Antezana-Paz, p. 16; Zondag report, p. 11; ECLA report, pp. 249, 264 (Table 188).

90. Based on ECLA report, p. 254. Other estimates show between $\frac{1}{2}$ per cent (Zondag report, p. 74) and 2 per cent (Keenleyside report, p. 53; Osborne, p. 111) under cultivation, but it is not clear whether these percentages refer to total land area or to the area of potentially usable land.

91. ECLA report, p. 250; Zondag report, p. 145.
92. Delio Jaramillo A., "La Reforma Agraria: La F.A.O., Bolivia y Guatemala," *La Nueva Economía,* I (October, 1961), pp. 587, 594. For evidence of the communist inspiration of the Mexican agrarian reform, see citations in Eder, "Urban Concentration, Agriculture, and Agrarian Reform," *Annals of the American Academy of Political and Social Science,* CCCLX (July, 1965), 27-47.
93. Land Tenure Center, *The Progress of Land Reform in Bolivia,* Discussion Paper 2 (Madison, Wis.: Land Tenure Center, University of Wisconsin, May, 1963), pp. 4-7, 11-13. According to an article published by the Royal Institute of International Affairs, Dr. Flores was a member of the staff of the U.S. Operations Mission in Bolivia, assigned to assist the Bolivian Land Reform Organization in its operations (*The World Today,* II (April, 1965), 182). This report was presumably based on the fact that the USOM/Bolivia, under its then director, worked very closely with Dr. Flores on the agrarian reform project. Castro Ferragut, an IDB official, notes that "a *minifundio* structure, equally undesirable and harmful, has spread" (Land Tenure Center, *The Progress of Land Reform in Bolivia,* p. 7).
94. Jaramillo, pp. 591, n. 2, 595, 598-99, 605-9, 613-14, 618; cf. Zondag report, p. 79.
95. Agnese Nelms Lockwood, *Indians of the Andes* (New York: Carnegie Endowment for International Peace, 1956), p. 378; cf. Zondag report, p. 81. The salt patches on the pasture lands around Cochabamba made the countryside, when seen from the air, appear to be covered with snow. The explanation of their origin is based on a conversation with Ross Moore, Director, USOM/Bolivia.
96. Dwight B. Heath, "Land Reform in Bolivia," *Inter-American Economic Affairs,* XII (1959), 3-27.
97. Lockwood, pp. 372, 379; Zondag report, p. vii.
98. Address to National Workers' Congress (Congreso Nacional de Trabajadores), *La Nación,* June 4, 1957.
99. Cf. Zondag report, pp. 77, 80, 81, 207; ECLA report, p. 270. A decennial *Festschrift* lauds President Paz-Estenssoro for having raised "the slaves of yesterday" to the dignity of human beings. Raul A. García, *Diez Años de Reforma Agraria en Bolivia: 1953-63* (La Paz: Dirección Nacional de Informaciones, 1963), pp. 11, 76.
100. Interview with Associated Press correspondent Richard G. Massock, quoted from Ostria-Gutiérrez, p. 198; Paz-Estenssoro, *Mensaje al Congreso,* 1956, p. 150. The figures from the farewell address of President Paz to Congress do not

coincide with figures given by U.S. sources. Zondag places U.S. aid, from July, 1953, through June, 1956, at $46,817,000 in food and fibers, including an estimated $8 million in U.S. surplus agricultural commodities, plus $13,296,000 in development assistance (Zondag report, Table LII, p. 270). However, these figures represent cost to the U.S. (the C.C.C.). The market value, supplied to me by USOM/Bolivia, was $34.1 million in commodities and $18.3 in development assistance, partly cash and partly the cost of services. The total value of U.S. aid for those fiscal years, and projected for the fiscal year ending June 30, 1957, according to the same source, was: 1954 — $9.4 million; 1955 — $20 million; 1956 — $23 million ($3 million taken from the 1957 allowance); 1957 — $18.6 million. The cost to the C.C.C. was at least $8.9 million higher (data incomplete for 1956).

101. Report signed by K. K. Henness, Director of Extension. SAI had been headed in that year by William J. Green, who returned to the United States in May, 1955, and was succeeded by Elton M. Smith, whose fine work I had an opportunity of observing in 1956-57.

102. USOM/Bolivia, *Point IV in Bolivia 1942-1960* (La Paz, 1960), p. 9.

103. See ECLA report, pp. 271-72; Zondag report, pp. 82, 182-85, 282. Ernest J. Sánchez, a bilingual U.S. citizen from New Mexico, headed the supervised credit activities.

104. Zondag report, pp. 78, 142-45, 188-89, 254-55; ECLA report, p. 250.

105. USOM/Bolivia, *Point IV in Bolivia;* Zondag report, pp. 186-87 (education); 187-88 (health and sanitation); 189-90 (public administration); 192, 282.

106. Zondag report, pp. 191, 192, 282.

Part II

1. Meeting with President Paz, June 8, 1956.
2. Meeting of organizing group, July 19, 1956.
3. Meetings of organizing group, July 5, 19, 1956.
4. Meeting of organizing group, July 5, 1956.
5. Meeting of organizing group, July 5, 1956.
6. Meetings of organizing group, July 5, 19, 1956.
7. Osborne, p. 61. See, for example, *La Nación* (the government paper), June 10, 1956, attributing the inflation to the Chaco War.
8. Ford, Bacon & Davis, Inc., *Mining Industry of Bolivia* (La Paz, 1956), especially Vol. II, p. 23. See *El Diario*, July 24, 25, 26,

27, 1956 (articles by Jose Sorneo, former Inspector General of the Central Bank) as an example of the theory that inflation was due to structural causes.

9. Article by Humberto Fossati, *El Diario*, July 31, 1956; conversations with Antezana-Paz, June and July, 1956. See also Antezana, pp. 19 and 36, for discussion of inflation forces up to 1954.

10. Zondag report, pp. 22, 225-31; Antezana-Paz, conversations, June and July, 1956.

11. Zondag report, pp. 41-43, 54, 168, 172; cf. Antezana, p. 17.

12. Zondag report, Annex to chap. III, p. 11; Osborne, p. 126; Keenleyside report, p. 12.

13. ECLA report, pp. 67, 74-76.

14. Metal exports in millions of dollars; value of boliviano in cents:

Year	Exports	Exchange Rate	Year	Exports	Exchange Rate	Year	Exports	Exchange Rate
1918	68.7	41.5	1931	16.0	‡35.4	1944	73.0	1.8
1919	40.7	35.4	1932	8.1	‡32.5	1945	73.9	1.5
1920	46.0	32.4	1933	14.6	‡21.2	1946	65.4	1.6
1921	14.0	22.9	1934	29.1	‡19.8	1947	75.2	1.5
1922	25.6	28.7	1935	43.5	‡23.9	1948	111.2	1.1
1923	31.2	31.1	1936	24.0	‡23.5	1949	99.0	0.82
1924	32.3	29.6	1937	32.9	4.1	1950	90.0	0.56
1925	*39.3	†36.5	1938	25.4	2.9	1951	145.6	0.50
1926	*41.4	†36.5	1939	31.9	2.3	1952	137.3	0.41
1927	*43.9	†36.5	1940	48.3	1.6	1953	109.8	0.11
1928	*39.5	†36.5	1941	58.3	1.8	1954	100.8	0.054
1929	44.3	‡36.0	1942	63.4	2.0	1955	97.9	0.025
1930	31.6	‡35.9	1943	78.1	1.9	1956	§87.6	§0.016

*Converted from bolivianos of a par value of 18 pence to dollars at the rate of 36.5 cents per boliviano. All export figures taken from various issues of the Central Bank *Bulletin*.

†Approximate values from the Kemmerer report. All other foreign exchange rates taken from various issues of the Central Bank *Bulletin*.

‡These are the "official free rates"; the free market rates were not available.

§Exports for 1956 are based on exports for the first four months multiplied by three. The foreign exchange rate for 1956 is the Central Bank free rate for May 31, 1956.

15. Dollar exports of metals and U.S. cents per boliviano shown in note 14 above. Bank note circulation from various issues of Central Bank *Bulletin*, viz. (in millions of bolivianos): 1918 — 26.0; 1919 — 26.9; 1920 — 33.9; 1921 — 27.4; 1922 — 24.4; 1923 — 26.5. Ratios (1918 base) computed by slide rule.

16. Bolivianos per dollar based on figures shown in note 14. Bank note circulation, see note 15, and following figures from Central Bank *Bulletin* (in millions):

1929	45	1936	210	1943	1,075	1950	3,327
1930	32	1937	252	1944	1,253	1951	3,967
1931	27	1938	288	1945	1,541	1952	6,214
1932	38	1939	369	1946	1,608	1953	11,600
1933	54	1940	476	1947	1,747	1954	20,049
1934	84	1941	642	1948	2,100	1955	39,198
1935	146	1942	818	1949	2,434	1956	54,937 (April 30)

17. Based on figures shown in notes 14 and 16, except for the cost of living in La Paz, which is taken from Central Bank *Bulletin* (1936 = 100), viz.: 1950 — 1,858; 1951 — 2,358; 1952 — 3,086; 1953 — 7,784; 1954 — 15,463; 1955 — 26,115; 1956 (May 31) — 43,500. Converted to 1951 = 100.

18. Translated from ECLA report, pp. 71, 73n.

19. Nestor Ortuño, Finance Ministry bureau chief, and Jorge Larrea, director of disbursements, are to be credited with this work. The data condensed in Table 3 bear the initials of Dr. Larrea, JLT; the data on government departments in Table 2 bear the initials NM. This fact is mentioned because too often the anonymous civil servants who do the work in government are ignored. In this case, the data compiled represented a truly Herculean labor. It may be the only case in which the budgeted or actual receipts and expenditures of a country operating on a multiple currency system have ever been tabulated on a realistic basis.

20. Central Bank, *Statistical Supplement*, XIV (December, 1956), 3.

21. This was not a regularly convened meeting of the council, but a special meeting at the presidential palace, attended by the President, the Ministers of Foreign Affairs, Finance, Economy, and Mines, and the author, with no secretary present.

22. The estimate of diversion of U.S. aid, and of inflationary impact, is based on conversations with Ross Moore, chief of U.S. Operations Mission; figures for 1955-56 counterpart funds and proceeds of sales are from USOM.

23. Bank note circulation from Central Bank; see note 20 above.

24. Zondag report, Tables LII, LIII, pp. 270, 271; periods chosen allow for a six-month lag between aid and counterpart.

25. *Pick's Currency Yearbook*, 1955.

26. Zondag report, Table LI, p. 269.

27. Report of Arthur Karasz, August, 1953.

28. Conversation with President Siles, October 16, 1956.

29. Fossati-Rangel report for the Coordination and Planning Commission.

30. Conversation with Eduardo Arze-Quiroga, July, 1956. ECLA places agricultural production at between $67.4 and $78.9 million, basing its estimate on *Servicio Agrícola Interamericano* estimates (ECLA report, Table 177, p. 251). Ross Moore, chief of the U.S. Operations Mission, considered that the production of subsistence farmers was somewhat underestimated, but he placed total agricultural production as "certainly under $100 million" before stabilization.

31. Private meeting with President-elect Siles, August 2, 1956.

32. Argentine *folkloristas* will recognize the latter proverb as paraphrased from *Martin Fierro* by José María Hernández (1834-86), but it is widely quoted throughout Latin America, and dates back to classical Greece, perhaps earlier.

33. Wilhelm Roepke, *Economics of the Free Society,* trans. Patrick M. Boardman (Chicago: Regnery, 1963), pp. 109-110.

34. Zondag report, Appendix I, p. 273.

35. See Zondag report, Annex to chap. iii, pp. 3, 5, for discussion of surcharges *(recargos)* and *revertibles;* Annex I to chap. iv for discussion of export licensing. See also ECLA report, pp. 78, 79.

36. It may be noted that this concept of free enterprise, free trade, and free foreign exchange, as the basis for a viable stabilization program, had been advocated by a Bolivian businessman even before the Revolution brought inflation to its galloping stage. Shortly after enactment of the stabilization program, *Última Hora* (January 11, 1957) called the attention of its readers to the "amazing" similarities between the ideas expressed by Aurelio Murillo in 1951 and those embodied in the program. See his pamphlet, *Donde Vamos con el Dirigismo Parcial?* (La Paz: En Marcha, 1951). While Murillo's little pamphlet scarcely purports to be a plan or a program, he appears to be one of the few Bolivians who realized how essential it was to establish a free market economy, even pointing out the necessity of reducing customs duties to eliminate smuggling, which was one of the aims of the completed program.

37. Antezana, pp. 40, 41; International Monetary Fund, *Annual Report* (Washington, D.C., 1954).

Part III

1. CONFERENCES IN WASHINGTON: *State Department* — Henry F. Holland, William Briggs, Maurice M. Bernbaum, Jack C. Corbett, James Corbett, Siegfried Garbuney, Harold Randall, A. M. Rosenson, Roy R. Rubottom, Jr., John Topping, Harry R. Turkel, Philip Williams, John Parke Young; *International*

Cooperation Administration — D. A. Fitzgerald, Henry J. Randall, De Witt L. Sage, Leonard Woods, Harry W. Yoe (Rollin S. Atwood was absent at the time, but I conferred with him in May and November); *Treasury Department* — W. Randolph Burgess, Andrew N. Overby, Charles Harley, Herman Koenig, Fred B. Smith, George H. Willis; *International Monetary Fund* — H. Merle Cochran, Jorge del Canto, Ivar Rooth, Frank A. Southard, Jr.; and others. CONFERENCES IN NEW YORK: *Foreign Bondholders Protective Council, Inc.* — Dana G. Munro, Kenneth M. Spang; *United Nations* — Hugh L. Keenleyside, Gustavo Martínez-Cabaña, Arthur Goldschmidt, Myer Cohen, Henry Cabot Lodge, Jr., Nathaniel King; *Chemical Corn Exchange Bank* — Harold H. Helm (Vice-Chairman), Isaac B. Grainger (Executive Vice-President), Charles E. Rance (Vice-President); *Colonial Trust Company* — Arthur S. Kleeman, President; *First National City Bank* — John F. Cannon, Jr. (Assistant Vice-President), Leo N. Shaw (Vice-President); *Grace National Bank* — Ralph S. Stillman, President; *Manufacturers Trust Company* — Horace Flanagan (Vice-President), Andrew L. Gomory (Executive Vice-President), John L. O'Halloran (Vice-President); and others.

2. Foreign Bondholders Protective Council, Inc., *Report 1955 Through 1957* (New York, 1957), pp. 35-43. Interest is computed from the data in that volume at the rates applicable to the respective bond issues for $17\frac{1}{2}$ years and for 26 years.

3. Central Bank, *Bulletin*, XXIV (January-June, 1953), 20, 58-60.

4. As of October 31, 1956, governmental debt to the Central Bank alone amounted to Bs. 204.6 billion (ECLA report, p. 70). By December total governmental debt was probably close to Bs. 250 billion.

5. *Última Hora,* September 21, 1956; *La Nación* and *El Diario,* September 22.

6. *El Diario,* September 24, 1956; *New York Times,* September 23, pp. 1, 39; September 24, p. 3; September 25, p. 15; September 26, p. 13; September 27, p. 15.

7. This alleged "promise" was supposedly made in July, 1956, at the meeting of hemisphere presidents in Panama; see *La Nación,* July 25, 1956, and *El Diario,* July 26, for alleged "promises" given by President Eisenhower as well as by Milton Eisenhower. A series of cables exchanged between the author, the Ambassador, and the State Department had very narrowly defined the statements to be made by President Eisenhower at that meeting, in order not to jeopardize the stabilization program; but of course there was nothing we could do to restrain the President's brother in his informal conversations.

8. *The Wine is Bitter* (New York: Doubleday, 1963), pp. 88-89, 274-96.
9. *Bolivia: 10 Años de Revolución,* p. 257.
10. *Farewell to Foggy Bottom* (New York: McKay, 1964), pp. 295-96.
11. *Última Hora,* October 30, 1956.
12. *Ibid.,* October 25, 1956.
13. Those present at the meeting at the house of John and Elaine Ohmans included: Arturo Ruescas, Edwin A. Moller, Hernando Poppe, Aníbal Aguilar, and Fuad Mujaes. The support of the stabilization program by the Departmental Federation of Chauffeurs and the Bolivian Confederation of Chauffeurs, representing the various transport workers' unions, is reported in *El Diario,* October 20, 1956.
14. *El Diario* and *La Nación,* October 27, 1956, and November 6, 7, 8, 9, 10, 11, 13, 1956. The meetings with the senators, labor leaders, and the MNR Political Committee, were arranged by the President. The meeting of the Political Committee was under the chairmanship of José Cuadros-Quiroga. Dr. Costanzo and Francisco Saenz of the IMF Mission accompanied me on this occasion to demonstrate the solidarity between our two missions and to help answer questions. I informed the group that the stabilization rate would probably not be over Bs. 13,000 (the then current free rate), but substantially higher than the official Bs. 190 rate. That announcement certainly must have confused the speculators. Others present were: Senators Federico Álvarez-Plata and Rubén Julio; Gastón Araoz, *Interventor* of the MNR Comando (Praetorian guard); and Señora Ela Campero de Davila of the MNR, whose role I can only surmise. Following the meeting, the Political Committee met with President Siles (*El Diario,* November 8, 1956) and pledged their support of the stabilization program, thanks largely to the efforts of Cuadros-Quiroga and Álvarez-Plata, or so I understand.
15. The wage-freezing decree and wage increases were approved by the council, calling as well for an employment freeze in government (i.e., that no vacancies would be filled). The decree was dated November 8 and published in *El Diario,* November 11, 1956.
16. *La Nación* and *El Diario,* October 18, 1956.
17. The ECLA report (p. 99) gives an "economically active" population of 1,210,000, of which 308,000 workers are employed in industries other than agriculture or service industries, or as artisans. The Zondag report (p. 217) shows a working population of 1,351,000, and 307,000 in other than agricultural, forestry, professional, domestic, and personal service activities.

The 150,000 figure for wage earners was used by President Siles (see above, p. 707, n *47*), while a 170,000 figure was used in Stabilization Council discussions, p. 449.

18. Meetings with Peter Antonelli, head of the Ford, Bacon & Davis Mining Survey Mission, October 23, 1956; with Raúl Gutiérrez-Granier, President, COMIBOL, October 25.

19. ECLA report, p. 20.

20. YPFB was represented at most of the Council meetings by the Acting President, Alberto Arze-Quiroga; the Vice-President of YPFB, Juan Luis Gutiérrez-Granier; the General Manager, Eduardo Hinojosa; Assistant General Manager, Alfonso Romero-Loza; Exploration Manager, Engineer Mauri; Operations Manager, Jorge Aldazoza; Administrative Manager, Luis Frías; and Inspector General, Clemente Dabalillo.

21. The Stabilization Council meetings were attended by the Director General of Railways, Gustavo Méndez, and Chief Engineer Gualberto Olmos.

22. The Stabilization Council meetings were attended by Alfonso Gumucio-Reyes, president of the Bolivian Development Corporation, and Joaquín Lemoine, General Manager.

23. The council meetings were attended by Jorge Salazar, President of the Mining Bank; Pablo Biggeman, General Manager; Alfredo Álvarez, Commercial Manager.

24. The Stabilization Council meetings were attended by Dr. Luis Bedregal-Rodo, General Manager of the CNSS.

25. Enacted as Decree 4539, December 15, 1956.

26. Decree 4540, December 15, 1956.

27. Decree 4541, December 15, 1956.

28. Decree 4545, December 15, 1956.

29. E.g., *El Diario*, October 30, 1956.

30. Figures supplied by the Finance Minister June 4, 1957, as of May 15. Included in a memorandum prepared by me, June 19, 1957, and issued by the Bolivian Embassy in Washington to the New York banks, August 15, 1957, in explanation of Bolivia's default on its commercial debts (Appendix V).

31. O. Ernest Moore, "The Stabilization of the Bolivian Peso," *Public Finance*, XIII (1958), 43, 57-58.

32. Decree 4538, December 15, 1956, arts. 37, 38.

33. Council meetings in November, 1956, attended by Raul Gutiérrez-Granier, Goosen Broesma, and Mario Vernaza; conferences with Peter Antonelli, chief of the FBD Mission, and with Gutiérrez and Broesma, in October, 1956.

34. B.L.S. wholesale commodity price index, converted to 1940 base.

35. The other members of the mission were Messrs. John R. Woodley (who remained in La Paz until August, 1957, to

cooperate with the National Monetary Stabilization Council and Central Bank), C. David Finch, Francisco R. Saenz, and Margaret Aspinwall. According to the press, the mission was met at the airport by high officials of the Finance Ministry, the Central Bank, and the U.N. Mission (*El Diario,* October 14, 1956). In actual fact, they were met only by Ernest Moore and Mr. and Mrs. George Eder. Whether or not the slight was intentional, they were doubtless thankful for the oxygen tanks we brought them and for the informality of the reception, which enabled them to retire to their hotel and recover from the 13,000-foot altitude before settling down to their strenuous undertaking.

Part IV

1. Press conference November 29, 1956; *El Diario,* November 30.
2. Letter, November 17, 1956, signed by Franklin Antezana-Paz.
3. Conference, November 18, 1956, with Ernest Moore and Roger Freeman, U.S. Financial Mission; Ross Moore, chief of USOM/Bolivia; Economic Counsellor Eugene Gilmore; Second Secretary Thomas Shields.
4. Taxes paid by Big Three taken from Fossati-Rangel report for National Planning and Coordination Commission, January-June, 1956, p. 109.
5. E.g., *El Diario,* November 24, 26, December 12, 1956; *Última Hora,* November 23, 1956, and December 1, 11, 1956; *La Nación,* December 12, 1956.
6. Speeches supporting the stabilization program were made by the following officials:

President Hernán Siles-Zuazo by radio, *La Nación,* November 28; to Congress, *Última Hora,* November 29; to the Association of Printing Trades, *La Nación,* November 29; and to the Army, *La Nación,* December 1. Juan Lechín-Oquendo, *La Nación,* November 27; *Última Hora,* November 29. Finance Minister Hugo Moreno-Córdova, *El Diario,* November 24, 30; *La Nación,* November 28. Secretary General of the FSTMB, Mario Torres-Calleja, and Minister of Mines Jorge Tamayo-Ramos, *El Diario,* November 26; *La Nación,* November 30, December 1. Minister of Economy Carlos Morales-Guillén, *La Nación,* November 29, 30. Minister of Labor Abel Ayoroa-Argandoña, *El Diario,* November 30. José Cuadros-Quiroga, Secretary General of the National Policy Committee of the MNR, *La Nación,* December 6.

Policy statements supporting the program were made by:

Bolivian Mine Workers' Federation, *La Nación*, November 29, December 1, *El Diario*, November 30, *Última Hora*, December 1. Federation of Industrial Employees, *La Nación*, November 29. National Manufacturers Association, (Remberto Capriles-Rico, President), *La Nación*, November 26, *Última Hora*, December 7. Bar Association, *El Diario*, November 30.

7. Brother Carlos Anasagasti, Titular Bishop of Caltadria and Apostolic Vicar of the Beni, *La Nación*, November 26; Brother José C. Rosenhammer, Apostolic Vicar of Chiquitos, *La Nación*, December 9, 1956.

8. *La Nación*, December 5, 1956.

9. Cable sent November 28, 1956. The cable from Ernest Moore was dated November 23, while the cable from Finance Minister Moreno-Córdova was dated November 24; but I was in New York from November 25 (Sunday) to November 27, and the messages were not delivered until November 28 and 29, respectively.

10. Dr. Antezana later informed the Stabilization Council that, in the letter officially filed with the IMF, he had been requested to delete this expression of gratitude on the ground that an international institution should not acknowledge indebtedness to an individual. The account of the proceedings before the IMF Board is based on Dr. Antezana's report to the Stabilization Council.

11. IMF *Annual Report*, 1954, pp. 132, 134-35; 1957, p. 125.

12. See list of banks and bankers, p. 716, n *1*.

13. Press release, June 17, 1958, Foreign Bondholders Protective Council, Inc.

14. *El Diario*, November 24, 1956.

15. Letter from Roger A. Freeman, December 5, 1956, to President Siles.

16. *La Nación*, *El Diario*, December 12, 1956.

17. The President's radio address, together with the text of Decrees 4538 and 4541, appeared in the press on December 17, 1956.

18. *La Nación*, *El Diario*, *Última Hora*, December 17, 1956.

19. *Ibid.*, December 20, 1956.

20. *Ibid.*, December 27, 1956.

21. *Ibid.*, December 17, 1956.

22. My telegram (unclassified) to the Secretary of State, December 19, 1956.

23. All La Paz papers, December 17-22, 1956.

24. *El Diario*, *La Nación*, December 17, 1956.

25. *La Nación*, December 17, 19; *Última Hora*, December 20, 1956.

26. *El Diario*, December 18, 1956.

27. *Última Hora*, December 18, 1956.

28. *El Diario,* December 19, 1956.
29. *La Nación,* December 20, 1956. *El Diario,* which supported the stabilization program from the beginning, reported (December 19) "the natural anxiety of the people" at the time. See Articles 34-38 of the Bolivian Constitution for a definition of the powers of the President under a state of siege.
30. My letter to President Siles, December 21, 1956. This concept of equating prosperity with abundance, and abundance with production, was suggested by a friend in Argentina, William Cook, an American businessman. I used it to good effect in all my speeches: "We all want to be prosperous...," concluding with an exhortation to increase productivity.
31. *La Nación,* December 25, 1956.
32. The statements quoted here and in the following three paragraphs were made by Minister of Labor Abel Ayoroa-Argandoña, Minister of Public Works Carlos F. Tovar-Baldivieso, Minister of Mines Jorge Tamayo-Ramos, Finance Minister Hugo Moreno-Córdova, and Executive Vice-President of the Planning Commission Miguel Gisbert-Nogué.
33. Decree 4538, December 15, 1956, Art. 30.
34. *Ibid.,* Art. 31.
35. *El Diario,* December 23, 1956. Statement by Dr. José Lucio Alvéstegui, President, National Mining Association.
36. The committee consisted of Ing. Gustavo Méndez, Director of Government Railways; Ing. Marcelino Guzmán, Chief of the Bureau of Municipal Electrical Services; Mario Vernaza, a director of COMIBOL; Dr. Santiago Sologuren, Legal Adviser to the Council; and, at the suggestion of President Siles, Dr. José Valdivieso.
37. *Última Hora,* December 20, 1956.
38. *El Diario,* December 20, 1956.
39. *La Nación,* December 30, 1956.
40. *El Pueblo,* December 22, 27, 1956.
41. *La Nación,* December 24, 1956.
42. *Última Hora,* December 24, 1956.
43. *La Nación,* December 27, 1956. The following day the same paper carried an editorial urging everyone to work harder and produce more to ensure the success of the new economic program.
44. See *La Nación,* December 27, 28, 1956, and *El Diario,* December 28, for an account of the COB convention.
45. *New York Times,* December 29, 30, 1956; La Paz papers, December 28-30.
46. *La Nación, El Diario, Última Hora,* December 29-31, 1956; January 3-5, 1957.
47. *El Diario,* December 29, 1956.

48. *La Nación, El Diario, El Pueblo,* January 1, 1957.
49. Roepke, *Economics of the Free Society,* pp. 247-49.

Part V

1. Law of December 6, 1957.
2. Zondag report, p. 172.
3. See decree, as published in *La Nación,* January 25; *El Diario,* February 1, 1957. The date of the decree remained unchanged, January 24, 1957, despite the subsequent correction.
4. Decree-law May 8, 1957; *El Diario,* May 16.
5. Zondag report, p. 172.
6. Decree-law 4592, February 27, 1957 (*La Nación,* February 28, March 15).
7. Letter reported to have been drafted by Jean Peset for the signature of Director of Revenues Medinacelli.
8. Testimony of Mayor Jaime Otero-Calderón.
9. Decree-law, February 27, 1957 (*La Nación,* February 28).
10. Mario Torres-Calleja, General Secretary of the FSTMB, had been appointed Minister of Mines to replace Jorge Tamayo-Ramos, who in turn replaced Carlos Morales-Guillén as Minister of Economy. Mario Vernaza-Perou, a director of COMIBOL, had cooperated with Tamayo in drafting the original tax schedule. The U.N. mining expert, André Gratacap, was highly regarded in all circles.
11. Decree-law February 14 (*El Diario,* February 15).
12. Letter from Deputy Nicolás Bernal.
13. Report by Eduardo Arze-Quiroga, Subsecretary of Foreign Affairs.
14. Decree-law enacted March 28 (*La Nación,* March 29).
15. See statement to this effect by Minister of Finance (*La Nación,* January 10, 1957).
16. The ECLA report, published prior to the tariff revision, comments on the shortcomings of the December 15, 1956, tariff and mentions that the council was in the process of preparing new rate schedules, without, however, pointing out that the December tariff had been drafted on the advice of U.N. experts (ECLA report, p. 84; p. 136).
17. In *La Nación,* May 10, 1957, the Finance Minister gives a figure of 2,000 *relojes* as having passed through customs, but the figure actually received from the Collector of Customs at the council meeting was 378. Possibly the larger figure includes clocks (*relojes* can mean either); the Swiss figure of 102,523 is for watches alone.

18. The norms were later given to the press by the Finance Minister (*La Nación,* May 10, 1957).

19. Some changes were recommended by the council later, while the bill was still pending in the Cabinet; e.g., a 20 per cent duty on rice and flour, April 3; a reduction in the duty on glass, April 5.

20. Consultation with Fernando Gasser, La Bélgica mill, and with Bolivian Development Corporation about the Guabirá mill.

21. Meeting with Ñuflo Chávez-Ortiz, April 11, 1957.

22. The Finance Minister reported to the council that only changes of secondary importance were made; i.e., a 75 per cent general limit for the protection of industry instead of 60 per cent, minor changes for rice and tobacco, and the changes in the automobile and watch duties referred to in the text. The decree was published in *La Nación,* May 8, 1957.

23. Petitions of Forestry Export Association and Bolivian Soap Manufacturers Association (*Última Hora,* May 25, 1957).

24. *El Diario,* August 30.

25. Keenleyside report, pp. 32-33, 38-39.

26. Zondag report, pp. 172-73.

27. Keenleyside report, p. 33.

28. Jasper S. Costa, *Some Aspects of Revenue Administration in Bolivia* (Washington, D.C.: International Cooperation Administration, 1958), p. 49.

29. American Embassy *Quarterly Economic Summary* A-354, October 31, 1963, p. 9.

30. For a description of budgetary procedures and practices, and prior budgets, see Zondag report, pp. 26-28, 227-28; Keenleyside report, pp. 22-24, 29-32.

31. The budget, as published in *La Nación,* February 15, 1957, shows an increase of Bs. 22.8 billion above the figures in Table 4, but the actual increase was Bs. 36 billion.

32. The phrase in quotation marks refers to a statement made by Harry R. Turkel, a State Department official accompanying the Collins mission.

33. Letter from Ross Moore to Hugo Moreno-Cordova, April 2, 1957.

34. Decree, March 15, 1957. Note that Bolivia had maintained a separate foreign exchange budget since 1954, but as the government accounts and part of the private sector accounts were carried at the official rate of Bs. 190 to the dollar, those budgets were meaningless and misleading (see Zondag report, p. 251).

35. Testimony of Dr. Antezana and others before the Stabilization Council.

36. Decree 4337, March 8, 1956 (see Zondag report, pp. 35-37).

Also Decree 4445, July 5, 1956; Central Bank, 28th *Annual Report*, 1956, p. 39.

37. To be sure, Hamlet would "take arms against a sea of troubles," but I prefer to mix my own metaphors.

38. Decree 4559, January 22, 1957 (*La Nación*, January 23, 1957).

39. The Superintendent of Banks, Victor Maldonado-Arce, attended the meeting to assist the council in its deliberations. Representing the banks, in defense of their petition, were Rufo Miranda B. (Manager, Banco Mercantil), Oswaldo Siles (Manager, Banco Popular del Perú), Hugo Zuazo-Rivera (Manager, Crédito Hipotecario de Bolivia), Jorge A. Saenz (President of same), Enrique Arellano (Manager, Banco Nacional), Assistant Manager Forgues of the Banco Comercial é Industrial, Fernando Viaña (Assistant Manager, Banco Colombo-Boliviano). See report of Ernest Moore in answer to the published petition of the bankers (*Última Hora*, February 8, 1957).

40. Decree, February 14, 1957 (*La Nación*, February 15); Circular C.5/57, Superintendency of Banks, February 1, 1957; *La Nación*, February 18.

41. Central Bank regulation, April 8, 1957 (*El Diario*, April 9).

42. Decree 4582, February 14, 1957, repealing Decree 4337, March 8, 1956 (Central Bank, 29th *Annual Report*, 1957, pp. 46, 126).

43. Decree 4648, May 14, 1957 (*La Nación*, May 16); editorial, *El Diario*, May 16; Central Bank, 29th *Annual Report*, 1957, pp. 137-38.

44. See Zondag report, pp. 34-35.

45. Keenleyside report, pp. 16-18; see also Zondag report, pp. 180-81.

46. *Última Hora*, September 3, 1957. The quotations are from O. Ernest Moore, "The Stabilization of the Bolivian Peso," *Public Finance*, XIII (1958), 63.

47. Minister of Mines Tórres' status as an agent is confirmed by his statement to the Stabilization Council that he had cleared a certain point with Lechín and believed that Lechín would accept the proposal made by the council.

48. At the March 12 meeting, the Finance Minister reported that $319,000 in merchandise was en route to Bolivia, or in customs, that had been purchased with exchange bought on the free market, probably at Bs. 12,000-Bs. 14,000 to the dollar; in addition, a further $781,000 of merchandise had been imported since stabilization with exchange previously purchased on the free market at approximately those rates. The Minister of Economy reported that approximately $5 million was outstanding in uncashed *revertibles, remanentes,* and *bonos de sobreproducción,* of which $2.6 million would be used for the payment of salaries to foreign *técnicos* and for the payment of

commissions, all payable in foreign exchange; $1.4 million for imports of materials and supplies and $1 million for machinery. At a later meeting, the General Manager of the Mining Bank, Pablo Biggeman, reported that foreign exchange payments due at the Bs. 190 rate to private mines for shipments made prior to stabilization, or payments still outstanding for *bonos de sobreproducción*, amounted to $1,269,000, of which $643,000 would be used for the importation of vehicles and parts, $248,000 for materials, supplies, and tools, and $378,000 for machines. Also due and pending payment were $1,750,000 in *remanentes*, a total on both accounts of approximately $3 million. This figure did not include amounts due to the agricultural sector. Ten days later, however, the Assistant General Manager of the Bank, Rafael Montenegro, gave completely different figures which are not reported here, as they do not even add up correctly.

49. Agenda for April 3, 1957, meeting. Many of the agenda items were held over for later meetings but, per contra, new problems were constantly arising so that the council was never able to catch up with its agenda, at least during my term of office.

50. Decree 4598, March 15, 1957; Resolution, April 6, 1957 (*La Nación*, April 7, 1957; Central Bank, 29th *Annual Report*, 1957, p. 129).

51. Decree, May 13, 1957, Art. 7 (*El Diario*, May 15, 1957).

52. *Ibid.*, Arts. 1-5.

53. The cooperative was the Cooperativa Industrial Boliviana, S.A., of Cochabamba, and Bolivians will have no difficulty in identifying the persons involved. The $37,000 advance represented a 50 per cent credit on exports to Brazil for trade agreement dollars. Eventually, the export tax on Brazil nuts was eliminated entirely; Decree 6378, February 20, 1963 (Central Bank, 35th *Annual Report*, 1963).

54. The matter was first brought up in January by the head of the Planning Commission, Miguel Gisbert-Nogué, and the Minister of Mines, Mario Torres-Calleja. To avoid possible misunderstanding in Bolivia, it must be added that another highly reputable attorney, Dr. Luis Adolfo Siles, was down in the accounts for a fee of $250 a month for several months; he is not the lawyer listed as the recipient of the $3,000 fee.

55. Decree, January 22, 1957 (*La Nación*, January 23, 1957).

56. Decree 4709, August 14, 1957 (Central Bank, 29th *Annual Report*, 1957, p. 143). See editorial in *Última Hora*, September 7, 1957. At that, the tax was less than the 12 per cent insisted upon by the labor ministers, but countered by the last-ditch resistance of the Finance Minister.

Part VI

1. Preliminary report to the council on a memorandum prepared by Peter Antonelli, Chief, FBD Mission, and José Parrado, Superintendent of Economic Studies, COMIBOL; conference with Raúl Gutiérrez-Granier (President of COMIBOL), Jorge Tamayo-Ramos (Minister of Economy, former Minister of Mines), Goosen Broesma (General Manager, COMIBOL), Peter Antonelli, and Parrado.
2. COMIBOL figures prepared March 12, 1957; revised by me, March 20; six months figures compiled by me, April 15, from COMIBOL accounts.
3. Conference with Gutiérrez and Broesma, May 10, 1957.
4. Credits authorized by the Stabilization Council: February 12, 1957 (Bs. 3.5 billion in addition to Bs. 6.5 billion authorized in 1956); February 21 (Bs. 6.5 billion); March 22 (Bs. 10 billion); April 12 (Bs. 7 billion); May 22 (Bs. 10 billion).
5. Council meeting at the presidential palace, resumed at COMIBOL office; present were Raúl Gutiérrez, Goosen Broesma, Mario Vernaza (COMIBOL director), Emilio Carvajal (Vice-President), José Parrado (Superintendent of Economic Studies), Herbert Weiss (Manager, Catavi mines), Manuel Flores (Manager, Huanuni mine), Alberto Heighton (Manager, Colquiri mine), and, later, Luis Bedregal-Rodo (Manager, CNSS), and José Cuadros-Quiroga (Minister of Government).
6. Present at council meeting: Goosen Broesma, Mario Vernaza, Emilio Carvajal, Sinforoso Cabrera (workers' commissar), Lucio Vega (Manager, San José mine), Raul Bohrt (Business Superintendent, San José mine), and a labor leader from the Pulacayo mine.
7. FBD report, Vol. III, pp. 77, 79.
8. *Ibid.*, p. 40.
9. *Última Hora,* June 19, 1957; translation by the author.
10. Zondag report, p. 101.
11. Conference with President Siles, January 14, 1957.
12. Meeting with Raúl Gutiérrez, February 21, 1957. Gutiérrez' high opinion of the former purchasing agent of COMIBOL is confirmed in the Zondag report, p. 101.
13. Present for the Mining Bank at the council meeting: Mario Alarcón-Lahore (Acting President); Pablo Biggeman (General Manager); Alfredo Álvarez (Administrative Manager); Rafael Montenegro (Assistant General Manager).
14. *Última Hora,* January 29.
15. *Última Hora,* March 11, 1957; *El Diario,* March 12. Pablo Biggeman and Rafael Montenegro were present for the Mining Bank at the council meeting.

16. Present for the Mining Bank: Jorge Salazar-Mostajo (President) and Pablo Biggeman (General Manager).

17. The assault on the Mining Bank officials is from a speech by President Siles, June 13, 1957 (*La Nación,* June 14). The protest of the bank employees appeared in *En Marcha,* June 6, 1957. None of the three more serious organs of the press *(El Diario, La Nación, Última Hora)* appears to have carried the workers' denial of these charges. *En Marcha* was the organ of the Movimiento Nacional Revolucionario; its Codirector, Luis Peñaloza, supported President Siles against the attacks of the COB and was shortly thereafter elevated to the presidency of the Central Bank. See also *El Diario,* June 2, 1957, showing how utterly discredited and useless the Mining Bank had become.

18. *The Bolivian National Revolution,* p. 172.

19. Note from Fundición Volcán, S.A., to the council, asking payment of the MIAG drafts.

20. The new President of the Development Corporation was Joaquín Lemoine, formerly the General Manager.

21. Testimony of Renán Castrillo, President of the Chamber of Deputies, and Ranolfo Mulloja, Mayor of Villa Montes.

22. Luis Bedregal-Rodo, General Manager, testifying for CNSS; Juan Luis Gutiérrez-Granier, President, testifying for YPFB. At later council meetings, Germán Butrón-Márquez (President of the Administrative Council of CNSS and Secretary General of the COB) was also present.

23. Letter to Luis Bedregal-Rodo, May 16, 1957, listing precise data required.

24. Average rate from IMF, *International Financial Statistics,* X (September, 1957), 54.

25. Germán Butrón-Márquez, *Observaciones de la C.N.S.S. a los Planteamientos de Mr. Eder* (La Paz: Caja Nacional de Seguridad Social, 1957), p. 44; *El Diario,* August 8, 1957.

26. Butrón-Márquez, p. 49.

27. *Ibid.,* pp. 82, 6. The account of Butrón's connection with *Vanguardia* is based on Alexander, *Bolivian National Revolution,* p. 52.

28. *El Diario,* June 19, 1957; *El Diario,* June 2, 1957; *Última Hora,* June 4; *En Marcha,* June 6.

29. The International Labor Organization actuary referred to, Louis de Battista, together with another U.N. adviser, Ángelo de Tuddo, were those principally responsible for the Bolivian social security structure and for the increase in charges to the 1957 levels (*Última Hora,* June 4, 1957; Butrón-Marquez, pp. 18, 96). See Keenleyside report, p. 98, for account of the

chaotic social security legislation prior to the reforms initiated by those advisers.

30. Guillermo Alborta-Velasco, *El Flágelo de la Inflación Monetaria en Bolivia, País Monoproductor* (Madrid: Ed. Romanica, 1963), p. 379.

31. Statement of Luis Bedregal-Rodo, General Manager of CNSS, to the Stabilization Council; statements of Raúl Gutiérrez-Granier, President of COMIBOL, and of President Siles.

32. *La Nación,* May 8, 1957; Decree, January 24, 1957.

33. Juan Luis Gutiérrez-Granier, President, and Eduardo Hinojosa, General Manager, appearing for YPFB.

34. YPFB represented by Eduardo Hinojosa, General Manager; José Candia, Administrative Manager; Guzmán de Aguilar, General Auditor.

35. Letter and memoranda from Norbert A. Bogdan, January 8, 1957; acknowledged February 25, 1957.

36. The letter, dated April 17, 1957, is marked "Personal and Confidential," so that I do not feel warranted in divulging the name of the bank or writer, although the fact is that the letter reveals a degree of understanding of and sympathy with the Bolivian situation that could only redound to their credit. I replied on May 14, and received a further informative acknowledgement dated May 23.

37. Central Bank Directors present: René Gómez-García, Hugo de la Rocha, Jorge Muller, Max Escobari, Hector Mendieta, Carlos Meave, Enrique Arellano; also Victor Romero, Assistant Manager of the monetary department. The presence of these gentlemen is not to be taken as implying that they had any political or personal interest in the transaction in question.

38. Quoted by Alborta-Velasco (pp. 382-84) from Hugo Moreno-Córdova, *Informe de Labores de 1956 a 1960,* p. 7. The statistical table referred to in the preceding paragraph was submitted by the Finance Minister on June 4, 1957. It was signed by L. C. Tapia and purports to show total debt as of May 15, 1957. However, the Central Bank reported outstanding guaranteed drafts of $33 million, of which $5 million were said to cover orders that had been cancelled (although the drafts had not been withdrawn from circulation), leaving outstanding obligations with the *aval* or other guaranty of the Central Bank of $28 million. Of this amount, so far as I could determine, in consultation with the Finance Minister and the president of the Central Bank, only the Markus, Arpic, and Titeux drafts were included in the Finance Ministry statement, so that the difference ($20,928,000) is entered in the table as additional guaranteed indebtedness (presumably covering imports by other than

government enterprises or departments and hence not included in the Finance Ministry tabulation).

39. The U.S. Treasury official referred to is Charles Harley, in charge of Bolivian stabilization fund matters for that department. Some time later, I received a telegram from the State Department going more fully into the legal aspects of the attachment of government or Central Bank funds, in the United Kingdom as well as in the United States, and in part qualifying their previous advice in the light of the possibility that a court might hold that the Central Bank funds were not in reality held in its account as an agent for the Bolivian government but represented a deposit belonging to COMIBOL. Note that if the stabilization plan had been strictly adhered to, that is, if the proceeds of all COMIBOL exports had gone to the Central Bank acting on behalf of the government, this question could never have arisen.

40. Meeting at the presidential palace, May 30, 1957: President Siles, Finance Minister Moreno, Minister of Economy Tamayo, Central Bank President Antezana, Planning Commission head Gisbert, and I.

41. Meeting with Ambassador Victor Andrade, July 30, 1957.

42. Letter, June 18, 1957, from Nicholas L. Deak, President, Deak & Co., Inc., New York City.

43. Present at the meeting for the Foreign Office: Dr. Eduardo Arze-Quiroga, Under Secretary of Foreign Affairs, and Dr. René Jordán-Pando. Present for the Bolivian Commission for the Study of the Brazilian Treaty: General René Gonzales-Tórrez, Dr. Wenceslao Gonzales-Cortez, Dr. Humberto Céspedes-Paz, Ing. Alfonso Balderrama, Carlos Boada, Alfredo Álvarez, José Morales-Guillén, Luis Reyes. Present for YPFB: Ing. Eduardo Hinojosa, Juan Luis Gutiérrez-Granier. Present for tin and lead smelters and exporters: Mario Vernaza, Max Torrico-del Castillo.

44. Editorial, *El Diario*, April 3, 1957, commenting on statement by Salim Chacur, perhaps the best-known member of the Levantine business community in Bolivia.

45. José Candia appeared as representative of YPFB; Jorge Salazar-Mostajo (President) and Antonio Mariscal (Acting Manager) for the Mining Bank; Dr. René Jordán-Pando (Director of the Economics Department) for the Foreign Office, accompanied by Luis Reyes, a former officer of the Central Bank, who had taken part in the treaty dollar arrangements.

46. *Última Hora*, February 8, 1957.

47. *La Nación*, January 23, 1957.

48. Letter from William Ketner, January 14, 1957, that placed 1957 requests at:

SAI (Agricultural Service)   Bs. 5,569,762,000
SCBAC (Roads Service)   13,185,573,620
SCISP (Health Service)   2,135,233,880
SCIDE (Education Service)   1,150,000,000
Total   Bs. 22,040,569,500

49. *El Diario,* November 11, 1958.
50. Council meetings attended by Ross Moore, USOM Director; Henry N. Cooper, Controller; Edward Marasciulo, Program Chief.
51. American Council on Education, *International Handbook of Universities* (2d ed., Washington: American Council on Education, 1962); Keenleyside report, p. 118; ECLA report, p. 94. The universities were located in La Paz, Cochabamba, Sucre, Santa Cruz, Tarija, Potosí, and Oruro. See Franz Tamayo, *Creación de la Pedagogia Nacional* (2d ed., La Paz: *El Diario,* 1944). For a survey of education prior to the Revolution, see Raymond H. Nelson, *Education in Bolivia* (Washington, D.C.: Federal Security Agency, 1949).
52. *Presencia,* June 13, 1957, placed the salary of a *media cátedra* (part-time professor) at Bs. 60,000 a month. In 1929, when the boliviano was worth 36 cents U.S., a salary of Bs. 600 a month ($216) provided a decent living. The president of the Central Bank, Dr. Antezana, recalls that he felt quite prosperous when, as a young man with a Sorbonne degree, he was offered a professorship at the University of San Andrés in La Paz.
53. Decrees 4540/1, December 15, 1956.
54. *La Nación,* March 22, 1957.
55. The meeting with Kenneth M. Spang, president, and Dana G. Munro, vice-president, of the Bondholders Council, took place the afternoon of December 6, 1956, and Gisbert and I had to be in Washington the following day for execution of the loan stand-by agreement with the Treasury Department. Because of the extreme pressure of time, there was merely an exchange of memoranda with pencilled corrections embodying the substance of the agreement. As a consequence, there were certain points of misunderstanding which remained to be cleared up when the Bondholders Council presented its definitive draft and proposed press release to the Bolivian Ambassador, who would be charged with executing the definitive agreement, viz.: (1) The Bondholders Council draft showed a "one per cent per annum" interest payment for 1957; Gisbert had specified a one-half per cent payment for 1957. The result was identical, as the payment would only be on interest coupons due during the second semester but, from the viewpoint of public acceptance in Bolivia, the distinction was vital.

(2) The Bondholders' draft showed payments at the 1 per cent rate only through the May, 1959, coupon, whereas our understanding was that it would be for the full 1958 and 1959 calendar years. (3) The proposed press release omitted Bolivia's right to increase sinking fund payments, which had been agreed to. (4) The proposed press release stated that the agreement embodied "the same schedule of rates as proposed in the earlier plan"; this was true in the sense that interest would be raised in successive steps from one per cent per annum to $1\frac{1}{2}$ to 2 and finally to 3 per cent, but the period within which it would reach each successive increase was strung out six months longer than under the earlier plan, and the amount of matured interest condoned was 50 per cent greater than under the previous plan. For political reasons in Bolivia, it was essential that the arrangements negotiated by Gisbert be made to appear substantially more favorable to Bolivia than those agreed to in 1948, as indeed they were. Fortunately, the Bondholders Council accepted Gisbert's and my understanding of the agreement, and it is clear that there was complete good faith on both sides, although, for a time, some of the Stabilization Council members, ever suspicious of "Wall Street," thought that the Bondholders Council had attempted to pull a fast one, or that either I or Gisbert had exaggerated the latter's success as a negotiator (my letter to Kenneth Spang, December 28, 1956). When the arrangement was finally announced, *Time* (June 24, 1957) characterized it as "the leanest agreement ever signed by the [Bondholders'] Council."

56. *Orientación,* June 22, 1957.
57. *El Diario, La Nación,* June 24, 1957. I had not, until then, known of the publication of the article and, of course, refused to confirm or deny the truth of the story (*El Diario,* June 24). The newspaper versions contained one minor error, that the vice-president's proposal was to buy the bonds at 35 per cent of par. The figure should have been 28.6 per cent. It may be that the correction had not been inserted in the original draft. In any event, I could hardly have corrected this error without acknowledging the authenticity of the quotation. The profit on the transaction would have been approximately $460,000 (p. 437n).
58. *El Diario,* June 26, 1957; *Intransigencia,* Vol. I, No. 1 (July, 1957).
59. *Última Hora,* June 24, 1957 (evening paper). The threat was relayed to me by a member of the Cabinet.
60. *El Diario, La Nación,* June 25, 1957.
61. *Última Hora,* June 26, 1957; *La Nación,* June 28; *Última Hora,* July 2; *El Diario,* July 27; *Última Hora,* August 1, 2; *La Nación,*

El Diario, August 2; *La Nación, El Diario,* August 4; *La Nación,* August 5; *El Diario, La Nación,* August 6; *El Diario,* August 13.

62. *La Nación, El Diario,* June 12, 1957; *Presencia,* June 15. The decree bears the date of May 24, 1957, but it was not released to the press until later. See Decree 4657-2 (Central Bank, 29th *Annual Report,* 1957, pp. 40, 136, 139).

63. Announcement by Foreign Bondholders Protective Council, Inc., June 17, 1958; *New York Times,* same date; *New York Times,* October 8, 1960.

64. The first committee had been formed by Supreme Resolution, April 22, 1954. President Siles' committee was formed by Supreme Resolution of December 7, 1956. Others on that committee were Moisés Ocampo, an engineer, and Dr. Raúl Bohrt-Parodi, representing labor. The Patiño group, aside from Dr. Mariaca, was composed of Luis Ballivián-Saracho, Valerio Delgado, Franz Naeser, and Luis Arnald, all well qualified (*El Diario,* March 20, 1957). See also Central Bank, 31st *Annual Report,* 1959, p. 62.

65. *La Nación, El Diario,* March 19, 1957.

66. Central Bank, 31st *Annual Report,* 1959, pp. 61-62. Agreement ratified by Supreme Resolution 60427, October 20, 1953.

67. Decree 5866, August 31, 1961, approving the Triangular Plan, Art. 5 (a). Taken from Central Bank, 33d *Annual Report,* 1961, p. 203. The arrangements are classified and not available to the public in the United States. See p. 747, n *53.*

68. The President of YPFB, Juan Luis Gutiérrez-Granier, the General Manager, Eduardo Hinojosa, and the Administrative Manager, José Candia, appeared on behalf of the company. Jorge Tamayo-Ramos was still Minister of Mines at the time. Other price reductions (for U.S. aid commodities) were made in June, 1957 (*Última Hora,* July 1, 1957).

69. *La Nación, El Diario,* January 9, 1957. The Director General of Labor at the time was Adolfo Cárdenas-Dick. The Minister of Labor was Abel Ayoroa-Argandoña.

70. *La Nación, El Diario,* January 10, 1957; editorial, *Última Hora,* January 10. Letter from Ross Moore, Director, USOM/Bolivia, to the president of the Central Bank, January 11, 1957, with follow-up February 12, advising of the deposit of $500,000 in the FRBNY in addition to the $2 million initial ICA deposit in the Stabilization Fund account.

71. The new Labor Minister was Félix Lara.

72. The representatives of the Confederation of Bank Employees who attended the council meeting were: José Luis Jofré, René Gómez-García, Honorato Branes, Eduardo Rodríguez, Avelino Duchén-de Córdova, Carlos Jahnsen, and Guillermo Limpias.

At one meeting, Jofré expressed his appreciation of my courtesy and that of the council in explaining so fully the purposes and exigencies of the stabilization program, but on the following day he stated that he simply could not go back to his *bases* (the rank and file) and admit that he had come out of the negotiations empty-handed. Later, however, the confederation came out strongly in support of the stabilization program, and against the COB resolutions (*El Diario,* June 19, 1957).

73. Statement by Minister of Mines, Mario Torres-Calleja, *La Nación,* May 8, 1957; statement by Minister of Public Works, Ramón Claure-Calvi, and editorial, *El Diario,* May 17; *Última Hora,* May 17, 1957.

74. Council meetings in June, 1957; *El Diario,* June 26.

75. *El Diario,* July 6, 1957. The Minister of Public Works and Communications, Ramón Claure-Calvi, took his orders from Lechín and not from the President.

76. Witnesses before the council at January, February, and March meetings: Mayor Jaime Otero-Calderón (La Paz); Director General of Railways Gustavo Méndez; Humberto Taboada, Manager, Electrical Cooperative of Sucre; Víctor Castro M., Secretary, Railway Workers' Confederation; Richard H. Dobson, Managing Director, The Antofagasta (Chili) & Bolivia Railway Co., Ltd.; G. M. Wilson, General Manager, Bolivia Railway Co., Ltd.; T. V. Woods, General Manager, and Albert Moore, Accountant, Guaqui-La Paz Railway; Luis Sepúlveda-Merino and Arnaldo Hopplin, representing Chilean Section, Arica-La Paz Railway; Luis Augusto Soux, Manager, Potosí Electric Company; Robinson, representative, Southern Railway of Peru, Ltd.; Rudge, representative, Peruvian Corporation, Ltd.

77. Attack on Antezana-Paz by Rafael Otazo, delegate to the Second National Workers' Congress, *La Nación,* June 15, 1957. Much to my relief, Dr. Antezana was kept on the council to June 21, the last meeting I attended before returning to the U.S. The entire Central Bank Board of Directors was later forced out under the same political pressure (*El Diario,* July 24). For Peñaloza's background in the *Tupac Amaru* group, and the Trotskyite POR, see Alexander, *The Bolivian National Revolution,* pp. 29-30.

78. *El Diario,* February 25, 1957; *Última Hora,* March 15, 1957.

79. *La Nación,* June 14, 1957.

80. *Última Hora,* January 10, 1957.

81. *El Diario, La Nación,* January 12; *Última Hora,* January 15; *Visión,* January 18; *El Diario,* January 27; *Última Hora,* January 28, 1957.

82. *Presencia,* January 19; *El Diario,* January 15, 16; *El Pueblo,* January 13; *Última Hora,* January 15, 1957.

83. Memorandum to President Siles, January 23, 1957. At the council meeting, President Siles expressed his regret at the vicious personal attacks against me by the Railway Workers' Federation of Oruro and others and his deep appreciation, as well as that of the council, for my services, but he did not come to my defense in public.

84. *Última Hora,* January 14. I later tried to get USOM/Bolivia to send this reporter, Guillermo Monje, at his request, to the United States on a goodwill and informational visit (August 14, 1957), but I was informed that neither ICA nor other agencies had funds for such proposes, which seems strange considering that thousands of less qualified visitors have been sent on similar tours. Professor Alexander, certainly no right-wing sympathizer, confirms my observation that it was the union leaders and politicians, no longer able to profit from the Bs. 190 exchange rate, who lost out from stabilization (*The Bolivian National Revolution,* p. 211).

85. *El Diario,* January 15, 1957; *Última Hora,* January 16, February 19; later comments, *El Diario,* May 4, *Última Hora,* June 7. My comment was borne out by an editorial in *Última Hora,* May 3, to the effect that the labor leaders were accustomed to gaining patronage through the distribution of quotas *(cupos),* and that since stabilization many labor organizations and especially "collectives" were disgruntled because there were no longer any *cupos.*

86. *La Nación,* April 7, 1957.

87. *La Nación, El Diario,* April 10, 1957; *La Nación, El Diario,* April 17, 1957.

88. Those present at the presidential palace at the 11:00 a.m. conference on April 17, 1957, were: Dr. Hernán Siles-Zuazo (President); Manuel Barrau-Pelaez (Minister of Foreign Affairs); Roberto Méndez-Tejada (Minister of Justice, Government, and Immigration); Jorge Tamayo-Ramos (Minister of National Economy); Mario Torres-Calleja (Minister of Mines and Petroleum); José Cuadros-Quiroga (Minister of Agriculture and Colonization); Dr. Gabriel Arze-Quiroga (Minister of Hygiene and Public Health); General Julio Prado (Minister of National Defense); Félix Lara (Minister of Labor and Social Welfare); Dr. Franklin Antezana-Paz (President of the Central Bank); Miguel Gisbert-Nogué (Executive Vice-President of the National Commission of Coordination and Planning); Dr. Federico Álvarez-Plata (member of the Central Political Committee of the MNR); Dr. Aníbal Aguilar *(idem.);* Rubén Julio *(idem.);* Dr. John R. Woodley (IMF representative); Ernest Moore (Financial Adviser, U.S. Financial Mission); and I. (The La Paz papers on April 18, reported the presence of the foreign experts but not the complete list of the Bolivians.)

89. *El Diario, La Nación,* April 26, 1957.
90. *La Nación, El Diario, Última Hora,* May 2, 1957; *El Diario,* May 4. Simultaneously with Lechín's speech, *Última Hora,* May 2, carried an equally detailed criticism of Lechín by Tito Bulacios-Nina, one of the original leaders of the Revolution.
91. *La Nación, El Diario,* May 19, 1957. Rumors prior to December, 1956, were that the boliviano would drop to Bs. 40,000; *La Nación,* January 21, 1957.
92. *La Nación, El Diario, Última Hora,* May 26, 27, 28, 29, 30, 1957.
93. E.g., attacked by columnist, *Última Hora,* May 30; by CNSS, June 7; by *El Pueblo,* June 1; supported by *La Nación, El Diario, Última Hora,* May 27, 28, 29, 30, June 4; by *Presencia,* May 30; by Humberto Fossati, *La Nación,* June 3. See *New York Times,* May 26.
94. Manifesto dated May 26, but published for the first time in *La Nación,* June 7, 1957.
95. *La Nación, El Diario,* June 6, 1957.
96. Lechín's statement to COB, *La Nación,* June 12, 1957; Siles' speech, *El Diario, La Nación,* June 14; Siles' report to Congress, *El Diario, La Nación,* August 9; *Presencia,* June 13; editorial, *La Nación,* June 13.
97. *Última Hora,* June 12, 13, 1957. Editorial, *Última Hora,* June 13, asking how it is possible to have a "controlled inflation."
98. *Última Hora,* June 12, 1957, the Chávez draft; *Última Hora,* June 12, 13, *El Diario,* June 12, the Trotskyite (POR) content of the manifesto; *La Nación, El Diario,* June 13, the final COB platform.
99. *El Diario, La Nación,* June 8, 9, 11, 12, 13, 15, 16, 17, 18, 19, 20, 22, 23, 25, 27, 30, July 5; *Última Hora,* June 13, 19; *La Nación,* August 5, 16, 30, September 6, 8, 10. See also *La Nación, El Diario,* May 23, for first announcement of labor support.
100. *La Nación,* June 9, 10, 11, 1957.
101. *La Nación,* June 13, 1957; *La Nación, El Diario, Última Hora,* June 14, 15; *El Diario,* June 16.
102. *Time,* June 17, 1957; *La Nación,* June 18.
103. *Anales del Congreso,* V (Bogotá, November 13, 1962), pp. 1978-88. The statement that Keynes agreed that socialism is the "road to serfdom" is based on a letter from Keynes to Hayek; Harrod, *The Life of John Maynard Keynes* (New York: Harcourt, Brace, 1951), p. 436.
104. Paz-Estenssoro, p. 149; Keenleyside report, p. v.
105. *Foreign Aid and Foreign Policy* (New York: St. Martin's Press, 1964), pp. 222-23.
106. The documentary source of this information may be classified;

however, the information was confirmed in conversations with ICA officials in Washington, Embassy officers in La Paz, and by Henry F. Holland (August 8, 1956, en route to New York). As to the Keynesian bias of Dr. Paz, see his speech, February, 1954, quoted by Powelson, *Latin America: Today's Economic and Social Revolution* (New York: McGraw-Hill Book Co., 1964), p. 233. As to the Keynesian theories of Karasz, see p. 479 n.

107. *Observations on Fiscal and Monetary Activities in Bolivia,* a report of the U.N. Technical Assistance Administration, September 27, 1954, to Sune Carlson, by Henry Bloch, Director, Fiscal Division, United Nations.

108. Arthur Karasz, "Inflación y Depresión en Términos de Desequilibrio entre Producción y Consumo," *Revista del Derecho,* VI (March, 1954), pp. 150-56. The recommendation that future note issues of the Central Bank be limited to Bs. 400 million a month is taken from an unpublished report by Karasz (April, 1953) in which he advised devaluation of the boliviano and expressed the belief that the currency circulation would thereafter become stabilized within the course of a year.

109. According to the President of COMIBOL, Raúl Gutiérrez, Karasz had at first opposed nationalization of the Big Three mines, but later advocated it.

110. Bolivians were almost unanimous in blaming Karasz for the 1953-56 policies and disasters (*El Diario,* June 12, 20, 1956; articles by Humberto Fossati, July 27, 28; *Última Hora,* July 30, August 2; conversations with businessmen and with members of the Stabilization Council, at various times). I pointed out the unfairness of this attitude at a farewell luncheon given to Karasz by the President and Directors of the Central Bank at the Hotel Copacabana, La Paz, July 25, 1956.

111. Conference with Arthur Karasz, June 7, 1956, from my report to Washington, June 21, 1956; statement of Karasz to board of directors of the Central Bank, April 23, 1956, to the effect that COMIBOL would require a $5-$6 a pound for tin to operate in the black (*El Diario,* June 20, 1956).

112. My letter to John B. Hollister, April 15, 1957. Hollister's retirement from ICA, *New York Times,* September 13, 1957, p. 1. Conversation with ICA evaluation officer, October 1, 1957. None of my reports reached Henry Holland or John Hollister, and very few reports ever reached Rollin Atwood (in charge of all Latin American operations for ICA) or Henry Randall (Bolivian desk officer for ICA), according to conversations with those gentlemen between November 30 and December 7, 1956. I had taken special precautions to ensure that the April 15, 1957, report to Hollister would get proper attention, but it

never got above the "working level people" in State or ICA (letter to William T. Briggs, State Department, April 13; reply, April 24, 1957).

113. *El Diario,* January 16, 1957. Sir Arthur and Lady Tyndall (and probably Dr. Zouteweij) left La Paz February 28, 1957. Meetings with Sir Arthur Tyndall and Hubertus Zouteweij: at British Embassy, with Ambassador Sir James Thyne Henderson, January 19; at my residence, January 21, with Ambassador Gerald Drew, Secretary of Embassy Herbert Leggett, and Ernest Moore.

114. *La Nación,* May 17, 1957. My translation.

115. ECLA report, pp. 82-83. My translation. The other ECLA economist to confer with me on March 8, 1957, and after was Pedro Vuskovic-Bravo.

116. ECLA report, pp. 83-84.

117. E.g., *La Nación, El Diario,* May 30, 31 (Dr. Prebisch's talk at University of San Andrés); *La Nación,* June 2, 1957.

118. ECLA report, p. 83. The data in Figure 8 were compiled from the most authoritative sources then available. Bank note circulation was taken from Central Bank figures, converted into dollars at the average rate of exchange for each year. U.S. aid figures for calendar years were provided by Cornelius Zondag, economist, USOM/Bolivia. The figures for the increases in short-term debts were provided by the Minister of Finance and President of the Central Bank. The loss of gold and foreign exchange reserves figure is taken from Central Bank statistics. The $12\frac{1}{2}$ per cent allowance for exploration, development, and replacement of equipment was computed on the basis of statements by the experts of the Ford, Bacon & Davis mission and others that $12\frac{1}{2}$ to 15 per cent on gross receipts would be a reasonable allowance (discussion with Max Coleman, FBD, and Mr. Zabriskie, COMIBOL geologist, June 10, 1956; later discussion with Goosen Broesma, COMIBOL, and Federico Ahlfeld, geologist). The mineral export total is the official export figure.

119. The figures used in the left-hand section of Figure 9 were provided by the Central Bank; those in the right-hand section are from *International Financial Statistics,* based on Central Bank figures.

120. The indices used in Figure 10 are relatives computed by me (December 31, 1956 = 100), based on figures taken from the IMF *International Financial Statistics,* September, 1957, March, 1958, and June, 1958, representing data as of the end of the respective months, viz.:

	Bolivianos per Dollar	Cost of Living 1953 = 100	Bank Note Circulation (In Billions)
1956			
December	7,745	2,800	160.02
1957			
January	7,500	2,840	159.46
February	7,525	2,580	179.71
March	7,725	2,640	183.12
April	7,725	2,550	189.37
May	7,740	2,300	191.94
June	8,375	2,260	170.43
July	8,525	2,260	175.98
August	8,700	2,190	177.91
September	8,655	2,200	173.34
October	8,720	2,320	177.07
November	8,625	2,370	180.96
December	8,565	2,420	220.70

The third column above represents total bank note circulation. Bank notes in the hands of the public were less, e.g., Bs. 148.81 billion at the end of December, 1956; Bs. 170.0 at the end of February, 1957; Bs. 169.5 at the end of June, 1957. The latter figures would doubtless represent a truer picture of the inflationary pattern (see Jaime Rodríguez-Rivadeneira, Chief of the Section of Economic and Statistical Studies, Central Bank, *El Diario*, June 28, 1957), but the figures for total note liability were more easily available on an up-to-date basis.

121. There was not the slightest doubt that the cause of the drop in the boliviano was Lechín's attack of June 5 and other speeches at the COB Congress (*Última Hora*, June 7, 8; *La Nación*, June 8; *El Diario*, June 8; *New York Times*, June 10, 1957). I refused to comment in answer to queries from the reporters, other than to say that the higher quotation for dollars was due to an increase in the demand, "and you will have to draw your own conclusions as to the reasons for that demand" (*Última Hora*, June 10, 1957).

122. IMF *Annual Report*, 1958, pp. 72, 116. The percentage changes given in the IMF report are misleading in view of the overwhelming preponderance of the government sector. Actually the government debt to the banks increased by Bs. 19.5 billion from June 30 to November 30, 1957; the private sector debt by Bs. 11.7 billion (*International Financial Statistics*, June, 1958; see also *Time*, June 17, 1957; *La Nación*, June 18).

123. Central Bank, 31st *Annual Report*, 1959, p. 36.

124. *Dirección de Estadística* figures used in speech by President Siles, June 4 (*La Nación,* June 5, 1957).
125. *La Nación,* June 7; later table published in *La Nación,* June 17, 1957.
126. Table published in *La Nación,* June 16; figures attributed expressly to Dr. Woodley by President Siles in speech, June 13 (*La Nación,* June 14, 1957).
127. *El Diario,* December 15, 1958; Central Bank, 29th *Annual Report,* 1957, pp. 23-24.
128. IMF *Annual Report,* 1959, pp. 110-11. Government borrowing from the Central Bank (*International Financial Statistics,* June 1958) increased from Bs. 301.6 billion on November 30, 1957, to Bs. 399.4 billion on December 31. Note issue increased by Bs. 39.7 in the same period. The Bs. 58.1 billion difference between the increase in government debt and the increase in note issue was reflected in the loss of an equivalent amount of dollars from the stabilization fund.
129. Information provided by knowledgeable mining engineers; confirmed by IMF *Annual Report,* 1958, p. 115, on the use of existing ore stocks.
130. Figures from same source as those in Table 13, p. 503.
131. *El Diario,* July 27, 1957.
132. American Smelting and Refining Co.; American Zinc, Lead and Smelting Co.; Anaconda Co.; Cerro de Pasco Corp.; International Nickel Co.; Kennecott Copper Corp.; National Lead Co.; National Steel Corp.; Newmont Mining Corp.; United States Steel Corp.
133. Dr. Carlos H. Valdez-Molina, "Algunos Planteamientos en Torno a la Crisis en Bolivia," *Minería Boliviana,* III (September, 1957), 56-57.
134. Central Bank, 34th *Annual Report,* 1962, pp. 42-43.
135. *La Nación,* January 19; *El Diario,* February 1, 1957.
136. *Última Hora,* January 28, 31; ECLA report, pp. 84, 135, 138.
137. IMF *International Financial Statistics,* June, 1958, cited for both import and export figures.
138. ECLA report, pp. 82, 257; see also pp. 256, 269.
139. Polls published in *La Nación,* January 20, March 22, April 18, 29, May 23, June 11, 29; *El Diario,* March 20; *Última Hora,* May 23, 1957.
140. *El Pueblo,* February 2, June 1; *Unidad,* February 27, 1957.
141. *El Diario,* June 14; *Última Hora,* June 13; *La Nación,* June 11, 1957. See also editorials in *Última Hora,* January 26, June 24, 26; *El Diario,* January 4; *La Nación,* January 13, 19, 28, all supporting the stabilization program; likewise the witty comments in *Presencia* (Roman Catholic), June 13, including a hilarious public opinion poll. Translations by me.

142. *New York Times*, August 7, 1959; *Time*, August 19.
143. Letter from the National Chamber of Commerce, June 24, 1957, signed by Aníbal Ormachea, President, and René Candia-Navarro, Manager. Translation by me.
144. *The Bolivian National Revolution*, pp. viii, 52, 207-8. The notes, pp. 285-94, indicate that Alexander's trip to Bolivia as an ICA "employee" took place between June 9 and August 1, 1957.
145. *El Diario*, September 1, 1957.
146. First National City Bank of New York, *Monthly Economic Letter*, May,1957, pp. 57-59, reprinted in *Última Hora*, June 22; *The Guaranty Survey*, May,1958, pp. 9-10.

Part VII

1. *New York Times*, January 25, 1958, p. 5; May 7, p. 11; May 8, p. 28; May 15, p. 11; May 16, p. 10, May 22, p. 14; May 28, p. 9; July 24, p. 8; September 14, p. 34; Juan de Onís, "Falange permitted to hold its first convention since 1952," September 16, p. 10; September 17, p. 6; October 22, p. 15; October 23, p. 5; October 24, p. 28; October 28, p. 7; November 14, p. 54.
2. *New York Times*, March 3, 1959, p. 8; March 4, pp. 1, 11; March 5, pp. 1, 4, 30; March 6, p. 10; March 7, p. 9; March 8, p. IV-4; March 9, p. 15; March 10, p. 14; March 12, p. 15; March 13, p. 8; March 14, p. 3; March 15, p. 1; March 16, p. 39; March 17, p. 2; March 20, p. 8; March 21, p. 2; March 22, p. IV-3; March 23, p. 30; March 31, p. 3; April 5, p. 24; April 7, p. 32; April 20, pp. 1, 4; April 21, pp. 16, 3 and 34; June 27, p. 2; June 28, p. 23; July 8, p. 12. Quoted phrase from Patch, "Bolivia: U.S. Assistance in a Revolutionary Setting," p. 136.
3. Humberto Fossati R., President, Central Bank, 32d *Annual Report*, 1960, March 14, 1961, p. 33 (my translation).
4. *Ibid.*, pp. lxxix, ciii; Law 60, December 20, 1960; *New York Times*, January 13, 1960, p. 70; February 20, p. 4; Juan de Onís, "Guevara-Arze takes refuge in U.S. Embassy," February 25; March 20, p. 15; March 21, p. 9; March 22, p. 17; April 17, p. 23; April 23, p. 6; April 26, p. 5; April 30, p. 4; June 6, p. 1; June 7, pp. 16, 34; June 17, p. 4; July 30, p. 4; "Change in Constitution," August 9; November 17, p. 13; November 22, p. 10; December 21, p. 25; December 22, p. 3; December 24, p. 3; December 26, p. 2; December 27, p. 25; December 28, p. 5. See Powelson, *Latin America...*, pp. 246-47, on USSR aid; and *El Diario*, September 25, 1962 (quoted from Amado Canelas O., *Nacionalización de las Minas de Bolivia: Historia de*

una Frustración [La Paz: Librería Altiplano, 1963], pp. 278-79), on Ñuflo Chávez' counteroffer.

5. *New York Times,* January 6, 1961, p. 3; January 25, p. 8; March 1, p. 47; March 4, p. 6; March 6, p. 14; May 13, p. 6; May 15, p. 1; June 12, p. 7; June 25, p. 3; September 15, p. 5; September 16, p. 5; September 21, p. 2; September 22, 1963, p. 3; *HAR,* XVI (September, 1963), 899; *HAR,* XVI (November, 1963), 1085; Alborta-Velasco, p. 343, on the robbery of COMIBOL and aftermath.

6. *New York Times,* January 22, 1961, p. III-1; June 11, p. III-1; July 31, 1962, p. 41.

7. Statement of Foreign Minister José Fellman-Velarde who "felt compelled to explain" in order to "maintain the respect of our people" (*HAR,* XVI [September, 1963], 898-99). Details of credit in Central Bank, 35th *Annual Report,* 1963, pp. 177-79; de Lesseps S. Morrison, *Latin American Mission* (New York: Simon and Schuster, 1965), p. 245*n.*

8. *New York Times,* April 14, 1963, p. 41; August 5, p. 8; September 22, p. 3; October 23, p. 4; October 24, p. 6; October 25, p. 2; October 26, pp. 9, 2; December 8, p. 1; December 14, p. 1; December 22, p. 16; *HAR,* XVI (September, 1963), 899-900; *HAR,* XVI (November, 1963), 1086. American Embassy, *Quarterly Economic Summary,* A-574 (February 7, 1964), p. 10; and A-354 (October 31, 1963), p. 11, are authority for labeling the labor leaders Federico Escobar and Ireneo Pimentel as communists.

9. American Embassy reports cited in note 8 above; Raúl Lema-Pelaez, Acting President, Central Bank, 34th *Annual Report,* 1962, p. 20 (translation by me).

10. Statement by Aníbal Aguilar-Peñarrieta; American Embassy, *Quarterly Economic Summary,* A-67 (August 13, 1964), p. 14.

11. *New York Times,* January 29, 1964, p. 14 (Edward C. Burks); May 30, p. 4 (Juan de Onís); June 1, p. 1 (Juan de Onís); the *Visión* letter, January 28, 1964.

12. *New York Times,* August 7, 1964, p. 2 (Juan de Onís); September 21, p. 1; September 23, p. 10; October 11, p. 25; October 30, p. 1; October 31, p. 7; November 1, p. 3; November 2, p. 9 (Richard Eder); November 4, p. 41; November 5, p. 1; November 6, p. 17; November 10, p. 2 (Henry Raymont); November 14, p. 12 (Henry Raymont); *London Bank,* XXX (February 20, 1965), p. 131; biographical sketch of General Barrientos: *New York Times,* November 10, 1964, p. 2; Heath, "Revolution and Stability in Bolivia."

13. *New York Times,* May 2, 1965, p. 2 (Juan de Onís); May 10, p. 16; May 18, p. 10; May 19, p. 4; May 20, p. 14 (Henry Raymont); May 23, p. 4 (Henry Raymont); May 24, p. 1 (Henry

Raymont); May 25, p. 1 (Henry Raymont); May 26, p. 1 (Henry Raymont); May 27, p. 1 (A.P. dispatch); May 28, p. 1; May 29, p. 3 (Henry Raymont); June 1, p. 3 (Henry Raymont); *The Wall Street Journal,* January 12, 1966, p. 16 (Norman Gall); *Ann Arbor News,* May 17, 1965, p. 18 (UPI dispatch); May 18, p. 2 (A.P. dispatch); *London Bank,* XXX (April 3, 1965), p. 278.

14. *London Bank* XXXI (January 22, 1966), p. 38; *London Bank,* XXXI (March 19, 1966), p. 148; *London Bank,* XXXI (June 25, 1966), p. 341; *London Bank,* XXXI (August 6, 1966), p. 424; *New York Times,* April 29, 1966, p. 12 (H. J. Maidenberg), July 2, 1966, p. 10; *Ann Arbor News,* July 5, 1966, p. 5 (Associated Press).

15. Gross domestic product (in millions of dollars at 1958 constant prices):

	1952	1956	1957	1958	1959	1960	1961	1962	1963	1964
Agriculture and livestock	113.1	104.2	110.7	121.5	128.6	121.9	131.9	136.4	151.4	154.3
Mining	58.3	46.1	47.4	32.7	31.2	33.8	37.7	35.5	36.5	41.3
Petroleum	2.1	13.1	14.7	14.2	13.3	14.6	13.2	14.2	16.7	17.7
Manufacturing	49.0	51.4	36.0	39.5	41.5	44.6	45.3	48.1	49.5	54.4
Construction	3.6	2.6	4.8	4.1	4.3	5.4	1.9	2.2	2.3	2.4
Commerce and finance	48.5	45.8	45.3	45.3	46.4	47.3	43.0	45.6	47.9	50.5
Transport	23.9	29.7	27.1	30.0	30.8	31.4	33.4	37.0	38.5	41.0
Government	55.0	26.0	20.7	27.1	28.0	31.9	32.5	34.5	36.5	37.8
Other services	34.3	35.9	36.2	36.8	37.7	38.6	42.5	43.5	44.8	47.1
Total (1952-63 base)	387.8	354.8	342.9	351.2	361.8	369.5	381.4	397.0	424.1	446.5
Total (1965 revision)				353.7	352.7	367.7	375.5	396.5	421.9	445.1

Sources: The 1957 figures from Bolivian Ten-Year Development Plan, *Planeamiento,* September, 1961, Table 1. The 1952, 1956, and 1958-62 figures from U.S. Aid, *Economic and Program Statistics,* 1964. In 1965, the National Planning and Coordination Administration revised the figures from 1957 on, on a basis that is not comparable with earlier estimates. For example, a large part of the petroleum industry expenditure has been removed from Petroleum and placed under Construction, and it would appear that over $25 million of sugar and other agriculture-based production has been taken from Agriculture and Livestock and placed under Manufacturing. The 1964 figures shown above have therefore been computed by percentages of change from 1963 to 1964, shown in the 1965 revised estimates, taken from *Economic and Program Statistics,* 1965.

16. *Bolivia: 10 Años de Revolución,* p. 177.

17. The 1963-64 data are from Department of Commerce, *International Commerce* (Washington: Bureau of Foreign and Domestic Commerce, December 21, 1964); and from *International Finance News Survey,* XVII (January 8, 1965), 7. See David G. Greene, "Revolution and the Rationalization of Reform in Bolivia," *Inter-American Economic Affairs,* XIX (Winter, 1965), 3-25.

18. American Embassy, *Quarterly Economic Summary*, A-354, October 31, 1963, p. 7.
19. American Embassy, *Quarterly Economic Summary*, A-67 (August 13, 1964), p. 9, and also references at note 18; and A-48 (August 11, 1965), p. 6.
20. Booz, Allen & Hamilton report to AID, October 31, 1963, pp. iv, 24-25, 42, 44. Tractor data from *London Bank*, XXX (May 29, 1965), 460.
21. See Jack Heller and Kenneth M. Kauffman, *Tax Incentives for Industry in Less Developed Countries* (Cambridge, Mass.: Harvard Law School, 1963). For an account of the unfair competition between the government sugar mill and the private mills, see pamphlet by Iturralde, *Consideraciones . . .*, pp. 19 ff.
22. *Bolivia: 10 Años de Revolución*, p. 57.
23. American Embassy, *Quarterly Economic Summary*, 574 (February 7, 1964), p. 5. Casto Ferragut, an IDB official, notes that a "*minifundio* structure, equally undesirable and harmful, has spread" (Land Tenure Center, *The Progress of Land Reform in Bolivia*, p. 7).
24. Powelson, *Latin America . . .*, p. 58.
25. *Bolivia: 10 Años de Revolución*, p. 70.
26. *El Diario*, March 1, 1964; from *International Financial News Survey*, XVI (May 1, 1964), 147; USAID *Economic and Program Statistics*, 1965, p. 37.
27. Average price of $1.28 for February, 1956; *International Financial Statistics*. The $1.008 average and other figures are from Figure 13 data.
28. Average prices of tin in New York, shown in Figure 13 (in cents U.S.) (see following page).
29. Advertisement by Bolivian government *New York Times*, October 2, 1958, p. 29; speech by Marcial Tamayo at U.N. Assembly, *New York Times*, October 3, p. 44; speech by Dillon at GATT, *New York Times*, October 17, p. 44; "Russia Breaks Tin Prices" ($86\frac{1}{2}$ cent price reached September 18) *Iron Age*, September 25, p. 146; Bolivian papers, September 19 to October 3, 1958; Central Bank, 30th *Annual Report*, 1958, Central Bank, June 30, 1959, p. 23; Guillermo Bedregal, *El Plan Nacional de Desarrollo y la Integración de la Industria Estañífera de Bolivia*, p. 33. An editorial in *El Diario*, October 3, 1958, however, stated that, although the government claimed that Russian dumping was the chief cause of Bolivia's troubles, it was only of secondary importance; the real cause was the low productivity of labor, strikes, and the exorbitant demands of the labor leaders.
30. October 29, 1964, high, $2.185, from *Iron Age*, November 5, 1964. February 14-23, 1951, high, $1.83, from *Iron Age*, February 22 and March 1, 1951. December 30, 1965, close from

Year	Price	Year	Price	Year	Price	Year	Price
1897	13.67	1917	61.802	1937	54.337	1957	96.4
1898	15.70	1918	88.750	1938	42.301	1958	95.0
1899	25.12	1919	63.328	1939	50.323	1959	102.0
1900	29.90	1920	48.273	1940	49.827	1960	101.3
1901	16.74	1921	29.916	1941	52.018	1961	113.1
1902	26.79	1922	32.554	1942	52.000	1962	114.5
1903	28.09	1923	42.664	1943	52.000	1963	116.7
1904	27.99	1924	50.176	1944	52.000	1964	157.8
1905	31.358	1925	57.893	1945	52.000	1965	176.3
1906	39.819	1926	65.285	1946	54.58		
1907	38.166	1927	64.353	1947	77.94		
1908	29.465	1928	50.427	1948	99.25		
1909	29.725	1929	45.155	1949	99.32		
1910	34.123	1930	31.694	1950	95.56		
1911	42.281	1931	24.467	1951	128.31		
1912	46.096	1932	22.017	1952	121.31		
1913	44.252	1933	39.110	1953	95.77		
1914	34.301	1934	52.191	1954	91.81		
1915	38.590	1935	50.420	1955	94.79		
1916	43.480	1936	46.441	1956	101.1		

Sources: Prices from 1897 through 1955 provided by Ford, Bacon & Davis, Inc. Prices from 1956 through 1965 from *International Financial Statistics*. Five-year averages on the chart were computed by me.

Iron Age, January 6, 1966. Tailings contract from *London Bank,* **XXX** (December 11, 1965), 1082.

31. Metal exports (in thousands of metric tons):

Year	Tin	Lead	Zinc	Total
1951	33.7	30.6	30.5	122.9
1952	32.5	30.0	35.6	121.2
1953	35.4	23.8	24.0	99.2
1954	29.3	18.2	20.4	82.5
1955	28.4	19.1	21.3	85.7
1956	27.3	21.6	17.1	74.8
1957	28.2	26.3	19.7	n.a.
1958	18.0	22.8	14.2	n.a.
1959	24.3	22.0	3.4	n.a.
1960	19.7	21.5	4.0	59.8
1961	20.7	20.3	5.3	69.0
1962	21.8	18.6	3.6	70.2
1963	23.1	20.2	4.6	80.5
1964	24.4	17.7	9.8	n.a.

Sources: Data for 1951-55 from Central Bank, *Monthly Statistical Supplement;* 1956-64 data from *International Financial Statistics.*

32. The material in this and the following paragraphs, except as otherwise noted, is from FBD report, Vol. 3, pp. 20, A-14, 15, A-17, A-18, A-23, A-24.

33. COMIBOL, *Operación Triangular*, p. 3.

34. *Journal of Commerce*, April 21, 1965; from *International Financial News Survey*, XVII (May 7, 1965), 168. *London Bank*, XXX (May 29, 1965), 460. Col. Lechín was accompanied by Col. Eduardo Mendez-Pereira, Minister of Mines (*ibid.*, April 3, 1965, p. 277). COMIBOL was authorized to call for bids on Matilde mine on February 9, 1962, according to *Bolivia: 10 Años de Revolución*, p. 39. The data on the various mines is from the FBD report.

35. *Operación Triangular*, p. 32.

36. Decree, February 3, 1961; *Bolivia: 10 Años de Revolución*, p. 39.

37. *London Bank*, XXX (October 2, 1965), 868.

38. The 1961 royalty rates ran as high as 26.26 per cent on high-content concentrates at $1.40 prices; see Central Bank, 33d *Annual Report*, 1961, p. 201. They were cut approximately 30 per cent on April 1, 1964, but were still based on a cumbersome and burdensome structure that greatly hampered the private mines (see *Operación Triangular*, p. 20).

39. Decree 5729, March 10, 1961 (Central Bank, 33d *Annual Report*, 1961, p. 203).

40. Concession approved, December 3, 1957; *Bolivia: 10 Años de Revolución*, p. 39. Concession data from American Embassy, *Quarterly Economic Summary*, A-67 (August 13, 1964). Production and tax figures from International Mining Corporation, *Annual Reports*, 1964 and 1965.

41. *Journal of Commerce*, April 21, 1965, from *International Financial News*, XVII (May 14, 1965), 176. The Planning Board had previously reported (in 1962) that five private mining enterprises had gone into Bolivia since stabilization (*Bolivia: 10 Años de Revolución*, p. 45), viz.: Schiavi Compañía (investment $668,670); Mitsubishi Metal Mining (copper — investment $8,770,000); SYMAF (a Belgian company, tin — investment $550,000); F. Kanematsu Co., Ltd. (copper, tin, gold, silver — investment $5,300,000); Nitto Mining (copper — investment n.a.).

42. Standard & Poor's *Corporation Records*; *London Bank*, XXIX (November 14, 1964), 969; Tidewater Oil Co., *Annual Report*, 1965.

43. Official export figures from *London Bank*, XXX (October 2, 1965), 868.

44. Central Bank, 32d *Annual Report*, 1960, p. 28; 1962 quota from 34th *Annual Report*, 1962, p. 19.

45. This paragraph and the four following paragraphs, except as otherwise noted, are based on *Operación Triangular*, pp. 2, 25, 27-28.

46. 3d *Annual Report*, Social Progress Trust Fund, Inter-American Development Bank; Art. 7, Memorandum of Understanding, June 9, 1961 (Triangular Plan).

47. IMF, *Annual Report*, 1958, pp. 110-11.

48. *Operación Triangular*, p. 5.

49. The contract provisions in this and the following paragraph are taken from Central Bank, 33d *Annual Report*, 1961, p. 203.

50. Negotiations between Guillermo Bedregal-Gutiérrez, COMIBOL President, and the FSTMB broke down when the latter refused to allow dismissal of the communist labor leaders, Ireneo Pimentel and Federico Escobar, and refused to permit dismissal of more than 650 miners, while COMIBOL insisted on dismissing 1,050 in implementation of the Triangular Plan (*Hispanic American Report*, XVI [September, 1963], 898).

51. COMIBOL report from *Operación Triangular*, pp. 7, 25. Critical opinion from Canelas, *Nacionalización de las Minas de Bolivia: Historia de una Frustración*, pp. 201-28, 259-62. Letter from Broesma, April 17, 1963, published in *El Diario*, October 20, 1963. In a talk to the University of Oruro faculty and students, Broesma attributed the Triangular Plan to U.S. alarm at Castro in Cuba and the USSR offer of $150 million to Bolivia (Canelas, p. 200).

52. *London Bank*, XXX (April 13, 1965), 278. American Embassy, *Quarterly Economic Summary*, August 11, 1965, p. 7. *El Diario*, October 5, 1965, May 3, 1966, reported in *International Financial News Survey*, XVI (November 19, 1965), 427; XVIII (May 27, 1966), 179. See also *El Diario*, June 4 and 8, 1966, reported in *International Financial News Survey*, XVIII (July 15, 1966), 236.

53. I was offered the opportunity of inspecting classified material in conference with AID and State Department officials in Washington, November 17, 1964, but regulations would have entailed execution of an application whose terms would have inhibited freedom of action. It was therefore deemed preferable to use such material as might be available from other sources, even though fragmentary. On October 14, 1965, the Assistant Director of Development (Bolivia-Chile) at AID gave me copies of the Triangular Agreement Memorandum of Understanding, June 9, 1961, and Supplementary Understandings down to October 11, 1965, but these do not contain the crucial provisions referred to in the text of this book, which have been taken from the Central Bank report cited in note 49. However, paragraphs 8, 9, and 10 of the June 9, 1961, Memorandum

reveal that such arrangements would be negotiated by IDB "with the advice of the governmental participants," and these arrangements appear to be still classified *in the United States* (see note 62, below).

54. Central Bank, 35th *Annual Report,* 1963, p. 44.
55. ECLA, *Economic Survey of Latin America 1954* (New York: United Nations, 1955), p. 128.
56. American Embassy *Annual Economic and Financial Review,* 1954-55, April 6, 1956, section by M. R. Barnebey. Zondag report, p. 13. The primary objective of the tin smelter as a Revolutionary imperative was made clear in conferences with MNR officials. FBD report, Vol. V, pp. 5, 6, 50. See also Vol. I, summary; Vol. II, pp. 2, 6, 115; Vol. III, pp. 3, 4, 5, 13, 27, 40, 69, 73, 78, 82, 92, 93, 115; Vol. IV, pp. 1, 3, 84-86; Vol. V, pp. 2, 4, 5, 19, 50; Vol. VII, p. 35; Vol. I, p. 32.
57. Powelson, *"Planeamiento Para el Desarrollo Económico," Revista de la Facultad de Sciencias Económicas,* June, 1964, p. 104.
58. Decree 6504, June 21, 1963 (Central Bank, 35th *Annual Report,* 1963).
59. FBD report, Vol. V, p. 4. The two local smelters were Empresa de Fundición HORMENT and Fundición de Estaño de Oruro, S.A. Decree 6370, February 8, 1963, expressly "authorized" COMIBOL, the Mining Bank, and the medium-sized mines to sell a greater percentage of their concentrates to those smelters (Central Bank, 35th *Annual Report,* 1963), but, apparently, the authorization was in fact an obligation, judging by the permissive provisions of the 1965 Mining Code.
60. *London Bank,* **XXIX** (May 30, 1964), 440.
61. Mining Code summary from *London Bank,* **XXX** (October 2, 1965), 868.
62. *Ibid.,* September 5, 1964, p. 742. Conference in USAID/ Washington, November 17, 1964, with Alex Firfer, Allen Gordon, and Lawrence Petersen.
63. *London Bank,* **XXX** (April 3, 1965), p. 278; (May 29, 1965), p. 460; *Globe & Mail,* Toronto, August 1, 1966, p. 24, quoting from *Financial Times,* London.
64. Decree 5558, September 2, 1960; Central Bank, 32d *Annual Report,* 1960, p. lxxxii. Profit and loss figures from USAID, *Economic and Program Statistics,* 1965, p. 29.
65. This and the following two paragraphs in the text based on the De Golyer and MacNaughton, Inc. report, March, 1964, pp. 3-5, 8-9, 16, 19, 21, 23, 25-27, 31-32, 35, 41-42, 47, except as otherwise indicated. Prior De G. & M. reports were dated September 26, 1960, and May 22, 1962.
66. *London Bank,* **XXX** (April 3, 1965), pp. 277-78; *Journal of*

Commerce, April 21, from *International Financial News Survey*, XVII (April 30, 1965), 160; *New York Times*, August 16, 1966, p. 12 (Juan de Onís).

67. This paragraph in the text (except as indicated for YPFB production) is based on Gulf Oil Corporation, *Annual Reports* for 1964 and 1965, and *Interim Report*, August 5, 1966, and on J. H. Carmical, *New York Times*, October 4, 1964, p. III-1.

68. De Golyer and MacNaughton, p. 39. *London Bank*, XXXI (September 17, 1966), p. 512.

69. American Embassy, *Quarterly Economic Summary*, A-354 (October 31, 1963), p. 13.

70. Compañía Petrolera Boliviana Shell, S.A. ($3,067,716 plus Bs. 3,887 million); Bolivia-California Petroleum Company ($2,554,132 plus Bs. 533 million); Bolivian Petroleum Company ($247,133); Central Bank, 31st *Annual Report*, 1959, p. 71. Also Andes Oil Co., Ltd. (representing Pure Oil Co.); Standard Oil of Ohio; Hancock Oil Co.; Chaco Petroleum Corp. (a subsidiary of Tennessee Gas Transmission Co.); Lyon Oil Co.; Murphy Corp.; Union Oil & Gas Corp. of Louisiana (from *Wall Street Journal*, December 24, 1958).

71. *International Commerce*, March 22, 1965; from *International Financial News Survey*, XVII (April 2, 1965), 127.

72. New York *Journal of Commerce*, May 7, 1964; from *International Financial News Survey*, XVI (May 15, 1964), 164; Banco Industrial, *Annual Report*, 1964.

73. USAID, *Economic and Program Statistics*, 1965, p. 36.

74. Decree 5600, October 11, 1960; Central Bank, 32d *Annual Report*, 1960, p. lxxxix.

75. *Planeamiento*, September, 1961 (the organ of the National Planning Board).

76. Resumé of aims from Guillermo Bedregal, *El Plan Nacional de Desarrollo y la Integración de la Industria Estañífera de Bolivia*, p. 13.

77. *Planeamiento*, p. 42-A, Table 5.

78. Decree 6310, December 6, 1962, from Central Bank, 34th *Annual Report*, 1962, p. 212. IDB, *Annual Report*, 1963, p. 60.

79. Central Bank, 32d *Annual Report*, 1960, p. 56; 34th *Annual Report*, 1962, p. 45. *Bolivia: 10 Años de Revolución*, p. 108, claims that the cost was $1,439,351 plus Bs. 4,107 billion, omitting the counterpart funds, and adds the information that the plant is run jointly by the Development Corporation, the mayor of Sucre, and the University of Sucre. Data for 1963 from American Embassy, *Quarterly Economic · Summary*, A-574 (February 7, 1964), p. 3. Fives-Lille data from *London Bank*, Vol. XXI (June 25, 1966), p. 341. See also *London Bank*, Vol. XXXI (September 17, 1966), p. 511 on IADB loan to cement plant.

80. *Bolivia: 10 Años de Revolución*, p. 68.

81. *London Bank*, **XXX** (April 3, 1965), 277.

82. American Embassy, *Quarterly Economic Summary*, A-67 (August 13, 1964), p. 10. See also Raymond E. Crist, "Bolivians Trek Eastward," *The Americas*, April 16, 1963, pp. 33-38; and James L. Tigner, "The Ryukyans in Bolivia," *Hispanic-American Historical Review*, May, 1963, pp. 206-29; *London Bank*, **XXX** (December 11, 1965), 1082.

83. IDB, *Annual Report*, 1963, pp. 86, 89, 95, 106; 1962, pp. 28, 64, 88, 102, 115; 1961, pp. 40, 90, 94; *New York Times*, June 12, 1961, p. 7.

84. Joint IDA-IDB press release, July 24, 1964, from *International Financial News Survey*, XVI (August 6, 1964). Other development projects, under the auspices of the Development Corporation and other government agencies, vary from such minor expenditures as the construction of a small electric power plant for the gold placer miners' cooperative at Tipuani (Juan de Onís, *New York Times*, August 16, 1964, p. 24) to the 430 miles of roads and highways recommended by the USOM/Bolivia at an estimated cost of some $16 million (USOM, Engineering & Transportation Division, *Red de Caminos Nacionales* [La Paz: USOM/Bolivia, 1961]). That highway plan, with its established order of priorities, has been superseded by a new emergency plan of highway construction to the COMIBOL and YPFB mining and oil areas, in particular the Tatarenda oil field recently developed by YPFB (*London Bank*, **XXX** [April 3, 1965]; *Journal of Commerce*, April 21, 1965; from *International Financial News Survey*, XVII [April 31, 1965], 160). The private mines and oil companies are required to construct their own access roads, so that these outlays constitute a subsidy to government enterprises that does not appear in the company profit and loss accounts.

85. IDB release 64/3603, November, 1964; IDB *Annual Report*, 1965, pp. 67, 88-89, 128.

86. *London Bank*, **XXX** (May 29, 1965), 460.

87. American Embassy, *Quarterly Economic Summary*, A-574 (February 7, 1964), p. 9; A-67 (August 13, 1964), p. 12; A-48 (August 11, 1965), pp. 5-6.

88. *HAR*, XVI (September, 1963), 898-99.

89. Law 147, December 29, 1961; Decree 5979, January 26, 1962; both from Central Bank, 34th *Annual Report*, 1962, pp. 172, 171, respectively.

90. Escott Reid, "Rich Lands, Poor Lands," *Finance and Development*, II (March, 1965), 21.

91. *London Bank*, **XXX** (October 2, 1965), 867.

92. See announcements, *Financial Times*, April 3, 1962, May 22,

1964, for material contained in this and the following paragraphs in the text, which has, however, been supplemented by other sources which are known to be reliable.

93. G. M. Wilson, the General Manager, was considered one of the most capable railway men stationed in South America. Certainly no one had greater problems to contend with or bore them with greater aplomb. R. H. Dobson, the Managing Director of the parent company in London, made visits to La Paz in 1957 and 1958 to take part in the negotiations with the government, and to confer with the Stabilization Council. Data for 1966 from *London Bank,* Vol. XXI (June 25, 1966), p. 342.

94. Data from *London Bank,* XXIX (December 26, 1964), 1100; American Embassy, *Quarterly Economic Summary,* A-48 (August 11, 1965), p. 5; and USAID, *Economic and Program Statistics,* 1965, p. 29.

95. Luis Peñaloza, Summary Proceedings, *IMF Annual Meeting, 1959.*

96. Law 48, December 16, 1960, from Central Bank, 32d *Annual Report,* 1960, p. xcviii.

97. This synopsis of what businessmen require as an incentive for investment in Latin America is based on replies to a questionnaire sent out by the Citizens Advisory Committee, United States Senate Committee on Banking and Currency, 83rd Congress, 1st Session (1953) and tabulated by George Jackson Eder, as the Reporting Member of the Subcommittee, under the title "The Expansion of Private Foreign Investments" (published in Columbia Society of International Law, *United States Trade and Investment in Latin America* [New York: Columbia University School of Law, 1963], pp. 279-95).

98. Decree 6481, May 31, 1963; Central Bank, 35th *Annual Report,* 1963. *London Bank,* XXX (December 11, 1965), 1082; *London Bank,* XXXI (June 25, 1966), p. 341.

99. Keenleyside report, p. 3.

100. ECLA report, pp. 88-98.

101. American Embassy, *Quarterly Economic Summary,* A-48 (August 11, 1965), pp. 2, 3, 7, and conversations with businessmen in New York in October, 1965.

102. American Embassy, *Quarterly Economic Summary,* A-67 (August 13, 1964), p. 8.

103. Decree 5311, September 29, 1959, from Central Bank, 31st *Annual Report,* 1959, p. 195. USOM, *Point IV in Bolivia: 1942-1960,* p. 9. Figures from mimeo release, USAID, Washington, 1964. See also Central Bank, 32d *Annual Report,* 1960, p. lxxxi.

104. American Embassy, *Quarterly Economic Summary,* A-354 (October 31, 1963); A-67 (August 13, 1964); Decrees 6556, August 22, 1963 (licensing); 6563, August 30 (duties); Decree

7054, February 17, 1965, revoked Decree 6556 in part; *London Bank,* XXX (May 29, 1965), 460; Central Bank, 35th *Annual Report,* 1963; *London Bank,* XXX (December 11, 1965), 1082.

105. Law 236, December 31, 1962. The private oil royalties are paid by the companies directly to the Central Bank to the order of the Committee of Public Works in the department where the oil is produced (Central Bank, 35th *Annual Report,* 1963).

106. Central Bank, 34th *Annual Report,* 1962, p. 135.

107. Decree 5939, December 8, 1961; from Central Bank, 33d *Annual Report,* 1961, p. 207; Decree 6171, July 27, 1962, from Central Bank, 34th *Annual Report,* 1962, p. 195.

108. *Bolivia: 10 Años de Revolución,* p. 195. USAID/Washington, mimeographed report, 1964.

109. Law 185, October 15, 1962, from Central Bank, 34th *Annual Report,* 1962, p. 207.

110. *New York Times,* October 8, 1960; January 22, 1961, p. III-1; June 11, p. III-1; July 31, 1962, p. 41; December 1, 1964, p. 61.

111. Foreign Bondholders Protective Council, Inc., May 22, 1964, press release; *Report 1962 through 1964,* pp. v, 9-10.

112. Minister of Labor; reported in *El Diario,* February 24, 1959.

113. See IMF, *Annual Report,* 1959, pp. 111, 138.

114. See Central Bank, 31st *Annual Report,* 1959, p. 36; 32d *Annual Report,* 1960, p. 34; for figures of drawings against the fund and cancellation of the Treasury stand-by.

115. On my departure, Ernest Moore was named Acting Executive Director of the National Monetary Stabilization Council (June-September, 1957), and was followed by Victor R. Rose as Executive Director (February, 1958-February, 1959). Rose was the last person to serve in that capacity, or as a foreign member of the council, but John P. Powelson (formerly with IMF; presently at the University of Pittsburgh) was appointed as an economist on the USOM/Bolivia staff in September, 1959, and in that capacity served as an adviser to the council for a year. Meanwhile, the original IMF resident representative, John R. Woodley (December, 1956-August, 1957) had been replaced by Herbert K. Zassenhaus (August, 1957-June, 1959). Later, Mr. Zassenhaus was replaced by George J. Clark (June, 1959-June, 1961), followed by Richard Richardson (June, 1961-August, 1962), Sergio Nicolau (August, 1962-August, 1963), and Marcello Caiola (March, 1964 to date). The arrivals and departures are noted in the La Paz papers on or shortly after the respective dates.

116. Juan de Onís, *New York Times,* September 19, 1958.

117. Central Bank, 30th *Annual Report,* 1958, pp. 23, 27-28.

118. *El Diario,* October 1, 1958, from *International Financial News Survey,* X (October 10, 1958).

119. See Joseph M. Guilfoyle, *Wall Street Journal*, December 24, 1958.

120. Central Bank, 30th *Annual Report*, 1958, pp. 53-54, on the treaty with Brazil, March 29, 1958; and Decree 5071, October 30, 1958, on the agreement with Argentina.

121. Decree 5134, January 20, 1959; Decree 5184, April 18, 1959; from Central Bank, 31st *Annual Report*, 1959, pp. 161, 171. Decree 5308, September 22, 1959, *ibid.*, p. 195.

122. IMF transaction rate from *International Financial Statistics*, XII (December, 1960), p. 62 *n*. Effective January 1, 1963, the IMF rate was established at 11.875 pesos (buying) and 11.885 pesos (selling), plus 2 per cent tax on sales to the private sector.

123. IMF, *Annual Report*, 1961, p. 28; 1962, pp. 16, 20-21; 1963, p. 15; 1964, p. 11. *International Financial News Survey*, XVII (March, 1965), table, pp. 4-5. Central Bank, 33d *Annual Report*, 1961, p. 26; 34th *Annual Report*, 1962, p. 22. *International Financial News Survey*, XVI (August 28, 1964), 1; *idem* (October 30, 1964), 392. *International Financial Statistics*, XIX (April, 1966).

124. Report of Executive Directors to the Board of Governors, IMF, on Tokyo meeting; *International Financial News Survey*, XVII (March 5, 1965), supplement; *idem*, XVIII (February 25, 1966), 1.

125.

Year	Pesos or Bolivianos per Dollar	Index	Cost of Living	Index	Money Supply	Index	Currency Circulation	Index
1956	7,760	*100*	2,800 (1953)	*100*	197	*100*	145.3	*100*
1957	8,865	*114*	2,420	*86*	291	*148*	212.5	*146*
1958	11,935	*154*	2,870	*102*	301	*152*	240.7	*166*
1959	11,885	*153*	3,160	*113*	386	*196*	320.6	*221*
1960	11,885	*153*	3,500	*125*	419	*212*	354.0	*244*
1961	11,885	*153*	3,760	*134*	496	*252*	414.3	*285*
1962	11,885	*153*	152 (1958)	*136*	556	*282*	460.1	*317*
1963	11.88	*153*	151	*135*	665	*338*	540.4	*372*
1964	11.88	*153*	167	*149*	803	*408*	657.7	*453*
1965	11.88	*153*	175	*154*	1,011	*514*	806.7	*555*

Note: Year-end figures, except for cost of living, which is the average for the month of December. All data from *International Financial Statistics*, except that the conversion from the 1953 base to the 1958 base for the cost of living has been computed on the basis of the average cost of living for 1958 (2,500 on the 1953 base; 100 on the 1958 base) and that all index figures, shown above in italics, have been computed on the basis of December 1956 = 100. The peso (shown in the first column for 1963-65) = 1,000 bolivianos. Money supply and circulation are in billions of bolivianos or millions of pesos.

126. USAID, *Economic and Program Statistics*, 1964, p. 30.

127. *International Financial Statistics*.

128. Decree 6161, July 13, 1962 (Central Bank, 34th *Annual Report*, 1962, pp. 22, 191). *London Bank*, XXIX (July 11, 1965), 566;

statement by Col. Juan José Torres-González, *London Bank,* XXIX (December 26, 1964), p. 1099. Also statements by Gen. René Barrientos-Ortuño and Lt. Col. Carlos Alcoreza-Melgarejo, *Bolivia,* January 1, 1965, p. 7.

129. *Última Hora,* January 22, 1960, commenting on U.S. Senate report on aid to Bolivia; *Presencia,* January 23, 1960.
130. Tad Szulc, *New York Times,* May 7, 1958, p. 11; *Hanson's Latin American Letter,* May 10; Juan de Onís, *New York Times,* September 14, p. 34; September 17, p. 6.
131. *American Metal Market,* October 3, 1958.
132. The *New York Times,* December 13, 1958, p. 23 and December 14, p. 14, reports Lechín's plea for money, but not his visit to Henry Holland.
133. *Foreign Aid and Foreign Policy,* p. 180.
134. Juan de Onís, *New York Times,* August 9, 1964, p. 10; Henry Raymont, *New York Times,* August 22, p. 1.
135. USAID, *Economic and Program Statistics 1965,* p. 31. Henry Raymont, *New York Times,* June 4, 1965, p. 7. Bolivian figures for 1964-65 from Table 21 converted at Pesos 11.88 per dollar.
136. FBD report, Vol. II, p. 4, and Zondag report, p. 99, on tungsten; on tin, p. 649*n.*
137.

Year	Billions of Bolivianos or Millions of Pesos	Thousands of Dollars	U. S. Grants and Loans — Commitments (Thousands of Dollars)
1954	...	$ 8,200	$12,197
1955	...	9,850	24,087
1956	...	8,260	23,829
1957	239.5	28,000	24,900
1958	231.6	19,500	24,300
1959	232.0	19,510	22,600
1960	264.5	22,240	15,100
1961	325.6	27,400	34,000
1962	392.2	33,000	35,500
1963	419.6	49,850	54,800
1964	512.9	60,920	72,100
1965 (budget)	608.5	72,290	16,500

Sources: Tax Collections: 1954-56, figures provided by Finance Minister; 1957, U.N., *Statistical Yearbook, 1963,* p. 582, converted at Bs. 8,565; 1958-65, *Economic and Program Statistics* (La Paz: USAID, 1965), p. 25, converted at Bs. 11,880 (or Pesos 11.88). U.S. grants and loans: 1954-58, Zondag report, p. 270; 1959-65, *Economic and Program Statistics,* 1964, 1965.

138. Agreement, July 20, 1962, between Bolivia, AID, and IDB; Central Bank, 34th *Annual Report,* 1962, p. 163. To implement this agreement, the regulations of the Mining Bank (established by decree of July 24, 1936) were revised by Decree 6408, March 22, 1963, while those of the Agricultural Bank (established by decree of February 11, 1942, amended by Decree 3839, September 23, 1954) were revised by Decree 6456, May 3, 1963; Central Bank, 35th *Annual Report,* 1963.

139. USAID press release published in *Washington Post Times & Herald,* June 25, 1964, p. C-2. The statements referred to as having been made by an official of USAID were made in conversation in Ann Arbor, Michigan.

140. Inquiry at the Export-Import Bank on October 14, 1965, confirmed the fact that no payments have been made since 1958. The facts are confirmed by comparison of the amounts outstanding shown in the annual Eximbank *Report to the Congress* for various years through June 30, 1965. Interest accumulated and defaulted is not computed in those reports, but may be calculated at $3\frac{1}{2}$ per cent on one defaulted loan that matured in June, 1964, and at $4\frac{3}{4}$ per cent on three other loans maturing in 1974 (the 1957 extensions are not shown in the annual reports). See June 30, 1959, *Report to Congress,* Vol. I, p. 191, for quoted comment.

141. American Embassy, *Quarterly Economic Summary,* A-574 (February 7, 1964), p. 9. *New York Times,* October 18, 1966, p. 4 (Juan de Onís).

142. *Idem,* A-67 (August 12, 1964), p. 6. International Mining Corporation, *Annual Report,* 1964.

143. USAID, *Economic and Program Statistics,* 1965, p. 33, supplemented by USOM, *Point IV in Bolivia 1942-1960,* p. 10. The figures in the two pamphlets do not tally; according to the latter, the 1952-61 outlay would be $26.3 million, while, according to the former, it would be $24.8 million.

144. U.S. Congress, Senate, Committee on Government Operations, *Administration of United States Foreign Aid Program in Bolivia,* Senate Report No. 1030, 86th Cong., 2d Sess.,January 20, 1960, pp. 17-22.

145. P. N. Rosenstein-Rodan, "Notes on the Theory of the Big Push," in *Economic Development for Latin America,* ed. Howard S. Ellis and Henry Wallich (London: Macmillan Co., 1962), p. 57.

146. *Foreign Aid and Foreign Policy,* pp. 208-9.

147. Conversation, October 11, 1965, with G. A. Costanzo, Senior Vice-President and George J. Clark, Assistant Vice-President,

First National City Bank, New York. There was, of course, a direct incentive for establishment of the branch, in that U.S. aid and P.L. 480 funds must by law be deposited in an American bank, if available (*New York Times,* H. J. Maidenberg, January 8, 1966, p. 29).

148. Statement by President of Military Junta, Gen. René Barrientos-Ortuño; Finance Minister Lt. Col. Carlos Alcoreza-Melgarejo; in interview in presence of IMF representative Marcello Caiola; *Bolivia,* January 1, 1965, p. 7. *New York Times,* July 2, 1966, p. 4 (Richard Eder).

149. Speeches by Guillermo Lora, at University of Oruro, January 29, 1957, and at University of San Andrés (La Paz), December 20, 1957; from *La Estabilización — Una Impostura.* COMIBOL President Guillermo Bedregal, *Problemas de Infraestructura,* in particular pp. 27-29. Guillermo Alborta Velasco, *El Flágelo de la Inflación Monetaria en Bolivia,* pp. 295-96.

150. *Economics of the Free Society,* p. 249.

151. *London Bank,* **XXX** (October 2, 1965), p. 867. The appellation of "anarcho-syndicalist" is from Alborta-Velasco, *El Flágelo de la Inflación Monetaria en Bolivia,* p. 338. American Embassy, *Quarterly Economic Summary,* August 11, 1965, p. 1.

152. *Bolivia,* January 1, 1965, p. 5.

153. Jeremy Bentham, *Works,* Vol. X, p. 142; based on Joseph Priestley, *Essay on Government.* In an ideal world, of course, where the rule of "the greatest happiness of the greatest number" prevails, Michigan would invariably beat Purdue, for there are certainly more students, faculty, and alumni who would rejoice at a Wolverine victory than would be dismayed by the Boilermakers' defeat.

154. See p. 466*n.*

BIBLIOGRAPHY

BIBLIOGRAPHY

Ahlfeld, Federico. *Mapa de los Yacimientos Minerales de Bolivia con una Memoria Explicativa*. Buenos Aires: Privately printed, 1946.

Ahlfeld, a German geologist, is generally considered to be the leading authority on Bolivia's mineral resources.

——. *Los Yacimientos Minerales de Bolivia*. La Paz: Privately printed, 1941.

Alborta-Velasco, Guillermo. *El Flágelo de la Inflación Monetaria en Bolivia, País Monoproductor*. Madrid: Ed. Románica, 1963.

Alexander, Robert Jackson. *A Primer of Economic Development*. New York: Macmillan Co., 1963.

——. *The Bolivian National Revolution*. New Brunswick, N.J.: Rutgers University Press, 1958.

An account by one who is "frankly sympathetic to what has been going on in Bolivia since April 9, 1952." A useful counterpoise to Ostria-Gutiérrez' right-wing account of the Revolution.

——. *The Venezuelan Democratic Revolution*. New Brunswick, N.J.: Rutgers University Press, 1964.

American Can Company. *Annual Report*. New York: American Can Co., 1965.

American Council on Education. *International Handbook of Universities*. 2d ed. Washington, D.C.: American Council on Education, 1962.

Antezana-Paz, Franklin. *La Política Monetaria de Bolivia*. La Paz: Banco Central de Bolivia, 1954.

Aramayo, Carlos Victor. *Memorandum Sobre los Problemas de la Industria Minera de Bolivia*. Madrid: Imprenta Gráficas Reunidas, 1956.

A reprint of a report written in 1946 by a shareholder in one of the Big Three mining companies. Enlightening and, on the whole, dispassionate. Aramayo was president of *La Razón,* an independent newspaper of La Paz which was suppressed and its properties confiscated by the Revolutionary Government.

Arnade, Charles W. *The Emergence of the Republic of Bolivia*. Gainesville, Fla.: University of Florida Press, 1957.

Arntz, Helmut (ed.). *Germany Reports*. 2d ed. Bonn: Press and Information Office of the Federal German Government, 1955.

Arthur Andersen & Co. *Tax and Trade Guide: France*. New York: Arthur Andersen & Co., 1961.

759

Ayala Z., Alfredo. *Historia General y de Bolivia.* La Paz: Ed. Don Bosco, 1958.

Baer, Werner, and Kerstenetzky, Isaac (eds.). *Inflation and Growth in Latin America.* Homewood, Ill.: Richard D. Irwin, 1964.

Bank of London & South America, Ltd. *Fortnightly Review.* London: Bank of London & South America, Ltd.

An invaluable report on trade, financial, foreign exchange, and economic matters in general, including new legislation. Cited in this book as *London Bank.*

Baudin, Louis. *El Imperio Socialista de los Incas.* Translated from the French by José Antonio Arze. 4th ed. Santiago, Chile: Empresa Editora Zig-Zag, 1955.

Bedregal, Guillermo. *El Plan Nacional de Desarrollo y la Integración de la Industria Estañifera de Bolivia.* La Paz: Corporación Minera Boliviana, 1962.

———. *Problemas de Infraestructura.* La Paz: Corporación Minera Boliviana, 1962.

This book concludes that the monetary stabilization program has failed to cure Bolivia's infrastructure problems.

Bentham, Jeremy. *The Works of Jeremy Bentham.* Edinburgh: John Bowring, 1843.

Blakeslee, George H. (ed.). *Latin America.* New York: G. E. Stechert, 1924.

Bloch, Henry S. *Observations on Fiscal and Monetary Activities in Bolivia.* La Paz: U.N. Technical Assistance Administration, 1954. (Hectograph.)

Cited in this book as the Bloch report.

Bloomfield, Arthur I. *Speculative and Flight Movements of Capital in Postwar International Finance.* Princeton, N.J.: Princeton University Press, 1954.

Bohan, Merwin L. *Report of the U.S. Economic Mission to Bolivia.* La Paz: U.S. Economic Mission, 1942.

Cited in this book as the Bohan report.

Bolivia: 10 Años de Revolución. La Paz: Dirección Nacional de Informaciones, 1962.

Booz, Allen & Hamilton, Inc. *Report to AID on the Feasibility of Expanding Sociedad Industrial Azucarera la Esperanza, S.A.* La Paz: Booz, Allen & Hamilton, Inc., 1963.

Brandenburg, Frank R. *The Making of Modern Mexico.* Englewood Cliffs, N.J.: Prentice-Hall, 1964.

The author's analysis of the Mexican experience shows that corruption in Bolivia is not unique in Latin America.

Bresciani-Turroni, Costantino. *The Economics of Inflation: A Study of Currency Depreciation in Post-War Germany.* Translated by Millicent E. Sayers with a foreword by Lionel Robbins. London: Allen & Unwin, 1937.

The definitive study of hyperinflation and subsequent stabilization in Germany following World War I.

Briggs, Ellis. *Farewell to Foggy Bottom.* New York: David McKay Co., 1964.

Butrón-Márquez, Germán. *Observaciones de la C.N.S.S. a los Planteamientos de Mr. Eder.* La Paz: Caja Nacional de Seguridad Social, 1957.

Cairnes, John Elliott. *Some Leading Principles of Political Economy Newly Expounded.* London and New York: Harper's, 1874.

Canelas O., Amado. *Nacionalización de las Minas de Bolivia: Historia de una Frustración.* La Paz: Librería Altiplano, 1963.

Carrasco, Manuel. *Simón E. Patiño, un Prócer Industrial.* Paris: Jean Grassin, 1960.

Cassell, Gustav. *Money and Foreign Exchange after 1914.* New York: Macmillan Co., 1922.

Chamberlin, William Henry. *The German Phoenix.* New York: Duell, Sloan & Pearce, 1963.

Columbia Society of International Law. *United States Trade and Investment in Latin America.* New York: Columbia University School of Law, 1963.

Corporación Minera Boliviana. *Operación Triangular.* La Paz: Corporación Minera Boliviana, March, 1964.

Constitución Política del Estado. La Paz: Gisbert y Cia., 1955.

Continental Can Company. *Annual Report.* New York: Continental Can Co., 1965.

Costa, Jasper S. *Some Aspects of Revenue Administration in Bolivia.* Washington, D.C.: International Cooperation Administration, 1958. (Mimeographed.)

Costanzo, Gesualdo A. *Programas de Estabilización Económica en América Latina.* Mexico City: Centro de Estudios Monetarios Latinamericanos, 1961.

Council on Foreign Relations. *Social Change in Latin America Today.* New York: Harper & Bros., 1960.

Crist, Raymond E. "Bolivians Trek Eastward," *The Americas,* April, 1963, pp. 33-38.

Daly, Rex. *Appraisal of Pakistan's Second Five-Year Plan.* Karachi: U.S. Agency for International Development, 1960.

Los Decretos del 14 de Mayo de 1953. La Paz: Ediciones S.P.I.C., 1953.

De Golyer and MacNaughton, Inc., *Report to USAID on YPFB.* Dallas, Texas: De Golyer and MacNaughton, Inc., 1964.

Dorrance, Graeme S. "The Effect of Inflation upon Economic Development," in *IMF Staff Papers,* Washington, D.C., 1963.

Dubois, Jules. *Operation America.* New York: Walker & Co., 1963.
The story of the communist plan for Latin America, this book presents a sensational rather than a balanced account.

Duguid, Julian. *Green Hell*. New York: Century, 1931.

Economic Commission for Latin America. *Economic Survey of Latin America 1954*. New York: United Nations, 1955.

Eder, Francis Xavier. *Descriptio Provinciae Moxitarum in Regno Peruano*. Budapest: Typis Universitatis, 1791.
    A posthumously published report by the Administrator of the Society of Jesus in Bolivia and Eastern Peru.

Eder, George Jackson. "Effect of Gold Price Changes upon Prices for Other Commodities," *Journal of the Royal Statistical Society*, CI, Part I (1938), 173-87.

————. "The Expansion of Private Foreign Investments," in Columbia Society of International Law, *United States Trade and Investment in Latin America*, pp. 279-95.

————. "Urban Concentration, Agriculture, and Agrarian Reform," *Annals of the American Academy of Political and Social Science*, CCCLX (July, 1965), 27-47.

Eisenhower, Milton. *The Wine is Bitter*. New York: Doubleday & Co., 1963.

Ellis, Howard S., and Wallich, Henry C. (eds.). *Economic Development for Latin America*. London: Macmillan Co., 1962.

Erhard, Ludwig. *Germany's Comeback in the World Market*. Translated by W. H. Johnston. London: Allen & Unwin, 1954.

————. *Prosperity Through Competition*. Translated by Edith Temple Roberts and John B. Wood. New York: Frederick A. Praeger, 1958.

Falcon, Walter P. "Farmer Response to Price in a Subsistance Economy: The Case of West Pakistan," *American Economic Review*, LIV (May, 1964), 580-81.

Farr's Manual of Sugar Companies. 34th ed. New York: Farr & Co., 1958.

Feis, Herbert. *Foreign Aid and Foreign Policy*. New York: St. Martin's Press, 1964.

Ferragut, Casto. *The Progress of Land Reform in Bolivia*. Discussion Paper No. 2. Madison, Wis.: Land Tenure Center, University of Wisconsin, 1963.

Field, Carter. *Bernard Baruch*. New York: McGraw-Hill Book Co., 1944.

Finot, Enrique. *Nueva Historia de Bolivia*. 2d ed. La Paz: Gisbert y Cia., 1954.

Flornoy, Bertrand. *Cuzco, ou le Socialisme chez les Inka*. Paris: La Nef, 1946.

————. *The World of the Inca*. Garden City, N.Y.: Doubleday & Co., 1958.

Ford, Bacon & Davis, Inc. *The Mining Industry of Bolivia*. La Paz: Ford, Bacon & Davis, 1956.
    Cited in this book as FBD report.

Fossati, Humberto, and Rangel, Domingo Alberto. *Estudio Econó-mico*. La Paz: Comisión Nacional de Coordinación y Planea-miento, 1956.
> Cited in this book as Fossati-Rangel report.
Franco-Guachalla, Alfredo. *En Torno a la Cuestión Social*. La Paz: Ministry of Labor, n.d.
Friedman, Milton, and Schwartz, Anna Jacobson. *A Monetary History of the United States, 1867-1960*. Princeton, N.J.: Princeton University Press, 1963.
Furtado, Celso. *Development and Underdevelopment*. Translated by W. de Aguiar and Eric C. Drysdale. Berkeley, Calif.: University of California Press, 1964.
Galbraith, John Kenneth. *Economic Development*. Cambridge, Mass.: Harvard University Press, 1964.
García, Raúl Alfonso. *Diez Años de Reforma Agraria en Bolivia: 1953-1963*. La Paz: Dirección Nacional de Informaciones, 1963.
Garcilaso-de la Vega. *Comentarios Reales de los Incas*. 2d ed. Buenos Aires: Emecé Editores, 1945.
> The classical work on the Incas and their conquest, written in the years 1609-17.
Gilmore, Raymond W. "Fauna and Ethnozoology of South America," in *Handbook of South American Indians* (Bureau of American Ethnology Bulletins, No. 143 [7 vols.; Washington, D.C., 1946-50]), VI, 438-39.
Goodrich, Carter. *The Economic Transformation of Bolivia*. Ithaca, N.Y.: Cornell University Press, 1955.
Graham, Frank D. "Achilles' Heels in Monetary Standards," *American Economic Review*, XXX (March, 1940), 16-32.
———. *The Cause and Cure of "Dollar Shortage."* Princeton, N.J.: Princeton University Press, 1949.
Greene, David G. "Revolution and the Rationalization of Reform in Bolivia," *Inter-American Economic Affairs*, XIX (Winter, 1965), 3-25.
Grunwald, Joseph. "The Structuralist School on Price Stability and Development," in Hirschman, Albert O. (ed.), *Latin American Issues: Essays and Comments*. New York: Twentieth Century Fund, 1961.
Gulf Oil Corporation. *Annual Report*. Pittsburgh, Pa.: Gulf Oil Corp., 1963, 1964, 1965.
Handbook of South American Indians. Edited by Julian H. Steward. (Smithsonian Institution, Bureau of American Ethnology Bulletin No. 143 [7 vols.; Washington, D.C., 1946-50].)
> Vol. II, *The Andean Civilizations;* Vol. III, *The Tropical Forest Tribes;* and Vol. VI, *Physical Anthropology, Linguistics, and Cultural Geography of South American Indians* are relevant to Bolivia and are the most authoritative studies of that area in their fields.

Hanson, Simon G. "The Alliance for Progress: The Third Year," *Inter-American Economic Affairs,* XVIII (Spring, 1965), 12.

Harrod, R. F. *The Life of John Maynard Keynes.* New York: Harcourt, Brace, 1951.

Hatcher, Harlan. *Revolutions of Aspiration.* Detroit, Mich.: Wayne State University Press, 1963.

Heath, Dwight B. "The Aymara Indians and Bolivia's Revolutions," *Inter-American Economic Affairs,* XIX (Spring, 1966), 31-40.

————. "Land Reform in Bolivia," *Inter-American Economic Affairs,* XII (Spring, 1959), 3-27.

   This penetrating study of the subject will shortly be superseded by the forthcoming volume *Land Reform and Social Revolution in Bolivia,* by Professor Heath, Hans C. Buechler, and Charles J. Erasmus, which will be the outstanding ethnological study in that area.

————. "Revolution and Stability in Bolivia," *Current History,* XLIX (December, 1962), 328ff.

Heilbroner, Robert. *The Great Ascent.* New York: Harper & Row, 1963.

————. *The Worldly Philosophers.* 2d ed. New York: Simon & Schuster, 1961.

Heller, Jack, and Kauffman, Kenneth M. *Tax Incentives for Industry in Less Developed Countries.* Cambridge, Mass.: Harvard Law School, 1963.

Hernández, José Mariá. *El Gaucho Martín Fierro.* Buenos Aires: Viau, 1937.

Higgins, Benjamin. *Economic Development: Principles, Problems, and Policies.* New York: W. W. Norton & Co., Inc., 1959.

Hirschman, Albert O. *The Strategy of Economic Development.* 2d ed. New Haven, Conn.: Yale University Press, 1961.

Hosmann, Elena. *Ambiente de Altiplano.* Buenos Aires: Editorial Peuser, 1945.

Hughes, Jonathan Roberts Tyson. *The Vital Few.* Boston, Mass.: Houghton Mifflin Co., 1966.

Hull, Cordell. *The Memoirs of Cordell Hull.* New York: Macmillan Co., 1948.

Huntington, Ellsworth. "The Adaptability of the White Man to Tropical America," in Blakeslee, George H. (ed.), *Latin America* (New York: G. E. Stechert, 1924), p. 368.

International Bank for Reconstruction and Development. *Some Techniques of Development Lending.* Washington, D.C.: International Bank for Reconstruction and Development, 1960.

International Labor Office. *Labor Problems in Bolivia.* Montreal: International Labor Office, 1943.

International Mining Corporation. *Annual Report.* New York: International Mining Corp., 1963, 1964, 1965.

International Monetary Fund. *Summary Proceedings, 1959 Annual Meeting*. Washington, D.C.: International Monetary Fund, 1959.

Iturralde, L., Luis. *Consideraciones sobre el Momento Actual de la Industria Azucarera Nacional*. La Paz: Editorial e Imprenta Artística, 1956.

Jaramillo, Delio. "La Reforma Agraria: La F.A.O., Bolivia y Guatemala," *La Nueva Economía*, I (October, 1961), 587-634.

Joslin, David. *A Century of Banking in Latin America*. London: Oxford University Press, 1963.

Karasz, Arturo. "Inflación y Depresión en Términos de Desequilibrio entre Producción y Consumo," *Revista del Derecho*, VI (March, 1954), 113-73.

Kemmerer, Edwin Walter. *Informe Kemmerer y Proyectos de Ley para la Reorganización del Banco de la Nación Boliviana, y Otros Proyectos*. La Paz: Finance Ministry, 1927.
Cited in this book as the Kemmerer report.

———. *Kemmerer on Money*. London: George Routledge & Sons, Ltd., 1934.
In its time considered an authoritative and outstanding brief treatise on the subject. Kemmerer was the most successful of all U.S. financial advisers in Latin America in the 1920's.

Keynes, John Maynard. *The Economic Consequences of the Peace*. New York: Harcourt Brace and Howe, 1920.

———. *The General Theory of Employment, Interest and Money*. New York: Harcourt, Brace, 1936.

Kimber, Albert W. *Foreign Dollar Bonds*. New York: White Weld and Co., 1951.

Kindleberger, Charles P. *Economic Development*. New York: McGraw-Hill Book Co., 1958.

Klein, Herbert S. "The Creation of the Patiño Tin Empire," *Inter-American Economic Affairs*, XIX (Autumn, 1965), 3-23.

Krishna, Raj. "Farm Supply Response in India-Pakistan," *Economic Journal*, LXXXIII (September, 1963), 477-87.

Leonard, Olen E. *Bolivia: Land, People, and Institutions*. Washington, D.C.: Scarecrow Press, 1952.

———. *Canton Chullpas: A Socioeconomic Study in the Cochabamba Valley of Bolivia*. Washington, D.C.: U.S. Department of Agriculture (Foreign Agricultural Report No. 27), 1948.

———. *Santa Cruz: A Socioeconomic Study of an Area in Bolivia*. Washington, D.C.: U.S. Department of Agriculture (Foreign Agricultural Report No. 31), 1948.

Lewis, William Arthur. *The Theory of Economic Growth*. Homewood, Ill.: Richard D. Irwin, 1955.

Lockwood, Agnese Nelms. *Indians of the Andes*. New York: Carnegie Endowment for International Peace, 1956.

Lora, Guillermo. *La Estabilización — Una Impostura.* La Paz: Editorial "Masas," 1960.

This book is a violent attack by the Partido Obrero Revolucionario (Trotskyite) leader on Eder and Siles personally, as well as on the stabilization program.

Marsh, Margaret A. *The Bankers in Bolivia.* New York: Vanguard Press, 1928.

Marshall, Alfred. *Principles of Economics.* 8th ed. London: Macmillan Co., 1925.

Mason, Edward S. *Economic Planning in Underdeveloped Areas.* New York: Fordham University Press, 1958.

Mason, J. Alden. "Languages of South American Indians," in *Handbook of South American Indians* (Bureau of American Ethnology Bulletins, No. 143 [7 vols.; Washington, D.C., 1946-50]), VI, 224.

Mason, Perry. *"Cash Flow" Analysis and the Funds Statement.* Accounting Research Study No. 2. New York: American Institute of Certified Public Accountants, 1961.

McBride, George McCutcheon. *The Agrarian Indian Communities of Highland Bolivia.* New York: Oxford University Press, 1921.

McQueen, Charles A. *The Bolivian Public Debt.* (Bureau of Foreign and Domestic Commerce, Trade Information Bulletin No. 194 [Washington, D.C., 1924].)

———. *Bolivian Public Finance.* (Bureau of Foreign and Domestic Commerce, Trade Promotion Series No. 6 [Washington, D.C., 1925].)

Contains materials now out of print and not easily available elsewhere.

Mendoza-López, Vicente. *Las Finanzas en Bolivia y la Estrategia Capitalista.* La Paz: Escuela Tipográfica Salesiana, 1940.

Metal Statistics, 1960. New York: American Metal Market, 1960.

Moore, O. Ernest, "The Stabilization of the Bolivian Peso," *Public Finance,* XIII (1958), 43-68.

Moreno-Córdova, Hugo. *Informe de Labores de 1956 a 1960.* La Paz: Ministerio de Hacienda, 1961.

Morrison, de Lesseps S. *Latin American Mission.* New York: Simon & Schuster, 1965.

Murillo, Aurelio R. *Donde Vamos con el Dirigismo Parcial?* 2d ed. La Paz: En Marcha, 1957.

Naciones Unidas. *Análisis y Proyecciones del Desarrollo Económico: IV — El Desarrollo Económico de Bolivia.* Mexico City: Publ. Naciones Unidas 58.II. G.2, 1958.

Cited in this book as the ECLA report.

Nelson, Raymond H. *Education in Bolivia.* Washington, D.C.: Office of Education, Federal Security Agency, 1949.

Nicoletopoulos, George. "Stand-by Arrangements," *Finance and Development,* III (December, 1964), 193.

Norr, Martin, and Kerlan, Pierre. *Taxation in France.* (Harvard Law School World Tax Series.) Chicago: Commerce Clearing House, 1966.

Nurkse, Ragnar. *Problems of Capital Formation in Underdeveloped Countries.* New York: Oxford University Press, 1957.

Olson, R. O. "Impact and Implications of Foreign Surplus Disposal on Underdeveloped Economies," *Journal of Farm Economics,* LI (December, 1960), 1042-45.

Ortega y Gasset, José. *La Rebelión de las Masas.* Madrid: Revista de Occidente, 1930.

Osborne, Harold. *Bolivia: A Land Divided.* 2d ed. London: Oxford University Press, 1955.

    The best concise (but well-informed and thorough) survey of Bolivia's history, land, people, and economy.

Ostria-Gutiérrez, Alberto. *The Tragedy of Bolivia.* Translated by Eithne Golden. New York: Devin-Adair Co., 1958.

    Un Pueblo en La Cruz, translated, condensed, and toned down for the English reader. Some additions have been made to the Spanish version (1956) to include a brief reference to the 1956-57 monetary stabilization.

————. *Un Pueblo en La Cruz.* 2d ed. Santiago, Chile: Editorial del Pacífico, 1956.

    An account of the origins and performance of the Movimiento Nacional Revolucionario of Bolivia by an opponent of the regime.

Patch, Richard W. "Bolivia: U.S. Assistance in a Revolutionary Setting," in Council on Foreign Relations, *Social Change in Latin America Today,* pp. 108-76.

Paz-Estenssoro, Víctor. *Mensaje del Presidente de la República.* La Paz: Ediciones S.P.I.C., 1956.

Peñaloza, Luis. *Historia Económica de Bolivia.* 2 vols. La Paz: Imprenta El Progreso, 1953-54.

    A Party-oriented economic history of Bolivia by the codirector of the MNR newspaper, *En Marcha,* who was appointed to the presidency of the Central Bank in mid-1957.

Pick's Currency Yearbook. New York: Pick's World Currency Report.

Powelson, John P. *Latin America: Today's Economic and Social Revolution.* New York: McGraw-Hill Book Co., 1964.

————. "Planeamiento para el Desarrollo Económico," *Revista de la Facultad de Sciencias Económicas,* June, 1964, p. 104.

Powelson, John P., and Solow, Anatole A. "Urban and Rural Development in Latin America," *Annals of the American Academy of Political and Social Science,* CCCLX (July, 1965), 58.

Prescott, William H. *History of the Conquest of Peru.* Philadelphia, Pa.: J. B. Lippincott Co., 1879.

Priestley, Joseph. *Essay on the First Principles of Government.* 2d ed. London: Johnson, 1771.

Rangel, Domingo Alberto. *Venezuela: País Ocupado.* La Paz: Editorial Juventud, 1955.

Reid, Escott. "Rich Lands, Poor Lands," *Finance and Development,* II (March, 1965), 21.

Reuss, Frederick G. *Fiscal Policy for Growth Without Inflation: The German Experiment.* Baltimore, Md.: Johns Hopkins Press, 1963.

Richey's Reference Handbook for Builders, Architects, and Construction Engineers. New York: Simmons-Boardman Publishing Co., 1951.

Roepke, Wilhelm. *Economics of the Free Society.* Translated by Patrick M. Boarman. Chicago, Ill.: Henry Regnery Co., 1963.

Rogers, James Harvey. *The Process of Inflation in France 1914-1927.* New York: Columbia University Press, 1929.
    Written late in 1927, the book does not cover the *de jure* stabilization of the franc in 1928 and its consequences.

Rosenbloom, Morris V. *Peace Through Strength.* New York: Farrar, Straus & Young, 1953.

Rosenstein-Rodan, P. N. "Notes on the Theory of the Big Push," in Ellis, Howard S., and Wallich, Henry C. (eds.), *Economic Development for Latin America.* London: Macmillan Co., 1962.

Rostow, Walt W. *Economics of Take-Off into Sustained Growth.* New York: St. Martin's Press, 1963.

Rueff, Jacques. *The Age of Inflation.* Translated by A. H. Meeus and F. G. Clarke. Chicago, Ill.: Henry Regnery Co., 1964.

Sauer, Carl O. "Cultivated Plants of South and Central America," in *Handbook of South American Indians* (Bureau of American Ethnology Bulletins, No. 143 [7 vols.; Washington, D.C., 1946-50]), VI, 496, 513.

Sayre, Joel. *Rackety-Rax.* New York: Alfred A. Knopf, 1932.

Schacht, Hjalmar Horace Greeley. *The Stabilization of the Mark.* Translated by Ralph Butler. New York: The Adelphi Co., 1927.

Schlesinger, Eugene Richard. *Multiple Exchange Rates and Economic Development.* Princeton, N.J.: Princeton University Press, 1952.

Schumpeter, J. A. *The Theory of Economic Development.* Cambridge, Mass.: Harvard University Press, 1934.

Solomon, Anthony Morton, Krause, Frank W., and Fieleke, Norman S. *The Finances of the Public Sector of Bolivia.* Washington, D.C.: U.S. Agency for International Development, 1963. (Mimeographed.)

Steggerda, Morris. "Anthropometry of South American Indians," in *Handbook of South American Indians* (Bureau of American

Ethnology Bulletins, No. 143 [7 vols.; Washington, D.C., 1946-50], VI, 63-68.

Tamayo, Franz. *Creación de la Pedagogia Nacional.* 2d ed. La Paz: El Diario, 1944.

Tennessee Gas Transmission Company (now Tenneco). *Annual Report.* Houston, Texas: Tennessee Gas Transmission Co., 1965.

Tidewater Oil Company. *Annual Report.* Los Angeles, Calif.: Tidewater Oil Co., 1965.

Tigner, James Lawrence. "The Ryukyuans in Bolivia," *Hispanic-American Historical Review,* XLIII (May, 1963), 206-29.

Trotsky, Leon (Lev Davidovich Bronshtein). *El Proceso de Moscú.* Mexico City: Nueva Era, 1937.

———. *La Revolución Traicionada.* Buenos Aires: Claridad, 1938.

———. *La Revolución Permanente.* Buenos Aires: Mar Dulce, n.d.

———. *Por los Estados Unidos Socialistas de América Latina.* Buenos Aires: Coyoacán, 1961.

Trumbull, Robert. *The Scrutable East.* New York: David McKay Co., 1965.

Tully, Andrew, and Britten, Milton. *Where Did Your Money Go? The Foreign Aid Story.* New York: Simon & Schuster, 1964.

United Nations, Economic and Social Council. *Report of the Commission of Enquiry on the Coca Leaf* (E/1666, E/CN. 7/AC.2/1, 1950). Lake Success, N.Y.: United Nations, 1950.

United Nations. *Report of the United Nations Mission of Technical Assistance to Bolivia* (II.B.5, 1951). New York: United Nations, 1951.

   Cited in this book as the Keenleyside report, this is the best general economic survey of Bolivia prepared up to 1950.

USAID/Bolivia. *Economic and Program Statistics.* La Paz: USAID/Bolivia, 1964, 1965.

United States Army. *Area Handbook for Bolivia.* Washington, D.C.: American University (Special Operations Research Office), 1963.

USOM/Bolivia, Engineering & Transportation Division. *Red de Caminos Nacionales.* La Paz: USOM/Bolivia, 1961.

USOM/Bolivia, *Point Four in Bolivia 1942-1960.* La Paz: USOM/Bolivia, 1960.

U.S. Senate. *Administration of National Security, Hearings before the Subcommittee on National Security Staffing and Operations of the Committee on Government Operations,* Part 2. 88th Cong., 1st Sess., June 14 and 17, 1963.

———. *Administration of National Security, The American Ambassador; A Study Submitted by the Subcommittee on National Security to the Committee on Government Operations.* 88th Cong., 2d Sess., 1964.

———, Committee on Government Operations. *Administration of*

United States Foreign Aid Programs in Bolivia. Senate Report No. 1030. 86th Cong., 2d Sess., January 20, 1960.

————. National Stockpile and Naval Petroleum Reserves Subcommittee of the Committee on Armed Services. *Inquiry into the Strategic and Critical Material Stockpiles of the United States.* 87th Cong., 2d Sess., 1961.

————, Subcommittee on Foreign Aid, Senate Committee on Foreign Affairs. *Technical Cooperation in the Andes Countries of South America.* 85th Cong., 1st Sess., March 5, 1957.

U.S. Tariff Commission. *Economic Controls and Commercial Policy in Bolivia.* Washington, D.C.: U.S. Tariff Commission, 1946.

Valdez-Molina, Carlos H. "Algunos Planteamientos en Torno a la Crisis en Bolivia," *Minería Boliviana,* III (September, 1957), 55-63.

Veblen, Thorstein. *Theory of the Leisure Class.* London: Allen & Unwin, 1924.

Vernon, Raymond. *The Dilemma of Mexico's Development.* Cambridge, Mass.: Harvard University Press, 1963.

Wallas, Graham. *The Great Society.* London: Macmillan Co., 1914.

Walston, Henry D. L. G. *Agriculture under Communism.* Chester Springs, Pa.: Dufour Editions, 1962.

Wheatley, John. *An Essay on the Theory of Money and Principles of Commerce,* Vol. I. London: Cadell & Davies, 1807.

Woodley, W. John R. "Multiple Currency Practices," *Fund and Bank Review: Finance and Development,* III (June, 1966), 113-19.

Zondag, Cornelius H. *The Bolivian Economy, 1952-65: The Revolution and Its Aftermath.* New York: Frederick A. Praeger, 1966.

This book was not available for reference in the present volume, but copious reference is made to Zondag's 1956 mimeographed report, which was the best economic study available up to the date of its publication.

————. *Problems in the Economic Development of Bolivia.* La Paz: U.S. Operations Mission, 1956. (Mimeographed.)

Cited in this book as the Zondag report.

INDEX

Note — Newspapers, newspaper correspondents, and official and periodical publications in general are listed in Index only when directly quoted or cited in text, not where mentioned solely as the source of news or factual material. Books and articles are indexed under the names of their authors and only when specifically cited in text. (See Bibliography for complete citations.)

Chauffeurs, Departmental Federation of (Federación Departmental de Choferes), 716n*13*

Chávez-Ortiz, Ñuflo (Vice-President): background, 29, 32; conferences with, 137-38, 172, 175-76, 722n*21;* participation in drafting stabilization program, 88n, 137-38, 156, 175-76, 468; repudiation of stabilization program, 470, 699, 734n*98;* investment code, 695; obstructs new customs tariff, 331-32, 388; defies Siles, 33, 704n*36;* blocks foreign bond agreement, 435-39, 465, 491, 562, 563n, 577, 679-80, 696, 730n*57;* resigns office, 439-41; asks U.S.S.R. aid, 521; mentioned, 33, 102, 164, 169, 175, 273, 303, 313, 404, 426, 462, 494, 512, 739n*4*

Chávez-Ortiz, Omar (Senator), 426

Chemical Corn Exchange Bank, 382-83, 386, 416, 714n*1*

Chile, 585, 661, 672

Chilean Development Bank, 352

Chilean State Railways (Ferrocarriles del Estado), 66, 732n*76*

Christian Democratic Community (Comunidad Demócrata Cristiana), 526

Church support of stabilization, 242. *See also* Mozzoni, Mgr. Humberto; Anasagasti, Carlos; Rosenhammer, José C.

CIA (Central Intelligence Agency), 280

Civil Aviation Administration, 118

Civil service: recommended reduction in, 630, 643-45, 691; control over filling vacancies, 272. *See also* Wages

Clark, George J. (IMF representative, La Paz, 1959-61; now vice-president, First National City Bank), xii, 750n*115*, 753n*147*

Classified material: availability outside of U.S., 548, 551, 598, 731n*67*, 745n*53*, 753n*138;* "Triangular Plan," 445, 545n, 731n*67*, 745n*53;* tin smelters, 551; other, 479, 598, 734n*106*, 753n*138;* tele-

grams transposed, 244n; Stabilization Council minutes not confidential, 151-52; IMF conversations, 89n, 245; confidential letters, 727n*36;* names concealed, 11n, 160, 519n, 247-50, 124-25

Claure-Calvi, Ramón (Minister of Public Works and Communication), 450-51, 454, 732nn*73,75*

Clay, General Lucius duB. (Military Governor, U.S. Zone, Germany), 306n

CNSS. *See* National Social Security Administration

Coalición de Organismos Sindicales y Partidos de Izquierda. *See* COSPI

COB (Central Obrera Boliviana, Bolivian Workers Confederation): 26, 33, 226, 523, 525; National Executive Committee, 29, 93, 138, 471; National Convention (First National Workers Congress), 283, 300-301, 458-61, 720n*44;* Second National Workers Congress, 403, 405, 455-56, 458, 464-73, 495, 501, 511n, 513, 548n, 710n*98,* 732n*77;* denounced, 264, 523; delegates support stabilization, 471-72, 511n; Workers' Congress attacks stabilization, 471, 734n*98;* mentioned, 91, 137, 238, 242, 299-300, 321, 405, 440-41, 462, 731n*72*

Cochabamba: municipality of, 450-51, 657, 681-82; region and department, 523, 525, 555, 561, 653, 656, 710n*95;* Cochabamba-Santa Cruz highway. *See* Bolivian Development Corporation projects (highways)

Cochran, H. Merle (deputy managing director, IMF), 714n*1*

Co-Government (Co-Gobierno), 33, 91, 96, 152, 226, 238, 300, 311, 334, 356, 369, 417n, 460

Cohen, Myer (UN Secretariat), 714n*1*

Cole, G. D. H. *See* Socialism and communism

Colegio de Abogados. *See* Bar Association

Coleman, Max (engineer, FBD mission to Bolivia), 736n*118*

Cooperativa Eléctrica de Sucre. *See* Electrical Cooperative of Sucre

Cooperativa Industrial Poliviana, S.A., 724n53

Corbett, Jack C. (director, Office of International Financial and Development Affairs, State Department), 714n1

Corbett, James (Department of State; formerly Assistant Chief, Finance & Investment Division, Bureau of Foreign & Domestic Commerce), 714n1

Corporación Boliviana de Fomento. *See* Bolivian Development Corporation

Corporación Minera de Bolivia (Bolivian Mining Corporation). *See* COMIBOL

Corporación Nacional de Fundiciones. *See* National Smelter Corporation

Corruption (including questionable practices that may or may not involve corruption): traditional, 28-29, 31, 602-3, 607, 609, 612; private sector, 152, 175, 429-30, 508, 612; engendered by quotas, foreign exchange and other controls, 30-31, 37, 38-40, 106, 112, 126, 135, 217, 300, 328n, 355-60, 424n, 485, 568, 733n85; engendered by high taxes, 323-24; engendered by U.S. aid, 121-22, 203-4, 430, 501n, 593, 609; curbed by stabilization, 283-84, 302, 485, 513; bags, 364, 365n, 392; Bolivian Development Corporation, 62-64, 328n, 399-401, 649, 654-57; Brazil nuts, 36-37, 359-60, 508, 669, 724n53; bulldozers, 657; chauffeurs' union, 682; coca leaves, 321n, 521; COMIBOL, 53-54, 391-93, 725nn10-12; *cuperos* (quota recipients), 275-78, 299-300; foreign bonds, 437, 730n57; government operations, general, 65n, 76, 214n; government purchases, 152, 244, 391-93, 409, 501n, 634; locomotives, 157, 288, 411, 662; Min-

ing Bank, 57, 120, 175-76, 270n, 288-89, 396, 726n17; mining concession, 362; MNR "cell," 170; National Social Security Administration, 404-5, 467; *políticos* and labor leaders, 37, 39-40, 53, 121-22, 170n, 175-77, 299-302, 328n, 333-34, 392-93, 396, 405, 409, 429, 454-55, 467, 501n, 522, 654, 656-57, 669, 726n17, 733n84,85; their unpaid debts to Central Bank, 122, 351, 501n; Reyes cattle project, 655-56; Santa Cruz water pipes, 410-11; Sucre cement plant, 656-57; smugglers, 333-34; truck of the month, 30-31; Venezuelan loan, proposed, 124, 158, 169, 176-77; Villa Montes irrigation project, 654-55; YPFB, 60. *See also* Black markets and marketeers; Smuggling

Corumbá-Santa Cruz Railway:smuggling, 39; "white elephant," 66-67, 567; debt to Brazil, 61, 67, 421, 490, 585, 660n

COSPI (Coalición de Organismos Sindicales y Partidos de Izquierda — Coalition of Labor Unions and Parties of the Left), 25

Costanzo, Gesualdo A. (head, IMF Mission to Bolivia; later, executive vice-president, First National City Bank): background, 167, stabilization in Greece, 124-25, 476; stabilization in Bolivia, 88, 120, 167-68, 227, 237, 245, 705n45; mentioned, 160, 162n, 180, 583, 716n14, 753n147

Cost of living: index numbers, 41, 189 (table), 499-501, 587, 590 (table), 591, 713n17, 736n120 (table), 751n125 (table); charts, 111, 496, 588; elimination of below-cost commissaries, 183-85, 189-91, 227-29, 500, 585, 641, 644; consumption estimates, 183, 189-91, 643; new index study recommended, 636, 646-47; mentioned, 150, 579, 636. *See also* Prices

Counterpart funds: food and other commodity shipments, 35, 112,

"Forty Points." *See* Stabilization program

Fossati-Rocha, Humberto (economist, National Planning and Coordination Commission): background, 115n, 165; suggested as Secretary General, Stabilization Council, 115n, 164; cooperation with Council, 115; economic views, 100, 165n, 481n, 734n*93*, 735n*110;* appointed president, Central Bank, 115n; mentioned, 156, 712n*9,* 718n*4,* 739n*3. See also* National Planning and Coordination Commission, economic studies

France: operations in Bolivia, 250n, 316n, 367n, 565; exports financed by U.S., 565; ambassador to Bolivia, 565

Franco-Guachalla, Alfredo (Minister of Labor), 508n

Free enterprise system: advocated, 94, 143, 612, 636(19), 699, 714n*36;* superiority over government enterprise, 195, 539, 554, 566, 612, 667, 696; government competition, 94, 532, 540n, 545, 551, 607, 628, 649-50, 742n*21;* taxes and other impediments to, 368n, 478n, 539, 540n, 545, 551, 601, 607, 649-50; mentioned, 341, 557n, 669, 686

Freeman, Roger A. (member, U.S. Financial Mission to Bolivia): background and appointment, 162-63; Stabilization Council meetings, 162-63, 262, 426; resignation, 163; tax recommendations, 260-61, 294-96, 313, 316n, 340-41, 719n*15;* mentioned, 243, 324, 670n, 718n*3*

Free-market economy, 88, 106, 125n, 135, 175, 220, 268, 276-80, 286, 289, 299, 303, 305-6, 365, 459, 466n, 469, 478n, 479, 499-500, 512, 530, 613, 631, 633-34, 643-44, 658-59, 687, 696, 699, 714n*36*

Frente de la Revolución Bolivian. *See* Bolivian Revolutionary Front

Frías, Luis (administrative manager, YPFB), 717n*20*

FSB (Falange Socialista Boliviana), 519n, 520

FSTMB (Federación Sindical de Trabajadores Mineros de Bolivia — Bolivian Mine Workers' Federation): background, 24, 26, 33; supports stabilization program, 177, 242, 718n*6;* causes trouble, 52-53, 274, 283, 440, 522, 523-25, 594, 745n*50;* attacks stabilization program, 300; mentioned, 96, 462-63, 542

Fundación Universitaria Simón Patiño, 50n

Fund for Special Operations, 433n, 563n, 564

Fundición de Estaño de Oruro, S.A., 746n*59*

Fundición Volcán, S.A., 726n*19*

Gall, Norman (*Wall Street Journal* correspondent), 740n*13*

Garbuney, Siegfried (State Department official), 714n*1*

Gasser, Fernando (president, Industrias "La Belgica," S.A., sugar mill), 722n*20*

GATT, 536

General Bureau of Iron and Steel, 565

General Services Administration, 445, 536n

Geography, 3-4, 7-11

German businessmen in Bolivia, 355n

Germany, Federal Republic of: stabilization of mark, 99-100, 125n, 127n, 305-6; basis of recovery, 305-7, 602; operations in Bolivia, 544-49, 560, 562, 564; exports and services financed by U.S., 544, 548, 560, 564

Gilmore, Eugene, Jr. (Counsellor of Embassy, La Paz), 138, 238, 280, 718n*3*

Gisbert-Nogué, Miguel (vice-president and chief executive of National Planning and Coordination Commission): background, 258; participation in organizing Stabilization Council, 88n, 94, 104-5, 137-38, 617; participation in Council discussions, 151-52, 176n, 194,

Investment in Bolivia (Instituto para la Promoción de Inversiones en Bolivia). *See* Investment
Instituto Boliviano de Encuestas de Opinión Pública. *See* Bolivian Institute of Public Opinion Polls
Instituto para la Promoción de las Inversiones en Bolivia. *See* Institute for the Promotion of Investment in Bolivia
Insurance companies, 645
Inter-American Committee for the Alliance for Progress, 565
Inter-American Development Bank: promotion of land reform, 74; loans, general, 521, 560n, 561-64, 597n, 598; futile infrastructure financing, 433n, 597n, 599-600, 753n*138;* COMIBOL financing, *passim* 543-49, 745nn*46,53;* capitalization, 563n; mentioned, 166, 559-60, 747n*79*
Inter-American Monetary Union (proposal), 646
Interest rates: regulation of, 219, 342, 345, 347; high rates as curb on inflation, 346-47; low rates for economic development, 346; mentioned, 398. *See also* Bank credit regulations
International Bank for Reconstruction & Development: loan possibilities (1956-57), 121, 187-88, 194, 196, 255, 456-57, 678, 696-97; mission to Bolivia, 255, 679-80; loans blocked by government bond default, 188, 255, 435-37, 562-63, 679-80, 696; mentioned, 167, 456-57, 558, 599n. *See also* International Development Association
International Cooperation Administration: contract with, v-vi, 701n*3;* constructive measures, 60, *passim* 75-83, 351, 670; stabilization fund, 141, 247-50, 427, 677, 680; inefficiency and blunders, 163n, 247-50, 697n, 733n*84,* 735n*112;* mentioned, 88, 142, 146-48, 155, 167, 258, 274, 362, 393, 498, 513, 626, 714n*1. See also* Agency for International Development; Point IV;

USOM/Bolivia; Washington, bureaucracy in
International Development Association, 558n, 562-63
International Development Services, 81
International Labor Organization: mission to Bolivia, 482-83; social security, 405, 726n*29;* mentioned, 647, 688
International Metal Processing Corporation, 536
International Mining Corporation, 191, 270, 541, 600, 744n*40,* 753n*142*
International Monetary Fund: 1953 stabilization attempt, 42-43, 135; IMF mission recommended in "Fifty Step Plan," 147, 150, 637(27); 1956 and subsequent missions, 88-89, 167-68, 220-21, 232, 237, 474, 717n*35,* 750n*115;* regulations, 240, 296, 632, 642; national quotas, 585-86; drawings and standby agreements, 586, 672, 680; application for loan and loan procedures, 180n, 237, 245-46, 674, 678, 680, 718n*2,* 719n*10;* blamed by Bolivians, 246n, 266, 273, 677; activities considered confidential, 89n, 245; mentioned, 88, 141-43, 149, 151, 155, 160, 163, 167-69, 178, 180, 187n, 216, 218, 239-240, 242, 245, 253, 258, 274, 320, 458, 485, 628, *passim* 635-46, 659, 662-63, 714n*1,* 716n*14,* 737n*122,* 751n*124,* 754n*148. See also* Stabilization fund
International Nickel Co., 738n*132*
International Telephone and Telegraph Corporation, 444n. *See also* Union Allumetière
International Tin Agreement. *See* Tin
Investment: government, 157, 558n, 560-67, 570, 697; private, 60, 94, 157, 505, 559, 567-70, 636(20), 637(23), 667, 678, 694-96, 749n*97;* climate, 94, 157-58, 505, 568-69, 601, 637(23,26), 647, 673, 694-95, 699, 749n*97;* Investment Code, 148,

Laski, Harold. *See* Socialism and communism

Lead, 537, 539, 743n*31*

Lechín-Oquendo, Juan (executive director, COB; leader of FSTMB; President of Senate; later, Vice-President of Bolivia): revolutionary activities and background, 24-25, 27-29, 461, 522n; Trotskyite and communist affiliations, 24, 26, 520, 522, 525, 559, 594, 703n*31;* power in FSTMB, COB, miners' militia, 24, 32, 300-301, 462, 732n*75;* conferences with, 137-38, 172-76; participation in drafting stabilization program, 137-38, 156, 172-73, 175-76, 185, 220-21, 226-31, 234, 262-63, 301, 468; support of program, 138, 152, 242, 282-83, 718n*6;* causes trouble, 282-83, 300-301, 368-69, 440, 452, 501n, 686; repudiation of program, 300, 468, 499, 511n, 519, 699, 734nn*90,96,* 737n*121;* attacks on Siles, Eder, 274, 459-63, 467-69, 734nn*90,96;* political activities, 1957-64, 301n, 303, 520-25, 559, 594, 699, 752n*132;* alleged coca smuggling, 321n; attacked by mob, 472, 524; hunger strike, 524; mentioned, 96, 102, 159, 164, 169, 171, 198, 200, 273-74, 300-303, 313, 319-20, 357, 362, 387, 404, 426, 439, 443, 464, 481, 494, 503, 678. *See also* COB; COMIBOL; FSTMB

Lechín-Suárez, Juan (Army colonel, president of COMIBOL), 538, 744n*34*

Leggett, Herbert (U.S. Secretary of Embassy in La Paz), 736n*113*

Legislation, Latin America, draftmanship, 70, 95, 137, 259n, 260, 586, 694-95. *See also* Congress

Lema-Pelaez, Raul, 740n*9*

Lemoine, Joaquín (general manager, later president, Bolivian Development Corporation): Guabirá sugar mill, 399, 648; attacks stabilization program, 513; mentioned, 398ff, 717n*22,* 726n*20*

Liberty National Bank (now National Bank of Washington), 383

Limpias, Guillermo (director, Confederation of Bank Employees), 731n*72*

Liquor and tobacco taxes. *See* Taxes, by categories

Lloyd Aereo Boliviano, S.A., 36-37, 59, 69, 118, 194, 200, 298, 359, 454, 564-65

Loans, "soft" and "hard." *See* United States aid (fallacy of distinction between loans and grants)

Lodge, Henry Cabot, Jr. (American Ambassador to the UN), 714n*1*

Lomax, Sir John (British Ambassador to Bolivia), 152

London School of Economics and Political Science, 475, 476n, 478n, 485

Longhorn Tin Smelter, 51, 707n*62*

Longon, Luigi (Italian communist), 525

Lora, Guillermo (leader of POR; Trotskyist party), 754n*149*

Lovett, Robert Abercrombie (Under-Secretary of State), 147n

Luce, Henry R. (publisher, *Time*), 11n, 519-20n

Lyon Oil Company, 747n*70*

McClellan, John L. (Senator, Democrat, Arkansas), 598n, 656

McCloy, John J. *See* American Overseas Finance Corporation

Macdonald, Thomas H. (former Director of the Bureau of Public Roads), 82

Machacamarca mine, 524

Madrejones oil fields and concession, 417n, 554

Maidenberg, H. J. (*New York Times* correspondent), 741n*14,* 753n*147*

Maldonado-Arce, Víctor (Superintendent of Banks), 723n*39*

Mannesmann, A. G. *See* Companhía Ferro Brasileiro

Mansfield, Lord. *See* Holman v. Johnson

Mansfield, Michael Joseph (Senator, Democrat, Montana), 39n, 242